THE FASCINATING FIELD OF ANTHROPOLOGY COMES ALIVE WITH

The Essence of Anthropology . . .

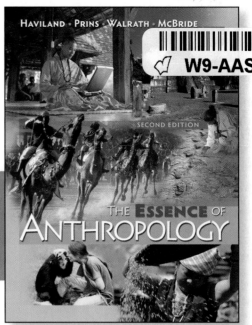

HAVILAND · PRINS · WALRATH · McBRIDE

SECOND EDITION

THE **ESSENCE** OF ANTHROPOLOGY

W9-AAS-169

This streamlined, clearly written text presents an integrated, holistic perspective

This book's nationally acclaimed author team makes it easy for students to understand anthropology's key concepts and their great relevance to today's complex world. Throughout this fascinating book, students discover so much about themselves, their culture, and today's globalized world. The book presents three themes that form a cohesive framework for understanding the factors that shape human behavior and beliefs. Those themes (how every culture, past and present, is an integrated and dynamic system of adaptation to internal and external factors; the connection between human culture and human biology; and the impact of globalization on peoples and cultures around the world) help student master the concepts of anthropology.

With an emphasis on social justice issues, environmental issues, and visual observation, the Second Edition of *The Essence of Anthropology* helps students explore the latest findings on today's hot topics in areas such as basic genetics, evolutionary theory, primate research, remote sensing, and sociolinguistics.

Engaging learning tools and features like these help students understand the relevance of anthropology to the world around them:

• *Biocultural Connections* features illustrate how cultural and biological processes work together to shape human evolution and the various ways humans face the challenges of existence.

• *Original Studies* and *Anthropology Applied* boxes focus on particularly interesting examples, helping students develop a deeper insight into the meaning and relevance of anthropological research.

• *Visual Essence* and *Visual Counterpoint* sections graphically demonstrate major concepts.

• The book includes new emphasis on social justice and environmental issues, and the importance of thinking ethically.

• New *Visual Counterpoint* photos have been added that present thought-provoking cross-cultural comparisons.

A dynamic assortment of teaching and learning tools accompanies your adoption of this text! Take a look inside . . .

RESOURCES FOR INSTRUCTORS

Online Instructor's Manual

Contains chapter outlines, learning objectives, key terms and concepts, and lecture suggestions, as well as test questions, including multiple-choice, true-false, and essay questions. Available at the password-protected portion of the Companion Website.

Power**Lecture**™

PowerLecture with ExamView®

ISBN-10: 0-495-60272-8
ISBN-13: 978-0-495-60272-9

A complete all-in-one reference for instructors, the **PowerLecture** CD contains Microsoft® PowerPoint® slides of images from the text, zoomable art, image library, PowerPoint lecture slides that outline the main points of each chapter, Google™ Earth coordinates, videos, Microsoft® Word files of the Test Bank and Instructor's Manual, and ExamView testing software that allows instructors to create, deliver, and customize tests and study guides (both print and online) in minutes.

ALSO AVAILABLE FOR STUDENTS

Classic Readings in Cultural Anthropology, Second Edition

by Gary Ferraro
ISBN: 0-495-50736-9
ISBN-13: 978-0-495-50736-9

Presenting an array of historical and contemporary works instrumental to the field's thought and research, Ferraro's reader provides selections that support the major topics covered in your cultural anthropology course, including new readings on globalization, politics and social control, economics, language and communication, and marriage and family.

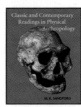

Classic and Contemporary Readings in Physical Anthropology

by M. K. Sandford with Eileen M. Jackson
ISBN-10: 0-495-51014-9
ISBN-13: 978-0-495-51014-7

This new reader presents classic and contemporary articles on key issues dealing with the nature of science, evolution and heredity, primate behavior, human evolution, and modern human variation.

Telecourse Study Guide

ISBN-10: 0-495-83695-8
ISBN-13: 978-0-495-83695-7

Introduces the central concepts, concerns, and research methods of anthropology to students taking the off-campus course, *Anthropology: The Four Fields.* This **Study Guide** contains a chapter preview, learning objectives, viewing notes to accompany the video lessons, questions to consider, key terms and concepts, a summary, and review questions.

Wadsworth Case Studies

Case Studies in Cultural Anthropology

Edited by George Spindler and Janice E. Stockard

This series offers a diverse array of case studies that emphasize culture change and the factors influencing change, in the peoples depicted. Now, Wadsworth presents a selection of over 60 classic and contemporary ethnographies in this series, representing geographic and topical diversity.

Case Studies on Contemporary Social Issues

John A. Young, Series Editor
This series explores how anthropology is used today in understanding and addressing problems faced by human societies around the world. Each case study in this acclaimed series examines an issue of socially recognized importance in the historical, geographical, and cultural context of a particular region of the world.

ONLINE RESOURCES TAKE STUDENTS BEYOND THE TEXT FOR INTERACTIVE STUDY

Anthropology Resource Center
ISBN-10: 0-495-12743-4 • ISBN-13: 978-0-495-12743-7

This online center offers a wealth of information and useful tools for both instructors and students in all four fields of anthropology. Students will find interactive maps, learning modules, video exercises, *Cross-Cultural Miscues, Meet the Scientists,* and more. For instructors, the Anthropology Resource Center includes a gateway to time-saving teaching tools, such as image banks, sample syllabi, and more. To get started with the **Anthropology Resource Center,** students and instructors are directed to **www.cengage.com/anthropology** where they can create an account through iChapters.com.

At the **Anthropology Resource Center,** students also have access to:
- **Research Online:** A guide to using the web to enhance the study of anthropology.
- **Applying Anthropology:** Developed by Gary Ferraro, this web tour of applied anthropology leads students to useful information on careers, graduate school programs in applied anthropology, and internships. They will also find real-world examples of working anthropologists applying the skills and methods of anthropology to help solve serious world problems.
- **Earthwatch Journal:** A Wadsworth exclusive journal of articles from the well-respected Earthwatch Institute.

For Instructors:
Supplement your resources with a community share-bank of digital images organized by key course concepts, and a syllabus integrating the ARC with the Second Edition of *The Essence of Anthropology.*

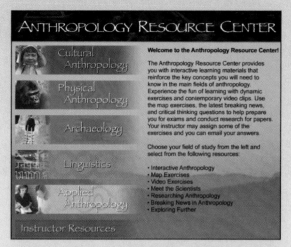

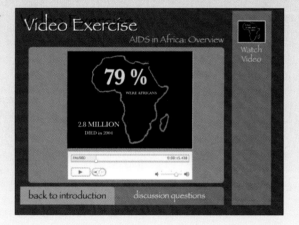

Companion Website
www.cengage.com/anthropology/haviland

This site provides students with basic learning resources—including tutorial quizzes, a final exam, learning objectives, Web links, flash cards, crossword puzzles, and more!

WebTUTOR

WebTutor™ ToolBox on WebCT® or Blackboard

Please contact your Cengage Learning representative for ordering information.

Creating an engaging e-learning environment is easier than ever with **WebTutor™ ToolBox.** Save time building or Web-enhancing your course, posting course materials, incorporating multimedia, tracking progress, and more with this customizable, engaging course management tool. **WebTutor ToolBox** saves you time and enhances your students' learning—pairing advanced course management capabilities with text-specific learning tools.

DELIVER ENGAGING LECTURES THAT SPARK CLASSROOM DISCUSSION WITH THESE EXCITING VIDEOS

ABC Videos

Launch your lectures with exciting video clips from the award-winning news coverage of ABC. Addressing topics covered in a typical course, these videos are divided into short segments—perfect for introducing key concepts in contexts relevant to students' lives. Ask your Cengage Learning representative for a listing of available videos.

AIDS in Africa DVD
ISBN-10: 0-495-17183-2
ISBN-13: 978-0-495-17183-6

The **AIDS in Africa** DVD features enlightening films that will expand your students' global perspective on the topic of HIV/AIDS, as well as of gender, faith, culture, and poverty. The documentary series focuses on the new democracy of Namibia and the many actions that are being taken to control HIV/AIDS. Included are four documentary films created by the Project Pericles scholars at Elon University: (1) *Young Struggles, Eternal Faith* focuses on caregivers in the faith community; (2) *The Shining Lights of Opuwo* shows how young people share their messages of hope through song and dance; (3) *The Measure of Our Humanity: HIV/AIDS in Namibia* deals with poverty and the nation's struggles; and (4) *You Wake Me Up* is a story of two HIV-positive women and their acts of courage that help other women learn to survive.

Visual Anthropology Video

From *Documentary Educational Resources* and Wadsworth, this 60-minute video features clips from over 30 new and classic anthropological films. It is a highly effective and engaging lecture launcher.

Wadsworth Anthropology Video Library

Qualified adopters may select full-length videos from an extensive library of excellent video sources drawn from *Films for the Humanities and Sciences.*

To create your perfect course package, contact your Wadsworth Cengage Learning sales representative, or visit **www.cengage.com/anthropology/haviland** for more information

The Essence of Anthropology

Second Edition

WILLIAM A. HAVILAND
Professor Emeritus, University of Vermont

HARALD E. L. PRINS
Kansas State University

DANA WALRATH
University of Vermont

BUNNY MCBRIDE
Kansas State University

WADSWORTH
CENGAGE Learning

Australia • Brazil • Japan • Korea • Mexico • Singapore • Spain • United Kingdom • United States

The Essence of Anthropology, Second Edition
William A. Haviland, Harald E. L. Prins, Dana Walrath, Bunny McBride

Editorial Director, West Coast: Marcus Boggs

Developmental Editor: Lin Gaylord

Editorial Assistant: Arwen Petty

Marketing Communications Manager: Tami Strang

Content Project Manager: Jerilyn Emori

Creative Director: Rob Hugel

Art Director: Caryl Gorska

Print Buyer: Karen Hunt

Rights Acquisitions Account Manager, Text: Mardell Glinski Shultz

Rights Acquisitions Account Manager, Image: Robyn Young

Production Service: Joan Keyes, Dovetail Publishing Services

Text Designer: Lisa Buckley

Photo Researcher: Billie Porter

Copy Editor: Jennifer Gordon

Cover Designer: Larry Didona

Cover Image: Clockwise from top left: ©Jonny Le Fortune/zefa/Corbis, ©Jan Butchofsky-Houser/Corbis, ©Kenneth Garrett/National Geographic Stock, ©Petitalot Eric/Belpress/Andia/drr.net, ©Susan Kuklin/Photo Researchers, Inc., ©James Kegley/drr.net

Compositor: Pre-Press PMG

For product information and technology assistance, contact us at **Cengage Learning Customer & Sales Support, 1-800-354-9706**

For permission to use material from this text or product, submit all requests online at **www.cengage.com/permissions**. Further permissions questions can be e-mailed to **permissionrequest@cengage.com**.

Library of Congress Control Number: 2008941129

Student Edition:

ISBN-13: 978-0-495-59981-4

ISBN-10: 0-495-59981-6

Wadsworth
10 Davis Drive
Belmont, CA 94002-3098
USA

Cengage Learning is a leading provider of customized learning solutions with office locations around the globe, including Singapore, the United Kingdom, Australia, Mexico, Brazil, and Japan. Locate your local office at: **www.cengage.com/international.**

Cengage Learning products are represented in Canada by Nelson Education, Ltd.

To learn more about Wadsworth, visit **www.cengage.com/wadsworth.**

Purchase any of our products at your local college store or at our preferred online store **www.ichapters.com.**

Printed in the United States of America
1 2 3 4 5 6 7 13 12 11 10 09

Dedicated to David and Pia Mayburg-Lewis, founders of Cultural Survival. Their tireless efforts on the behalf of indigenous peoples and human rights continue to inspire.

ABOUT THE AUTHORS

While distinct from one another, all four members of this author team share overlapping research interests and a similar vision of what anthropology is (and should be) about. For example, all are "true believers" in the four-field approach to anthropology and all have some involvement in applied work.

WILLIAM A. HAVILAND is Professor Emeritus at the University of Vermont, where he founded the Department of Anthropology and taught for thirty-two years. He holds a Ph.D. in Anthropology from the University of Pennsylvania. He has carried out original research in archaeology in Guatemala and Vermont; ethnography in Maine and Vermont; and physical anthropology in Guatemala. This work has been the basis of numerous publications in various national and international books and journals, as well as in media intended for the general public. His books include *The Original Vermonters*, coauthored with Marjorie Power, and a technical monograph on ancient Maya settlement. He also served as technical consultant for the award-winning telecourse, *Faces of Culture*, and is coeditor of the series *Tikal Reports*, published by the University of Pennsylvania Museum of Archaeology and Anthropology.

Besides his teaching and writing, Dr. Haviland has lectured to numerous professional as well as non-professional audiences in Canada, Mexico, Lesotho, South Africa, and Spain, as well as in the United States. A staunch supporter of indigenous rights, he served as expert witness for the Missisquoi Abenakis of Vermont in an important court case over aboriginal fishing rights. Awards received by Dr. Haviland include being named University Scholar by the Graduate School of the University of Vermont in 1990, a Certificate of Appreciation from the Sovereign Republic of the Abenaki Nation of Missisquoi, St. Francis/Sokoki Band in 1996, and a Lifetime Achievement Award from the Center for Research on Vermont in 2006. Now retired from teaching, he continues his research, writing, and lecturing from the coast of Maine. His latest book is *At the Place of the Lobsters and Crabs* (2009).

HARALD E. L. PRINS (Ph.D., New School, 1988) is a University Distinguished Professor of Anthropology at Kansas State University. Born in the Netherlands, he studied and taught at various universities in Europe and the United States. He has done extensive fieldwork among indigenous peoples in South and North America, published many dozens of articles in half a dozen languages, authored *The Mi'kmaq: Resistance, Accommodation, and Cultural Survival* (1996), co-authored *Asticou's Island Domain: Wabanaki Indians at Mount Desert Island, 1500–2000* (2007), and co-edited several books and special journal volumes. Also trained in film, he co-authored the documentary *Our Lives in Our Hands* (1986) and the award-winning *Oh, What a Blow that Phantom Gave Me!* (2003). Dr. Prins has won his university's most prestigious undergraduate teaching awards, held the Coffman Chair for University Distinguished Teaching Scholars (2004–05), and was honored as Professor of the Year for the State of Kansas by the Carnegie Foundation for the Advancement of Teaching in 2006. He served as expert witness in Native rights cases in the U.S. Senate and various Canadian courts, and was instrumental in the successful federal recognition and land claims of the Aroostook Band of Micmacs (1991). Dr. Prins served as president of the Society for Visual Anthropology and visual anthropology editor of the *American Anthropologist,* and is a Research Associate at the Smithsonian Institution.

DANA WALRATH (Ph.D., University of Pennsylvania, 1997) is Assistant Professor of Family Medicine at the University of Vermont and a Women's Studies affiliated faculty member. She specializes in medical and biological anthropology with principal interests in biocultural aspects of reproduction, the cultural context of biomedicine, genetics, and evolutionary medicine. She directs an innovative educational program at the University of Vermont's College of Medicine that brings anthropological theory and practice to first-year medical students. Before joining the faculty at the University of Vermont in 2000, she taught at the University of Pennsylvania and Temple University. Her research has been supported by the National Science Foundation, Health Resources and Services Administration, the Centers for Disease Control, and the Templeton Foundation. Dr. Walrath's publications have appeared in *Current Anthropology, American Anthropologist, American Journal of Physical Anthropology*, and several biomedical journals. Her work was included in the recent volumes *Feminist Anthropology: Past, Present, and Future* (2006) and *The Social Archaeology of Funerary Remains* (2006). An active member of the Council on the Anthropology of Reproduction, she has also served on a national committee to develop women's health-care learning objectives for medical education. She leads the development of the HEAL project, an innovative local initiative to improve health care for low-income Vermonters, including refugees and immigrants.

BUNNY MCBRIDE (M.A., Columbia University, 1980) is an award-winning author specializing in cultural anthropology, indigenous peoples, international tourism, and nature conservation issues. Published in dozens of national and international print media, she has reported from Africa, Europe, China, and the Indian Ocean. Highly rated as a teacher, she served as visiting anthropology faculty at Principia College, the Salt Institute for Documentary Field Studies, and since 1996 as adjunct lecturer of anthropology at Kansas State University. McBride's many publications include *Women of the Dawn* (1999), *Molly Spotted Elk: A Penobscot in Paris* (1995), and *Asticou's Island Domain: Wabanaki Indians at Mount Desert Island, 1500–2000* (co-authored, 2007). The Maine state legislature awarded her a special commendation for significant contributions to Native women's history (1999). A community activist and researcher for the Aroostook Band of Micmacs (1981–91), McBride assisted this Maine Indian community in its successful efforts to reclaim lands, gain tribal status, and revitalize cultural traditions. McBride has curated various museum exhibits based on her research, most recently *Journeys West: The David & Peggy Rockefeller American Indian Art Collection*. Currently, she is working on a series of museum exhibitions and serving as oral history advisor for the Kansas Humanities Council and board member of the Women's World Summit Foundation, based in Geneva, Switzerland.

BRIEF CONTENTS

DETAILED CONTENTS

CHAPTER 15
Spirituality, Religion, and the Supernatural 296

CHAPTER 16
Global Changes and the Role of Anthropology 316

FEATURES CONTENTS

PREFACE

It has been a joy to work on this second edition of *The Essence of Anthropology*. Fueled with feedback from students and faculty, we have built on the strengths and tended to any flaws identified in the first edition. Mostly, reviewers asked us to sharpen our aim to present four-field anthropology to undergraduates in a text that is reader-friendly and to the point. In short, they called for an even shorter text, but one that still does justice to the breadth and depth of the discipline. We took the challenge seriously, determined to craft a book that is lighter in weight, but not "lightweight."

As with the first edition, the word *essence* served as our guiding principle—alerting us to reach for content that covers anthropology's classical foundations and modern ramifications without getting carried away by too many details or examples. We aimed for an engaging, quick-moving narrative that gives anthropology majors a solid basis for more advanced coursework while sowing seeds of awareness in all students concerning cultural and biological diversity. Keeping this in mind, we honed our narrative, trimming the length of most chapters by about 10 percent. In addition, we cut two chapters ("Field Methods in Archaeology and Paleoanthropology" and "Processes of Change"), incorporating their most essential information into other chapters. The result is a streamlined 16-chapter textbook that we hope is as engaging for students and teachers as it was for us as researchers and writers.

Of course the text has been thoroughly updated. Also, for those unfamiliar with the Haviland et al. textbook series, it is worth noting that this edition of *Essence*, like the first, stands on the substantial shoulders of our *Anthropology: The Human Challenge* (the discipline's leading introductory textbook for more than three decades).

OUR MISSION

Time and time again, we have observed that most students enter an introductory anthropology class intrigued by the general subject but with little more than a vague sense of what it is all about. Thus, the first and most obvious task of our text is to provide a thorough introduction to the discipline—its foundations as a domain of knowledge and its major insights into the rich diversity of humans as a culture-making species.

In doing this, we draw from the research and ideas of a number of traditions of anthropological thought, exposing students to a mix of theoretical perspectives and methodologies. Such inclusiveness reflects our conviction

that different approaches offer distinctly important insights about human biology, behavior, and beliefs.

If most students start out with only a vague sense of what anthropology is, they often have less clear—and potentially more problematical—views of the superiority of their own species and culture. A secondary task for this text, then, is to prod students to appreciate the rich complexity and breadth of human diversity. Along with this is the task of helping them understand why there are so many differences and similarities in the human condition, past and present.

Debates regarding globalization and notions of progress, the "naturalness" of the mother-father-child(ren) nuclear family, new genetic technologies, and how gender roles relate to biological variation all benefit greatly from the fresh and often fascinating insights gained through anthropology. This probing aspect of the discipline is perhaps the most valuable gift we can pass on to those who take our classes. If we, as teachers and textbook authors, do our jobs well, students will gain a wider and more open-minded outlook on the world and a critical but constructive perspective on human origins and on their own biology and culture today. To borrow a favorite line from the famous poet T. S. Eliot, "And the end of all our exploring will be to arrive where we started and know the place for the first time" ("Four Quartets").

There has never been as great a need for students to acquire the anthropological tools to allow them to escape culture-bound ways of thinking and acting and to gain tolerance and respect for other ways of life. Thus, we have written this text, in large part, to help students make sense of our increasingly complex world and to navigate through its interrelated biological and cultural networks with knowledge and skill, whatever professional path they take.

A DISTINCTIVE APPROACH

Two key factors distinguish *Essence* from other introductory anthropology texts: our integrative presentation of the discipline's four fields and a trio of unifying themes that tie the book together and help keep students focused.

Integration of the Four Fields

Unlike traditional texts that present anthropology's four fields—archaeology, linguistics, cultural anthropology, and physical anthropology—as if they were separate or independent, our book takes an integrative approach. This reflects the comprehensive character of our discipline, a domain of knowledge where members of our species are studied in their totality—as social creatures biologically evolved with the inherent capacity for learning and sharing culture by means of symbolic communication. This approach also reflects our collective experience as practicing anthropologists who recognize that we cannot fully understand humanity in all its fascinating complexity unless we see the systemic interplay among environmental, physiological, material, social, ideological, psychological, and symbolic factors, both past and present.

For analytical purposes, however, we discuss physical anthropology as distinct from archaeology, linguistics, and sociocultural anthropology. Accordingly, there are separate chapters that focus primarily on each field, but the book repeatedly demonstrates how the different perspectives together provide a more complete picture of humankind. Among many examples of this integrative approach, Chapter 7, "Modern Human Diversity," discusses the social context of race and cultural practices that have impacted the human genome. Similarly, material concerning linguistics appears not only in Chapter 9, "Language and Communication," but in "Living Primates" (Chapter 3), "Human Evolution" (Chapter 4), and "The Emergence of Cities and States" (Chapter 6). These chapters include material on the linguistic capabilities of apes, the emergence of human language, and the origin of writing. In addition, every chapter includes a Biocultural Connection feature to further illustrate the interplay of biological and cultural processes in shaping the human experience.

Unifying Themes

In our own teaching, we recognize the value of marking out unifying themes that help students see the big picture as they grapple with the great array of concepts and information encountered in the study of human beings. In *Essence* we employ three such themes.

1. **Systemic adaptation:** *We emphasize that every culture, past and present, is an integrated and dynamic system of adaptation that responds to a combination of internal and external factors, including influences of the environment.*

2. **Biocultural connection:** *We highlight the integration of human culture and biology in the steps humans take to meet the challenges of survival.* The theme of biocultural connection runs throughout the text—as a thread in the main narrative and in a boxed feature that highlights this connection with a topical example for each chapter.

3. **Globalization:** *We track the emergence of globalization and its disparate impact on various peoples and cultures around the world.* While European colonization was a global force for centuries, leaving a significant—often devastating—footprint on the affected peoples in Asia, Africa, and the Americas, decolonization began about 200 years ago and became a worldwide wave in the mid-1900s. Since the 1960s, however, political and economic hegemony has taken a new and fast-paced form—namely, globalization (in many ways, a phenomenon that expands on imperialism). Both forms of global domination—colonialism and globalization—are examined in *Essence*, culminating in the final chapter where we apply the concept of structural power to globalization, discussing it in terms of hard and soft power and linking it to structural violence.

PEDAGOGY

The Essence of Anthropology features a range of learning aids, in addition to the three unifying themes described above. Each pedagogical piece plays an important role in the learning process—from clarifying and enlivening the material to revealing relevancy and aiding recall.

Accessible Language and a Cross-Cultural Voice

What could be more basic in pedagogy than clear communication? In addition to our standing as professional anthropologists, all four co-authors devote time to addressing audiences outside of our profession. Using that experience in the writing of our textbooks, we make a point of cutting through unnecessary jargon to speak directly to students. Manuscript reviewers have recognized this, noting that even the most difficult concepts are presented in accessible and straightforward prose that is easy for today's first- and second-year college students to understand, without being dumbed down. Where technical terms are necessary, they appear in bold type, are carefully defined in the narrative, and are defined again in the running glossary in simple, clear language. There is also a complete glossary of these terms at the end of the book.

To make the narrative more accessible to students, we have broken it up into smaller bites, shortening the length of the paragraphs. We have also inserted additional subheads to provide visual cues to help students track what has been read and what is coming next.

Accessibility involves not only clear writing enhanced by visual cues, but also a broadly engaging voice or style. The voice of *Essence* is distinct among introductory texts in the discipline, for it has been written from a cross-cultural perspective. We avoid the typical Western "we/they" voice in favor of a more inclusive one that will resonate with both Western and non-Western students and professors. Moreover, the book highlights the theories and work of anthropologists from all over the world. Finally, its cultural examples come from industrial and postindustrial societies as well as nonindustrial ones.

Strong Visuals

Haviland et al. texts repeatedly garner high praise from students and faculty for having a rich array of visuals, including maps, photographs, and figures. This is important since humans—like all primates—are visually oriented, and a well-chosen image may serve to "fix" key information in a student's mind. Unlike some competing texts, all of our visuals are in color, enhancing their appeal and impact. This new edition of *Essence* features two more photographs per chapter than our first edition, and we have enlarged many of these images to increase their impact.

New in this edition is the Visual Essence feature—opening each chapter with an especially compelling photograph accompanied by a paragraph that prods students to take a deep look at the photo, while establishing in broad strokes the essence of that particular chapter. As authors with strong backgrounds in the visual arts and communication, we are keenly aware of the pull and power of images—especially for this generation of students who are so enculturated in visual media. Through the Visual Essence introducing each chapter, we aim to help students see the anthropological details of each photograph and glimpse the essence of the chapter they are beginning.

Thought-Provoking Questions for Reflection

Each chapter closes with Questions for Reflection designed to stimulate and deepen thought, trigger class discussion, and link the material to the student's own life.

Clarifying Chapter Outlines and Closing Summaries

At the beginning of each chapter, we include an outline of key topics that sets up a mental framework for the material covered. And at the end of each chapter, we provide a bulleted summary that recaps the more important ideas presented in the chapter. These summaries are handy study guides for reviewing the chapter content.

Engaging Original Studies

Selected from ethnographies and other original works by anthropologists or written expressly for Haviland et al., these studies present concrete examples that bring specific concepts to life and convey the passion of their authors. Each study sheds additional light on an important anthropological concept or subject area found in the chapter where it appears. Notably, each Original Study is integrated within the flow of the chapter narrative, signaling students that the content is not extraneous or supplemental.

Featured in eleven chapters, these studies cover a range of topics: "Fighting HIV/AIDS in Africa: Traditional Healers on the Front Line" by Suzanne Leclerc-Madlala; "Ninety-Eight Percent Alike: What Our Similarity to Apes Tells Us about Our Understanding of Genetics" by Jonathan Marks; "Reconciliation and Its Cultural Modification in Primates" by Frans B. M. de Waal; "The Real Dirt on Rainforest Fertility" by Charles C. Mann; "A Feckless Quest for the Basketball Gene" by Jonathan Marks; "Language and the Intellectual Abilities of Orangutans" by H. Lyn White Miles; "The Blessed Curse" by R. K. Williamson; "Arranging Marriage in India" by Serena Nanda; "African Burial Ground Project" by Michael Blakey; "Healing among the Ju/'hoansi of the Kalahari" by Marjorie Shostak; and "Standardizing the Body: The Question of Choice" by Laura Nader.

Relevant Anthropology Applied Features

These succinct and compelling profiles illustrate anthropology's wide-ranging relevance in today's world and give students a glimpse into a variety of the careers anthropologists enjoy. Featured in six of the chapters, they include: "Forensic Anthropology: Voices for the Dead"; "Stone Tools for Modern Surgeons"; "Action Archaeology and the Community at El Pilar" by Anabel Ford; "New Houses for Apache Indians" by George S. Esber; "Agricultural Development and the Anthropologist" by Ann Kendall; and "Dispute Resolution and the Anthropologist" about William Ury.

Biocultural Connection Features

Appearing in every chapter, this feature illustrates how cultural and biological processes interact to shape human biology, beliefs, and behavior. It reflects the integrated biocultural approach central to the field of anthropology today. The sixteen features (several of them new) include: "The Anthropology of Organ Transplantation"; The Social Impact of Genetics on Reproduction"; "Nonhuman Primates and Human

Disease"; "Evolution and Human Birth"; "Breastfeeding, Fertility, and Beliefs"; "Social Stratification and Diseases of Civilization: Tuberculosis"; "Paleolithic Prescriptions for Today's Diseases"; "Pig Lovers and Pig Haters" by Marvin Harris; "The Biology of Human Speech"; "Down Syndrome Across Cultures" by Katherine A. Dettwyler; "Surviving in the Andes: Aymara Adaptation to High Altitude"; "Marriage Prohibitions in the United States" by Martin Ottenheimer; "Maori Origins: Ancestral Genes and Mythical Canoes"; "Gender, Sex, and Human Violence"; "Peyote Art: Divine Visions among the Huichol"; and "Toxic Breast Milk Threatens Arctic Culture."

The Barrel Model of Culture

To support the theme of systemic and dynamic adaptation, we use the "barrel model" of culture—depicted as a simple but telling drawing (Figure 8.2) that shows the interrelatedness of economic, social, and ideological factors within a cultural system, along with the outside influences of environment, climate, and other societies. Throughout the second half of the book, examples are linked back to this point and this image, ensuring that students catch the concept that every culture is an integrated and dynamic system of adaptation that responds to a combination of internal and external factors.

Integrated Gender Coverage

In contrast to many introductory texts, *Essence* integrates rather than separates gender coverage. Thus, material on gender-related issues is included in every chapter, emphasizing the fact that concepts and issues surrounding gender are almost always too complicated to remove from their context. Moreover, this integration demonstrates the pervasive significance of gender considerations in all human activity.

The inclusion of gender in the book's "biological" chapters allows students to grasp the analytic distinction between sex and gender, illustrating the subtle influence of gender norms on biological theories about sex difference. Gender-related material ranges from discussions of gender roles in evolutionary discourse and studies of nonhuman primates, to intersexuality, homosexual identity, same-sex marriage, and female genital mutilation. Through a steady drumbeat of such coverage, this edition avoids ghettoizing gender to a single chapter that is preceded and followed by resounding silence. And, overall, it provides considerably more gender-related material than the single chapter on the topic that most books contain. Also of note is an effort to avoid male-centered language in our descriptions.

Glossary as You Go

The running glossary is designed to catch the student's eye, reinforcing the meaning of each newly introduced term. It is also useful for chapter review, as the student may readily isolate the new terms and their definitions. A complete glossary is also included at the back of the book. In the glossaries each term is defined in clear, understandable language. As a result, less class time is required for going over terms, leaving instructors free to pursue matters of greater interest.

CHAPTER HIGHLIGHTS

The pedagogical features described above strengthen each of the sixteen chapters in *The Essence of Anthropology* by serving as threads that tie the text together and help students feel the holistic nature of the discipline. In addition, the engaging presentation of the concepts themselves provides students with a solid foundation in the principles and practices of anthropology today. The chapter highlights presented below offer a preview.

Chapter 1: The Essence of Anthropology

The opening chapter introduces students to the holistic discipline of anthropology, the unique focus of each of its subdisciplines, and the common philosophical and methodological approaches they share. This second edition has an expanded integrated methods section that replaces separate discussions that appeared scattered throughout the text in the previous edition. This approach emphasizes the commonalities of anthropological fieldwork while providing an overview of practices specific to each subdiscipline. The integrated discussion allows professors to cover methods early in the semester at the appropriate depth for their classrooms and also encourages students to see the links among all kinds of anthropological fieldwork. This approach also allows for an expanded discussion of ethics in anthropological research and the history of the development of anthropological ethics.

The chapter also has expanded its introduction to the subdisciplines of archaeology with coverage of technological innovations in archaeology and discussion of subspecializations, such as historical archaeology, zoo archaeology, bioarchaeology, and ethnobotany. The introduction to linguistics has been expanded to reflect the broad range of social and cultural topics that can be investigated through language. Two boxed features help illustrate the interconnection of biology and culture in the human experience: Suzanne Leclerc-Madlala's compelling Original Study, "Fighting HIV/AIDS in Africa: Traditional Healers on the Front Line," and a Biocultural Connection highlighting Margaret Lock's work on the anthropology of organ transplantation. An Anthropology Applied feature on forensic anthropology and archaeology illustrates the importance of forensics in the investigations of international human rights abuses. The chapter closes with a section titled "Anthropology and Globalization," in which we show the relevance of anthropology to several of today's most significant social and political issues.

Chapter 2: Biology and Evolution

This chapter provides clear but simple explanations of evolutionary processes at the population, individual, and molecular levels. Several new or updated figures enhance the chapter to make these biological processes all the more accessible. We integrate cultural and biological approaches through the historical exploration of the genetics revolution and have included the work of prominent scientists such as Rosalind Franklin, Charles Lyell, and Thomas Malthus that had not appeared in the previous edition.

The chapter's expanded Biocultural Connection, "The Social Impact of Genetics on Reproduction," features the work of cultural anthropologist Rayna Rapp and provides students with concrete examples of the influence of genetics on people's lives. Similarly, the Original Study "Ninety-Eight Percent Alike: What Our Similarity to Apes Tells Us about Our Understanding of Genetics" by biological anthropologist Jonathan Marks illustrates that scientific data are interpreted within human contexts. This Original Study is tied into our discussion of the alternative classificatory schemes (*hominin* versus *hominid*), allowing students to see that the schemes differ depending upon whether classification is based on genetic criteria or morphology. We include this discussion for two reasons: First, in the popular press students will notice that both *hominid* (*New York Times*) and *hominin* (*National Geographic*) are used. Second, practicing anthropologists such as their professors may prefer one term over the other. Having this discussion in the book makes the text compatible with both classificatory approaches. A simple, elegant table defining the various taxonomic levels accompanies this discussion.

Chapter 3: Living Primates

Here we survey the amazing diversity found in the biology and behavior of the major living primate groups, and we frame this discussion in terms of primate conservation. The statistics on primate extinction from the 2008 International Primatological Society Congress have been included along with a broad discussion of conservation that emphasizes globalization and habitat loss. While the chapter focuses particularly on the African ape species since they are most closely related

to humans, students will gain a broad understanding of the mammalian primate pattern of adaptation and the distinctions among the five major primate groups. For simplicity we employ the traditional grade distinction between prosimians and anthropoid primates (rather than the strepsirhine/haplorhine dichotomy) in our survey of diversity among living primates; we do, however, explain both systems to help students develop critical and abstract thinking by comparing those two approaches.

Content-rich figures help convey a great deal of material without excessive length. Gender issues are featured through the important perspectives of female primatologists and a balanced focus on both male and female primates in contemporary field studies. New research on cooperation among females that are not genetically related challenge kin selection theories; we also include studies on the visual spatial skills of chimps. Primatologist Frans de Waal's fascinating Original Study "Reconciliation and Its Cultural Modification in Primates" offers an excellent example of how primatologists have reworked older theories—in this case, the emphasis on aggression and male dominance hierarchies. Jane Goodall's work to protect the rights of chimpanzees used in biomedical research is featured in the chapter's Biocultural Connection.

Chapter 4: Human Evolution

This chapter begins with a discussion of the general principles and theories of macroevolution and a picture of how paleoanthropologists go about reconstructing evolutionary relationships and behavior in the past. New and revised figures help students grasp concepts like geological time, continental drift, climate change, and comparative anatomy. We have expanded our discussions of the self-correcting nature of science and the false notion of "biological progress" in this edition, as these ideas are critical to the analyses of cultures that follow in later chapters. Our streamlined overview of mammalian primate evolution concentrates on the essence of the fossil record during the last 5–8 million years, while including important new discoveries such as the 10-million-year-old fossils ancestral to gorillas.

We provide a solid overview of bipedalism and of the diversity among the australopithecines without getting bogged down in nomenclature. We explain that paleoanthropologists can take either a "lumping" or a "splitting" approach to the fossil record. Examining the genus *Homo*, we show the increasing importance of culture as a means of solving the challenges of existence as seen in the remains of ancient stone tools, hearths, dwellings, and art, and in the spread of humans from Africa to Asia and Europe. We provide students with an overview of the two major competing theories of modern human origins (recent African origins and multiregional hypothesis), and we explore the disputed place of the Neandertals in the process. Our goal here is to show how paleoanthropologists engage in debate as they reconstruct the past rather than come out in favor of one of these hypotheses. The chapter's Biocultural Connection, "Evolution and Human Birth," discusses the influence of contemporary gender roles and associated biomedical birth practices on theories of the evolution of human birth. The Anthropology Applied feature, "Stone Tools for Modern Surgeons," demonstrates the sophistication of ancient technology through their contemporary use in operating rooms.

Chapter 5: The Neolithic Revolution: The Domestication of Plants and Animals

The revolutionary Neolithic period ushered in a way of life that radically differed from the human trajectory up to this point. This chapter focuses on the major cultural changes of the Neolithic revolution—the domestication of plants and animals and settlements into villages. We examine theories to account for these cultural changes, provide a vocabulary with which students can understand the different mechanisms of change, and present a survey of the independent changes throughout the globe. Charles Mann's work on the New World and Jared Diamond's framework for understanding this revolution are included.

A discussion of differences in the rates of biological and cultural change provides students with a framework for thinking about human health—past, present, and future. The Biocultural Connection featuring the work of Melvin Konner and Carol Worthman on ovulation and breastfeeding practices among the Ju/'hoansi provides a concrete example of the interaction of cultural practice and human biology relevant to the Neolithic. A compelling Original Study, "The Real Dirt on Rainforest Fertility," describes the work in the Amazon by an international team of archaeologists that is making significant contributions to our understanding of farming practices in the past and to increasing the productivity of rainforest soil today.

Chapter 6: The Emergence of Cities and States

The framework used for this chapter's exploration of the emergence of cities and states is that many of today's problems of urban life and organized states originated in the earliest expressions of these novel social forms. We present the ancient monuments throughout the globe most readily associated with the field of archaeology, while exploring a range of theories that account for their development. Cities and states are not presented as a more advanced phase of cultural development, but rather as an emerging social system with its own

positive and negative features. Negative features include the environmental consequences and the production of stratified societies in which some classes of people have a greater share of resources than others. Positive features include the various vocational specializations characteristic of cities and states that foster technological and other developments.

The chapter presents a case study on the great Maya city Tikal, including a new figure that maps out the central city; this case study provides perspective on how archaeologists use the data they recover to reconstruct past behavior and beliefs. The practical knowledge that can be derived from archaeological study is emphasized in the Anthropology Applied feature, "Action Archaeology and the Community at El Pilar." This updated feature describes Anabel Ford's work to establish an international preserve known as a peace park (spanning Belize and Guatemala) and sustainable ecotourism surrounding El Pilar, the Maya site she discovered. A Biocultural Connection illustrates the relationship between poverty and disease that began with the earliest socially stratified societies and continues today.

Chapter 7: Modern Human Diversity: Race and Racism

We ground this exploration of human biological diversity in a discussion of how power relations rooted in colonialism and slavery have influenced the way this diversity has been portrayed. We use a historical approach to help students understand why race is not a valid biological category when applied to humans. The work of Linnaeus, Blumenbach, and Samuel Morton forms part of our discussion of the intellectual history of the classification of humans into a series of racial types. Revealing the role of 19th- and early 20th-century physical anthropology in maintaining these false racial hierarchies, we show that discrete human races do not exist. We also show the vital roles of anthropologists such as Franz Boas and Ashley Montagu in debunking biological race.

Having established the falsehood of biological race, we provide students with a framework for the appropriate study of human biological variation using clines. Global variation in skin pigmentation is presented as an example of adaptation to a specific environment. This discussion helps students see the difference between the legitimate study of human biological variation and the ways that social beliefs about biological difference can turn into racism. Jonathan Marks's Original Study, "The Feckless Quest for the Basketball Gene," reinforces these concepts. Closing the chapter, we examine the effects of the environment on human biological variation through several examples of microevolutionary change related to human health. A Biocultural Connection, "Paleolithic Prescriptions for Today's Diseases," introduces students to evolutionary medicine, which applies knowledge from human evolutionary history to health problems today.

Chapter 8: The Characteristics of Culture

Here we address anthropology's core concept of culture, exploring the term and its significance for individuals and societies. Elaborating on culture as the medium through which humans handle the problems of existence, we mark out its characteristics: Culture is learned, shared, based on symbols, integrated, and dynamic. The chapter includes discussions on culture and adaptation; the functions of culture; culture, society, and the individual; ethnocentrism; and culture change in the age of globalization. Special features include a new Biocultural Connection by Marvin Harris, "Pig Lovers and Pig Haters," and an Anthropology Applied, "New Houses for Apache Indians," updated by anthropologist George Esber who describes his role in designing culturally appropriate homes for a Native American community.

Also in this chapter is our original illustration of the barrel model of culture, which conveys the integrative and dynamic nature of culture. This model also introduces the concepts of infrastructure, social structure, and superstructure.

Chapter 9: Language and Communication

One of humankind's most distinctive characteristics is language, a sophisticated means of communication through which culture is transmitted from one generation to the next. In this chapter we investigate the nature of language and the three branches of linguistic anthropology—descriptive linguistics, historical linguistics, and the study of language in its social and cultural settings (ethnolinguistics and sociolinguistics). We look at language and gender, as well as processes of language divergence and language loss and revival, including a discussion of UNESCO's Initiative B@bel. We also look at language distribution on the Internet.

We discuss body language (proxemics and kinesics), paralanguage, and tonal languages (which comprise 70 percent of the world's languages), as well as the origins of language and the emergence of writing. The latter takes readers from traditional speech performatives and memory devices to Egyptian hieroglyphics to the conception and spread of the alphabet to the 2003–2012 Literacy Decade established by the United Nations. Finally, Chapter 9 presents two features—the popular Original Study on "Language and the Intellectual Ability of Orangutans" updated by its author, H. Lyn White Miles, and an illustrated Biocultural Connection on "The Biology of Human Speech."

Chapter 10: Social Identity, Personality, and Gender

Every culture teaches children the behavior that is expected of them as members of their community; this socialization ensures that individuals growing up in a community will contribute to its survival. Since adult personality is in large part the product of life experiences, the ways children are raised and educated significantly shape their later selves.

This chapter looks at individual identity within a sociocultural context. We survey a range of issues: the concept of self, enculturation and the behavioral environment, social identity through personal naming, the development of personality, the concepts of group and modal personality, and the idea of national character. The section on naming features a new ethnographic example of Navajo naming and the First Laugh ceremony with a photo. A substantial section titled "Alternative Gender Models from a Cross-Cultural Perspective" provides a thought-provoking historical overview of intersexuality, transsexuality, and transgendering, including current statistics on the incidence of intersexuality worldwide. Our discussion of normal and abnormal personality in social context offers a new subsection on *sadhus,* holy men in Hindu culture, and the mental disorders section includes a discussion of anorexia nervosa. The Biocultural Connection by Katherine Dettwyler, "Down Syndrome Across Cultures," provides a poignant account of this phenomenon, and R. K. Williamson offers a stirring Original Study on intersexuality, "The Blessed Curse."

Chapter 11: Subsistence and Exchange

Here we investigate the various ways humans meet their basic needs and how societies use culture to adapt to the environment. This connects to the subject matter of economic systems—the production, distribution, and consumption of goods—also covered in the chapter. We begin with a discussion of adaptation, followed by profiles on modes of subsistence in which we look at food-foraging and food-producing societies—pastoralism, crop cultivation, and industrialization. Under the heading "Subsistence and Economics," we delve into such matters as the control of resources (natural, technological, labor) and types of labor division (gender, age, cooperative labor, craft specialization). A section on distribution and exchange defines various forms of reciprocity (with a detailed, illustrated description of the Kula ring), along with redistribution (including a potlatch account) and market exchange. We also touch on leveling mechanisms and feature two new boxed features: a fascinating Biocultural Connection, "Surviving in the Andes: Aymara Adaptation to High Altitude," and an Anthropology Applied on agricultural development and anthropology.

Chapter 12: Sex, Marriage, and Family

This chapter looks at marriage and family in their various forms and the roles they play in meeting the challenges of human existence—from creating alliances that help ensure survival to regulating sexual activity to balance sexual desires with the need for stability and security. Exploring the close interconnection among sexual reproductive practices, marriage, family, and household, we discuss the household as the basic building block in a culture's social structure, the center where child rearing—as well as shelter, economic production, consumption, and inheritance—is commonly organized. And we explain that the core of the household usually consists of some form of family—people who are married to each other and/or a group of relatives stemming from the parent–child bond and the interdependence of men and women.

Particulars addressed in this chapter include the incest taboo, endogamy and exogamy, dowry and bride-price, cousin marriage, same-sex marriage, divorce, residence patterns, and non-family households. The chapter also includes a discussion contrasting past and present Christian and Muslim Shariah laws concerning the regulation of sexual relations; a passage on how new reproductive technologies (NRTs) are affecting the ways humans think about and form families; and definitions of marriage, family, nuclear family, and extended family that have been updated to encompass current situations around the world.

The chapter ends with a section titled "Marriage, Family, and Household in Our Globalized and Technologized World," which includes new material on migrant labor households. Also noteworthy are Serena Nanda's popular Original Study, "Arranging Marriage in India," and a Biocultural Connection on "Marriage Prohibitions in the United States," revised and updated by its author, Martin Ottenheimer.

Chapter 13: Kinship and Other Methods of Grouping

In most cultural systems, solutions to many organizational challenges (such as defense, resource allocation, and labor) are beyond the scope of family and household and require broader cooperative efforts based on kinship and other forms of grouping that help ensure material and emotional security. This chapter looks at the various forms of descent groups and the roles descent plays as an integrated feature in a cultural system. We present examples concerning lineages, clans, phratries, and moieties, followed by illustrations of a representative range of kinship systems and their kinship terminologies. A substantial section on grouping beyond kinship includes discussions of grouping by gender, age, and common interest.

The chapter next considers grouping based on social hierarchy, which leads into our much revised discussion of castes. We explore the historical context and role of caste in India's Hindu culture and present similar situations from other parts of the world. The chapter ends with a brief commentary on the role globalization plays in both increasing and decreasing social stratification. Special features include archaeologist Michael Blakey's "African Burial Ground Project" Original Study (which builds upon the Biocultural Connection on this topic featured in the last edition of *Essence*) and a new Biocultural Connection, "Maori Origins: Ancestral Genes and Mythical Canoes," which comes with an eye-catching photo and locator map.

Chapter 14: Politics, Power, and Violence

Inevitably, social living entails friction, which can escalate to anxiety and violence, undermining our need for structure and security. Thus, every society requires some means for resolving conflicts and preventing the breakdown of social order. This chapter investigates these issues as they present themselves within a range of uncentralized and centralized political systems—from kin-ordered bands and tribes, to chiefdoms and states. We explore the question of power, the intersection of politics and religion, and issues of political leadership and gender.

Discussing the maintenance of order, we look at internalized and externalized controls, along with social control through witchcraft and through law. We mark the functions of law and the ways different societies deal with crime—including new sentencing laws in Canada based on traditional Native American restorative justice techniques such as the Talking Circle. Then, shifting our focus from maintaining order within a society to political organization and external affairs, we discuss warfare and present a historical look at armed conflicts among humans. A new section, "Domination and Repression," considers the global inequities born of colonialism and features subsections on acculturation, ethnocide, and genocide. The chapter concludes with a new section, "Resistance to Domination and Repression," with subsections about violent and nonviolent resiΩstance. Special features in this chapter include a Biocultural Connection, "Gender, Sex, and Human Violence," and an Anthropology Applied box, "Dispute Resolution and the Anthropologist" about William Ury.

Chapter 15: Spirituality, Religion, and the Supernatural

We open this chapter with a discussion of the role of religion and spirituality (including a global overview of religions today), followed by a description of the anthropological approach to religion and a new section on myth. We then discuss beliefs concerning supernatural beings and powers: gods and goddesses, ancestral spirits, animism, animatism, and sacred spaces. A new section, "Performing Religion and Spirituality," overarches subsections on religious specialists (priests and priestesses, as well as shamans) and rituals and ceremonies (rites of passage and rites of intensification). Ethnographic examples include male initiation rites among Aborigines and female initiation rites among the Mende in West Africa, Navajo Indian sandpainting ceremonies, and Ju'hoansi trance dance healing rituals.

A section on shamanism explores the origins of the term and presents our shamanic complex model of how these healings take place. A substantial section on religion, magic, and witchcraft highlights Ibibio witchcraft. Touching on religion and culture change, this chapter introduces revitalization movements. We conclude the chapter with a very brief new section titled "Persistence of Religion and Spirituality." Special features here include a new Biocultural Connection on Huichol peyote art and an Original Study by Marjorie Shostak about Ju/'hoansi healers and the trance dance.

Chapter 16: Global Changes and the Role of Anthropology

Our final chapter—rich with global maps depicting pollution, migrations, and energy consumption—zeroes in on numerous global challenges confronting the human species today. It prompts students to use the anthropological tools they have learned to think critically about these issues and to help bring about a future in which humans live in harmony with one another and with the nature that sustains us all.

We begin with two new sections: "Modernization in the Age of Globalization" and "A Global Transnational Culture." The chapter offers a succinct historical tracing of human movement and interaction across the globe from 500 years ago through today's era of globalization. Under the heading "Structural Power in the Age of Globalization," we define and illustrate the term *structural power* and its two branches—hard power (military and economic might) and soft power (media might that gains control through ideological influence). The section on hard power includes a detailed, illustrated discussion of the rise of global corporations, and the section on soft power looks at our global media environment. We then address problems of structural violence—from pollution and global warming to epidemics of hunger and obesity, as well as psychological problems caused by powerful marketing messages that shape cultural standards concerning the ideal human body. We also investigate the roles structural power and violence play in internal and external migrations, touching on the lives of refugees, migrant workers, and diasporic communities. Special features include Laura Nader's Original Study, "Standardizing the Body: The Question of

Choice," and a new Biocultural Connection, "Toxic Breast Milk Threatens Arctic Culture." This chapter brings the book to a close with an encouraging note about anthropology's potential for helping to solve practical problems on local and global levels.

SUPPLEMENTS

The Essence of Anthropology, second edition, comes with a comprehensive supplements program to help instructors efficiently create an effective learning environment both inside and outside the classroom and to aid students in mastering the material.

Supplements for Instructors

Online Instructor's Manual with Test Bank for *The Essence of Anthropology*, Second Edition

The Instructor's Manual offers detailed chapter outlines, lecture suggestions, key terms, and student activities such as *InfoTrac® College Edition* exercises and *Anthropology Resource Center* exercises. In addition, there are over 75 chapter test questions including multiple choice, true-false, fill-in-the-blank, short answer, and essay. (ISBN: 0-495-60271-X)

PowerLecture® with ExamView (Windows/Macintosh) for *The Essence of Anthropology*, Second Edition

This easy-to-use tool includes preassembled Microsoft PowerPoint presentations using charts, graphs, line art, and images with a new zoom feature, from the book. PowerLecture® also features ExamView® testing software. Create, deliver, and customize tests and study guides (both print and online) in minutes with this easy-to-use assessment and tutorial system. ExamView® offers both a Quick Test Wizard and an Online Test Wizard that guide you step-by-step throughout the process of creating tests, while its unique "WYSWYG" capability allows you to see the test you are creating on screen exactly as it will print or display online. You can build tests of up to 250 questions using up to 12 question types. Using ExamView's complete word-processing capabilities, you can enter an unlimited number of new questions or edit existing questions. (ISBN: 0-495-60272-8)

WebTutor Toolbox for Blackboard® Printed Access Card *or* WebTutor Toolbox for WebCT® Printed Access Card for *The Essence of Anthropology*, Second Edition

WebTutor Toolbox provides access to all the content of this text's rich Book Companion website from within your course management system. Robust communication tools—such as course calendar, asynchronous discussion, real-time chat, a whiteboard, and an integrated e-mail system—make it easy for your students to stay connected to the course. (WebTutor Toolbox for Blackboard, ISBN: 0-495-83697-4; WebTutor Toolbox for WebCT, ISBN: 0-495-83696-6)

Wadsworth Anthropology Video Library

Qualified adopters may select full-length videos from an extensive library of offerings drawn from such excellent educational video sources as *Films for the Humanities and Sciences*. Please ask your Cengage sales consultant for information on these videos.

ABC Anthropology Video Series

This exclusive video series was created jointly by Wadsworth and ABC for the anthropology course. Each video contains approximately 60 minutes of footage originally broadcast on ABC within the past several years. The videos are broken into short 2- to 7-minute segments, perfect for classroom use as lecture launchers or to illustrate key anthropological concepts. An annotated table of contents accompanies each video, providing descriptions of the segments and suggestions for their possible use within the course. (ISBN: 0-495-83704-0)

Visual Anthropology Video

Bring engaging anthropology concepts to life with this dynamic 60-minute video from Documentary Educational Resources and Wadsworth Publishing. Video clips highlight key scenes from more than thirty new and classic anthropological films that serve as effective lecture launchers. This video is only available to instructors. (ISBN: 0-534-56651-0)

AIDS in Africa DVD

Southern Africa has been overcome by a pandemic of unparalleled proportions. This documentary series focuses on the new democracy of Namibia and the many actions that are being taken to control HIV/AIDS. Included in this series are four documentary films created by the Periclean Scholars at Elon University: (1) *Young Struggles, Eternal Faith,* which focuses on caregivers in the faith community; (2) *The Shining Lights of Opuwo,* which shows how young people share their messages of hope through song and dance; (3) *A Measure of Our Humanity,* which describes HIV/AIDS as an issue related to gender, poverty, stigma, education, and justice; and (4) *You Wake Me Up,* a story of two women who are HIV positive and their acts of courage helping other women learn to survive. Cengage/Wadsworth is excited to offer these award-winning films to instructors for use in class. When presenting topics such as gender, faith, culture, poverty, and so forth, the films will be enlightening for students and will expand their global perspective of HIV/AIDS. (ISBN: 0-495-17183-2)

Online Resources for Instructors and Students

Website for *The Essence of Anthropology,* Second Edition

Go to http://www.cengage.com/anthropology and click on *The Essence of Anthropology,* Second Edition, to reach the website that accompanies this book. This website offers many study aids, including tutorial quizzes for each chapter, a practice final exam, learning objectives, web links, flashcards, crossword puzzles, and more! (ISBN: 0-495-60273-6)

Anthropology Resource Center

This hands-on online center offers a wealth of information and useful tools for both instructors and students in all four fields of anthropology: cultural anthropology, physical anthropology, archaeology, and linguistics. It includes interactive maps, learning modules, video exercises, breaking news in anthropology, and more! For the instructor, an Image Bank of photos for instructional use only is provided, as well as a sample syllabus for easy integration of exercises from the *Anthropology Resource Center* into your course. (ISBN-10: 0-495-39454-8 | ISBN-13: 978-0-495-39454-9)

Turnitin Originality Checker

Turnitin provides an originality check of student papers; it offers a simple solution for instructors who want a strong deterrent against plagiarism, as well as encouragement for students to employ proper research techniques. Access is available for packaging with each copy of this book. For more information go to www.ichapters.com. (ISBN: 1-413-03018-1 [one semester])

InfoTrac® College Edition

Give your students access to an entire library's worth of reliable sources with InfoTrac College Edition, an online university library of more than 5,000 academic and popular magazines, newspapers, and journals. (ISBN: 0-534-55853-4)

Supplements for Students

Telecourse Study Guide for *The Essence of Anthropology,* Second Edition

This accompanies the video course, *Anthropology: The Four Fields,* and introduces the central concepts, concerns, and research methods of cultural anthropology to students, taking the course off-campus. This Study Guide contains a chapter preview, learning objectives, viewing notes to accompany the video lessons, questions to consider, key terms and concepts, a summary, and review questions. (ISBN: 0-495-83695-8)

Case Studies and Readings

Case Studies in Cultural Anthropology, edited by George Spindler and Janice E. Stockard

This volume offers a diverse array of case studies that emphasize culture change and the factors influencing change in the peoples depicted. New topics include *Challenging Gender Norms: Five Genders among the Bugis in Indonesia* by Sharyn Graham Davies (ISBN: 0-495-09280-0) and *Hawaiian Fisherman* by Ed Glazier, which looks at the social, political and economic aspects of fishing in Hawaii (ISBN: 0-495-00785-4). Visit www.cengage.com/anthropology for a complete listing of all case studies.

Case Studies on Contemporary Social Issues, edited by John A. Young

This volume offers a variety of case studies that explore how anthropology is used today in understanding and addressing problems faced by human societies around the world. Barry S. Hewlett and Bonnie L. Hewlett explore the cultural practices and politics affecting the spread of disease in their new case study entitled *Ebola, Culture and Politics: The Anthropology of an Emerging Disease* (ISBN 0-495-00918-0); James F. Eder explores livelihood and resource management as a result of global changes in the Philippines in the new case study, *Migrants to the Coasts: Livelihood, Resource Management, and Global Change in the Philippines* (ISBN: 0-495-09524-9); and Michael Ennis-McMillan explores water resource management in *A Precious Liquid: Drinking Water and Culture in the Valley of Mexico* (ISBN 0-534-61285-7). Visit www.cengage.com/anthropology for a complete listing of all case studies.

Case Studies in Archaeology, edited by Jeffrey Quilter

These engaging accounts of cutting-edge archaeological techniques, issues, and solutions—as well as studies discussing the collection of material remains—range from site-specific excavations to types of archaeology practiced. Visit www.cengage.com/anthropology for a complete listing of all case studies.

Classic and Contemporary Readings in Physical Anthropology, edited by Mary K. Sandford with Eileen M. Jackson

This accessible reader includes twenty-three selections that help students examine the question, "What does it mean to be human?" The book's collection of classic and contemporary readings stresses the importance of scientific principles and methods, including the applications of new technology, and covers five main areas of interest: the nature of science, evolution and heredity, primate behavior, human evolution, and modern human variation. (ISBN: 0-495-51014-9)

Classic Readings in Cultural Anthropology, Second Edition, edited by Gary Ferraro

Practical and insightful, this concise and accessible reader presents a core selection of historical and contemporary works that have been instrumental in shaping anthropological thought and research over the past decades. Readings are organized around eight topics that closely mirror most introductory textbooks and are selected from scholarly works on the basis of their enduring themes and contributions to the discipline. (ISBN: 0-495-50736-9)

Globalization and Change in Fifteen Cultures: Born in One World, Living in Another, edited by George Spindler and Janice E. Stockard

In this volume, fifteen case study authors write about culture change in today's diverse settings around the world. Each original article provides insight into the dynamics and meanings of change, as well as the effects of globalization at the local level. (ISBN: 0-534-63648-9)

Current Perspectives: Readings from InfoTrac® College Edition: Cultural Anthropology and Globalization

Ideal to supplement your cultural anthropology textbook, this new reader will evoke lively classroom discussions about the real-world challenges and opportunities of globalization. Selected articles about globalization are drawn from InfoTrac® College Edition's vast database of full-length, peer-reviewed articles from more than 5,000 top academic journals, newsletters, and periodicals. (ISBN: 0-495-00810-9)

Modules in Cultural and Physical Anthropology

Each free-standing module is actually a complete text chapter, featuring the same quality of pedagogy and illustration that are contained in Wadsworth/Cengage Learning anthropology texts.

Medical Anthropology in Applied Perspective, by Lynn Sikkink

Medical anthropology has become an ever-broadening field that is both interdisciplinary and applied, and many students will go to work in this field, whether it is in health care, medical research, childbirth, or development. This module introduces students to a variety of ways medical anthropologists work in the areas of illness and healing, food and nutrition, birth and reproduction, and health care. (ISBN-10: 0-495-10017-X | ISBN–13: 978-0-495-10017-1)

Human Environment Interactions: New Directions in Human Ecology, by Cathy Galvin

Cathy Galvin provides students with an introduction to the basic concepts in human ecology, before discussing cultural ecology, human adaptation studies, human behavioral ecology—including material on systems approaches and cognitive and critical approaches—and political ecology. She concludes the module with a discussion of resilience and global change as a result of human–environment interactions today and the tools used. (ISBN: 0-534-62071-X)

Evolution of the Brain: Neuroanatomy, Development, and Paleontology, by Daniel D. White

The human species is the only species that has ever created a symphony, written a poem, developed a mathematical equation, or studied its own origins. The biological structure that has enabled humans to perform these feats of intelligence is the human brain. This module explores the basics of neuroanatomy, brain development, lateralization, and sexual dimorphism and provides the fossil evidence for hominid brain evolution. (ISBN-10: 0-495-12903-8 | ISBN-13: 978-0-49512-9035)

Forensic Anthropology Module: A Brief Review, by Diane France

Diane France provides information on forensic anthropology in various situations: the myths and realities of the search for human remains in crime scenes; forensic anthropology in the courtroom; some of the special challenges of mass fatality incidents, such as plane crashes and terrorist acts; and what students should consider if they want to purse a career in forensic anthropology. (ISBN: 0-534-58812-3)

Molecular Anthropology Module, by Leslie Knapp

Leslie Knapp explores how molecular genetic methods are used to understand the organization and expression of genetic information in humans and nonhuman primates. Students will learn about the common laboratory methods used to study genetic variation and evolution in molecular anthropology. Examples are drawn from up-to-date research on human evolutionary origins and comparative primate genomics to demonstrate that scientific research is an ongoing process with theories frequently being questioned and reevaluated. (ISBN: 0-534-62069-8)

These resources are available to qualified adopters, and ordering options for student supplements are flexible. Please consult your local Cengage sales consultant for more information or to evaluate examination copies of any of these resources or to receive product demonstrations. You may also contact the Wadsworth Academic Resource Center at 800-423-0563 or visit us at academic.cengage.com. Additional information is also available at academic.cengage.com/anthropology/Haviland.

ACKNOWLEDGMENTS

In this day and age, no textbook comes to fruition without extensive collaboration. Beyond the shared endeavors of our author team, this book owes its completion to a wide range of individuals, from colleagues in the discipline to those involved in the production process. We are particularly grateful for the exceptional group of manuscript reviewers listed below. They provided detailed and thoughtful feedback that helped us to hone and re-hone our narrative.

> Beverly A. Davenport, University of North Texas
> Gloria Gozdzik, West Virginia University
> Gregory S. Gullette, Georgia State University
> David B. Halmo, University of Wisconsin, Parkside
> Patricia Jolly, University of Northern Colorado
> Susan M. Kenyon, Butler University
> Gabriele Kohpahl, California State University, Northridge
> Sarah W. Neusius, Indiana University of Pennsylvania
> Luz N. Perez Prado, University of Texas, San Antonio
> Janet Rafferty, Mississippi State University

We carefully considered and made use of the wide range of comments provided by these individuals. Our decisions on how to utilize their suggestions were influenced by our own perspectives on anthropology and teaching, combined with the priorities and page limits of this text. Thus, neither our reviewers nor any of the other anthropologists mentioned here should be held responsible for any shortcomings in this book. They should, however, be credited as contributors to many of the book's strengths.

Thanks, too, go to colleagues who provided material for some of the Original Study, Biocultural Connection, and Anthropology Applied features in this text: Michael Blakey, Katherine A. Dettwyler, George Esber, Anabel Ford, Marvin Harris, Ann Kendall, Suzanne Leclerc-Madlala, Margaret Lock, Charles C. Mann, Jonathan Marks, H. Lyn White Miles, Laura Nader, Serena Nanda, Martin Ottenheimer, Marjorie Shostak, William Ury, Frans B. M. de Waal, and R. K. Williamson.

We have debts of gratitude to office workers in our departments for their cheerful help in clerical matters: Karen Rundquist and Katie Weaver. And to research librarian extraordinaire Nancy Bianchi and colleagues Yvette Pigeon, Scott Waterman, Robert Gordon, Martin Ottenheimer, Harriet Ottenheimer, Jeffrey Ehrenreich, Michael Wesch, Tiffany Kershner, and Laura Bathurst for engaging in lively discussions of anthropological and pedagogical approaches. Also worthy of note here are the introductory anthropology teaching assistants who, through the years, have shed light for us on effective ways to reach new generations of students.

Our thanksgiving inventory would be incomplete without mentioning individuals at Wadsworth/Cengage Learning who helped conceive this text and bring it to fruition. Special gratitude goes to senior development project manager Lin Marshall Gaylord for her vision, anthropological knowledge, and unique longevity as our key publishing contact. Our thanks also go out to Wadsworth's skilled and enthusiastic editorial, marketing, design, and production team: Marcus Boggs (West Coast editorial director), Andrew Keay (media editor), Arwen Petty (editorial assistant), Erin Abney and Liana Monari (assistant editors), as well as Jerilyn Emori (content project manager) and Caryl Gorska (art director).

In addition to all of the above, we have had the invaluable aid of several most able freelancers, including Joan Keyes of Dovetail Publishing Services; Lisa Buckley of Buckley Design; Carol Reitz, proofreader; Jenna Gray at Pre-Press PMG of PreMedia Global, Inc.; and our expert and enthusiastic photo researcher Billie Porter, who was always willing to go the extra mile to find the most telling and compelling photographs. We are especially thankful to have had the opportunity to work once again with copyeditor Jennifer Gordon, whose keen eye and kind manner keep our t's crossed and our temperaments steady.

And finally, all of us are indebted to family members who have not only put up with our textbook preoccupation but cheered us on in the endeavor. Dana had the tireless support and keen eye of husband Peter Bingham—along with the varied contributions of their three sons Nishan, Tavid, and Aram Bingham. As coauthor spouses under the same roof, Harald and Bunny have picked up slack for each other on every front to help this project move along smoothly. And, as always, Bill (and the entire team) extends great gratitude to his spouse Anita de Laguna Haviland, who remains remarkably interested in and attentive to the production of the book.

VISUAL ESSENCE

Part of being human is our fascination with ourselves. Where did we come from? Why do we act in certain ways? What makes us tick? While some answer these questions with biological mechanisms and others with social or spiritual explanations, the discipline of anthropology addresses them through a holistic, integrated approach. Anthropology considers human culture and biology, in all times and places, as inextricably intertwined, each affecting the other in important ways. This photograph, taken in a specialized maternity clinic in Gujarat, India, provides a case in point. Since commercial surrogacy—the practice of paying a woman to carry someone else's fetus to term—became legal in India in 2002, wealthy childless people from all over the globe travel to India for this service. Chosen by foreigners because of their healthy drug-free lifestyle and lower cost, Indian women take on extra biological risk to allow others to reproduce their genes. Numerous biological and cultural complexities surround the lives of every individual involved.

The Essence of Anthropology

1

THE ANTHROPOLOGICAL PERSPECTIVE

Anthropology is the study of humankind in all times and places. Of course many other research disciplines are concerned in one way or another with humans. For example, anatomy and physiology focus on our species as biological organisms. The social sciences are concerned with human relationships, while the humanities examine artistic and philosophical achievements in human cultures. Anthropology is distinct because of its focus on the interconnections and interdependence of all aspects of the human experience in all places, in the present and deep into the past, well before written history. This unique, broad **holistic perspective** equips anthropologists to address that elusive thing we call human nature.

Anthropologists welcome the contributions of researchers from other disciplines and in return offer their own findings for the benefit of these other disciplines. Anthropologists do not expect to know as much about the structure of the human eye as anatomists or as much about the perception of color as psychologists. As synthesizers, however, they are prepared to understand how these bodies of knowledge relate to color-naming practices in different societies. Because they look for the broad basis of ideas and practices without limiting themselves to any single social or biological aspect, anthropologists can acquire

anthropology The study of humankind in all times and places
holistic perspective A fundamental principle of anthropology, that the various parts of human culture and biology must be viewed in the broadest possible context in order to understand their interconnections and interdependence

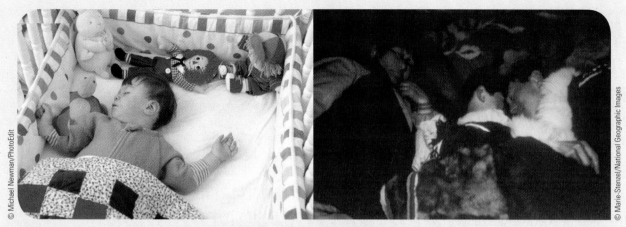

The photo on the right shows a Nenet family sleeping together in their *chum* (reindeer-skin tent). Nenet people are arctic reindeer pastoralists living in Siberia. Although infants in the United States typically sleep apart from their parents, cross-cultural research shows that co-sleeping, of mother and baby in particular, is the rule.

an especially expansive and inclusive overview of the complex biological and cultural organism that is the human being.

The holistic perspective also helps anthropologists stay keenly aware of ways that their own cultural ideas and values may impact upon their research. As the old saying goes, people often see what they believe, rather than what appears before their eyes. By maintaining a critical awareness of their own assumptions about human nature—checking and rechecking the ways their beliefs and actions might be shaping their research—anthropologists strive to gain objective knowledge about people. With this in mind, anthropologists aim to avoid the pitfalls of **ethnocentrism**, a belief that the ways of one's own culture are the only proper ones. Thus, anthropologists have contributed

ethnocentrism The belief that the ways of one's own culture are the only proper ones
culture-bound Theories about the world and reality based on the assumptions and values of one's own culture
applied anthropology The use of anthropological knowledge and methods to solve practical problems, often for a specific client
medical anthropology A specialization in anthropology that brings theoretical and applied approaches from cultural and biological anthropology to the study of human health and disease
physical anthropology Also known as biological anthropology. The systematic study of humans as biological organisms
molecular anthropology A branch of biological anthropology that uses genetic and biochemical techniques to test hypotheses about human evolution, adaptation, and variation

uniquely to our understanding of diversity in human thought, biology, and behavior, as well as to our understanding of the many things humans have in common.

While other social sciences have predominantly concentrated on contemporary peoples living in North American and European (Western) societies, anthropologists have traditionally focused on non-Western peoples and cultures. Anthropologists work with the understanding that to fully access the complexities of human ideas, behavior, and biology, *all humans*, wherever and whenever, must be studied. A cross-cultural and long-term evolutionary perspective distinguishes anthropology from other social sciences. This approach guards against the danger that theories of human behavior will be **culture-bound**—that is, based on assumptions about the world and reality that come from the researcher's own particular culture.

As a case in point, consider the fact that infants in the United States typically sleep apart from their parents. To people accustomed to multi-bedroom houses, cribs, and car seats, this may seem normal, but cross-cultural research shows that "co-sleeping," of mother and baby in particular, is the rule. Further, the practice of sleeping apart favored in Western industrialized societies dates back only about 200 years.

Recent studies have shown that separation of mother and infant in Western societies has important biological and cultural consequences. For one thing, it increases the length of the infant's crying bouts. Some mothers incorrectly interpret their infants' tears as a deficiency in breast milk and switch to feeding them bottled formula, proven to be less healthy. In extreme cases, the crying may provoke physical abuse. But the benefits of co-sleeping go beyond significant reductions in crying: The higher frequency and longer duration of each feeding for breast fed babies stimulates their brain development. They are apparently less susceptible to sudden infant death syndrome (SIDS or "crib death"). There are benefits to the mother as well: Frequent nursing prevents early ovulation after childbirth, it promotes loss of weight gained during pregnancy, and nursing mothers get at least as much sleep as mothers who sleep without their infants.[1]

These benefits may lead one to ask: Why do so many mothers continue to sleep apart from their infants? In North America the cultural values of independence and consumerism come into play. To begin building individual identities, babies are provided with rooms (or at least space) of their own. This room of one's own also provides parents with a place for the toys, furniture, and other paraphernalia associated with "good" and "caring" parenting in North America.

ANTHROPOLOGY AND ITS FIELDS

Individual anthropologists tend to specialize in one of four fields or subdisciplines: physical (biological) anthropology, cultural anthropology, linguistic anthropology, or archaeology (Figure 1.1). Some anthropologists consider archaeology and linguistics as part of the broader study of human cultures, but archaeology and linguistics also have close ties to biological anthropology.

Figure 1.1 **The Four Fields of Anthropology**
Note that the divisions between them are not sharp, indicating that their boundaries overlap.

---

[1]Barr, R. G. (1997, October). The crying game. *Natural History*, 47. Also, McKenna, J. J. (2002, September–October). Breastfeeding and bedsharing. *Mothering*, 28–37.

For example, while linguistic anthropology focuses on the cultural aspects of language, it has deep connections to the evolution of human language and the biological basis of speech and language studied within physical anthropology.

Each of anthropology's fields may take a distinct approach to the study of humans, but all gather and analyze data that are essential to explaining similarities and differences among humans, across time and space. Moreover, all of them generate knowledge that has numerous practical applications. Individuals within each of the four fields practice **applied anthropology**, which entails the use of anthropological knowledge and methods to solve practical problems. Applied anthropologists do not offer their perspectives from the sidelines. Instead, they actively collaborate with the communities where they work—setting goals, solving problems, and conducting research together. In this book, examples of how anthropology contributes to solving a wide range of the challenges humans face appear in Anthropology Applied features.

One of the earliest contexts in which anthropological knowledge was applied to a practical problem was the international public health movement that began in the 1920s. This marked the beginning of **medical anthropology**—a specialization that brings theoretical and applied approaches from the fields of cultural and biological anthropology to the study of human health and disease. The work of medical anthropologists sheds light on the connections between human health and political and economic forces, both locally and globally. Examples of this specialization appear in some of the Biocultural Connections featured in this text, including the one presented in this chapter, "The Anthropology of Organ Transplantation."

Physical Anthropology

Physical anthropology, also called *biological anthropology*, focuses on humans as biological organisms. Traditionally, biological anthropologists concentrated on human evolution, primatology, growth and development, human adaptation, and forensics. Today, **molecular anthropology**, or the anthropological study of genes and genetic relationships, contributes significantly to the contemporary study of human biological diversity. Comparisons among groups separated by time, geography, or the frequency of a particular gene can reveal how humans have adapted and where they have migrated. As experts in the anatomy of human bones and tissues, physical anthropologists lend their knowledge about the body to applied areas such as gross anatomy laboratories, public health, and criminal investigations.

Biocultural Connection

The Anthropology of Organ Transplantation

In 1954, the first organ transplant occurred in Boston when surgeons removed a kidney from one identical twin to place it inside his sick brother. Though some transplants rely upon living donors, routine organ transplantation largely depends on the availability of organs obtained from individuals who have died.

From an anthropological perspective, the meanings of death and the body vary cross-culturally. While death could be said to represent a particular biological state, social agreement about this state's significance is of paramount importance. Anthropologist Margaret Lock has explored differences between Japanese and North American acceptance of the biological state of "brain death"

and how it affects the practice of organ transplants.

Brain death relies upon the absence of measurable electrical currents in the brain and the inability to breathe without technological assistance. The brain-dead individual, though attached to machines, still seems alive with a beating heart and pink cheeks. North Americans find brain death acceptable, in part, because personhood and individuality are culturally located in the brain. North American comfort with brain death has allowed for the "gift of life" through organ donation and subsequent transplantation.

By contrast, in Japan the concept of brain death is hotly contested, and organ transplants are rarely performed. The Japanese do not incorporate a

mind–body split into their models of themselves and locate personhood throughout the body rather than in the brain. They resist accepting a warm pink body as a corpse from which organs can be "harvested." Further, organs cannot be transformed into "gifts" because anonymous donation is not compatible with Japanese social patterns of reciprocal exchange.

Organ transplantation carries far greater social meaning than the purely biological movement of an organ from one individual to another. Cultural and biological processes are tightly woven into every aspect of this new social practice.

(Based on Margaret Lock (2001). Twice dead: Organ transplants and the reinvention of death. *Berkeley: University of California Press)*

Paleoanthropology

Human evolutionary studies (known as **paleoanthropology**) focus on biological changes through time to understand how, when, and why we became the kind of organisms we are today. In biological terms, we humans are primates, one of the many kinds of mammals. Because we share a common ancestry with other primates, most specifically apes, paleoanthropologists look back to the earliest primates (65 or so million years ago), or even the earliest mammals (225 million years ago), to reconstruct the complex path of human evolution. Paleoanthropology, unlike other evolutionary studies, takes a **biocultural** approach focusing on the interaction of biology and culture.

The fossilized skeletons of our ancestors allow paleoanthropologists to reconstruct the course of human evolutionary history. They compare the size and shape of these fossils to one another and to the bones of living species. With each new fossil discovery, paleoanthropologists have another piece to add to human evolutionary history. Biochemical and genetic studies add

considerably to the fossil evidence. As we will see in later chapters, genetic evidence establishes the close relationship between humans and ape species—chimpanzees, bonobos, and gorillas. Genetic analyses indicate that the distinctive human line originated 5 to 8 million years ago. Physical anthropology therefore deals with much greater time spans than archaeology or other branches of anthropology.

Primatology

Studying the anatomy and behavior of the other primates helps us understand what we share with our closest living relatives and what makes humans unique. Therefore, **primatology**, or the study of living and fossil primates, is a vital part of physical anthropology. Primates include the Asian and African apes, as well as monkeys, lemurs, lorises, and tarsiers.

Biologically, humans are members of the ape family—large-bodied, broad-shouldered primates with no tail. Detailed studies of ape behavior in the wild indicate that the sharing of learned behavior is a significant part of their social life. Increasingly, primatologists designate the shared, learned behavior of nonhuman apes as *culture.* For example, tool use and communication systems indicate the elementary basis of language in some ape societies. Primate studies offer scientifically grounded perspectives on the behavior of our ancestors, as well as greater appreciation and respect for the

paleoanthropology The study of the origins and predecessors of the present human species
biocultural Focusing on the interaction of biology and culture
primatology The study of living and fossil primates

Though Jane Goodall originally began her studies of chimpanzees to shed light on the behavior of our distant ancestors, the knowledge she has amassed through over forty years in the field has reinforced how similar we are. In turn, she has devoted her career to championing the rights of our closest living relatives.

abilities of our closest living relatives. As human activity encroaches on all parts of the world, many primate species are endangered. Primatologists often advocate for the preservation of primate habitats so that these remarkable animals will be able to continue to inhabit the earth with us.

Human Growth, Adaptation, and Variation

Another specialty of physical anthropologists is the study of human growth and development. Anthropologists examine biological mechanisms of growth as well as the impact of the environment on the growth process. For example, Franz Boas, a pioneer of American anthropology of the early 20th century, compared the heights of immigrants who spent their childhood in "the old country" to the increased heights obtained by their children who grew up in the United States. Today, physical anthropologists study the impacts of disease, pollution, and poverty on growth. Comparisons between human and nonhuman primate growth patterns can provide clues to the evolutionary history of humans. Detailed anthropological studies of the hormonal, genetic, and physiological bases of healthy growth in living humans also contribute significantly to the health of children today.

Studies of human adaptation focus on the capacity of humans to adapt or adjust to their material environment—biologically and culturally. This branch of physical anthropology takes a comparative approach to humans living today in a variety of environments. Humans are remarkable among the primates in that they now inhabit the entire earth. Though cultural adaptations make it possible for humans to live in some environmental extremes, biological adaptations also contribute to survival in extreme cold, heat, and high altitude.

Some of these biological adaptations are built into the genetic makeup of populations. The long period of human growth and development provides ample opportunity for the environment to shape the human body. *Developmental adaptations* are responsible for some features of human variation such as the enlargement of the right ventricle of the heart to help push blood to the lungs among the Quechua Indians of highland Peru. *Physiological adaptations* are short-term changes in response to a particular environmental stimulus. For example, a woman who normally lives at sea level will undergo a series of physiological responses, such as the increased production of the red blood cells that carry oxygen, if she suddenly moves to a high altitude. All of these kinds of biological adaptation contribute to present-day human variation.

Human differences include visible traits such as height, body build, and skin color, as well as biochemical factors such as blood type and susceptibility to certain diseases. Still, we remain members of a single species. Physical anthropology applies all the techniques of modern biology to achieve fuller understanding of human variation and its relationship to the different environments in which people have lived. Physical anthropologists' research on human variation has debunked false notions of biologically defined races, a notion based on widespread misinterpretation of human variation.

Anthropology *Applied*   Forensic Anthropology: Voices for the Dead

Forensic anthropology is the identification of skeletal remains for legal purposes. Law enforcement authorities call upon forensic anthropologists to use skeletal remains to identify murder victims, missing persons, or people who have died in disasters, such as plane crashes. Forensic anthropologists have also contributed substantially to the investigation of human rights abuses in all parts of the world by identifying victims and documenting the cause of their death.

Among the best-known forensic anthropologists is Clyde C. Snow. He has been practicing in this field for over forty years, first for the Federal Aviation Administration and more recently as a freelance consultant. In addition to the usual police work, Snow has studied the remains of General George Armstrong Custer and his men from the 1876 battlefield at Little Big Horn, and in 1985, he went to Brazil, where he identified the remains of the notorious Nazi war criminal Josef Mengele.

He was also instrumental in establishing the first forensic team devoted

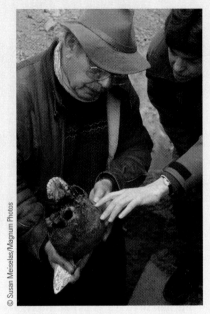

Physical anthropologists do not just study fossil skulls. Here Clyde Snow holds the skull of a Kurd who was executed by Iraqi security forces. Snow specializes in forensic anthropology and is widely known for his work identifying victims of state-sponsored terrorism.

© Susan Meiselas/Magnum Photos

to documenting cases of human rights abuses around the world. This began in 1984 when he went to Argentina at the request of a newly elected civilian government to help with the identification of remains of the *desaparecidos*, or "disappeared ones," the 9,000 or more people who were eliminated by government death squads during seven years of military rule. A year later, he returned to give expert testimony at the trial of nine junta members and to teach Argentineans how to recover, clean, repair, preserve, photograph, x-ray, and analyze bones. Besides providing factual accounts of the fate of victims to their surviving kin and refuting the assertions of "revisionists" that the massacres never happened, the work of Snow and his Argentinean associates was crucial in convicting several military officers of kidnapping, torture, and murder.

Since Snow's pioneering work, forensic anthropologists have become increasingly involved in the investigation of human rights abuses in all parts of the world, from Chile to Guatemala, Haiti, the Philippines, Rwanda, Darfur,

forensic anthropology Subfield of applied physical anthropology that specializes in the identification of human skeletal remains for legal purposes

cultural anthropology Also known as social or sociocultural anthropology. The study of customary patterns in human behavior, thought, and feelings. It focuses on humans as culture-producing and culture-reproducing creatures

culture A society's shared and socially transmitted ideas, values, and perceptions, which are used to make sense of experience and generate behavior and are reflected in that behavior

ethnography A detailed description of a particular culture primarily based on fieldwork

fieldwork The term anthropologists use for on-location research

participant observation In ethnography, the technique of learning a people's culture through social participation and personal observation within the community being studied, as well as interviews and discussion with individual members of the group over an extended period of time

ethnology The study and analysis of different cultures from a comparative or historical point of view, utilizing ethnographic accounts and developing anthropological theories that help explain why certain important differences or similarities occur among groups

Forensic Anthropology

One of the many practical applications of physical anthropology is **forensic anthropology**: the identification of human skeletal remains for legal purposes. Although they are called upon by law enforcement authorities to identify murder victims, forensic anthropologists also investigate human rights abuses such as systematic genocide, terrorism, and war crimes. These specialists use details of skeletal anatomy to establish the age, sex, population affiliation, and stature of the deceased. Forensic anthropologists can also determine whether the person was right- or left-handed, exhibited any physical abnormalities, or had experienced trauma. While forensics relies upon differing frequencies of certain skeletal characteristics to establish population affiliation, it is nevertheless false to say that all people from a given population have a particular type of skeleton. (See the Anthropology Applied feature to read about the work of several forensic anthropologists and forensic archaeologists.)

Iraq, Bosnia, and Kosovo. Meanwhile, they continue to do important work for more typical clients. In the United States these clients include the Federal Bureau of Investigation and city, state, and county medical examiners' offices.

Forensic anthropologists specializing in skeletal remains commonly work closely with forensic archaeologists. The relation between them is rather like that between a forensic pathologist, who examines a corpse to establish time and manner of death, and a crime scene investigator, who searches the site for clues. While the forensic anthropologist deals with the human remains—often only bones and teeth—the forensic archaeologist controls the site, recording the position of all relevant finds and recovering any clues associated with the remains. In Rwanda, for example, a team assembled in 1995 to investigate a mass atrocity for the United Nations included archaeologists from the U.S. National Park Service's Midwest Archaeological Center. They performed the standard archaeological procedures of mapping the site, determining its boundaries, photographing and recording all surface finds, and excavating, photographing, and recording skeletons and associated materials buried in mass graves.[a]

In another example, Karen Burns of the University of Georgia was part of a team sent to northern Iraq after the 1991 Gulf War to investigate alleged atrocities. On a military base where there had been many executions, she excavated the remains of a man's body found lying on its side facing Mecca, conforming to Islamic practice. Although there were no intact clothes, two threads of polyester used to sew clothing were found along the sides of both legs. Although the threads survived, the clothing, because it was made of natural fiber, had decayed. "Those two threads at each side of the leg just shouted that his family didn't bury him," says Burns.[b] Proper though his position was, no Islamic family would bury their own in a garment sewn with polyester thread; proper ritual would require a simple shroud.

In recent years two major anthropological analyses of skeletal remains have occurred in New York City, dealing with both past and present atrocities. Amy Zelson Mundorff, a forensic anthropologist for New York City's Office of the Chief Medical Examiner, was injured in the September 11, 2001, terrorist attack on the World Trade Center. Two days later she returned to work to supervise and coordinate the management, treatment, and cataloguing of people who lost their lives in the attack.

Just a short walk awa[...] workers in lower Manh[...] a 17th- and 18th-cent[...] ground in 1991 (see Chapter 1[...]. chaeological investigation of the burial ground revealed the horror of slavery in North America, showing that even young children were worked so far beyond their ability to endure that their spines were fractured. Biological archaeologist Michael Blakey, who led the research team, notes: "Although bioarchaeology and forensics are often confused, when skeletal biologists use the population as the unit of analysis (rather than the individual), and incorporate cultural and historical context (rather than simply ascribing biological characteristics), and report on the lifeways of a past community (rather than on a crime for the police and courts), it is bioarchaeology rather than forensics."[c]

Thus, several kinds of anthropologists analyze human remains for a variety of purposes contributing to the documentation and correction of atrocities committed by humans of the past and present.

[a]Conner, M. (1996). The archaeology of contemporary mass graves. SAA Bulletin, 14(4), 6, 31.

[b]Cornwell, T. (1995, November 10). Skeleton staff. Times Higher Education, 20.

[c]Blakey, M. (2003, October 29). Personal communication.

Cultural Anthropology

Cultural anthropology (also called *social* or *sociocultural anthropology*) is the study of patterns of human behavior, thought, and feelings. It focuses on humans as culture-producing and culture-reproducing creatures. Thus, in order to understand the work of the cultural anthropologist, we must clarify the meaning of "culture." The concept is discussed in detail in Chapter 8, but for our purposes here, we may think of **culture** as the (often unconscious) standards by which societies—structured groups of people—operate. These standards are socially learned, rather than acquired through biological inheritance. The manifestations of culture may vary considerably from place to place, but no person is "more cultured" in the anthropological sense than any other.

Cultural anthropology has two main components: ethnography and ethnology. An **ethnography** is a detailed description of a particular culture primarily based on **fieldwork**, which is the term all anthropologists use for on-location research. Because the hallmark of ethnographic fieldwork is a combination of social participation and personal observation within the community being studied, as well as interviews and discussions with individual members of a group, the ethnographic method is commonly referred to as **participant observation**. Ethnographies provide the information used to make systematic comparisons among cultures all across the world. Known as **ethnology**, such cross-cultural research allows anthropologists to develop theories that help explain why certain important differences or similarities occur among groups.

Ethnography

Through participant observation—residing in a community, sharing in activities including meals, learning how to speak and behave acceptably, and personally experiencing their habits and customs—the ethnographer is able to understand the culture of the society in which or she is doing fieldwork more fully than a nonparticipant researcher ever could. Being a participant observer does not mean that the anthropologist must join in a people's quarrels or fights in order to study a culture in which conflict is prominent; but by living in a community where violence is common, the ethnographer should be able to understand how aggression fits into the overall cultural framework. The ethnographer must observe carefully to gain an overview without placing too much emphasis on one part at the expense of another. Only by discovering how all aspects of a culture—its social, political, economic, and religious practices and institutions—relate to one another can the ethnographer begin to understand the cultural system. An ethnographer's most essential tools are notebooks, pen/pencil, camera, tape recorder, and, increasingly, a laptop computer. Most important of all, he or she needs flexible social skills.

The popular image of ethnographic fieldwork is that it occurs among people who live in far-off, isolated places. To be sure, much ethnographic work has been done in the remote villages of Africa or South America, the islands of the Pacific Ocean, the Indian tribal reservations of North America, the deserts of Australia, and so on. However, as the discipline of anthropology developed, Western industrialized societies also became a legitimate focus of anthropological study. Some of this shift occurred as scholars from non-Western cultures became anthropologists. Ethnographic fieldwork has transformed from expert Western anthropologists studying people in "other" places to collaborations among anthropologists from all parts of the world and the varied communities in which they work. Today, anthropologists from all around the globe employ the same research techniques that were used in the study of non-Western peoples to explore such diverse subjects as religious movements, street gangs, land rights, schools, marriage practices, conflict resolution, corporate bureaucracies, and health-care systems in Western cultures.

Ethnology

Largely descriptive in nature, ethnography provides the raw data needed for ethnology—the branch of cultural anthropology that involves cross-cultural comparisons and theories that explain differences or similarities among groups. Intriguing insights into one's own beliefs and practices may come from cross-cultural comparisons. Consider, for example, the amount of time spent on domestic chores by industrialized peoples and traditional food foragers (people who rely on wild plant and animal resources for subsistence). Anthropological research has shown that food foragers work far less at domestic tasks and other subsistence pursuits compared to people in industrialized societies. Urban women in the United States who were not working for wages outside their homes put 55 hours a week into their housework—this despite all the "labor-saving" dishwashers, washing machines, clothes dryers, vacuum cleaners, food processors, and microwave ovens. In contrast, aboriginal women in Australia devoted 20 hours a week to their chores.[2] Nevertheless, consumer appliances have become important indicators of a high standard of living in the United States due to the widespread belief that household appliances reduce housework and increase leisure time.

Considering such cross-cultural comparisons, one may think of ethnology as the study of alternative ways of doing things. But more than that, by making systematic comparisons, ethnologists seek to arrive at scientific conclusions concerning the function and operation of cultural practices in all times and places. Today cultural anthropologists contribute to applied anthropology in a variety of contexts ranging from business to education to health care to governmental interventions to humanitarian aid.

Linguistic Anthropology

Perhaps the most distinctive feature of the human species is language. Although the sounds and gestures made by some other animals—especially apes—may serve functions comparable to those of human language, no other animal has developed a system of symbolic communication as complex as that of humans. Language allows people to preserve and transmit countless details of their culture from generation to generation.

The branch of anthropology that studies human languages is called **linguistic anthropology**. Although it shares data and methods with the discipline of linguistics, it differs in that it uses these to answer anthropological questions. When this field began, it emphasized the documentation of languages of cultures under ethnographic study—particularly those whose future seemed precarious. Mastery of Native American languages—with grammatical structures so different from the

---

linguistic anthropology The study of human languages
discourse An extended communication on a particular subject

[2]Bodley, J. H. (1985). *Anthropology and contemporary human problems* (2nd ed., p. 69). Palo Alto, CA: Mayfield.

Indo-European and Semitic languages to which Euramerican scholars were accustomed—prompted the notion of *linguistic relativity*. This refers to the idea that linguistic diversity reflects not just differences in sounds and grammar but differences in ways of looking at the world. For example, the observation that the language of the Hopi Indians of the American Southwest had no words for *past, present,* and *future* led the early proponents of linguistic relativity to suggest that the Hopi people had a unique conception of time.[3] Similarly, the observation that English-speaking North Americans use a number of slang words—such as *dough, greenback, dust, loot, bucks, change, paper, cake, moolah, benjamins,* and *bread*—to refer to money could be a product of linguistic relativity. The profusion of names helps to identify a thing of special importance to a culture. Similarly, the importance of money within North American culture is also evident in the equation of money with time in phrases such as "time is money," "a waste of time," and "spend some time."

Complex ideas and practices integral to a culture's survival can also be reflected in language. For example, among the Nuer, a nomadic group that travels with grazing animals throughout southern Sudan, a baby born with a visible deformity is not considered a human baby. Instead it is called a baby hippopotamus. This name allows for the safe return of the "hippopotamus" to the river where it belongs. Such infants would not be able to survive in Nuer society, and so linguistic practice is compatible with the compassionate choice the Nuer have had to make.

The notion of linguistic relativity has been challenged by theorists who propose that the human capacity for language is based on biological universals that underlie all human thought. Recently, Stephen Pinker has even suggested that, at the universal biological level, thought is nonverbal.[4] A holistic anthropological approach considers language as dependent on both a biological basis shared by all humans and specific cultural patterning.

In order to examine anthropological questions through linguistic analyses, linguistic anthropologist Dell Hymes developed a framework that focused on specific speech events.[5] Such events form a **discourse** or an extended communication on a particular subject. Within a speech event or series of events, the researcher can focus on features such as the physical and psychological setting, the participants, the purpose, the sequence, and social rules. For example, linguistic anthropologists may deal with the relationship between language and the social roles/identity within a society. How does financial status, age, or gender affect the way individuals use their culture's language? The linguistic anthropologist might examine whether the tendency for females in the United States to end statements with an upward inflection, as though the statement were a question, reflects a pattern of male dominance in this society. Because members of any culture may use a variety of different registers and inflections, the ones they choose to use at a specific instance to express their thoughts convey particular meanings.

Linguistic anthropologists also focus on the socialization process through which an individual becomes part of a culture. Children take on this fundamental task as they grow and develop, but it can be seen in adults as well. Adults may need to assimilate because of a geographic move or because they are taking on a professional identity. First-year medical students, for example, amass 6,000 new vocabulary words and a series of linguistic conventions as they begin to take on the role of a physician.

As with the anthropological perspective on culture, language is similarly regarded as alive, malleable, and changing. Online tools such as Urban Dictionary track the changes in North American slang, and traditional dictionaries include new words and usages each year. These language changes have important implications as linguistic anthropologists track them to increase our understanding of the human past. By working out relationships among languages and examining their spatial

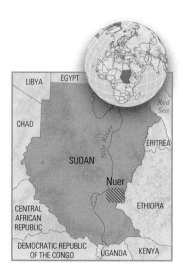

---

[3]Whorf, B. (1946). The Hopi language, Toreva dialect. In *Linguistic structures of Native America*. New York: Viking Fund.

[4]Pinker, S. (1994). *The language instinct: How the mind creates language*. New York: William Morrow.
[5]Hymes, D. (1974). *Foundations in sociolinguistics: An ethnographic approach*. Philadelphia: University of Pennsylvania Press.

distributions, linguistic anthropologists may estimate how long the speakers of those languages have lived where they do. By identifying those words in related languages that have survived from an ancient ancestral tongue, anthropological linguists can also suggest not only where, but how, the speakers of the ancestral language lived. Such work has shown, for example, linguistic ties between geographically distant groups such as the people of Finland and Turkey.

Linguistic anthropology is practiced in a number of applied settings. For example, linguistic anthropologists have collaborated with ethnic minorities in the revival of languages suppressed or lost during periods of oppression by another ethnic group. Anthropologists have helped to create written forms of languages that previously existed only orally. These examples of applied linguistic anthropology represent the kind of true collaboration that is characteristic of anthropological research today.

Archaeology

Archaeology is the branch of anthropology that studies human cultures through the recovery and analysis of material remains and environmental data. Such material products include tools, pottery, hearths, and enclosures that remain as traces of cultural practices in the past, as well as human, plant, and marine remains, some of which date back 2.5 million years. The arrangement of these traces, as much as the traces themselves, reflects specific human ideas and behavior. For example, shallow, restricted concentrations of charcoal that include oxidized earth, bone fragments, and charred plant remains, located near pieces of fire-cracked rock, pottery, and tools suitable for food preparation, indicate cooking and food processing. Such remains can reveal much about a people's diet and subsistence practices. Together with skeletal remains, these material remains help archaeologists reconstruct the biocultural context of past human lifeways. Archaeologists organize this material through time and use it to explain cultural variability and culture change through time.

archaeology The study of human cultures through the recovery and analysis of material remains and environmental data
bioarchaeology The archaeological study of human remains, emphasizing the preservation of cultural and social processes in the skeleton
cultural resource management A branch of archaeology concerned with survey and/or excavation of archaeological and historical remains threatened by construction or development and policy surrounding protection of cultural resources

Because archaeological research is explicitly tied to unearthing material remains in particular environmental contexts, a variety of innovations in the geographical and geological sciences have been readily incorporated into archaeological research. Innovations such as geographic information systems (GIS), remote sensing, and ground penetrating radar (GPR) complement traditional explorations of the past through archaeological digs.

Archaeologists can reach back for clues to human behavior far beyond the mere 5,000 years to which historians are confined by their reliance on written records. Calling this time period "prehistoric" does not mean that these societies were less interested in their history or that they did not have ways of recording and transmitting history. It simply means that written records do not exist. That said, archaeologists are not limited to the study of societies without written records; they may study those for which historic documents are available to supplement the material remains. In most literate societies, written records are associated with governing elites rather than with farmers, fishers, laborers, or slaves, and therefore they include the biases of the ruling classes. In fact, according to James Deetz, a pioneer in historical archaeology of the Americas, in many historical contexts, "material culture may be the most objective source of information we have."[6]

Archaeological Subspecializations

While archaeologists tend to specialize in particular culture zones or time periods, connected with particular regions of the world, a number of topical subspecializations also exist. **Bioarchaeology**, for example, is the archaeological study of human remains, emphasizing the preservation of cultural and social processes in the skeleton. For example, mummified skeletal remains from the Andean highlands in South America preserve not only this burial practice but also provide evidence of some of the earliest brain surgery ever documented. In addition, these bioarchaeological remains exhibit skull deformation techniques that distinguish nobility from other members of society.

Other archaeologists specialize in *ethnobotany*, studying how people of a given culture made use of indigenous plants. Still others specialize in *zooarchaeology*, tracking the animal remains recovered in archaeological excavations.

Although most archaeologists concentrate on the past, some of them study material objects in contemporary settings. One example is the Garbage Project,

[6]Deetz, J. (1977). *In small things forgotten: The archaeology of early American life* (p. 160). Garden City, NY: Anchor Press/Doubleday.

founded by William Rathje at the University of Arizona in 1973. This anthropological study of household waste of Tucson residents continues to produce thought-provoking information about contemporary social issues. For example, when surveyed by questionnaires, only 15 percent of households report the consumption of beer but no household reported more than eight cans a week. Analysis of garbage from the same area showed that some beer was consumed in over 80 percent of the households, and 50 percent of households discarded more than eight cans per week.

In addition to providing actual data on beer consumption, the Garbage Project has tested the validity of research survey techniques, upon which sociologists, economists, other social scientists and policymakers rely heavily. The tests show a significant difference between what people *say* they do and what the garbage analysis shows they *actually* do. Ideas about human behavior based on simple survey techniques therefore may be seriously in error.

Cultural Resource Management

While archaeology may conjure up images of ancient pyramids and the like, much archaeological fieldwork is carried out as **cultural resource management**. What distinguishes this work from traditional archaeological research is that it is part of activities legislated to preserve important aspects of a country's prehistoric and historic heritage. For example, in the United States, if the transportation department of a state government plans to replace an inadequate highway bridge, steps have to be taken to identify and protect any significant prehistoric or historic resources that might be affected by this new construction. Since passage of the Historic Preservation Act of 1966, the National Environmental Policy Act of 1969, and the Archaeological and Historical Preservation Act of 1974, cultural resource

management is required for any construction project that is partially funded or licensed by the U.S. government. As a result, the field of cultural resource management has flourished. Many archaeologists are employed by such agencies as the Army Corps of Engineers, the National Park Service, the U.S. Forest Service, and the U.S. Natural Resource Conservation Service to assist in the preservation, restoration, and salvage of archaeological resources.

When cultural resource management work or other archaeological investigation unearths Native American cultural items or human remains, federal laws come into the picture again. The Native American Graves Protection and Repatriation Act (NAGPRA), passed in 1990, provides a process for the return of these remains to lineal descendants, culturally affiliated Indian tribes, and Native Hawaiian organizations. NAGPRA has become central to the work of anthropologists who study Paleo-Indian cultures in the United States. The Kennewick Man controversy highlights some of the ethics debates surrounding NAGPRA.

In addition to working in all the capacities mentioned, archaeologists also consult for engineering firms to help them prepare environmental impact statements. Some of these archaeologists operate out of universities and colleges, while others are on the staff of independent consulting firms. When state legislation sponsors any kind of archaeological work it is referred to as *contract archaeology*.

ANTHROPOLOGY, SCIENCE, AND THE HUMANITIES

With its broad scope of subjects and methods, anthropology has sometimes been called the most humane of the sciences and the most scientific of the humanities—a designation that most anthropologists accept with pride. Given their intense involvement with people of all times and places, anthropologists have amassed considerable information about human failure and success, weakness and greatness—the real stuff of the humanities. While anthropologists steer clear of a "cold" impersonal scientific approach that reduces people and the things they do and think to mere numbers, their quantitative studies have contributed substantially to the scientific study of the human condition. But even the most scientific anthropologists always keep in mind that human societies are made up of individuals with rich assortments of emotions and aspirations that demand respect.

Beyond this, anthropologists remain committed to the proposition that one cannot fully understand another culture by simply observing it; as the term *participant*

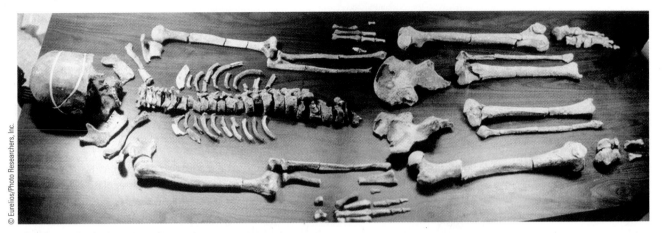

© Eurelios/Photo Researchers, Inc.

"The Ancient One" and the "Kennewick Man" both refer to the 9,300-year-old skeletal remains that were found in 1996 near Kennewick, Washington. Surrounded by controversy since its discovery, Kennewick Man is among the earliest ever made in the western hemisphere and has great potential to advance scientific understanding of ancient lifeways and migration patterns in the Americas. Because Kennewick Man was found within their ancestral homelands, a group of Native American tribes claimed the remains under the Native American Graves Protection and Repatriation Act (NAGPRA). Viewing these human bones as belonging to an ancestor, they wish to return them to the earth in a respectful ceremony. Scientists challenged this in federal court, and in 2004, the scientists were granted permission to continue research and analysis of the remains. Doug Owsley, the forensic anthropologist from the Smithsonian Institution who is leading the research team, has said that scientific investigation is yielding even more information than expected. Because conflicting worldviews are at the center of this controversy, it is unlikely that it will be easily resolved.

observation implies, one must *experience* it as well. This same commitment to fieldwork and to the systematic collection of data, whether it is qualitative or quantitative, is also evidence of the scientific side of anthropology. Anthropology is an **empirical** social science based on observations or information about humans taken in through the senses and verified by others rather than on intuition or faith. But anthropology is distinguished from other sciences by the diverse ways in which scientific research is conducted within this discipline.

Science, a carefully honed way of producing knowledge, aims to reveal and explain the underlying logic, the structural processes that make the world "tick." The creative scientific endeavor seeks testable explanations for observed phenomena, ideally in terms of the workings of hidden but unchanging principles or laws. Two basic ingredients are essential for this: imagination and skepticism. Imagination, though having the potential to lead us astray, helps us recognize unexpected ways phenomena might be ordered and to

think of old things in new ways. Without it, there can be no science. Skepticism allows us to distinguish fact (an observation verified by others) from fancy, to test our speculations, and to prevent our imaginations from running away with us.

In their search for explanations, scientists do not assume that things are always as they appear on the surface. After all, what could be more obvious than the earth staying still while the sun travels around it every day?

Like other scientists, anthropologists often begin their research with a **hypothesis** (a tentative explanation or hunch) about the possible relationships between certain observed facts or events. By gathering various kinds of data that seem to ground such suggested explanations on evidence, anthropologists come up with a **theory**— an explanation supported by a reliable body of data. In their effort to demonstrate linkages between *known* facts or events, anthropologists may discover *unexpected* facts, events, or relationships. An important function of theory is that it guides us in our explorations and may result in new knowledge. Equally important, the newly discovered facts may provide evidence that certain explanations, however popular or firmly believed to be true, are unfounded. When the evidence is lacking or fails to support the suggested explanations, promising hypotheses or attractive hunches must be dropped. In other words, anthropology relies on empirical evidence. Moreover, no scientific theory—no matter how widely

empirical Based on observations of the world rather than on intuition or faith
hypothesis A tentative explanation of the relationships between certain phenomena
theory In science, an explanation of natural phenomena, supported by a reliable body of data
doctrine An assertion of opinion or belief formally handed down by an authority as true and indisputable

accepted by the international community of scholars—is beyond challenge.

It is important to distinguish between scientific theories—which are always open to future challenges born of new evidence or insights—and doctrine. A **doctrine**, or dogma, is an assertion of opinion or belief formally handed down by an authority as true and indisputable. For instance, those who accept a creationist doctrine on the origin of the human species as recounted in sacred texts or myths do so on the basis of religious authority, conceding that such views may be contrary to genetic, geological, biological, or other explanations. Such doctrines cannot be tested or proved one way or another: They are accepted as matters of faith.

Straightforward though the scientific approach may seem, its application is not always easy. For instance, once a hypothesis has been proposed, the person who suggested it is strongly motivated to verify it, and this can cause one to unwittingly overlook negative evidence and unanticipated findings. This is a familiar problem in all science as noted by paleontologist Stephen Jay Gould: "The greatest impediment to scientific innovation is usually a conceptual lock, not a factual lock."[7] Because culture provides humans with their concepts and shapes our very thoughts, it can be challenging to frame hypotheses or develop interpretations that are not culture-bound. By encompassing both humanism and science, the discipline of anthropology can draw on its internal diversity to overcome conceptual locks.

FIELDWORK

All anthropologists think about whether their culture may have shaped the scientific questions they ask. In so doing, they rely heavily on a technique that has been successful in other disciplines: They immerse themselves in the data to the fullest extent possible. In the process, anthropologists become so thoroughly familiar with even the smallest details that they can begin to recognize underlying patterns in the data, many of which might have been overlooked. Recognition of such patterns enables the anthropologist to frame meaningful hypotheses, which then may be subjected to further testing or validation in the field. Within anthropology, fieldwork provides additional rigor to the concept of total immersion in the data.

While fieldwork was introduced above in connection with cultural anthropology, it is characteristic of *all* the anthropological subdisciplines. Archaeologists and paleoanthropologists excavate in the field. A biological anthropologist interested in the effects of globalization on nutrition and growth will live in the field among a community of people to study this question. A primatologist might live among a group of chimpanzees or baboons just as a linguist will study the language of a community by living in that community. Fieldwork, being immersed in another culture, challenges the anthropologist to be constantly aware of the ways that cultural factors influence the research questions. Anthropological researchers self-monitor through constantly checking their own biases and assumptions as they work; they present these self-reflections along with their observations, a practice known as *reflexivity*.

Unlike many other social scientists, anthropologists usually do not go into the field armed with prefigured questionnaires. Though they will have completed considerable background research and some tentative hypotheses, anthropologists recognize that many of the best discoveries are made by maintaining an open mind. As fieldwork proceeds, anthropologists sort out their observations, sometimes by formulating and testing limited or low-level hypotheses, or by intuition. The anthropologist works closely with the community so that the research process can become a collaborative effort. The results are constantly checked for consistency, for if the parts fail to fit together in a manner that is consistent, then the anthropologist knows that a mistake may have been made and that further inquiry is necessary. Validity or the reliability of a researcher's conclusions is established through the replication of observations and/or experiments by another researcher. Thus, it becomes obvious if one's colleague has "gotten it right."

Traditional validation by others is uniquely challenging in anthropology because observational access is often limited. Access to a particular research site can be constrained by a number of factors. Difficulties of travel, obtaining permits, insufficient funding, or social, political, and environmental conditions can hamper the process, and what may be observed in a certain context at a certain time may not be at others, and so on. Thus, one researcher cannot easily confirm the reliability or completeness of another's account. For this reason, anthropologists bear a special responsibility for accurate reporting. In the final research report, she or he must be clear about several basic things: Why was a particular location selected as a research site? What were the research objectives? What were the local conditions during fieldwork? Which local individuals provided the key information and major insights? How were the data collected and recorded? How did the researcher check his/her own biases? Without such background information, it is difficult for others to judge the validity of the account and the soundness of the researcher's conclusions.

On a personal level, fieldwork requires the researcher to step out of his or her cultural comfort zone

[7]Gould, S. J. (1989). *Wonderful life* (p. 226). New York: Norton.

into a world that is unfamiliar and sometimes unsettling. Anthropologists in the field are likely to face a host of challenges—physical, social, mental, political, and ethical. They may have to deal with the physical challenge of adjusting to unaccustomed food, climate, and hygiene conditions. Typically, anthropologists in the field struggle with such mental challenges as loneliness, feeling like a perpetual outsider, being socially clumsy and clueless in their new cultural setting, and having to be alert around the clock because anything that is happening or being said may be significant to their research. Political challenges include the possibility of unwittingly letting oneself be used by factions within the community, or being viewed with suspicion by government authorities who may suspect the anthropologist is a spy. And there are ethical dilemmas: what to do if faced with a cultural practice one finds troubling, such as female circumcision; how to deal with demands for food supplies and/or medicine; the temptation to use deception to gain vital information; and so on.

At the same time, fieldwork often leads to tangible and meaningful personal, professional, and social rewards, ranging from lasting friendships to vital knowledge and insights concerning the human condition that make positive contributions to people's lives. Something of the meaning of anthropological fieldwork—its usefulness and its impact on researcher and subject—is conveyed in the following Original Study by Suzanne Leclerc-Madlala, an anthropologist who left her familiar New England surroundings nearly twenty-five years ago to do AIDS research among Zulu-speaking people in South Africa. Her research interest has changed the course of her own life, not to mention the lives of individuals who have AIDS/HIV and the type of treatment they receive.

Original Study

Fighting HIV/AIDS in Africa: Traditional Healers on the Front Line

Suzanne Leclerc-Madlala

In the 1980s, as a North American anthropology graduate student at George Washington University in Washington, DC, I met and married a Zulu-speaking student from South Africa. It was the height of apartheid, and upon moving to that country I was classified as "honorary black" and forced to live in a segregated township with my husband. The AIDS epidemic was in its infancy, but it was clear from the start that an anthropological understanding of how people perceive and engage with this disease would be crucial for developing interventions. I wanted to learn all that I could to make a difference, and this culminated in earning a Ph.D. from the University of Natal on the cultural construction of AIDS among the Zulu. The HIV/AIDS pandemic in Africa became my professional passion.

Faced with overwhelming global health-care needs, the World Health Organization passed a series of resolutions in the 1970s promoting collaboration between traditional and modern medicine. Such moves held a special relevance for Africa where traditional healers typically outnumber practitioners of modern medicine by a ratio of 100 to 1 or more. Given Africa's

disproportionate burden of disease, supporting partnership efforts with traditional healers makes sense. But what sounds sensible today was once considered absurd, even heretical. For centuries Westerners generally viewed traditional healing as a whole lot of primitive mumbo jumbo practiced by witchdoctors with demonic powers who perpetuated superstition. Yet, its practice survived. Today, as the African continent grapples with an HIV/AIDS epidemic of crisis proportion, millions of sick people who are either too poor or too distant to access modern health care are proving that traditional healers are an invaluable resource in the fight against AIDS.

Of the world's estimated 40 million people currently infected by HIV, 70 percent live in sub-Saharan Africa, and the vast majority of children left orphaned by AIDS are African. From the 1980s onward, as Africa became synonymous with the rapid spread of HIV/AIDS, a number of prevention programs involved traditional healers. My initial research in South Africa's KwaZulu-Natal province—where it is estimated that 36 percent of the population is HIV infected—revealed that traditional Zulu

healers were regularly consulted for the treatment of sexually transmitted disease (STD). I found that such diseases, along with HIV/AIDS, were usually attributed to transgressions of taboos related to birth, pregnancy, marriage, and death. Moreover, these diseases were often understood within a framework of pollution and contagion, and like most serious illnesses, ultimately believed to have their causal roots in witchcraft.

In the course of my research, I investigated a pioneer program in STD and HIV education for traditional healers in the province. The program aimed to provide basic biomedical knowledge about the various modes of disease transmission, the means available for prevention, the diagnosing of symptoms, the keeping of records, and the making of patient referrals to local clinics and hospitals.

Interviews with the healers showed that many maintained a deep suspicion of modern medicine. They perceived AIDS education as a one-way street intended to press them into formal health structures and convince them of the superiority of modern medicine. Yet, today, few of the 6,000-plus KwaZulu-Natal healers who have been trained in AIDS education say they would opt for less collaboration; most want to have more.

Treatments by Zulu healers for HIV/AIDS often take the form of infusions of bitter herbs to "cleanse" the body, strengthen the blood, and remove misfortune and "pollution." Some treatments provide effective relief from common ailments associated with AIDS such as itchy skin rashes, oral thrush, persistent diarrhea, and general debility. Indigenous plants such as *unwele* (*Sutherlandia frutescens*) and African potato (*Hypoxis hemerocallidea*) are well-known traditional medicines that have proven immunoboosting properties. Both have recently become available in modern pharmacies packaged in tablet form. With modern anti-retroviral treatments still well beyond the reach of most South Africans, indigenous medicines that can delay or alleviate some of the suffering caused by AIDS are proving to be valuable and popular treatments.

Knowledge about potentially infectious bodily fluids has led healers to change some of their practices. Where porcupine quills were once used to give a type of indigenous injection, patients are now advised to bring their own sewing needles to consultations. Patients provide their own individual razor blades for making incisions on their skin, where previously healers reused the same razor on many clients. Some healers claim they have given up the practice of biting clients' skin to remove foreign objects from the body. It is not uncommon today, especially in urban centers like Durban, to find healers proudly displaying AIDS training certificates in their inner-city "surgeries" where they don white jackets and wear protective latex gloves.

Politics and controversy have dogged South Africa's official response to HIV/AIDS. But back home in the

© Kerry Cullinan

Medical anthropologist Suzanne Leclerc-Madlala visits with "Doctor" Koloko in KwaZulu-Natal, South Africa. This Zulu traditional healer proudly displays her official AIDS training certificate.

waddle-and-daub, animal-skin-draped herbariums and divining huts of traditional healers, the politics of AIDS holds little relevance. Here the sick and dying are coming in droves to be treated by healers who have been part and parcel of community life (and death) since time immemorial. In many cases traditional healers have transformed their homes into hospices for AIDS patients. Because of the strong stigma that still plagues the disease, those with AIDS symptoms are often abandoned or sometimes chased away from their homes by family members. They seek refuge with healers who provide them with comfort in their final days. Healers' homes are also becoming orphanages as healers respond to what has been called the "third wave" of AIDS destruction: the growing legions of orphaned children.

The practice of traditional healing in Africa is adapting to the changing face of health and illness in the context of HIV/AIDS. But those who are suffering go to traditional healers not only in search of relief for physical symptoms. They go to learn about the ultimate cause of their disease—something other than the immediate cause of a sexually transmitted "germ" or "virus." They go to find answers to the "why me and not him" questions, the "why now" and

"why this." As with most traditional healing systems worldwide, healing among the Zulu and most all African ethnic groups cannot be separated from the spiritual concerns of the individual and the cosmological beliefs of the community at large. Traditional healers help to restore a sense of balance between the individual and the community, on one hand, and between the individual and the cosmos, or ancestors, on the other hand. They provide health care that is personalized, culturally appropriate, holistic, and tailored to meet the needs and expectations of the patient. In many ways it is a far more satisfactory form of healing than that offered by modern medicine.

Traditional healing in Africa is flourishing in the era of AIDS, and understanding why this is so requires a shift in the conceptual framework by which we understand, explain, and interpret health. Anthropological methods and its comparative and holistic perspective can facilitate, like no other discipline, the type of understanding that is urgently needed to address the AIDS crisis.

(By Suzanne Leclerc-Madlala. Adapted in part from S. Leclerc-Madlala (2002). Bodies and politics: Healing rituals in the democratic South Africa. *In V. Faure (Ed.),* Les cahiers de 'l'IFAS, *No. 2. Johannesburg: The French Institute)*

FIELD METHODS

While fieldwork and the comparative method cut across all anthropological fields, some particular methods are characteristic only of paleoanthropology and archaeology with their focus on humans and their ancestors in the distant past. Other methods are typical of research focused on the cultures of contemporary societies. Some additional methods particular to primatology and linguistic anthropology will be described in Chapters 3 and 9, respectively.

Archaeological and Paleoanthropological Methods

Archaeologists and paleoanthropologists face a dilemma. The only way to thoroughly investigate our past is to excavate sites where biological and cultural remains are found. Unfortunately, excavation results in the site's destruction. Thus, anthropologists attempt to excavate in such a way that the location and context of everything recovered, no matter how small, are precisely recorded. Without these records, knowledge that can be derived from physical and cultural remains diminishes dramatically.

Archaeologists work with **artifacts**, any object fashioned or altered by humans—a flint scraper, a basket, an axe, or such things as house ruins or walls. An artifact expresses a facet of human culture. Because it is something that someone made, archaeologists like to say that an artifact is a product or representation of human behavior and beliefs, or, in

artifact Any object fashioned or altered by humans
material culture The durable aspects of culture such as tools, structures, and art
fossil The preserved remains of plants and animals that lived in the past
soil marks Stains that show up on the surface of recently plowed fields that reveal an archaeological site
middens A refuse or garbage disposal area in an archaeological site
grid system A system for recording data in three dimensions from an archaeological excavation
datum point The starting, or reference, point for a grid system
relative dating In archaeology and paleoanthropology, designating an event, object, or fossil as being older or younger than another
absolute or chronometric dating In archaeology and paleoanthropology, dates for archaeological or fossil materials based on solar years, centuries, or other units of absolute time

more technical terms, artifacts are **material culture**. Artifacts are not considered in isolation; rather, they are integrated with biological and ecological remains to provide a context that permits reconstruction of past lifeways. Some of the oldest biological remains have survived through the process of fossilization. Broadly defined, a **fossil** is any trace or impression of an organism that has been preserved in the earth's crust from past geologic time. Fossilization typically involves the hard parts of an organism. Bones, teeth, shells, horns, and the woody tissues of plants are the most successfully fossilized materials. Although the soft parts of an organism are rarely fossilized, the casts or impressions of footprints, brains, and even whole bodies have sometimes been found. Entirely preserved fossil skeletons dating from before the cultural practice of burial about 100,000 years ago are exceedingly rare.

Because dead animals quickly attract meat-eating scavengers and bacteria that cause decomposition, they rarely survive long enough to become fossilized. For an organism to become a fossil, it must be covered by some protective substance soon after death. The materials surrounding the physical remains gradually harden, forming a protective shell around the skeleton of the organism. The internal cavities of bones or teeth and other parts of the skeleton fill in with mineral deposits from the sediment immediately surrounding the specimen. Then the external walls of the bone decay and are replaced by calcium carbonate or silica.

Sites

Where are artifacts and fossils found? Places containing archaeological remains of previous human activity are known as *sites*. There are many kinds of sites, and sometimes it is difficult to define their boundaries, for remains may be strewn over large areas. Sites are even found underwater. Some examples of sites identified by archaeologists and paleoanthropologists are hunting campsites, from which hunters went out to hunt game; kill sites, in which game was killed and butchered; village sites, in which domestic activities took place; and cemeteries, in which the dead, and sometimes their belongings, were buried.

Locating and mapping archaeological sites are vital aspects of archaeological and paleoanthropological investigation. Many sites, particularly very old ones, frequently lie buried underground covered by layers of sediment deposited since the site was in use. Most sites are revealed by the presence of artifacts. But as we go back in time, the association of skeletal and cultural remains becomes less likely. Physical remains dating from before 2.5 million years ago are found without any associated cultural remains.

While chance may play a crucial role in a site's discovery, survey techniques in which the archaeologist explores and maps large geographic areas allow researchers to plot the sites available for excavation. A survey can be made from the ground, but more common today is the use of remote sensing techniques. Aerial photographs have been used by archaeologists to find sites since the 1920s. They are still widely used today along with more recent technological innovations such satellite mapping and ground penetrating radar (GPR) mentioned above.

Climate and geography can impact the discovery of archaeological and paleoanthropological sites. In open areas, sites are visible from the ground by mounds or **soil marks** or stains showing up on the surface of recently plowed fields. In forested regions changes in vegetation provide evidence of a site. For example, the topsoil of ancient storage and refuse pits is often richer in organic matter than that of the surrounding areas, and so it grows distinctive vegetation. At Tikal, an ancient Maya site in Guatemala, breadnut trees usually grow near the remains of ancient houses, so that archaeologists can use these trees to help guide their search.

Sometimes natural processes, such as soil erosion or droughts, expose sites or fossils. For example, in eastern North America and other areas where shellfish consumption was common, **middens**, prehistoric refuse mounds filled with shells, have been exposed by erosion along coastlines or river banks. As will be seen below, erosion and other geological processes have played a key role in fossil discovery.

Excavation and Analysis

Once an investigator identifies a site likely to contribute to the research agenda, the next step is to plan and carry out excavation. To begin, the land is cleared, and the places to be excavated are plotted as a **grid system**. The surface of the site is divided into squares of equal size, and each square is numbered and marked with stakes. Each object found may then be located precisely in the square from which it came. (Remember, context is everything!) The starting point of a grid system may be a large rock, the edge of a stone wall, or an iron rod sunk into the ground. This starting point, located precisely in three dimensions, is also known as the reference or **datum point**. At a large site covering several square miles, the plotting may be done in terms of individual structures, numbered according to the square of the "giant grid" in which they are found. In a gridded site, each square is dug separately with great care. Trowels are used to scrape the soil, and screens are used to sift all the loose soils so that even the smallest artifacts, such as flint chips or beads, are recovered.

The paleoanthropologist excavating fossils must be particularly skilled in the techniques of geology, or have ready access to geological expertise, because a fossil is of little value unless its place in the sequence of rocks that contain it can be determined. Surgical skill and caution are required to remove a fossil from its burial place without damage. An unusual combination of tools and materials is usually included in the kit of the paleoanthropologist—pickaxes, enamel coating, burlap for bandages, and sculpting plaster.

Both the fossil and the earth immediately surrounding it, or the matrix, are removed as a single block and brought to a laboratory. There, many more painstaking hours will be required to separate the fossil from the surrounding matrix. Before leaving the discovery area, the investigator makes a thorough sketch map of the terrain and pinpoints the find on geological maps to aid future investigators.

For both paleoanthropology and archaeology, at least three hours of laboratory work correspond to a single hour of excavation time. A wide variety of molecular and chemical techniques provide evidence about the context and nature of the recovered remains. Establishing the date of remains is particularly vital for the reconstruction of our past.

Remains can be dated by noting their position in the earth, by measuring the amount of chemicals contained in fossil bones and artifacts, or through association with other plant, animal, or cultural remains. These methods are known as **relative dating** techniques because they do not establish precise dates for remains but rather the relationship among a series of remains by using geological principles to place remains in chronological order. **Absolute dating** or **chronometric dating** (from the Latin for "measuring time") methods provide actual dates calculated in years "before the present" (BP). These methods rely upon advances in the disciplines of chemistry and physics that use properties such as rates of decay of radioactive elements. These elements may be present in the remains themselves or in the surrounding soil. Absolute dating methods scientifically establish actual dates for the major events of geological and evolutionary history. By comparing dates and remains across a variety of sites, anthropologists can reconstruct human origins, migrations, and technological developments.

Many relative and absolute dating techniques are available but each has certain weaknesses. Ideally, archaeologists and paleoanthropologists try to utilize as many methods as are appropriate, given the materials available and the funds at their disposal. By doing so, they significantly reduce the risk of error. Several of the most frequently employed dating techniques are presented in Table 1.1.

TABLE 1.1   ABSOLUTE AND RELATIVE DATING METHODS USED BY ARCHAEOLOGISTS AND PALEOANTHROPOLOGISTS

Dating Method	Time Period	Method's Process	Drawbacks
Stratigraphy	Relative only	Based on the law of superposition, which states that lower layers or strata are older than a higher stratum	Site specific; natural forces, such as earthquakes, and human activity, such as burials, disturb stratigraphic relationships
Fluorine analysis	Relative only	Compares the amount of fluorine from surrounding soil absorbed by specimens after deposition	Site specific
Faunal and floral series	Relative only	Sequencing remains into relative chronological order based on an evolutionary sequence established in another region with reliable absolute dates; called *palynology* when done with pollen grains	Dependent upon known relationships established elsewhere
Seriation	Relative only	Sequencing cultural remains into relative chronological order based on stylistic features	Dependent on known relationships established elsewhere
Dendrochronology	About 3,000 years before present (BP) maximum	Compares tree growth rings preserved in a site with a tree of known age	Requires ancient trees of known age
Radiocarbon	Accurate <50,000 BP	Compares the ratio of radioactive carbon 14 (^{14}C) (with a half-life of 5,730 years) to stable carbon 12 (^{12}C) in organic material	Increasingly inaccurate when assessing remains from more than 50,000 years ago
Potassium argon (K-Ar)	>200,000 BP	Compares the amount of radioactive potassium (^{40}K with a half-life of 1.25 billion years) to stable argon (^{40}Ar)	Requires volcanic ash; requires cross-checking due to contamination from atmospheric argon
Amino acid racemization	40,000–180,000 BP	Compares the change in the number of proteins in a right- versus left-sided three-dimensional structure	Amino acids leached out from soil variably cause error
Thermoluminescence	Possibly up to 200,000 BP	Measures the amount of light given off due to radioactivity when sample heated to high temperatures	Technique developed for recent materials such as Greek pottery; not clear how accurate the dates will be for older remains
Electron spin resonance	Possibly up to about 200,000 BP	Measures the resonance of trapped electrons in a magnetic field	Works with tooth enamel, not yet developed for bone; problems with accuracy
Fission track	Wide range of times	Measures the tracks left in crystals by uranium as it decays; good cross-check for K-Ar technique	Useful for dating crystals only
Paleomagnetic reversals	Wide range of times	Measures orientation of magnetic particles in stones and links them to whether magnetic field of earth pulled toward the north or south during their formation	Large periods of normal or reversed magnetic orientation require dating by some other method; some smaller events are known to interrupt the sequence
Uranium series	40,000–180,000	Measures the amount of uranium decaying in cave sites	Large error range

Ethnographic Methods

For the archaeologist and paleoanthropologist, fieldwork must take place where material and physical remains are located. For the ethnographic researcher, the entire world is a potential field site. The research problem or question can drive the choice of field site.

Anthropologists prepare for fieldwork by studying theoretical, historical, ethnographic, and any other literature relevant to the research problem to be investigated as well as studying all that has previously been documented about the particular culture they wish to study. Having delved into the existing literature, they may then formulate a theoretical framework and research question to guide them in their fieldwork. If possible, ethnographers make a preliminary trip to the field site before moving there for more extended research.

Because anthropologists must be able to communicate with the people they have chosen to study, they will also have to learn the people's language. Many of the 6,000 languages currently spoken in the world have already been recorded and written down, especially during the past hundred years or so. Therefore, anthropologists may learn many different languages prior to their fieldwork.

In the Field

When participating in an unfamiliar culture, anthropologists are often helped by one or more generous individuals in the village or neighborhood. They may also be taken in by a family; through participation in the daily routine of a household, they will soon become familiar with the community's basic shared cultural features.

Anthropologists may also formally enlist the assistance of **key consultants**—members of the society being studied—who provide information that helps researchers understand the meaning of what they observe. (Early anthropologists referred to such individuals as "informants.") Just as parents guide a child toward proper behavior, so do these insiders help researchers unravel the "mysteries" of what at first is a strange and puzzling world. To compensate local individuals for their help in making the anthropologists feel welcome in the community and gain access to the treasure troves of inside information, fieldworkers may thank them for their time and expertise with goods, services, or cash.

Asking questions is fundamental to ethnographic fieldwork and takes place in **informal interviews** (unstructured, open-ended conversations in everyday life) and **formal interviews** (structured question–answer sessions carefully notated as they occur and based on prepared questions). Informal interviews may be carried out anytime and anywhere—on horseback, in a canoe, by a cooking fire, during ritual events, while walking through the community, and so on. Such casual exchanges are essential, for it is often in these conversations that people share most freely. Moreover, questions put forth in formal interviews typically grow out of cultural knowledge and insights gained during informal ones.

Getting people to open up requires dropping all assumptions and cultivating the ability to ask questions and to *really* listen. Questions generally fall into one of two categories: broad, *open-ended questions*, such as, "Can you tell me about your childhood?" and *closed questions* seeking specific pieces of information, such as, "Where and when were you born?"

Researchers employ numerous **eliciting devices**—activities and objects used to draw out individuals and encourage them to recall and share information. For example, an ethnographic researcher may take and share photographs of cultural objects or activities and ask locals to explain what they see in the pictures.

Because many anthropologists still do fieldwork among traditional peoples in all corners of the earth, they may find themselves in distant places about which there is little detailed geographic knowledge. Therefore ethnographers frequently construct maps of the area under study that document the cultural meaning given to particular geographic features. Satellite geographic information systems (GIS) serve the ethnographer as they do the archaeologist and the paleoanthropologist.

The Ethnography

After collecting ethnographic information, the next challenge is to piece together all that has been gathered into a coherent whole that accurately describes the culture.

---

key consultants Members of the society being studied who provide information that helps the researchers understand the meaning of what they observe. Early anthropologists referred to such individuals as informants

informal interview An unstructured, open-ended conversation in everyday life

formal interview A structured question–answer session, carefully notated as it occurs and based on prepared questions

eliciting devices Activities and objects used to draw out individuals and encourage them to recall and share information

Traditionally, ethnographies are detailed written descriptions that document the culture under study in terms of the research question at hand. Ethnographers may focus on topics such as the circumstances and place of fieldwork itself; historical background; the community or group today; its natural environment, settlement patterns, subsistence practices, networks of kinship relations, and other forms of social organization; marriage and sexuality; economic exchanges; political institutions; myths, sacred beliefs, and ceremonies; and current developments. These may be illustrated with photographs and accompanied by maps, kinship diagrams, and figures showing social and political organizational structures, settlement layout, floor plans of dwellings, seasonal cycles, and so on.

Sometimes ethnographic research is documented not only in writing but also with sound recordings, on film or digital media. Visual records may be used not only for documentation and illustration, but also for analysis or as a means of gathering additional information in interviews. Moreover, motion picture or video footage shot for the sake of documentation and research may also be edited into a documentary film or a digital ethnography, which provides an accurate visual representation of the ethnographic subject.[8]

ANTHROPOLOGY'S COMPARATIVE METHOD

The end product of anthropological research, if properly carried out, is a coherent statement about a people that provides an explanatory framework for understanding the beliefs, behavior, or biology of those who have been studied. And this, in turn, is what permits the anthropologist to frame broader hypotheses about human beliefs, behavior, and biology. A single instance of any phenomenon is generally insufficient for supporting a plausible hypothesis. Without some basis for comparison, the hypothesis grounded in a single case may be no more than a particular historical coincidence. On the other hand, a single case may be enough to cast doubt on, if not refute, a theory that had previously been held to be valid. For example, the discovery in 1948 that aborigines living in Australia's northern Arnhem Land put in an average workday of less than 6 hours, while living well above a level of bare sufficiency, was enough to call into question the widely accepted notion that food-foraging peoples are so preoccupied with finding scarce food that they lack time for any of life's more pleasurable activities. The observations made in the Arnhem Land study have since been confirmed many times over in various parts of the world.

Hypothetical explanations of cultural and biological phenomena may be tested through comparison of archaeological, biological, linguistic, historical, and/or ethnographic data for several societies found in a particular region. Carefully controlled comparison provides a broader basis for drawing general conclusions about humans than does the study of a single culture or population.

A key resource for cross-cultural comparison is the **Human Relations Area Files (HRAF)**, a vast collection of cross-indexed ethnographic and archaeological data catalogued by cultural characteristics and geographic location. Initiated at Yale University in the mid-1900s, this ever-growing data bank classifies more than 700 cultural and biocultural characteristics and includes nearly 400 societies, past and present, from all around the world. Archived in about 300 libraries (on microfiche and/or online) and approaching a million pages of information, the HRAF facilitates comparative research on almost any cultural feature imaginable—warfare, subsistence practices, settlement patterns, birth practices, marriage, rituals, and so on.

Ideally, theories in anthropology are generated from worldwide comparisons or comparisons across species or through time. The cross-cultural researcher examines a global sample of societies in order to discover whether or not hypotheses proposed to explain cultural phenomena or biological variation are universally applicable. The cross-cultural researcher depends upon data gathered by other scholars as well as his or her own. These data can be in the form of written accounts, artifacts and skeletal collections housed in museums, published descriptions of these collections, or recently constructed databases that allow for cross-species comparisons of molecular structure of specific genes or proteins.

Human Relations Area Files (HRAF) A vast collection of cross-indexed ethnographic, biocultural, and archaeological data catalogued by cultural characteristics and geographic location. Archived in about 300 libraries (on microfiche or online)

informed consent Formal recorded agreement to participate in the research. Federally mandated for all researchers in the United States and Europe

---

[8]See Collier, J., & Collier, M. (1986). *Visual anthropology: Photography as a research method.* Albuquerque: University of New Mexico Press; el Guindi, F. (2004). *Visual anthropology: Essential method and theory.* Walnut Creek, CA: Altamira Press.

QUESTIONS OF ETHICS

The kinds of research carried out by anthropologists, and the settings within which they work, raise a number of important moral questions about the potential uses and abuses of our knowledge. In the early years of the discipline, many anthropologists documented traditional cultures they assumed would disappear due to disease, warfare, or acculturation imposed by colonialism, growing state power, or international market expansion. Some worked as government anthropologists, gathering data used to formulate policies concerning indigenous peoples or even to help predict the behavior of enemies during wartime. After the colonial era ended in the 1960s, anthropologists began to establish a code of ethics to ensure their research does not harm the groups they study.

This code grapples with questions such as: Who will utilize our findings and for what purposes? Who decides what research questions are asked? Who, if anyone, will profit from the research? For example, in the case of research on an ethnic or religious minority whose values may be at odds with dominant mainstream society, will governmental or corporate interests use anthropological data to suppress that group? And what of traditional communities around the world? Who is to decide what changes should, or should not, be introduced for community "betterment"? And who defines what constitutes betterment—the community, a national government, or an international agency like the World Health Organization? What are the limits of cultural relativism when a traditional practice is considered a human rights abuse globally?

Today, many universities require that anthropologists, like other researchers, communicate in advance the nature, purpose, and potential impact of the planned study to individuals who provide information—and obtain their **informed consent** or formal recorded agreement to participate in the research. Of course, this requirement is easier to fulfill in some societies or cultures than in others, as most anthropologists recognize. When it is a challenge to obtain informed consent, or even impossible to precisely explain the meaning and purpose of this concept and its actual consequences, anthropologists may protect the identities of individuals, families, or even entire communities by altering their names and locations. For example, when Dutch anthropologist Anton Blok studied the Sicilian mafia, he did not obtain the informed consent of this violent secret group but opted not to disclose their real identities.[9] Anthropologists deal with matters that are private and sensitive, including things that individuals would prefer not to have generally known about them. How does one write about such important but delicate issues and at the same time protect the privacy of the individuals who have shared their stories?

The dilemma facing anthropologists is also recognized in the preamble of the American Anthropological Association's Code of Ethics, first formalized in 1971 and modified in its current form in 1998. This document outlines the various ethical responsibilities and moral obligations of anthropologists, including this central maxim: "Anthropological researchers must do everything in their power to ensure that their research does not harm the safety, dignity, or privacy of the people with whom they work, conduct research, or perform other professional activities."

The AAA ethics statement is an educational document that lays out the rules and ideals applicable to anthropologists in all the subdisciplines. While the AAA has no legal authority, it does issue policy statements on research ethics questions as they come up. For example, recently the AAA recommended that field notes from medical settings should be protected and not subject to subpoena in malpractice lawsuits. This honors the ethical imperative to protect the privacy of individuals who have shared their stories with anthropologists.

Emerging technologies have ethical implications that impact anthropological inquiry. For example, the ability to sequence and patent particular genes has led to debates about who has the right to hold a patent—the persons from whom the particular genes were obtained or the researcher who studies the genes? Similarly, as seen in the Kennewick Man controversy mentioned earlier, the ethics of ownership when it comes to ancient remains are particularly thorny. Given the radical changes taking place in the world today, a scientific understanding of the past has never been more important. Do ancient remains belong to the scientist, to the people living in the region under scientific investigation, or to whoever happens to have possession of them? Market forces convert these remains into very expensive collectibles and lead to systematic mining of archaeological and fossil sites. Collaborations between local people and scientists not only preserves the ancient remains from market forces, but also honors the connections of indigenous people to the places and remains under study.

To sort out the answers to all of the above questions, anthropologists recognize that they have special obligations to three sets of people: those whom they study, those who fund the research, and those in the profession who expect us to publish our findings so that they may be used to increase our collective knowledge. Because fieldwork requires a relationship of trust between fieldworkers and the community in which they work, the anthropologist's first responsibility clearly is to the people who have shared their stories and the greater community. Everything possible must be done to protect their physical, social, and psychological welfare and to honor their dignity and privacy. This task is frequently complex. For example, telling the story of a people gives information both to relief agencies who

---

[9]Blok, A. (1974). *The Mafia mafia of a Sicilian village 1860–1960*. New York: Harper & Row.

might help them and to others who might take advantage of them.

While anthropologists regard as basic a people's right to maintain their own culture, any connections with outsiders can endanger the cultural identity of the community being studied. To surmount these obstacles, anthropologists frequently collaborate with and contribute to the communities in which they are working, allowing the people being studied to have some say about how their stories are told.

ANTHROPOLOGY AND GLOBALIZATION

A holistic perspective and a long-term commitment to understanding the human species in all its variety are the essence of anthropology. Thus, anthropology is well equipped to grapple with an issue that has overriding importance for all of us at the beginning of the 21st century: **globalization**. This term refers to worldwide interconnectedness, evidenced in global movements of natural resources, trade goods, human labor, finance capital, information, and infectious diseases. Although worldwide travel, trade relations, and information flow have existed for several centuries, the pace and magnitude of these long-distance exchanges have picked up enormously in recent decades; the Internet, in particular, has greatly expanded information exchange capacities.

The powerful forces driving globalization are technological innovations, cost differences among countries, faster knowledge transfers, and increased trade and financial integration among countries. Touching almost everybody's life on the planet, globalization is about economics as much as politics, and it changes human relations and ideas as well as our natural environments. Even geographically remote communities are quickly becoming more interdependent through globalization.

Doing research in all corners of the world, anthropologists are confronted with the impact of globalization on human communities wherever they are located. As participant observers, they describe and try to explain how individuals and organizations respond to the massive changes confronting them. Anthropologists may also find out how local responses sometimes change the global flows directed at them. Dramatically increasing every year, globalization can be a two-edged sword. It may generate economic growth and prosperity, but it also undermines long-established institutions. Generally, globalization has brought significant gains to higher-educated groups in wealthier countries, while doing little to boost developing countries and actually contributing to the erosion of traditional cultures. Upheavals born of globalization are key causes for rising levels of ethnic and religious conflict throughout the world.

Obviously, since all of us now live in a global village, we can no longer afford the luxury of ignoring our neighbors, no matter how distant they may seem. In this

The consumption habits of people in more temperate parts of the world are threatening the lifestyle of people from circumpolar regions. As global warming melts the polar ice caps, traditional ways of life, such as building an igloo as this Inuit man is doing, in Iqaluit, the capital of the Canadian territory of Nunavut, may become impossible. Therefore, the Inuit people consider global warming a human rights issue.

© The Canadian Press (Kevin Frayer)

age of globalization, anthropology may not only provide humanity with useful insights concerning diversity, but it may also assist us in avoiding or overcoming significant problems born of that diversity. In countless social arenas, from schools to businesses to hospitals, anthropologists have done cross-cultural research that makes it possible for educators, businesspeople, and doctors to do their work more effectively.

For example, in the United States today, discrimination based on notions of race continues to be a serious issue affecting economic, political, and social relations. Far from being the biological reality it is supposed to be, anthropologists have shown that the concept of race (and the classification of human groups into higher and lower racial types) emerged in the 18th century as an ideological vehicle for justifying European dominance over Africans and American Indians. In fact, differences of skin color are simply surface adaptations to different climactic zones and have nothing to do with physical or mental capabilities. Indeed, geneticists find far more biological variation *within* any given human population than *among* them. In short, human "races" are divisive categories based on prejudice, false ideas of differences, and erroneous notions of the superiority of one's own group. Given the importance of this issue, race will be discussed further in Chapter 7.

A second example involves the issue of same-sex marriage. In 1989, Denmark became the first country to enact a comprehensive set of legal protections for same-sex couples, known as the Registered Partnership Act. At this writing, more than a half-dozen other countries and some individual states within the United States have passed similar laws, variously named, and numerous countries around the world are considering or have passed legislation providing people in homosexual unions the benefits and protections afforded by marriage.[10] In some societies—including Spain, Canada, Belgium, and the Netherlands—same-sex marriages are considered socially acceptable and allowed by law, even though opposite-sex marriages are far more common. As individuals, countries, and states struggle to define the boundaries of legal protections they will grant to same-sex couples, the anthropological perspective on marriage is useful. Anthropologists have documented same-sex marriages in human societies in various parts of the world, where they are regarded as acceptable under appropriate circumstances. Homosexual behavior occurs in the animal world just as it does among humans.[11] The key difference between people and other animals is that human societies possess beliefs regarding homosexual behavior, just as they do for heterosexual behavior. An understanding of global variation in marriage patterns and sexual behavior does not dictate that one pattern is more right than another. It simply illustrates that all human societies define the boundaries for social relationships.

A final example relates to the common confusion of *nation* with *state*. Anthropology makes an important distinction between these two: States are politically organized territories that are internationally recognized, whereas nations are socially organized bodies of people who share ethnicity—a common origin, language, and cultural heritage. For example, the Kurds constitute a nation, but their homeland is divided among several states: Iran, Iraq, Turkey, and Syria. The international boundaries among these states were drawn up after World War I, with little regard for the region's ethnic groups or nations. Similar processes have taken place throughout the world, especially in Asia and Africa, often making political conditions in these countries inherently unstable. As we will see in later chapters, states and nations rarely coincide, nations being split among different states, and states typically being controlled by members of one nation who commonly use their control to gain access to the land, resources, and labor of other nationalities within the state. Most of the armed conflicts in the world today, such as the many-layered conflicts in the Caucasus Mountains of Russia's southern borderlands, are of this sort and are not mere acts of "tribalism" or "terrorism," as commonly asserted.

As these examples show, ignorance about other peoples and their ways is a cause of serious problems throughout the world. Anthropology offers a way of looking at and understanding the world's peoples—insights that are nothing less than basic skills for survival in this age of globalization.

---

[10]Merin, Y. (2002). *Equality for same-sex couples: The legal recognition of gay partnerships in Europe and the United States.* Chicago: University of Chicago Press. "Court says same-sex marriage is a right." (2004, February 5). *San Francisco Chronicle.* Up-to-date overviews and breaking news on the global status of same-sex marriage are posted on the Internet by the Partners Task Force for Gay & Lesbian Couples at www.buddybuddy.com.

globalization Worldwide interconnectedness, evidenced in global movements of natural resources, trade goods, human labor, finance capital, information, and infectious diseases

---

[11]Kirkpatrick, R. C. (2000). The evolution of human homosexual behavior. *Current Anthropology, 41,* 384.

Chapter Summary

■ Anthropologists are concerned with the objective and systematic study of humankind in all times and places. Unique among the sciences and humanities, anthropology has long emphasized the study of non-Western societies and a holistic approach, which aims to formulate theoretically valid explanations and interpretations of human diversity based on detailed studies of all aspects of human biology, behavior, and beliefs in all known societies, past and present.

■ Anthropology contains four major fields: physical anthropology, cultural anthropology, linguistic anthropology, and archaeology. Physical anthropologists focus on humans as biological organisms; they particularly emphasize tracing the evolutionary development of the human animal and studying biological variation within the species today. Cultural anthropologists study humans in terms of their cultures, the often-unconscious standards by which social groups operate. Linguists, who study human languages, may deal with the description of a language, with the history of languages, or how languages are used in particular social settings. Archaeologists study human cultures through the recovery and analysis of material remains and environmental data.

■ Within all of anthropology's subdisciplines, one can find applied anthropologists who utilize the discipline's unique research methodology toward solving practical problems. Forensics is an example of applied physical anthropology. Language preservation is an example of applied linguistic anthropology.

■ Fieldwork is characteristic of all the anthropological subdisciplines. Fieldwork provides a unique perspective because of the complete immersion it entails. Fieldwork in archaeology and paleoanthropology includes finding sites where remains are buried through survey methods, excavating for skeletal and material remains, and analyzing the material in the laboratory. In the lab, materials are placed in the complete environmental, temporal, and cultural context. Some cultural anthropologists are ethnographers, who do a particular kind of hands-on fieldwork known as participant observation. They produce a detailed record of a specific culture in writing (and/or visual imagery) known as an ethnography. Other cultural anthropologists are also ethnologists, who study, analyze, and construct theories about cultures from a comparative or historical point of view, utilizing ethnographic accounts. Often, they focus on a particular aspect of culture, such as religious or economic practices.

■ The comparative method is key to all branches of anthropology. Anthropologists make broad comparisons among peoples and cultures—past and present. They also compare related species and fossil groups.

■ Anthropological research raises a number of important ethical questions about the potential uses and abuses of anthropological knowledge and the ways that it is obtained. The anthropological code of ethics, first formalized in 1971 and continually revised, outlines the moral and ethical responsibility of anthropologists to the people whom they study, to those who fund the research, and to the profession as a whole.

■ Due to a tradition of studying the connections between diverse peoples over time, anthropology is uniquely positioned to study globalization in a world increasingly connected through recent technological advancements.

■ Unique among the sciences and humanities, anthropology has long emphasized the study of non-Western societies and a holistic approach, which aims to formulate theoretically valid explanations and interpretations of human diversity based on detailed studies of all aspects of human biology, behavior, and beliefs in all known societies, past and present.

■ In anthropology, the humanities, social sciences, and natural sciences come together into a genuinely humanistic science. Anthropology's link with the humanities can be seen in its concern with people's beliefs, values, languages, arts, and literature—oral as well as written—but above all in its attempt to convey the experience of living in different cultures. As part of both the sciences and the humanities, anthropology has essential insights to offer the modern world, particularly in this era of globalization when understanding our neighbors in the global village has become a matter of survival for all.

Questions for Reflection

1. Anthropology uses a holistic approach to explain all aspects of human beliefs, behavior, and biology. How might anthropology challenge your personal perspective on the following questions: Where did we come from? Why do we act in certain ways? What makes us tick?

2. From the holistic anthropological perspective, humans have one leg in culture and the other in nature. Are there examples from your life that illustrate the interconnectedness of human biology and culture?

3. Globalization can be described as a two-edged sword. How does it foster growth and destruction simultaneously?

4. The textbook definitions of *state* and *nation* are based on scientific distinctions between both organizational types. However, this distinction is commonly lost in everyday language. Consider, for instance, the names *United States of America* and the *United Nations*.

5. The Biocultural Connection in this chapter contrasts different cultural perspectives on "brain death," while the Original Study features a discussion about traditional Zulu healers and their role in dealing with AIDS victims. What do these two accounts suggest about the role of applied anthropology in dealing with cross-cultural health issues around the world?

Key Terms

anthropology
holistic perspective
ethnocentrism
culture-bound
applied anthropology
medical anthropology
physical anthropology
molecular anthropology
paleoanthropology
biocultural
primatology
forensic anthropology

cultural anthropology
culture
ethnography
fieldwork
participant observation
ethnology
linguistic anthropology
discourse
archaeology
bioarchaeology
cultural resource
  management

empirical
hypothesis
theory
doctrine
artifact
material culture
fossil
soil marks
middens
grid system
datum point

relative dating
absolute or chronometric
  dating
key consultants
informal interview
formal interview
eliciting devices
Human Relations Area
  Files (HRAF)
informed consent
globalization

glasses a day

got milk?

VISUAL ESSENCE

Among the primates, humans are the only species capable of inhabiting the entire globe. Over the course of our evolutionary history, both culture and biology have contributed to our ability to adapt to a very wide range of environments. In terms of biological evolution, adaptation consists of changes over time in the genetic makeup of populations. Forces in the environment, through the process of natural selection, bring about these changes. But for humans, in addition to forces that derive solely from nature, the environment includes elements that people shape through their cultural practices. For example, unlike the vast majority of human adults globally, Kevin Garnett, formerly of the Timberwolves, can "get milk" because some of his genetic ancestors had a tradition of dairying. Only populations with this cultural tradition possess high frequencies of the genes required to continue digesting milk into adulthood. Encoded in their genes, the ability to digest milk has remained in the descendents of these populations even if today they no longer practice dairying. Natural selection is one of the four evolutionary forces that account for the diversity of all life on earth today.

Biology and Evolution

2

EVOLUTION AND CREATION STORIES

A common part of the mythology of most peoples is a story explaining the appearance of humans on earth. The accounts of creation recorded in the Bible's Book of Genesis, for example, explain human origins. A vastly different example, serving the same function, is the traditional belief of the Nez Perce, American Indians native to eastern Oregon and Idaho. For the Nez Perce, humanity is the creation of Coyote, a trickster-transformer inhabiting the earth before humans. Coyote chased the giant beaver monster Wishpoosh over the earth, leaving a trail to form the Columbia River. When Coyote caught Wishpoosh, he killed him, dragged his body to the riverbank, and cut it into pieces, each body part transforming into one of the various peoples of this region. The Nez Perce were made from Wishpoosh's head, thus conferring on them great intelligence and horsemanship.[1]

Creation stories depict the relationship between humans and the rest of the natural world, sometimes reflecting a deep connection among people, other animals, and the earth. In the traditional Nez Perce creation story, groups of people derive from specific body parts—each possessing a special talent and relationship with a particular animal. By contrast, the story of creation depicted in the Book of Genesis emphasizes human uniqueness and the concept of time. Creation is depicted as a series of actions occurring over the course of six days. God's final act of creation is to fashion the first human from the earth in his own image before the seventh day of rest.

Evolution, the major organizing principle of the biological sciences, also accounts for the diversity of life on earth. Theories of evolution provide mechanisms for change and explanations for how the variety of organisms, both in the past and today, came into being. However, evolution differs from creation stories in that

---

[1]Clark, E. E. (1966). *Indian legends of the Pacific Northwest* (p. 174). Berkeley: University of California Press.

it explains the diversity of life in consistent scientific language, using testable ideas (hypotheses). Contemporary scientists make comparisons among living organisms to test hypotheses drawn from evolutionary theory. Through their research, scientists have deciphered the molecular basis of evolution and the mechanisms through which evolutionary forces work on populations of organisms. Though scientific theories of evolution treat humans as biological organisms, at the same time historical and cultural processes also shape evolutionary theory and our understanding of it.

THE CLASSIFICATION OF LIVING THINGS

The development of biology and its central concept, evolution, provides an excellent example of the ways that historical and cultural processes can shape scientific thought. As the exploitation of foreign lands by European explorers changed their prevailing approach to the natural world, discovery of new life forms challenged the previously held notion of fixed unchanging life on earth.

Before this time, Europeans organized living things and inanimate objects alike into a ladder or hierarchy known as the Great Chain of Being, an approach to nature first developed by Aristotle in ancient Greece over 2,000 years ago. The categories were based upon visible similarities, and one member of each category was considered its "primate" (from the Latin *primus*), meaning the first or best of the group. For example, the primate of rocks was the diamond, the primate of birds was the eagle, and so forth. Humans were at the very top of the ladder, just below the angels.

This classificatory system was in place until Carolus Linnaeus developed the *Systema Naturae*, or system of nature, in the 18th century to classify the diversity of

From *Lindauer Bilderbogen no. 5*, edited by Friedrich Boer. Jan Thorbecke Verlag, Sigmaringen, West Germany.

A professor of medicine and botany in Sweden, Carolus Linnaeus, who created the first comprehensive system of living things, also prepared and prescribed medicinal plants, as did other physicians of the time. He arranged for his students to join the major European voyages so they could bring back new medicinal plants and other life forms. Through his observations of the bloom times of some plant species, Linnaeus proposed a "flower clock" that could show the time of day according to whether blossoms of particular species were open or shut.

living things collected and brought to Europe on seafaring vessels from all parts of the globe. Linnaeus's compendium reflected a new understanding of life on earth and of the place of humanity among the animals.

Linnaeus noted the similarity among humans, monkeys, and apes, classifying them together as **primates**. Not the first or the best of the animals on earth, primates are just one of several kinds of **mammal**, animals having body hair or fur who suckle or nurse their young. In other words, Linnaeus classified living things into a series of categories that are progressively more inclusive on the basis of internal and external visual similarities. **Species**, the smallest working units in biological classificatory systems, are reproductively isolated populations or groups of populations capable of interbreeding to produce fertile offspring. Species are subdivisions of larger, more inclusive groups, called **genera** (singular, **genus**). Humans, for example, are classified in the genus *Homo* and species *sapiens*.

Linnaeus based his classificatory system on the following criteria:

1. Body structure: A Guernsey cow and a Holstein cow are the same species because they have identical body structure. A cow and a horse do not.

primates The group of mammals that includes lemurs, lorises, tarsiers, monkeys, apes, and humans

mammals The class of vertebrate animals distinguished by bodies covered with fur, self-regulating temperature, and in females milk-producing mammary glands

species The smallest working unit in the system of classification. Among living organisms, species are populations or groups of populations capable of interbreeding and producing fertile viable offspring

genus, genera (pl.) In the system of plant and animal classification, a group of like species

taxonomy The science of classification

analogies In biology, structures possessed by different organisms that are superficially similar due to similar function; without sharing a common developmental pathway or structure

2. Body function: Cows and horses give birth to live young. Although they are different species, they are closer than either cows or horses are to chickens, which lay eggs and have no mammary glands.

3. Sequence of bodily growth: At the time of birth—or hatching out of the egg—young cows and chickens resemble their parents in their body plan. They are therefore more closely related to each other than either one is to the frog, whose tadpoles undergo a series of changes before attaining the basic adult form.

Modern **taxonomy**, or the science of classification (from the Greek for "naming divisions"), while retaining the structure of the Linnaean system, is based on more than body structure, function, and growth. Today, scientists also compare protein structure and genetic material to construct the relationships among living things. Such molecular comparisons can even be aimed at parasites, bacteria, and viruses, allowing scientists to classify or trace the origins of particular diseases, such as SARS (sudden acute respiratory syndrome) or HIV (human immunodeficiency virus). An emphasis on genetics rather than morphology has led to a reworking of taxonomic designation in the human family, among others, as is described in Table 2.1.

Cross-species comparisons identify anatomical features of similar function as **analogies**, while anatomical features that have evolved from a common ancestral

---

TABLE 2.1 THE CLASSIFICATION OF HUMANS

Taxonomic Category	Category to Which Humans Belong	Biological Features Used to Define and Place Humans in This Category
Kingdom	Animalia	Humans are animals. We do not make our own food (as plants do) but depend upon intake of living food.
Phylum	Chordata	Humans are chordates. We have a notochord (a rodlike structure of cartilage) and nerve chord running along the back of the body as well as gill slits in the embryonic stage of our life cycle.
Subphylum*	Vertebrata	Humans are vertebrates possessing an internal backbone, with a segmented spinal column.
Class	Mammalia	Humans are mammals, warm-blooded animals covered with fur, possessing mammary glands for nourishing their young after birth.
Order	Primates	Humans are primates, a kind of mammal with a generalized anatomy, relatively large brains, and grasping hands and feet.
Suborder	Anthropoidea	Humans are anthropoids, social, daylight-active primates.
Superfamily	Hominoid	Humans are hominoids with broad, flexible shoulders and no tail. Chimps, bonobos, gorillas, orangutans, gibbons, and siamangs are also hominoids.
Family Subfamily	Hominid Hominin	Humans are hominids. We are hominoids from Africa, genetically more closely related to chimps, bonobos, and gorillas than to hominoids from Asia. Some scientists use "hominid" to refer only to humans and their ancestors. Others include chimps and gorillas in this category, using the subfamily "hominin" to distinguish humans and their ancestors from chimps and gorillas and their ancestors. The two taxonomies differ according to emphasis on genetic versus morphological similarities. Those who use "hominin" do so to emphasize the genetic relationship among humans, chimps, and gorillas. Those who refer to humans and their ancestor as "hominids" give preference to the similarities in body shape among chimpanzees, gorillas, and orangutans.
Genus Species	*Homo* *sapiens*	Humans have large brains and rely on cultural adaptations to survive. Ancestral fossils are placed in this genus and species depending upon details of the skull shape and interpretations of their cultural capabilities. Genus and species names are always italicized.

*Most categories can be expanded or narrowed by adding the prefix "sub" or "super." A family could thus be part of a superfamily and in turn contain two or more subfamilies.

feature are called **homologies**. For example, the hand of a human and the wing of a bat evolved from the forelimb of a common ancestor, though they have acquired different functions: The human hand and bat wing are homologous structures. During their early embryonic development, homologous structures arise in a similar fashion and pass through similar stages before differentiating. The wings of birds and butterflies look similar and have a similar function (flying): These are analogous, but not homologous, structures because they do not follow the same developmental sequence.

Through careful comparison and analysis of organisms, Linnaeus and his successors have grouped species into genera and into even larger groups such as families, orders, classes, phyla, and kingdoms. Each taxonomic level is distinguished by characteristics shared by all the organisms in the group.

THE DISCOVERY OF EVOLUTION

Just as European seafaring and exploitation brought about an awareness of the diversity of life across the earth, construction and mining, which came with the onset of industrialization in Europe, brought about an awareness of change in life forms through time. As work like cutting railway lines or quarrying limestone became commonplace, fossils, or preserved remains, of past life forms were brought into the light.

At first, the fossilized remains of elephants and giant saber-toothed tigers in Europe were interpreted according to religious doctrine. For example, the early 19th-century theory of *catastrophism* championed by French paleontologist and anatomist George Cuvier invoked natural events like the Great Flood of the Book of Genesis to account for the disappearance of these species in European lands. During this same time period, British geologist Sir Charles Lyell championed *uniformitarianism*,

a theory that was not compatible with biblical interpretations. This theory accounts for variation in the earth's surface through the gradual accumulation, over extremely long periods of time, of minute changes, brought about by the same natural processes, such as erosion, that are immediately observable. The time depth required for uniformitarianism was not compatible with the most literal interpretations of the Bible, in which the earth is a mere six thousand or so years old.

With industrialization, Europeans became more comfortable with the ideas of change and progress. In hindsight, it seems inevitable that someone would hit upon the idea of evolution. So it was that, by the start of the 19th century, many naturalists had come to accept the idea that life had evolved, even though they were not clear about how it happened. It remained for Charles Darwin (1809–1882) to formulate a theory that has withstood the test of time.

Grandson of Erasmus Darwin (a physician, scientist, poet, and originator of a theory of evolution himself), Charles Darwin began the study of medicine at the University of Edinburgh, Scotland. Finding himself unfit for this profession, he went to Christ's College, Cambridge, to study theology. He then left Cambridge to take the position of companion to Captain Robert FitzRoy on the *H.M.S. Beagle*, which was about to embark on an expedition to various poorly mapped parts of the world. The voyage lasted for almost five years, taking Darwin along the coasts of South America, to the Galapagos Islands, across the Pacific to Australia, and then across the Indian and Atlantic oceans to South America before returning to England in 1836.

Observing the tremendous diversity of living creatures as well as the astounding fossils of extinct animals, Darwin began to note that species varied according to the environments they inhabited. The observations he made on this voyage, his readings of Lyell's *Principles of Geology* (1830), and the arguments he had with the orthodox and dogmatic FitzRoy all contributed to the ideas culminating in Darwin's most famous book, *On the Origin of Species*. This book, published in 1859, over twenty years after he returned from his voyage, described a theory of evolution accounting for change within species and for the emergence of new species in purely naturalistic terms.

Darwin added observations from English farm life and intellectual thought to the ideas he began to develop on the *Beagle*. He paid particular attention to domesticated animals and farmers' practice of breeding their stock to select for specific traits. Darwin's theoretical breakthrough derived from an essay by economist Thomas Malthus (1766–1834), which warned of the potential consequences of increased human population, particularly of the poor. Malthus observed that animal

---

homologies In biology, structures possessed by two different organisms that arise in similar fashion and pass through similar stages during embryonic development, though they may possess different functions

natural selection The evolutionary process through which factors in the environment exert pressure, favoring some individuals over others to produce the next generation

genes Portions of DNA molecules that direct the synthesis of specific proteins

law of segregation The Mendelian principle that variants of genes for a particular trait retain their separate identities through the generations

law of independent assortment The Mendelian principle that genes controlling different traits are inherited independently of one another

populations, unlike human populations, remained stable, due to an overproduction of young followed by a large proportion of animal offspring not surviving to maturity. Darwin wrote in his autobiography, "it at once struck me that under these circumstances favourable variations would tend to be preserved, and unfavourable ones to be destroyed. The results of this would be the formation of a new species. Here, then I had at last got a theory by which to work."[2]

Darwin combined his observations into the theory of **natural selection** as follows: All species display a range of variation, and all have the ability to expand beyond their means of subsistence. It follows that, in their "struggle for existence," organisms with variations that help them to survive in a particular environment will reproduce with greater success than those without them. Thus, as generation succeeds generation, nature selects the most advantageous variations, and species evolve. So obvious did the idea seem in hindsight that Thomas Henry Huxley, one of the era's most prominent scientists, remarked, "How extremely stupid of me not to have thought of that."[3]

However straightforward the idea of evolution by natural selection may appear, the theory was (and is) a source of considerable controversy. Two problems plagued Darwin's theory throughout his career. First, how did variation arise in the first place? Second, what was the mechanism of heredity by which variable traits could be passed from one generation to the next? Ironically, some of the information Darwin needed, the basic laws of heredity, were available by 1866, through the experimental work of Gregor Mendel (1822–1884), a Roman Catholic monk, working in the monastery gardens in Brno, a city in today's Czech Republic.

Mendel, who was raised on a farm, possessed two particular talents: a flair for mathematics and a passion for gardening. As with all farmers of his time, Mendel had an intuitive understanding of biological inheritance. He went a step farther, though, in that he recognized the need for theoretical explanations. Thus, at age 34, he began careful breeding experiments in the monastery garden, starting with pea plants.

Over 8 years, Mendel planted over 30,000 plants, controlling their pollination, observing the results, and figuring out the mathematics behind it all. This allowed him to predict the outcome of hybridization, or breeding that combined distinct varieties of the same species, over successive generations, in terms of basic laws of heredity. Though his findings were published in 1866 in a respected scientific journal, no one recognized

the importance of Mendel's work during his lifetime. In 1900, cell biology had advanced to the point where rediscovery of Mendel's laws was inevitable, and in that year three European botanists, working independently of one another, rediscovered not only the laws but also Mendel's original paper. With this rediscovery, the science of genetics began. Still, it would be another 53 years before the molecular mechanisms of heredity, and the discrete units of inheritance, would be discovered. Today, a comprehensive understanding of heredity, molecular genetics, and population genetics supports Darwinian evolutionary theory.

HEREDITY

In order to understand how evolution works, one has to have some understanding of the mechanics of heredity, because heritable variation constitutes the raw material for evolution. Our knowledge of the mechanisms of heredity is fairly recent; most of the fruitful research into the molecular level of inheritance has taken place in the past five decades. Although some aspects remain puzzling, the outlines by now are clear.

The Transmission of Genes

While today we define a **gene** as a portion of the DNA molecule containing a sequence of base pairs that encodes a particular protein, the molecular basis of the gene was not known at the turn of the 20th century when biologists coined the term from the Greek word for "birth." Mendel had deduced the presence and activity of genes by experimenting with garden peas to determine how various traits are passed from one generation to the next. Specifically, he discovered that inheritance was *particulate*, rather than *blending,* as Darwin and many others thought. That is, the units controlling the expression of visible traits come in pairs, one from each parent, and retain their separate identities over the generations rather than blending into a combination of parental traits in offspring. This was the basis of Mendel's first **law of segregation**, which states that pairs of genes separate and keep their individuality and are passed on to the next generation, unaltered. Another of his laws—that of **independent assortment**—states that different traits (under the control of distinct genes) are inherited independently of one another.

Mendel based his laws on statistical frequencies of observed characteristics, such as color and texture in generations of plants. His inferences about the mechanisms of inheritance were confirmed through the discovery of the cellular and molecular basis of inheritance in the first half of the 20th century. When **chromosomes**, the

[2]Darwin, C. (1887). *Autobiography*. Reprinted in *The life and letters of Charles Darwin* (1902). F. Darwin (Ed.). London: John Murray.
[3]Quoted in Durant, J. C. (2000, April 23). Everybody into the gene pool. *New York Times Book Review*, 11.

British scientist Rosalind Franklin's pioneering work in x-ray crystal photography played a vital role in unlocking the secret of the genetic code in 1953. Without her permission, Franklin's colleague Maurice Wilkins showed one of her images to James Watson. In his book *The Double Helix,* Watson wrote, "The instant I saw the picture my mouth fell open and my pulse began to race." While her research was published simultaneously in the prestigious journal *Nature* in 1953 alongside that of James Watson, Francis Crick, and Maurice Wilkins, only the gentlemen received the Nobel Prize for the double-helix model of DNA in 1962.

© Vittorio Luzzati/National Portrait Gallery, London

cellular structures containing the genetic information, were discovered at the start of the 20th century, they provided a visible vehicle for transmission of traits proposed in Mendel's laws.

It was not until 1953 that James Watson and Francis Crick found that genes are actually portions of molecules of deoxyribonucleic acid (**DNA**)—long strands of which form chromosomes. DNA is a complex molecule with an unusual shape, rather like two strands of a rope twisted around each other with ladderlike steps between the two strands. Alternating sugar and phosphate molecules form the backbone of these strands connected to each other by four base pairs: adenine, thymine, guanine, and cytosine (usually written as A, T, G, and C). Connections between the strands occur between so-called complementary pairs of bases (A to T, G to C; see Figure 2.1). Sequences of three complementary bases specify the sequence of

chromosomes In the cell nucleus, the structures visible during cellular division containing long strands of DNA combined with a protein
DNA Deoxyribonucleic acid. The genetic material consisting of a complex molecule whose base structure directs the synthesis of proteins
chromatid One half of the "X" shape of chromosomes visible once replication is complete. Sister chromatids are exact copies of each other
alleles Alternate forms of a single gene
genome The complete structure sequence of DNA for a species
mitosis A kind of cell division that produces new cells having exactly the same number of chromosome pairs, and hence copies of genes, as the parent cell

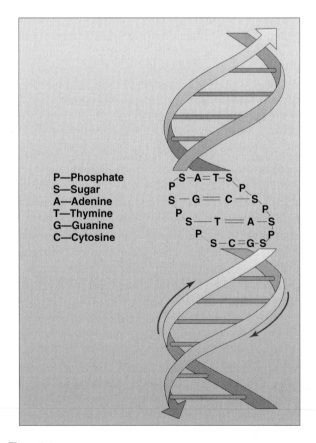

P—Phosphate
S—Sugar
A—Adenine
T—Thymine
G—Guanine
C—Cytosine

Figure 2.1

This diagrammatic representation of a portion of deoxyribonucleic acid (DNA) illustrates its twisted ladderlike structure. Alternating sugar and phosphate groups form the structural sides of the ladder. The connecting "rungs" are formed by pairings between complementary bases—adenine with thymine and cytosine with guanine.

amino acids in protein synthesis. This arrangement also confers upon genes the unique property of being able to replicate or make exact copies of themselves. The term **chromatid** refers to one half of the "X" shape of chromosomes visible once replication is complete. Sister chromatids are exact copies of each other.

Genes and Alleles

A sequence of chemical bases on a molecule of DNA (a gene) constitutes a recipe for making proteins. As science writer Matt Ridley puts it, "Proteins . . . do almost every chemical, structural, and regulatory thing that is done in the body: they generate energy, fight infection, digest food, form hair, carry oxygen, and so on and on."[4] Almost everything in the body is made of or by proteins.

There are alternate forms of genes, known as **alleles**. For example, the gene for a human blood type in the A-B-O system refers to a specific portion of a DNA molecule on chromosome 9, and corresponds to

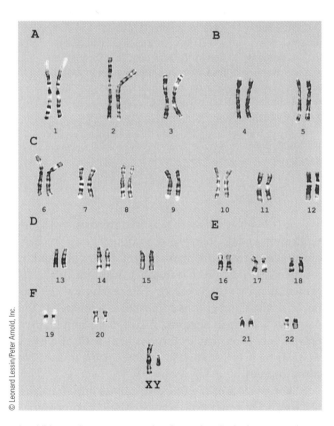

© Leonard Lessin/Peter Arnold, Inc.

In addition to the twenty-two pairs of somatic or body chromosomes, humans possess one pair of sex chromosomes. Pictured here is the pair found in the normal male phenotype: a larger X chromosome and smaller Y. The female phenotype is determined by the presence of two X chromosomes. Offspring inherit an X chromosome from their mothers but either an X or a Y from their fathers, resulting in approximately equal numbers of male and female offspring in subsequent generations. Though the Y chromosome is critical for differentiation into a male phenotype, compared to other chromosomes the Y is tiny and carries little genetic information.

[4]Ridley, M. (1999). *Genome: The autobiography of a species in 23 chapters* (p. 40). New York: HarperCollins.

alternate forms that determine the specific blood type (the A allele and B allele). Genes, then, are not really separate structures, as had once been imagined, but locations, like dots on a map. These genes provide the recipe for the many proteins that keep us alive and healthy.

The human **genome**—the complete sequence of human DNA—contains 3 billion chemical bases, with about 20,000 to 25,000 genes, a number similar to that found in most mammals. Of the 3 billion bases, humans and mice are about 90 percent identical. Both species have a mere three times as many genes as does the fruit fly, but half the number of genes found in the rice plant. In other words the number of genes or base pairs does not explain every difference among organisms. At the same time, those 20,000 to 25,000 human genes account for only 1 to 1.5 percent of the entire genome, indicating that scientists still have far more to learn about how genes work. Frequently, genes themselves are split by long stretches of DNA that are not part of the known protein code. The 1,062 bases of the A-B-O blood group gene, for example, are interrupted by five such stretches. In the course of protein production, these stretches of DNA are metaphorically snipped out and left on the cutting room floor.

Cell Division

In order to grow and maintain good health, the body cells of an organism must divide and produce new cells. Cell division is initiated when the chromosomes replicate, forming a second pair that duplicates the original pair of chromosomes in the nucleus. To do this, the DNA "unzips" between the base pairs—adenine from thymine and guanine from cytosine—following which each base on each now-single strand attracts its complementary base, reconstituting the second half of the double helix. Each new pair is surrounded by a membrane and becomes the nucleus that directs the activities of a new cell. This kind of cell division is called **mitosis**. As long as no errors are made in this replication process, cells within organisms can divide to form daughter cells that are exact genetic copies of the parent cell.

Like most animals, humans reproduce sexually. One reason sex is so "popular," from an evolutionary perspective, is that it provides opportunity for genetic variation. All animals contain two copies of each chromosome, having inherited one from each parent. In humans this involves twenty-three pairs of chromosomes. Sexual reproduction can bring beneficial alleles together, purge the genome of harmful ones, and allow beneficial alleles to spread without being held back by the baggage of disadvantageous variants of other genes. While human societies have always regulated sexual reproduction in some ways, the science of genetics has had a tremendous impact on social aspects of reproduction as seen in this chapter's Biocultural Connection.

Biocultural Connection

The Social Impact of Genetics on Reproduction

While pregnancy and childbirth have been traditional subjects for cultural anthropological study, the genetics revolution has raised new questions for the biocultural study of reproduction. At first glance, the genetics revolution has simply expanded biological knowledge. Individuals today, compared to a hundred years ago, can now see their own genetic makeup even to the level of base pair sequence. A deeper look illustrates that this new biological knowledge has the capacity to profoundly transform cultures. In many cultures, the social experience of pregnancy and childbirth has changed dramatically as a result of the genetic revolution. New reproductive technologies allow for the genetic assessment of fertilized eggs and embryos (the earliest stage of animal development), with far-reaching social consequences.

These new reproductive technologies have also become the object of anthropological study as cultural anthropologists study the social impact of biological knowledge. Over the past twenty years, anthropologist Rayna

Rapp has studied the social impact of prenatal (before birth) genetic testing in North America.[a] Her work illustrates how biological knowledge is generated and interpreted by humans every step of the way.

Prenatal genetic testing is conducted most frequently through amniocentesis, a technique developed in the 1960s through which fluid, containing cells from the developing embryo, is drawn from the womb of a pregnant woman. The chromosomes and specific genes are then analyzed for abnormalities. Rapp traces the development of amniocentesis from an experimental procedure to one routinely used in pregnancy in North America. For example, today pregnant women over the age of 35 routinely undergo this test because certain genetic conditions are associated with older maternal age. Trisomy 21 or Down syndrome, in which individuals have an extra 21st chromosome, can be easily identified through amniocentesis.

Through ethnographic study, Rapp shows that a biological fact (such as

an extra 21st chromosome) is open to diverse interpretations and reproductive choices by "potential parents." She also illustrates how genetic testing may lead to the labeling of disabled people as undesirable, pitting women's reproductive rights against the rights of the disabled. During their second trimester, women are guaranteed the right to decide whether to terminate or continue a pregnancy after diagnosis of a genetic anomaly. Following this brief window, the law protects the rights of disabled individuals with these same anomalies. Individual women must negotiate a terrain in which few rules exist to guide them. New reproductive technology has created an utterly novel social situation.

Rapp's anthropological investigation of the social impact of amniocentesis illustrates the complex interplay between biological knowledge and cultural practices.

[a]Rapp, R. (1999). *Testing women, testing the fetus: The social impact of amniocentesis in America (The Anthropology of Everyday Life)*. New York: Routledge.

Sexual reproduction increases genetic diversity, which in turn has contributed to a multitude of adaptations among sexually reproducing species such as humans. When new individuals are produced through sexual reproduction, the process involves the merging of two cells, one from each parent. If two regular body cells, each containing twenty-three pairs of chromosomes, were to merge, the result would be a new individual with forty-six pairs of chromosomes; such an individual surely could not survive. But this increase in chromosome number does not occur, because the sex cells that join to form a new individual are the product of a different kind of cell division, called **meiosis**.

---

meiosis A kind of cell division that produces the sex cells, each of which has half the number of chromosomes found in other cells of the organism

homozygous Refers to a chromosome pair that bears identical alleles for a single gene

heterozygous Refers to a chromosome pair that bears different alleles for a single gene

genotype The alleles possessed for a particular trait

Although meiosis begins like mitosis, with the replication and doubling of the original genes in chromosomes through the formation of sister chromatids, it proceeds to divide that number into four new cells rather than two (Figure 2.2). Thus each new cell has only half the number of chromosomes compared to the parent cell. Human eggs and sperm, for example, have only twenty-three single chromosomes (half of a pair), whereas body cells have twenty-three pairs, or forty-six chromosomes.

The process of meiotic division has important implications for genetics. Because paired chromosomes are separated, two different types of new cells will be formed; two of the four new cells will have one half of a pair of chromosomes, and the other two will have the second half of the original chromosome pair. At the same time, corresponding portions of one chromosome may "cross over" to the other one, somewhat scrambling the genetic material compared to the original chromosomes. Sometimes, the original pair is **homozygous**, possessing identical alleles for a specific gene. For example, if in both chromosomes

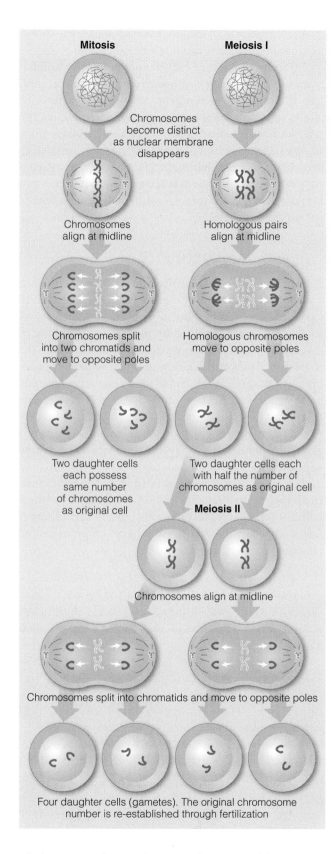

Mitosis / **Meiosis I**

Chromosomes become distinct as nuclear membrane disappears

Chromosomes align at midline

Homologous pairs align at midline

Chromosomes split into two chromatids and move to opposite poles

Homologous chromosomes move to opposite poles

Two daughter cells each possess same number of chromosomes as original cell

Two daughter cells each with half the number of chromosomes as original cell

Meiosis II

Chromosomes align at midline

Chromosomes split into chromatids and move to opposite poles

Four daughter cells (gametes). The original chromosome number is re-established through fertilization

Figure 2.2

Each chromosome consists of two sister chromatids, which are exact copies of each other. During mitosis, these sister chromatids separate into two identical daughter cells. In meiosis, the cell division responsible for the formation of gametes, the first division halves the chromosome number. The second meiotic division is essentially like mitosis and involves the separation of sister chromatids. Chromosomes in red came from one parent; those in blue came from the other. Meiosis results in four daughter cells that are not identical.

half of the new cells will contain only the B allele; the offspring have a 50–50 chance of getting either one. It is impossible to predict any single individual's **genotype**, or genetic composition, but (as Mendel originally discovered) statistical probabilities can be established.

What happens when a child inherits the allele for type O blood from one parent and that for type A from the other? Will the child have blood of type A, O, or some mixture of the two? Figure 2.3 illustrates some of the possible outcomes. Many of these questions were answered by Mendel's original experiments.

Mendel discovered that certain alleles are able to mask the presence of others; one allele is dominant, whereas the other is recessive. Actually, it is the traits that

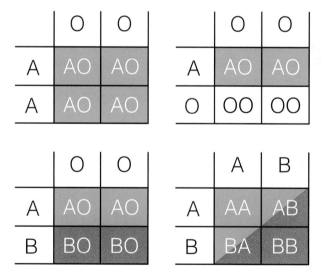

Figure 2.3

These four Punnett squares (named for British geneticist Reginald Punnett) illustrate some of the possible phenotypes and genotypes of offspring within the A-B-O system. Each individual possesses two alleles within this system, and together these two alleles constitute the individual's genotype. "Phenotype" refers to the physical characteristic expressed by the individual. The alleles of one parent are listed on the left-hand side of the square, while the other parent's alleles are listed across the top. The potential genotypes of offspring are listed in the colored squares by letter. Phenotypes are indicated by color: blue indicates the type A phenotype; orange indicates the B phenotype. Individuals with one A and one B allele have the AB phenotype and make both blood antigens. Individuals with the O phenotype have two O alleles.

of the original pair the gene for A-B-O blood type is represented by the allele for type A blood, then all new cells will have the A allele. But if the original pair is **heterozygous**, with the A allele on one chromosome and the allele for type B blood on the other, then

are dominant or recessive rather than the alleles themselves; geneticists merely speak of dominant and recessive alleles for the sake of convenience. Thus, one might speak of the allele for type A blood as being dominant to the one for type O. An individual whose blood type genes are heterozygous, with one A and one O allele, will have type A blood. In other words, the heterozygous condition (AO) will show exactly the same physical characteristic, or **phenotype**, as the homozygous (AA), even though the two have a somewhat different genetic composition, or genotype. Only the homozygous recessive genotype (OO) will show the phenotype of type O blood.

The **dominance** of one allele does not mean that the **recessive** one is lost or in some way blended. A type A heterozygous parent (AO) will produce sex cells containing both A and O alleles. (This is an example of Mendel's law of segregation, that alleles retain their separate identities.) Recessive alleles can be handed down for generations before they are matched with another recessive allele in the process of sexual reproduction and show up in the phenotype. The presence of the dominant allele simply masks the expression of the recessive allele.

All of the traits Mendel studied in garden peas showed this dominant–recessive relationship, and so for some years it was believed that this was the only relationship possible. Later studies, however, have indicated that patterns of inheritance are not always so simple. In some cases, neither allele is dominant; they are both codominant. An example of co-dominance in human heredity can be seen also in the inheritance of blood types. Type A is produced by one allele; type B by another.

A heterozygous individual will have a phenotype of AB, because neither allele can dominate the other.

The inheritance of blood types points out another complexity of heredity. Although each of us has at most two alleles for any given gene, the number of possible alleles for that gene that may be found in a population is by no means limited to two. Certain traits have three or more allelic forms. For example, over one hundred alleles exist for **hemoglobin**, the blood protein that carries oxygen. Only one allele can appear on each of the two homologous chromosomes, so each individual is limited to two genetic alleles.

Polygenetic Inheritance

So far, we have spoken as if all the traits of organisms are determined by just one gene. However, most physical traits—such as height, skin color, or susceptibility to disease—are controlled by multiple genes. In such cases, we speak of **polygenetic inheritance**, where the respective alleles of two or more genes influence phenotype. For example, several individuals may have the exact same height, but because there is no single height gene that determines an individual's size, unraveling the genetic underpinnings of 5 foot 3 inches or 160 centimeters cannot be done neatly. Characteristics subject to polygenetic inheritance exhibit a continuous range of variation in their phenotypic expression that does not correspond to simple Mendelian rules. As U.S. biological anthropologist Jonathan Marks demonstrates in the following Original Study, the relationship between genetics and continuous traits remains a mystery.

Original Study

Ninety–Eight Percent Alike: What Our Similarity to Apes Tells Us about Our Understanding of Genetics

Jonathan Marks

It's not too hard to tell Jane Goodall from a chimpanzee. Goodall is the one with long legs and short arms, a prominent forehead, and whites in her eyes. She's the one with a significant amount of hair only on her head, not all over her body. She's the one who walks, talks, and wears clothing.

A few decades ago, however, the nascent field of molecular genetics recognized an apparent paradox: However easy it may be to tell Jane Goodall from a chimpanzee on the basis of physical characteristics, it is considerably harder to tell them apart according to their genes.

More recently, geneticists have been able to determine with precision that humans and chimpanzees are over 98 percent identical genetically, and that figure has become one of the most well-known factoids in the popular scientific literature. It has been invoked to argue that we are simply a third kind of chimpanzee, together with the common chimp and the rarer bonobo; to claim

human rights for nonhuman apes; and to explain the roots of male aggression.

Using the figure in those ways, however, ignores the context necessary to make sense of it. Actually, our amazing genetic similarity to chimpanzees is a scientific fact constructed from two rather more mundane facts: our familiarity with the apes and our unfamiliarity with genetic comparisons.

To begin with, it is unfair to juxtapose the differences between the bodies of people and apes with the similarities in their genes. After all, we have been comparing the bodies of humans and chimpanzees for 300 years, and we have been comparing DNA sequences for less than 20 years. Now that we are familiar with chimpanzees, we quickly see how different they look from us. But when the chimpanzee was a novelty, in the 18th century, scholars were struck by the overwhelming similarity of human and ape bodies. And why not? Bone for bone, muscle for muscle, organ for organ, the bodies of humans and apes differ only in subtle ways. And yet, it is impossible to say just how physically similar they are. Forty percent? Sixty percent? Ninety-eight percent? Three-dimensional beings that develop over their lifetime don't lend themselves to a simple scale of similarity.

Genetics brings something different to the comparison. A DNA sequence is a one-dimensional entity, a long series of A, G, C, and T subunits. Align two sequences from different species and you can simply tabulate their similarities; if they match 98 out of 100 times, then the species are 98 percent genetically identical.

But is that more or less than their bodies match? We have no easy way to tell, for making sense of the question "How similar are a human and a chimp?" requires a frame of reference. In other words, we should be asking: "How similar are a human and a chimp, compared to what?" Let's try and answer the question. How similar are a human and a chimp, compared to, say, a sea urchin? The human and chimpanzee have limbs, skeletons,

bilateral symmetry, a central nervous system; each bone, muscle, and organ matches. For all intents and purposes, the human and chimpanzee aren't 98 percent identical, they're 100 percent identical.

On the other hand, when we compare the DNA of humans and chimps, what does the percentage of similarity mean? We conceptualize it on a linear scale, on which 100 percent is perfectly identical, and 0 percent is totally different. But the structure of DNA gives the scale a statistical idiosyncrasy. Because DNA is a linear array of those four bases—A, G, C, and T—only four possibilities exist at any specific point in a DNA sequence. [See Figure 2.1.] The laws of chance tell us that two random sequences from species that have no ancestry in common will match at about one in every four sites.

Thus, even two unrelated DNA sequences will be 25 percent identical, not 0 percent identical. (You can, of course, generate sequences more different than that, but greater differences would not occur randomly.) The most different two DNA sequences can be, then, is 75 percent different. Now consider that all multicellular life on earth is related. A human, a chimpanzee, and the banana the chimpanzee is eating share a remote common ancestry, but a common ancestry nevertheless. Therefore, if we compare any particular DNA sequence in a human and a banana, the sequence would have to be more than 25 percent identical. For the sake of argument, let's say 35 percent. In other words, your DNA is over one-

third the same as a banana's. Yet, of course, there are few ways other than genetically in which a human could be shown to be one-third identical to a banana.

That context may help us to assess the 98 percent DNA similarity of humans and chimpanzees. The fact that our DNA is 98 percent identical to that of a chimp is not a transcendent statement about our natures but merely a decontextualized and culturally interpreted datum.

Moreover, the genetic comparison is misleading because it ignores qualitative differences among genomes. Genetic evolution involves much more than simply replacing one base with another. Thus, even among such close relatives as human and chimpanzee, we find that the chimp's genome is estimated to be about 10 percent larger than the human's; that one human chromosome contains a fusion of two small chimpanzee chromosomes; and that the tips of each chimpanzee chromosome contain a DNA sequence that is not present in humans.

In other words, the pattern we encounter genetically is actually quite close to the pattern we encounter anatomically. In spite of the shock the figure of 98 percent may give us, humans are obviously identifiably different from, as well as very similar to, chimpanzees. The apparent paradox is simply a result of how mundane the apes have become, and how exotic DNA still is.

(By Jonathan Marks (2000, May 12). 98% alike (what our similarity to apes tells us about our understanding of genetics). The Chronicle of Higher Education, *B7. Reprinted by permission)*

EVOLUTION, INDIVIDUALS, AND POPULATIONS

At the level of the individual, the study of genetics shows how traits are transmitted from parent to offspring, enabling a prediction about the chances that any given individual will display some phenotypic characteristic. At the level of the group, the study of genetics takes on additional significance, revealing how evolutionary processes account for the diversity of life on earth.

phenotype The observable or testable appearance of an organism that may or may not reflect a particular genotype due to the variable expression of dominant and recessive alleles

dominance The ability of one allele for a trait to mask the presence of another allele

recessive An allele for a trait whose expression is masked by the presence of a dominant allele

hemoglobin The protein that carries oxygen in the red blood cells

polygenetic inheritance Two or more genes contribute to the phenotypic expression of a single characteristic

A key concept in genetics is that of the **population**, or a group of individuals within which breeding takes place. **Gene pool** refers to all the genetic variants possessed by members of a population. It is within populations that natural selection takes place, as some members contribute a disproportionate share of the next generation. Over generations, the relative proportions of alleles in a population change (biological evolution) according to the varying reproductive success of individuals within that population. In other words, at the level of population genetics, **evolution** can be defined as changes in allele frequencies in populations. This is also known as *microevolution*. Four evolutionary forces—mutation, gene flow, genetic drift, and natural selection—are responsible for the genetic changes that underlie the biological variation present in species today. As we shall see, variation is at the heart of evolution. These evolutionary forces create and pattern diversity.

Mutation

The ultimate source of evolutionary change is **mutation** of genes because mutation constantly introduces new variation. Although some mutations may be harmful or beneficial to individuals, most mutations are neutral. But in an evolutionary sense, random mutation is inherently positive, as it provides the ultimate source of new genetic variation. New body plans—such as walking on two legs compared to knuckle-walking like our closest relatives, chimpanzees and gorillas—ultimately depended on genetic mutation. A random mutation might create a new allele that creates a modified protein that makes a new biological task possible. Without the variation brought in through random mutations, populations cannot change over time in response to changing environments.

For sexually reproducing species like humans, the only mutations of any evolutionary consequence are those occurring in sex cells, since these cells form future generations. Mutations may arise whenever copying

mistakes are made during cell division. This may involve a change in a single base of a DNA sequence or, at the other extreme, relocation of large segments of DNA, including entire chromosomes. As you read this page, the DNA in each cell of your body is being damaged.[5] Fortunately, DNA repair enzymes constantly scan DNA for mistakes, slicing out damaged segments and patching up gaps. These repair mechanisms prevent diseases like cancer and ensure that we get a faithful copy of our parental inheritance. Genes controlling DNA repair therefore form a critical part of any species' genetic makeup.

Because no species has perfect DNA repair, new mutations arise continuously, so that all species continue to evolve. Geneticists have calculated the rate at which various types of mutant genes appear. In human populations, they run from a low of about five mutations per million sex cells formed, in the case of a gene abnormality that leads to the absence of an iris in the eye, to a high of about a hundred per million, in the case of a gene involved in a form of muscular dystrophy. The average is about thirty mutants per million. Environmental factors may increase the rate at which mutations occur. These include certain dyes, antibiotics, and chemicals used in the preservation of food. Radiation, whether of industrial or solar origin, represents another important cause of mutations. There is even evidence that stress can increase mutation rates, increasing the diversity necessary for selection if successful adaptation is to occur.[6]

In humans, as in all multicellular animals, the very nature of genetic material ensures that mutations will occur. For instance, the fact that genes are split by stretches of DNA that are not a part of that gene increases the chances that a simple "editing" mistake in the process of copying DNA will cause mutations. To cite one example, no fewer than fifty such segments of DNA fragment the gene for collagen—the main structural protein of the skin, bones, and teeth. One result of this seemingly inefficient situation is that it becomes possible to shuffle the gene segments themselves like a deck of cards, putting together new proteins with new functions. Although individuals may suffer as a result, mutations also confer versatility at the population level, making it possible for an evolving species to adapt more quickly to environmental changes. It is important to realize that mutations occur randomly and thus do not arise out of need for some new adaptation.

---

population In biology, a group of similar individuals that can and do interbreed
gene pool All the genetic variants possessed by members of a population
evolution Changes in allele frequencies in populations. Also known as microevolution
mutation Chance alteration of genetic material that produces new variation
genetic drift Chance fluctuations of allele frequencies in the gene pool of a population
founder effects A particular form of genetic drift deriving from a small founding population not possessing all the alleles present in the original population

---

[5]Culotta, E., & Koshland, D. E., Jr. (1994). DNA repair works its way to the top. *Science, 266*, 1926.
[6]Chicurel, M. (2001). Can organisms speed their own evolution? *Science, 292*, 1824–1827.

20th Century Fox/The Kobal Collection/Hayes, Kerry

In evolutionary terms, mutations serve as the ultimate source of all new genetic variation. A generally positive force, most mutations have minimal effects or are neutral. Nevertheless, human-produced mutagens—such as pollutants, preservatives, cigarette smoke, radiation, and even some medicines—increasingly threaten people in industrial societies. While the negative effects of mutation are evident in the clear link between cigarette smoke and cancer, the positive side of mutation has been fictionalized in the special talents of the X-Men.

Genetic Drift

The evolutionary force of **genetic drift** refers to chance fluctuations of allele frequencies in the gene pool of a population. These changes at the population level come about due to random events at the individual level. Over the course of a lifetime, each individual is subject to a number of random events affecting its survival. For example, an individual squirrel in good health and possessed of a number of advantageous traits may be killed in a chance forest fire; a genetically well-adapted baby cougar may not live longer than a day if its mother gets caught in an avalanche, whereas the weaker offspring of a mother that does not die may survive. In a large population, such accidents of nature are unimportant; the accidents that preserve individuals with certain alleles will be balanced out by the accidents that destroy them. However, in small populations, such averaging out may not be possible. Some alleles may become overrepresented in a population due to chance events.

Because human populations today are so large, we might suppose that human beings are unaffected by genetic drift. But a chance event, like a rock slide that kills five individuals from a small town, with a population of say 10,000, could significantly alter the frequencies of alleles in the local gene pool.

A particular kind of genetic drift, known as **founder effects**, may occur when an existing population splits up into two or more new ones, especially if one of these new populations is founded by a particularly small number of individuals. In such cases, it is unlikely that the gene frequencies of the smaller population will be representative of those of the larger one. Isolated island populations may possess limited variability due to founder effects.

An interesting example can be seen on the Pacific Ocean island of Pingelap in Micronesia, where 5 percent of the population is completely color-blind, a condition known as *achromatopsia*. This is not the "normal" red-green color blindness that affects 8 to 20 percent of males in most populations but rather a complete inability to see color. The high frequency of achromotopsia occurred sometime around 1775 after a typhoon swept through the island, reducing its total population to only twenty individuals. Among the survivors was a single individual who was heterozygous for this condition. After a few generations, this gene became fully embedded in the expanding population. Today a full 30 percent

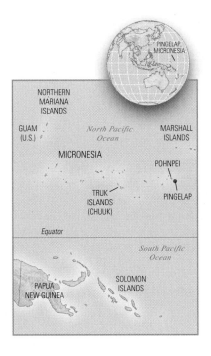

of the island's inhabitants are carriers compared to a mere .003 percent seen in the United States.[7]

Genetic drift is likely to have been an important factor in human evolution, because until 10,000 years ago all humans were food foragers generally living in relatively small, self-contained populations. Whenever biological variation is observed, whether it is the distant past or the present, it is always possible that chance events of genetic drift can account for the presence of this variation.

Gene Flow

Another factor that brings change to the gene pool of a population is **gene flow**, or the introduction of new alleles from nearby populations. Interbreeding allows "road-tested" genes to flow into and out of populations, thus increasing the total amount of variation present within the population. Migration of individuals or groups into the territory occupied by others may lead to gene flow. Geographic factors also affect gene flow. For example, if a river separates two populations of small mammals, preventing interbreeding, these populations will begin to accrue random genetic differences due to their isolation. If the river changes course and the two populations can interbreed freely, new alleles that may have been present in only one population will now be present in both populations due to gene flow.

Among humans, social factors—such as mating rules, intergroup conflict, and our ability to travel great distances—affect gene flow. For example, the last five hundred years have seen the introduction of alleles into Central and South American populations from both the Spanish colonists and the Africans whom Europeans imported as slaves. More recent migrations of people from East Asia have added to this mix. When gene flow is present, variation within populations increases. Throughout the history of human life on earth, gene flow has been important because it keeps populations from developing into separate species.

---

gene flow The introduction of alleles from the gene pool of one population into that of another

adaptation A series of beneficial adjustments to the environment

sickle-cell anemia An inherited form of anemia caused by a mutation in the hemoglobin protein that causes the red blood cells to assume a sickle shape

---

[7]Sacks, O. (1998). *Island of the Colorblind*. New York: Knopf.

Natural Selection

Although gene flow and genetic drift may produce changes in the allele frequency of a population, that change would not necessarily make the population better adapted to its biological and social environment. Natural selection, the evolutionary force described by Darwin, accounts for adaptive change. **Adaptation** is a series of beneficial adjustments to the environment. Adaptation is not an active process but rather the outcome of natural selection. As we will explore throughout this textbook, humans can adapt to their environment through culture as well as biology. When biological adaptation occurs at a genetic level, natural selection is at work.

Natural selection refers to the evolutionary process through which genetic variation at the population level is shaped to fit local environmental conditions. In other words, instead of a completely random selection of individuals whose traits will be passed on to the next generation, there is selection by the forces of nature. In the process, the frequency of genetic variants for harmful or nonadaptive traits within the population is reduced while the frequency of genetic variants for adaptive traits is increased. Over time, changes in the genetic structure of the population are visible in the biology or behavior of a population, and such genetic changes can result in the formation of new species.

The adaptability of organic structures and functions, no matter how much a source of wonder and fascination, nevertheless falls short of perfection. This is so because natural selection can only work with what the existing store of genetic variation provides; it cannot create something entirely new. Variation protects populations from dying out or species from going extinct in changing environments. In the words of one evolutionary biologist, evolution is a process of tinkering, rather than design. Often tinkering involves balancing beneficial and harmful effects of a specific allele in a specific environment as the following case study of sickle-cell anemia illustrates.

The Case of Sickle-Cell Anemia

Among human beings, a particularly well-studied case of an adaptation paid for by the misery of many individuals brings us to the example of **sickle-cell anemia**, a painful disease in which the oxygen-carrying red blood cells change shape (sickle) and clog the finest parts of the circulatory system. This disorder first came to the attention of geneticists in Chicago when it was observed that most North Americans who suffer from it are of

African ancestry. Investigation traced the abnormality to populations that live in a clearly defined belt across central Africa where the sickle-cell allele is found at surprisingly high frequencies. Geneticists were curious to know why such a harmful hereditary disability persisted in these populations.

According to the theory of natural selection, any alleles that are harmful will tend to disappear from the group, because the individuals who are homozygous for the abnormality generally die—are "selected out"—before they are able to reproduce. Why, then, had this seemingly harmful condition remained in populations from central Africa?

The answer to this mystery began to emerge when it was noticed that the areas with high rates of sickle-cell anemia are also areas in which a particularly deadly form of malaria is common (Figure 2.4). This severe form of malaria causes many deaths or, in those who survive, high fevers that significantly interfere with their reproductive abilities. Moreover, it was discovered that hemoglobin abnormalities are also found in people living in parts of the Arabian Peninsula, Greece, Algeria, Syria, and India, all regions where malaria is (or was) common. Further research established that while individuals with hemoglobin abnormalities can still contract malaria, hemoglobin abnormalities are associated with

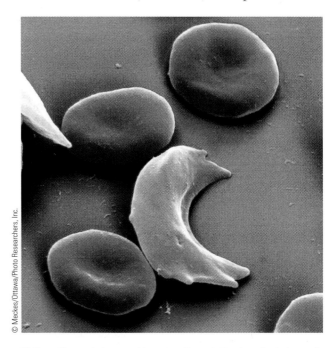

Sickle-cell anemia is caused by a genetic mutation in a single base of the hemoglobin gene resulting in abnormal hemoglobin, called hemoglobin S. Those afflicted by the disease are homozygous for the allele S, and all their red blood cells "sickle." Co-dominance is observable with the sickle and normal alleles. Heterozygotes make 50 percent normal hemoglobin and 50 percent sickle hemoglobin. Shown here is a sickle hemoglobin red blood cell among normal red blood cells.

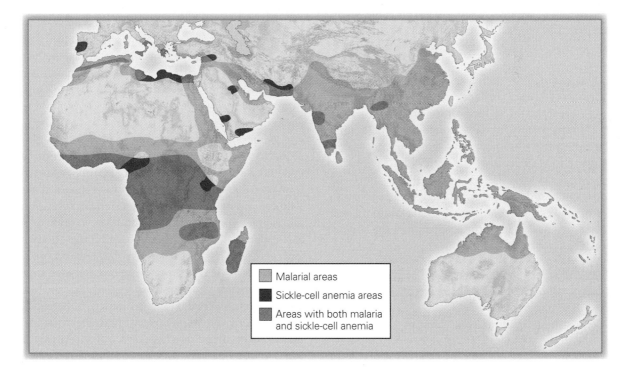

Figure 2.4 Malaria Map

The allele that, in homozygotes, causes sickle-cell anemia makes heterozygotes resistant to falciparum malaria. Thus, the allele is most common in populations native to regions where this strain of malaria is common.

an increased ability to survive the effects of the malarial parasite; it seems that the effects of the abnormal hemoglobin in limited amounts were less injurious than the effects of the malarial parasite.

Thus, selection favored heterozygous individuals with normal and sickling hemoglobin. The mutation that causes hemoglobin to sickle consists of a change in a single base of DNA, so it can arise readily by chance. The loss of alleles for abnormal hemoglobin caused by the death of those homozygous for it (from sickle-cell anemia) was balanced out by the loss of alleles for normal hemoglobin, as those homozygous for normal hemoglobin were more likely to die from malaria.

This example also points out how adaptations tend to be specific; the abnormal hemoglobin was an adaptation to environments in which the malarial parasite flourished. When individuals adapted to malarial regions came to regions relatively free of malaria, what had been an adaptive characteristic became an injurious one. Without malaria, the abnormal hemoglobin becomes comparatively disadvantageous. Although the rates of sickle-cell trait are still relatively high among African Americans—about 9 percent show the sickling trait—this represents a significant decline from the approximately 22 percent who are estimated to have shown the trait when the first African captives were shipped across the Atlantic and sold as slaves. A similar decline in the sickle-cell allele would occur over the course of several generations in malarial zones if this deadly disease were brought under control.

This example also illustrates the important role culture may play even with respect to biological adaptation. In Africa, the severe form of malaria was not a significant problem until humans abandoned food foraging for farming a few thousand years ago. In order to farm, people had to clear areas of the natural forest cover. In the forest, decaying vegetation on the forest floor had imparted an absorbent quality to the ground so that the heavy rainfall of the region rapidly soaked into the soil. But once stripped of its natural vegetation, the soil lost this quality.

Furthermore, the forest canopy was no longer there to break the force of the rainfall, and so the impact of the heavy rains tended to compact the soil further. The result was that stagnant puddles commonly formed after rains, providing the perfect

breeding environment for the type of mosquito that is the host to the malarial parasite. These mosquitoes then began to flourish and transmit the malarial parasite to humans. Thus, humans unwittingly created the kind of environment that made a hitherto disadvantageous trait, the abnormal hemoglobin associated with sickle-cell anemia, advantageous. While the biological process of evolution accounts for the frequency of the sickle-cell allele, cultural processes shape the environment to which humans adapt.

ADAPTATION AND PHYSICAL VARIATION

While the relationship between sickle-cell disease and malaria provides us with a neat example of a genetic adaptation to a particular environment, continuous traits controlled by many genes can be studied in terms of adaptation to a particular environment as well. However, this tends to be more complex. Because specific examples of adaptation can be difficult to prove at times, scientists sometimes suggest that their colleagues' scenarios about adaptation are "Just So" stories.

Anthropologists study biological diversity in terms of **clines**, or the continuous gradation over space in the form or frequency of a trait. The spatial distribution or cline for the sickle-cell allele allowed anthropologists to identify the adaptive function of this gene in a malarial environment. Clinal analysis of a continuous trait such as body shape, which is controlled by a series of genes, allows anthropologists to interpret human global variation in body build as an adaptation to climate.

Generally, people long native to regions with cold climates tend to have greater body bulk (not to be equated with fat) relative to their extremities (arms and legs) than do people native to regions with hot climates, who tend to be relatively tall and slender. Interestingly, tall, slender bodies show up in human evolution as early as 2 million years ago. A person with larger body bulk and relatively shorter extremities may suffer more from summer heat than someone whose extremities are relatively long and whose body is slender. But the person will conserve needed body heat under cold conditions. A bulky body tends to conserve more heat than a less bulky one because it has less surface area relative to volume. In hot, open country, by contrast, people benefit from a long, slender body that can get rid of excess heat quickly. A small slender body can also promote heat loss due to a high surface area to volume ratio.

clines Gradual changes in the frequency of an allele or trait over space

In addition to these sorts of very long-term effects that climate may have imposed on human variation, climate can also contribute to human variation through its impact on the process of growth and development (developmental adaptation). For example, some of the physiological mechanisms for withstanding cold or dissipating heat have been shown to vary depending upon the climate an individual experiences as a child. Individuals spending their youth in very cold climates develop circulatory system modifications that allow them to remain comfortable at temperatures people from warmer climates cannot tolerate. Similarly, hot climate promotes the development of a higher density of sweat glands, creating a more efficient system for sweating to keep the body cool.

Cultural processes complicate studies of body build and climatic adaptation. For example, dietary differences particularly during childhood will cause variation in body shape through their effect on the growth process. Another complicating factor is clothing. Much of the way people adapt to cold is cultural, rather than biological. For instance, Inuit peoples of northern Canada live in an Arctic region where much of the year is very cold. To cope with this, they long ago developed efficient clothing to keep the body warm. Because of this, the Inuit (and other Eskimos) are provided with what amount to artificial tropical environments inside their clothing. Such cultural adaptations allow humans to inhabit the entire globe.

Some anthropologists have suggested that variation in such features as face and eye shape relate to climate. For example, biological anthropologists once proposed that the flat facial profile and round head, common in populations native to East and Central Asia, as well as Arctic North America, derive from adaptation to very cold environments. Though these features are common in Asian and Native American populations, considerable physical variation exists within each population. Some individuals who spread to North America from Asia have a head shape that is more common among Europeans. Such variation lies at the heart of the Kennewick Man controversy described in Chapter 1.

In biological terms, evolution is responsible for all that humans share as well as the broad array of human diversity. Evolution is also responsible for the creation of new species over time. Primatologist Frans de Waal has said, "Evolution is a magnificent idea that has won over essentially everyone in the world willing to listen to scientific arguments."[8] We will return to the topic of human evolution in chapters that follow, but first we will look at the other living primates in order to understand the kinds of animals they are, what they have in common with humans, and what distinguishes the various forms.

Chapter Summary

■ In the 18th century, Carolus Linnaeus devised a system to classify the great variety of living things then known. On the basis of similarities in body structure, body function, and sequence of bodily growth, he grouped organisms into small groups, or species. Modern taxonomy still uses his basic system but now looks at such characteristics as chemical reactions of blood, protein structure, and the makeup of the genetic material itself. These new kinds of data have led to the revision of some existing taxonomies. Although Linnaeus regarded species as fixed and unchangeable, this idea was challenged by the discovery of fossils, the idea of progress, and the many continuities among different species.

■ Charles Darwin formulated a theory of evolution in 1859 as descent with modification occurring as a population adapts to its environment through natural selection. A population is a group of interbreeding individuals. While natural selection works upon individuals, evolution occurs at the population level as changes occur in the frequencies of certain alleles or traits.

■ Genes, the units of heredity, are segments of molecules of DNA (deoxyribonucleic acid), and the entire sequence of DNA is known as the genome. DNA is a complex molecule resembling two strands of rope twisted around each other with ladderlike rungs connecting the two strands. The sequence of bases along the DNA molecule directs the production of proteins. Proteins, in turn, constitute specific identifiable traits such as blood type. Just about everything in the human body is made of or by proteins, and human DNA provides the instructions for the thousands of proteins that keep us alive and healthy. DNA molecules have the unique property of being able to produce exact copies of themselves. As long as no errors are made in the process of

---

[8]de Waal, F. (2001). Sing the song of evolution. *Natural History,* *110* (8), 77.

replication, new daughter cells will be exact genetic copies of the parent cell.

■ DNA molecules are located on chromosomes, structures found in the nucleus of each cell. Chromosomes consist of two sister chromatids, which are exact copies of each other. Each kind of organism has a characteristic number of chromosomes, which are usually found in pairs in sexually reproducing organisms. Humans have twenty-three pairs. Different versions or alternate forms of a gene for a given trait are called alleles. The total number of different alleles of genes available to a population is called its gene pool.

■ Mitosis, one kind of cell division that results in new cells, begins when the chromosomes (hence the genes) replicate, forming a duplicate of the original pair of chromosomes in the nucleus. Sister chromatids separate during mitosis and form identical daughter cells. Meiosis is related to sexual reproduction; it begins with the replication of original chromosomes, but these are divided into four cells, in humans each containing twenty-three single chromosomes. The normal human number of twenty-three pairs of chromosomes is re-established when an egg and sperm unite in the fertilization process.

■ In the late 19th century Gregor Mendel discovered the particulate nature of heredity and that some dominant alleles are able to mask the presence of recessive alleles. The allele for type A blood in humans, for example, is dominant to the allele for type O blood. Alleles that are both expressed when present are termed co-dominant. For example, an individual with the alleles for type A and type B blood has the AB blood type.

■ Phenotype refers to the physical characteristics of an organism, whereas genotype refers to its genetic composition. Two organisms may have different genotypes but the same phenotype. An individual with type A blood phenotype may possess either the AO or the AA genotype.

■ Four evolutionary forces—mutation, genetic drift, gene flow, and natural selection—affect the genetic structures of populations. Evolution at the level of population genetics is change in allele frequencies, which is also known as micro-evolution. The ultimate source of genetic variation is mutation, changes in DNA that may be helpful or harmful to the organism. Although mutations are inevitable given the nature of cellular chemistry, environmental factors—such as heat, chemicals, or radiation—can increase the mutation rate. The effect of random events on the gene pool of a small population is called genetic drift. Genetic drift may have been an important factor in human evolution because until 10,000 years ago humans lived in small isolated populations. Gene flow, the introduction of new variants of genes from nearby populations, distributes new variation to all populations and serves to prevent speciation.

■ Natural selection is the evolutionary force involved in adaptive change. It reduces the frequency of alleles for harmful or maladaptive traits within a population and increases the frequency of alleles for adaptive traits. A well-studied example of adaptation through natural selection in humans is inheritance of the trait for sickling red blood cells. The sickle-cell trait, caused by the inheritance of an abnormal form of hemoglobin, is an adaptation to life in regions in which malaria is common. In these regions, the sickle-cell trait plays a beneficial role, but in other parts of the world, the sickling trait is no longer advantageous, while the associated sickle-cell anemia remains injurious. Geneticists predict that as malaria is brought under control, within several generations there will be a decline in the number of individuals who carry the allele responsible for sickle-cell anemia.

■ Physical anthropologists have determined that some human physical variation appears related to climatic adaptation. People native to cold climates tend to have greater body bulk relative to their extremities than individuals from hot climates; the latter tend to be relatively tall and slender. Studies involving body build and climate are complicated by other factors such as the effects on physique of diet and clothing.

Questions for Reflection

1. Humans can adapt to the environments they inhabit through biological and cultural means. But humans also shape their environments through a variety of cultural practices. What changes do you see occurring in the environment today due to human action? How do you imagine humans will adapt to these changes?

2. The social meanings of science can challenge the place of other belief systems. Is it possible for spiritual and scientific models of human nature to coexist? How do you personally reconcile science and religion?

3. The discovery of the structure and function of the DNA molecule affects individuals and societies in many ways. Has the scientific understanding of the human genetic code challenged your conception of what it means to be human? How much of your life is dictated by the structure of DNA? And what will be the social consequences of depicting humans as entities programmed by their DNA?

4. The frequency of the sickle-cell allele in populations provides a classic example of adaptation on a genetic level. Describe the benefits of this deadly allele. Are mutations good or bad?

5. Why is the evolution of continuous traits more difficult to study than the evolution of a trait controlled by a single gene?

Key Terms

primates	analogies
mammals	homologies
species	natural selection
genus, genera (pl.)	genes
taxonomy	law of segregation

law of independent
   assortment
chromosomes
DNA
chromatid
alleles
genome

mitosis
meiosis
homozygous
heterozygous
genotype
phenotype
dominance

recessive
hemoglobin
phenotypic inheritance
population
gene pool
evolution
mutation

genetic drift
founder effects
gene flow
adaptation
sickle-cell anemia
clines

VISUAL ESSENCE Other primates have long fascinated humans due to our many shared anatomical and behavioral characteristics. Our similarities are visible in the way these Japanese macaques, a species of Old World monkey, enjoy a hot tub on a cold day, much in the same way that a human would. Our differences have had devastating consequences for our closest living relatives in the animal world. No primates other than humans threaten the survival of others on a large scale. As a result of human destruction of primate habitats and hunting of primates for bush-meat or souvenirs, nearly 50 percent of the known 634 primate species and subspecies are threatened with extinction in the next decade. Anthropologists study other primates because their biology and behavior are so close to those of humans, but they also work to ensure that these primates do not go extinct due to human actions.

Living Primates

3

The diversity of life on earth attests to the fact that living organisms solve the challenge of survival in many ways. In evolutionary terms, survival means reproducing subsequent generations of the species and avoiding extinction. Over the course of countless generations, each species has followed its own unique journey, an evolutionary history including random turns as well as patterned adaptation to the environment. Because new species are formed as populations diverge from one another, closely related species resemble one another due to recent common ancestry. In other words, closely related species have shared part of their evolutionary journey together. With each step living creatures can only build on what already exists, making today's diversity a product of tinkering with ancestral body plans, behaviors, and physiology.

In this chapter we will look at the biology and behavior of the primates, the group of animals to which humans belong. By doing so, we will gain a firmer understanding of those characteristics we share with other primates, as well as those that distinguish us from them and make us distinctively human. Studying communication and tool use among our primate cousins today, for example, can help anthropologists reconstruct how and why humans developed as they did.

METHODS AND ETHICS IN PRIMATOLOGY

Just as anthropologists employ diverse methods to study humans, primatologists today use a variety of methods to study the biology, behavior, and evolutionary history of our closest living relatives. Some primatologists concentrate on the comparative anatomy of ancient skeletons, while others trace evolutionary relationships by studying the comparative physiology and genetics of living species. Primatologists study the biology and behavior of living primates both in their natural habitats and in captivity in zoos, primate research colonies, or learning laboratories.

Primates are often caught in the wild and killed for bush-meat or even for souvenirs. Others are captured and sold as pets. These two monkeys hug each other, perhaps for comfort, while caged in a marketplace in Medan, Indonesia. Primatologists have worked extensively to protect primates in their natural habitats and have argued that the same basic rights that are guaranteed to humans should be extended to our closest living relatives in the animal kingdom.

© Associated Press

The classic image of a primatologist is someone like Jane Goodall, a world-renowned British researcher who has devoted her career to in-depth observation of chimpanzees in their natural habitat in Tanzania. While documenting the range and nuance of chimpanzee behavior, she has also championed primate habitat conservation and humane treatment of primates in captivity. This philosophy of conservation and preservation is basic to primatology and has led to additional innovations in research methods. For example, primatologists have developed a number of noninvasive methods that allow them to link primate biology and behavior in the field while minimizing physical disruption. Primatologists gather shedded hair, feces, and other body secretions left by the primates in the environment for later analysis in the laboratory. These analyses provide invaluable information about characteristics such as diet or genetic relatedness among a group of individuals.

Work with captive animals provides more than knowledge about the basic biology of primates. It has also allowed primatologists to document the humanity of our closest living relatives. Many of the amazing linguistic and conceptual abilities of primates became known through studies of captive animals. Individual primatologists have devoted their careers to working with one or several primates in captivity, teaching them to communicate through pictures on a computer screen or American Sign Language. While it is recognized that even compassionate captivity imposes stress on primates, it is hoped that the knowledge gained through these studies will contribute ultimately to primate conservation and survival as human understanding of our closest living relatives increases.

At first glance it might seem that work with captive animals is inherently less "humane" when compared to field studies. However, field studies also raise important ethical issues for primatologists to consider. Primatologists must maintain an awareness of how their presence affects the behavior of the group. For example, does becoming tolerant of human observers make the primates more vulnerable? Primates habituated to humans commonly range beyond established wilderness preserves and come in close contact with other humans who may be more interested in hunting than observation. Contact between primates and humans can also expose endangered primates to infectious diseases carried by humans. Whether working with primates in captivity or in the field, primatologists must seriously consider the well-being of the primates they study.

PRIMATES AS MAMMALS

Biologists classify humans within the primate order, a subgroup of the class Mammalia. The other primates include lemurs, lorises, tarsiers, monkeys, and apes. Humans—together with chimpanzees, bonobos, gorillas, orangutans, gibbons, and siamangs—form the hominoids, colloquially known as apes, a superfamily within the primate order. Biologically speaking, as hominoids, humans are apes!

The primates are only one of several different kinds of mammals, such as rodents, carnivores, and ungulates (hoofed mammals). Primates, like other mammals, are intelligent animals, having more in the way of brains than reptiles or other kinds of vertebrates. This increased brain power, along with the mammalian pattern of growth and development, forms the biological basis of the flexible behavior patterns typical of mammals. In most species, the young are born live, the egg being retained within the womb of the female until the embryo achieves an advanced state of growth. Once born, the young receive milk from their mothers' mammary glands, the structure from which the class Mammalia gets its name. During this period of infant dependency, young mammals learn many of the things they will need for survival as adults. Primates in general and apes in particular have a very long period of infant and childhood dependency in which the young learn the ways of their social group. Thus, mammalian primate biology is central to primate behavioral patterns.

Relative to other members of the animal kingdom, mammals are highly active. This activity is made possible by a relatively constant body temperature, an efficient respiratory system featuring a separation between the nasal (nose) and mouth cavities (allowing them to breathe while they eat), a diaphragm to assist in drawing in and letting out breath, and an efficient

four-chambered heart that prevents mixing of oxygenated and deoxygenated blood. Primates possess a skeleton in which the limbs are positioned beneath the body, rather than out at the sides, for easy flexible movement. The bones of the limbs have joints constructed to permit growth in the young while simultaneously providing strong, hard joint surfaces that will stand up to the stresses of sustained activity. Mammals stop growing when they reach adulthood, whereas reptiles continue to grow through their lives.

Mammals and reptiles also differ in terms of their teeth. Reptiles possess identical, pointed, peglike teeth, whereas mammals have teeth specialized for particular purposes: incisors for nipping, gnawing, and cutting; canines for ripping, tearing, killing, and fighting; premolars that may either slice and tear or crush and grind (depending on the kind of animal); and molars for crushing and grinding (Figure 3.1). This enables mammals to eat a wide variety of food—an advantage to them, since they require more food than reptiles to sustain their high activity level. But they pay a price: Reptiles have unlimited tooth replacement throughout their lives, whereas mammals are limited to two sets. The first set serves the immature animal and is replaced by the "permanent" or adult teeth. The specializations of mammalian teeth allow species and evolutionary relationships to be identified through dental comparisons.

Evidence from ancient skeletons indicates the first mammals appeared over 200 million years ago as small

Providing milk to young via mammary glands distinguishes mammals from other animals. Nursing young individuals is an important part of the general mammalian tendency to invest high amounts of energy into rearing relatively few young at a time. The pattern in reptiles is to lay many eggs that hatch independently, with the young fending for themselves.

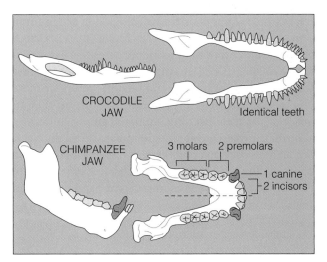

Figure 3.1

The crocodile jaw, like jaws of all reptiles, contains a series of identical teeth. If a tooth breaks or falls out, a new tooth will emerge in its place. Mammals, by contrast, possess precise numbers of specialized teeth, each with a particular shape characteristic of the group, as indicated on the chimpanzee jaw: Incisors in front are shown in blue, canines behind in red, followed by two premolars and three molars in yellow (the last being the "wisdom teeth" in humans).

nocturnal (active at night) creatures. The earliest primatelike creatures came into being about 65 million years ago when a new mild climate favored the spread of dense tropical and subtropical forests over much of the earth. The change in climate and habitat, combined with the sudden extinction of dinosaurs, favored mammal diversification, including the evolutionary development of **arboreal** (tree-living) mammals from which primates evolved.

The ancestral primates possessed biological characteristics that allowed them to adapt to life in the forests. Their relatively small size enabled them to use tree branches not accessible to larger competitors and predators. Arboreal life opened up an abundant new food supply. The primates were able to gather leaves, flowers, fruits, insects, birds' eggs, and even nesting birds, rather than having to wait for them to fall to the ground. Natural selection favored those who judged depth correctly and gripped the branches tightly. Those individuals who survived life in the trees passed on their genes to the succeeding generations. Although the earliest primates were nocturnal, today most primate species are **diurnal** (active in the day). The transition to diurnal life in the trees involved important biological adjustments that helped shape the biology and behavior of humans today.

PRIMATE CHARACTERISTICS

While the living primates are a varied group of animals, they do share a number of features. We humans, for example, can grasp, throw things, and see in three dimensions because of shared primate characteristics. Compared to other mammals, primates possess a relatively unspecialized anatomy, whereas their behavioral patterns are diverse and flexible. Many primate characteristics are useful in one way or another to arboreal, or tree-dwelling, animals, although (as any squirrel knows) they are not essential to life in the trees. For animals preying upon the many insects living on the fruit and flowers of trees and shrubs, however, primate characteristics such as manipulative hands and keen

nocturnal Active at night and at rest during the day
arboreal Living in the trees
diurnal Active during the day and at rest at night
binocular vision Vision with increased depth perception from two eyes set next to each other allowing their visual fields to overlap
stereoscopic vision Complete three-dimensional vision (or depth perception) from binocular vision and nerve connections that run from each eye to both sides of the brain allowing nerve cells to integrate the images derived from each eye

vision would have been enormously adaptive. Life in the trees along with the visual predation of insects played a role in the evolution of primate biology.

Primate Dentition

While mammalian teeth are more specialized than those of reptiles (recall Figure 3.1), the varied primate diet—shoots, leaves, insects, and fruits—requires relatively unspecialized teeth, compared to those found in other mammals. The evolutionary trend for primate dentition has been toward a reduction in the number and size of the teeth. The earliest primates as well as many species of mammals alive today possess more incisors, premolars, and molar teeth than living primates. The canine teeth of most of the primates, especially males, are daggerlike and useful for ripping into tough foods. Canines also serve well in social communication. Adult males display their large canines in order to assert their dominance.

Sensory Organs

The primates' adaptation to arboreal life involved changes in the form and function of their sensory organs. The sense of smell was vital for the earliest ground-dwelling, night-active mammals. It enabled them to operate in the dark, to sniff out their food, and to detect hidden predators. However, for active tree life during daylight, good vision is a better guide than smell in judging the location of the next branch or tasty morsel. Accordingly, the sense of smell declined in primates, while vision became highly developed.

Travel through the trees demands judgments concerning depth, direction, distance, and the relationships of objects hanging in space, such as vines or branches. Monkeys, apes, and humans achieved this through binocular stereoscopic color vision (Figure 3.2), the ability to see the world in the three dimensions of height, width, and depth. **Binocular vision** (in which two eyes sit next to each other on the same plane so that their visual fields overlap) together with nerve connections that run from each eye to both sides of the brain confer complete depth perception characteristic of three-dimensional or **stereoscopic vision**. This arrangement allows nerve cells to integrate the images derived from each eye. Increased brain size in the visual area in primates and a greater complexity of nerve connections also contribute to stereoscopic color vision.

Tree-living primates also possess an acute sense of touch. An effective feeling and grasping mechanism helps keep them from falling and tumbling while speeding through the trees. The early mammals from which

© Iven DeVore/Anthro-Photo

Though the massive canine teeth of some male primates are serious weapons, they are more often used to communicate rather than to draw blood. Raising his lip to "flash" his canines, this baboon will get the young members of his group in line right away. Over the course of human evolution, overall canine size decreased, as did differences in canine size between males and females.

The Primate Brain

An increase in brain size, particularly in the cerebral hemispheres—the areas supporting conscious thought—occurred in the course of primate evolution. In monkeys, apes, and humans, the cerebral hemispheres completely cover the cerebellum, the part of the brain that coordinates the muscles and maintains body balance. One of the most significant outcomes of this development is the flexibility seen in primate behavior. Rather than relying on reflexes controlled by the cerebellum, primates constantly react to a variety of features in the environment. Messages from the hands and feet, eyes and ears, as well as from the sensors of balance, movement, heat, touch, and pain, are simultaneously relayed to the cerebral cortex.

Obviously the cortex had to evolve considerably in order to receive, analyze, and coordinate these impressions and transmit the appropriate response back to the motor nerves. The enlarged, responsive cerebral cortex provides the biological basis for flexible behavior patterns found in all primates, including humans.

The emphasis on vision in primates described above corresponded to changes in the primate brain. Reptiles possess nerve cells in the backs of their eyes that process visual information. All mammals, by contrast, process visual messages in the brain, which allows this information to be integrated with other sensory information: sound, touch, taste, position sense, and smell.

It is also likely that primates' insect predation in an arboreal setting played a role in the enlargement of the

Primary receiving area for visual information

Figure 3.2

Monkeys, apes, and humans possess binocular stereoscopic vision. Binocular vision refers to overlapping visual fields due to forward-facing eyes. Three-dimensional or stereoscopic vision comes from binocular vision and the transmission of information from each eye to both sides of the brain.

primates evolved possessed tiny touch-sensitive hairs at the tips of their hands and feet. In primates, sensitive pads backed up by nails on the tips of the animals' fingers and toes replaced these hairs.

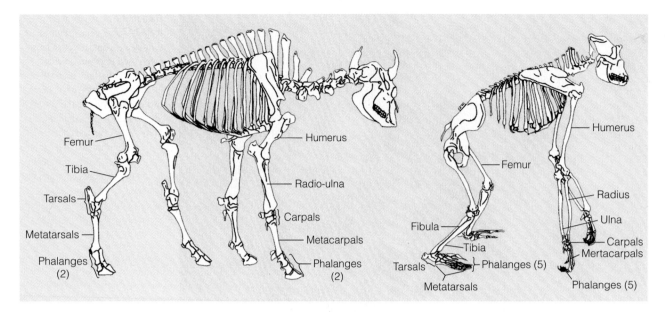

Figure 3.3

All primates possess the same ancestral vertebrate limb pattern as seen in reptiles and amphibians, consisting of a single upper long bone, two lower long bones, and five radiating digits (fingers and toes), as seen in this gorilla (right) skeleton. Other mammals such as bison (left) have a modified version of this pattern. In the course of evolution bison have lost all but two of their digits, which form their hooves. The second long bone in the lower part of the limb is reduced. Note also the joining of the skull and vertebral column in these skeletons. In bison (as in most mammals) the skull projects forward from the vertebral column, but in semi-erect gorillas, the vertebral column is further beneath the skull.

brain. This behavior pattern would have required great agility and motor coordination, which would favor development of these areas of the brain. Interestingly, the parts of the brain responsible for higher mental faculties developed in an area alongside the motor centers of the brain.[1]

---

opposable Able to bring the thumb or big toe in contact with the tips of the other digits on the same hand or foot in order to grasp objects

prosimians A subdivision within the primate order based on shared anatomical characteristics that includes lemurs, lorises, and tarsiers

anthropoids A subdivision within the primate order based on shared anatomical characteristics that includes New World monkeys, Old World monkeys, and apes (including humans)

strepsirhines A subdivision within the primate order based on shared genetic characteristics; includes lemurs and lorises

haplorhines A subdivision within the primate order based on shared genetic characteristics; includes tarsiers, New World monkeys, Old World monkeys, and apes (including humans)

---

[1]Romer, A. S. (1945). *Vertebrate paleontology* (p. 103). Chicago: University of Chicago Press.

The Primate Skeleton

The skeleton gives vertebrates—animals with internal backbones—their basic shape or silhouette, supports the soft tissues, and helps protect vital internal organs (Figure 3.3). Some evolutionary trends are evident in the primate skeleton. For example, as primates relied increasingly on vision rather than smell, the eyes rotated forward to become enclosed in a protective layer of bone. Simultaneously, the snout reduced in size. The opening at the base of the skull for passage of the spinal cord assumed a more forward position, reflecting some degree of upright posture rather than a constant four-footed stance.

The limbs of the primate skeleton follow the same basic ancestral plan seen in the earliest vertebrates. The upper portion of each arm or leg has a single long bone, the lower portion has two bones, and then hands or feet with five radiating digits. Many other animals possess limbs specialized to optimize a particular behavior, such as running. The generalized limb pattern allows for flexible movements by primates.

In nearly all of the primates, the big toe and thumb are **opposable**, making it possible to grasp and manipulate objects such as sticks and stones with both the hands and feet. Humans and their direct ancestors are the only exceptions, having lost the opposable big toe. Other aspects of primate skeletal variation include the shape of the collarbone (clavicle), which varies among primate groups depending upon their pattern of locomotion. Monkeys move about on all fours and so have narrow bodies with short collarbones. In the apes, a long collarbone orients the arms at the side rather than at the front of the body, allowing for heightened flexibility. With their broad flexible shoulder joints, apes can hang suspended from tree branches and swing from tree to tree.

The retention of the flexible vertebrate limb pattern in primates was a valuable asset to evolving humans. It was, in part, having hands capable of grasping that enabled our own ancestors to manufacture and use tools and thus alter the course of their evolution. Today our ape anatomy allows humans to do things as varied as throw a baseball at lightning speed or weave intricate patterns from threads suspended on wide looms.

LIVING PRIMATES

Except for a few species of monkeys who live in temperate climates and humans who inhabit the entire globe, the living primates inhabit warm areas of the world. We will briefly explore the diverse biology and behavior of five natural groupings of contemporary primates: (1) lemurs and lorises, (2) tarsiers, (3) New World monkeys (monkeys native to Central and South America), (4) Old World monkeys (monkeys native to Africa and Eurasia), and (5) apes.

Traditionally, primatologists grouped lemurs, lorises, and tarsiers together as **prosimians** (from the Latin for "before monkeys") based on morphological similarities they share with the most ancient primates. They placed monkeys, apes, and humans together as **anthropoids** (from the Greek for "humanlike"). Recent molecular evidence has shown that tarsiers are more closely related to monkeys, apes, and humans than to lemurs and lorises. Thus, a molecular approach divides the primates into two groups called the **strepsirhines** (lemurs and lorises) and the **haplorhines** (tarsiers, monkeys, apes, and humans). For the purposes of this chapter, which emphasizes the entire adaptive package of primate groups, dividing the primates into prosimians and anthropoids makes sense. The anatomy and behavior of the prosimians most closely resemble the nocturnal behavioral pattern of the earliest primates. The anthropoid primates tend to be larger, active in the daytime, and live in large social groups. The anthropoids out-competed diurnal prosimians in regions where both kinds of primate co-exist.

Lemurs and Lorises

Lemurs are restricted to the island of Madagascar (off the east coast of Africa), while lorises range from Africa to southern and eastern Asia. The lorises, like the ancestral primates, are all nocturnal, or active at night, and arboreal. On Madagascar, where there was no competition from anthropoid primates until humans arrived, lemurs diversified substantially, with many lemur species becoming ground-dwelling and diurnal, or active during the day. The fossil evidence from Madagascar shows that some lemurs even reached very large sizes.

All living prosimian species are small, with none larger than a good-sized dog. In general body outline, they resemble rodents and insect-eating animals, with short pointed snouts, large pointed ears, and big eyes. In the anatomy of the upper lip and snout, lemurs and lorises resemble nonprimate mammals, in that the upper lip is bound down to the gum, and the naked skin on the nose around the nostrils is moist and split. They also have long tails. The striped tail of a ring-tailed lemur is somewhat like the tail of a raccoon.

Lemurs and lorises have typical primate "hands," although they use them in pairs, rather than one at a time. Sensitive pads and flattened nails are located at the tips of the fingers and toes, and they retain a claw on their second toe, sometimes called a "grooming claw," which they use for scratching and cleaning. Lemurs and lorises possess another unique structure for grooming: a dental comb made up of the lower incisors and canines that projects forward from the jaw and that can be run through their fur. Though lemurs and lorises have retained a number of ancestral characteristics typical of the earliest fossil primates and the insectivores from which primates evolved, it is incorrect to think of them as "less evolved"; they have simply taken a unique evolutionary path since their divergence from the other primates.

Over the course of their evolutionary history, primates came to rely more on their vision than on their sense of smell. Prosimians, who were the earliest group of primates to appear, maintain their primary reliance on smell. On the island of Madagascar, home to many species of diurnal ground-dwelling lemurs, such as the ring-tailed lemur, the prosimians mark their territory and communicate through "smelly" messages left for others with a squirt from glands located on their wrists. Though prosimians appeared before the anthropoids in primate evolution, and retain many ancestral features such as their dependence on smell, they are no less evolved. Outside of Madagascar, prosimians remained arboreal and nocturnal due to competition from monkeys and apes.

Tarsiers

Outwardly, and in their nocturnal habit, tarsiers resemble the lemurs and lorises. Genetically, however, they are more closely related to monkeys and apes. In the structure of the nose and lips, and the part of the brain governing vision, tarsiers resemble monkeys.

Tarsiers are mainly nocturnal insect eaters. The head, eyes, and ears of these kitten-sized arboreal creatures are huge in proportion to the body, making them well adapted for nocturnal life. If human faces had eyes with the same proportions as tarsiers, our eyes would be approximately the size of oranges. Tarsiers have the remarkable ability to turn their heads 180 degrees, so they can see where they have been as well as where they are going.

Tarsiers, like some lemurs and lorises, possess longer hind limbs than their front limbs, allowing them to move from tree to tree by vertical clinging and leaping. First they hang onto the trunk of one tree in an upright

With their large eyes, tarsiers are well adapted for nocturnal life. If human faces had eyes with the same proportions as tarsiers, our eyes would be approximately the size of oranges. In their nocturnal habit and outward appearance, tarsiers resemble lemurs and lorises. Genetically, however, they are more closely related to monkeys and apes, causing scientists to rework the suborder divisions in primate taxonomy to reflect this evolutionary relationship.

prehensile Having the ability to grasp
brachiation Using the arms to move from branch to branch, with the body hanging suspended beneath the arms

position, with their long legs curled up tightly like springs and their heads twisted to look in the direction they are moving. They propel themselves into the air, do a "180," and land facing the trunk on their tree of choice. Tarsiers are named for the elongated tarsal, or foot bone, that provides these tiny animals leverage for jumps of 6 feet or more.

Anthropoids: Monkeys and Apes

Monkeys, apes, and humans resemble one another more than any of these groups resemble lemurs, lorises, or tarsiers. Humans are remarkably like monkeys but even more like the other apes in their appearance.

New World monkeys live in tropical forests of South and Central America. All are arboreal with long

Grasping hands and three-dimensional vision enable primates like these South American monkeys to lead active lives in the trees. In some New World monkey species, a grasping or prehensile tail makes life in the trees even easier. The naked skin on the undersides of their tails resembles the sensitive skin found at the tips of our fingers and is even covered with whorls like fingerprints. This sensory skin allows New World monkeys to use their tails as a fifth limb.

tails. Some groups of New World monkeys possess **prehensile** or grasping tails, which they use as a fifth limb. The naked skin on the undersides of their tails resembles the sensitive skin found at the tips of our fingers and is even covered with whorls like fingerprints. These and other features distinguish the New World monkeys from the Old World monkeys, apes, and humans. Old World monkeys and apes, including humans, have a 40-million-year shared evolutionary history in Africa that is distinct from the course taken by anthropoid primates in the tropical Americas.

The Old World monkeys, divided from the apes at the taxonomic level of superfamily, possess nonprehensile tails. They may live on the ground or in the trees, using a quadrapedal or four-footed pattern of locomotion on the ground or a palms-down position in the trees. Their bodies are narrow with hind limbs and forelimbs of equal length and relatively fixed and sturdy shoulder, elbow, and wrist joints. Old World monkey species range from the tropical regions of Africa and Asia to Gibraltar off the southern coast of Spain to as far north as Japan.

Baboons, a kind of Old World monkey, have been of particular interest to paleoanthropologists because some baboon species live in environments similar to those in which humans may have originated. These baboons have abandoned trees (except for sleeping and refuge) and are largely terrestrial, living in the savannahs, deserts, and highlands of Africa. They have long, fierce faces and eat a diet consisting of leaves, seeds, insects, and lizards. They live in large, well-organized troops comprised of related females and adult males that have transferred out of other troops.

Small and Great Apes

The other apes (the hominoid superfamily) are the closest living relatives we humans have in the animal world. They include gibbons, siamangs, orangutans, gorillas, chimpanzees, and bonobos. Apes (including humans) are large, tail-less, wide-bodied primates. All apes possess a shoulder anatomy specialized for hanging suspended below tree branches, although among apes only gibbons and talented gymnasts swing from branch to branch in the pattern known as **brachiation**. At the opposite extreme are gorillas, which generally climb trees, using their hands and feet to grip the trunks and branches. While smaller gorillas may swing from branch to branch, in larger individuals swinging is limited to leaning outward while reaching for fruit and clasping a limb for support. Still, most of their time is spent on the ground. All apes except humans and their immediate ancestors possess arms that are longer than their legs.

© Peter Drowne/Color-Pic, Inc.

All apes, including humans, possess widely spaced flexible shoulder joints for hanging suspended below the branches or swinging from branch to branch. Gibbons are the masters of the swinging form of locomotion called brachiation (from the Latin for "arm motion"). Large apes, such as this orangutan, move slowly through the lower branches using their long arms to span great distances.

In moving on the ground, the African apes "knuckle-walk" on the backs of their hands, resting their weight on the middle joints of the fingers. They stand erect when reaching for fruit, looking over tall grass, or doing any activity where they find an erect position advantageous. Though apes can walk on two legs (bipedally) for short periods of time, the structure of the ape pelvis is not well suited to support the weight of the torso and limbs for more than several minutes.

Standing about 3 feet high, gibbons and siamangs, the small apes that are native to Southeast Asia and Malaya, have compact, slim bodies with extraordinarily long arms compared to their short legs. Although their usual form of locomotion is brachiation, they can run erect, holding their arms out for balance. Gibbon and siamang males and females are similar in size, living in social groups of two adults and offspring.

community A unit of primate social organization composed of fifty or more individuals who inhabit a large geographical area together

dominance hierarchies An observed ranking system in primate societies ordering individuals from high (alpha) to low standing corresponding to predictable behavioral interactions including domination

Orangutans are found in Borneo and Sumatra. They are considerably taller than gibbons and siamangs and are much heavier, as are the other great apes. In the closeness of the eyes and facial prominence, an orangutan looks humanlike. The people of Sumatra gave orangutans their name, "man of the forest," using the Malay term *orang*, which means "human." On the ground, orangutans walk with their forelimbs in a fists-sideways or a palms-down position. They are, however, more arboreal than the African apes. Although sociable by nature, the orangutans of upland Borneo spend most of their time alone (except in the case of females with young), as they have to forage over a wide area to obtain sufficient food. By contrast, fruits and insects are sufficiently abundant in the swamps of Sumatra to sustain groups of adults and permit coordinated group travel. Thus, gregariousness is a function of the richness of their habitat.[2]

Gorillas, found in tropical Africa, are the largest of the apes; an adult male can weigh over 450 pounds, with females about half that size. The body is covered with a thick coat of glossy black hair, and mature males have a silvery gray upper back. There is a strikingly human

[2]Normile, D. (1998). Habitat seen as playing larger role in shaping behavior. *Science, 279,* 1454.

look about the face, and like humans, gorillas focus on things in their field of vision by directing the eyes rather than moving the head. Gorillas are mostly ground dwellers, but the lighter females and young may sleep in trees in carefully constructed nests. Because of their weight, adult males spend less time in the trees but raise and lower themselves among the tree branches when searching for fruit. Gorillas knuckle-walk, using all four limbs with the fingers of the hand flexed, placing the knuckles instead of the palm of the hand on the ground. They stand erect to reach for fruit, to see something more easily, or to threaten perceived sources of danger with their famous chest-beating displays. Though known for these displays to protect the members of their troop, adult male "silverback" gorillas are the gentle giants of the forest. As vegetarians, gorillas devote a major portion of each day to eating volumes of plant matter to sustain their massive bodies. Although gorillas are gentle and tolerant, bluffing is an important part of their behavioral repertoire.

Chimpanzees and bonobos are two closely related species of the same genus (*Pan*), bonobos being lesser known and restricted in their distribution to the rainforests of the Democratic Republic of Congo. Common chimpanzees, by contrast, are widely distributed in the forested portions of sub-Saharan Africa. Long-time favorites in zoos and circuses, chimpanzees are regarded as particularly quick and clever. Nevertheless, all four great apes are of equal intelligence, despite some differences in cognitive styles. More arboreal than gorillas, but less so than orangutans, chimpanzees and bonobos forage on the ground much of the day, knuckle-walking like gorillas. At sunset, they return to the trees, where they build their nests. Chimps build their nests over a wide area, whereas bonobos prefer to build their nests close to one another.

PRIMATE BEHAVIOR

Primates adapt to their environments through a wide variety of behaviors. Primates are social animals, living and traveling in groups that vary in size from species to species. In many primate species, including humans, adolescence is a time during which individuals change the relationships they have had with the group they have known since birth. Among primates this change takes the form of migration of either males or females to new social groups.

Young apes spend more time reaching adulthood than do most other mammals. During this lengthy period of growth and development, they learn the behaviors of their social group. While biological factors play a role in the duration of primate dependency, many of the specific behaviors learned during childhood derive solely from the traditions of the group. The behavior of primates, particularly apes, provides anthropologists with clues about the earliest development of human culture.

Primatologists have carried out many studies of ape behavior in the animals' natural habitats, seeking models to help reconstruct the behavior of evolving humans. While no living primate lives exactly as our ancestors did, these studies have revealed remarkable variation and sophistication in ape behavior. Primatologists increasingly interpret these variations as cultural because they are learned rather than genetically programmed or instinctive. We shall concentrate on the behavior of two closely related African species of chimpanzee: common chimpanzees and bonobos.

Chimpanzee and Bonobo Behavior

Like nearly all primates, chimpanzees and bonobos are highly social animals. Among chimps, the largest social organizational unit is the **community**, usually composed of fifty or more individuals who collectively inhabit a large geographical area. Rarely, however, are all of these animals together at one time. Instead, they are usually found ranging singly or in small subgroups consisting of adult males, or females with their young, or males and females together with their young. In the course of their travels, subgroups may join forces and forage together, but sooner or later these will break up again into smaller units. Typically, when some individuals split off others join, so the composition of subunits shifts frequently.

Relationships among individuals within some of the ape communities studied are relatively harmonious. In the past, primatologists believed that male **dominance hierarchies**, in which some animals outrank and can dominate others, formed the basis of primate social structures. They noted that physical strength and size play a role in determining an animal's rank. By this measure males generally outrank females. However, the male-biased cultures of many primatologists may have contributed to this theoretical perspective with its emphasis on domination through superior size and strength. Male dominance hierarchies seemed "natural" to these early researchers.

With the benefit of detailed field studies over the last forty years, including cutting-edge research by primatologists such as Jane Goodall, the nuances of primate social behavior and the importance of female primates have been documented. High-ranking female chimpanzees may dominate low-ranking males. And among bonobos, female rank determines the social order of the group far more than male rank. While greater strength and size do contribute to an animal's higher rank, several other factors also come into play in determining its social position. These include the rank of its mother, which is largely determined through her cooperative social behavior and how effectively each individual animal creates alliances with others.

On the whole, bonobo females form stronger bonds with one another than do chimpanzee females. Moreover, the strength of the bond between mother and son interferes with bonds among males. Bonobo males defer to females in feeding, and alpha (high-ranking) females have been observed chasing alpha males; such males may even yield to low-ranking females, particularly when groups of females form alliances.[3] Further, allied females will band together to force an aggressive male out of the community. This is particularly interesting in light of the fact that bonobo females are cooperating even though they are not genetically related to one another.[4]

The emphasis on social ranking, competition, and attack behavior by Western primatologists may have derived in part from the values of Western cultures. By contrast, Japanese primatologist Kinji Imanishi, who initiated field studies of bonobos in the early 20th century, investigated and demonstrated the importance of social cooperation rather than competition. Likewise, Dutch primatologist Frans de Waal's research, highlighted in the following Original Study, shows that reconciliation after an attack may be even more important from an evolutionary perspective than the actual attack.

Original Study

Reconciliation and Its Cultural Modification in Primates

Frans B. M. de Waal

Despite the continuing popularity of the struggle-for-life metaphor, it is increasingly recognized that there are drawbacks to open competition, hence that there are sound evolutionary reasons for curbing it. The dependency of social animals on group life and cooperation makes aggression a socially costly strategy. The basic dilemma facing many animals, including humans, is that they sometimes cannot win a fight without losing a friend.

This photo shows what may happen after a conflict—in this case between two female bonobos. About 10 minutes after their fight, the two females approach each other, with one clinging to the other and both rubbing their clitorises and genital swellings together in a pattern known as genito-genital (or GG) rubbing. This sexual contact, typical of bonobos, constitutes a so-called reconciliation. Chimpanzees, which are closely related to bonobos (and to us: Bonobos and chimpanzees are our closest animal relatives), usually reconcile in a less sexual fashion, with an embrace and mouth-to-mouth kiss.

There is now evidence for reconciliation in more than twenty-five different primate species, not just in apes but also in many monkeys. The same sorts of studies have been conducted on human children in the schoolyard, and of course children show reconciliation as well. Researchers have even found reconciliation in dolphins, spotted

© Amy Parish/Anthro-Photo

Two adult female bonobos engage in so-called GG rubbing, a sexual form of reconciliation typical of this species.

---

[3]de Waal, F., Kano, T., & Parish, A. R. (1998). Comments. *Current Anthropology, 39,* 408, 410, 413.

[4]Gierstorfer, C. (2007). Peaceful primates, violent acts. *Nature, 447,* 7.

hyenas, and some other nonprimates. Reconciliation seems widespread: A common mechanism found whenever relationships need to be maintained despite occasional conflict.[a, b]

The definition of reconciliation used in animal research is a friendly reunion between former opponents not long after a conflict. This is somewhat different from definitions in the dictionary, primarily because we look for an empirical definition that is useful in observational studies—in our case, the stipulation that the reunion happen not long after the conflict. There is no intrinsic reason that a reconciliation could not occur after hours or days, or, in the case of humans, generations.

Let me describe two interesting elaborations on the mechanism of reconciliation. One is *mediation.* Chimpanzees are the only animals to use mediators in conflict resolution. In order to be able to mediate conflict, one needs to understand relationships outside of oneself, which may be the reason why other animals fail to show this aspect of conflict resolution. For example, if two male chimpanzees have been involved in a fight, even on a very large island as where I did my studies, they can easily avoid each other, but instead they will sit opposite from each other, not too far apart, and avoid eye contact. They can sit like this for a long time. In this situation, a third party, such as an older female, may move in and try to solve the issue. The female will approach one of the males and groom him for a brief while. She then gets up and walks slowly to the other male, and the first male walks right behind her.

We have seen situations in which, if the first male failed to follow, the female turned around to grab his arm and make him follow. So the process of getting the two males in proximity

seems intentional on the part of the female. She then begins grooming the other male, and the first male grooms her. Before long, the female disappears from the scene, and the males continue grooming: She has in effect brought the two parties together.

There exists a limited anthropological literature on the role of conflict resolution, a process absolutely crucial for the maintenance of the human social fabric in the same way that it is crucial for our primate relatives. In human society, mediation is often done by high-ranking or senior members of the community, sometimes culminating in feasts in which the restoration of harmony is celebrated.[c]

The second elaboration on the reconciliation concept is that it is not purely instinctive, not even in our animal relatives. It is a learned social skill subject to what primatologists now increasingly call "culture" (meaning that the behavior is subject to learning from others as opposed to genetic transmission[d]). To test the learnability of reconciliation, I conducted an experiment with young rhesus and stumptail monkeys.

Not nearly as conciliatory as stumptail monkeys, rhesus monkeys have the reputation of being rather aggressive and despotic. Stumptails are considered more laid-back and tolerant. We housed members of the two species together for 5 months. By the end of this period, they were a fully integrated group: They slept, played, and groomed together. After 5 months, we separated them again, and measured the effect of their time together on conciliatory behavior. The research controls—rhesus monkeys who had lived with one another, without any stumptails—showed absolutely no change in the tendency to reconcile. Stumptails showed a high rate of reconciliation, which was also expected, because they also do so if living together. The most interesting group was the

experimental rhesus monkeys, those who had lived with stumptails.

These monkeys started out at the same low level of reconciliation as the rhesus controls, but after they had lived with the stumptails, and after we had segregated them again so that they were now housed only with other rhesus monkeys who had gone through the same experience, these rhesus monkeys reconciled as much as stumptails do. This means that we created a "new and improved" rhesus monkey, one that made up with its opponents far more easily than a regular rhesus monkey.[e]

This was in effect an experiment on social culture: We changed the culture of a group of rhesus monkeys and made it more similar to that of stumptail monkeys by exposing them to the practices of this other species. This experiment also shows that there exists a great deal of flexibility in primate behavior. We humans come from a long lineage of primates with great social sophistication and a well-developed potential for behavioral modification and learning from others.

(By Frans B. M. de Waal, Living Links, Yerkes National Primate Research Center, Emory University)

[a]de Waal, F. B. M. (2000). Primates—A natural heritage of conflict resolution. *Science, 28,* 586–590.

[b]Aureli, F., & de Waal, F. B. M. (2000). *Natural conflict resolution.* Berkeley: University of California Press.

[c]Reviewed by Frye, D. P. (2000). Conflict management in cross-cultural perspective. In F. Aureli & F. B. M. de Waal, *Natural conflict resolution* (pp. 334–351). Berkeley: University of California Press.

[d]See de Waal, F. B. M. (2001). *The ape and the sushi master.* New York: Basic Books, for a discussion of the animal culture concept.

[e]de Waal, F. B. M., & Johanowicz, D. L. (1993). Modification of reconciliation behavior through social experience: An experiment with two macaque species. *Child Development, 64,* 897–908.

The social sophistication characteristic of primates is evident in behaviors that at first glance might seem wholly practical. For example, **grooming**, the ritual cleaning of another animal to remove parasites and other matter from its skin or coat, is a common pastime for both chimpanzees and bonobos. Besides serving hygienic purposes, it can be a gesture of friendliness, closeness, appeasement, reconciliation, or even submission. Bonobos and chimpanzees have favorite grooming partners. Group sociability, an important behavioral trait undoubtedly also found among human ancestors, is further expressed in embracing, touching,

grooming The ritual cleaning of another animal's skin and fur to remove parasites and other matter and the joyous welcoming of other members of the ape community.

Group protection and coordination of group efforts are facilitated by visual and vocal communication, including special calls for warnings, threats, and gathering. Prior to the 1980s most primates were thought to be vegetarian while humans alone were considered meat-eating hunters. Pioneering research by Jane Goodall, among others, revealed that the diets of monkeys and apes were extremely varied. Goodall's fieldwork among chimpanzees in their natural habitat at Gombe, a wildlife reserve on the eastern shores of Lake Tanganyika in Tanzania, revealed that these apes supplement their primary diet of fruits and other plant foods with insects and meat. Even more surprising, she found that in addition to killing small invertebrate animals for food, they also hunted and ate monkeys. Goodall observed chimpanzees grabbing adult red colobus monkeys and flailing them to death.[5] Since her pioneering work, other primatologists have documented hunting behavior in baboons and capuchin monkeys, among others.

Chimpanzee females sometimes hunt, but males do so far more frequently. When on the hunt, they may spend up to two hours watching, following, and chasing intended prey. Moreover, in contrast to the usual primate practice of each animal finding its own food, hunting frequently involves teamwork to trap and kill prey, particularly when hunting for baboons. Once a potential victim has been isolated from its troop, three or more adult chimps will carefully position themselves so as to block off escape routes while another pursues the prey. Following the kill, most who are present get a share of the meat, either by grabbing a piece as chance affords or by begging for it.

Whatever the nutritional value of meat, hunting is not done purely for dietary purposes, but for social and sexual reasons as well. U.S. anthropologist Craig Stanford, who has been doing fieldwork among the chimpanzees of Gombe since the early 1990s, found that these sizable apes (100-pound males are common) frequently kill animals weighing up to 25 pounds and eat much more meat than previously believed. Their preferred prey is the red colobus monkey that shares their forested habitat. Annually, chimpanzee hunting parties at Gombe kill about 20 percent of these monkeys, many of them babies, often shaking them out of the tops of 30-foot trees. They may capture and kill as many as seven victims in a raid. These hunts usually take place during the dry season when plant foods are less readily available and when females display genital swelling, which signals that they are ready to mate. On average, each chimp at Gombe eats about a quarter-pound of meat per day during the dry season. For female chimps, a supply of protein-rich food helps support the increased nutritional requirements of pregnancy and lactation.

Somewhat different chimpanzee hunting practices have been observed in West Africa. At Tai National Park in the Ivory Coast, for instance, chimpanzees engage in highly coordinated team efforts to chase monkeys hiding in very tall trees in the dense tropical forest. Individuals who have especially distinguished themselves in a successful hunt see their contributions rewarded with more meat. Recent research shows that bonobos in Congo's rainforest also supplement their diet with meat obtained by means of hunting. Although their behavior resembles that of the chimpanzees, there are crucial differences.

Among bonobos, hunting is primarily a female activity. Also, female hunters regularly share carcasses with other females, but less often with males. Even when the most dominant male throws a tantrum nearby, he may still be denied a share of meat.[6] Female bonobos behave in much the same way when it comes to sharing other foods such as fruits.

ovulation Moment when an egg released from the ovaries into the womb is receptive for fertilization

---

[5]Goodall J. (1986). *The chimpanzees of Gombe: Patterns of behavior.* Cambridge, MA: Belknap Press.

[6]Ingmanson, E. J. (1998). Comment. *Current Anthropology, 39,* 409.

humans) sexuality goes far beyond male–female mating for purposes of biological reproduction. Primatologists have observed virtually every possible combination of ages and sexes engaging in a remarkable array of sexual activities, including oral sex, tongue-kissing, and massaging each other's genitals. Male bonobos may mount each other, or one may rub his scrotum against that of the other. They have also been observed "penis fencing"—hanging face to face from a branch and rubbing their erect penises together as if crossing swords. Among females, genital rubbing is particularly common. As described in this chapter's Original Study, the primary function of most of this sex, both hetero- and homosexual, is to reduce tensions and resolve social conflicts. Since the documentation of a variety of sexual activities among bonobos, field studies by primatologists working with other species are now recording a variety of sexual behaviors among these species as well.

Reproduction and Care of Young

Most mammals mate only during specified breeding seasons occurring once or twice a year, but many primate species are able to breed at any time during the course of the year. The average adult female monkey or ape spends most of her adult life either pregnant or nursing her young, times at which she is not sexually receptive. Apes generally nurse each of their young for about four years. After her infant is weaned, she will become pregnant again. Human societies modify the succession and timing of pregnancy and lactation by a variety of cultural means.

Among most (but not all) primates, females generally give birth to one infant at a time. Natural selection may have favored single births among primate tree dwellers because the primate infant, which has a highly developed grasping ability (the grasping reflex can also be seen in human infants), must be transported about by its mother, and more than one clinging infant would seriously encumber her as she moved about the trees.

Primates follow a pattern of bearing few young but devoting more time and effort to the care of each individual offspring. Compared to other mammals such as mice, which pass from birth to adulthood in a matter of weeks, primates spend a great deal of time growing up. As a general rule, the more closely related to humans the primate species is, the longer the period of infant and childhood dependency. For example, a lemur is dependent upon its mother for only a few months after birth, while an ape is dependent for four or five years. A chimpanzee infant cannot survive if its mother dies before it reaches the age of 4

The sexual practices of chimpanzees and bonobos differ as much as their hunting strategies. For chimps, sexual activity—initiated by either the male or the female—occurs primarily during the periods when females signal their fertility through genital swelling. By most human standards, chimp sexual behavior is promiscuous. A dozen or so males have been observed to have as many as fifty copulations in one day with a single female. Dominant males try to monopolize sexually receptive females, although cooperation from the female is usually required for this to succeed. An individual female and a lower-ranking male sometimes form a temporary bond, leaving the group together for a few private days during the female's fertile period. Thus, dominant males do not necessarily father all (or even most) of the offspring in a social group. Social success, achieving alpha male status, does not translate neatly into the evolutionary currency of reproductive success.

Concealed Ovulation

In contrast to chimpanzees, bonobos (like humans) do not limit their sexual behavior to times of female fertility. Whereas the genitals of chimpanzee females are swollen only at times of fertility, female bonobo genitals are perpetually swollen. The constant swelling, in effect, conceals the females' **ovulation**, or moment when an egg released into the womb is receptive for fertilization. Ovulation is also concealed in humans, by the constant absence of genital swelling.

Concealed ovulation in humans and bonobos may play a role in the separation of sexual activity for social reasons and pleasure from the purely biological task of reproduction. In fact, among bonobos (as among

at the very least. During the juvenile period, young primates are still dependent upon the larger social group rather than on their mothers alone, using this period for learning and refining a variety of behaviors. If a juvenile primate's mother dies, he or she may be adopted by an older male or female member of the social group.

The long interval between births, particularly among the apes, results in small population sizes among our closest relatives. A female chimpanzee, for example, does not reach sexual maturity until about the age of 10, and once she produces her first live offspring, there is a period of five or six (on average 5.6) years before she will bear another. Thus, assuming that none of her offspring die before adulthood, a female chimpanzee must survive for at least twenty or twenty-one years just to maintain the size of chimpanzee populations at existing levels. In fact, chimpanzee infants and juveniles do die from time to time, and not all females live full reproductive lives. These chance events, combined with the long intervals between births, help explain why apes are far less abundant in the world today than are monkeys. Habitat destruction and hunting contribute further to declining ape populations.

A long slow period of growth and development, particularly among the hominoids, also provides opportunities. For example, bonobo and chimpanzee dependence on learned social behavior is related to their extended period of childhood development. Born without built-in responses dictating specific behavior in complex situations, the young chimp or bonobo, like the young human, learns how to strategically interact with others and even manipulate them for his or her own benefit—by trial and error, observation, imitation, and practice. Young primates make mistakes along the way, learning to modify their behavior based on the reactions of other members of the group. Each member of the community has a unique physical appearance and personality. Youngsters learn to match their interactive behaviors according to each individual's social position and temperament. Anatomical features such as a free upper lip (unlike lemurs or cats, for example) allow monkeys and apes varied facial expression, contributing to greater communication among individuals.

Communication

Primates, like many animals, vocalize. They have a great range of calls that are often used together with movements of the face or body to convey a message. Observers have not yet established the meaning of all the sounds, but a good number have been distinguished, such as warning calls, threat calls, defense calls, and gathering calls. The behavioral reactions of other animals hearing the call have also been studied. Among bonobos and chimpanzees, vocalizations are emotional. Much of these species' communication takes place by the use of specific gestures and postures. Indeed, a number of these, such as kissing and embracing, are in virtually universal use today among humans as well as apes.

Primatologists have classified numerous kinds of chimpanzee vocalizations and visual communication signals. Facial expressions convey emotional states such as distress, fear, or excitement. Numerous distinct vocalizations or calls have been associated with a variety of sensations. For example, chimps will smack their lips or clack their teeth to express pleasure with sociable body contact. Calls labeled "pant-hoots" can be differentiated into specific types used for arrival of individuals or inquiring. Together, these facilitate group protection, coordination of group efforts, and social interaction in general. One form of communication appears to be unique to bonobos: the use of trail markers. When foraging, the community breaks up into smaller groups, rejoining again in the evening to nest together. To keep track of each party's whereabouts, those in the lead will, at the intersections of trails or where downed trees obscure trails, deliberately stomp down the vegetation to indicate their direction, or rip off large leaves and place them carefully for the same purpose. Thus, they all know where to come together at the end of the day.[7]

Experiments with captive apes, carried out over several decades, reveal that their communication abilities exceed what they make use of in the wild. In some of these experiments, bonobos and chimpanzees have been taught to communicate using symbols, as in the case of Kanzi, a bonobo who uses a keyboard. Other chimpanzees, gorillas, and orangutans have been taught American Sign Language. Although this research provoked controversy, in part because it challenged notions of human uniqueness, it has become evident that apes are capable of understanding language quite well, even using rudimentary grammar. They are able to generate original utterances, ask questions, distinguish naming something from asking for it, develop original ways to tell lies, coordinate their actions, and even spontaneously teach language to others. Even though they cannot literally *speak,* it is now clear that all of the great ape

---

tool An object used to facilitate some task or activity

[7]Recer, P. (1998, February 16). Apes shown to communicate in the wild. *Burlington Free Press,* 12A.

species can develop *language skills* to the level of a 2- to 3-year-old human child.[8] Interestingly, a Japanese research team led by primatologist Tetsuro Matsuzawa, recently demonstrated that chimps can outperform college students at a computer-based memory game that tests relative ability to take a "quick mental snapshot" of the environment. The researchers propose that some of this spatial skill was lost to make brain space for human language.[9]

Use of Objects as Tools

Young chimpanzees also learn other functional behaviors from adults, such as how to make and use tools. A **tool** may be defined as an object used to facilitate some task or activity. Beyond deliberately modifying objects to make them suitable for particular purposes, chimps can to some extent modify them to regular patterns and may even prepare objects at one location in anticipation of future use at another place. For example, chimps have been observed selecting a long, slender branch, stripping off its leaves, and carrying it on a "fishing" expedition to a termite nest. Reaching their destination, they insert the stick into the nest, wait a few minutes, and then pull it out to eat the insects clinging to it.

There are numerous examples of chimpanzees using tools: They use leaves as wipes or sponges to get drinking water out of a hollow. Large sticks may serve as clubs or as missiles (as may stones) in aggressive or defensive displays. Recently a chimp group in Senegal has even been observed fashioning sticks into spears and using them to hunt.[10] Stones are used as hammers and anvils to crack open certain kinds of nuts. Twigs are used as toothpicks to clean teeth as well as to extract loose baby teeth. Chimps use these dental tools not just on themselves but on other individuals as well.[11]

Bonobos in the wild have not been observed making and using tools to the extent that chimpanzees do. However, their use of large leaves as trail markers may be considered a form of tool use. Tool-making

© Martin Harvey/Peter Arnold, Inc.

Chimps use a variety of tools in the wild. Here a chimp is using a long stick stripped of its side branches to fish for termites. Chimps will select a stick when still quite far from a termite mound and modify its shape on their way to the snacking spot.

capabilities have also been demonstrated by a captive bonobo who independently made stone tools remarkably similar to the earliest tools made by our own ancestors.

As researchers uncover increasing evidence of the remarkable behavioral sophistication and intelligence of chimpanzees and other apes—including a capacity for conceptual thought previously unsuspected by most scientists—the widespread practice of caging our primate cousins and exploiting them for entertainment or medical experimentation becomes increasingly controversial. The Biocultural Connection discusses this complex issue.

THE QUESTION OF CULTURE

The more we learn of the behavior of our nearest primate relatives, the more we become aware of the importance to chimps of learned, socially shared

---

[8]Lestel, D. (1998). How chimpanzees have domesticated humans. *Anthropology Today, 12*(3); Miles, H. L. W. (1993). Language and the orangutan: The "old person" of the forest. In P. Cavalieri & P. Singer (Eds.), *The great ape project* (pp. 45–50). New York: St. Martin's Press.

[9]Inoue, S., & Matsuzawa, T. (2007). Working memory of numerals in chimpanzees. *Current Biology, 17, 23,* 1004–1005; Callaway, E. (2007, December 3). Chimp beats students at computer game. Published online: *Nature,* doi:10.1038/news.2007.317.

[10]Hopkin, M. (2007, February 22). Chimps make spears to catch dinner. Published online: *Nature,* doi:10.1038/news070219–11.

[11]McGrew, W. C. (2000). Dental care in chimps. *Science, 288,* 1747.

Biocultural Connection

Nonhuman Primates and Human Disease

Biological similarities among humans, apes, and Old World monkeys have led to the extensive use of these nonhuman primate species in biomedical research, aimed at preventing or curing disease in humans. A cultural perspective that separates humans from our closest living relatives is necessary for this research to occur. Those who fully support these research efforts state that biomedical research in a limited number of chimpanzees or rhesus macaques lessens human suffering and spares human lives. Through testing with chimpanzees, scientists have successfully developed vaccines for hepatitis B and hepatitis C. These vaccines, along with current work on vaccines for HIV, are often cited as sufficient reasons to continue such research. Others, such as primatologist Jane Goodall, vehemently disagree with this approach. Goodall emphasizes that cultural processes

determine the place of animals within biomedical research. She advocates elimination of the cultural distinction between humans and our closest relatives for purposes of biomedical research.

Some biomedical research disturbs animals minimally. For example, DNA can be extracted from the hair naturally shed by living primates, allowing for cross-species comparisons of disease genes. To facilitate this process, primate cell repositories have been established for researchers to obtain samples of primate DNA. Other biomedical research is far more invasive to the individual primate. For example, to document the infectious nature of kuru, a disease closely related to mad cow disease, the extract from the brains of sick humans was injected into the brains of living chimpanzees. A year and a half later, the chimpanzees began to sicken. They had the same classic features of kuru—uncontrollable

spasticity, seizures, dementia, and ultimately death.

The biological similarities of humans and other primates leading to such research practices derive from a long, shared evolutionary history. By comparison, the cultural rules that allow our closest relatives to be the subjects of biomedical research are relatively short-lived. As Jane Goodall has said, "Surely it should be a matter of moral responsibility that we humans, differing from other animals mainly by virtue of our more highly developed intellect and, with it, our greater capacity for understanding and compassion, ensure that the medical progress slowly detaches its roots from the manure of nonhuman animal suffering and despair. Particularly when this involves the servitude of our closest relatives."[a]

[a]Goodall, Jane. (1990). *Through a window: My thirty years with the chimpanzees of Gombe.* Boston: Houghton Mifflin.

practices and knowledge. This raises the question: Do chimpanzees, bonobos, and the other apes have culture? The answer appears to be yes. The detailed study of ape behavior has revealed variation among groups in use of tools and patterns of social engagement that seem to derive from the traditions of the group rather than a biologically determined script. Humans share with the other apes an ability to learn the complex but flexible patterns of behavior particular to a social group during a long period of childhood dependency.

Primate Behavior and Human Evolution

In Western societies there has been an unfortunate tendency to erect what paleontologist Stephen Jay Gould referred to as "golden barriers" that set us apart from the rest of the animal kingdom.[12] It is unfortunate, for

it blinds us to the fact that a continuum exists between "us" and "them" (other animals). We have already seen that the physical differences between humans and apes are largely differences of degree, rather than kind.

It now appears that the same is true with respect to behavior. As primatologist Richard Wrangham once put it,

> Like humans, [chimpanzees] laugh, make up after a quarrel, support each other in times of trouble, medicate themselves with chemical and physical remedies, stop each other from eating poisonous foods, collaborate in the hunt, help each other over physical obstacles, raid neighboring groups, lose their tempers, get excited by dramatic weather, invent ways to show off, have family traditions and group traditions, make tools, devise plans, deceive, play tricks, grieve, and are cruel and are kind.[13]

---

[12]Quoted in de Waal, F. (2001). *The ape and the sushi master* (p. 235). New York: Basic Books.

[13]Quoted in Mydens, S. (2001, August 12). He's not hairy, he's my brother. *New York Times*, sec. 4, 5.

This is not to say that we are "just" another ape; obviously, "degree" does make a difference. While the continuities between us and our primate kin reflect a common evolutionary heritage, our more recent evolution has taken us in a somewhat different direction. By looking at the range of behaviors displayed by contemporary apes and other primates, we may find clues to the practices and capabilities possessed by our own ancestors as their evolutionary path diverged from those of the other African apes. Human intellectual capacity for compassion has roots in our mammalian primate heritage. If it is granted that our closest living relatives, among other co-inhabitants of our planet, have an inherent right to survive, then it is imperative that humanity applies our compassion and intelligence toward ensuring their survival.

Primate Conservation

At present, nearly 50 percent of the known primate species and subspecies face extinction in the next decade.[14] In Asia, the statistics are even more alarming with more than 70 percent of species threatened and at least 80 percent at risk in Indonesia and Vietnam. Included among them are all of the great apes, as well as such formerly widespread and adaptable species as rhesus macaques. In the wild these animals are threatened by habitat destruction caused by economic development (farming, lumbering, cattle ranching, rubber tapping), as well as by hunters and trappers who pursue them for food, trophies, research, or as exotic pets. Primatologists have long known the devastating effects of habitat destruction through slash-and-burn agriculture. Recent studies also document the powerful impact of human hunting of primates for bush-meat or traditional medicines.

Further, it is not just traditional practices such as the burning and clearing of tropical forests that are destroying primate habitats. Globalization is exerting a profound impact on local conditions. For example, the mineral (coltan) that is used in cell phones is mined primarily from gorilla habitats in the Democratic Republic of Congo. As the world is increasingly cell phone dependent, new roads are constructed into gorilla habitats. On the positive side a global emphasis on recycling cell phones will reduce the amount of new coltan needed. War also impacts primate habitats significantly, even after a war has ended. Hunters may use the automatic weapons left over from human conflicts in their pursuit of bush-meat.

Further, because monkeys and apes are so closely related to humans, they are regarded as essential for biomedical research in which humans cannot be used (as just discussed in the Biocultural Connection). While most primates in laboratories are bred in captivity, an active trade in live primates still threatens their local extinction.

Because of their vulnerability, the conservation of primates has become a matter of urgency. Traditional conservation efforts emphasized habitat preservation above all else. Primatologists are calling for new efforts that educate local communities to curtail hunting primates for food and medicine to complement existing habitat preservation efforts. Primatologists work to maintain some populations in the wild, either by establishing preserves where animals are already living or by moving populations to places where suitable habitat exists. This approach requires constant monitoring and management to ensure that sufficient space and resources remain available.

Primatologists also maintain captive breeding colonies that provide the kind of physical and social environment that encourages psychological and physical well-being, as well as reproductive success. Primates in zoos and laboratories do not successfully reproduce when deprived of such amenities as opportunities for climbing, materials to use for nest building, others with whom to socialize, and places for privacy. While such amenities contribute to the success of breeding colonies in captivity, ensuring the survival of our closest living relatives in suitable natural habitats is a far greater challenge that humans must meet in the years to come.

The good news is the results of conservation efforts are beginning to show. For example, the population size of the mountain gorilla (*Gorilla beringei beringei*) is increasing, even with the political chaos of Rwanda, Uganda, and the Democratic Republic of Congo, due to intense conservation programs. Western lowland gorilla populations are also on the rise. Similarly, tamarin monkey populations in Brazil have stabilized despite being on the brink of extinction thirty years ago, demonstrating the effectiveness of the conservation initiatives put into place. According to primatologist Sylvia Atsalis, "The presence alone of scientists has been shown to protect primates, acting as a deterrent to habitat destruction and hunting. The more people we can send, the more we can help to protect endangered primates."[15]

---

[14]Kaplan, M. (2008, August 5). Almost half of primate species face extinction. Published online: *Nature,* doi:10.1038/news.2008.1013.

[15]Ibid.

Chapter Summary

■ Primatologists work to protect our closest living relatives while studying them using methods that are minimally invasive.

■ Primates, like most mammals, are intelligent animals whose young are born live and nourished with milk from their mothers. Like other mammals, they maintain constant body temperature and have respiratory and circulatory systems that will sustain high activity levels. Their skeleton and teeth also resemble those of other mammals, although there are differences of detail.

■ Primates can be divided into five natural groupings: (1) lemurs and lorises, (2) tarsiers, (3) New World monkeys, (4) Old World monkeys, and (5) apes, including humans. Lemurs, lorises, and tarsiers are sometimes grouped together as prosimians because they share a series of anatomical characteristics, while monkeys, apes, and humans are considered anthropoid or humanlike primates. Because genetic evidence indicates that tarsiers are more closely related to the monkeys and apes, the primate order can also be divided into strepsirhines (lemurs and lorises) and haplorhines (tarsiers, monkeys, apes, and humans).

■ Prosimians are more dependent on the sense of smell than anthropoids, and where competition from anthropoids is present, they are nocturnal arboreal creatures. Nearly all anthropoids are diurnal, exploiting a wide range of habitats and expressing considerable behavioral flexibility and variation.

■ Primates show a number of characteristics that developed as adaptations to insect predation and life in the trees. These adaptive characteristics include a generalized set of teeth, suited to eating insects but also a variety of fruits and leaves. These teeth are fewer in number and set in a smaller jaw than in most mammals. Other adaptations that developed in the course of primate evolution include binocular stereoscopic vision, or depth perception, and an intensified sense of touch, particularly in the hands.

■ This combination of developments had an effect upon the primate brain, resulting in larger size and greater complexity in later-appearing species. There were also changes in the primate skeleton: in particular, a reduction of the snout, an enlargement of the braincase, and numerous adaptations for upright posture and flexibility of limb movement.

■ The primate reproductive pattern can be characterized by fewer offspring born to each female and a longer period of infant dependency compared to most mammals. This period of dependency allows young primates to learn the behaviors of its group.

■ The apes are humans' closest relatives. Apes include gibbons, siamangs, orangutans, gorillas, bonobos, and chimpanzees. In their outward appearance, the apes seem to resemble one another more than they do humans, but their genetic structure and biochemistry reveal that the African apes, bonobos, chimpanzees, and gorillas are closer to humans than they are to orangutans, gibbons, and siamangs.

■ The social life of primates is complex. Primates are social animals, and most species live and travel in groups. Frequently individuals transfer to new groups at adolescence. In many primate species, both males and females can be organized into dominance hierarchies. In the case of females, high rank is associated with enhanced reproductive success. In males, however, high rank does not necessarily confer a reproductive advantage.

■ A characteristic primate activity is grooming, which is a sign of closeness between individuals. Among chimpanzees, sexual interaction between adults of opposite sex generally takes place only when a female is in estrus. In bonobos, however, constant swelling of the female's genitals suggests constant estrus, whether or not she is actually fertile. A consequence of this concealed ovulation in bonobos is a separation of sexual activity from the biological task of reproduction. Among bonobos, sex between both opposite- and same-sex individuals serves as a means of reducing tensions, as in the genital rubbing that frequently takes place between females.

■ Primates have elaborate systems of communication based on vocalizations and gestures. In addition, bonobos employ trail signs to communicate their whereabouts to others.

■ The diet of most primates is made up of a variety of fruits, leaves, and insects, but bonobos and chimpanzees (and some other primate species) sometimes hunt, kill, and eat animals as well. Among chimps, most hunting is done by males and may require considerable teamwork. By contrast, it is usually the female bonobo who hunts. Once a kill is made, the meat is generally shared with other animals.

■ Among chimpanzees and the other apes, learned behavior is especially important. From adults, juveniles learn to use a variety of tools and substances for various purposes. Innovations made by one individual may be adopted by other animals, standardized, and passed on to succeeding generations. Because practices are learned, socially shared, and often differ from one group to another, we may speak of chimpanzee culture.

■ Nearly 50 percent of all primate species and subspecies are threatened with extinction in the next decade. Human actions, such as global flows of technology and commodities and local political and social conditions, threaten the other primates. Intense conservation efforts have produced good effects and urgently need reinforcement in order to protect our closest living relatives in the animal kingdom.

Questions for Reflection

1. In the 21st century many primates species are threatened with extinction. Why is it so important to prevent this from happening?

2. Considering some of the trends seen among the primates, such as increased brain size or reduced tooth number, why is it incorrect to say that some primates are more evolved than others? Are humans more evolved than chimpanzees?

3. Given the variation seen in the specific behaviors of chimp and bonobo groups, is it fair to say that our close relatives possess culture?

4. Many primate species, particularly apes, are endangered today. Though some features of ape biology may be responsible for apes' limited population size, humans, with ever-expanding populations, share these same biological features. Besides life cycle biology, what factors are causing endangerment of primates, and how can humans work to prevent the extinction of our closest living relatives?

Key Terms

nocturnal
arboreal
diurnal
binocular vision
stereoscopic vision
opposable
prosimians
anthropoids
strepsirhines

haplorhines
prehensile
brachiation
community
dominance hierarchies
grooming
ovulation
tool

VISUAL ESSENCE

Over the past 5 million years, humans evolved from a small-brained African ape species able to walk on two legs to a species with complex culture inhabiting the entire globe. As seen in these skulls of various human ancestors, arranged from most ancient on the left to most recent on the right, brain size also increased dramatically over the course of time. This increase, however, began only 2.5 million years ago and coincides with the first appearance of stone tools in the archaeological record. Together these changes mark the appearance of the genus *Homo*. Paleoanthropologists trace the complex story of how we became fully human, true members of the species *Homo sapiens*. They use fossils such as these, as well as archaeological and laboratory data, and make use of observations about the other primates and humans living today to reconstruct our evolutionary history. This understanding of how we came to be not only contributes substantially to our understanding of who we are but may even shed some light on our future.

Human Evolution

4

As well as being scholars, anthropologists attempting to piece together the puzzle of human evolution must be imaginative thinkers and patient detectives, for the available evidence is often scant or full of misleading and even contradictory clues. The quest for the origins of humans from more ancient species has elements of a detective story; it involves mysteries concerning the emergence of humanity, none of which have been completely resolved. Unanswered questions remain: Which ancestors were the first to walk on two legs? Which were the first with human-sized brains? Who were the first to use tools, the first to use fire, the first to actually use sounds to produce what we call language?

Because each new discovery contributes to resolving the puzzle of human evolution, the order of discovery is important. Each new fossil, stone tool, painted cave wall, or laboratory result has the potential to reconfigure our understanding of human evolutionary history. Although all discoveries impact evolutionary studies, the role of culture in human evolution makes unraveling our past particularly complex.

Differences in the rates of biological and culture change account for some of the complications and debates relating to human evolutionary history. Cultural practices and technologies can change rapidly with innovations occurring during the lifetime of individuals. By contrast, because it depends upon genetically inherited traits, biological change requires many generations. Paleoanthropologists try to decipher whether an evident culture change in the past corresponds to a major biological change, such as the appearance of a new species. The biological evidence for new species often consists of small changes in the shape or size of the skull. When we take into account the variation present today within the species *Homo sapiens*, we can see why reconciling the relation between differences in skulls and culture change is often a source of debate within paleoanthropology.

U.S. anthropologist Misia Landau has noted that the story of human evolution follows the narrative form of a heroic epic because of the role culture plays in human evolution. The hero, or evolving human, is faced with a series of natural challenges that cannot be overcome from a strictly biological standpoint. Endowed with the gift of intelligence, the hero can meet these challenges and become fully human. In this narrative, culture separates humans from other evolving animals. This narrative may unintentionally imply a notion of progress, but in biological terms there is no such thing as progress. While it is true that the evolution of culture was critical to our becoming the kind of species we are today, it did not "improve" us biologically. Each species has followed its own evolutionary course over millions of years, changing through time in directions that ensured its biological success. We continue to share this planet with some of these species, while others who were biologically successful for a time, surviving for millions of years, have since gone extinct.

MACROEVOLUTION AND THE PROCESS OF SPECIATION

While microevolution refers to changes in the allele frequencies of populations, **macroevolution** focuses on the formation of new species (**speciation**) and on the evolutionary relationships between groups of species. The term *species* is usually defined as a population or group of populations that is capable of interbreeding and producing viable, fertile offspring. In other words, species are reproductively isolated. The bullfrogs in one farmer's pond are the same species as those in a neighboring pond, even though the two populations may never actually interbreed; in theory, they are capable of doing so if they are brought together. This definition, however, is not entirely satisfactory because isolated populations may be in the process of evolving into different species, and it is hard to tell exactly when they become biologically distinct. The microevolutionary forces of mutation, gene flow, genetic drift, and natural selection can lead to macroevolutionary change as species diverge.

macroevolution Evolution above the species level
speciation The process of forming new species
cladogenesis Speciation through a branching mechanism whereby an ancestral population gives rise to two or more descendant populations
anagenesis A sustained directional shift in a population's average characteristics
punctuated equilibria A model of macroevolutionary change that suggests evolution occurs via long periods of stability or stasis punctuated by periods of rapid change
continental drift According to the theory of plate tectonics, the movement of continents embedded in underlying plates on the earth's surface in relation to one another over the history of life on earth

Certain factors, known as isolating mechanisms, can separate breeding populations and lead to the appearance of new species. Because isolation prevents gene flow, changes that affect the gene pool of one population cannot be introduced into the gene pool of the other. Random mutation may introduce new alleles in one of the isolated populations but not in the other. Genetic drift and natural selection may affect the two populations in different ways. Over time, as the two populations come to differ from each other, speciation occurs in a branching fashion known as **cladogenesis**. Speciation can also happen without branching, as a single population accumulates sufficient new mutations over time to be considered a separate species. This process is known as **anagenesis** (Figure 4.1). Speciation is inferred in the fossil record when a group of organisms takes on a different appearance over time.

Because speciation is a process, it can occur at various rates. Speciation through the process of adaptive change to the environment as proposed in Darwin's *Origin of Species* (1859) is generally considered to occur at a slow rate. In this model, speciation happens as organisms become more adapted to their environments. Sometimes, however, speciation can occur quite rapidly. For example, a genetic mutation such as one involving a key regulatory gene can lead to the formation of a new body plan. Such genetic accidents may involve material that is broken off, transposed, or transferred from one chromosome to another. Genes that regulate the growth and development of an organism may have a major effect on its adult form. Scientists have discovered certain key genes called *homeobox genes* that are responsible for large-scale effects on the growth and development of the

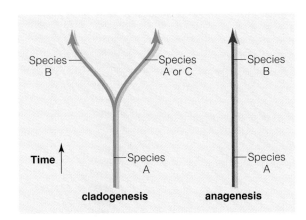

Figure 4.1 **Cladogenesis and Anagenesis**
Cladogenesis occurs as different populations of an ancestral species become reproductively isolated. Through drift and differential selection, the number of descendant species increases. By contrast, anagenesis can occur through a process of variational change that takes place as small differences in traits that (by chance) are advantageous in a particular environment accumulate in a species' gene pool. Over time, this may produce sufficient change to transform an old species into a new one. Genetic drift may also account for anagenesis.

organism. If a new body plan happens to be adaptive, natural selection will maintain this new form during long periods of time rather than promoting change.

Paleontologists Stephen Jay Gould and Niles Eldredge proposed that speciation occurs in a pattern of **punctuated equilibria** or the alternation between periods of rapid speciation and times of stability. Often, this conception of evolutionary change is contrasted with speciation through adaptation sometimes referred to as *Darwinian gradualism*. A close look at the genetics and the fossil record indicates that both models of evolutionary change are important.

It may be difficult to determine whether variation preserved in the fossil record presents evidence of separate species. How can we tell whether two sets of fossilized bones represent species that were capable of interbreeding and producing fertile, viable offspring? To approximate an answer to this question, paleoanthropologists use as many sources of data as possible to check the proposed evolutionary relationships. Paleoanthropologists use genetic and biochemical data, along with observations about the biology and behavior of living groups, to support theories about speciation in the past. Thus, reconstructing evolutionary relationships draws on much more than bones alone.

Even with this rich array of scientific knowledge to draw upon, prevailing beliefs and biases can influence the interpretation of fossil finds. Fortunately the self-correcting nature of scientific investigation allows evolutionary lineages to be redrawn in light of all new discoveries. This aspect of science is one of its greatest strengths. As technological innovations allow for new experiments, new investigations, and new discoveries that in turn reveal new aspects of the mysteries of life on earth, scientists develop theories and test hypotheses consistent with the complete data available. The reliance of science upon data and testable hypotheses is in fact what distinguishes it from storytelling.

MAMMALIAN PRIMATE EVOLUTION

Humans have a long evolutionary history as mammals and primates that set the stage for the cultural beings we are today. Evidence from ancient skeletons indicates the first mammals appeared over 200 million years ago as small nocturnal creatures.

In the time since the appearance of the first mammals, the earth itself has changed considerably. During the past 200 million years, the position of the continents has shifted through a process called **continental drift**. This process accounts for the re-arrangement of the adjacent land masses through the theory of plate tectonics (Figure 4.2). According to this theory, the

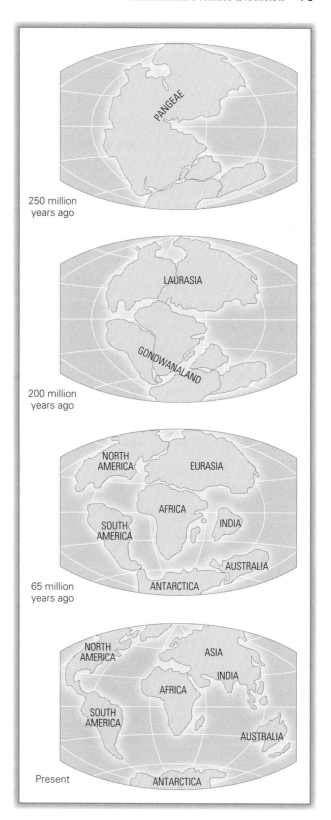

Figure 4.2

Continental drift is illustrated by the position of the continents during several geological periods. At the time of the extinction of the dinosaurs, 65 million years ago, the seas opened up by continental drift, creating isolating barriers between major land masses. About 23 million years ago, at the start of the geological time period known as the Miocene epoch, African and Eurasian land masses reconnected.

continents, embedded in platelike segments of the earth, move their positions as the edges of the underlying plates are created or destroyed. Plate movements are also responsible for geological phenomena such as earthquakes, volcanic activity, and mountain formation. Continental drift is important for understanding the distribution of fossil primate groups whose history we will now explore. The shifting orientation of the earth's continents is also responsible for the climatic changes in the environment that affected the course of evolution for primates and other living things.

The earliest primatelike mammals came into being about 65 million years ago when a new, mild climate favored the spread of dense tropical and subtropical forests over much of the earth. The change in climate and habitat, combined with the sudden extinction of dinosaurs, favored mammal diversification, including the evolutionary development of arboreal mammals from which primates evolved. Fossil evidence indicates that the earliest primates began to develop around 65 million years ago, when the mass extinction of the dinosaurs opened new ecological niches, or ways of life within a complete environmental system, for mammals. By 60 million years ago, primates inhabited North America and Eurasia (Europe and Asia), which at that time were joined together as the "supercontinent" Laurasia and separated from Africa. The earliest primates were small nocturnal insect eaters adapted to life in the trees.

By about 40 million years ago, diurnal anthropoid primates appeared, and fossil evidence indicates that Old World and New World species had separated by about this time. Many of the Old World anthropoid species became ground dwellers. By about 23 million years ago, at the start of the geological epoch known as the Miocene (Figure 4.3), the first fossil apes or hominoids began to appear in Asia, Africa, and Europe; hominoids are the broad-shouldered tailless primates that include all living and extinct apes and humans. The word *hominoid* comes from the Latin roots *Homo* and *Homin* (meaning "human being") and the suffix *oïdes* ("resembling"). As a group, hominoids get their name from their resemblance to humans. While some of these ancient primates were relatively small, others were larger than present-day gorillas.

It was also during the Miocene that the African and Eurasian land masses made direct contact. For most of the preceding 100 million years, the Tethys Sea—a continuous body of water that joined what are now the Mediterranean Sea and the Black Sea to the Indian

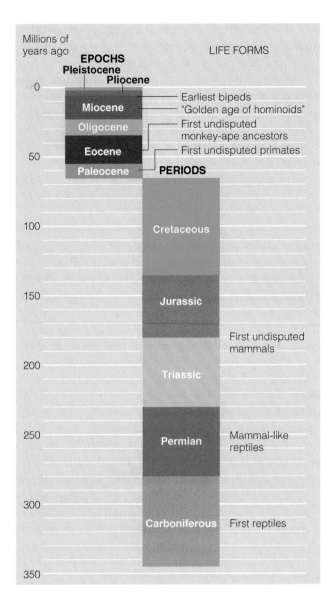

Figure 4.3

This timeline highlights the major milestones in the course of mammalian primate evolution that ultimately led to humans and their ancestors. The Paleocene, Eocene, Oligocene, and Miocene Epochs are subsets of the Tertiary Period. The Quaternary Period begins with the Pleistocene and continues today.

Ocean—barred migration between Africa and Eurasia. Connection of these land masses through what is now the Middle East allowed Old World primate groups such as African apes to expand their ranges into Eurasia. The climatic changes set into motion during the Miocene epoch may have played a role in the success of the human line once it originated. In particular, the drying of the eastern third of Africa may have opened new ecological niches for our ancestors.

Miocene fossil remains of apes from this time period have been found from the caves of China, to the forests of France, to eastern Africa where the earliest

bipedalism A special form of locomotion on two feet found in humans and their ancestors

fossil remains of bipeds have been found. So varied and ubiquitous were the fossil apes of this period that some primatologists have labeled the Miocene the "golden age of the hominoids." In the waning years of the Miocene, one of these apes began the evolutionary line ancestral to humans.

HUMAN EVOLUTION

Humans and their ancestors are distinct among the hominoids for **bipedalism**—a special form of locomotion on two feet. Larger brains and bipedal locomotion constitute the most striking differences between contemporary humans and our closest primate relatives. Although we might like to think that it is our larger brains that make us special among fellow primates, it is now clear that bipedalism appeared at the beginning of the ancestral line leading to humans and played a pivotal role in setting us apart from the apes. Brain expansion came later.

In the past thirty years, genetic and biochemical studies have confirmed that the African apes—chimpanzees, bonobos, and gorillas—are our closest living relatives (Figure 4.4). By comparing genes and proteins among all the apes, scientists have estimated that gibbons, followed by orangutans, were the first to diverge from a very ancient common ancestral line. At some time between 5 and 8 million years ago (mya), humans, chimpanzees, and gorillas began to follow separate evolutionary courses. Chimpanzees later diverged into two separate species: the common chimpanzee and the bonobo.

The First Bipeds

Between 5 and 15 million years ago, various kinds of hominoids lived throughout Africa and Eurasia. One of these apes living in Africa between 5 and 8 million years ago was a direct ancestor to the human line. Fossil evidence for early African apes from the late Miocene is relatively rare because the forested environments these apes inhabited were not conducive to fossilization. Nevertheless, the fossil evidence, such as the recent discovery of a 10-million-year-old ape thought to be ancestral to gorillas, supports the genetic evidence.[1] This specimen suggests that the human–chimp–gorilla split occurred about 2 million years earlier than previously thought. Other discoveries have begun to fill in the fossil record from this critical time period, such as the 6-million-year-old *Orrorin*—meaning "original man"—fossils discovered in Kenya in 2001.[2] Also, a beautifully preserved 6- to 7-million-year-old skull nicknamed *Toumai*—meaning "hope for life"—was discovered in Chad, Central Africa, in 2002.[3] It too has been suggested as the original human ancestor.

For a hominoid fossil to be definitively classified as part of the human evolutionary line, certain evidence of bipedalism is required. Bipedalism is associated with anatomical changes literally from head to toe (Figure 4.5). Evidence of walking on two feet is preserved in the skull

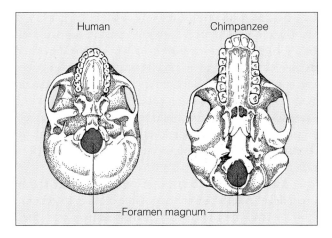

Figure 4.5 **Foramen Magnum**
Bipedialism can be inferred from the position of the foramen magnum, the large opening at the base of the skull. Note its relatively forward position on the human skull (left) compared to the chimp skull.

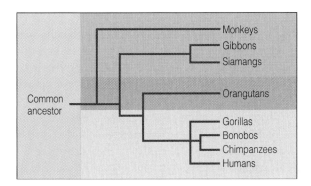

Figure 4.4
The relationship among monkeys, apes, and humans can be established by comparing molecular similarities and differences. Although chimpanzees, gorillas, and orangutans physically resemble one another more than any of them resemble humans, molecular evidence indicates that humans are most closely related to the African ape species. Using a "molecular clock," scientists date the split between the human and African ape lines to between 5 and 8 million years ago. Over the past few years, several important fossil finds dating from between 5 and 7 million years ago have been discovered that support the molecular evidence.

[1]Suwa, G., et al. (2007, August 23). A new species of great ape from the late Miocene epoch in Ethiopia. *Nature, 448,* 921–924. Published online: doi:10.1038/nature06113.
[2]Senut, B., et al. (2001). First hominid from the Miocene (Lukeino formation, Kenya). *C. R. Academy of Science, Paris, 332,*137–144.
[3]Brunet, M., et al. (2002). A new hominid from the Upper Miocene of Chad, Central Africa. *Nature, 418,* 145–151.

because balancing the skull above the spinal column in an upright posture requires a skull position relatively centered above the spinal column. The spinal cord leaves the skull at its base through an opening called the *foramen magnum* (Latin for "big opening"). In a knuckle-walker like a chimp, the foramen magnum is placed more toward the back of the skull, whereas in a biped it is in a more forward position.

Extending down from the skull of a biped, the spinal column makes a series of convex and concave curves that together maintain the body in an upright posture by positioning the body's center of gravity above the legs rather than forward. The curves correspond to the neck (cervical), chest (thoracic), lower back (lumbar), and pelvic (sacral) regions of the spine, respectively (Figure 4.6). In a chimp, the shape of the spine follows a single arching curve. Interestingly, at birth the spines of human babies have a single arching curve as seen in adult apes. As they mature the curves characteristic of bipedalism appear—the cervical curve at about 3 months on average, a time when babies begin to be able to hold up their own heads, and the lumbar curve at around 12 months, a time when many babies begin to walk.

The shape of the pelvis also differs considerably between bipeds and other apes. Rather than an elongated shape following the arch of the spine as seen in chimps, the biped pelvis is wider and foreshortened so that it can provide structural support for the upright body. With a wide bipedal pelvis, the lower limbs would be oriented away from the body's center of gravity if the thigh bones (femora) did not angle in toward each other from the hip to the knee, a phenomenon described as "kneeing-in." (Notice how your own knees and feet can touch when standing while your hip joints remain widely spaced.) This angling does not continue past the knee to the shin bones (tibia), which are oriented vertically. The resulting knee joint is not symmetrical, allowing the thigh and shin bones to meet despite their different orientations.

Another characteristic of bipeds is their stable arched feet and the absent opposable big toe. In general, humans and their ancestors possess shorter toes than the other apes.

These anatomical features allow paleoanthropologists to "diagnose" bipedal locomotion even in fragmentary remains, such as the top of the shin bone or the base of a skull. In addition, bipedal locomotion can also

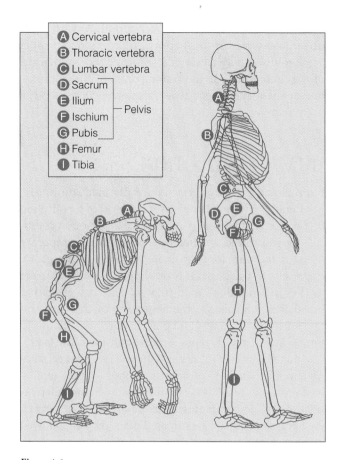

- (A) Cervical vertebra
- (B) Thoracic vertebra
- (C) Lumbar vertebra
- (D) Sacrum ⎤
- (E) Ilium ⎥
- (F) Ischium ⎥— Pelvis
- (G) Pubis ⎦
- (H) Femur
- (I) Tibia

Figure 4.6

Notice the single continuous curve in the chimp backbone and the elongated pelvis. In humans the four vertebral regions make a series of concave and convex curves to position the skull above the legs. Also, the pelvis is more basin-shaped. Notice too the differences in the lengths of the arms and legs and the placement where the cervical vertebra meet the skull base.

be established through fossilized footprints, preserving not so much the shape of foot bones but the characteristic stride used by humans and their ancestors. In fact, bipedal locomotion is a process of shifting the body's weight from one foot to the other as the nonsupporting foot swings forward.

The most dramatic confirmation of walking ability in early human ancestors comes from Laetoli, Tanzania, in East Africa, where 3.6 million years ago three individuals walked across newly fallen volcanic ash. Because it was damp, the ash took the impressions of their feet, and these were sealed beneath subsequent ash falls until discovered in 1978. The shape of the footprints and the linear distance between each step are quite human.

All early bipeds are not necessarily direct ancestors of later humans. Consider, for example, fossils of the genus *Ardipithecus* (literally, "ground ape" in the Afar language) that lived between 4.4 and 5.8 million years ago. Found in Ethiopia, East Africa, this genus was much smaller than a modern chimpanzee, but it was chimpanzeelike

Australopithecus The genus including several species of early bipeds from southern and eastern Africa living between about 1.1 and 4.3 million years ago, one of whom was directly ancestral to humans

Fossilized footprints were preserved in volcanic ash at the 3.6-million-year-old Tanzanian site of Laetoli. As shown here, the foot of a living human fits right inside this ancient footprint, which shows the characteristic pattern of bipedal walking.

© Andrew Hill/Anthro-Photo

in other features, such as the shape and enamel thickness of its teeth. On the other hand, a partially complete skeleton of one *Ardipithecus* individual suggests that unlike chimpanzees, and like all other species in the human line, this creature was bipedal. Given the combination of bipedalism and chimpanzeelike characteristics, many paleoanthropologists consider it a side branch of the human evolutionary tree. Fossil evidence shows that over the next several million years, many bipedal species inhabited Africa—making it more accurate to refer to an evolutionary bush rather than a tree.

Bipedalism is considered an important adaptive feature in the more open country known as *savannah*—grasslands with scattered trees and groves.[4] A biped could not run as fast as a quadruped but could keep up a steady pace over long distances in search of food and water without tiring. With free hands, a biped could take food to places where it could be eaten in relative safety and could carry infants rather than relying on the babies hanging on for themselves. Bipeds could use their hands to wield sticks or other objects in threat displays and to protect themselves against predators. (Other apes can do this but only for short bursts of time.) Also, erect posture is better suited for endurance running, as it exposes a smaller area of the body to the direct heat of the sun than a quadrupedal position, helping to prevent overheating on the open savannah. Furthermore, a biped, with its head held high, could see farther, spotting food as well as predators from a distance.

Australopithecines

Between 4 and 5 million years ago, the environment of eastern and southern Africa was a mosaic of open country with pockets of closed woodland. Scholars propose that some early bipeds inhabited some of the woodland pockets. Later human ancestors inhabited the savannah and are assigned to one or another species of the genus *Australopithecus* (from Latin *australis,* meaning "southern," and Greek *pithekos,* meaning "ape"). Scholarly judgments vary on just how many species there were in Africa between about 1.1 and 4.3 million years ago. For our purposes, it suffices to refer to them collectively as "australopithecines."

Although adapted fully to bipedalism, curved toe bones and relatively long arms indicate australopithecines had not given up tree climbing altogether. One reason may be that sparsely distributed trees continued to be important places of refuge on the African savannah, a land teeming with dangerous predatory animals. Chimpanzees today build their night nests in trees, suggesting a habit that may have been part of the australopithecine pattern as well. In addition, trees provide rich sources of food such as fruits, seeds, and nuts. A bipedal stance may have also been advantageous for obtaining food in trees, a technique employed by orangutans today.[5]

[4] Lewin, R. (1987). Four legs bad, two legs good. *Science, 235,* 969.

[5] Thorpe, S. K. S., Holder, R. L., & Crompton, R. H. (2007). Origin of human bipedalism as an adaptation for locomotion on flexible branches. *Science, 316,* 1328–1331; Kaplan, M. (2007, May 31). Upright orangutans point way to walking. Published online: doi:10.1038/news070528–8.

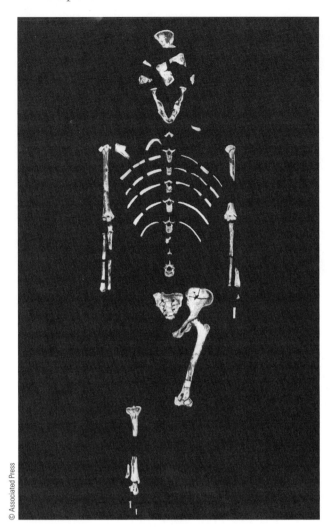

© Associated Press

A 40 percent complete skeleton, "Lucy" (named after the Beatles' song "Lucy in the Sky with Diamonds"—popular at the time of discovery) indicates that these australopithecine ancestors were bipedal. This adult female *Australopithecus* was only 3½ feet tall, typical of the small size of female australopithecines. By understanding the shapes of bones, paleoanthropologists have reconstructed an entire skeleton from the fragmentary remains that were discovered.

The earliest definite australopithecine fossils date back 4.2 million years,[6] whereas the most recent ones are only about 1 million years old. They have been found up and down the length of eastern Africa

robust australopithecines Several species within the genus *Australopithecus* who lived from 1.1 to 2.5 million years ago in eastern and southern Africa; known for the rugged nature of their chewing apparatus (large back teeth, large chewing muscles, and bony ridge on their skull tops for the insertion of these large muscles)

gracile australopithecines Member of the genus *Australopithecus* possessing a more lightly built chewing apparatus; likely had a diet that included more meat than that of the robust australopithecines

[6]Wolpoff, M. (1996). *Australopithecus:* A new look at an old ancestor. *General Anthropology, 3*(1), 2.

from Ethiopia to South Africa and westward into Chad (Figure 4.7).

Among the later australopithecines, a number of species had particularly large back teeth and correspondingly large muscles and bones associated with chewing. Collectively, these species are considered **robust australopithecines** because of the rugged nature of their chewing apparatus, which also included modifications on the skull for the insertion of the large chewing muscles. The robust australopithecines inhabited both eastern and southern Africa until about 1 million years ago when they appear to have gone extinct. Based on their teeth and the chemicals preserved in their bones, the robust australopithecines appear to have had diets that included considerable vegetable matter. They are contrasted with the **gracile australopithecines**, which possessed a more delicate chewing apparatus and were likely to have had a diet that included more meat. The first skull in the series at the opening of this chapter is from a typical gracile australopithecine. The proliferation of bipedal species indicates that this new mode of locomotion was very successful.

None of the australopithecines were as large as most modern humans, although all were much more muscular for their size. Males seem to have been significantly

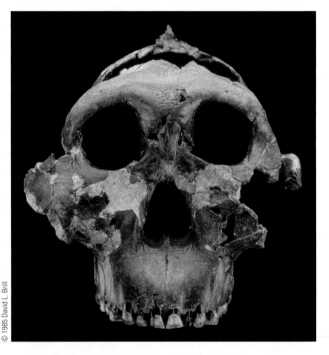

© 1985 David L. Brill

Robust australopithecines had extremely large cheek teeth (molars) compared to the size of their front teeth. They also had large chewing muscles and a bony ridge on the top of their skulls for the attachment of those large muscles. If you place your own hands on the sides of your skull above your ears while opening and closing your jaw, you can feel where your chewing muscles attach to your skull. By moving your hands toward the top of your skull, you can feel where these muscles end in humans.

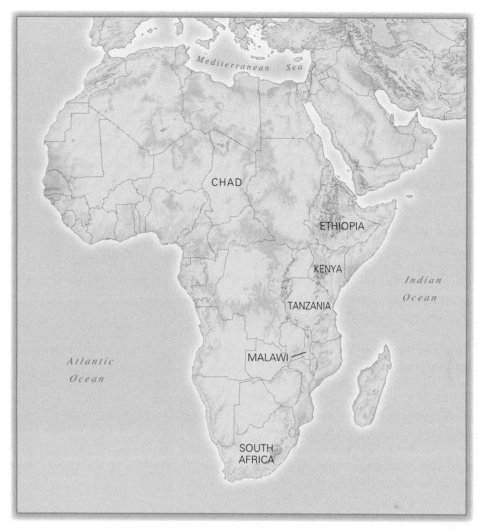

Figure 4.7
Australopithecine fossils have been found in South Africa, Malawi, Tanzania, Kenya, Ethiopia, and Chad. In the Miocene the Eurasian and African continents made contact at the eastern and western ends of what now is the Mediterranean Sea. As these land masses met, "rifting" also occurred, gradually raising the elevation of the eastern third of Africa. The dryer climates that resulted may have played a role in human evolution in the distant past. In the present this rifting also created excellent geological conditions for finding fossils.

larger than females, with size differences between the sexes less than those found in living apes such as gorillas and orangutans but greater than those among living humans. Taking their relative body size into consideration, australopithecines possessed brains comparable to those of modern African apes. However, the shape of the jaw and some aspects of the teeth were more like those of modern humans than they were like those of apes.

To survive in their savannah environment, early bipeds may have tried out supplementary sources of food on the ground, as they likely did around the time when the first members of the genus *Homo* appeared about 2.5 million years ago. In addition to plant foods, the major new source was animal protein. This was not protein from monkey meat obtained as a result of coordinated hunting parties, like those of the chimpanzees and bonobos of today, but rather the fatty marrow and leftover edible flesh that remained in and on the bones of dead animals.

Homo habilis

On the savannah, it is difficult for a primate with a humanlike digestive system to satisfy its protein requirements from available plant resources. Chimpanzees have a similar problem today when out on the savannah. In this environment, they spend more than a third of their time going after insects like ants and termites while also searching for eggs and small vertebrate animals. Not only are such animal foods easily digestible, but they provide high-quality proteins that contain all the essential amino acids, the building blocks of protein, in just the right percentages. No single plant food does this by itself. Only the right combination of plants can supply the balance of amino acids provided by meat alone.

Our ancestors probably solved their dietary problems in much the same way that chimps on the savannah do today but with one key difference. For more efficient utilization of animal protein, our ancestors probably used sharp tools rather than dagger-like teeth for scavenging meat and later for butchering carcasses.

The earliest identifiable tools consist of a number of stone implements made by striking sharp-edged flakes from the surface of a stone core. In the process, cores were transformed into choppers. These flakes and choppers, first discovered in Olduvai Gorge in Tanzania, are known as implements in the **Oldowan** tool tradition. They mark the beginning of the **Lower Paleolithic**, or Old Stone Age, a very long period spanning from approximately 200,000 to 2.5 million years ago. The earliest tools of this sort, which were recently found in Ethiopia, are perhaps even 2.6 million years old.

Before this time, australopithecines probably used tools such as heavy sticks to dig up roots or ward off animals, unmodified stones to hurl as weapons or to crack open nuts and bones, and simple carrying devices made of hollow gourds or knotted plant fibers. These tools, however, are not traceable in the archaeological record.

Since the late 1960s, a number of sites in southern and eastern Africa have been discovered with fossil remains of a lightly built biped with a body all but indistinguishable from that of the earlier australopithecines, except that the teeth are smaller, and the brain is significantly larger relative to body size. Furthermore, the inside of the skull shows a pattern in the left cerebral hemisphere that in contemporary humans is associated with language. Although this does not conclusively indicate language use, it suggests a marked advance in information-processing capacity over that of australopithecines. Since major brain-size increase and tooth-size reduction are important trends in the evolution of the genus *Homo*, paleoanthropologists

© 1999 David L. Brill

The oldest stone tools, dated to between 2.5 and 2.6 million years ago, were discovered in Gona, Ethiopia, by Ethiopian paleoanthropologist Sileshi Semaw.

designated these fossils as a new species: ***Homo habilis*** ("handy man").[7] Significantly, the earliest fossils to exhibit these trends appeared around 2.5 million years ago, coincident with the earliest evidence of stone tool making.

Interpreting the Fossil Record

When paleoanthropologists from the 1960s and 1970s depicted the lifeways of early *Homo*, they concentrated on "man the hunter," a tough guy with a killer instinct wielding tools on a savannah teeming with meat, while the female members of the species stayed at home tending their young. However, this theoretical reconstruction of ancient human life is seriously flawed. There is insufficient evidence to support this view, and it reflects a male-centered bias in both the discipline's earlier accounts and in the ethnographic record of still-existing foraging cultures used for comparative purposes.

Oldowan The first stone tool industry beginning between 2.5 and 2.6 million years ago

Lower Paleolithic Old Stone Age beginning with the earliest Oldowan tools spanning from about 200,000 or 250,000 to 2.6 million years ago

Homo habilis "Handy man." The first fossil members of the genus *Homo* appearing 2.5 million years ago, with larger brains and smaller faces than australopithecines

---

[7]Leakey, L. S. B., Tobias, P. B., & Napier, J. R. (1964). A new species of the genus *Homo* from Olduvai Gorge. *Nature, 202*, 7–9. (Some have argued that *H. habilis* was too varied to be considered a single species.)

Evolution and Human Birth

Because biology and culture have always shaped human experience, it can be a challenge to separate the influences of each of these factors on human practices. For example, in the 1950s, paleoanthropologists developed the theory that human childbirth is particularly difficult compared to birth in other mammals. This theory was based in part on the observation of a "tight fit" between the human mother's birth canal and the baby's head, though several other primates also possess similarly tight fits between the newborn's head or shoulders and the birth canal. Nevertheless, changes in the birth canal associated with bipedalism were held responsible for difficult birth in humans.

At the same historical moment, North American childbirth practices were changing. In one generation from the 1920s to the 1950s, birth shifted from the home to the hospital. In the process childbirth was transformed from something a woman normally accomplished at home, perhaps with the help of a midwife or relatives, into the high-tech delivery of a neonate (the medical term for a newborn) with the assistance of medically trained personnel. During the 1950s women were generally fully anesthetized during the birth process. Paleoanthropological theories mirrored the cultural norms, providing a scientific explanation for the change in North American childbirth practices.

As a scientific theory, the idea of especially difficult human birth stands on shaky ground. No fossil neonates have ever been recovered, and only a handful of complete pelves (the bones forming the birth canal) exist. Instead, scientists must examine the birth process in living humans and nonhuman primates to reconstruct the evolution of the human birth pattern. Cultural beliefs and practices, however, shape every aspect of birth. Cultural factors determine where a birth occurs, the actions of the individuals present, and beliefs about the nature of the experience.

When paleoanthropologists of the 1950s and 1960s asserted that human childbirth is more difficult than birth in other mammals, they may have been drawing upon their own North American cultural beliefs that childbirth is dangerous and belongs in a hospital. A quick look at global neonatal mortality statistics indicates that in countries such as the Netherlands and Sweden, healthy, well-nourished women give birth successfully outside of hospitals as they did throughout human evolutionary history. In other countries, deaths related to childbirth reflect malnutrition, infectious disease, and the low social status of women, rather than an inherently faulty biology.

Until the 1960s, most anthropologists doing fieldwork among foragers stressed the role of male hunters and underreported the significance of female gatherers in providing food for the community. As anthropologists became aware of their own biases, they began to set the record straight, documenting the vital role of "woman the gatherer" in provisioning the social group in foraging cultures, past and present. (See the Biocultural Connection above for another example of gender and paleoanthropological interpretation.) Uncovering biases is as important as any new discovery for interpreting the fossil record.

Tools, Food, and Brain Expansion

New evidence suggests that early humans depended more on scavenging than on hunting. Indeed, microscopic analysis of cut marks on fossil bones, which commonly overlie marks made by the teeth of carnivores, suggests that the lightly built *Homo habilis* may have been a *tertiary scavenger*: third in line to feed off an animal killed by a predator. Tool-wielding ancestors could break open the shafts of long bones to get at the fat and protein-rich marrow inside. Recently, it has been suggested that evolving humans may even have been prey themselves and that the selective pressure imposed by predators played a role in brain expansion.[8]

Many scenarios proposed for the adaptation of early *Homo*—such as the relationship among tools, food, and brain expansion—rely upon a feedback loop between brain size and behavior. The behaviors made possible by larger brains confer advantages to large-brained individuals, contributing to their increased reproductive success. Over time, gene frequencies shift such that variants with larger brains become more common in successive generations, and the population gradually evolves to acquiring a larger-brained form.

Paleoanthropologists debate whether the evolution of the genus *Homo* from australopithecine ancestors was a gradual or sudden process or some combination of the two. Recently, researchers at the University of Pennsylvania announced discovery of a genetic mutation, shared by all humans but absent in apes, that acts to prevent growth of powerful jaw muscles.

Applying the theory of punctuated equilibria or sudden evolutionary transformation (discussed earlier in this chapter), they calculate that the mutation arose sometime

---

[8]Hart, D., & Sussman, R. W. (2005). *Man the hunted: Primates, predators, and human evolution*. Boulder, CO: Westview Press.

between 2.1 and 2.7 million years ago, the period when *H. habilis* first appeared. They argue that without heavy jaw muscles attached to the outside of the braincase, a significant constraint to brain growth was removed. In other words, humans may have developed large brains as an accidental byproduct of jaw-size reduction.[9] Natural selection added to the effects of the sudden change of the jaw through the gradual brain expansion that continued in the genus *Homo* until some 200,000 years ago. By then, brain size had approximately tripled and reached the levels of today's humans. Tool making preserved in the archaeological record provides us with tangible data concerning our ancestors' cultural abilities fitting with the simultaneous biological expansion of the brain.

Beginning with *H. habilis* in Africa around 2.5 million years ago, human evolution followed a sure course of increasing brain size relative to body size and increasing cultural development, each acting upon and thereby promoting the other.

Homo erectus

Shortly after 2 million years ago, by which time *Homo habilis* and Oldowan tools had become widespread in Africa, a new species, **Homo erectus** ("upright man"), appeared on that continent. Unlike *H. habilis,* however, *H. erectus* did not remain confined to Africa. In fact, evidence of *H. erectus* fossils almost as old as those discovered in Africa have been found in the Caucasus Mountains of Georgia (between Turkey and Russia), south-central China, and on the island of Java, Indonesia. These fossils indicate that it was not long before members of the genus *Homo* spread widely throughout much of Asia and eventually Europe as well (Figure 4.8).

The emergence of *H. erectus* as a new species in the long course of human evolution coincided with the beginning of the Pleistocene epoch, which spanned from 10,000 to 1.8 million years ago. During this time of periodic global cooling, Arctic cold conditions and abundant

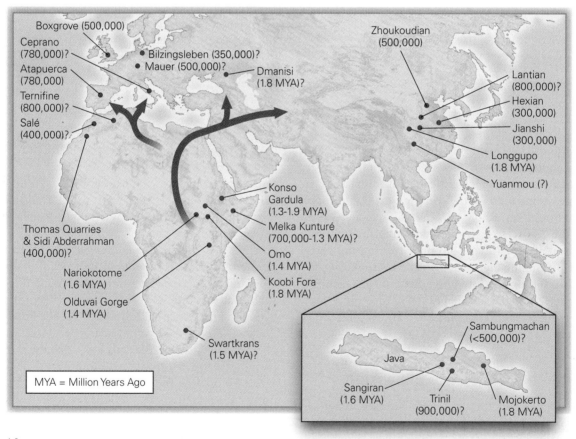

Figure 4.8

Sites, with dates, at which *Homo erectus* remains have been found. The arrows indicate the proposed routes by which *Homo* spread from Africa to Eurasia. The question marks indicate the uncertain dating for particular sites.

---

[9]Stedman, H. H., et al. (2004). Myosin gene mutation correlates with anatomical changes in the human lineage. *Nature, 428,* 415–418.

snowfall in the earth's northern hemisphere created vast ice sheets that temporarily covered much of Eurasia and North America. These fluctuating major glacial periods often lasted tens of thousands of years, separated by intervening warm periods. During interglacial periods, the world warmed up to the point that the ice sheets melted and sea levels rose, but sea levels were generally much lower than today, exposing large surfaces of low-lying lands now under water.

The Pleistocene epoch, with its dramatic climatic shifts is the time during which humans—from *H. erectus* to *H. sapiens*—evolved and spread all across the globe. Confronted by environmental changes due to climatic fluctuations or movements into different geographic areas, our early human ancestors were constantly challenged to make biological and, more especially, cultural adaptations in order to survive and successfully reproduce. In the course of this long evolutionary process, random mutations introduced new characteristics into evolving populations in different regions of the world. As we shall see below, whether one or all of these populations contributed to modern humanity is one of the great debates of paleoanthropology.

The principle of natural selection was at work on humans as it was on all forms of life, favoring the perpetuation of certain characteristics within particular environmental conditions. At the same time, other characteristics that conferred no particular advantage or disadvantage also appeared by random mutation in geographically removed populations. The end result was a gradually growing physical variation in the genus *Homo*. In this context, it is not surprising that *H. erectus* fossils found in Africa, Asia, and Europe reveal levels of physical variation not unlike those seen in modern human populations living across the globe today. Many paleoanthropologists believe that the physical variation in the genus *Homo* was too great to consider all these specimens a single species, instead splitting *H. erectus* into a variety of distinct species.

Available fossil evidence indicates that *H. erectus* had body size and proportions similar to modern humans, though with heavier musculature. Differences in body size between the sexes diminished considerably compared to earlier bipeds, perhaps to facilitate successful childbirth.[10] Based on fossil skull evidence, *H. erectus* average brain size fell within the higher range of *H. habilis* and within the lower range of modern human brains. The dentition was fully human, though relatively large by modern standards. As one might expect, given its larger brain, *H. erectus* outstripped its predecessors in cultural abilities.

In Africa and most of Eurasia, the Oldowan chopper was replaced by the more sophisticated hand axe. At first the hand axes—shaped by regular blows giving them a larger and finer cutting edge than chopper tools—were probably all-purpose implements for food procurement and processing, and defense. But *H. erectus* also developed cleavers (like hand axes but without points) and various scrapers to process animal hides for bedding and clothing. In addition, this early human relied on flake tools used "as is" to cut meat and process vegetables, or refined by "retouching" into points and borers for drilling or punching holes in materials. Improved technological efficiency is also evident in *H. erectus'* use of raw materials.

Instead of making a few large tools out of big pieces of stone, *Homo erectus* placed a new emphasis on smaller tools, thus economizing their raw materials. Some of these raw materials continue even today to have practical value, as the Anthropology Applied feature illustrates.

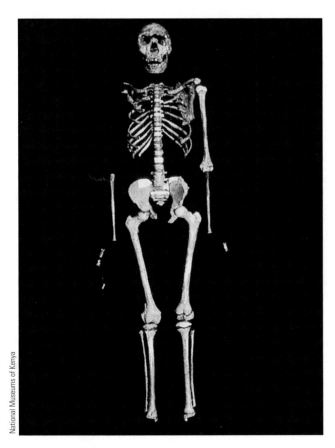

National Museums of Kenya

One of the oldest and certainly one of the most complete *Homo erectus* fossils is the "Nariokotome Boy" from Lake Turkana, Kenya. Though the remains are those of a tall adolescent boy, its pelvis has been used to reconstruct the evolution of human birth.

Homo erectus "Upright man." A species within the genus *Homo* first appearing just after 2 million years ago in Africa and ultimately spreading throughout the Old World

---

[10]Hager, L. (1989). The evolution of sex differences in the hominid bony pelvis. Ph.D. dissertation, University of California, Berkeley.

Anthropology *Applied*   Stone Tools for Modern Surgeons

When anthropologist Irven DeVore of Harvard University was to have some minor melanomas removed from his face, he did not leave it up to the surgeon to supply his own scalpels. Instead, he had graduate student John Shea make a scalpel. Making a blade of obsidian (a naturally occurring volcanic glass) by the same techniques used by Upper Paleolithic people to make blades, he then hafted this in a wooden handle, using melted pine resin as glue and then lashing it with sinew. After the procedure, the surgeon reported that the obsidian scalpel was superior to metal ones.[a]

DeVore was not the first to undergo surgery in which stone scalpels were used. In 1975, Don Crabtree, then at Idaho State University, prepared the scalpels that his surgeon would use in Crabtree's heart surgery. In 1980, Payson Sheets at the University of Colorado

prepared obsidian scalpels that were used successfully in eye surgery. And in 1986, David Pokotylo of the Museum of Anthropology at the University of British Columbia underwent reconstructive surgery on his hand with blades he himself had made (the hafting was done by his museum colleague, Len McFarlane).

The reason for these uses of scalpels modeled on ancient stone tools is that the anthropologists realized that obsidian is superior in almost every way to materials normally used to make scalpels: It is 210 to 1,050 times sharper than surgical steel, 100 to 500 times sharper than a razor blade, and 3 times sharper than a diamond blade (which not only costs much more, but cannot be made with more than 3 mm of cutting edge). Obsidian blades are easier to cut with and do less damage in the process (under a microscope, incisions made

with the sharpest steel blades show torn ragged edges and are littered with bits of displaced flesh).[b] As a consequence, the surgeon has better control over what she or he is doing, and the incisions heal faster with less scarring and pain. Because of the superiority of obsidian scalpels, Sheets went so far as to form a corporation in partnership with Boulder, Colorado, eye surgeon Dr. Firmon Hardenbergh. Together, they developed a means of producing cores of uniform size from molten glass, as well as a machine to detach blades from the cores.

[a] Shreeve, J. (1995). *The Neandertal enigma: Solving the mystery of modern human origins* (p. 134). New York: William Morrow.

[b] Sheets, P. D. (1987). Dawn of a New Stone Age in eye surgery. In R. J. Sharer & W. Ashmore (Eds.), *Archaeology: Discovering our past* (p. 231), Palo Alto, CA: Mayfield.

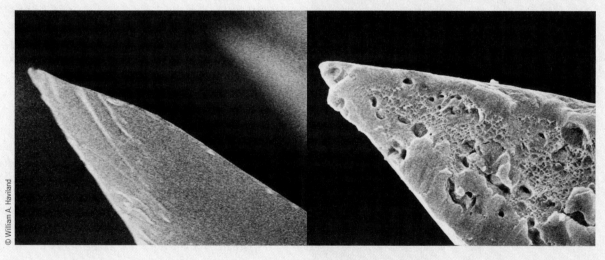

© William A. Haviland

These electron micrographs of the tips of an obsidian blade (left) and a modern steel scalpel (right) illustrate the superiority of the obsidian.

Remains found in southern Africa also suggest that *Homo erectus* may have learned to use fire by 1 million years ago. Fire gave our human ancestors more control over their environment. It permitted them to continue activities after dark and provided a means to frighten away predators. It supplied them with the warmth and

light needed for cave dwelling, and it enabled them to cook their food. The ability to modify food culturally through cooking may have played a role in the reduction of the tooth size and jaws of later fossil groups since raw food is tougher and requires more chewing. However, cooking does more than this. It detoxifies a number of otherwise poisonous plants. In addition, it alters substances in plants, allowing important vitamins, minerals, and proteins to be absorbed from the gut rather than passing unused through the intestines. And, finally, it makes high-energy complex carbohydrates, such as starch, digestible.

In addition, without controlled use of fire, it is unlikely that early humans could have moved successfully into regions where winter temperatures regularly dropped below 50 degrees Fahrenheit (10 degrees Celsius)—as they must have in northern China or the mountain highlands of central Asia, or most of Europe, where the genus *Homo* spread some 780,000 years ago. Although considerable variation exists, studies of modern humans indicate that most people can remain reasonably comfortable down to 50 degrees Fahrenheit with minimal clothing so long as they keep active. Below that temperature, hands and feet cool to the point of pain. In short, when our human ancestors learned to employ fire to warm and protect themselves and to cook their food, they dramatically increased their geographic range and nutritional options.

With *H. erectus* we also begin to have evidence of organized hunting as the means for procuring meat, animal hides, horn, bone, and sinew. Early evidence demonstrating the hunting technology of these ancestors includes 400,000-year-old wooden spears discovered in a peat bog (what was originally marsh or swamp land) in northern Germany, although it is likely that evolving humans had begun to hunt before then. Increased organizational ability may also be indicated in prehistoric sites such as Ambrona in Spain, where it has been proposed that fires were used to drive a variety of large animals (including elephants) into a swamp for killing,[11] though natural grass fires have been proposed as an alternative explanation.

With *H. erectus,* then, we find a clearer manifestation than before of the complex interplay of biological, cultural, and ecological factors. Changes in social organization and technology paralleled an increase in brain size and complexity and a reduction in tooth and jaw size. The appearance of cultural adaptations such as controlled use of fire, cooking, and more complex tool kits may have facilitated language development. Analysis of the tools made by early *Homo* indicates that the toolmakers were overwhelmingly right-handed, handedness being a trait associated with language abilities. Moreover, the size of the opening for the nerve that controls tongue movement, so important for spoken language, is comparable to that of modern humans. Improvements

in communication and social organization brought about by language undoubtedly contributed to better methods for food gathering and hunting, to a population increase, and to territorial expansion. Continuous biological and culture change through natural selection in the course of hundreds of thousands of years gradually transformed *H. erectus* into the next emerging species: *Homo sapiens.*

Lumpers or Splitters

At various sites in Africa, Asia, and Europe, a number of fossils have been found that date to between roughly 200,000 and 400,000 years ago. The best population sample, bones of about thirty individuals of both sexes and all ages (but none older than about 40), comes from Atapuerca, a 400,000-year-old site in Spain. Overall, these bones depict a mixture of characteristics of *Homo erectus* with those of early *Homo sapiens,* exactly what one would expect of fossil remains transitional between the two. For example, brain size overlaps the upper end of the *H. erectus* range and the lower end of the range for *H. sapiens.*

Whether one chooses to call these or any other contemporary fossils early *H. sapiens,* late *H. erectus,* or *Homo antecessor,* as did the Spanish anthropologists who discovered them, is more than a name game. Fossil names indicate researchers' perspectives about evolutionary relationships among groups. When specimens are given separate species names, it signifies that they form part of a reproductively isolated group. But were they isolated? Some argue that the evidence does not support such an assumption. There are two basic approaches to naming species in the fossil record: lumping and splitting.

This textbook takes the lumping approach because it is simpler and emphasizes general trends that are appropriate for an introduction to the field. Some paleoanthropologists have the perspective that viewing the fossil record with such detailed biological determinations is arbitrary. Arguing that it is impossible to demonstrate whether or not a collection of ancient bones and teeth represents a distinctive species, they also tend to be "lumpers," placing more or less similar-looking fossil specimens together in more inclusive groups. "Splitters," by contrast, focus on the variation in the fossil record, interpreting fine-grained differences in the shape of skeletons or skulls as evidence of distinctive biological species with corresponding cultural capacities. Referring to the variable shape of the bony ridge above ancient eyes, South African paleoanthropologist Philip Tobias has quipped, "Splitters will create a new species at the drop of a brow ridge." Splitting has the advantage of specificity, whereas lumping has the advantage of simplicity.

---

[11]Freeman, L. G. (1992). *Ambrona and Torralba: New evidence and interpretation.* Paper presented at the 91st Annual Meeting, American Anthropological Association.

VISUAL **COUNTERPOINT**

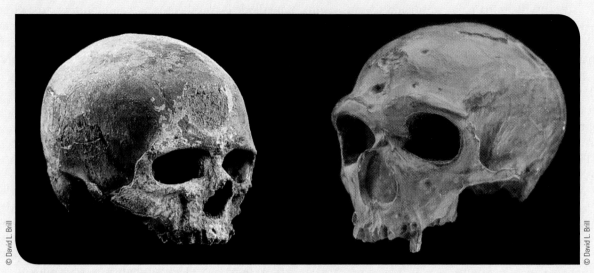

At the same time that Neandertals were first discovered in the late 19th century, other fossil specimens known as Cro-Magnons were found near Neandertal sites in southwestern France. At the time of their discovery, they were thought to be two distinct ancient forms of a similar age. The invention of dating techniques allowed scientists to learn that Neandertals and Cro-Magnons did not co-exist. With a high forehead, the more recent Cro-Magnon skull (left) is more like contemporary Europeans than the older Neanderthal skull (right) with its prominent brow ridge and sloping forehead. In addition, some have proposed that cultural continuity in diet can be inferred between Cro-Magnons and contemporary French people. The Cro-Magnon skull has evidence of a fungal infection, perhaps from eating tainted mushrooms. Mushrooms are a delicacy in this region to this day. While Cro-Magnons are clearly the ancestors of contemporary humans, the exact relationship between Neandertals and living people today is one of the great debates of paleoanthropology.

The Neandertals

Closer to the present, the fossil record provides us with many more human specimens compared to earlier periods. The record is particularly rich when it comes to **Neandertals**, perhaps the most controversial ancient members of the genus *Homo*. Typically, they are represented as the classic "cave men," stereotyped in Western popular media and even in museum displays as wild and hairy club-wielding brutes.

Based on abundant fossil evidence, we now know that Neandertals were extremely muscular members of the genus *Homo* living from about 30,000 to approximately 125,000 years ago in Europe and parts of Asia. Although they had modern-sized brains, Neandertal faces and skulls were quite different from those of later fossilized remains, which are referred to as anatomically modern humans. Their large noses and teeth

Neandertals A distinct group within the genus *Homo* inhabiting Europe and Southwest Asia from approximately 30,000 to 125,000 years ago
Mousterian The tool industry of the Neandertals and their contemporaries of Europe, Southwest Asia, and northern Africa from 40,000 to 125,000 years ago

projected forward more than is the case with modern humans.

Neandertals generally had a sloping forehead and prominent bony brow ridges over their eyes, a receding chin, and on the back of the skull a bony mass provided for attachment of powerful neck muscles. These features, while not exactly in line with modern ideals of European beauty, are also common in Norwegian and Danish skulls dating to about 1,000 years ago—the time of the Vikings[12]—and can be seen to a certain degree in some living humans today. Nevertheless, these anatomical similarities do little to negate the popular image of Neandertals as cave-dwelling brutes. Their rude reputation may also derive from the time of their discovery, as the first widely publicized Neandertal skull was found in 1856, well before scientific theories to account for human origins had gained acceptance.

This odd-looking old skull, found in Germany's Neander "Valley" (*tal* in German), took scientists by surprise. Initially, they explained its extraordinary features as evidence of some disfiguring disease in an invading "barbarian" from the east who had crawled into a deep

[12]Ferrie, H. (1997) An interview with C. Loring Brace. *Current Anthropology, 38*, 861.

cave to die. Although we now know that many aspects of the Neandertals' unique skull shape and body form represent their biological adaptation to an extremely cold climate, and that their brain size and capacity for cultural adaptation were noticeably superior to those of earlier members of the genus *Homo*, Neandertals are still surrounded by controversy.

A Separate Species?

Were Neandertals a separate species that became extinct about 30,000 years ago? Or were they a subspecies of *Homo sapiens*? And if they were not a dead end, an unsuccessful side branch in human evolution, did they actually contribute to our modern human gene pool? In that case, so the argument goes, their direct descendants walk the earth now. The place of Neandertals in human evolutionary history is a highly contentious issue.

With their large brain size, the Neandertal capacity for cultural adaptation was predictably superior to what it had been in earlier species. Neandertals' extensive use of fire, for example, was essential to survival in the cold climate of Europe during the various glacial periods. They lived in small bands or single-family units, both in the open and in caves, probably communicating through language. Evidence of deliberate burials of the deceased among Neandertals reflects a measure of ritual behavior in their communities.

Moreover, the fossil remains of an amputee discovered in Iraq and an arthritic man excavated in France imply that Neandertals cared for the disabled, something not seen previously in the human fossil record. The tool-making tradition of all but the latest Neandertals is called the **Mousterian** tradition after a site (Le Moustier) in the Dordogne region of southern France. *Mousterian* refers to a tradition of the Middle Paleolithic or Middle Stone Age tool industries of Europe and southwestern Asia, generally dating from about 40,000 to 125,000 years ago.

Although considerable variability exists, Mousterian tools are generally lighter and smaller than those of earlier traditions. While previous industries obtained only two or three flakes from an entire stone core, Mousterian toolmakers obtained many smaller flakes, which they skillfully retouched and sharpened. Their tool kits also contained a greater variety of tool types than the earlier ones: hand axes, flakes, scrapers, borers, notched flakes for shaving wood, and many types of points that could be attached to wooden shafts to make spears. This variety of tools facilitated more effective use of food resources and enhanced the quality of clothing and shelter. Mousterian stone tools were used by *all* people, Neandertals and their contemporaries elsewhere, including Europe, western Asia, and North Africa, during this time period. By the time that classic Neandertals were disappearing between 30,000 and 40,000 years ago, their technology was comparable to the tool complexes used by anatomically modern *H. sapiens* during that same period.[13]

The Genus *Homo* Elsewhere

Meanwhile, archaic *H. sapiens* variants without the mid-facial projection and massive muscle attachments on the back of the skull common among Neandertals inhabited other parts of the world. Human fossil skulls found near the Solo River in Java are a prime example. Dates for these specimens range from about 27,000 to 200,000 years ago. The fossils, with their modern-sized brains, display certain features of *H. erectus* combined with those of archaic as well as more modern *H. sapiens*.

Further, a controversial discovery on the Indonesian island of Flores illustrates that geographic isolation can account for an unusual amount of variation in morphology for members of the genus *Homo*. A small-bodied, small-brained adult specimen—dated to between 18,000 and 38,000 years ago, no more than 1 meter (3 feet) tall with humanlike skull and teeth—was designated as the new species *Homo floresiensis* in 2004.[14]

The paleoanthropologists who discovered this specimen, along with discoveries of stone tools and the bones of other animal species dated back to 90,000 years ago, suggest that *Homo floresiensis* is "the end product of a long period of evolution on a comparatively small island where environmental conditions placed small body size at a selective advantage."[15] Some paleoanthropologists argue that the skeleton represents an individual with the disease condition of microcephaly (small headedness) and a variety of other medical conditions. However, recent studies indicate that the ratio of brain size to body size in this specimen is like an australopithecine, while the shape of the brain, as preserved on the inside of the skull, is like a dwarf version of *Homo erectus*.[16] Additional discoveries in the region have supported this theory.

Fossils from various parts of Africa, the most famous being a skull from Kabwe in Zambia, also show a combination of ancient and modern traits. Finally, similar remains have been found at several places in China. For these members of the genus *Homo*, improved cultural adaptive abilities relate to the fact that the brain had achieved modern size. These specimens are generally classified as archaic *Homo sapiens*. Like Neanderthals

---

[13]Mellars, P. (1989). Major issues in the emergence of modern humans. *Current Anthropology, 30,* 356–357.

[14]Brown, P., et al. (2004). A new small bodied hominin from the Late Pleistocene of Flores, Indonesia. *Nature, 431,* 1055–1061.

[15]Brown, et al., p. 1060.

[16]Falk, D., et al. (2005). The brain of LB1, *Homo floresiensis*. *Science, 308,* 242–245.

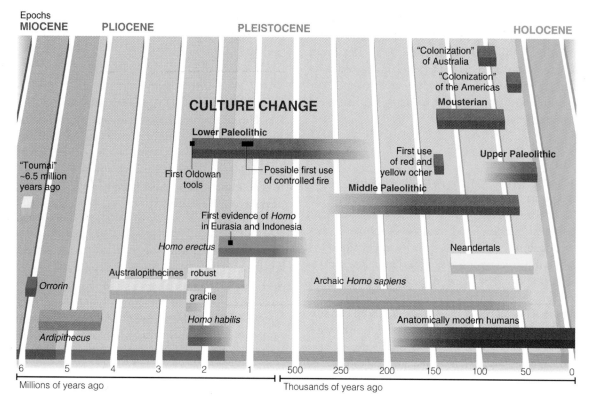

Figure 4.9

Paleoanthropologists debate the exact relationship among the bipedal species along with the number of species that existed over the past 5 to 8 million years. This timeline takes a "lumping" approach, limiting the number of fossil groups presented. The time spans for the Lower, Middle, and Upper Paleolithic vary tremendously by region. Note also that the time scale is expanded for the most recent 250,000 years.

they are large-brained, but their skull shape is different from that of later specimens.

Such a brain made possible not only sophisticated technology but also conceptual thought of considerable intellectual complexity. Decorative pendants and objects with carved and engraved markings also appear in the archaeological record from this period. Objects were also commonly colored with pigments such as manganese dioxide and red or yellow ocher. The ceremonial burial of the dead and nonutilitarian decorative objects provide additional evidence supporting theoretical arguments in favor of symbolic thinking and language use in these ancient populations.

Establishing the relationship between anatomical change and culture change over the course of human evolutionary history is complex (Figure 4.9). Beginning around 200,000 years ago, individuals with a somewhat more anatomically modern human appearance began to appear in Africa and southwestern Asia. While the earliest of these fossils are associated with the Mousterian tool industries used by the Neandertals, over time new tool industries and other forms of cultural expression

appeared. Whether these changes in skull shape are linked with superior cultural abilities is at the heart of the modern human origins debate.

THE UPPER PALEOLITHIC

A veritable explosion of tool types and other forms of cultural expression beginning about 40,000 years ago constitutes what is known as the **Upper Paleolithic** transition. Upper Paleolithic tool kits include increased prominence of "blade" tools: long, thin, precisely shaped pieces of stone demonstrating the considerable skill of their creators. The Upper Paleolithic, lasting until about 10,000 years ago, marks the beginning of behavioral modernity. It is best known from archaeological evidence found in Europe where numerous distinctive tool complexes from successive time periods have been documented. In addition, the European archaeological record from this period is rich with cave wall paintings, engravings, and bas-relief sculptures as well as many portable nonutilitarian artifacts.

In Upper Paleolithic times, humans began to manufacture tools for more effective hunting, fishing, and gathering. Cultural adaptation also became more highly specific and regional, thus enhancing human chances for survival under a wide variety of

Upper Paleolithic The last part (10,000 to 40,000 years ago) of the Old Stone Age, featuring tool industries characterized by long slim blades and an explosion of creative symbolic forms

environmental conditions. Instead of manufacturing all-purpose tools, Upper Paleolithic populations inhabiting a wide range of environments—mountains, marshlands, tundra, forests, lake regions, river valleys, and seashores—all developed specialized devices suited to the resources of their particular habitat and to the different seasons. In the Upper Paleolithic humans found ways and means to cross icy Arctic regions and open water to reach places never previously inhabited by humans. Humans reached Australia between 40,000 and 60,000 years ago and the Americas between about 15,000 and 30,000 years ago.

This degree of regional specialization required improved manufacturing techniques. The blade method of manufacture, invented by archaic *H. sapiens* and later used widely in Europe and western Asia, required less raw material than before and resulted in smaller and lighter tools with a better ratio between weight of flint and length of cutting edge. The pressure-flaking technique—in which a bone, antler, or wooden tool is used to press off small flakes from a larger flake or blade—gave the Upper Paleolithic toolmaker greater control over the shape of the tool than was possible with percussion flaking.

Invented by Mousterian toolmakers, the *burin* (a stone tool with chisel-like edges) came into common use in the Upper Paleolithic. The burin provided an excellent means of working bone and antler into tools such as fishhooks and harpoons. The spear-thrower or *atlatl* (a Nahuatl word used by Aztec Indians in Mexico, referring to a wooden device, 1 to 2 feet long, with a hook on the end for throwing a spear) also appeared at this time. By effectively elongating the arm, the atlatl gave hunters increased force behind the throw.

In addition to the creativity evident in their tools and weapons, Upper Paleolithic people produced representational artwork. In some regions, tools and weapons were engraved with beautiful animal figures; pendants were made of bone and ivory, as were female figurines; and small sculptures were modeled out of clay. Spectacular paintings and engravings depicting humans and animals of this period have been found on the walls of caves and rock shelters in southwestern Europe, Australia, and Africa.

Rock Painting of a Bull and Horses, c. 17,000 B.C., Prehistoric Caves of Lascaux, Dordogne, France/ The Bridgeman Art Library

These 17,000-year-old images, painted on a wall in the multi-chambered Lascaux Cave in the Dordogne region of southwestern France, were discovered in 1940 by four teenage boys. In addition to the Ice Age animals depicted here—horses, wild ox, rhino, and bison—the chambers of Lascaux feature renderings of many other recognizable species. The carved and painted interiors of such caves were often deep underground and difficult to reach. Upper Paleolithic artists burned animal fat in sandstone lamps to light their way. In 1963 Lascaux Cave was closed to the public because carbon dioxide from the breath of thousands of visitors was damaging the ancient paintings. The French government built an exact replica of the cave so that visitors can still experience the wonder of these ancient works.

The southern African rock art tradition spanned 27,000 years and lasted into historic times; from this continuity, we know that much of it depicts artists' visions when in altered states of consciousness related to spiritual practices. Along with the animals, the art also includes a variety of geometric motifs reminiscent of visual hallucinations spontaneously generated by the human nervous system when in a trancelike state.

Australian cave art, some of it older than European cave art and also associated with trancing, includes similar motifs. The occurrence of the same geometric designs in the cave art of Europe suggests trancing was a part of these prehistoric foraging cultures as well. Some suggest that geometric motifs in Paleolithic art were interpreted as stylized human figures and patterns of descent. Although speculative, the great importance of kinship in all historically known communities of hunters, fishers, and gatherers at least makes such a suggestion plausible.

Whether or not a new kind of human, anatomically modern with correspondingly superior intellectual and creative abilities, is responsible for this cultural explosion is hotly debated within paleoanthropology. After all, new kinds of humans were not associated with subsequent "cultural explosions" such as the Neolithic revolution (Chapter 5). The biological and cultural evidence preserved in fossil and archaeological records does not tell a simple story.

THE MODERN HUMAN ORIGINS DEBATE

On a biological level, the modern human origins debate can be distilled to a question of whether one, some, or all populations of the archaic groups played a role in the evolution of modern *H. sapiens*. Those supporting the **multiregional hypothesis** argue that the fossil evidence suggests a simultaneous local transition from *H. erectus* to modern *H. sapiens* throughout all the parts

multiregional hypothesis The hypothesis that modern humans originated through a process of simultaneous local transition from *Homo erectus* to *Homo sapiens* throughout the inhabited world

recent African origins hypothesis The hypothesis that all modern people are derived from one single population of archaic *Homo sapiens* from Africa who migrated out of Africa after 100,000 years ago, replacing all other archaic forms due to their superior cultural capabilities. Also called the Eve or out of Africa hypothesis

of the world inhabited by early members of the genus *Homo*. By contrast, those supporting the **recent African origins hypothesis** (also known as the *Eve* or *out of Africa hypothesis*) argue that all anatomically modern humans living today descend directly from one more recent single population of archaic *H. sapiens* in Africa. This hypothesis asserts that improved cultural capabilities allowed members of this group to replace other archaic human forms as they began to spread out of Africa some time after 100,000 years ago. So while both models place human origins firmly in Africa, the first argues that our human ancestors began moving into Asia and Europe as early as 1.8 million years ago, whereas the second maintains that anatomically modern *H. sapiens* evolved only in Africa, completely replacing other members of the genus *Homo* as they spread throughout the world.

For many years, the recent African origins hypothesis relied upon genetic evidence. In particular, genetic evidence is said to point to a single mother or "Eve" for all anatomically modern humans by tracing human origins through DNA that is found in the mitochondria—a cellular structure that is maternally inherited. Until recently, the absence of good fossil evidence from Africa has been a major problem for the recent African origins hypothesis. In 2003, however, skulls of two adults and one child (discovered in 1997 in the Afar region of Ethiopia) described as anatomically modern were reconstructed and dated to 160,000 years ago.[17] The discoverers of these fossils called them *Homo sapiens idaltu* (meaning "elder" in the local Afar language). Convinced that they have conclusively demonstrated the recent African origins hypothesis, they argue that their latest evidence verifies that Neandertals represent a dead-end side branch of human evolution.

Though the recent African origins hypothesis is the mainstream position, not every scholar supports it. Among those with opposing views are Chinese and Australian paleoanthropologists, who generally favor the multiregional hypothesis in part because it fits better with the fossil discoveries from Australia and Asia.

By contrast, the recent African origins hypothesis depends more upon the interpretation of genetic evidence, fossils, and cultural remains from Europe, Africa, and southwestern Asia. Proponents of multiregionalism critique this model on several grounds. For example, the molecular evidence upon which it is based has been strongly criticized as more recent genetic

---

[17]White, T., et al. (2003). Pleistocene *Homo sapiens* from the Middle Awash, Ethiopia. *Nature, 423,* 742–747.

studies indicate that Africa was not the sole source of DNA in modern humans.[18]

Recent African origins proponents argue that anatomically modern people co-existed for a time with archaic populations until the superior cultural capacities of the moderns resulted in extinction of the archaic peoples. This may help explain its popularity with Western scholars, as it resonates with European experience of colonial expansion; the difference is that Africa rather than Europe is the origin of the supposedly superior people. It also harmonizes with the historical discomfort of considering Neandertals as fully human.

It has been argued that evidence from Europe, where Neandertals and "anatomically moderns" co-existed between 30,000 and 40,000 years ago, supports a model of co-existence and replacement. However, defining some fossils as either Neandertal or anatomically modern is difficult. The latest Neandertals show features (such as chins) more commonly seen in anatomically modern humans, while "early moderns" show features (such as brow ridges and bony masses at the back of the skull) reminiscent of Neandertals.

This mix of modern and Neandertal features is so evident in a child's skeleton recently found in Portugal as to lead several specialists to regard it as clear evidence of hybridization, or successful sexual mating between both human populations.[19] Other specialists argue that some of the modern-appearing features are simply due to the fact that this specimen is a child. But if this child is a hybrid, it would mean that the two human forms belonged to one single species rather than to separate ones. Multiregionalists argue that the simplest way to account for all this evidence is to consider these fossils as belonging to a single varied population, with some individuals showing features more typical of Neandertals than others. They cite archaeological evidence that the cultural achievements of late Neandertals were not fundamentally different from those of "early moderns,"[20] as well as evidence that the culture of these European "early moderns" developed in Europe[21] and was not introduced from outside, as recent African origins proponents assert.

Nevertheless, by 30,000 years ago, many of the distinctive anatomical features seen in archaic groups like Neandertals seem to disappear from the fossil record in Europe. Instead, individuals with higher foreheads, smoother brow ridges, and more distinct chins seem to have had Europe to themselves. However, if one looks at the full range of contemporary human variation across the globe, one can find living people who do not meet the anatomical definition of modernity proposed in the recent African origins model.[22]

The modern human origins debate raises fundamental questions about the complex relationship between biological and cultural human variation. As we reviewed the human fossil record throughout this chapter, inferences were made about the cultural capabilities of our ancestors partially based on biological features. For instance, the argument of a significantly increased brain size of *Homo habilis* 2.5 million years ago compared to earlier australopithecines was used to support the claim that these ancestors were capable of more complex cultural activities, including the manufacture of stone tools. Can we make the same kinds of assumptions about other more recent biological developments? Can we say that only anatomically modern humans with higher foreheads and reduced brow ridges were capable of making sophisticated tools and beautiful art due to fundamental biological difference?

Supporters of the multiregional hypothesis argue we cannot. They argue instead that the human evolutionary history consists of a long period of a single evolving human species without geographically distinct biological types. Paleoanthropologists looking at the fossil evidence can recognize distinctive suites of features possessed by fossil groups, but whether these groups constitute distinct species or variation within a single species is far more difficult to determine.

Without isolation, gene flow tends to keep populations from differentiating into distinct species. As we shall see in the following chapters, since the end of the Ice Age into today's era of globalization, most populations did not live in extreme isolation. The integrating effects of gene flow have become so powerful that dramatic regional variations for suites of traits no longer exist.

Whatever the path in the more recent years of our long evolutionary history, we have become an amazingly diverse and yet still unified single species inhabiting the entire earth.

[18]Templeton, A. R. (1995). The "Eve" hypothesis: A genetic critique and reanalysis. *American Anthropologist, 95*(1), 51–72; Gibbons, A. (1997). Ideas on human origins evolve at anthropology gathering. *Science, 276*, 535–536; Pennisi, E. (1999). Genetic study shakes up out of Africa theory. *Science, 283*, 1828.

[19]Holden, C. (1999). Ancient child burial uncovered in Portugal. *Science, 283*, 169.

[20]d'Errico, F., et al. (1998). Neandertal acculturation in Western Europe? *Current Anthropology, 39*, 521. See also Henry, D. O., et al. (2004). Human behavioral organization in the Middle Paleolithic: Were Neandertals different? *American Anthropologist, 107*(1), 17–31.

[21]Clark, G. A. (2002). Neandertal archaeology: Implications for our origins. *American Anthropologist, 104*(1), 50–67.

[22]Wolpoff, M., & Caspari, R. (1997). *Race and human evolution* (pp. 344–345, 393). New York: Simon & Schuster.

Chapter Summary

■ Macroevolution focuses on the formation of new species (speciation) and on the evolutionary relationships between groups of species. Speciation can occur in a branching fashion known as cladogenesis or without branching (anagenesis), as a single population accumulates sufficient new mutations over time to be considered a separate species. Microevolutionary forces of mutation, gene flow, genetic drift, and natural selection can lead to macroevolutionary change, but the tempo of evolutionary change varies. A mutation in a regulatory gene can bring about rapid change. The punctuated equilibrium model proposes that macroevolution is characterized by long spans of relative stability with periods of rapid change interspersed.

■ Climate changes led to the appearance of primates about 65 million years ago, following a mass extinction of dinosaurs. These primates were small, arboreal, nocturnal, insect eaters. Old World and New World species separated by about 40 million years ago. Many of the Old World anthropoid species became ground dwellers. About 23 million years ago, hominoids, the broad-shouldered tailless primates that include all living and extinct apes and humans, began to appear throughout Asia, Africa, and Europe. Genetic studies have confirmed that the African apes—chimpanzees, bonobos, and gorillas—are our closest living relatives. Larger brains and bipedal locomotion constitute the most striking differences between humans and our closest primate relatives. Bipedalism preceded brain expansion and played a pivotal role in setting us apart from the apes.

■ The earliest members of the bipedal human line diverged from the African apes (chimpanzees, bonobos, and gorillas) sometime between 5 and 8 million years ago. Best known are the australopithecines, well equipped for generalized foraging in a relatively open savannah environment. Although many theories propose that bipedalism reinforced brain expansion by freeing the hands for activities other than locomotion, the increase in brain size did not appear in human evolutionary history until much later with the appearance of the genus *Homo*.

■ With the first members of genus *Homo—Homo habilis—* about 2.5 million years ago, stone tools begin to appear in the archaeological record. Possible earlier tools made of perishable materials such as plant fibers are not preserved. Throughout the course of the evolution of the genus *Homo*, the critical importance of culture as the human mechanism for adaptation imposed selective pressures favoring a larger brain, which in turn made possible improved cultural adaptation.

■ *Homo erectus*, appearing about 2 million years ago, had a brain close in size to that of modern humans and sophisticated behaviors including controlled use of fire for warmth, cooking, and protection. *H. erectus* remains are found throughout Africa, Asia, and Europe, reaching the colder northern areas about 780,000 years ago. The technological efficiency of *H. erectus* is evidenced in improved tool making—first the hand axe and later specialized tools for hunting, butchering, food processing, hide scraping, and defense. Hunting

techniques developed by *H. erectus* reflected a considerable advance in organizational ability.

■ Between 200,000 and 400,000 years ago, evolving humans achieved the brain capacity of contemporary *Homo sapiens*. Apparently several local variations of the genus *Homo* existed around this time period, including the Neandertals. Their capacity for cultural adaptation was considerable, doubtless because large brains made sophisticated technology and conceptual thought possible. Those who lived in Europe used fire extensively in their Arctic climate, lived in small bands, and communicated through language. Remains testify to ritual behavior and caretaking for the aged and infirm. Determining the place of Neandertals in the human evolutionary line is one of the major debates of paleoanthropology.

■ Evidence indicates that at least one population of archaic *H. sapiens* evolved into modern humans. Whether this involved the biological evolution of a new species with improved cultural capabilities or a simultaneous worldwide process involving all archaic forms remains one of the most contentious issues in paleoanthropology. The recent African origins hypothesis proposes that modern humans evolved in Africa about 200,000 years ago, replacing other populations as they spread throughout the globe. The multiregional hypothesis proposes that humans originated in Africa some 2 million years ago and that ancient populations throughout the globe are all ancestors of modern humans unified as a single species maintained through gene flow.

■ The stone tool industries and artwork of Upper Paleolithic cultures surpassed any previously undertaken by humans. Cave paintings and rock art found in Spain, France, Australia, and Africa served a religious purpose and attest to a highly sophisticated aesthetic sensibility. Humans came to inhabit the entire globe during this period, developing watercraft and other technologies suitable for adaptation to a variety of environments.

■ Paleoanthropologists link changes in cultural capacity to changes in brain size and skull shape over most of the course of human evolutionary history. As we get closer to the present, and fossil specimens possess brains the size of contemporary humans, paleoanthropologists debate whether a particular skull shape can be linked to cultural abilities and a behavioral repertoire. With the gene flow that has existed since at least the end of the Ice Age, it is not possible to divide humans into a series of distinct types.

Questions for Reflection

1. Over the course of the past 2.5 million years, the fossil evidence shows that changes in skull shape came with increasing brain size; these changes are associated with culture in the form of the earliest stone tools, coordinated hunting efforts, the controlled use of fire, language, and eventually an explosion of innovations and symbolic expression in the Upper

Paleolithic. As our discussion gets closer to the present, how do the two major hypotheses for modern human origins relate skull size and shape to cultural differences? Can skull shape and size account for cultural differences among contemporary peoples?

2. Do you think evidence from a single bone is enough to determine whether an organism from the past was bipedal?

3. Paleoanthropologists can be characterized as either "lumpers" or "splitters" depending upon their approach to recognizing species in the fossil record. Which of these approaches do you prefer and why?

4. How do you feel about the possibility of having Neandertals as part of your ancestry? How might you relate the Neandertal debate to stereotyping or racism in contemporary society?

5. Do you think that gender has played a role in anthropological interpretations of the behavior of our ancestors and the

way that paleoanthropologists and archaeologists c
their research? Do you believe that feminism has a
play in the interpretation of the past?

Key Terms

macroevolution	Oldowan
speciation	Lower Paleolithic
cladogenesis	*Homo habilis*
anagenesis	*Homo erectus*
punctuated equilibria	Neandertals
continental drift	Mousterian
bipedalism	Upper Paleolithic
Australopithecus	multiregional hypothesis
robust australopithecines	recent African origins
gracile australopithecines	hypothesis

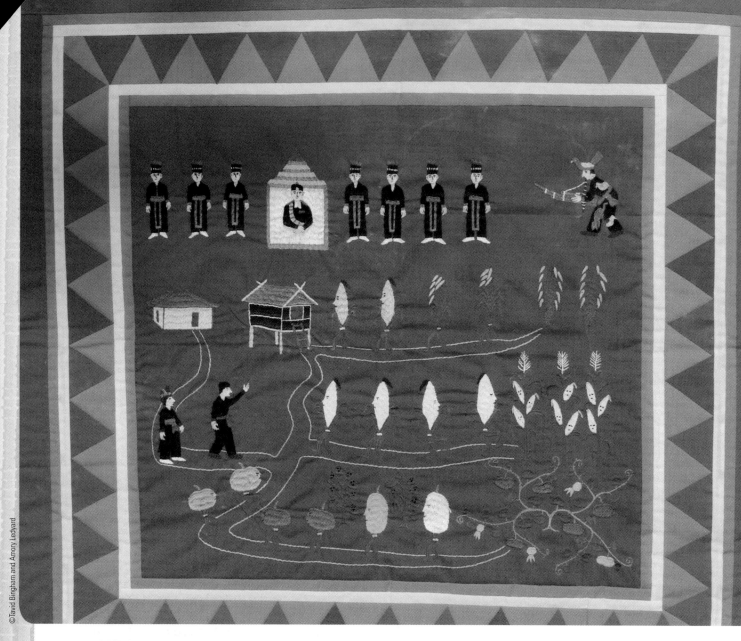

VISUAL ESSENCE This embroidery by Hmong artist Pangxiong Sirathasuk depicts not only her culture's story of the origins of farming—a way of life that began as early as 10,000 years ago—but also some of the consequences of this shift from food foraging to food production. According to Hmong folklore, the vegetables started out walking into villages. But they became disgusted with human greed and walked back to the fields, stating that humans in the future would have to work very hard to receive the earth's bounty. Farming and the domestication of animals, along with village life, mark the start of the Neolithic period. These cultural innovations solved some of the challenges of existence, but they also posed risks to human health, both in the past and in the present, and involved considerable labor. Diets limited by reliance on single crops sometimes led to malnutrition and even famine when these crops failed. Crowded living conditions and close contact with animals in Neolithic villages promoted the spread of infectious disease. This embroidery also shows that the innovations from one part of the world disseminated globally. While the traditional Hmong homeland is in Southeast Asia, the pumpkins and corn depicted here are crops that were originally domesticated in the Americas.

The Neolithic Revolution: The Domestication of Plants and Animals

5

Throughout the Paleolithic, people depended exclusively on wild sources of food for their survival. They hunted and trapped wild animals, fished and gathered shell-fish, eggs, berries, nuts, roots, and other plant foods, relying on their wits and muscles to acquire what nature provided. Whenever favored sources of food became scarce, people adjusted by increasing the variety of foods eaten and incorporating less desirable foods into their diets.

Over time, the subsistence practices of some people began to change in ways that radically transformed their way of life as they became food producers rather than food foragers.[1] For some human groups, food production was accompanied by a more sedentary existence, which in turn permitted a reorganization of the workload in society: Some individuals could be freed from the food quest to devote their energies to other tasks. Over the course of thousands of years, these changes brought about an unforeseen way of life. With good reason, the **Neolithic** era (literally, the "new stone" age), when this change took place, has been called a revolutionary one in human history.

Neolithic The New Stone Age; prehistoric period beginning about 10,000 years ago in which peoples possessed stone-based technologies and depended on domesticated crops and/or animals

---

[1]Rindos, D. (1984). *The origins of agriculture: An evolutionary perspective* (p. 99). Orlando: Academic Press.

THE MESOLITHIC ROOTS OF FARMING AND PASTORALISM

As seen in the previous chapter, by the end of the Paleolithic, humans spread throughout the globe. During this period much of the northern hemisphere was covered with glaciers. By 12,000 years ago, warmer climates prevailed, and these glaciers receded, causing changes in human habitats globally. As sea levels rose throughout the world, many areas that had been dry land during periods of glaciation—such as the Bering Strait, parts of the North Sea, and an extensive land area that had joined the eastern islands of Indonesia to mainland Asia—flooded.

In some northern regions, warmer climates brought about particularly marked changes, allowing the replacement of barren tundra with forests. In the process, the herd animals—upon which northern Paleolithic peoples had depended for much of their food, clothing, and shelter—disappeared from many areas. Some, like the caribou and musk ox, moved to colder climates; others, like the mammoths, died out completely. In the new forests, animals were often more solitary in their habits. As a result, large cooperative hunts were less productive than before. Diets shifted to abundant plant foods as well as fish and other foods in and around lakes, bays, and rivers. In Europe, Asia, and Africa, this transitional period between the Paleolithic and the Neolithic is called the **Mesolithic**, or Middle Stone Age. In the Americas, comparable cultures are referred to as **Archaic cultures**.

New technologies accompanied the changed post-glacial environment. People began manufacturing new kinds of ground stone tools, shaped and sharpened by grinding the tool against sandstone, often using sand as an additional abrasive. Once shaped and sharpened, these stones were set into wooden or sometimes antler handles to make effective axes and adzes, cutting tools with a sharp blade set at right angles to a handle. Although such implements take longer to make, they are less prone to breakage under heavy-duty usage than those made of chipped stone. Thus, they were helpful in clearing forest areas and in the woodwork needed for the creation of dugout canoes and skin-covered boats. Evidence for the presence of seaworthy watercraft at Mesolithic sites indicates that human foraging for food took place on the open water as well as the land. Thus, it was possible to make use of deep-water resources along with those of coastal areas, rivers, and lakes.

The **microlith**, a small but hard, sharp, blade, was the characteristic tool of the Mesolithic. Although a microlithic ("small stone" tools) tradition existed in Central Africa by about 40,000 years ago,[2] such tools did not become common elsewhere until the Mesolithic. Microliths could be mass produced because they were small, easy to make, and could be fashioned from sections of blades. These small tools could be attached to arrow or other tool shafts by using melted resin (from pine trees) as a binder. Microliths provided Mesolithic people with an important advantage over their Upper Paleolithic forebears: The small size of the microlith enabled them to devise a wider array of composite tools made out of stone and wood or bone. Thus, they could make sickles, harpoons, arrows, knives, and daggers by fitting microliths into slots in wood, bone, or antler handles. Later experimentation with these forms led to more sophisticated tools and weapons such as bows to propel arrows.

Dwellings from the Mesolithic provide evidence of a somewhat more settled lifestyle during this period. People subsisting on a dietary mixture of wild game, seafood, and plants in the now milder forested environments of the north did not need to move regularly over large geographic areas in pursuit of migratory herds.

In the warmer parts of the world, wild plant foods were more readily available, and so their collection complemented hunting in the Upper Paleolithic more than had been the case in the colder northern regions. Hence, in areas like Southwest Asia, the Mesolithic represents less of a changed way of life than was true in Europe. Here, the important **Natufian culture** flourished.

The Natufians lived between 10,200 and 12,500 years ago at the eastern end of the Mediterranean Sea

---

Mesolithic The Middle Stone Age of Europe, Asia, and Africa beginning about 12,000 years ago

Archaic cultures Term used to refer to Mesolithic cultures in the Americas

microlith A small blade of flint or similar stone, several of which were hafted together in wooden handles to make tools; widespread in the Mesolithic

Natufian culture A Mesolithic culture living in the lands that are now Israel, Lebanon, and western Syria, between about 10,200 and 12,500 years ago

innovation Any new idea, method, or device that gains widespread acceptance in society

primary innovation The creation, invention, or discovery by chance of a completely new idea, method, or device

secondary innovation The deliberate application or modification of an existing idea, method, or device

domestication An evolutionary process whereby humans modify, either intentionally or unintentionally, the genetic makeup of a population of plants or animals, sometimes to the extent that members of the population are unable to survive and/or reproduce without human assistance

---

[2]Bednarik, R. G. (1995). Concept-mediated marking in the Lower Paleolithic. *Current Anthropology, 36,* 606.

in caves, rock shelters, and small villages with stone- and mud-walled houses. They are named after the Wadi en-Natuf, a ravine near Jerusalem, Israel, where the remains of this culture were first found. They buried their dead in communal cemeteries, usually in shallow pits without any other objects or decorations. A small shrine is known from one of their villages, a 10,500-year-old settlement at Jericho in the Jordan River Valley. Basin-shaped depressions in the rocks found outside homes and plastered storage pits beneath the floors of the houses indicate that the Natufians were the earliest Mesolithic people known to have stored plant foods. Certain tools found among Natufian remains bear evidence of their use to cut grain. These Mesolithic sickles consisted of small stone blades set in straight handles of wood or bone.

The new way of life of the various Mesolithic and Archaic cultures generally provided supplies of food sufficiently abundant to permit people in some parts of the world to live in larger and more sedentary groups. They became village dwellers, and some of these settlements went on to expand into the first farming villages, towns, and ultimately cities.

THE NEOLITHIC REVOLUTION

The Neolithic, or New Stone Age, derives its name from the polished stone tools that are characteristic of this period. But more important than the presence of these tools is the cultural transition from a foraging economy based on hunting, gathering, and fishing to one based on food production, representing a major change in the subsistence practices of early peoples. While many of the early food producers became village dwellers, other groups used Neolithic tools and settled in villages while still maintaining a foraging lifestyle as some groups do into the present. The Neolithic revolution was by no means smooth or instantaneous; in fact, the switch to food production spread over many centuries—even millennia—and was a direct outgrowth of the preceding Mesolithic. Where to draw the line between the two periods is not always clear.

The ultimate source of all culture change is **innovation**: any new idea, method, or device that gains widespread acceptance in society. **Primary innovation** is the creation, invention, or discovery by chance of a completely new idea, method, or device. A **secondary innovation** is a deliberate application or modification of an existing idea, method, or device.

An example of a primary innovation is the discovery that firing clay makes it permanently hard. Presumably, accidental firing of clay occurred frequently in ancient cooking fires—but a chance occurrence is of no account unless someone perceives an application of it. This perception took place about 25,000 years ago, when people began making figurines of fired clay. However, it was not until around 10,000 years ago that people recognized a highly practical application of fired clay and began using it to make pottery containers and cooking vessels.

The accidental discoveries responsible for primary innovations are not generated by environmental change or some other need, nor are they necessarily adaptive. They are, however, given structure by the cultural context. Thus, the outcome of the discovery of fired clay by migratory food foragers 25,000 years ago was very different from what it was when discovered later by more settled farmers in Southwest Asia, where it set off a cultural chain reaction as one invention led to another at the start of the Neolithic.

The shift to relatively complete reliance on domesticated plants and animals took several thousand years. While this transition has been particularly well studied in Southwest Asia, archaeological evidence for food production also exists from other parts of the world such as China and Central America and the Andes at similar or somewhat earlier dates. The critical point is not which region invented farming first, but rather the independent but more or less simultaneous invention of food production throughout the globe.

Domestication: What Is It?

Domestication is a process whereby humans modify, either intentionally or unintentionally, the genetic makeup of a population of plants or animals, sometimes to the extent that members of the population are unable to survive and/or reproduce without human assistance. Domestication is essentially a special case of interdependence between different species frequently seen in the natural world, where one species depends on another (that feeds upon it) for its protection and reproductive success.

According to U.S. evolutionary biologist, geographer, and all-around theorist Jared Diamond, humans are not the only species known to domesticate another. Certain ants native to the American tropics grow fungi in their nests, and these fungi provide the ants with most of their nutrition. Like human farmers, the ants add manure to stimulate fungal growth and eliminate competing weeds, both mechanically and through use of antibiotic herbicides. The fungi are protected and ensured reproductive success while providing the ants with a steady food supply.[3]

---

[3]Diamond, J. (1998). Ants, crops, and history. *Science, 281,* 1974–1975.

In plant–human interactions, domestication ensures the plants' reproductive success while providing humans with food. Selective breeding eliminates thorns, toxins, and bad-tasting chemical compounds, which in the wild had served to ensure a plant species' survival, at the same time producing larger, tastier edible parts attractive to humans. U.S. environmentalist Michael Pollan suggests that domesticated plant species successfully exploit human desires to out-compete other plant species and considers "agriculture as something grasses did to people to conquer trees."[4]

Evidence of Early Plant Domestication

Domesticated plants generally differ from their wild ancestors in ways favored by humans, including increased size, at least of edible parts; reduction or loss of natural means of seed dispersal; reduction or loss of protective devices such as husks or distasteful chemical compounds; loss of delayed seed germination (important to wild plants for survival in times of drought or other temporarily adverse conditions); and development of simultaneous ripening of the seed or fruit.

For example, wild cereals have a very fragile stem, whereas domesticated ones have a tough stem. Under natural conditions, plants with fragile stems scatter their seed for themselves, whereas those with tough stems do not. When the grain stalks were harvested, their soft stems would shatter at the touch of sickle or flail, and many of their seeds would be lost. Inevitably, though unintentionally, most of the seeds that people harvested would have been taken from the tough plants. Early domesticators probably also tended to select seed from plants having few husks or none at all—eventually breeding them out—because husking prior to pounding the grains into meal or flour required extra labor.

Many of the distinguishing characteristics of domesticated plants can be seen in remains from archaeological sites. Paleobotanists can often tell the fossil of a wild plant species from a domesticated one, for example, by studying the shape and size of various plant structures.[5]

Evidence of Early Animal Domestication

Domestication also produced changes in the skeletal structure of some animals. For example, the horns of

© 1995 Reprinted with Permission from W. C. Galinat. The New York Botanical Garden.

A   B   C

W.C. Galinat

Increased size of edible parts is a common feature of domestication. The large ear of corn or maize (C) that we know today is a far cry from the tiny ears (about an inch long) characteristic of 5,500-year-old maize (B). Maize may have arisen when a simple gene mutation transformed male tassel spikes of the wild grass called teosinte (A) into the small, earliest versions of the female maize ear. Teosinte, a wild grass from highland Mexico, is far less productive than maize and does not taste very good. Like most plants that were domesticated, it was not a favored food for foraging people. Domestication transformed it into something highly desirable.

---

[4]Pollan, M. (2001). *The botany of desire: A plant's-eye view of the world*. New York: Random House.

[5]Gould, S. J. (1991). *The flamingo's smile: Reflections in natural history* (p. 368). New York: Norton.

wild goats and sheep differ from those of their domesticated counterparts. Some types of domesticated sheep have no horns altogether. Similarly, the size of an animal or its parts can vary with domestication as seen in the smaller size of certain teeth of domesticated pigs compared to those of wild ones.

A study of age and sex ratios of butchered animals at an archaeological site may indicate whether animal domestication was practiced. Investigators have determined that if the age and/or sex ratios at the site differ from those in wild herds, the imbalances are due to domestication. Archaeologists documented a sharp rise in the number of young male goats killed at 10,000-year-old sites in the Zagros Mountains of Iran. Evidently people were slaughtering the young males for food and saving the females for breeding. Although such herd management does not prove that the goats were fully domesticated, it does indicate a step in that direction.[6] Similarly, the archaeological sites in the Andean highlands, dating to around 6,300 years ago, contain evidence that these animals were penned up, indicating the beginning of domestication.

Beginnings of Domestication

Scientists still do not have all the answers about how and why domestication took place. Nonetheless, three observations help us to understand how the switch to food production may have taken place.

The first of these observations is that the transition to food production did not come about from discoveries, such as that seeds, if planted, grow into plants. Contemporary food foragers are perfectly aware of the role of seeds in plant growth, that plants grow better under certain conditions than others, and so forth. Jared Diamond aptly describes contemporary food foragers as "walking encyclopedias of natural history with individual names for as many as a thousand or more plant and animal species, and with detailed knowledge of those species' biological characteristics, distribution, and potential uses."[7] What's more, they frequently apply their knowledge to actively manage the resources on which they depend. For example, indigenous people living in northern Australia deliberately alter the runoff channels of creeks to flood extensive tracts of land, converting them into fields of wild grain. Indigenous Australians choose to continue to forage while also managing the land.

Second, the switch from food foraging to food production does not free people from hard work. In fact, available ethnographic data indicate just the opposite— that farmers, by and large, work far longer hours compared to most food foragers.

Finally, food production is not necessarily a more secure means of subsistence than food foraging. Seed crops in particular—of the sort originally domesticated in Southwest Asia, Central America, and the Andean highlands—are highly productive but not stable from an ecological perspective because of low species diversity. Without constant human attention, their productivity suffers.

For these reasons, it is little wonder that food foragers do not necessarily regard farming and animal husbandry as superior to hunting, gathering, or fishing. Thus, some people in the world have continued as food foragers into the present. However, it has become increasingly difficult for them, because food-producing peoples (including postindustrial societies) have deprived them of more and more of the land base necessary for their way of life. For food foragers, as long as existing practices work well, there is no need to abandon them, especially if they provide an eminently satisfactory way of life. Noting that food foragers have more time for play and relaxation than food producers, U.S. anthropologist Marshall Sahlins has labeled hunter-gatherers the "the original affluent society."[8] Farming brings with it a whole new system of relationships that disturbs an age-old balance between humans and nature.

WHY HUMANS BECAME FOOD PRODUCERS

In view of what has been said so far, we may well ask: Why did any human group abandon food foraging in favor of food production?

Several theories have been proposed to account for this change in human subsistence practices. One older theory, championed by Australian archaeologist V. Gordon Childe, is the desiccation, or oasis, theory, which is based on environmental determinism. Its proponents advanced the idea that the glacial cover over Europe and Asia caused a shift in rain patterns from Europe to northern Africa and Southwest Asia. When the glaciers retreated northward, so did the rain patterns. As a result, northern Africa and Southwest Asia became dryer, and people were forced to congregate at oases for water. Because of the relative food scarcity in such an environment, necessity drove people to collect the wild grasses and seeds growing around the oases, congregating in a part of Southwest Asia known as the Fertile Crescent (Figure 5.1). Eventually they had to cultivate the grasses to provide enough

---

[6]Zeder, M. A., & Hesse, B. (2000). The initial domestication of goats (*Capra hircus*) in the Zagros Mountains 10,000 years ago. *Science, 287,* 2254–2257.

[7]Diamond, J. (1997). *Guns, germs, and steel* (p. 143). New York: Norton.

[8]Sahlins, M. (1972). *Stone age economics.* Chicago: Aldine.

Figure 5.1 The Fertile Crescent of Southwest Asia and the Area of Natufian Culture

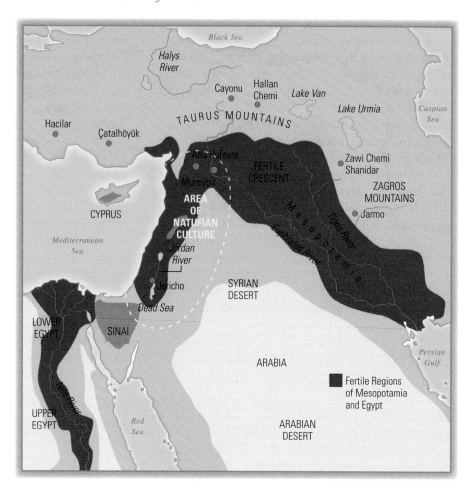

food for the community. According to this theory, animal domestication began because the oases attracted hungry animals, such as wild goats, sheep, and also cattle, which came to graze on the stubble of the grain fields and to drink. Finding that these animals were often too thin to kill for food, people began to fatten them up.

Although Childe's oasis theory can be critiqued on a number of grounds and many other theories have been proposed to account for the shift to domestication, it remains historically significant as the first scientifically testable explanation for the origins of food production. Childe's theory set the stage for the development of archaeology as a science. Later theories developed by archaeologists built on Childe's ideas and took into account the role of chance environmental circumstances of the specific region along with other specific cultural factors that may be driving change.

The Fertile Crescent

Present evidence indicates that the earliest plant domestication took place gradually in the Fertile Crescent, the long arc-shaped sweep of river valleys and coastal plains extending from the Upper Nile (Sudan) to the Lower Tigris (Iraq). Archaeological data suggest the domestication of rye as early as 13,000 years ago by people living at a site (Abu Hureyra) east of Aleppo, Syria, although wild plants and animals continued to be their major food sources. Over the next several millennia they became full-fledged farmers, cultivating rye and wheat.[9] By 10,300 years ago, others in the region were also growing crops.

The domestication process was a consequence of a chance convergence of independent natural events and other cultural developments.[10] The Natufians, whose culture we looked at earlier in this chapter, illustrate this process. These people lived at a time of dramatically changing climates in Southwest Asia. With the end of the last glaciation, temperatures not only became significantly warmer but markedly seasonal as well. Between 6,000 and 12,000 years ago, the region experienced the most extreme seasonality in its history,

---

[9]Pringle, H. (1998). The slow birth of agriculture. *Science, 282,* 1446–1449.

[10]McCorriston, J., & Hole, F. (1991). The ecology of seasonal stress and the origins of agriculture in the Near East. *American Anthropologist, 93,* 46–69.

with dry summers significantly longer and hotter than today. As a consequence of increased evaporation, many shallow lakes dried up, leaving just three in the Jordan River Valley. At the same time, the region's plant cover changed dramatically. Those plants best adapted to environmental instability and seasonal dryness were annuals, including wild cereal grains and legumes (such as peas, lentils, and chickpeas). Because they complete their life cycle in a single year, annuals can evolve very quickly under unstable conditions. Moreover, they store their reproductive abilities for the next wet season in abundant seeds, which can remain dormant for prolonged periods.

The Natufians, who lived where these conditions were especially severe, adapted by modifying their subsistence practices in two ways: First, they probably burned the landscape regularly to promote browsing by red deer and grazing by gazelles, the main focus of their hunting activities. Second, they placed greater emphasis on the collection of wild seeds from the annual plants that could be effectively stored to see people through the dry season. The importance of stored foods, coupled with the scarcity of reliable water sources, promoted more sedentary living patterns, reflected in the substantial villages of late Natufian times. The reliance upon seeds in Natufian subsistence was made possible by the fact that they already possessed sickles (originally used to cut reeds and sedges for baskets) for harvesting grain and grinding stones for processing a variety of wild foods.[11]

The use of sickles to harvest grain turned out to have important consequences, again unexpected, for the Natufians. In the course of harvesting, it was inevitable that many easily dispersed seeds would be lost at the harvest site, whereas those from plants that did not readily scatter their seeds would be mostly carried back to where people processed and stored them.[12]

The periodic burning of vegetation carried out to promote the deer and gazelle herds may have also affected the development of new genetic variation. Heat is known to affect mutation rates. Also, fire removes individuals from a population, which changes the genetic structure of a population drastically and quickly. With seeds for nondispersing variants being carried back to settlements, it was inevitable that some lost seeds would germinate and grow there on dump heaps and other disturbed sites (latrines, areas cleared of trees, or burned-over terrain).

Many of the plants that became domesticated were "colonizers," variants that do particularly well in disturbed habitats. Moreover, with people becoming increasingly sedentary, disturbed habitats became more extensive as resources closer to settlements were depleted over time. Thus, variants of plants particularly susceptible to human manipulation had more opportunities to flourish where people were living. Under such circumstances, it was inevitable that eventually people would begin to actively promote their growth, even by deliberately sowing them. Ultimately, people realized that they could play a more active role in the process by deliberately trying to breed the strains they preferred. With this, domestication may be said to have shifted from a process that was unintentional to one that was intentional.

The development of animal domestication in Southwest Asia seems to have proceeded along somewhat similar lines in the hilly country of southeastern Turkey, northern Iraq, and the Zagros Mountains of Iran. Large herds of wild sheep and goats, as well as much environmental diversity, characterized these regions. From the flood plains of the valley of the Tigris and Euphrates rivers, for example, travel to the north or east takes one into high country through three other zones: first steppe; then oak and pistachio woodlands; and, finally, high plateau country with grass, scrub, or desert vegetation. Valleys that run at right angles to the mountain ranges afford relatively easy access across these zones. Today, a number of peoples in the region still graze their herds of sheep and goats on the low steppe in the winter and move to high pastures on the plateaus in the summer.

Moving back in time prior to the domestication of plants and animals, we find the region inhabited by peoples whose subsistence pattern, like that of the Natufians, was one of food foraging. Distinct plants were found in each ecological zone, and because of the variation in altitude, plant foods matured at different times in different zones. Many animal species were hunted for meat and hides by these people, most notably the hoofed animals: deer, gazelles, wild goats, and wild sheep. Their bones are far more common in human refuse piles than those of other animals. This is significant, for most of these animals naturally move back and forth from low winter pastures to high summer pastures. People followed these animals in their seasonal migrations, making use along the way of other wild foods in the zones through which they passed: palm dates in the lowlands; acorns, almonds, and pistachios higher up; apples and pears higher still; wild grains maturing at different times in different zones; woodland animals in the forested zone between summer and winter grazing lands. All in all, it was a rich, varied fare.

The archaeological record indicates that, at first, animals of all ages and sexes were hunted by the people of the Southwest Asian highlands. But, beginning about 11,000 years ago, the percentage of immature sheep eaten increased to about 50 percent of the total. At the same time, the percentage of females among animals

[11]Olszewski, D. I. (1991). Comment. *Current Anthropology, 32,* 43.

[12]Blumer, M. A., & Byrne, R. (1991). The ecological genetics and domestication and the origins of agriculture. *Current Anthropology, 32,* 30.

eaten decreased. (Feasting on male lambs increases yields by sparing the females for breeding.) This marks the beginning of human management of sheep. As this management of flocks became more efficient, sheep were increasingly shielded from the effects of natural selection, allowing variants preferred by humans to have increased reproductive success. Variants attractive to humans did not arise out of need but at random, as mutations do. But then humans selectively bred the varieties they favored. In such a way, those features characteristic of domestic sheep—such as greater fat and meat production, excess wool, and so on—began to develop. By 9,000 years ago, the shape and size of the bones of domestic sheep had become distinguishable from those of wild sheep. At about the same time, similar developments were taking place in southeastern Turkey and the lower Jordan River Valley, where pigs were the focus of attention.[13]

Some researchers have recently linked animal domestication to the development of fixed territories and settlements. Without a notion of resource ownership, they suggest that hunters would not be likely to postpone the short-term gain of killing prey for the long-term gain of continued access to animals in the future.[14] Eventually, animal species domesticated in one area were introduced into areas outside their natural habitat.

To sum up, the domesticators of plants and animals sought only to maximize the food sources available to them. They were not aware of the long-term and revolutionary cultural consequences of their actions. But as the process continued, the productivity of the domestic species increased relative to wild species. Thus, they became increasingly more important to subsistence, resulting in further domestication and further increases in productivity.

Other Centers of Domestication

In addition to Southwest Asia, the domestication of plants and, in some cases, animals took place independently in Southeast Asia, parts of the Americas (Central America, the Andean highlands, the tropical forests of South America, and eastern North America), northern China, and Africa (Figure 5.2). In China, domestication of rice was under way along the middle

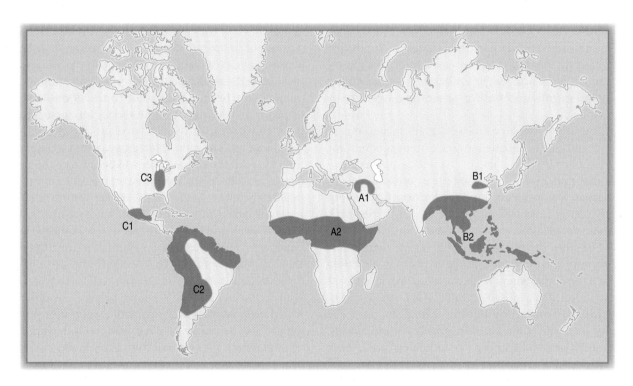

Figure 5.2
Early plant and animal domestication took place in such widely scattered areas as Southwest Asia (A1), Central Africa (A2), China (B1), Southeast Asia (B2), Central America (C1), South America (C2), and North America (C3).

vegeculture The cultivation of domesticated root crops, such as yams and taro
horticulture Cultivation of crops carried out with simple hand tools such as digging sticks or hoes

[13]Pringle, p. 1448.

[14]Alvard, M. S., & Kuznar, L. (2001). Deferred harvest: The transition from hunting to animal husbandry. *American Anthropologist, 103*(2), 295–311.

Yangtze River by about 11,000 years ago.[15] It was not until 4,000 years later, however, that domestic rice dominated wild rice to become the dietary staple.

In Southeast Asia, decorations on pottery dated to sometime between 5,000 and 8,800 years ago document rice as the earliest species to be domesticated. This region, however, is primarily known for the domestication of root crops, most notably yams and taro. Root crop farming, or **vegeculture**, typically involves the growing of many different species together in a single field. Because this approximates the complexity of the natural vegetation, vegeculture tends to be more stable than seed crop cultivation. Propagation or breeding of new plants typically occurs through vegetative means—the planting of cuttings—rather than the planting of seeds.

In the Americas, the domestication of plants began about as early as it did in these other regions. One species of domestic squash may have been grown as early as 10,000 years ago in the coastal forests of Ecuador; at the same time another species was being grown in an arid region of highland Mexico.[16] Evidently, these developments were independent of each other. The ecological diversity of the highland valleys of Mexico, like the hill country of Southwest Asia, provided an excellent environment for domestication. Movement of people through a variety of ecological zones as they changed altitude brought plant and animal species into new habitats, providing opportunities for "colonizing" species and humans alike.

Domestication in the Andean highlands of Peru, another environmentally diverse region, emphasized root crops, the best known being potatoes (of which about 3,000 varieties were grown, versus the mere 250 grown today in North America). South Americans also domesticated guinea pigs, llamas, alpacas, and ducks, whereas people in the Mexican highlands never did much with domestic livestock. They limited themselves to dogs, turkeys, and bees. American Indians living north of Mexico developed some of their own indigenous domesticates. These included local varieties of squash and sunflower.

Ultimately, American Indians domesticated over 300 food crops, including two of the four most important ones in the world today: potatoes and maize (the other two are wheat and rice). In fact, 60 percent of the crops grown in the world today were first cultivated by America's indigenous peoples, who not only remain the developers of the world's largest array of nutritious foods but are also the primary contributors to the world's varied cuisines.[17] After all, where would Italian cuisine be without tomatoes? Thai cooking without peanuts? Northern European cooking without potatoes? Small wonder American Indians have been called the world's greatest farmers.[18]

As plant species became domesticated, **horticultural** societies came into being. These are small communities of gardeners working with simple hand tools and using neither irrigation nor the plow. Horticulturists typically cultivate a variety of crops in small gardens they have cleared by hand. The sophistication of the ancient farming methods as used by Indians in the Amazon rainforest is evident in the research conducted by an international team of archaeologists and other scientists. These ancient methods, which left behind rich dark soils, may have important applications for humans today, as explained in this chapter's Original Study. Reviving these ancient soil-enrichment techniques could contribute to better global management of rainforests and climate today.

Original Study

The Real Dirt on Rainforest Fertility
Charles C. Mann

IRANDUBA, AMAZÔNAS STATE, BRAZIL—Above a pit dug by a team of archaeologists here is a papaya orchard filled with unusually vigorous trees bearing great clusters of plump green fruit. Below the surface lies a different sort of bounty: hundreds, perhaps thousands, of burial urns and millions of pieces of broken ceramics, all from an almost unknown people who flourished here before the conquistadors.

But surprisingly, what might be most important about this central Amazonian site is not the vibrant orchard or the extraordinary outpouring of ceramics but the dirt under the trees and around the ceramics. A rich, black soil known locally as *terra preta do Indio* (Indian dark earth), it sustained large settlements on these lands for 2 millennia, according to the Brazilian-American archaeological team working here.

Throughout Amazonia, farmers prize *terra preta* for its great productivity—some farmers have worked it for years with minimal fertilization. Such long-lasting fertility is an anomaly in the tropics. Despite the exuberant growth of rainforests, their red and yellow soils are notoriously poor: weathered, highly acidic, and low in organic matter and essential nutrients. In these oxisols, as they are known, most carbon and

[continued]

[15]Pringle, p. 1449.
[16]Pringle, p. 1447.

[17]Weatherford, J. (1988). *Indian givers: How the Indians of the Americas transformed the world* (pp. 71, 115). New York: Fawcett Columbine.
[18]Weatherford, p. 95.

[continued]

nutrients are stored not in the soil, as in temperate regions, but in the vegetation that covers it. When loggers, ranchers, or farmers clear the vegetation, the intense sun and rain quickly decompose the remaining organic matter in the soil, making the land almost incapable of sustaining life—one reason ecologists frequently refer to the tropical forest as a "wet desert."

Because *terra preta* is subject to the same punishing conditions as the surrounding oxisols, "its existence is very surprising," says Bruno Glaser, a chemist at the Institute of Soil Science and Soil Geography at the University of Bayreuth, Germany. "If you read the textbooks, it shouldn't be there." Yet according to William I. Woods, a geographer at Southern Illinois University, Edwardsville, *terra preta* might cover as much as 10 percent of Amazonia, an area the size of France. More remarkable still, *terra preta* appears to be the product of intensive habitation by precontact Amerindian populations. "They practiced agriculture here for centuries," Glaser says. "But instead of destroying the soil, they improved it—and that is something we don't know how to do today."

In the past few years, a small but growing group of researchers—geographers, archaeologists, soil scientists, ecologists, and anthropologists—has been investigating this "gift from the past," as *terra preta* was called by the late anthropologist James B. Petersen, a founding member of the Iranduba team. By understanding how indigenous groups created Amazonian dark earths, these researchers hope, today's scientists might be able to transform some of the region's oxisols into new *terra preta*. Indeed, experimental programs to produce "*terra preta* nova" have already begun. Population pressure and government policies are causing rapid deforestation in the tropics, and poor tropical soils make much of the clearing as economically nonviable in the long run as it is ecologically damaging.

THE GOOD EARTH

Terra preta is scattered throughout Amazonia, but it is most frequently found on low hills overlooking rivers—the kind of terrain on which indigenous

groups preferred to live. According to Eduardo Neves, an archaeologist at the University of São Paulo who is part of the Iranduba team, the oldest deposits date back more than 2,000 years and occur in the lower and central Amazon; *terra preta* then appeared to spread to cultures upriver. By AD 500 to 1000, he says, "it appeared in almost every part of the Amazon Basin."

Typically, black-soil regions cover 1 to 5 hectares, but some encompass 300 hectares or more. The black soils are generally 40 to 60 centimeters deep but can reach more than 2 meters. Almost always they are full of broken ceramics. Although they were created centuries ago—probably for agriculture, researchers such as Woods believe—patches of *terra preta* are still among the most desirable land in the Amazon. Indeed, *terra preta* is valuable enough that locals sell it as potting soil. To the consternation of archaeologists, long planters full of *terra preta*, complete with pieces of pre-Columbian pottery, greet visitors to the airport in the lower Amazon town of Santarém.

As a rule, *terra preta* has more "plant-available" phosphorus, calcium, sulfur, and nitrogen than surrounding oxisols; it also has much more organic matter, retains moisture and nutrients better, and is not rapidly exhausted by agricultural use when managed well.

The key to *terra preta*'s long-term fertility, Glaser says, is charcoal: *Terra preta* contains up to 70 times as much

as adjacent oxisols. "The charcoal prevents organic matter from being rapidly mineralized," Glaser says. "Over time, it partly oxidizes, which keeps providing sites for nutrients to bind to." But simply mixing charcoal into the ground is not enough to create *terra preta*. Because charcoal contains few nutrients, Glaser says, "high nutrient inputs via excrement and waste such as turtle, fish, and animal bones were necessary." Special soil microorganisms are also likely to play a role in its persistent fertility, in the view of Janice Thies, a soil ecologist who is part of a Cornell University team studying *terra preta*. "There are indications that microbial biomass is higher in *terra preta*," she says, which raises the possibility that scientists might be able to create a "package" of charcoal, nutrients, and microfauna that could be used to transform oxisols into *terra preta*.

SLASH-AND-CHAR

Surprisingly, *terra preta* seems not to have been created by the "slash-and-burn" agriculture famously practiced in the tropics. In slash-and-burn, farmers clear and then burn their fields, using the ash to flush enough nutrients into the soil to support crops for a few years; when productivity declines, they move on to the next patch of forest. Glaser, Woods, and other researchers believe that the long-ago Amazonians created *terra preta* by a process that Christoph Steiner, a University of Bayreuth soil scientist, has dubbed "slash-and-char."

Instead of completely burning organic matter to ash, in this view, ancient farmers burned it only incompletely, creating charcoal, then stirred the charcoal directly into the soil. Later they added nutrients and, in a process analogous to adding sourdough starter to bread, possibly soil previously enriched with microorganisms. In addition to its potential benefits to the soil, slash-and-char releases much less carbon into the air than slash-and-burn, which has potential implications for climate change.

(Charles C. Mann, Science, 297, 920–923. Copyright © by the American Association for the Advancement of Science. Reprinted by permission)

Considering the separate innovations of plant domestication, it is interesting to note that in all cases people developed the same categories of foods. Everywhere, starchy grains (or root crops) are accompanied by one or more legumes: wheat and barley with peas, chickpeas, and lentils in Southwest Asia; maize with various kinds of beans in Mexico, for example. Together the amino acids (building blocks of proteins) in these starch and legume combinations provide humans with sufficient protein. The starchy grains are the core of the diet and are eaten at every meal in the form of bread, some sort of food wrapper (like a tortilla), or a gruel or thickening agent in a stew along with one or more legumes. Being rather bland, these sources of carbohydrates and proteins are invariably combined with flavor-giving substances that help the food go down.

In Mexico, for example, the flavor enhancer par excellence is the chili pepper; in other cuisines it may be a bit of meat or fat, a dairy product, or mushrooms. Anthropologist Sidney Mintz refers to this as the *core-fringe-legume pattern* (CFLP), noting that only recently has it been upset by the worldwide spread of processed sugars and high-fat foods.[19]

FOOD PRODUCTION AND POPULATION SIZE

Human population has been growing steadily since the Neolithic. The exact relationship between population growth and food production is similar to the old chicken and egg question. Some assert that population growth creates pressures that result in innovations such as food production while others suggest that population growth is a consequence of food production. As already noted, domestication inevitably leads to higher yields, and higher yields make it possible to feed more people, albeit at the cost of more work.

While increased dependence on farming is associated with increased fertility across human populations,[20] the reasons behind this illustrate the complex interplay between human biology and culture in all human activity. Some researchers have suggested that the availability of soft foods for infants brought about by farming promoted population growth. In humans, frequent breastfeeding has a dampening effect on mothers' ovulation, inhibiting pregnancy in nursing

mothers who breastfeed exclusively. Because breastfeeding frequency declines when soft foods are introduced, fertility tends to increase.

However, it would be overly simplistic to limit the explanation for changes in fertility to the introduction of soft foods. Many other pathways can also lead to fertility changes. For example, among farmers, numerous children are frequently seen as assets to help out with the many household chores. Further, it is now known that sedentary lifestyles and diets emphasizing a narrow range of resources characteristic of the Neolithic led to growing rates of infectious disease and higher mortality. High infant mortality may well have led to a cultural value placed on increased fertility. In other words, the relationship between farming and fertility is far from simple, as explored in this chapter's Biocultural Connection.

THE SPREAD OF FOOD PRODUCTION

Paradoxically, although domestication increases productivity, it also increases instability. This is so because those varieties with the highest yields become the focus of human attention, while other varieties are less valued and ultimately ignored. As a result, farmers become dependent on a rather narrow range of resources, compared to the wide range utilized by food foragers. Today, this range is even narrower. Modern agriculturists rely on a mere dozen species for about 80 percent of the world's annual tonnage of all crops.[21]

This dependence upon fewer varieties means that when a crop fails, for whatever reason, farmers have less to fall back on than do food foragers. Furthermore, the likelihood of failure is increased by the common farming practice of planting crops together in one locality, so that a disease contracted by one plant can easily spread to others. Moreover, by relying on seeds from the most productive plants of a species to establish next year's crop, farmers favor genetic uniformity over diversity. The result is that if some virus, bacterium, or fungus is able to destroy one plant, it will likely destroy them all. This is what happened in the terrible Irish potato famine of 1845–1850, which caused the deaths of about 1 million people due to hunger and disease and forced another 2 million to abandon their homes and emigrate. The population of Ireland dropped from 8 million people before the Great Famine to only 5 million after the famine was over.

---

[19]Mintz, S. (1996). A taste of history. In W. A. Haviland & R. J. Gordon (Eds.), *Talking about people* (2nd ed., pp. 81–82). Mountain View, CA: Mayfield.

[20]Sellen, D. W., & Mace, R. (1997). Fertility and mode of subsistence: A phylogenetic analysis. *Current Anthropology, 38,* 886.

[21]Diamond, *Guns, germs, and steel,* p. 132.

Biocultural Connection

Breastfeeding, Fertility, and Beliefs

Cross-cultural studies indicate that farming populations tend to have higher rates of fertility than hunter-gatherers. These differences in fertility were calculated in terms of the average number of children born per woman and through the average number of years between pregnancies or birth spacing. Hunter-gatherer mothers have their children about four to five years apart while some contemporary farming populations not practicing any form of birth control have another baby every year and a half.

For many years this difference was interpreted as a consequence of nutritional stress among the hunter-gatherers. This theory was based in part on the observation that humans and many other mammals require a certain percentage of body fat in order to reproduce successfully. The theory was also grounded in the mistaken cultural belief that the hunter-gatherer lifestyle, supposedly inferior to that of "civilized" people, could not provide adequate nutrition for closer birth spacing. Detailed studies by anthropologists Melvin Konner and Marjorie Shostak,

among the !Kung or Ju/'hoansi (pronounced "zhutwasi") people of the Kalahari Desert in southern Africa, disproved this theory, revealing instead a remarkable interplay between cultural and biological processes in human infant feeding.[a, b]

The detailed observations of Ju/'hoansi infant-feeding practices were combined with studies of hormonal levels in nursing Ju/'hoansi mothers conducted by Carol Worthman. Ju/'hoansi mothers do not believe that babies should be fed on schedules, as recommended by some North American child-care experts, nor do they believe that crying is "good" for babies. Instead, they respond rapidly to their infants and breastfeed them whenever the infant shows any signs of fussing during both the day and night. The resulting pattern is breastfeeding in short, very frequent bouts. Together the ethnographic and laboratory studies document that this pattern of breastfeeding stimulates the body to suppress ovulation, or the release of a new egg into the womb for fertilization. The hormonal signals from nipple stimulation through breastfeeding control

the process of ovulation. Thus, the average number of years between children among the Ju/'hoansi is not a consequence of nutritional stress. Instead, Ju/'hoansi infant-feeding practices and beliefs directly affect the biology of fertility.

[a]Konner, M., & Worthman, C. (1980). Nursing frequency, gonadal function, and birth spacing among !Kung hunter-gatherers. *Science, 207,* 788–791.

[b]Shostak, M. (1983). *Nisa: The life and words of a !Kung woman.* New York: Random House.

The Irish potato famine illustrates how the combination of increased productivity and vulnerability may contribute to the geographic spread of farming. Time and time again in the past, population growth, followed by crop failure, has triggered movements of people from one place to another, where they have reestablished their familiar subsistence practices. Thus, once farming came into existence, it was more or less guaranteed that it would spread to neighboring regions through such migrations. From Southwest Asia, for instance, farming spread northeastward eventually to all of Europe, westward to North Africa, and eastward to India. Domesticated variants also spread from China

and Southeast Asia westward. Those who brought crops to new locations brought other things as well, including languages, beliefs, and new alleles for human gene pools. This spread of certain ideas, customs, or practices from one culture to another is known as **diffusion**.

A similar diffusion occurred from West Africa to the southeast, creating the modern far-reaching distribution of speakers of Bantu languages. Crops including sorghum (so valuable today it is grown in hot, dry areas on all continents), pearl millet, watermelon, black-eyed peas, African yams, oil palms, and kola nuts (source of modern cola drinks) were first domesticated in West Africa but began spreading eastward by 5,000 years ago. Between 2,000 and 3,000 years ago, Bantu speakers with their crops reached the continent's east coast and a few centuries later reached deep into what is now the country of South Africa.

diffusion The spread of certain ideas, customs, or practices from one culture to another

CULTURE OF NEOLITHIC SETTLEMENTS

A number of Neolithic settlements have been excavated, particularly in Southwest Asia. The structures, artifacts, and food debris found at these sites have revealed much about the daily activities of their former inhabitants as they pursued the business of making a living. Perhaps the best known of these sites is Jericho, an early farming community in the Jordan River Valley of Palestine.

Jericho: An Early Farming Community

Excavations at the Neolithic settlement that later grew to become the biblical city of Jericho revealed the remains of a sizable farming community inhabited as early as 10,350 years ago. Here, in the Jordan River Valley, crops could be grown almost continuously due to the presence of a bounteous spring and the rich soils of an Ice Age lake that had dried up some 3,000 years earlier. In addition, flood-borne deposits originating in the Judean highlands to the west regularly renewed the fertility of the soil.

To protect their settlement against floods and associated mudflows, as well as invaders, the people of Jericho built massive stone walls around the settlement.[22] Within these walls (6½ feet wide and 12 feet high), as well as a large rock-cut ditch (27 feet wide and 9 feet deep), an estimated 400 to 900 people lived in houses of mud brick with plastered floors arranged around courtyards. In addition to these houses, a stone tower that would have taken 100 people 104 days to build was located inside one corner of the wall, near the spring. A staircase inside it probably led to a mud-brick building on top. Nearby were mud-brick storage facilities as well as peculiar structures of possible ceremonial significance. A village cemetery also reflects the sedentary life of these early people. Nomadic groups, with few exceptions, rarely buried their dead in a single central location.

Close contact between the farmers of Jericho and other villages is indicated by common features in art, ritual, use of prestige goods, and burial practices. Other evidence of trade consists of obsidian and turquoise from Sinai as well as marine shells from the coast, all discovered inside the walls of Jericho.

[22] Bar-Yosef, O. (1986). The walls of Jericho: An alternative interpretation. *Current Anthropology, 27,* 160.

Neolithic Material Culture

Various innovations in the realms of tool making, pottery, housing, and clothing characterized life in Neolithic villages. All of these are examples of material culture.

Tool Making

Early harvesting tools were made of wood or bone into which razor-sharp flint blades were inserted. Later tools continued to be made by chipping and flaking stone, but during the Neolithic period, stone that was too hard to be chipped was ground and polished for tools. People developed scythes, forks, hoes, and simple plows to replace their basic digging sticks. Mortars and pestles were used to grind and crush grain. Later, when domesticated animals became available for use as draft animals, plows were redesigned. Along with the development of diverse technologies, individuals acquired specialized skills for creating a variety of craft specialties including leatherworks, weavings, and pottery.

Pottery

Hard work on the part of those producing the food would also support other members of the society who could then apply their skills and energy to various craft specialties such as pottery. In the Neolithic, different forms of pottery were created for transporting and storing food, water, and various material possessions. Because pottery vessels are impervious to damage by insects, rodents, and dampness, they could be used for storing small grains, seeds, and other materials. Moreover, food could be boiled in pottery vessels directly over the fire rather than by such ancient techniques as dropping stones heated directly in the fire into the food being cooked. Pottery was also used for pipes, ladles, lamps, and other objects; some cultures even used large vessels for disposal of the dead. Significantly, pottery containers remain important for much of humanity today.

Widespread use of pottery, which is made of clay and fired in very hot ovens, is a good, though not foolproof, indication of a sedentary community. It is found in abundance in all but a few of the earliest Neolithic settlements. Its fragility and weight make it less practical for use by nomads and hunters, who more typically use woven bags, baskets, and animal hide containers. Nevertheless, there are some modern nomads who make and use pottery, just as there are farmers who lack it. In fact, food foragers in Japan were making pottery vessels by 13,000 years ago, long before they were being made in Southwest Asia.

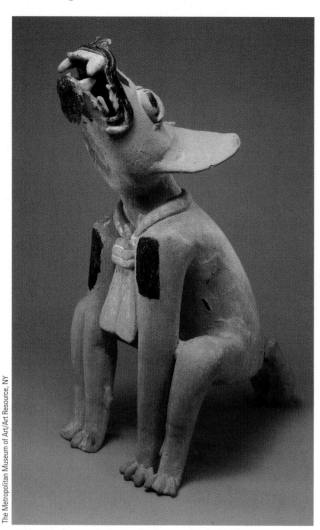

The Metropolitan Museum of Art/Art Resource, NY

Ancient pottery provides evidence of animal domestication as well as the craft specializations that developed as a consequence of the Neolithic revolution. This howling canine came from Remojadas, a culture that flourished between 1000 and 2100 years ago along the Gulf Coast of present day Mexico. Dogs, one of the few species domesticated in Mesoamerica, were frequently incorporated into vessels or free-standing pieces such as this hollow ceramic figure.

The manufacture of pottery requires artful skill and some technological sophistication. To make a useful essel requires knowledge of clay: how to remove impurities from it, how to shape it into desired forms, and how to dry it in a way that does not cause cracking. Proper firing is tricky as well; clay must be heated

Neolithic revolution Domestication of plants and animals by peoples with stone-based technologies, beginning about 10,000 years ago and leading to radical transformations in cultural systems; sometimes referred to as the Neolithic transition

Mesoamerica The region encompassing southern Mexico and northern Central America

sufficiently so that it will harden and resist future disintegration from moisture, but care must be taken to prevent the object from cracking or even exploding as it heats and later cools down.

Pottery is decorated in various ways. For example, designs can be engraved on the vessel before firing, or special rims, legs, bases, and other details may be made separately and fastened to the finished pot. Painting is the most common form of pottery decoration, and there are literally thousands of painted designs found among the pottery remains of ancient cultures.

Housing

Food production and the new sedentary lifestyle brought about another technological development—house building. Permanent housing is of limited interest to most food foragers who frequently are on the move. Cave shelters, pits dug in the earth, and simple lean-tos made of hides and wooden poles serve the purpose of keeping the weather out. In the Neolithic, however, dwellings became more complex in design and more diverse in type. Some were constructed of wood, while others included more elaborate shelters made of stone, sun-dried brick, or branches plastered together with mud or clay.

Although permanent housing frequently goes along with food production, there is evidence that substantial housing could exist without food production. For example, on the northwestern coast of North America, people lived in substantial houses made of heavy planks hewn from cedar logs, yet their food consisted entirely of wild plants and animals, especially salmon and sea mammals.

Clothing

During the Neolithic, for the first time in human history, clothing was made of woven textiles. The raw materials and technology necessary for the production of clothing came from several sources: flax and cotton from farming; wool from domesticated sheep, llamas, or goats; silk from silk worms. Human invention contributed the spindle for spinning and the loom for weaving.

Social Structure

Evidence of all the economic and technological developments listed thus far has enabled archaeologists to draw certain inferences concerning the organization of Neolithic societies. Although indication of ceremonial activity exists, little evidence of a centrally organized and directed religious life has been found. Burials, for example, show a marked absence of social differentiation. Early Neolithic graves were rarely constructed of or covered by stone slabs and rarely included elaborate objects. Evidently, no person had attained the kind of exalted status that would have required an elaborate funeral. The smallness of most villages and the absence of elaborate buildings suggest that the inhabitants knew one another very well and were even related, so that most of their relationships were probably highly personal ones, with equal emotional significance.

The general picture that emerges is one of a relatively egalitarian society with minimal division of labor but some development of new and more specialized social roles. Villages seem to have been made up of several households, each providing for most of its own needs. The organizational needs of society beyond the household level were probably met by kinship groups.

Neolithic Cultures in the Americas

In the Americas the shape and timing of the **Neolithic revolution** (sometimes called the *Neolithic transition*) differed compared to other parts of the world. For example, Neolithic agricultural villages were common in Southwest Asia between 8,000 and 9,000 years ago, but similar villages did not appear in the Americas until about 4,500 years ago, in **Mesoamerica** (the region from central Mexico to Costa Rica) and the Andean highlands. Moreover, pottery, which developed in Southwest Asia shortly after plant and animal domestication, did not emerge in the Americas until about 4,500 years ago. The potter's wheel was not used by early Neolithic people in the Americas. Instead, elaborate pottery was manufactured by hand. Looms and the hand spindle appeared in the Americas about 3,000 years ago.

None of these absences indicate any backwardness on the part of Native American peoples, many of whom, as we have already seen, were highly sophisticated farmers and plant breeders. Rather, the effectiveness of existing practices was such that they continued to be satisfactory. When food production developed in Mesoamerica and the Andean highlands, it did so wholly independently of Europe and Asia, with different crops, animals, and technologies.

Outside Mesoamerica and the Andean highlands, hunting, fishing, and the gathering of wild plant foods remained important elements in the economy of Neolithic peoples in the Americas. Apparently, most American Indians continued to emphasize a food-foraging rather than a food-producing mode of life, even though maize and other domestic crops came to be cultivated just about everywhere that climate permitted. The Indian lifeways were so effective, so well integrated into a complete cultural system, and so environmentally stable that for many of these groups the change to food production was unnecessary. It was only the disease and domination set into motion with the appearance of European explorers that devastated these stable cultures.[23]

THE NEOLITHIC AND HUMAN BIOLOGY

Although we tend to think of the invention of food production in terms of its cultural consequences, it obviously had a biological impact as well. From studies of human skeletons from Neolithic burials, physical anthropologists have found evidence for a somewhat lessened mechanical stress on peoples' bodies and teeth. Although there are exceptions, the teeth of Neolithic peoples generally show less wear, their bones are less robust, and osteoarthritis (the result of stressed joint surfaces) is not as marked as in the skeletons of Paleolithic and Mesolithic peoples.

On the other hand, there is clear evidence for a marked deterioration in health and mortality. Skeletons from Neolithic villages show evidence of severe and chronic nutritional stress as well as pathologies related to infectious and deficiency diseases. High-starch diets led to increased dental decay during the Neolithic as well. Scientists have recently documented dental drilling of teeth in a 9,000-year-old Neolithic site in Pakistan.[24] This resembles the high frequency of dental decay seen in contemporary populations when they switch from a varied hunter-gatherer diet to a high-starch diet. As we will explore in Chapter 7, for populations adapted genetically to the hunter-gatherer diet, a shift away from this diet frequently leads to the development of diabetes.

Domestication encourages a sedentary lifestyle with the great potential for overpopulation relative to the resource base. Under these conditions, even minor environmental fluctuations can lead to widespread

[23] Mann, C. C. (2005). *1491: New revelations of the Americas before Columbus.* New York: Knopf.
[24] Coppa, A., et al. (2006). Early Neolithic tradition of dentistry. *Nature, 440,* 755–756.

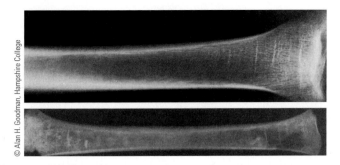

Harris lines near the ends of these youthful thigh bones, found in a prehistoric farming community in Arizona, are indicative of recovery after growth arrest, caused by famine or disease.

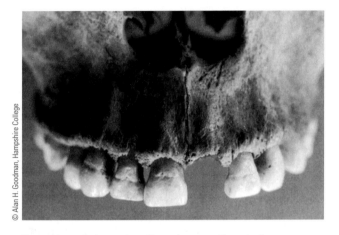

Enamel hypoplasias, such as those shown on these teeth, are indicative of arrested growth caused by famine or disease. These teeth are from an adult who lived in an ancient farming community in Arizona.

hunger and malnutrition. Evidence of stress and disease increased proportionally with population density and the reliance on intensive agriculture.[25] Further, the crowded conditions in settlements and competition among settlements for resources also led to increased mortality due to warfare.

For the most part, the crops on which Neolithic peoples came to depend were selected for their higher productivity and storability rather than nutritional

---

agriculture Intensive crop cultivation, employing plows, fertilizers, and/or irrigation
pastoralism Breeding and managing migratory herds of domesticated grazing animals, such as goats, sheep, cattle, llamas, or camels

---

[25]Cohen, M. N., & Armelagos, G. J. (1984). *Paleopathology at the origins of agriculture.* Orlando: Academic Press; Goodman, A., & Armelagos, G. J. (1985). Death and disease at Dr. Dickson's mounds. *Natural History, 94*(9), 12–18.

balance. Moreover, as already noted, their nutritional shortcomings would have been exacerbated by their susceptibility to periodic failure, particularly as populations grew in size. Thus, the worsened health and higher mortality of Neolithic peoples are not surprising. Some have gone so far as to assert that the switch from food foraging to food production was the worst mistake that humans ever made!

Another key contributor to the increased incidence of disease and mortality was probably the new mode of life in Neolithic communities. Sedentary life in fixed villages brings with it sanitation problems as garbage and human waste accumulate. These are not a problem for small groups of people who move about from one campsite to another. Moreover, airborne diseases are more easily transmitted where people are gathered into villages. Farming practices also created the ideal environment for the species of mosquito that spreads malaria.

Another factor, too, was the close association between humans and their domestic animals, a situation conducive to the transmission of some animal diseases to humans. A host of life-threatening diseases—including smallpox, chicken pox, and in fact all of the infectious diseases of childhood that were not overcome by medical science until the latter half of the 20th century—were transmitted to humans through their close association with domestic animals (Table 5.1).

THE NEOLITHIC AND THE IDEA OF PROGRESS

Although the overall health of Neolithic peoples suffered as a consequence of this cultural shift, many view the transition from food foraging to food production as a great step upward on a ladder of progress. In part this interpretation is due to one of the more widely held beliefs of Western culture, that human history is basically a record of steady progress over time. To be sure, farming allowed people to increase the size of their populations, to live together in substantial sedentary communities, and to reorganize the workload in ways that permitted craft specialization. This is not progress in a universal sense but, rather, a set of cultural beliefs about the nature of progress. Each culture, after all, defines progress (if it does so at all) in its own terms.

Whatever the benefits of food production, however, a substantial price was paid. As anthropologists Mark Cohen and George Armelagos put it, "Taken as a whole, indicators fairly clearly suggest an overall decline in the quality—and probably in the

TABLE 5.1	DISEASES ACQUIRED FROM DOMESTICATED ANIMALS

Disease	Animal with Most Closely Related Pathogen
Measles	Cattle (rinderpest)
Tuberculosis	Cattle
Smallpox	Cattle (cowpox) or other livestock with related pox viruses
Influenza	Pigs, ducks
Pertussis ("whooping cough")	Pigs, dogs

Close contact with animals provides a situation in which variants of animal pathogens may establish themselves in humans. For example, humans have developed symptoms from infection with avian influenza (bird flu) following contact with domesticated birds.

Source: Diamond, J. (1997). *Guns, germs, and steel* (p. 207). New York: Norton

length—of human life associated with the adoption of agriculture."[26]

Rather than imposing ethnocentric notions of progress on the archaeological record, it is best to view the advent of food production as but one more factor contributing to the diversification of cultures, something that had begun in the Paleolithic. Although some societies continued to practice various forms of hunting, gathering, and fishing, others became horticultural.

Some horticultural societies developed **agriculture**. Technologically more complex than horticultural societies, agriculturalists practice intensive crop cultivation, employing plows, fertilizers, and possibly irrigation. They may use a wooden or metal plow pulled by one or more harnessed draft animals, such as horses, oxen, or water buffaloes, to produce food on larger plots of land. The distinction between horticulturalist and intensive agriculturalist is not always an easy one to make. For example, the Hopi Indians of the North American Southwest traditionally employed irrigation in their farming while at the same time using basic hand tools.

Pastoralism arose in environments that were too dry, too grassy, too steep, too cold, or too hot for effective horticulture or intensive agriculture. Pastoralists breed and manage migratory herds of domesticated grazing animals, such as goats, sheep, cattle, llamas, or camels. For example, the Russian steppes, with their heavy grass cover, were not suitable to farming without a plow, but they were ideal for herding. Thus, a number of peoples living in the arid grasslands and deserts that stretch from northwestern Africa into Central Asia kept large herds of domestic animals, relying on their neighbors for plant foods. Finally, some societies went on to develop civilizations—the subject of the next chapter.

Chapter Summary

■ The end of the glacial period saw great physical changes in human habitats. Sea levels rose, vegetation changed, and herd animals disappeared from many areas. The Mesolithic period marked a shift from big game hunting to the hunting of smaller game and gathering a broad spectrum of plants and aquatic resources. Increased reliance on seafood and plants made the Mesolithic a more sedentary period for many peoples. Ground stone tools, including axes and adzes, met the needs for new technologies in the postglacial world. Many Mesolithic tools in the Old World were made with microliths—small, hard, sharp blades of flint or similar stone that could be mass produced and hafted with others to produce implements like sickles. In the Americas, Archaic cultures are comparable to the Old World Mesolithic.

[26] Cohen, M. N., & Armelagos, G. J. (1984). Paleopathology at the origins of agriculture: Editors' summation. In *Paleopathology at the origins of agriculture* (p. 594). Orlando: Academic Press.

■ The change to food production took place independently and more or less simultaneously in various regions of the world. Along with food production, people became more sedentary, allowing a reorganization of the workload, so that some people could pursue other tasks. From the end of the Mesolithic, some human groups became larger and more permanent as people domesticated plants and animals. Other peoples retained food foraging, sometimes with a sedentary way of life.

■ A domesticated plant or animal is one that has become genetically modified as an intended or unintended consequence of human manipulation. Analysis of plant and animal remains at a site usually indicates whether its occupants were food producers. Wild cereal grasses, for example, typically have fragile stems, whereas cultivated ones have tough stems. Domesticated plants can also be identified because their edible parts are generally larger than those of their wild counterparts. Domestication produces skeletal changes in some animals. The horns of wild goats and sheep, for example, differ from those of domesticated ones. Age and sex imbalances in herd animals may also indicate manipulation by human domesticators.

■ The most probable theory to account for the Neolithic revolution is that domestication came about as a consequence of a chance convergence of separate natural events and cultural developments. This happened independently at basically the same time in Southwest and Southeast Asia, highland Mexico and Peru, South America's Amazon forest, eastern North America, China, and Africa. In all cases, however, people developed food complexes based on starchy grains and/or roots that were consumed with protein-containing legumes plus flavor enhancers.

■ Human population sizes have increased steadily since the Neolithic. Some scholars argue that pressure from increasing population size led to innovations such as intensive agriculture. Others suggest that these innovations allowed population size to grow.

■ Two major consequences of domestication are that crops become more productive but also more vulnerable. This combination periodically causes population size to outstrip food supplies, whereupon people are apt to move into new regions. In this way, farming has often spread from one region to another, as into Europe from Southwest Asia. Sometimes, food foragers will adopt the cultivation of crops from neighboring peoples in response to a shortage of wild foods.

■ Among the earliest known sites containing domesticated plants and animals are those of Southwest Asia. These sites were mostly small villages of mud huts with individual storage pits and clay ovens. There is evidence not only of cultivation and domestication but also of trade. At ancient Jericho, remains of tools, houses, and clothing indicate the oasis was occupied by Neolithic people as early as 10,350 years ago. At its height, Neolithic Jericho had a population of 400 to 900 people. Comparable villages developed independently in Mexico and Peru by about 4,500 years ago.

■ During the Neolithic, stone that was too hard to be chipped was ground and polished for tools. People developed scythes, forks, hoes, and plows to replace simple digging sticks. The Neolithic was also characterized by the extensive manufacture and use of pottery. The widespread use of pottery is a good indicator of a sedentary community. It is found in all but a few of the earliest Neolithic settlements. The manufacture of pottery requires knowledge of clay and the techniques of firing or baking. Other technological developments that accompanied food production and the sedentary life were the building of permanent houses and the weaving of textiles.

■ Archaeologists have been able to draw some inferences concerning the social structure of Neolithic societies. No evidence has been found indicating that religion or government was yet a centrally organized institution. Social organization was probably relatively egalitarian, with minimal division of labor and little development of specialized social roles.

■ The development of food production had biological, as well as cultural, consequences. New diets, living arrangements, and farming practices led to increased incidence of disease and higher mortality rates. Increased fertility, however, more than offset mortality, and globally human population has grown since the Neolithic.

Questions for Reflection

1. The changed lifeways of the Neolithic included the domestication of plants and animals as well as settlement into villages. What were the costs and benefits of this new way of life? Did the Neolithic set into motion problems that are still with us today?

2. Why do you think some people of the past chose not to make the change from food foraging to food producing? What problems existing in today's world have their origins in the lifeways of the Neolithic?

3. Though human biology and culture are always interacting, the rates of biological change and culture change uncoupled at some point in the history of our development. Think of examples of how the differences in these rates had consequences for humans in the Neolithic and in the present.

4. Why are the changes of the Neolithic sometimes mistakenly associated with progress? Why have the social forms that originated in the Neolithic come to dominate the earth?

5. Although the archaeological record indicates some differences in the timing of domestication of plants and animals in different parts of the world, why is it incorrect to say that one region was more advanced than another?

Key Terms

Neolithic	Natufian culture	domestication	Neolithic revolution
Mesolithic	innovation	vegeculture	Mesoamerica
Archaic cultures	primary innovation	horticulture	agriculture
microlith	secondary innovation	diffusion	pastoralism

VISUAL ESSENCE

With the emergence of cities and states, human societies began to develop organized central governments and a concentration of power that made it possible to build monumental structures such as the great pyramids of Egypt visible on the horizon in this photo of Cairo. But cities and states also ushered in a series of problems, many of which city dwellers still face. For example, social stratification, in which a ruling elite controls the means of subsistence and many other aspects of daily life, exploits many city dwellers and poor people in outlying areas. While the people of stratified societies are interdependent, the elite classes have disproportionate access to and control of all resources, including human labor. In Cairo, as in other big cities, housing, for example, is dramatically different for different social classes. While the elite live in luxurious homes, 5 million urban poor live illegally in tomb rooms of cemeteries known as the City of the Dead.

The Emergence of Cities and States

A walk down a busy street of a city such as New York or San Francisco brings us in contact with numerous activities essential to life in North American society. Sidewalks are crowded with people going to and from offices and stores. Heavy traffic of cars, taxis, and trucks periodically comes to a standstill. A brief two-block stretch may contain a grocery store; shops selling clothing, appliances, or books; a restaurant; a newsstand; a gasoline station; and a movie theater. Other features such as a museum, a police station, a school, a hospital, or a church distinguish some neighborhoods.

Each of these services or places of business is dependent on others from outside this two-block radius. A butcher shop, for instance, depends on slaughterhouses and beef ranches. A clothing store could not exist without designers, farmers who produce cotton and wool, and workers who manufacture synthetic fibers. Restaurants rely on refrigerated trucking and vegetable and dairy farmers. Hospitals need insurance companies, pharmaceutical companies, and medical equipment industries to function. All institutions, finally, depend on the public utilities—the telephone, gas, water, and electric companies. Although interdependence is not immediately apparent to the passerby, it is an important aspect of modern cities.

The interdependence of goods and services in a big city makes a variety of products readily available to people. But interdependence also creates vulnerability. If strikes, bad weather, or acts of violence cause one service to stop functioning, other services can deteriorate. At the same time, cities are resilient in their response to stresses. When one service breaks down, others take over its functions. During a long newspaper strike in New York City in the 1960s, for example, several new magazines were launched, and television networks expanded their coverage of news and events. This phenomenon resembles the recent flourishing of

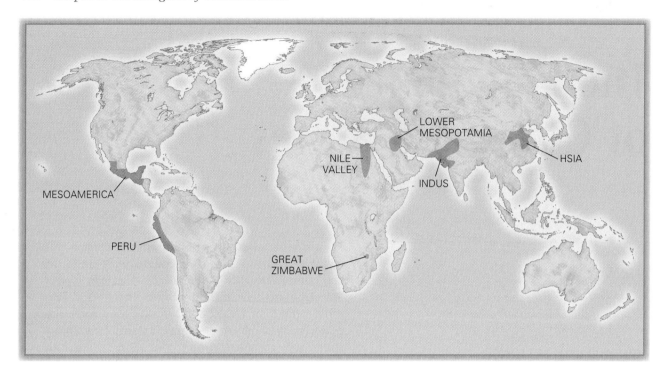

Figure 6.1

The major early civilizations sprang from Neolithic villages in various parts of the world. Those of the Americas developed wholly independently of those in Africa and Eurasia; Chinese civilization seems to have developed independently of Southwest Asia (including the Nile and Indus) civilizations.

reality television programs in the United States during the 2007–2008 Hollywood writers' strike. In many parts of the world, the violence of war has caused extensive damage to basic infrastructure, leading to the development of alternative systems to cope with everything from the most basic tasks such as procuring food to communication within global political systems. With the rise of the Internet and globalization, the interdependence of goods and services that used to be characteristic only of cities extends far beyond city limits.

On the surface, city life seems so orderly that we take it for granted; but a moment's reflection reminds us that the intricate fabric of city life did not always exist, and the concentrated availability of diverse goods is a very recent development in human history.

DEFINING CIVILIZATION

The word *civilization* comes from the Latin *civis,* which refers to one who is an inhabitant of a city, and *civitas,* which refers to the urban community in which one dwells. In everyday North American and European usage, the word *civilization* connotes refinement and progress and may imply judgments about cultures according to an ethnocentric standard. In anthropology, by contrast, the term has a more precise meaning that

> **civilization** In anthropology a type of society marked by the presence of cities, social classes, and the state

avoids culture-bound notions. As used by anthropologists, **civilization** refers to societies in which large numbers of people live in cities, are socially stratified, and are governed by a ruling elite working through centrally organized political systems called states. We shall elaborate on all of these points in the course of this chapter.

As Neolithic villages grew into towns, the world's first cities developed. This happened between 4,500 and 6,000 years ago, first in Mesopotamia (modern-day Iraq), then in Egypt's Nile Valley and the Indus Valley (today's India and Pakistan). In China, civilization was under way by 5,000 years ago. Independent of these developments in Eurasia and Africa, the first American Indian cities appeared in Peru around 4,000 years ago and in Mesoamerica about 2,000 years ago (Figure 6.1).

What characterized these first cities? Why are they called the birthplaces of civilization? The first feature of cities—and of civilization—is their large size and population.

But cities are more than overgrown towns. Consider the case of Çatalhöyük, a compact 9,500-year-old settlement in south-central Turkey.[1] The tightly

---

[1]Material on Çatalhöyük is drawn from Balter, M. (1998). Why settle down? The mystery of communities. *Science, 282,* 1442–1444; Balter, M. (1999). A long season puts Çatalhöyük in context. *Science, 286,* 890–891; Balter, M. (2001). Did plaster hold Neolithic society together? *Science, 294,* 2278–2281; Kunzig, R. (1999). A tale of two obsessed archaeologists, one ancient city and nagging doubts about whether science can ever hope to reveal the past. *Discover, 20*(5), 84–92.

packed houses for its more than 5,000 inhabitants left no room for streets. People traversed the roofs of neighboring houses and dropped through a hole in the roof to get into their own homes. While house walls were covered with all sorts of paintings and bas-reliefs, the houses were structurally similar to one another, and no known public architecture existed. People grew some crops and tended livestock but also collected significant amounts of food from wild plants and animals, never intensifying their agricultural practices. Evidence of a division of labor or of a centralized authority is minimal or nonexistent. It was as if several Neolithic villages were crammed together in one place at Çatalhöyük.

Archaeological evidence from early urban centers, by contrast, demonstrates organized planning by a central authority, technological intensification, and social stratification. For example, flood control and protection were vital components of the great ancient cities of the Indus River Valley, located in today's India and Pakistan. Mohenjo-Daro, an urban center at its peak some 4,500 years ago with a population of at least 20,000, was built on an artificial mound, safe from flood waters. Further, the streets of this densely populated city were laid out in a grid pattern and included individual homes with sophisticated drainage systems.

Ancient peoples incorporated their spiritual beliefs and social order into the cities they built. For example, the layout of the great Mesoamerican city Teotihuacan, founded 2,200 years ago, translated the solar calendar into a unified spatial pattern. The Street of the Dead—a grand north-south axis running from the Pyramid of the Moon and bordered by the Pyramid of the Sun and the royal palace compound—was deliberately oriented to an astronomical marker, east of true north. Ancient city planners even channeled the San Juan River to conform to the grid where it runs through the city. Surrounding this core were thousands of apartment compounds, separated from one another by a grid of narrow streets, maintaining the east-of-north orientation throughout the city. It is estimated that over 100,000 people inhabited this great city until its sudden collapse possibly in the 7th century.

Finally, clear evidence for both social and economic diversity exists in Teotihuacan. Some six levels of society can be recognized by variation in size and quality of apartment rooms. Those at and near the top of the social scale lived on or near the Street of the Dead. The Pyramid of the Sun along this avenue was built above a cave, which was seen as a portal to the underworld and as the home of deities associated with death. Teotihuacan artisans worked on exotic goods and raw materials imported from afar, and at least two neighborhoods housed people with foreign affiliations—one with Oaxaca, the other (the "merchant's quarter") with the Gulf and Maya lowlands. Farmers, whose labor in fields (some of them irrigated) supplied the food to fellow city dwellers, also resided in the city.[2]

Mohenjo-Daro and Teotihuacan, like other early cities throughout the globe, were far more than expanded Neolithic villages. Such great changes took place in the transition from village to city that the emergence of urban living is considered by some to be one of the great developments in human culture. The following case study gives us a glimpse of another of the world's ancient cities, including how archaeologists have studied it and how it may have grown from a smaller farming community.

TIKAL: A CASE STUDY

The ancient city of Tikal, one of the largest lowland Maya centers in existence, is situated in Central America about 300 kilometers north of Guatemala City. Tikal was built on a broad limestone terrace in a rainforest. Here the Maya settled 3,000 years ago. Because the Maya calendar can be precisely correlated with our own, it is known that their civilization flourished until 1,100 years ago.

At its height, Tikal covered about 120 square kilometers (km^2), and its center or nucleus was the Great Plaza, a large paved area surrounded by about 300 major structures and thousands of houses (Figure 6.2). Starting from a small, dispersed population, Tikal swelled to at least 45,000 people. By 1,550 years ago, its population density had reached 600 to 700 persons per square kilometer, which was three times that of the surrounding region.

Tikal and the surrounding region were intensively explored under the joint auspices of the University of Pennsylvania Museum and the Guatemalan government from 1956 through the 1960s. At the time, it was the most ambitious archaeological project undertaken in the western hemisphere.

In the first few years of the Tikal Project, archaeologists investigated only major temple and palace structures found in the vicinity of the Great Plaza, at the site's epicenter. But in 1959, aiming to gain a balanced view of Tikal's development and composition, they turned their attention to hundreds of small mounds that surrounded larger buildings and were thought to be the remains of dwellings. In a sense, this represented a shift in the practice of archaeology toward studying the complexities of everyday life. Imagine how difficult it would be to get a realistic view of life in a major city such as Washington, DC, or Beijing by looking only at their monumental public buildings. Similarly, a realistic view of Tikal cannot be reconstructed without examining the full range of ruins in the area.

[2]Cowgill, G. L. (1997). State and society at Teotihuacan, Mexico. *Annual Review of Anthropology, 26,* 129–161.

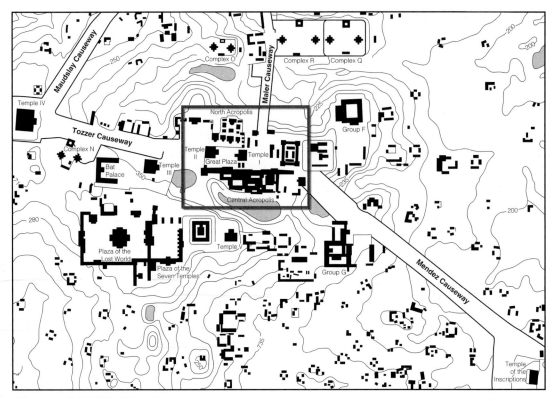

Figure 6.2

Tikal spreads far beyond the Great Plaza and the monumental buildings that have been largely excavated and are mapped here. Archaeologists used surveying techniques, test pits, and other strategies to fully define the city's boundaries and to understand the full spectrum of lifeways that took place there. The red outline in the center of the map delineates the royal court, royal burial ground, and central marketplace. In addition to what is pictured here, Tikal extends several kilometers outward in every direction.

The excavation of small structures, most of which were probably houses, permitted the estimation of Tikal's population size and density. This information allowed archaeologists to test the conventional assumption that the subsistence practices of the Maya inhabitants were inadequate to sustain large population concentrations.

Extensive excavation also provided a sound basis for a reconstruction of the everyday life and social organization of the Maya, a people who had been known almost entirely through the study of ceremonial remains. For example, differences in architecture, house construction, and associated artifacts and burials suggest differences in social class. Features of house distribution might reflect the existence of extended families or other types of kin groups. The excavation of both large and small structures revealed the social structure of the total population of Tikal.[3]

Surveying and Excavating the Site

Mapping crews extensively surveyed 6 square kilometers of forested land surrounding the Great Plaza, providing a preliminary map to guide the small-structure excavation process.[4] Aerial photography could not be used for this mapping, because the tree canopy in this area is often 30 meters (about 100 feet) above the ground, obscuring all but the tallest temples. Many of the small ruins are practically invisible even to observers on the ground. Four years of mapping revealed that ancient Tikal was far larger than the original 6 km[2] surveyed. More time and money allowed continued surveying of the area in order to fully define the city's boundaries and calculate its overall size.[5]

The initial excavation of six structures, two plazas, and a platform revealed new structures not visible before excavation, the architectural complexity of the structures, and an enormous quantity of artifacts that had to be washed and catalogued. Some structures were partially excavated, and some remained uninvestigated. Following this initial work, the archaeological team excavated over a hundred additional small structures in different parts of the site in order to ensure investigation of a representative sample. The team also sank

[3]Haviland, W. A. (2002). Settlement, society and demography at Tikal. In J. Sabloff (Ed.), *Tikal*. Santa Fe: School of American Research.

[4]Haviland, W. A., et al. (1985). *Excavations in small residential groups of Tikal: Groups 4F-1 and 4F-2*. Philadelphia: University Museum.
[5]Puleston, D. E. (1983). *The settlement survey of Tikal*. Philadelphia: University Museum.

numerous test pits in various other small-structure groups to supplement the information gained from more extensive excavations.

Evidence from the Excavation

Excavation at Tikal produced considerable evidence about the social organization, technology, and diversity in this ancient city, as well as the relationship between people in Tikal and other regions. For example, the site provides evidence of trade in nonperishable items. Granite, quartzite, hematite, pyrite, jade, slate, and obsidian all were imported, either as raw materials or finished products. Marine materials came from Caribbean and Pacific coastal areas. Tikal is located on top of an abundant source of chert (a flintlike stone used to manufacture tools), which may have been exported in the form of raw material and finished objects. Located between two river systems to the east and west, Tikal may have been on a major overland trade route between the two. Also, evidence for trade in perishable goods such as textiles, feathers, salt, and cacao indicates that there were full-time traders among the Tikal Maya.

In the realm of technology, specialized woodworking, pottery, obsidian, and shell workshops have been found. The skillful stone carving displayed on stone monuments suggests that occupational specialists did this work. The same is true of the fine artwork exhibited on ceramic vessels. Ancient artists had to envision what their work would look like after their pale, relatively colorless ceramics had been fired.

To control the large population, some form of bureaucratic organization must have existed in Tikal. From Maya written records (glyphs), we know that the government was headed by a hereditary ruling dynasty with sufficient power to organize massive construction and maintenance. This included a system of defensive ditches and embankments on the northern and southern edges of the city. The longest of these ran for a distance of perhaps 19 to 28 kilometers. Although we do not have direct evidence, there are clues to the existence of textile workers, dental workers, makers of bark cloth "paper," scribes, masons, astronomers, and other occupational specialists.

The religion of the Tikal Maya may have developed initially as a means to cope with the uncertainties of agriculture. Soils at Tikal are thin, and the only available water comes from rain that has been collected in reservoirs. Rain is abundant in season, but its onset tends to be unreliable. Conversely, the elevation of Tikal, high relative to surrounding terrain, may have caused it to be perceived as a "power place," especially suited for making contact with supernatural forces and beings.

The Maya priests tried not only to win over and please the deities in times of drought but also to honor them in times of plenty. Priests, the experts on the

© Nishan Bingham

Archaeologists have proposed that Tikal may have emerged as an important religious center due its relative altitude in the region. Today it is still an important religious center for local Maya, who gather in front of the acropolis for a traditional ceremony.

Maya calendar, determined the most favorable time to plant crops and were involved with other agricultural matters. This tended to keep people in or near the city. The population in and around Tikal depended upon their priests to influence supernatural beings and forces on their behalf, so that their crops would not fail.

As the population increased, land for agriculture became scarce, forcing the Maya to find new methods of food production that could sustain the dense population concentrated at Tikal. They added the planting and tending of fruit trees and other crops that could be grown around their houses in soils enriched by human waste (unlike houses at Teotihuacan, those at Tikal were not built close to one another). Along with increased reliance on household gardening, the Maya constructed artificially raised fields in areas that were flooded each rainy season. In these fields, crops could be intensively cultivated year after year, as long as they were carefully maintained. Measures were taken to maximize collection of water for the dry season, by converting low areas into reservoirs and constructing channels to carry runoff from plazas and other architecture into these reservoirs.

As these changes were taking place, a class of artisans, craftspeople, and other occupational specialists emerged to serve the needs of an elite consisting of the priesthood and a ruling dynasty. The Maya built

Anthropology Applied

Action Archaeology and the Community at El Pilar

Anabel Ford

Resource management and conservation are palpable themes of the day. Nowhere is this more keenly felt than the Maya forest, one of the world's most biodiverse areas and among the last terrestrial frontiers. Over the next two decades this area's population will double, threatening the integrity of the tropical ecosystems with contemporary development strategies. Curiously, in the past the Maya forest was home to a major civilization with at least three to nine times the current population of the region.

I began my work as an archaeologist in the Maya forest in 1972. I was interested in the everyday life of the Maya through the study of their cultural ecology—the multifaceted relationships of humans and their environment—rather than monumental buildings. Despite my interest in daily life in the forest, monumental buildings became a part of my work. While conducting a settlement survey in the forest, I discovered El Pilar, a Maya urban center

with temples and plazas covering more than 50 hectares. The observation that the ancient Maya evolved a sustainable economy in the tropics of Mesoamerica guided my approach to developing El Pilar.

Astride the contemporary border separating Belize and Guatemala, El

Pilar has been the focus of a bold conservation design for a binational peace park on a troubled border. My vision for El Pilar is founded on the preservation of cultural heritage in the context of the natural environment. With a collaborative and interdisciplinary team of local villagers, government administrators, and scientists, we have established the El Pilar Archaeological Reserve for Maya Flora and Fauna. Since 1993, the innovations of the El Pilar program have forged new ground in testing novel strategies for community participation in the conservation development of the El Pilar Reserve. This program touches major administrative themes of global importance: tourism, natural resources, foreign affairs, and rural development and education. Yet the program's impacts go further. Learning from and working with traditional Maya farmers, or forest gardeners, positively impacts agriculture, rural enterprise, and capacity building. There are

numerous temples, public buildings, and various kinds of houses appropriate to the distinct social classes of their society.

For several hundred years, Tikal was able to sustain its ever-growing population. When the pressure for food and land reached a critical point, population growth stopped. At the same time, warfare with other cities was becoming increasingly destructive. All of this is marked archaeologically by abandonment of houses on prime land in rural areas, by the advent of nutritional problems visible in skeletons recovered from burials, and by the construction of the previously mentioned defensive ditches and embankments. In other words, a period of readjustment set in, which must have been directed by an already strong central authority. Activities then continued as before, but without further population growth for another 250 years or so.

As this case study shows, excavations at Tikal demonstrated the splendor, the social organization, the belief systems, and the agricultural practices of

Bronze Age In the Old World, the period marked by the production of tools and ornaments of bronze; began about 5,000 years ago in China and Southwest Asia and about 500 years earlier in Southeast Asia

the ancient Maya civilization among other things. This chapter's Anthropology Applied feature illustrates a very different approach to another Maya site, just a day's walk from Tikal.

CITIES AND CULTURE CHANGE

If a person who grew up in a rural North American village today moved to Chicago, Montreal, or Los Angeles, she or he would experience a very different way of life. The same would be true for a Neolithic village dweller who moved into one of the world's first cities in Mesopotamia 5,500 years ago. Four basic changes mark the transition from Neolithic village life to life in the first urban centers: agricultural innovation, diversification of labor, central government, and social stratification.

Agricultural Innovation

Changes in farming methods distinguished early civilizations from Neolithic villages. The ancient Sumerians, for example, built an extensive system of dikes, canals, and reservoirs to irrigate their farmlands. With such a system, they could control water resources at

few areas untouched by the program's inclusive sweep, and more arenas can contribute to its evolution.

At El Pilar, I practice what I call "action archaeology," a pioneering conservation model that draws on lessons learned from the recent and distant past to benefit contemporary populations. For example, the co-evolution of Maya society and the environment provide clues about sustainability in this region today. At El Pilar we apply traditional forest gardening: an alternative to resource-diminishing plow and pasture farming methods. The forest survives and demonstrates resilience to impacts brought on by human expansion. The ancient Maya lived with this forest for millennia, and the El Pilar program argues there are lessons to be learned from that past.

The El Pilar Program recognizes the privilege it has enjoyed in forging an innovative community participatory process, in creating a unique management planning design, and in developing a new tourism destination. The success of local outreach at El Pilar can best be seen in the growth of the

© Rolox Awards for Excellence, Susan Gray

community organization Amigos de El Pilar (Friends of El Pilar). With groups based in both Belize and Guatemala, the Amigos de El Pilar have worked together with the El Pilar program to build an inclusive relationship between the community and the reserve that is mutually beneficial. The development of this dynamic relationship lies at the heart of the El Pilar philosophy—resilient and with the potential to educate communities, reform local-level resource management, and inform conservation designs for the Maya Forest.

(By Anabel Ford, Director of Mesoamerican Research Center, University of California, Santa Barbara. www.marc.ucsb.edu, www.espmaya .org, www.forestgardeners.org)

will; water could be held and then run off into the fields as necessary. Irrigation was an important factor affecting an increase of crop yields. Freedom from seasonal rain cycles allowed farmers to harvest more crops in one year. Increased crop yields, resulting from agricultural innovations, contributed to the high population densities of ancient civilizations.

Diversification of Labor

A diversification of labor was also characteristic of early civilizations. In a Neolithic village without irrigation or plow farming, every family member participated in the raising of crops. The high crop yields made possible by new farming methods and the increased population permitted a sizable number of people to pursue nonagricultural activities on a full-time basis.

Ancient public records document a variety of specialized workers. For example, an early Mesopotamian document from the old Babylonian city of Lagash (modern-day Tell al-Hiba, Iraq) lists the artisans, craftspeople, and others paid from crop surpluses stored in the temple granaries. These lists included coppersmiths, silversmiths, sculptors, merchants, potters, tanners, engravers, butchers, carpenters, spinners, barbers, cabinetmakers, bakers, clerks, and brewers.

With specialization came the expertise that led to the invention of new ways of making and doing things. In Eurasia and Africa, civilization ushered in what archaeologists often refer to as the **Bronze Age**, a period marked by the production of tools and ornaments made of this metal. Metals were in great demand for the manufacture of farmers' and artisans' tools, as well as for weapons. Copper and tin (the raw materials from which bronze is made) were smelted, or separated from their ores, then purified, and cast to make plows, swords, axes, and shields. Later, such tools were made from smelted iron. In wars, stone knives, spears, and slings could not stand up against metal spears, arrowheads, swords, helmets, or armor.

The indigenous civilizations of the Americas also used metals. In South America, copper, silver, and gold were used for tools as well as ceremonial and ornamental objects. The Aztecs and Maya used the same soft metals for ceremonial and ornamental objects while continuing to rely on stone for their everyday tools. To those who assume that metal is inherently superior, this seems puzzling. However, the ready availability of obsidian (a glass formed by volcanic activity), its extreme sharpness (many times sharper than the finest steel), and the ease with which it could be worked made it perfectly suited to their needs. Moreover, unlike bronze—and especially iron—copper, silver, and gold are soft metals and have limited

The construction of elliptical granite walls held together without any mortar at Great Zimbabwe in southern Zimbabwe, Africa, attests to the skill of the people who built these structures. When European explorers, unwilling to accept the notion of civilization in sub-Saharan Africa, discovered these magnificent ruins, they wrongly attributed them to white non-Africans. This false notion persisted until archaeologists demonstrated that these structures were part of a city with 12,000 to 20,000 inhabitants that served as the center of a medieval Bantu state.

practical use. Obsidian tools provide some of the sharpest cutting edges ever made. (See Chapter 4's Anthropology Applied, "Stone Tools for Modern Surgeons.")

Early civilizations developed extensive trade systems to procure the raw materials needed for their technologies. In many parts of the world, boats provided greater access to trade centers, transporting large loads of imports and exports between cities at less cost than if they had been carried overland. A one-way trip from the ancient Egyptian cities along the Nile River to the Mediterranean port city of Byblos in Phoenicia (not far from the present city of Beirut, Lebanon) took far less time by rowboat compared to the overland route. With a sailboat, it took even less time.

Egyptian kings, or pharaohs, sent expeditions south to Nubia (northern Sudan) for gold; east to the Sinai Peninsula for copper; to Arabia for spices and perfumes; to Asia for lapis lazuli (a blue semiprecious stone) and other jewels; north to Lebanon for cedar, wine, and funerary oils; and southwest to central Africa for ivory, ebony, ostrich feathers, leopard skins, cattle, and the captives they enslaved. Evidence of trading from Great Zimbabwe in southern Africa indicates that these trading networks extended throughout the Old World. Increased contact with foreign peoples through trade brought new information to trading economies, furthering the spread of innovations and even bodies of knowledge such as geometry and astronomy.

Central Government

The emergence of a governing elite also characterized early civilizations. The challenges new cities faced because of their size and complexity required a strong central authority. The governing elite saw to it that different interest groups, such as farmers or craft specialists, provided their respective services and did not infringe on one another.

Just as they do today, governments of the past ensured that cities were safe from their enemies by constructing fortifications and raising an army. They levied taxes and appointed tax collectors so that construction workers, the army, and other public expenses could be paid. They saw to it that merchants, carpenters, or farmers who made legal claims received justice according to standards of the legal system. They guaranteed safety for the lives and property of ordinary people and assured them that any harm done to one person by another would be justly handled. In addition, surplus food had to be stored for times of scarcity, and public works such as extensive irrigation systems or fortifications had to be supervised by competent, fair individuals. The mechanisms of government served all these functions.

Evidence of Centralized Authority

Evidence of centralized authority in ancient civilizations comes from such sources as law codes, temple records, and royal chronicles. Excavation of the city structures themselves provides additional evidence because they can show definite signs of city planning. The precise astronomical layout of the Mesoamerican city Teotihuacan, described earlier, attests to strong, centralized control.

Monumental buildings and temples, palaces, and large sculptures are usually found in ancient civilizations. For example, the Great Pyramid for the tomb of Khufu, the Egyptian pharaoh, is 755 feet long (236 meters) and 481 feet high (147 meters); it contains about 2.3 million stone blocks, each with an average weight of 2.5 tons. The Greek historian Herodotus reports that it took 100,000 men twenty years to build this tomb. Such gigantic structures could be built only because a powerful central authority could harness the considerable labor force, engineering skills, and raw materials necessary for their construction.

Another indicator of the existence of centralized authority is writing, or some form of recorded information. With writing, central authorities could disseminate information and store, systematize, and deploy memory for political, religious, and economic purposes.

Scholars attribute the initial motive for the development of writing in Mesopotamia to record keeping of state affairs. Writing allowed early governments to keep accounts of their food surplus, tribute records, and other business receipts. Some of the earliest documents appear to be just such records—lists of vegetables and animals bought and sold, tax lists, and storehouse inventories.

Before 5,500 years ago, records consisted initially of "tokens," ceramic pieces with different shapes indicative of different commercial objects. Thus, a cone shape could represent a measure of grain, or a cylinder could be an animal. As the system developed, tokens represented different animals; processed foods such as oil, trussed ducks, or bread; and manufactured or imported goods such as textiles and metal.[6] Ultimately, clay tablets with impressed marks representing objects replaced these tokens.

In the Mesopotamian city of Uruk in Iraq (which likely derives its modern country name from this ancient place), by 5,100 years ago a new writing technique emerged, in which writers used a reed stylus to make wedge-shaped markings on a tablet of damp clay. Originally, each marking stood for a word. Because most words in this language were monosyllabic, over time the markings came to stand for syllables.

Controversy surrounds the question of the earliest evidence of writing. Traditionally, the earliest writing was linked to Mesopotamia. However, in 2003 archaeologists working in the Henan Province of central China discovered signs carved into 8,600-year-old tortoise shells; these markings resemble later-written characters and predate the Mesopotamian evidence by about 2,000 years.[7]

In the Americas, writing systems came into use among various Mesoamerican peoples, but the Maya system was particularly sophisticated. The Maya writing system, like other aspects of Maya culture, appears to have roots in the earlier writing system of the Olmec civilization.[8] The Maya hieroglyphic system had less to do with keeping track of state properties than with extravagant

© Anita de Laguna Haviland

Carved monuments like this were commissioned by Tikal's rulers to commemorate important events in their reigns. Portrayed on this one is a king who ruled about 1,220 years ago. Such skilled stone carving could only have been accomplished by a specialist. The translation of the text shows that this monument recorded the dynastic genealogy of the Maya ruler portrayed on it.

celebrations of the accomplishments of their rulers. Maya lords glorified themselves by recording their dynastic genealogies, important conquests, and royal marriages; by using grandiose titles to refer to themselves; and by associating their actions with important astronomical events. Different though this may be from the record keeping of ancient Mesopotamia, all writing systems share a concern with political power and its maintenance.

The Earliest Governments

A king and his advisors typically headed the earliest city governments. Of the many ancient kings known, one stands out as truly remarkable for the efficient government organization and highly developed legal system characterizing his reign. This is Hammurabi, the Babylonian king who lived in Mesopotamia (modern Iraq) sometime between 3,700 and 3,950 years ago. From Babylon, the capital of his empire, he issued a set of laws now known as the Code of Hammurabi, notable for its thorough detail and standardization. It prescribed the correct form for legal procedures and determined penalties for perjury and false accusation. It contained laws applying to property rights, loans and debts, family rights, and even damages paid for malpractice by a physician. It defined fixed rates to be charged in various trades and branches of commerce and mechanisms to protect the poor, women, children, and slaves against injustice.

---

[6]Lawler, A. (2001). Writing gets a rewrite. *Science, 292,* 2419.

[7]Li, X., et al. (2003). The earliest writing? Sign use in the seventh millennium BC at Jiahu, Henan Province, China. *Antiquity, 77,* 31–44.

[8]Pohl, M. E. D., Pope, K. O., & von Nagy, C. (2002). Olmec origins of Mesoamerican writing. *Science. 298,* 1984–1987.

Officials had the code publicly displayed on huge stone slabs so that no one could plead ignorance. Even the poorest citizens were supposed to know their rights and responsibilities. Distinct social classes were clearly reflected in the law ("rule of law" does not necessarily mean "equality before the law"). For example, if an aristocrat put out the eye of a fellow aristocrat, the law required that his own eye be put out in turn; hence, the saying "an eye for an eye." However, if the aristocrat put out the eye of a commoner, the punishment was simply a payment of silver.[9]

While some civilizations flourished under a single ruler with extraordinary governing abilities, other civilizations possessed a widespread governing bureaucracy that was very efficient at every level. The government of the Inca empire is one such example.

The Inca civilization of Peru and its surrounding territories reached its peak 500 years ago, just before the arrival of the Spanish invaders. By 1525, it stretched 2,500 miles from north to south and 500 miles from east to west, making it at the time one of the largest empires on the face of the earth. Its population, which numbered in the millions, was composed of people of many different ethnic groups. In the achievements of its governmental and political system, Inca civilization surpassed every other civilization of the Americas and most of those of Eurasia. An emperor, regarded as the divine son of the Sun God, headed the government. Under him came the royal family, the aristocracy, imperial administrators, and lower nobility, and below them the masses of artisans, craftspeople, and farmers.

The empire was divided into four administrative regions, further subdivided into provinces, and so on down to villages and families. Government agricultural and tax officials closely supervised farming activities such as planting, irrigation, and harvesting. Teams of professional relay runners could carry messages up to 250 miles in a single day over a network of roads and bridges that remains impressive even today.

Considering the complexity of the Inca civilization, it is surprising that they had no known form of conventional writing. Instead, public records and historical chronicles were kept in the form of an ingenious coding system of colored strings with knots.

Social Stratification

The rise of large, economically diversified populations presided over by centralized governing authorities brought with it the fourth culture change characteristic of civilization: social stratification, or the emergence of social classes. For example, symbols of special status and privilege appeared in the ancient cities of Mesopotamia, where people were ranked according to the kind of work they did or the family into which they were born.

People who stood at or near the head of government were the earliest holders of high status. Although specialists of one sort or another—metal workers, tanners, traders, or the like—generally outranked farmers, such specialization did not necessarily bring with it high status. Rather, people engaged in these kinds of economic activities were either members of the lower classes or outcasts.[10] Merchants of the past could sometimes buy their way into a higher class. With time, the possession of wealth and the influence it could buy became in itself a requisite for high status, as it is in some contemporary cultures.

How do archaeologists know that different social classes existed in ancient civilizations? As described earlier, laws and other written documents, as well as archaeological features including dwelling size and location, can reflect social stratification.

It is also revealed by burial customs. Graves excavated at early Neolithic sites are mostly simple pits dug in the ground, containing few, if any, grave goods. **Grave goods** consist of things such as utensils, figurines, and personal possessions, symbolically placed in the grave for the deceased person's use in the afterlife. Early Neolithic grave sites reveal little variation, indicating essentially classless societies. Graves excavated in civilizations, by contrast, vary widely in size, mode of burial, and the number and variety of grave goods. This reflects a stratified society, divided into social classes. The graves of important persons contain not only various artifacts made from precious materials, but sometimes, as in some early Egyptian burials, the remains of servants evidently killed to serve their master in the afterlife.

Skeletons from the burials may also provide evidence of stratification. Age at death as well as presence of certain diseases can be determined from skeletal remains. In stratified societies of the past, the dominant groups usually lived longer, ate better, and

grave goods Items such as utensils, figurines, and personal possessions, symbolically placed in the grave for the deceased person's use in the afterlife

hydraulic theory The theory that explains civilization's emergence as the result of the construction of elaborate irrigation systems, the functioning of which required full-time managers whose control blossomed into the first governing body and elite social class

[9]Moscati, S. (1962). *The face of the ancient orient* (p. 90). New York: Doubleday.

[10]Sjoberg, G. (1960). *The preindustrial city* (p. 325). New York: Free Press.

Grave goods frequently indicate the status of deceased individuals in stratified societies. For example, China's first emperor was buried with 7,000 life-size terra cotta figures of warriors.

enjoyed an easier life than lower-ranking members of society, just as they do today.

THE MAKING OF STATES

From Africa to China to the South American Andes, ancient civilizations are almost always associated with magnificent palaces built high above ground, sculptures so perfect as to be unrivaled by those of today's artists, and engineering projects so vast and daring as to awaken in us a sense of wonder. These impressive accomplishments could indicate that civilization is better than other cultural forms, particularly when civilizations have come to dominate peoples with other social systems. But domination is more a reflection of aggression, size, and power than it is cultural superiority. In other words, the emergence of centralized governments, characteristic of civilizations, has allowed some cultures to dominate others and for civilizations to flourish. Anthropologists have proposed several theories to account for the transition from small, egalitarian farming villages to large urban centers in which population density, social inequality, and diversity of labor required a centralized government.

Ecological Approaches

Ecological approaches emphasize the role of the environment in the development of states. Among these, the irrigation or **hydraulic theory** holds that civilizations developed when Neolithic peoples realized that the best farming occurred in the fertile soils of river valleys, provided periodic flooding was controlled.[11] The centralized effort to control the irrigation process blossomed into the first governing body, elite social class, and civilization.

Another theory suggests that in regions of ecological diversity, trade is necessary to procure scarce resources. In Mexico, for example, trade networks distributed chilies grown in the highlands, cotton and beans from intermediate elevations, and salt from the coasts to people throughout the region. Some form of centralized authority developed to organize trade for the procurement of these commodities and to redistribute them.

A third theory developed by U.S. anthropologist Robert Carneiro suggests that states develop where populations are hemmed in by such environmental barriers as mountains, deserts, seas, or other human populations as

[11] Wittfogel, K. A. (1957). *Oriental despotism, a comparative study of total power.* New Haven, CT: Yale University Press.

Cahokia Mounds State Historic Site

The relative dearth of ancient monumental structures in North America has led some to inappropriately assume the superiority of Europeans, rather than as evidence of a successfully balanced cultural pattern of North American Native groups. Cahokia, located in Southern Illinois, was a city with an estimated population of 40,000 people dating from 650 to 1400. Cahokia's pyramid-shaped ceremonial mounds were larger in area than the great pyramids of Egypt. Until 1800, when Philadelphia surpassed it, Cahokia was the largest city in the land that is now the United States.

an outcome of warfare and conflict in these circumscribed regions.[12] As these populations grow, they have no space in which to expand, and so they begin to compete for increasingly scarce resources. Internally, this may result in the development of social stratification, in which an elite controls important resources to which lower classes have limited access. Externally, this leads to warfare and even conquest, which, to be successful, require elaborate organization under a centralized authority.

Problems exist with each of these ecological theories. Across the globe and through time, cultures can be found that do not fit these models. For example, some of the earliest large-scale irrigation systems developed in highland New Guinea, where strong centralized governments never emerged. North American Indians possessed trade networks that extended from Labrador in northeastern Canada to the Gulf of Mexico and the Yellowstone region of the Rocky Mountains and even to the Pacific without centralized control.[13] In many of the cultures that do not fit the theories of ecological determinism, neighboring cultures learned to co-exist rather than pursuing warfare to the point of complete conquest.

Although few anthropologists would deny the importance of the human–environment relationship, many are dissatisfied with approaches that do not take into account the beliefs and values that regulate the

interaction between people and their environment.[14] For example, as described in the case study of Tikal, while religion was tied to the earth in that the priests determined the most favorable time for planting crops, the beliefs and power relations that developed within Maya culture were not environmentally determined. Human societies past and present bring their beliefs and values into their interactions with the environment.

Action Theory

One criticism of the above theories is that they fail to recognize the capacity of ambitious, charismatic leaders to shape the course of human history. Accordingly, anthropologists Joyce Marcus and Kent Flannery have developed what they call **action theory**.[15] This theory acknowledges the relationship of society to the environment in shaping social and cultural behavior, but it also recognizes that forceful leaders strive to advance their positions through self-serving actions. In so doing, they may create change.

In the case of Maya history, for example, local leaders, who once relied on personal charisma for the economic and political support needed to sustain them in their positions, may have seized upon religion to solidify their power. Through religion they developed an ideology that endowed them and their descendants with supernatural ancestry and allowed themselves privileged access to the gods, on which their followers depended. In this case,

action theory The theory that self-serving actions by forceful leaders play a role in civilization's emergence

---

[12]Carneiro, R. L. (1970). A theory of the origin of the state. *Science, 169,* 733–738.

[13]Haviland, W. A., & Power, M. W. (1994). *The original Vermonters* (2nd ed., chs. 3 & 4). Hanover, NH: University Press of New England.

[14]Adams, R. M. (2001). Scale and complexity in archaic states. *Latin American Antiquity, 11,* 188.

[15]Marcus, J., & Flannery, K. V. (1996). *Zapotec civilization: How urban society evolved in Mexico's Oaxaca Valley.* New York: Thames & Hudson.

© AFP/Getty Images

East of Naples, Italy, dumping of toxic waste and the sheer volume of normal garbage have become serious environmental threats. Organized crime syndicates provide illegal, and less expensive, ways to dispose of toxic waste, which has led to a contamination of the environment and the foods produced there. There is concern that dioxin, asbestos, and other toxins may have made their way into the food supply, including into water buffalo milk that is used to make the gourmet treat buffalo mozzarella.

certain individuals could monopolize power and emerge as divine kings, using their power to subjugate any rivals.

As the above example makes clear, the context in which a forceful leader operates is critical. In the case of the Maya, the combination of existing cultural and ecological factors opened the way to the emergence of political dynasties. Thus, explanations of civilization's emergence are likely to involve multiple causes, rather than just one. Furthermore, we may also have the cultural equivalent of what biologists call *convergence,* where similar societies come about in different ways. Consequently, a theory that accounts for the rise of civilization in one place may not account for its rise in another.

CIVILIZATION AND ITS DISCONTENTS

Living in the context of civilization ourselves, we are inclined to view its development as a great step upward on a so-called ladder of progress. Whatever benefits civilization has brought, the culture changes it represents have produced new problems. Among them is the problem of waste disposal. In fact, waste disposal probably began to be a problem in settled, farming communities even before civilizations emerged. But as villages grew into towns and towns grew into cities, the problem became far more serious, as crowded conditions and the buildup of garbage and sewage created optimum environments for infectious diseases such as bubonic plague, typhoid, and cholera. Early cities therefore tended to be disease-ridden places, with relatively high death rates.

Genetically based adaptation to diseases may also have influenced the course of civilization. In northern

Europeans, for example, the mutation of a gene on chromosome 7 makes carriers resistant to cholera, typhoid, and other bacterial diarrheas.[16] Because of the mortality caused by these diseases, selection favored spread of this allele among northern Europeans. But, as with sickle-cell anemia, protection comes at a price. That price is cystic fibrosis, a usually fatal disease present in people who are homozygous for the altered gene.

The rise of towns and cities brought with it other acute infectious diseases. In a small population, diseases such as chicken pox, influenza, measles, mumps, pertussis, polio, rubella, and smallpox will kill or immunize so high a proportion of the population that the virus cannot continue to propagate. Measles, for example, is likely to die out in any human population with fewer than half a million people.[17] Hence, such diseases, when introduced into small communities, spread immediately to the whole population and then die out. Their continued existence depends upon the presence of a large population, as found in cities. Survivors possessed immunity to these deadly diseases.

Infectious disease played a major role in European colonization of the Americas. When Europeans with immunity to so-called Old World diseases came to the Americas for the first time, they brought these devastating diseases with them. Millions of Native Americans—who had never been exposed to the microbes that cause diseases such as influenza, smallpox, typhus, and measles—died as a result.

---

[16]Ridley, M. (1999). *Genome: The autobiography of a species in 23 chapters* (p. 142). New York: HarperCollins.

[17]Diamond, J. (1997). *Guns, germs, and steel* (p. 203). New York: Norton.

Biocultural Connection

Social Stratification and Diseases of Civilization: Tuberculosis

Before the discovery of antibiotics in the early 20th century, individuals infected with the bacteria causing the disease tuberculosis (TB) would invariably waste away and die. But before the development of cities, TB in humans was rare. The bacteria that cause TB cannot survive in the presence of sunlight and fresh air. Therefore, TB, like many other sicknesses, can be called a disease of civilization.

Before humans lived in dark, crowded urban centers, if an infected individual coughed and released the TB bacteria into the air, sunlight would prevent the spread of infection. But civilization affects disease in another powerful way. The social distribution of TB indicates that social stratification is as much a determinant of disease as any bacterium, past and present.

For example, Ashkenazi Jews of eastern Europe were forced into urban ghettos over several centuries, becoming especially vulnerable to the TB thriving in crowded, dark, confined neighborhoods. As we have seen with the genetic response to malaria (sickle cell and other abnormal hemoglobins) and bacterial diarrheas (the cystic fibrosis gene), TB triggered a genetic response in the form of the Tay-Sachs allele. Individuals heterozygous for the Tay-Sachs allele were protected from this disease.[a]

Unfortunately, homozygotes for the Tay-Sachs allele develop a lethal, degenerative condition that remains common in Ashkenazi Jews. Without the selective pressure of TB, the frequency of the Tay-Sachs allele would never have increased. Similarly, without the strict social rules confining poor Jews to the ghettos (compounded by rules about marriage), the frequency of the Tay-Sachs allele would never have increased. In recent times, cultural mechanisms such as prenatal and premarital genetic testing have resulted in a decrease in the frequency of the Tay-Sachs allele.

While antibiotics have reduced deaths from TB, resistant forms of the bacteria require an expensive regime of multiple drugs. Not only are poor individuals more likely to become infected with TB, they are also less likely to be able to afford expensive medicines required to treat this disease. For people in poor countries and for disadvantaged people in wealthier countries TB—like AIDS—can be an incurable, fatal, infectious disease. As Holger Sawert from the World Health Organization has said, "Both TB and HIV thrive on poverty." The difficult living conditions in urban slums promote the spread of infectious disease. Poverty also makes medical treatment inaccessible.

Before the social stratification accompanying the emergence of cities and states, as far as infectious microbes were concerned, all humans were the same.

[a]Ridley, M. (1999). *Genome: The autobiography of a species in 23 chapters* (p. 191). New York: HarperCollins.

Not until relatively recent times did public health measures reduce the risk of living in cities, and had it not been for a constant influx of rural peoples, areas of high population density might not have persisted. Europe's urban population, for example, did not become self-sustaining until the early 1900s.[18]

What led people to live in such unhealthy places? Most likely, people were attracted by the same things that lure people to cities today. Cities are vibrant, exciting places that provide people with new opportunities and protection in times of warfare. Of course, people's experience in the cities did not always live up to expectations, particularly for the poor, as described in this chapter's Biocultural Connection.

In addition to health problems, many early cities faced social problems strikingly similar to those found in cities all over the world today. Dense population and the inequalities of class systems and oppressive centralized governments created internal stress. The poor saw that the wealthy had all the things that they themselves lacked. It was not just a question of luxury items; the poor did not have enough food or space in which to live with comfort, dignity, and health.

Evidence of warfare in early civilizations is common. Cities were fortified. Ancient documents list battles, raids, and wars between groups. Cylinder seals, paintings, and sculptures depict battle scenes, victorious kings, and captured prisoners of war. Increasing population and the accompanying scarcity of fertile farming land often led to boundary disputes and quarrels between civilized states or between so-called tribal peoples and a state. When war broke out, people crowded into walled cities for protection and for access to irrigation systems.

What we would call development today—the transformation of rural open spaces into densely populated and built-up environments—posed similar problems in the past. At the Maya city of Copan, in the present-day country of Honduras, much of the fertile bottom lands along the Copan River were paved over as the city grew, making the people more and more dependent on food grown in the fragile soils of the valley slopes. This ultimately led to catastrophic soil loss through erosion and a breakdown of food production. Similarly, in ancient Mesopotamia, evaporation of water from extensive irrigation works resulted in a buildup of salt in the soil, ruining it for agricultural use.

---

[18]Diamond, p. 205.

It is discouraging to note that many of the problems associated with the first civilizations are still with us. Waste disposal, pollution-related health problems, crowding, social inequities, and warfare continue to be serious problems. Through the study of past civilizations, and through comparison of contemporary societies, we now stand a chance of understanding such problems. Such understanding represents a central part of the anthropologist's mission and can contribute to the ability of our species to transcend human-made problems.

Chapter Summary

■ The world's first cities grew out of Neolithic villages between 4,500 and 6,000 years ago—first in Mesopotamia, then in Egypt and the Indus Valley. In China, the process was under way by 5,000 years ago. Somewhat later, and completely independently, similar changes took place in Mesoamerica and the central Andes. Four basic culture changes mark the transition from Neolithic village life to life in civilized urban centers: agricultural innovation, diversification of labor, emergence of centralized government, and social stratification.

■ Agricultural innovation involved the development of new farming methods, such as irrigation, that increased crop yields. Agricultural innovations brought about other changes such as increased population size.

■ Diversification of labor occurred as a result of population growth in cities. Some people could provide sufficient food for others who devoted themselves fully to specialization as artisans and craftspeople. With specialization came the development of new technologies, leading to the beginnings of extensive trade systems. New knowledge disseminated as an outgrowth of technological innovation and increased contact with foreign peoples through trade. Sciences such as geometry and astronomy first developed within the early civilizations.

■ The emergence of a central government provided an authority to deal with the complex problems associated with cities. Evidence of a central governing authority comes from such sources as law codes, temple records, and royal chronicles. With the invention of writing, governments could keep records of their transactions and/or boast of their own power and glory. Additional evidence of centralized government comes from monumental public structures and signs of centralized planning. Typically, the first cities were headed by a king and his special advisors.

■ Social stratification, or the emergence of social classes, is another culture change characteristic of cities and states. Symbols of status and privilege appeared, and individuals were ranked according to the work they did or the position of their families. Archaeologists have been able to verify the existence of social classes in ancient civilizations by excavating graves to study burial customs, grave goods, and skeletons; by noting the size of dwellings in excavated cities; and by examining preserved records in writing and art.

■ A number of theories have been proposed to explain why cities and states developed. Ecological theories emphasize the interrelation of the actions of ancient people and their environment. According to these theories, civilizations developed as centralized governments began to control irrigation systems, trade networks, and/or scarce resources. While these factors coincide with the emergence of states, it is difficult to establish whether the environmental condition caused the culture changes. These theories omit the importance of the beliefs and values of the cultures of the past as well as the actions of forceful, dynamic leaders, whose efforts to promote their own interests may play a role in social change. Probably, several factors acted together, rather than singly, to bring about the emergence of cities and states.

■ Early cities were beset by many problems. Poor sanitation in early cities, coupled with large numbers of people living in close proximity, created environments in which infectious diseases were rampant. Early urban centers also faced social problems strikingly similar to those persisting in the world today. Dense population, class systems, and a strong centralized government created internal stress. Warfare was common; cities were fortified, and armies served to protect the state.

Questions for Reflection

1. In large-scale societies of the past and present, elite classes have disproportionate access to and control of all resources. Is this social stratification an inevitable consequence of the emergence of cities and states? How can the study of social stratification in the past contribute to the resolution of contemporary issues of social justice?

2. In previous chapters it was emphasized that human evolutionary history should not be thought of as progress. Why is it similarly incorrect to think of the shift from village to city to state as progress?

3. What are some of the ways that differences in social stratification are expressed in your community? Does your community have any traditions surrounding death that serve to restate the social differentiation of individuals?

4. With today's global communication and economic networks, will it be possible to shift away from social systems involving centralized governments or is a global centralized authority inevitable?

5. With many archaeological discoveries there is a value placed on "firsts," such as the earliest writing, the first city, or the earliest government. Given the history of the independent emergence of cities and states throughout the world, do you think that scientists should place more value on these events just because they are older?

Key Terms

civilization	hydraulic theory
Bronze Age	action theory
grave goods	

SOUTHERN WHITES ARE THE NEGROES' BEST FRIENDS BUT NO INTEGRATION

VISUAL ESSENCE Although "colored only" and "white only" schools, drinking fountains, waiting rooms, and so forth became illegal in the United States following the civil rights movement of the 1960s, racism still persists—not only in the United States but in many other countries. Racism is fueled by a folk belief that so-called racial groups are natural and separate divisions within our species based on visible physical differences. Biological evidence demonstrates that separate races do not exist. Broadly defined, geographic "racial" groupings differ from one another in only 7 percent of their genes. Having exchanged genes throughout evolutionary history, human populations continue to do so today. Instead of leading to the development of distinctive subspecies (biologically defined races), this genetic exchange has maintained all of humankind as a single species. While race functions as a social and political category that promotes inequality in some societies, it is a cultural construct without an objective scientific basis.

Modern Human Diversity: Race and Racism

From male to female, short to tall, light to dark, biological variation can be categorized in a number of ways, but in the end we are all members of the same species. Minute variations of our DNA give each of us a unique genetic fingerprint, yet this variation remains within the bounds of being genetically human. Visible differences among modern humans are expressed within the framework of biological features shared throughout the species, and as a species, humans vary.

Human genetic variation generally is distributed across the globe in a continuous fashion. From a biological perspective, this variation sometimes follows a pattern imposed by interaction with the environment through the evolutionary process of natural selection. At other times, the variation results from random genetic drift. The significance we give our biological variation, however, is always patterned because the way we perceive variation—in fact, whether we perceive it at all—is determined by culture. For example, in many Polynesian cultures, where skin color is not a determinant of social status, people pay little attention to this physical characteristic. By contrast, in countries such as the United States, Brazil, and South Africa, where skin color is a significant social and political category, it is one of the first things people notice.

Biological diversity, therefore, cannot be studied without an awareness of the cultural dimensions that shape the questions asked about diversity as well as the history of how this knowledge has been used. When European scholars first began their systematic study of human variation in the 18th and 19th centuries, they were concerned with documenting differences among human groups in order to divide them hierarchically into progressively "better types" of humans. Today, this hierarchical approach has been appropriately abandoned. Before exploring how contemporary biological variation is studied today, we will examine the effects of social ideas about race and racial hierarchy on the interpretation of biological variation, past and present.

THE HISTORY OF HUMAN CLASSIFICATION

Early European scholars tried to systematically classify *Homo sapiens* into subspecies, or races, based on geographic location and phenotypic features such as skin color, body size, head shape, and hair texture. The 18th-century Swedish naturalist Carolus Linnaeus originally divided humans into subspecies based on geographic location and classified all Europeans as "white," Africans as "black," American Indians as "red," and Asians as "yellow."

The German physician Johann Blumenbach (1752–1840) introduced some significant changes to this four-race scheme in the 1795 edition of his book *On the Natural Variety of Mankind*. Most notably this book formally put forth the notion of a hierarchy of human types. Based on a comparative examination of his human skull collection, Blumenbach judged as most beautiful the skull of a woman from the Caucasus Mountain range (located between the Black Sea and the Caspian Sea of southeastern Europe and southwestern Asia). It was more symmetrical than the others, and he saw it as a reflection of nature's ideal form: the circle. Surely, Blumenbach reasoned, this "perfect" specimen resembled God's original creation. Moreover, he thought that the living inhabitants of the Caucasus region were the most "beautiful" in the world. Based on these criteria, he concluded that this high mountain range, not far from the lands mentioned in the Bible, was the place of human origins.

Blumenbach determined that all light-skinned peoples in Europe and adjacent parts of western Asia and northern Africa belonged to the same race. On this basis, he dropped the "European" race label and replaced it with "Caucasian." Although he continued to distinguish American Indians as a separate race, he regrouped dark-skinned Africans as "Ethiopian"

and split those Asians not considered Caucasian into two separate races: "Mongolian" (referring to most inhabitants of Asia, including China and Japan) and "Malay" (indigenous Australians, Pacific Islanders, and others).

Convinced that Caucasians were closest to the original ideal humans supposedly created in God's image, Blumenbach ranked them as superior. The other races, he argued, were the result of "degeneration"; by moving away from their place of origin and adapting to different environments and climates, they had degenerated

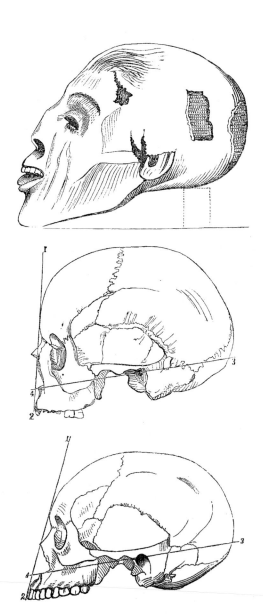

race In biology, the taxonomic category of subspecies that is not applicable to humans because the division of humans into discrete types does not represent the true nature of human biological variation. In some societies race is an important social category

The work of 19th-century Philadelphia physician Samuel Morton is an example of ideologically biased research conducted to justify popular prejudices about so-called racial hierarchies. His biased measurement of a series of skulls to demonstrate the supposed biological superiority of groups of people through features of skull shape and size was effectively challenged in Stephen Jay Gould's classic book *The Mismeasure of Man*.

physically and morally into what many Europeans came to think of as inferior races.[1]

We now clearly recognize the factual errors and ethnocentric prejudices embedded in Blumenbach's work, as well as others, with respect to the concept of race. Especially disastrous is the notion of superior and inferior races, as this has been used to justify brutalities ranging from repression to slavery to mass murder to genocide. It has also been employed to rationalize cruel mockery, as painfully illustrated in the tragic story of Ota Benga, a Twa pygmy man who in the early 1900s was caged in a New York zoo with an orangutan.

Captured in a raid in Congo, Ota Benga came into the possession of a North American businessman, Samuel Verner, looking for exotic "savages" for exhibition in the United States. In 1904, Ota and a group of fellow Twa were shipped across the Atlantic and exhibited at the World's Fair in Saint Louis, Missouri. About 23 years old at the time, Ota was 4 feet 11 inches in height and weighed 103 pounds. Throngs of visitors came to see displays of dozens of indigenous peoples from around the globe, shown in their traditional dress and living in replica villages doing their customary activities. The fair was a success for the organizers, and all the Twa pygmies survived to be shipped back to their homeland. Verner also returned to Congo and with Ota's help collected artifacts to be sold to the American Museum of Natural History in New York City.

In the summer of 1906, Ota came back to the United States with Verner, who soon went bankrupt and lost his entire collection. Left stranded in the big city, Ota was placed in the care of the museum and then taken to the Bronx Zoo and exhibited in the monkey house, with an orangutan as company. Ota's sharpened teeth (a cultural practice among his own people) were seen as evidence of his supposedly cannibal nature. After intensive protest, zoo officials released Ota from his cage and during the day let him roam free in the park, where he was often harassed by teasing visitors. Ota (usually referred to as a "boy") was then turned over to an orphanage for African American children. In 1916, upon hearing that he would never return to his homeland, he took a revolver and shot himself through the heart.[2]

The racist display at the Bronx Zoo a century ago was by no means unique. Just the tip of the ethnocentric iceberg, it was the manifestation of a powerful ideology in which one small part of humanity sought to demonstrate and justify its claims of biological and cultural superiority.

This had particular resonance in North America, where people of European descent colonized lands originally inhabited by Native Americans and then went on to exploit African slaves and (later) Asians imported as a source of cheap labor. Indeed, such claims, based on false notions of race, have resulted in the oppression and genocide of millions of humans because of the color of their skin or the shape of their skulls.

Fortunately, by the early 20th century, some scholars began to challenge the concept of racial hierarchies. Among the strongest critics was Franz Boas (1858–1942), a Jewish scientist who immigrated to the United States because of rising anti-Semitism in his German homeland and who became a founder of North America's four-field anthropology. As president of the American Association for the Advancement of Science, Boas criticized false claims of racial superiority in an important speech titled "Race and Progress," published in the prestigious journal *Science* in 1909. Boas's scholarship in both cultural and biological anthropology contributed to the depth of his critique.

Ashley Montagu (1905–1999), a student of Boas and one of the best-known anthropologists of his time, devoted much of his career to combating scientific racism. Born Israel Ehrenberg to a working-class Jewish family in England, he also felt the sting of anti-Semitism. After changing his name in the 1920s, he immigrated to the United States, where he went on to fight racism in his writing and in academic and public lectures. Of all his works, none is more important than his book *Man's Most Dangerous Myth: The Fallacy of Race*. Published in 1942, it took the lead in debunking the concept of clearly bounded races as a "social myth." The book has since gone through six editions, the last in 1998. Montagu's once controversial ideas have now become mainstream, and his text remains one of the most comprehensive treatments of its subject.

RACE AS A BIOLOGICAL CONCEPT

To understand why the "racial" approach to human variation has been so unproductive and even damaging, we must first understand the race concept in strictly biological terms. In biology, a **race** is defined as a subspecies, or a population of a species differing geographically, morphologically, or genetically from other populations of the same species.

Simple and straightforward though such a definition may seem, there are three very important things to note about it. First, it is arbitrary; there is no agreement on how many differences it takes to make a race.

---

[1]Gould, S. J. (1994). The geometer of race. *Discover, 15*(11), 65–69.
[2]Bradford, P. V., & Blume, H. (1992). *Ota Benga: The pygmy in the zoo*. New York: St. Martin's Press.

Fingerprint patterns of loops, whorls, and arches are genetically determined. Grouping people on this basis would place most Europeans, sub-Saharan Africans, and East Asians together as "loops," Australian aborigines and the people of Mongolia together as "whorls," and central Europeans and the Bushmen of southern Africa together as "arches."

For example, if one researcher emphasizes skin color while another emphasizes blood group differences, they will not classify people in the same way. Ultimately, it is impossible to reach agreement on the number of genes and precisely which ones are the most important for defining races.

The second thing to note about the biological definition of race is that it does not mean that any one race has exclusive possession of any particular variant of any gene or genes. In human terms, the frequency of a trait like the type O blood group, for example, may be high in one population and low in another, but it is present in both. In other words, populations are genetically "open," meaning that genes flow between them. Because populations are genetically open, no fixed racial groups can exist. The only reproductive barriers that exist for humans are the cultural rules some societies impose regarding appropriate mates.

Third, the biological definition of race does not apply to humans because the differences among individuals within a so-called racial population are greater than the differences among separate populations. Evolutionary biologist Richard Lewontin demonstrated this through genetic analyses in the 1970s. He compared the amount of genetic variation within populations and among so-called racial groups, finding a mere 7 percent of human variation existing among groups.[3] Indeed, the vast majority of genetic variation exists *within* groups. As the science writer James Shreeve puts it, "most of what separates me genetically from a typical African or Eskimo also separates me from another average American of European ancestry."[4] This follows from the fact of genetic openness of races; no one race has an exclusive claim to any particular form of a gene or trait.

Yao Ming, center for the Houston Rockets, receives his Special Olympics Global Ambassador jersey from athlete Xu Chuang (left) and Special Olympics East Asia President Dicken Yung. Standing side by side, these three individuals illustrate the wide range of variation in height seen within a single so-called racial category.

THE CONCEPT OF HUMAN RACES

While the biological race concept is not applicable to human variation, nevertheless race exists as a significant cultural category. Human groups frequently insert a false notion of biological difference into the cultural category of race to make it appear more factual and objective. In various ways, cultures define religious, linguistic, and ethnic groups as "races," thereby confusing linguistic and cultural traits with physical traits.

For example, in many Latin American countries, people are commonly classified as Indian, Mestizo (mixed), or Ladino (of Spanish descent). But despite the biological connotations of these terms, the criteria used for assigning individuals to these categories consist of things such as whether they wear shoes, sandals, or go barefoot; speak Spanish or an Indian language; live in a thatched hut or a European-style house; and so forth. Thus, an Indian—by speaking Spanish, wearing Western-style clothes, and living in a house in a non-Indian neighborhood—ceases to be an Indian, no matter how many "Indian genes" he or she may possess.

---

[3]Lewontin, R. C. (1972). The apportionment of human diversity. In T. Dobzhansky et al. (Eds.), *Evolutionary biology* (pp. 381–398). New York: Plenum Press.

[4]Shreeve, J. (1994). Terms of estrangement. *Discover, 15*(11), 60.

This sort of confusion of nonbiological characteristics with the biological notion of heredity is by no means limited to Latin American societies. To various extents, such confusion is found in most societies of Europe and North America. Take, for example, the fact that the racial categories used by the U.S. Census Bureau change with every census. The current large catch-all categories (white, black, American Indian or Alaskan Native, Asian, and Pacific Islander or native Hawaiian) include diverse peoples. Asian, for example, includes such different people as Chinese and East Indians, whereas native Hawaiian and Alaskan are far more restrictive. The Census Bureau also asks people to identify Hispanic ethnicity, a category that includes people who, in their countries of origin, might be classified as Indian, Mestizo, or Ladino. The addition of categories for native Hawaiians, Middle Easterners, and people who consider themselves multiracial does nothing to improve the situation.

To compound the confusion, inclusion in one or another of these categories is usually based on self-identification, which means that these are not biological categories at all. The observation that the purported race of an individual can vary over the course of his or her lifetime speaks to the fact that cultural forces shape the designation of membership in a particular racial category.[5]

In the United States, where race is a political and social determinant of health, health statistics are gathered by Census Bureau categories for the purposes of correcting health disparities among social groups. Unfortunately, the false biological concept of race is frequently inferred in these analyses. As a result, the increased risk of dying from a heart attack for African Americans compared to "whites" is attributed to biological differences rather than to health-care disparities or other social factors.

Similarly, medical genetics research is regularly oversimplified into the comparisons among the racial types defined in the 18th and 19th centuries. Whether this genetic research will avoid the trap of recreating false genetic types that do not reflect the true nature of human variation remains to be seen. The recent claims made for race-specific drugs and vaccines based on limited scientific data indicate that the social category of race may again be interfering with our understanding of the true nature of human genetic diversity.

To make matters worse, the confusion of social with biological factors is frequently combined with prejudices that then serve to exclude whole categories of people from certain roles or positions in society. For example, in colonial North America, a "racial" worldview that had antecedents in the unequal power relations between the English or Saxon "race" and the Irish or Celtic "race" in

© Schalkwijik/Art Resource, NY

In colonial Mexico, sixteen different *castas* ("castes") were named, giving specific labels to individuals who were various combinations of Spanish, Indian, and African ancestry. These paintings of *castas* are traditionally arranged from light to dark as a series and reflect an effort to impose hierarchy despite the fluid social system in place. In the United States the hierarchy was more rigid and the "one drop rule," also known as *hypodescent*, would ascribe the "lower" position to individuals if they had even one drop of blood from a grouping within the hierarchy.

Europe assigned American Indians and Africans imported as slaves to perpetual low status. A supposed biological inferiority was used to justify this low status, whereas access to privilege, power, and wealth was reserved for favored groups of European descent.[6]

Because of the colonial association of lighter skin with greater power and higher social status, people whose history includes domination by lighter-skinned Europeans have sometimes valued this phenotype. In Haiti, for example, the "color question" has been the dominant force in social and political life. Skin texture, facial features, hair color, and socioeconomic class collectively play a role in the ranking. According to Haitian anthropologist Michel-Rolph Trouillot, "a rich black becomes a mulatto, a poor mulatto becomes black."[7]

[5]Hahn, R. A. (1992). The state of federal health statistics on racial and ethnic groups. *Journal of the American Medical Association*, 267(2), 268–271.

[6]American Anthropological Association. (1998). Statement on "race." www.ameranthassn.org.

[7]Trouillot, M. R. (1996). Culture, color, and politics in Haiti. In S. Gregory & R. Sanjek (Eds.), *Race*. New Brunswick, NJ: Rutgers University Press.

These skulls, from the genocide war memorial in Rwanda, record some of the horror of the genocide that took place in this central African country in 1994. Over the course of only about a hundred days, a militia of the ruling Hutu majority brutally murdered close to 1 million ethnic Tutsis. With clear genocidal intent, systematic organization, and intense speed, Hutu actions, resembling those of the Nazi regime, remind us that genocide is far from a thing of the past. The global effects of the Rwandan genocide have been massive. Millions of Rwandans, both refugees and killers, now live in neighboring regions, disrupting the stability of these states. Through the United Nations and individual governments, the international community has recognized that it failed to act to prevent this genocide and collectively has taken steps toward maintaining peace in the region. The parallels between Rwanda and the current conflicts in Congo, Burundi, and Sudan are chilling.

The Nazis in Germany elevated a racialized world-view to state policy, with particularly evil consequences. The Nuremberg race laws of 1935 declared the superiority of the Aryan "race" and the inferiority of the Gypsy and Jewish "races." The Nazi doctrine justified, on supposed biological grounds, political repression and extermination. In all, 11 million people (Jews, Gypsies, homosexuals, and other so-called inferior people, as well as political opponents of the Nazi regime) were deliberately put to death.

Tragically, the Nazi Holocaust (from the Greek word for "wholly burnt" or "sacrificed by fire") is not unique in human history. Such genocides, programs of extermination of one group by another, have a long history that predates World War II and continues today. Recent and ongoing genocide in parts of South America, Africa, Europe, and Asia, like previous genocides, are accompanied by a rhetoric of dehumanization and a depiction of the people being exterminated as a lesser type of human.

Considering the problems, confusion, and horrendous consequences, it is small wonder that

racism A doctrine of superiority by which one group justifies the dehumanization of others based on their distinctive physical characteristics

most anthropologists have abandoned the race concept as being of no utility in understanding human biological variation. Instead, they have found it more productive to study *clines*, the distribution and significance of single, specific, genetically based characteristics and continuous traits related to adaptation. They examine human variation within small breeding populations, the smallest units in which evolutionary change occurs.

THE SOCIAL SIGNIFICANCE OF RACE: RACISM

Scientific facts, unfortunately, have been slow to change what people think about race. **Racism**, a doctrine of superiority by which one group justifies the dehumanization of others based on their distinctive physical characteristics, is not just about discriminatory ideas, values, or attitudes but is also a political problem. Indeed, politicians have often exploited this concept as a means to mobilizing support, demonizing opponents, and eliminating rivals. Racial conflicts result from social stereotypes, not scientific facts.

Race and Behavior

The assumption that behavioral differences exist among human "races" remains an issue to which many people still cling tenaciously. Throughout history, certain characteristics have been attributed to groups of people under a variety of names—national character, spirit, temperament—all of them vague and standing for a number of concepts unrelated to any biological phenomena. Common myths involve the coldness of Scandinavians or the rudeness of Americans or the war-like character of Germans or the lazy nature of Africans. Such unjust characterizations rely upon a false notion of biological difference.

To date, no inborn behavioral characteristic can be attributed to any group of people (which the nonscientist might term a "race") that cannot be explained in terms of cultural practices. If the Chinese happen to exhibit exceptional visual-spatial skills, it is probably because the business of learning to read Chinese characters requires a visual-spatial kind of learning, one that is not as necessary in mastering Western alphabets.[8] Similarly, the exclusion of "non-whites" from honors in the sport of golf (until Tiger Woods) had more to do with the social rules of country clubs and the sport's expense. All such differences or characteristics can be explained in terms of culture.

In the same vein, high crime rates, alcoholism, and drug use among certain groups can be explained with reference to culture rather than biology. Individuals alienated and demoralized by poverty, injustice, and unequal opportunity tend to abandon the traditional paths to success of the dominant culture because these paths are blocked. In a racialized society, poverty and all its ill consequences affect some groups of people much more severely than others.

Race and Intelligence

A question frequently asked by those unfamiliar with the fallacy of biological race in humans is whether some "races" are inherently more intelligent than others. First we must ask, what do we mean by the term *intelligence*? Unfortunately, there is no general agreement as to what abilities or talents actually make up what we call intelligence, even though some psychologists insist that it is a single quantifiable thing measured by IQ tests. Many more psychologists consider intelligence to be the product of the interaction of different sorts of cognitive abilities: verbal, mathematical-logical, spatial, linguistic,

musical, bodily kinesthetic, social, and personal.[9] Each may be thought of as a particular kind of intelligence, unrelated to the others. This being so, these types of intelligence must be independently inherited (to the degree they are inherited), just as height, blood type, skin color, and so forth are independently inherited. Thus, the various abilities that constitute intelligence are independently distributed like other phenotypic traits such as skin color and blood type.

But IQ tests themselves are not a fully valid measure of inborn intelligence. An IQ test measures performance (something that one does) rather than genetic disposition (something that the individual was born with). Performance reflects past experiences and present motivational state, as well as innate ability.

Though IQ tests are not a reliable measure of inborn intelligence, using them to prove the existence of significant differences in intelligence among human populations has been going on for at least a century. In the United States systematic comparisons of intelligence between "whites" and "blacks" began in the early 20th century and were frequently combined with data gathered by physical anthropologists about skull shape and size.

During World War I, for example, a series of IQ tests, known as Alpha and Beta, were regularly given to draftees. The results showed that the average score attained by Euramericans was higher than that obtained by African Americans. Even though African Americans from the urban northern states scored higher than Euramericans from the rural South, and some African Americans scored higher than most Euramericans, many people took this as proof of the intellectual superiority of "white" people. But all the tests really showed was that, on the average, "whites" outperformed "blacks" in the social situation of IQ testing. The tests did not measure intelligence per se, but the ability, conditioned by culture, of certain individuals to respond appropriately to certain questions conceived by Americans of European descent for comparable middle-class "whites." These tests frequently require knowledge of "white" middle-class values and linguistic behavior.

For such reasons, intelligence tests continue to be the subject of controversy. Many psychologists as well as anthropologists are convinced that they are of limited use, because they are applicable only to particular cultural circumstances. When cultural and environmental factors are held constant, African and European Americans tend to score equally well.[10]

---

[8]Chan, J. W. C., & Vernon, P. E. (1988). Individual differences among the peoples of China. In J. W. Berry (Ed.), *Human abilities in cultural context* (pp. 340–357). Cambridge, England: Cambridge University Press.

[9]Jacoby, R., & Glauberman, N. (Eds.). (1995). *The Bell Curve debate* (pp. 7, 55–56, 59). New York: Random House.

[10]Sanday, P. R. (1975). On the causes of IQ differences between groups and implications for social policy. In M. F. A. Montagu (Ed.), *Race and IQ* (pp. 232–238). New York: Oxford University Press.

Nevertheless some researchers still insist that significant differences in intelligence among human populations exist. Recent proponents of this view are Richard Herrnstein, a psychologist, and Charles Murray, a political scientist and longtime fellow of the American Enterprise Institute, a conservative think tank in the United States. Their argument, in a lengthy (and highly publicized) book entitled *The Bell Curve*, is that the difference in IQ scores between Americans of African, Asian, and European descent is primarily determined by genetic factors and therefore immutable.

Herrnstein and Murray's book has been justly criticized on many grounds, including violation of basic rules of statistics and their practice of utilizing studies, no matter how flawed, that appear to support their thesis while ignoring or barely mentioning those that contradict it. In addition, they are also wrong on purely theoretical grounds. Because genes are inherited independently of one another, whatever alleles that may be associated with intelligence bear no relationship with the ones for skin pigmentation or with any other aspect of human variation such as blood type.

Further, the expression of genes always occurs in an environment. Among humans, culture shapes all aspects of the environment. In the following Original Study, U.S. physical anthropologist Jonathan Marks extends the discussion of race and intelligence to stereotypes about athletic abilities of different so-called races.

Original Study

A Feckless Quest for the Basketball Gene

Jonathan Marks

You know what they say about a little knowledge. Here's some: The greatest sprinters and basketball players are predominantly black. Here's some more: Nobel laureates in science are predominantly white.

What do we conclude? That blacks have natural running ability, and whites have natural science ability? Or perhaps that blacks have natural running ability, but whites don't have natural science ability, because that would be politically incorrect?

Or perhaps that we can draw no valid conclusions about the racial distribution of abilities on the basis of data like these.

That is what modern anthropology would say.

But it's not what a new book, *Taboo: Why Black Athletes Dominate Sports and Why We're Afraid to Talk about It*, says. It says that blacks dominate sports because of their genes and that we're afraid to talk about it on account of a cabal of high-ranking politically correct postmodern professors—myself, I am flattered to observe, among them.

The book is a piece of good old-fashioned American anti-intellectualism (those dang perfessers!) that plays to vulgar beliefs about group differences of the sort we recall from *The Bell Curve* (1994). These are not, however, issues that anthropologists are "afraid to talk about"; we talk about them a lot. The author, journalist and former television producer Jon Entine, simply doesn't like what we're saying. But to approach the subject with any degree of rigor, as anthropologists have been trying to do for nearly a century, requires recognizing that it consists of several related questions.

First, how can we infer a genetic basis for differences among people? The answer: Collect genetic data. There's no substitute. We could document consistent differences in physical features, acts, and accomplishments until the Second Coming and be entirely wrong in thinking they're genetically based. A thousand Nigerian Ibos and a thousand Danes will consistently be found to differ in complexion, language, and head shape. The first is genetic, the second isn't, and the third we simply don't understand.

What's clear is that, developmentally, the body is sufficiently plastic that subtle differences in the conditions of growth and life can affect it profoundly. Simple observation of difference is thus not a genetic argument.

Which brings us to the second question: How can we accept a genetic basis for athletic ability and reject it for intelligence? The answer: We can't.

Both conclusions are based on the same standard of evidence. If we accept that blacks are genetically endowed jumpers because "they" jump so well, we are obliged to accept that they are genetically unendowed at schoolwork because "they" do so poorly.

In either case, we are faced with the scientifically impossible task of drawing conclusions from a mass of poorly controlled data. Controls are crucial in science: If every black schoolboy in America knows he's supposed to be good at basketball and bad at algebra, and we have no way to measure schoolboys outside the boundaries of such an expectation, how can we gauge their "natural" endowments? Lots of things go into the observation of excellence or failure, only one of which is genetic endowment.

But obviously humans differ. Thus, the last question: What's the relationship between patterns of human genetic variation and groups of people? The answer: It's complex.

All populations are heterogeneous and are built in some sense in opposition to other groups. Jew or Muslim, Hutu or Tutsi, Serb or Bosnian, Irish or English, Harvard or Yale—one thing we're certain of is that the groups of most significance to us don't correspond to much in nature.

Consider, then, the category "black athlete"—and let's limit ourselves to men here. It's broad enough to encompass Arthur Ashe, Mike Tyson, and Kobe Bryant.

When you read about the body of the black male athlete, whose body do you imagine? Whatever physical gift these men share is not immediately apparent from looking at them.

Black men of highly diverse builds enter athletics and excel.

Far more don't excel. In other words, there is a lot more to being black and to being a prominent athlete than mere biology. If professional excellence or overrepresentation could be regarded as evidence for genetic superiority, there would be strong implications for Jewish comedy genes and Irish policeman genes.

Inferring a group's excellence from the achievements of some members hangs on a crucial asymmetry: To accomplish something means that you had the ability to do it, but the failure to do it doesn't mean you didn't have

the ability. And the existing genetic data testify that known DNA variations do not respect the boundaries of human groups.

To be an elite athlete, or elite anybody, presumably does require some kind of genetic gift. But those gifts must be immensely diverse, distributed broadly across the people of the world—at least to judge from the way that the erosion of social barriers consistently permits talent to manifest itself in different groups of people.

In an interview with *The Philadelphia Daily News* in February, Mr. Entine observed that Jews are overrepresented among critics of the views he espouses. But is that a significantly Jewish thing? Or is it simply a consequence of the fact that among any group of American intellectuals you'll find Jews overrepresented because they are a well-educated minority? There's certainly no shortage of non-Jews who find the ideas in "Taboo" to be demagogic quackery.

Of course, Jewish academics may sometimes be speaking as academics,

not as Jews. Likewise black athletes may perform as athletes, not just as embodied blackness.

How easy it is to subvert Michael Jordan, the exceptional and extraordinary man, into merely the representative of the black athlete.

The problem with talking about the innate superiority of the black athlete is that it is make-believe genetics applied to naïvely conceptualized groups of people. It places a spotlight on imaginary natural differences that properly belongs on real social differences.

More important, it undermines the achievements of individuals as individuals. Whatever gifts we each have are far more likely, from what we know of genetics, to be unique individual constellations of genes than to be expressions of group endowments.

(By Jonathan Marks (2000, April 8). A feckless quest for the basketball gene. New York Times. Copyright © 2000 by the New York Times Co. Reprinted by permission)

Separating genetic components of intelligence (or any other continuous trait) from environmental contributors poses enormous problems.[11] Most studies of intelligence rely on comparisons between identical twins, genetically identical individuals raised in the same or different environments. Twin studies are plagued by a host of problems: inadequate sample sizes, biased subjective judgments, failure to make sure that "separated twins" really were raised separately, unrepresentative samples of adoptees to serve as controls, untested assumptions about similarity of environments. In fact, children reared by the same mother resemble her in IQ to the same degree, whether or not they share her genes.[12] Clearly, the degree to which intelligence is inherited through genes is far from understood.[13]

Undoubtedly, the effects of social environment are important for intelligence. This should not surprise us, as other genetically determined traits are influenced by environmental factors. Height in humans, for example,

has a genetic basis while also being dependent upon both nutrition and health status (severe illness in childhood arrests growth, and renewed growth never makes up for this loss). While it is possible to see the effects of the environment on growth, the exact relative contributions of genetic and environmental factors on either the height or the intelligence of an individual are unknown.

Nevertheless documentation of the importance of the environment in the expression of intelligence exposes further the problems with generalizations about IQ and "race." For example, IQ scores of all groups in the United States, as in most industrial and postindustrial countries, have risen some 15 points since World War II. In addition, the gap between Americans of African and European descent, for example, is narrower today than in the past. Other studies show impressive IQ scores for African American children from socially deprived and economically disadvantaged backgrounds who have been adopted into highly educated and prosperous homes. It is now known that underprivileged children adopted into such privileged families can boost their IQs by 20 points. It is also well known that IQ scores rise in proportion to the test-takers' amount of schooling. More such cases could be cited, but these suffice to make the point: A bias in IQ testing based on social class exists.

---

[11]Andrews, L. B., & Nelkin, D. (1996). The bell curve: A statement. *Science, 271*, 13.

[12]Lewontin, R. C., Rose, S., & Kamin, L. J. (1984). *Not in our genes* (pp. 100, 113, 116). New York: Pantheon.

[13]Lewontin, Rose, & Kamin, pp. 9, 121.

The assertion that IQ is biologically fixed and immutable is clearly false. Ranking human beings with respect to their intelligence scores in terms of "racial" difference is doubly false.

Over the past 2.5 million years, all populations of the genus *Homo* have adapted primarily through culture—actively inventing solutions to the problems of existence, rather than relying only on biological adaptation. Thus, we would expect a comparable degree of intelligence in all present-day human populations. The only way to be sure that individual human beings develop their innate abilities and skills to the fullest is to make sure they have access to the necessary resources and the opportunity to do so. This certainly cannot be accomplished if whole populations are assumed at the outset to be inferior.

HUMAN BIOLOGICAL DIVERSITY

Although the biological category of race is not valid when considering groups of humans, this is not to say that differences in various biological traits such as skin color do not exist. In fact, skin color provides an excellent example of the role of natural selection in shaping human variation.

Skin Color: A Case Study in Adaptation

Skin color is subject to great variation and is attributed to several key factors: the transparency or thickness of the skin; a copper-colored pigment called carotene; reflected color from the blood vessels (responsible for the rosy color of lightly pigmented people); and, most significantly, the amount of melanin (from *melas,* a Greek word meaning "black")—a dark pigment in the skin's outer layer. People with dark skin have more melanin-producing cells than those with light skin, but everyone (except albinos) has a measure of melanin. Exposure to sunlight increases melanin production, causing skin color to deepen.

Melanin is known to protect skin against damaging ultraviolet solar radiation;[14] consequently, dark-skinned peoples are less susceptible to skin cancers and sunburn than are those with less melanin. They also seem to be less susceptible to destruction of certain vitamins under intense exposure to sunlight. Because the highest concentrations of dark-skinned people tend to be found in the tropical regions of the world, it appears that natural selection has favored heavily pigmented skin as a protection against exposure where ultraviolet radiation is most constant.[15]

The inheritance of skin color involves several genes, each with several alleles, thus creating a continuous range of expression for this trait. In addition, the geographic distribution of skin color tends to be continuous (Figures 7.1 and 7.2). In northern latitudes, light skin has an adaptive advantage related to the skin's important biological function as the manufacturer of vitamin D through a chemical reaction dependent upon sunlight. Vitamin D is vital for maintaining the balance of calcium in the body. In northern climates with little sunshine, light skin allows enough sunlight to penetrate the skin and stimulate the formation of vitamin D, essential for healthy bones. Dark pigmentation interferes with this process. The severe consequences of vitamin D deficiency can be avoided through culture. Until recently, children in northern Europe and northern North America were regularly fed a spoonful of cod liver oil during the dark winter months. Today, pasteurized milk is often fortified with vitamin D.

Given what we know about the adaptive significance of human skin color, and the fact that, until 800,000 years ago, members of the genus *Homo* were exclusively creatures of the tropics, it is likely that lightly pigmented skins are a recent development in human history. Conversely, and consistent with humanity's African origins, darkly pigmented skins likely are quite ancient.

The enzyme tyrosinase, which converts the amino acid tyrosine into the compound that forms melanin, is present in lightly pigmented peoples in sufficient quantity to make them very "black." The reason it does not is that they have genes that inactivate or inhibit it.[16] Human skin, more liberally endowed with sweat glands and lacking heavy body hair compared to other primates, effectively eliminates excess body heat in a hot climate. This would have been especially advantageous to our ancestors on the savannah, who could have avoided confrontations with large carnivorous animals by carrying out most of their activities in the heat of the day. For the most part, tropical predators rest during this period, hunting primarily from dusk until early morning. Without much hair to cover their bodies, selection would have favored dark skin in our human ancestors. In short, based on available scientific evidence, all humans appear to have a "black" ancestry, no matter how "white" some of them may appear to be today.

---

[14]Neer, R. M. (1975). The evolutionary significance of vitamin D, skin pigment, and ultraviolet light. *American Journal of Physical Anthropology, 43,* 409–416.

[15]Branda, R. F., & Eatoil, J. W. (1978). Skin color and photolysis: An evolutionary hypothesis. *Science, 201,* 625–626.

[16]Wills, C. (1994). The skin we're in. *Discover, 15*(11), 79.

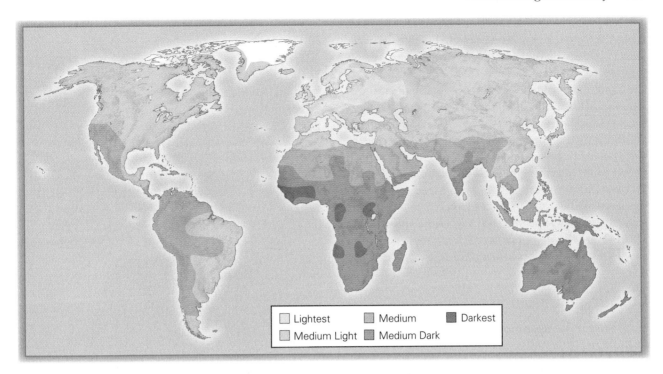

Lightest   **Medium**   **Darkest**
Medium Light   **Medium Dark**

Figure 7.1

This map illustrates the distribution of dark and light human skin pigmentation before 1492. Medium-light skin color in Southeast Asia reflects the spread into that region of people from southern China, whereas the medium darkness of people native to southern Australia is a consequence of their tropical Southeast Asian ancestry. Lack of dark skin pigmentation among tropical populations of Native Americans reflects their ancestry in Northeast Asia a mere 20,000 years ago.

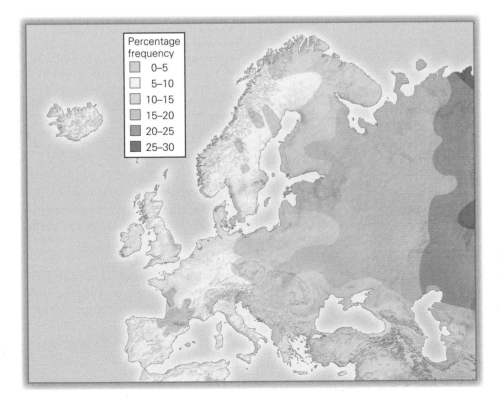

Percentage frequency
0–5
5–10
10–15
15–20
20–25
25–30

Figure 7.2

The east-west gradient in the frequency of the type B blood in Europe contrasts with the north-south gradient in skin color shown in Figure 7.1. Whatever genes are involved in the various abilities lumped together as intelligence must be independently assorted as well.

Obviously, one should not conclude that, because it may be a more recent development, lightly pigmented skin is better, or more highly evolved, than heavily pigmented skin. The latter is clearly better evolved to the conditions of life in the tropics or at high altitudes, although with cultural adaptations like protective clothing, hats, and more recently invented sunscreen lotions, lightly pigmented people can survive there. Conversely, the availability of supplementary sources of vitamin D allows more heavily pigmented people to do quite well far away from the tropics. In both cases, culture has rendered skin color differences largely irrelevant from a purely biological perspective. With time and with the efforts being made in many cultures today, skin color may eventually lose its social significance as well.

Culture and Biological Diversity

While cultural adaptation has reduced the importance of biological adaptation and physical variation, at the same time, cultural forces impose their own selective pressures. For example, take the reproductive fitness of individuals with diabetes—a disease with a known genetic predisposition. In North America and Europe today, where medication is relatively available, people with diabetes are as biologically fit as anyone else. However, if diabetics are denied access to the needed medication, as they are in many parts of the world, their biological fitness is lost and they die out. In fact, one's financial status affects one's access to medication, and so, however unintentional it may be, one's biological fitness may be decided by one's financial status.

Cultural factors can also contribute directly to the development of disease. For example, one type of diabetes is very common among overweight individuals who get little exercise—a combination that describes 61 percent of people from the United States today who are increasingly beset by this condition. As people from traditional cultures throughout the world adopt a Western high-sugar diet and activity pattern, the frequency of diabetes and obesity increases.

Another example of culture acting as an agent of biological selection has to do with lactose tolerance: the ability to digest **lactose**, the primary constituent of fresh milk. This ability depends on the capacity to make a particular enzyme, **lactase**.

Loss of traditional cultural practices brought about by forced reservation life has resulted in high rates of diabetes among American Indians. The Pima Indians of Arizona have the highest rates of diabetes in the world today. Diabetes was not a problem for the Pima before the plentiful high-carbohydrate diet and low activity patterns typical of American culture replaced their traditional lifeways. Despite the sociopolitical roots of this disease in their community, the Pima have participated in U.S. government-funded research aimed at both understanding the genetic origins of diabetes and finding effective treatment for it. Here a Pima woman prepares to give herself an insulin injection.

Most mammals as well as most human populations—especially Asian, Native Australian, Native American, and many (but not all) African populations—do not continue to produce lactase into adulthood. Failure to retain lactase production into adulthood causes gas pains and diarrhea for individuals who consume milk. Only 10 to 30 percent of Americans of African descent and 0 to 30 percent of adult Asians are lactose tolerant.[17] By contrast, lactase retention and lactose tolerance are normal for over 80 percent of adults of northern

lactose A sugar that is the primary constituent of fresh milk
lactase An enzyme in the small intestine that enables humans to assimilate lactose
thrifty genotype Human genotype that permits efficient storage of fat to draw on in times of food shortage and conservation of glucose and nitrogen

---

[17]Harrison, G. G. (1975). Primary adult lactase deficiency: A problem in anthropological genetics. *American Anthropologist, 77,* 815–819.

Biocultural Connection

Paleolithic Prescriptions for Today's Diseases

Though increased life expectancy is often hailed as one of modern civilization's greatest accomplishments, in some ways people in the "developed" world are far less healthy than our ancestors. Throughout most of our evolutionary history, humans led more physically active lives and ate a more varied low-fat diet than people do now. They did not drink or smoke. They spent their days scavenging or hunting for animal protein while gathering vegetable foods with some insects thrown in for good measure. They stayed fit through traveling great distances each day over the savannah and beyond.

Today humans may survive longer, but survival entails skyrocketing rates of obesity and chronic disease. Heart disease, diabetes, high blood pressure, and cancer plague individuals in wealthy industrialized nations. These diseases become global threats as Western diets and "couch potato" habits replace traditional lifeways.

Anthropologists Melvin Konner and Marjorie Shostak and physician Boyd Eaton have suggested that our Paleolithic ancestors have provided a prescription for a cure. They propose that as "stone-agers in a fast lane," people's health will improve by returning to the lifestyle to which their bodies are adapted.[a] Such Paleolithic prescriptions are an example of evolutionary medicine—a branch of medical anthropology that uses evolutionary principles to contribute to human health.

Evolutionary medicine bases its prescriptions on the idea that rates of culture change exceed the rates of biological change. Our food-forager physiology was shaped over millions of years, and our bodies are best adapted to this lifestyle. By contrast, the culture changes leading to contemporary lifestyles have occurred rapidly, in mere instants in evolutionary terms.

The downward trajectory for human health began with the earliest human village settlements some 10,000 years ago. While nutritional deficiencies and an increase in infectious diseases have troubled humans since the start of the Neolithic, the main health threats to humans have shifted over the past sixty years.

The invention of antibiotics has effectively controlled or eliminated many infectious diseases at the same time that decreased physical activity and increased calorie consumption have led to obesity and chronic disease. Returning to the lifestyle of our Paleolithic forebears—with high physical activity along with a diet characterized by moderate consumption of varied but unprocessed foods—we can substantially improve our health today.

[a]Eaton, S. B, Konner, M., & Shostak, M. (1988). Stone-agers in the fast lane: Chronic degenerative diseases in evolutionary perspective. *American Journal of Medicine, 84*(4), 739–749.

European descent. Eastern Europeans, Arabs, and some East Africans are closer to northern Europeans in lactase retention than they are to Asians and other Africans. Generally speaking, a high retention of lactase is found in populations with a long tradition of dairying. For them, fresh milk is an important dietary item. In such populations, selection in the past favored those individuals with the allele that confers the ability to assimilate lactose, selecting out those without this allele.

Because milk is associated with health in North American and European countries, powdered milk has long been a staple of economic aid to other countries. In fact, such practices work against the members of populations in which lactase is not commonly retained into adulthood. Those individuals who are not lactose tolerant are unable to utilize the many nutrients in milk. Frequently they also suffer diarrhea, abdominal cramping, and even bone degeneration, with serious results. In fact, the shipping of powdered milk to victims of South American earthquakes in the 1960s caused many deaths among them.

Among Europeans, lactose tolerance is linked with the evolution of a non-thrifty genotype as opposed to the **thrifty genotype** that characterized humans until about 6,000 years ago.[18] The thrifty genotype permits efficient storage of fat to draw on in times of food shortage. In times of scarcity individuals with the thrifty genotype conserve glucose (a simple sugar) for use in brain and red blood cells (as opposed to other tissues such as muscle), as well as nitrogen (vital for growth and health).

Regular access to glucose through the lactose in milk led to selection for the non-thrifty genotype as protection against adult-onset diabetes, or at least its onset relatively late in life (at a nonreproductive age). Populations that are lactose intolerant retain the thrifty genotype. As a consequence, when they are introduced to Western-style diets (characterized by abundance, particularly of foods high in sugar content), the incidence of obesity and diabetes skyrockets. This chapter's Biocultural Connection describes how a return to a Paleolithic lifestyle can reduce the prevalence of chronic

---

[18]Allen, J. S., & Cheer, S. M. (1996). The non-thrifty genotype. *Current Anthropology, 37*, 831–842.

health problems such as obesity, diabetes, and heart disease, regardless of genotype "thriftiness."

In view of the consequences for human biology of such seemingly benign innovations as dairying or farming, we may wonder about many recent practices—for example, the effects of increased exposure to radiation from use of x-rays, nuclear accidents, production of radioactive wastes, ozone depletion (which increases human exposure to solar radiation), and the like. In addition to exposure to radiation, humans also face increased exposure to other known mutagenic agents, including a wide variety of chemicals.

Hormone-disrupting chemicals are of particular concern because they interfere with the reproductive process. For example, in 1938 a synthetic estrogen known as DES (diethylstilbestrol) was developed and subsequently prescribed for a variety of ailments ranging from acne to prostate cancer. Moreover, DES was routinely added to animal feed. It was not until 1971, however, that researchers realized that DES causes vaginal cancer in young women. Subsequent studies have shown that DES causes problems with the male reproductive system and can produce deformities of the female reproductive tract of individuals exposed to DES in utero. DES mimics the natural hormone, binding with appropriate receptors in and on cells, and thereby turns on biological activity associated with the hormone.[19]

DES is not alone in its effects: At least fifty-one chemicals—many of them in common use—are now known to disrupt hormones, and even this could be the tip of the iceberg. Some of these chemicals mimic hormones in the manner of DES, whereas others interfere with other parts of the endocrine system, such as thyroid and testosterone metabolism. Included are such supposedly benign and inert substances as plastics widely used in laboratories and chemicals added to polystyrene and polyvinyl chloride (PVCs) to make them more stable and less breakable. These plastics are widely used in plumbing, food processing, and food packaging.

Hormone-disrupting chemicals are also found in many detergents and personal care products, contraceptive creams, the giant jugs used to bottle drinking water, and plastic linings in cans. About 85 percent of food cans in the United States are so lined. Similarly, the deleterious health consequences of the release of compounds from plastic wrap and plastic containers during microwaving are now known, though for years using plastic in the microwave was an acceptable cultural practice. Similarly, bisphenol-A (BPA)—a chemical widely used in the manufacturing of water bottles and baby bottles (hard plastics)—has recently been associated with higher rates

of chronic diseases such as heart disease and diabetes and has been shown to disrupt a variety of other reproductive and metabolic processes. Infants and fetuses are at the greatest risk from exposure to BPA.[20]

While there is consensus in the scientific community and governments are starting to take action (the Canadian government declared BPA a toxic compound), removing this compound from the food industry may be easier that ridding the environment of this contaminant. For decades billions of pounds of BPA have been produced each year, and in turn it has been dumped into landfills and into bodies of water. As with the Neolithic revolution and the development of civilization, each invention creates new challenges for humans.

The implications of all these developments are sobering. We know that pathologies result from extremely low levels of exposure to harmful chemicals. Yet, besides those used domestically, the United States exports millions of pounds of these chemicals to the rest of the world.[21] Hormone disruptions may be at least partially responsible for certain trends that have recently concerned scientists. These range from increasingly early onset of puberty in human females to dramatic declines in human sperm counts. With respect to the latter, some sixty-one separate studies confirm that sperm counts have dropped almost 50 percent from 1938 to 1990. Most of these studies were carried out in the United States and Europe, but some from Africa, Asia, and South America show that this is essentially a worldwide phenomenon. If this trend continues, it will have profound results.

One of the difficulties with predicting trends is that serious health consequences of new cultural practices are often not apparent until years or even decades later. By then, of course, these practices are fully embedded in the cultural system, and huge financial interests are at stake. Today, cultural practices, probably as never before, are currently having an impact on human gene pools.

It remains to be seen just what the long-term effects on the human species as a whole will be. Unquestionably, this impact is deleterious to those individuals whose misery and death are the price paid for many of the material benefits of civilization we enjoy today. The fact that poor people and people of color disproportionately bear these burdens demonstrates that racism and classism still exert their negative effects globally.

---

[19]Colburn, T., Dumanoski, D., & Myers, J. P. (1996). Hormonal sabotage. *Natural History, 3,* 45–46.

[20]Lang, I. A., et al. (2008). Association of urinary bisphenol A concentration with medical disorders and laboratory abnormalities in adults. *Journal of the American Medical Association, 300*(11), 1303–1310; vom Saal, F. S., & Myers, J. P. (2008). Bisphenol A and risk of metabolic disorders. *Journal of the American Medical Association, 300*(11), 1353–1355; and Richter, C. A., et al. (2007). In vivo effects of bisphenol A in laboratory rodent studies. *Reproductive Toxicology, 24*(2), 199–224.

[21]Colburn, Dumanoski, & Myers, p. 47.

Chapter Summary

■ Humans are a single, highly variable species inhabiting the entire globe. Though biological processes are responsible for human variation, the biological concept of race or subspecies cannot be applied to human diversity. Contemporary human variation does not exist as discrete racial types. Instead, individual traits appear in continuous gradations from one population to another without sharp breaks. In addition, because of the independent inheritance of individual traits and the genetic openness of human populations, the vast majority of human variation exists within populations rather than among populations. While anthropologists work actively to show that the biological concept of race is false when applied to human diversity, they recognize the significance of race as a sociopolitical category in many countries such as the United States, Haiti, Brazil, and South Africa.

■ Racism can be viewed solely as a social problem. Racial conflicts result from social stereotypes and not scientific facts. Racists of the past and present frequently invoke the notion of biological difference to support unjust social practices.

■ Notwithstanding the impossibility of defining biologically valid human "races," many people have assumed that biobehavioral differences among human races exist. These behavioral characteristics attributed to race can be explained in terms of experience as well as a hierarchical social order affecting the opportunities and challenges faced by different groups of people, rather than biology.

■ In the United States, intelligence or IQ testing was used in the 20th century to try to establish racial differences in intelligence. In addition to problems relating to the cultural and environmental specificity of these tests, comparisons among people divided according to the false biological category of race are unwarranted. Furthermore, at present, it is not possible to separate the inherited components of intelligence from those that are culturally acquired. There is still no consensus on what intelligence really is, but it is generally agreed that intelligence is made up of several different talents and abilities.

■ In many parts of the world, "race" is commonly thought of in terms of skin color. Subject to tremendous variation, skin color is a function of several factors: transparency or thickness of the skin, distribution of blood vessels, and amount of carotene and melanin in the skin. Exposure to sunlight increases the amount of melanin, darkening the skin. Natural selection has favored heavily pigmented skin as protection against the strong solar radiation of equatorial latitudes. In northern latitudes, natural selection has favored relatively depigmented skin, which can utilize relatively weak solar radiation in the production of vitamin D. Cultural factors such as selective mating, as well as geographic location, play a part in skin color distribution globally.

■ Although the human species has come to rely on cultural rather than biological adaptation for survival, human gene pools still change in response to external factors. Many of these changes are brought about by cultural practices; for example, peoples with a dairying tradition possess the ability to digest milk sugars (lactose) into adulthood and a non-thrifty genotype. Populations that are lactose intolerant retain the thrifty genotype. As a consequence, when they are introduced to Western-style diets (characterized by abundance, particularly of foods high in sugar content), the incidence of obesity and diabetes skyrockets.

■ Today hormone-disrupting chemicals, used in plastics and other industries, are of particular importance to human health because they interfere with the reproductive and metabolic process. They are also associated with higher rates of chronic diseases.

■ One of the difficulties with predicting trends is that serious health consequences of new cultural practices are often not apparent until years or even decades later. By then, of course, these practices are fully embedded in the cultural system.

Questions for Reflection

1. As a species humans are extremely diverse, and yet our biological diversity cannot be partitioned into discrete types, subspecies, or races. At the same time, race functions as a social and political category that imposes inequality in some societies. How have cultural beliefs about race affected the interpretation of biological diversity in the past? What are the cultural beliefs about biological diversity in your community today?

2. While we can see and scientifically explain population differences in skin color, why is it invalid to use the biological concept of subspecies or race when referring to humans? Can you imagine another species of animal, plant, or microorganism for which the subspecies concept makes sense?

3. Globally, health statistics are gathered by country. In addition, some countries such as the United States gather health statistics by "race." How are these two endeavors different and similar? Should health statistics be gathered by group?

4. How do you define the concept of intelligence? Do you think scientists will ever be able to discover the genetic basis of intelligence?

5. Cultural practices affect microevolutionary changes in the human species and often have dramatic effects on human health. As the world becomes increasingly interconnected, how should humans regulate these kinds of actions globally?

Key Terms

race	lactase
racism	thrifty genotype
lactose	

© Namit Arora

VISUAL ESSENCE Each culture is distinct, expressing its unique qualities in numerous ways—by the clothes we wear, the way we speak, what we eat, where we find our food, when we rest, and with whom we live. Although culture goes far beyond what meets the eye, it is inscribed everywhere we look. Here we see Rabari camel nomads ranging the Kutch desert in western India. Since regular movement is an essential part of their quest for survival, nearly everything they own is transportable and necessary. Moreover, the material possessions they make, use, and carry are well crafted and beautifully decorated with meaningful designs. The distinctive fabrics, forms, and colors of their objects and apparel mark the social identity of the group. Thus, these travelers are easily recognized as Rabari, even from a distance. Such particular and shared presentation of the self is one of many functions of culture.

The Characteristics of Culture

Students of anthropology are bound to find themselves studying a seemingly endless variety of human societies, each with its own distinctive environment and system of economics, politics, and religion. Yet for all this variety, these societies have one thing in common: Each is a group of people cooperating to ensure their collective survival and well-being. Group living and cooperation are impossible unless individuals know how others are likely to behave in any given situation. Thus, some degree of predictable behavior is required of each person within the society. In humans, it is culture that sets the limits of behavior and guides it along predictable paths that are generally acceptable to those who fall within the culture.

THE CONCEPT OF CULTURE

Anthropologists conceived the modern concept of culture toward the end of the 19th century. The first really clear and comprehensive definition came from the British anthropologist Sir Edward Tylor. Writing in 1871, he defined culture as "that complex whole which includes knowledge, belief, art, law, morals, custom, and any other capabilities and habits acquired by man as a member of society."

Recent definitions tend to distinguish more clearly between actual behavior and the abstract ideas, values, and perceptions of the world that inform that behavior. To put it another way, **culture** goes deeper than observable behavior; it is a society's shared and socially transmitted ideas, values, and perceptions, which are used to make sense of experience and generate behavior and are reflected in that behavior.

culture A society's shared and socially transmitted ideas, values, and perceptions, which are used to make sense of experience and generate behavior and are reflected in that behavior

CHARACTERISTICS OF CULTURE

Through the comparative study of many human cultures, past and present, anthropologists have gained an understanding of the basic characteristics evident in all of them: Every culture is socially learned, shared, based on symbols, integrated, and dynamic. A careful study of these characteristics helps us to see the importance and the function of culture itself.

Culture Is Learned

All culture is socially learned rather than biologically inherited. One learns one's own culture by growing up with it, and the process whereby culture is passed on from one generation to the next is called **enculturation**.

Most animals eat and drink whenever the urge arises. Humans, however, are enculturated to do most of their eating and drinking at certain culturally prescribed times and feel hungry as those times approach. These eating times vary from culture to culture, as does what is eaten, how it is prepared, how it is consumed, and where. To add complexity, food is used to do more than merely satisfy nutritional requirements. When used to celebrate rituals and religious activities, as it often is, food "establishes relationships of give and take, of cooperation, of sharing, of an emotional bond that is universal."[1]

Through enculturation every person learns socially appropriate ways of satisfying the basic biologically determined needs of all humans: food, sleep, shelter, companionship, self-defense, and sexual gratification. It is important to distinguish between the needs themselves, which are not learned, and the learned ways in which they are satisfied—for each culture determines in its own way how these needs will be met. For instance, a French Canadian fisherman's idea of a great dinner and a comfortable way to sleep may vary greatly from that of a Maasai nomadic herder in East Africa.

> **enculturation** The process by which a society's culture is passed on from one generation to the next and individuals become members of their society
> **society** An organized group or groups of interdependent people who generally share a common territory, language, and culture and who act together for collective survival and well-being
> **gender** The cultural elaborations and meanings assigned to the biological differentiation between the sexes

Learned behavior is exhibited in some degree by most, if not all, mammals. Several species may even be said to have elementary culture, in that local populations share patterns of behavior that, as among humans, each generation learns from the one before and that differ from one population to another. For example, research shows a distinctive pattern of behavior among lions of southern Africa's Kalahari Desert—behavior that fostered nonaggressive interaction with the region's indigenous hunters and gatherers and that each generation of lions passed on to the next.[2] Moreover, Kalahari lion culture changed over a thirty-year period in response to new circumstances. That said, it is important to note that not all learned behavior is cultural. For instance, a pigeon may learn tricks, but this behavior is reflexive, the result of conditioning by repeated training, not the product of enculturation.

Beyond our species, examples of cultural behavior are particularly evident among other primates. A chimpanzee, for example, will take a twig, strip it of all leaves, and smooth it down to fashion a tool for extracting termites from their nest. Such tool making, which juveniles learn from their elders, is unquestionably a form of cultural behavior once thought to be exclusively human. In Japan, macaque monkeys have learned the advantages of washing sweet potatoes before eating them and passed the practice on to the next generation. Within any given primate species, the culture of one population often differs from that of others, just as it does among humans. We have discovered both in captivity and in the wild that primates in general and apes in particular "possess a near-human intelligence, generally including the use of sounds in representational ways, a rich awareness of the aims and objectives of others, the ability to engage in tactical deception, and the ability to use symbols in communication with humans and each other."[3]

Growing human awareness and understanding concerning such traits in our primate relatives have spawned numerous movements to extend human rights to apes. The movement reached a milestone in 2008 when Spain's parliament approved a resolution committing the country to the "Declaration on Great Apes," extending some human rights to gorillas, chimpanzees, bonobos, and orangutans.[4]

---

[1]Caroulis, J. (1996). Food for thought. *Pennsylvania Gazette,* 95(3),16.

[2]Thomas, E. M. (1994). *The tribe of the tiger: Cats and their culture* (pp. 109–186). New York: Simon & Schuster.
[3]Reynolds, V. (1994). Primates in the field, primates in the lab. *Anthropology Today, 10*(2), 4.
[4]O'Carroll, E. (2008, June 27). Spain to grant some human rights to apes. *Christian Science Monitor.*

VISUAL COUNTERPOINT

In all human societies adults teach social roles and pass on cultural skills to the next generation. Here a North American mother introduces her child to the computer, and a Maya Indian mother in Guatemala shows her daughter how to handle a machete—useful for a multitude of tasks, from gardening to chopping food to cutting wood for fire and building.

Culture Is Shared

As a shared set of ideas, values, perceptions, and standards of behavior, culture is the common denominator that makes the actions of individuals intelligible to other members of their society. It enables them to predict how others are most likely to behave in a given circumstance, and it tells them how to react accordingly. **Society** may be defined as an organized group or groups of interdependent people who generally share a common territory, language, and culture and who act together for collective survival and well-being. The ways in which these people depend upon one another can be seen in such features as their economic, communication, and defense systems. They are also bound together by a general sense of common identity.

Because culture and society are such closely related concepts, anthropologists study both. Obviously, there can be no culture without a society. Conversely, there are no known human societies that do not exhibit culture. This cannot be said for all other animal species. Ants and bees, for example, instinctively cooperate in a manner that clearly indicates a remarkable degree of social organization, yet this instinctual behavior is not a culture.

Although a culture is shared by members of a society, it is important to realize that all is not uniform. For one thing, no two people share the exact same version of their culture. And there are bound to be other variations. At the very least, there is some difference between the roles of men and women. This stems from the fact that women give birth and men do not and that there are obvious differences between male and female reproductive anatomy and physiology. Every society gives cultural meaning to biological sex differences by explaining them in a particular way and specifying what their significance is in terms of social roles and expected patterns of behavior.

Because each culture does this in its own way, there can be tremendous variation from one society to another. Anthropologists use the term **gender** to refer to the cultural elaborations and meanings assigned to the biological differentiation between the sexes. So, although one's *sex* is biologically determined, one's *gender* is socially constructed within the context of one's particular culture.

Apart from sexual differences directly related to reproduction, any biological basis for contrasting gender roles has largely disappeared in modern industrial and postindustrial societies. (For example, hydraulic lifts used

© Randy Duchaine/Alamy

Newborn girls (under pink blankets) and boys (under blue blankets) in a U.S. hospital nursery. Euramerican culture requires that newborn infants be assigned a gender identity of either male or female. Yet, significant numbers of infants are born each year whose genitalia do not conform to cultural expectations. Because only two genders are recognized, the usual reaction is to make the young bodies conform to cultural requirements through gender assignment surgery that involves constructing male or female genitalia. This is in contrast to many Native American cultures in which more than two genders are recognized.[5]

to move heavy automobile engines in an assembly line eliminate the need for muscular strength in that task.) Nevertheless, all cultures exhibit at least some role differentiation related to biology—some far more so than others.

In addition to cultural variation associated with gender, there is also variation related to age. In any society, children are not expected to behave as adults, and the reverse is equally true. But then, who is a child and who is an adult? Again, although age differences are

---

subculture A distinctive set of ideas, values, and behavior patterns by which a group within a larger society operates, while still sharing common standards with that larger society

ethnic group People who collectively and publicly identify themselves as a distinct group based on cultural features such as common origin, language, customs, and traditional beliefs

ethnicity This term, rooted in the Greek word *ethnikos* ("nation") and related to *ethnos* ("custom"), is the expression of the set of cultural ideas held by an ethnic group

---

[5]For statistics on this, see Blackless, M., et al. (2000). How sexually dimorphic are we? Review and synthesis. *American Journal of Human Biology, 12,* 151–166.

"natural," cultures give their own meaning and timetable to the human life cycle.

Subcultures: Groups Within a Larger Society

Besides age and gender variation, there may be cultural variation among subgroups in societies that share an overarching culture. These may be occupational groups in societies where there is a complex division of labor, or social classes in a stratified society, or ethnic groups in some other societies. When such groups exist within a society, each functioning by its own distinctive standards of ideas, values, and behavior while still sharing some common standards, we speak of **subcultures**. The word *subculture* carries no suggestion of lesser status relative to the word *culture.*

Amish communities comprise one example of a subculture in North America. Specifically, they are an **ethnic group**—people who collectively and publicly identify themselves as a distinct group based on cultural features such as common shared origin, language, customs, and traditional beliefs. The Amish originated in western Europe during the Protestant revolution in the 16th century. Today members of this group number about 100,000 and live mainly in Pennsylvania, Ohio, Illinois, and Indiana in the United States, and in Ontario, Canada.

These rural pacifists base their lives on their traditional Anabaptist beliefs, which hold that only adult baptism is valid and that "true Christians" (as they define them) should not hold government office, bear arms, or use force. They prohibit marriage outside their faith, which calls for obedience to radical Christian teachings, including social separation from what they see as the wider "evil world" and rejection of material wealth as "vainglorious."

Valuing simplicity, hard work, and a high degree of neighborly cooperation, the Amish dress in a distinctive plain garb and even today rely on the horse for transportation as well as agricultural work.[6] Among themselves they usually speak a German dialect known as Pennsylvania Dutch (from *Deutsch,* meaning "German"). They use High German for religious purposes, although children learn English in school. Rejecting what they regard as "worldly" knowledge, Amish communities maintain their own schools to ensure that youngsters learn Amish social values as well as reading, writing, and arithmetic.

In sum, the Amish share the same **ethnicity**. This term, rooted in the Greek word *ethnikos* ("nation") and

---

[6]Hostetler, J., & Huntington, G. (1971). *Children in Amish Society.* New York: Holt, Rinehart & Winston.

The Amish people have held on to their traditional agrarian way of life in the midst of industrialized North American society. Their strong community spirit—reinforced by close social ties between family and neighbors, common language, traditional customs, and shared religious beliefs that set them apart from non-Amish people—is also expressed in a traditional barn raising, a large collective construction project.

related to *ethnos* ("custom"), is the expression of the set of cultural ideas held by an ethnic group.

Amish nonconformity to many standards of mainstream culture has frequently resulted in conflict with state authorities, as well as legal and personal harassment. Pressed to compromise, they have introduced "vocational training" beyond junior high to fulfill state requirements, while managing to retain control of their schools and maintain their way of life.

Confronted with economic challenges that make it impossible for most Amish groups to subsist solely on farming, some work outside their communities. Many more have established cottage industries and actively market homemade goods to tourists and other outsiders. Yet, while their economic separation from mainstream society has declined over the past four decades, their cultural separation has not.[7] They remain a reclusive community, more distrustful than ever of the dominant North American culture surrounding them and mingling as little as possible with non-Amish people.

The Amish are but one example of the way a subculture may develop and be dealt with by the larger culture within which it functions. Different as they are, the Amish actually put into practice many values that other North Americans respect in the abstract: thrift, hard work, independence, a close family life. The degree of tolerance

accorded to them, in contrast to some other ethnic groups, is also due in part to the fact that the Amish are "white" Europeans; they are defined as being of the same "race" as those who comprise dominant mainstream society. Although the concept of race has been shown to have no biological validity when applied to humans, it still persists as a powerful social classification. This can be seen in the common lack of tolerance shown toward American Indians, typically viewed as racially different by members of the dominant society.

Implicit in the discussion thus far is that subcultures may develop in different ways. On the one hand, a subculture such as the Amish in the United States may emerge when a community of immigrants retains some distinctive customs from the ancestral homeland while settling in a new society. On the other hand, American Indian subcultures are formerly independent cultural groups that underwent colonization by European settlers and were forcibly brought under the control of federal governments in the United States and Canada.

Although all American Indian groups have experienced enormous changes due to colonization, many have held on to traditions significantly different from those of the dominant Euramerican culture surrounding them, so that it is sometimes difficult to decide whether they remain as distinct cultures as opposed to subcultures. In this sense, *culture* and *subculture* represent opposite ends of a continuum, with no clear dividing line between them. The Anthropology Applied feature examines the intersection of culture and subculture with an example concerning Apache Indian housing.

---

[7]Kraybill, D. B. (2001). *The riddle of Amish culture* (pp. 1–6, 244, 268–269). Baltimore: Johns Hopkins University Press.

Anthropology Applied   New Houses for Apache Indians

George S. Esber

The United States, in common with other industrialized countries of the world, contains a number of more or less separate subcultures. Those who live by the standards of one particular subculture have their closest relationships with one another, receiving constant reassurance that their perceptions of the world are the only correct ones and coming to take it for granted that the whole culture is as they see it. As a consequence, members of one subculture frequently have trouble understanding the needs and aspirations of other such groups. For this reason anthropologists, with their special understanding of cultural differences, are frequently employed as go-betweens in situations requiring interaction between peoples of differing cultural traditions.

As an example, while I was still a graduate student in anthropology, one of my professors asked me to work with architects and a community of Tonto Apache Indians to research housing needs for a new Apache community. Although the architects knew of the cross-cultural differences in the use of space, they had no idea of how to get relevant information from the Indian

people. For their part, the Apaches had no explicit awareness of their needs, for these were based on unconscious patterns of behavior. For that matter, few people are consciously aware of the space needs for their own social patterns of behavior.

My task was to persuade the architects to hold back on their planning long enough for me to gather, through participant observation and a review of written records, the data from which Apache housing needs could be abstracted. At the same time, I had to overcome Apache anxieties over an outsider coming into their midst to learn about matters as personal as their daily lives as they are acted out, in and around their homes. With these hurdles overcome, I was able to identify and successfully communicate to the architects those features of Apache life having importance for home and community design. At the same time, discussions of my findings with the Apaches enhanced their own awareness of their unique needs.

As a result of my work, the Apaches moved into houses that had been designed with *their* participation,

for *their* specific needs. Among my findings was the realization that the Apaches preferred to ease into social interactions rather than to shake hands and begin interacting immediately, as is more typical of the Anglo pattern. Apache etiquette requires that people be in full view of one another so each can assess the behavior of others from a distance prior to engaging in social interaction with them. This requires a large, open living space. At the same time, hosts feel compelled to offer food to guests as a prelude to further social interaction. Thus, cooking and dining areas cannot be separated from living space. Nor is standard middle-class Anglo kitchen equipment suitable, since the need for handling large quantities among extended families requires large pots and pans, which in turn calls for extra-large sinks and cupboards. Built with such ideas in mind, the new houses accommodated long-standing native traditions.

(By George S. Esber. Adapted from Designing Apache houses with Apaches. (1987). In R. M. Wulff & S. J. Fiske (Eds.), Anthropological praxis: Translating knowledge into action. Boulder, CO: Westview Press. Updated by Esber 2007)

Pluralism

Our discussion raises the issue of the multi-ethnic or **pluralistic society** in which two or more ethnic groups or nationalities are politically organized into one territorial state but maintain their cultural differences. Pluralistic societies could not have existed before the first politically centralized states arose a mere 5,000 years ago. With the rise of the state, it became possible to bring about the political unification of two or more formerly independent societies, each with its own culture, thereby creating a more complex order that transcends the theoretical one culture–one society linkage.

pluralistic society A society in which two or more ethnic groups or nationalities are politically organized into one territorial state but maintain their cultural differences
symbol A sign, sound, emblem, or other thing that is arbitrarily linked to something else and represents it in a meaningful way

Pluralistic societies, which are common in the world today (Figure 8.1), all face the same challenge: They are comprised of groups that, by virtue of their high degree of cultural variation, are essentially operating by different sets of rules. Since social living requires predictable behavior, it may be difficult for the members of any one subgroup to accurately interpret and follow the different standards by which the others operate.

Unfortunately, the difficulty members of one subgroup within a pluralistic society may have making sense of the standards by which members of other groups operate can go far beyond mere misunderstanding. It can intensify to the point of anger and violence. There are many examples of troubled pluralistic societies in the world today, including Bolivia, Iraq, and Kenya, where central governments face major challenges in maintaining peace and lawful order.

Figure 8.1

Shown here are some of the ethnic groups of the Russian Federation, the dominant and by far the largest part of the former Union of Soviet Socialist Republics.

Culture Is Based on Symbols

Much of human behavior involves **symbols**—signs, sounds, emblems, and other things that are linked to something else and represent them in a meaningful way. Because often there is no inherent or necessary relationship between a thing and its representation, symbols are arbitrary, acquiring specific meanings when people agree on usage in their communications.

In fact, symbols—ranging from national flags to wedding rings to money—enter into every aspect of culture, from social life and religion to politics and economics. We are all familiar with the fervor and devotion that a religious symbol can elicit from a believer. An Islamic crescent, Christian cross, or a Jewish Star of David—as well as the sun among the Inca, a cow among the Hindu, a white buffalo calf among Plains Indians, or any other object of worship—may bring to mind years of struggle and persecution or may stand for a whole philosophy or creed.

The most important symbolic aspect of culture is language—using words to represent objects and ideas. Through language humans are able to transmit culture from one generation to another. In particular, language makes it possible to learn from cumulative, shared experience. Without it, one could not inform others about events, emotions, and other experiences to which they were not a party. Language is so important that an entire chapter in this book is devoted to the subject.

Culture Is Integrated

Culture, as we have seen, includes what people do for a living, the tools they use, the ways they work together, how they transform their environments and construct their dwellings, what they eat and drink, how they worship, what they believe is right or wrong, what gifts they exchange when, who they marry, and how they raise their children, bury their dead, and so on. Because these and all other aspects of a culture must be reasonably well integrated in order to function properly, anthropologists seldom focus on an individual feature in isolation. Instead, they view each in terms of its larger context and carefully examine its connections to related cultural features.

For purposes of comparison and analysis, anthropologists customarily imagine a culture as a well-structured system made up of distinctive parts that function together as an organized whole. While they may sharply distinguish each part as a clearly defined unit with its own characteristic features and special place within the larger system, anthropologists recognize that reality is a complex, intertwined entity, and divisions between cultural units are often blurry.

Broadly speaking, a society's cultural features fall within three categories: social structure, infrastructure, and superstructure. **Social structure** concerns rule-governed relationships—with all their rights and obligations—that hold members of a society together. Households, families, associations, and power relations, including politics, are all part of social structure. It establishes group cohesion and enables people to consistently satisfy their basic needs, including food and shelter for themselves and their dependents, by means of work. So, there is a direct relationship between a group's social structure and its economic foundation, which includes subsistence practices and the tools and other material equipment used to make a living.

Because subsistence practices involve tapping into available resources to satisfy a society's basic needs, this aspect of culture is known as **infrastructure**. Supported by this economic foundation, a society is also held together by a shared sense of identity and worldview. This collective body of ideas, beliefs, and values by which a group of people makes sense of the world—its shape, challenges, and opportunities—and their place in it is known as ideology or **superstructure**. Including religion and national ideology, it structures the overarching ideas that people in a society have about themselves and everything else that exists around them—and it gives meaning and direction to their lives. Influencing and reinforcing one another, and continually adapting to changing demographic and environmental factors, these three interdependent structures together form part of a cultural system (Figure 8.2).

A culture cannot endure if it does not deal effectively with basic challenges. It must include strategies for the production and distribution of goods and services considered necessary for life. To ensure the biological continuity of its members, it must also provide a social

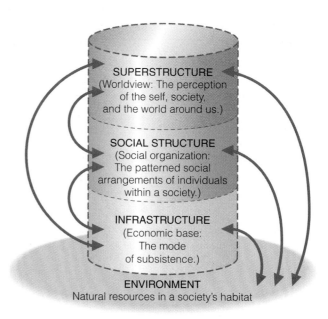

Figure 8.2 **The Barrel Model of Culture**
Every culture is an integrated and dynamic system of adaptation that responds to a combination of internal factors (economic, social, ideological) and external factors (environmental, climatic). Within a cultural system, there are functional relationships among the economic base (infrastructure), the social organization (social structure), and the ideology (superstructure). A change in one leads to a change in the others.

structure for reproduction and mutual support. It must offer ways to pass on knowledge and enculturate new members so they can assist one another and contribute to their community as well-functioning adults. It must facilitate social interaction and provide ways to avoid or resolve conflicts within their group as well as with outsiders.

Since a culture must support all aspects of life, as indicated in our barrel model, it must also meet the psychological and emotional needs of its members. This last function is met, in part, simply by the measure of predictability that each culture, as a shared design for thought and action, brings to everyday life. Of course it involves much more than that, including a worldview that helps individuals understand their place in the world and cope with upheavals. For example, every culture provides its members with certain customary ideas and rituals that enable them to think creatively about the meaning of life and death. Many cultures even make it possible for people to imagine an afterworld that no one has actually been to and returned from to tell about. Invited to suspend disbelief and engage in such imaginings, people find the means to deal with the grief of losing a loved one.

In addition to meeting all the challenges noted above, a culture must be able to change if it is to remain adaptive under shifting conditions.

social structure The rule-governed relationships—with all their rights and obligations—that hold members of a society together. This includes households, families, associations, and power relations, including politics

infrastructure The economic foundation of a society, including its subsistence practices and the tools and other material equipment used to make a living

superstructure A society's shared sense of identity and worldview. The collective body of ideas, beliefs, and values by which a group of people makes sense of the world—its shape, challenges, and opportunities—and their place in it. This includes religion and national ideology

Kapauku Culture as Integrated System

The integration of economic, social, and ideological aspects of a culture can be illustrated by the Kapauku Papuans, a mountain people of Western New Guinea, studied in 1955 by the North American anthropologist Leopold Pospisil.[8] The Kapauku economy relies on plant cultivation, along with pig breeding, hunting, and fishing. Although plant cultivation provides most of the people's food, it is through pig breeding that men achieve political power and positions of legal authority.

Among the Kapauku, pig breeding is a complex business. Raising a lot of pigs requires a lot of food to feed them. The primary fodder is sweet potatoes, grown in garden plots. According to Kapauku culture, certain garden activities and taking care of pigs are tasks that fall exclusively in the domain of women's work. So, to raise many pigs, a man needs numerous women in the household. Thus, in Kapauku society, multiple wives are not only permitted, they are highly desired. For each wife, however, a man must pay a bride price, and this can be expensive. Furthermore, wives have to be compensated for their care of the pigs. Put simply, it takes pigs, by which wealth is measured, to get wives, without whom pigs cannot be raised in the first place. Needless to say, this requires considerable entrepreneurship. It is this ability that produces leaders in Kapauku society.

The interrelatedness of the various parts of Kapauku culture is even more complicated. For example, one condition that encourages men to marry several women is a surplus of adult females, sometimes caused by loss of males through warfare. Among the Kapauku, recurring warfare has long been viewed as a necessary evil. By the rules of Kapauku warfare, men may be killed but women may not. This system works to promote the sort of imbalanced sex ratio that fosters the practice of having more than one wife. Having multiple wives tends to work best if all of them come to live in their husband's village, and so it is among the Kapauku. With this

arrangement, the men of a village are typically "blood" relatives of one another, which enhances their ability to cooperate in warfare. Considering all of this, it makes sense that Kapauku typically trace descent (ancestry) through men.

Descent reckoning through men, coupled with near-constant warfare, tends to promote male dominance. So it is not surprising to find that positions of leadership in Kapauku society are held exclusively by men, who appropriate the products of women's labor in order to play their political "games." Such male dominance is by no means characteristic of all human societies. Rather, as in the Kapauku case, it arises only under particular sets of circumstances that, if changed, will alter the way in which men and women relate to each other.

Culture Is Dynamic

Cultures are dynamic systems that respond to motions and actions within and around them. When one element within the system shifts or changes, the entire system strives to adjust, just as it does when an outside force applies pressure. To function adequately, a culture must be flexible enough to allow such adjustments in the face of unstable or changing circumstances.

All cultures are, of necessity, dynamic, but some are far less so than others. When a culture is too rigid or static and fails to provide its members with the means required for long-term survival under changing conditions, it is not likely to endure. On the other hand, some cultures are so fluid and open to change that they may lose their distinctive character. The Amish mentioned earlier in this chapter typically resist change as much as possible but are constantly making balanced decisions to adjust when absolutely necessary. North Americans in general, however, have created a culture in which change has become a positive ideal.

In sum, for a culture to function properly, its various parts must be consistent with one another. But consistency is not the same as harmony. In fact, there is often friction and potential for conflict within every culture—among individuals, factions, and competing institutions. Even on the most basic level of a society, individuals rarely experience the enculturation process in precisely the same way, nor do they perceive their reality in precisely identical fashion. Moreover, conditions may change, brought on by inside or outside forces.

A society will function reasonably well as long as its culture is capable of handling the daily strains and tensions. However, when a culture no longer provides adequate solutions or when its component parts are no longer consistent, a situation of cultural crisis ensues. Notably, the cultural system in stratified societies generally favors the ruling elite, while the groups scraping by on the

---

[8]Pospisil, L. (1963). *The Kapauku Papuans of west New Guinea.* New York: Holt, Rinehart & Winston.

Biocultural Connection

Pig Lovers and Pig Haters

Marvin Harris

In the Old Testament of the Bible, the Israelite's God (Yahweh) denounced the pig as an unclean beast that pollutes if tasted or touched. Later, Allah conveyed the same basic message to his prophet Muhammad. Among millions of Jews and Muslims today, the pig remains an abomination, even though it can convert grains and tubers into high-grade fats and protein more efficiently than any other animal.

What prompted condemnation of an animal whose meat is relished by the greater part of humanity? For centuries, the most popular explanation was that the pig wallows in its own urine and eats excrement. But linking this to religious abhorrence leads to inconsistencies. Cows kept in a confined space also splash about in their own urine and feces.

These inconsistencies were recognized in the 12th century by Maimonides, a widely respected Jewish philosopher and physician in Egypt, who said God condemned swine as a public health measure because pork had "a bad and damaging effect upon the body." The mid-1800s discovery that eating undercooked pork caused trichinosis appeared to verify Maimonides's reasoning. Reform-minded Jews then renounced the taboo, convinced that if well-cooked pork did not endanger public health, eating it would not offend God.

Scholars have suggested this taboo stemmed from the idea that the animal was once considered divine—but this explanation falls short since sheep, goats, and cows were also once worshiped in the Middle East, and their meat is enjoyed by all religious groups in the region.

I think the real explanation for this religious condemnation lies in the fact that pig farming threatened the integrity of the basic cultural and natural ecosystems of the Middle East. Until their conquest of the Jordan Valley in Palestine over 3,000 years ago, the Israelites were nomadic herders, living

bottom benefit the least. The difference may be measured in terms of material wealth as well as physical health.

CULTURE AND ADAPTATION

In the course of their evolution, humans, like all animals, have continually faced the challenge of adapting to their environment. As discussed in Chapter 2, the term *adaptation* refers to a gradual process by which organisms adjust to the conditions of the locality in which they live. Organisms adapt biologically as the frequency of advantageous alleles and their corresponding phenotypes increase in a population through a process known as *natural selection*. For example, body hair coupled with certain other physiological traits protects mammals from extremes of temperature; specialized teeth help them to procure the kinds of food they need; and so on. Short-term physiological responses to the environment—along with responses that become incorporated into an organism through interaction with the environment during growth and development—are other kinds of biological adaptations.

Humans, however, have increasingly come to depend on **cultural adaptation**, a complex of ideas, technologies, and activities that allows them to survive

> **cultural adaptation** A complex of ideas, activities, and technologies that enables people to survive and even thrive in their environment

and even thrive in their environment. Biology has not provided them with built-in fur coats to protect them in cold climates, but it has given them the ability to make their own coats, build fires, and construct shelters to shield themselves against the cold. They may not be able to run as fast as a cheetah, but they are able to invent and build vehicles that can carry them faster and further than any other creature. Through culture and its many constructions, the human species has secured not just its survival but its expansion as well—at great cost to other species and, increasingly, to the planet at large. By manipulating environments through cultural means, people have been able to move into a vast range of environments, from the icy Arctic to the searing Sahara Desert. They have even set foot on the moon.

This is not to say that everything that humans do they do *because* it is adaptive to a particular environment. For one thing, people do not just react to an environment as given; rather, they react to it as they perceive it, and different groups of people may perceive the same environment in radically different ways. They also react to things other than the environment: their own biological natures; their beliefs and attitudes; and the short- and long-term consequences of their behavior for themselves and other life forms that share their habitats. (See the Biocultural Connection feature for a particular cultural adaptation.) Although people maintain cultures to deal with problems, some cultural practices have proved to be maladaptive and have actually created new problems—such as toxic water

almost entirely from sheep, goats, and cattle. Like all pastoralists, they maintained close relationships with sedentary farmers who held the oases and the great rivers. With this mixed farming and pastoral complex, the pork prohibition constituted a sound ecological strategy. The pastoralists could not raise pigs in their arid habitats, and among the semi-sedentary farming populations pigs were more of a threat than an asset.

The basic reason for this is that the world zones of pastoral nomadism correspond to unforested plains and hills that are too arid for rainfall agriculture and that cannot easily be irrigated. The domestic animals best adapted to these zones are ruminants (including cattle, sheep, and goats), which can digest grass, leaves, and other cellulose foods more effectively than other mammals.

The pig, however, is primarily a creature of forests and shaded riverbanks. Although it is omnivorous, its best weight gain is from foods low in cellulose (nuts, fruits, tubers, and especially grains), making it a direct competitor of man. It cannot subsist on grass alone and is ill-adapted to the hot, dry climate of the grasslands, mountains, and deserts in the Middle East.

Among the ancient mixed farming and pastoralist communities of the Middle East, domestic animals were valued primarily as sources of milk, cheese, hides, dung, fiber, and traction for plowing. Goats, sheep, and cattle provided all of this, plus an occasional supplement of lean meat. From the beginning, therefore, pork must have been a luxury food, esteemed for its succulent, tender, and fatty qualities.

Between 4,000 and 9,000 years ago, the human population in the Middle East increased sixty-fold. Extensive deforestation accompanied this rise, largely due to damage caused by sheep and goat herds. Shade and water, the natural conditions appropriate for raising pigs, became ever more scarce, and pork became even more of a luxury.

The Middle East is the wrong place to raise pigs, but pork remains a luscious treat. People find it difficult to resist such temptations on their own. Hence Yahweh and Allah were heard to say that swine were unclean—unfit to eat or touch. In short, it was ecologically maladaptive to try to raise pigs in substantial numbers, and small-scale production would only increase the temptation. Better then, to prohibit the consumption of pork entirely.

(Excerpted from Marvin Harris (1989). Cows, pigs, wars, and witches: The riddles of culture *(pp. 35–60). New York: Vintage Books/Random House)*

and air caused by certain industrial practices, or North America's obesity epidemic brought on by the culture of cars, fast food, television, and personal computers.

A further complication is the relativity of any given adaptation: What is adaptive in one context may be seriously maladaptive in another. For example, the sanitation practices of food-foraging peoples—their toilet habits and methods of garbage disposal—are appropriate to contexts of low population densities and some degree of residential mobility. But these same practices become serious health hazards in the context of large, fully sedentary populations. Similarly, behavior that is adaptive in the short run may be maladaptive over the long run. Thus, the development of irrigation in ancient Mesopotamia (southern Iraq) made it possible over the short run to increase food production, but over time it favored the gradual accumulation of salts in the soils. This, in turn, contributed to the collapse of civilization there about 4,000 years ago. For a culture to be successful, it must produce collective human behavior that is generally adaptive to the natural environment.

CULTURE AND CHANGE

Cultures have always changed over time, although rarely as rapidly or as massively as many are doing today. Change takes place in response to such events as population growth, technological innovation, environmental crisis, the intrusion of outsiders, or modification of behavior and values within the culture. In our current age of globalization, we are witnessing a much accelerated pace of widespread and radical change, discussed in detail in the last chapter of this book.

While cultures must have some flexibility to remain adaptive, culture change can also bring unexpected and often disastrous results. For example, consider the relationship between culture and the droughts that periodically afflict so many people living in African countries just south of the Sahara Desert. The lives of some 14 million pastoral nomadic people native to this region are centered on cattle and other livestock, herded from place to place as required for pasturage and water. For thousands of years these people have been able to go about their business, efficiently utilizing vast areas of arid lands in ways that allowed them to survive severe droughts many times in the past. Unfortunately, their way of life is frowned upon by the central governments of modern states in the region because it involves moving back and forth across relatively new international boundaries, making the nomads difficult to track for purposes of taxation and other governmental controls.

Seeing nomads as a challenge to their authority, these governments have gone all out to stop them from ranging through their traditional grazing territories and to convert them into sedentary villagers. Imposed loss of mobility has resulted in overgrazing. The problem has been compounded by government efforts to press pastoralists into a market economy by

Pastoralists herd their grazing animals, moving slowly across vast territories in search of food. As nomadic peoples who depend on their mobility for survival, they may cross unmarked international borders. Difficult to control by central governments trying to impose taxes on them, these nomads face major obstacles in pursuing their customary way of life. No longer able to range through their traditional grazing territories due to government restrictions on land use, these African herders and their cattle are hit all the harder when droughts occur. So it is in this photo taken in Kenya, Africa where the combination of limited grazing lands and severe drought resulted in the death of many animals and turned others into "bones on hoofs."

© Tony Karumba/AFP/Getty Images

giving them incentives to raise many more animals than required for their own needs in order to have a surplus to sell and thus add to the tax base. This has led to overgrazing, erosion, and a lack of reserve pasture during recurring droughts. Thus, droughts are far more disastrous than previously. When one occurs, it jeopardizes the very existence of the nomads' traditional way of life.

CULTURE, SOCIETY, AND THE INDIVIDUAL

Ultimately, a society is no more than a union of individuals, all of whom have their own special needs and interests. To survive, it must succeed in balancing the immediate self-interest of its individual members against the needs and demands of the collective well-being of society as a whole. To accomplish this, a society offers rewards for adherence to its culturally prescribed standards. In most cases, these rewards assume the form of social approval. For example, in contemporary North American society a person who holds a good job, takes care of family, pays taxes, and does volunteer work in the neighborhood may be spoken of as a "model citizen" in the community. To ensure the survival of the group, each person must learn to postpone certain

ethnocentrism The belief that the ways of one's own culture are the only proper ones
cultural relativism The idea that one must suspend judgment of other people's practices in order to understand them in their own cultural terms

immediate personal satisfactions. Yet the needs of the individual cannot be suppressed too far or the result may be a degree of emotional stress and growing resentment that results in protest, disruption, and sometimes even violence.

Consider, for example, the matter of sexual expression, which, like anything that people do, is shaped by culture. Sexuality is important in every society, for it helps to strengthen cooperative bonds among members of society, ensuring the perpetuation of society itself. Yet sex can be disruptive to social living. If the issue of who has sexual access to whom is not clearly spelled out, competition for sexual privileges can destroy the cooperative bonds on which human survival depends. Uncontrolled sexual activity, too, can result in reproductive rates that cause a society's population to outstrip its resources. Hence, as it shapes sexual behavior, every culture must balance the needs of society against the individual's sexual needs and desires so that frustration does not build up to the point of being disruptive in itself.

Cultures vary widely in the way they go about this. On one end of the spectrum, societies such as the Amish in North America or the Muslim Brotherhood in Egypt have taken an extremely restrictive approach, specifying no sex outside of marriage. On the other end are such societies as the Norwegians in northern Europe, who generally accept premarital sex and often choose to have children outside marriage, or even more extreme, the Canela Indians in Brazil, whose social codes guarantee that, sooner or later, everyone in a given village has had sex with just about everyone of the opposite sex. Yet, even as permissive as the latter situation may sound, there are nonetheless strict rules as to how the system operates.[9] Not just in sexual matters, but in all life issues, cultures must strike a balance between the needs and desires of individuals and those of society as a whole.

ETHNOCENTRISM AND THE EVALUATION OF CULTURE

There are numerous highly diverse cultural solutions to the challenges of human existence. The question often arises, Which is best? Anthropologists have been intrigued to find that all cultures tend to see themselves as the best of all possible worlds. This is reflected in the way individual societies refer to themselves: Typically, a society's traditional name for itself translates roughly into "true human beings." In contrast, their names for outsiders commonly translate into various versions of "subhumans," including "monkeys," "dogs," "weird-looking people," "funny talkers," and so forth. Any adequately functioning culture regards its own ways in positive terms, and often as the only proper ones, a view known as **ethnocentrism**.

Anthropologists have been actively engaged in the fight against ethnocentrism ever since they started to study and actually live among traditional peoples with radically different cultures—thus learning by personal experience that these "others" were no less human than anyone else. Resisting the common urge to rank cultures, anthropologists have instead aimed to understand individual cultures and the general concept of culture. To do so, they have examined each culture on its own terms, aiming to discern whether or not the culture satisfies the needs and expectations of the people themselves. If a people practiced human sacrifice or capital punishment, for example, anthropologists asked about the circumstances that made the taking of human life acceptable according to that particular group's values.

The idea that one must suspend judgment on other peoples' practices in order to understand them in their own cultural terms is called **cultural relativism**. Only through such an approach can one gain a meaningful view of the values and beliefs that underlie the behaviors and institutions of other peoples and societies as well as clearer insights into the underlying beliefs and practices of one's own society.

Cultural relativism is essential as a research tool. However, employing it as a tool does not mean suspending judgment forever, nor does it require that anthropologists defend a people's right to engage in any cultural practice, no matter how destructive. All that is necessary is that we avoid *premature* judgments until we

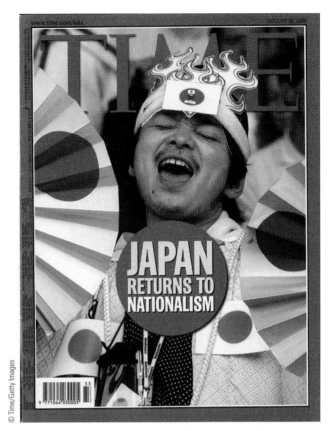

Japanese traditionally referred to their own people as a "divine nation," governed by the *mikado* (emperor) who was revered as a god. Today, a revival of Japanese nationalism is expressed by the restoration of controversial symbols in public places. These include singing (at public events and in some schools) the *kimigayo*, a hymn of praise to the divine emperor that served as Imperial Japan's national anthem. And the *hinomaru* (the rising sun flag), once raised by Japanese soldiers in conquered territories, increasingly is seen flying in public places and private homes. Historically associated with militant Japanese imperialism, these nationalist symbols reflect a tradition of ethnocentrism not unlike those of other nations claiming a divine association, as in "One Nation under God," "God's Own Country," "God's Chosen People," and "God's Promised Land."

have a full understanding of the culture in which we are interested. Then, and only then, may anthropologists adopt a critical stance and in an informed way consider the advantages and disadvantages particular beliefs and behaviors have for a society and its members. As the late British anthropologist David Maybury-Lewis emphasized, "one does not avoid making judgments, but rather postpones them in order to make informed judgments later."[10]

Forty years ago U.S. anthropologist Walter Goldschmidt devised a still-useful formula to help colleagues avoid the pitfalls of ethnocentrism without ending up in the "anything goes" position of cultural relativism

---

[9]Crocker, W. A., & Crocker, J. (1994). *The Canela, bonding through kinship, ritual and sex* (pp. 143–171). Fort Worth: Harcourt Brace.

[10]Maybury-Lewis, D. H. P. (1993). A special sort of pleading. In W. A. Haviland & R. J. Gordon (Eds.), *Talking about people* (2nd ed., p. 17). Mountain View, CA: Mayfield.

pushed to absurdity.[11] In his view the important question to ask is, How well does a given culture satisfy the physical and psychological needs of those whose behavior it guides?

Specific indicators are to be found in the nutritional status and general physical and mental health of its population; the incidence of violence, crime, and delinquency; the demographic structure, stability, and tranquility of domestic life; and the group's relationship to its resource base. The culture of a people who experience high rates of malnutrition (including obesity), violence, crime, delinquency, suicide, emotional disorders and despair, and environmental degradation may be said to be operating less well than that of another people who exhibit few such problems. In a well-working culture, people "can be proud, jealous, and pugnacious, and live a very satisfactory life without feeling '*angst*,' '*alienation*,' '*anomie*,' '*depression*,' or any of the other pervasive ills of our own inhuman and civilized way of living."[12] When traditional ways of coping no longer seem to work, and people feel helpless to shape their own lives in their own societies, symptoms of cultural breakdown become prominent.

In short, a culture is essentially a maintenance system to ensure the continued well-being of a group of people. Therefore, it may be deemed successful as long as it secures the survival of a society in a way that its members find to be reasonably fulfilling. What complicates matters is that any society is made up of groups with different interests, raising the possibility that some people's interests may be served better than those of others. Therefore, a culture that is quite fulfilling for one group within a society may be less so for another.

For this reason, anthropologists must always ask, *Whose* needs and *whose* survival are best served by the culture in question? Only by looking at the overall situation can a reasonably objective judgment be made as to how well a culture is working. But anthropologists today recognize that few peoples still exist in total or near-total isolation and understand that globalization affects the dynamics of culture change in almost every

Image credit (vertical): © Clay McLachlan/Reuters/Corbis

A high rate of crime and delinquency is one sign that a culture is not adequately satisfying a people's needs and expectations. This San Quentin Prison cell block can be seen as such evidence. It is sobering to note that 25 percent of all imprisoned people in the world are incarcerated in the United States. In the past ten years the country's jail and prison population jumped by more than 600,000—from 1.6 to 2.2 million. Ironically, people in the United States think of their country as "the land of the free," yet it has the highest incarceration rate in the world (724 per 100,000 inhabitants).

corner of our global village. Accordingly, as will be detailed in many of the following chapters, we must widen our scope and develop a truly worldwide perspective that enables us to appreciate cultures as increasingly open and interactive (and sometimes reactive) systems.

Chapter Summary

■ Culture, to the anthropologist, is a society's shared and socially transmitted ideas, values, and perceptions, which are used to make sense of experience and generate behavior and are reflected in that behavior. Culture cannot exist without society: an organized group or groups of interdependent people who generally share a common territory, language, and culture and who act together for collective survival and well-being. Culture, which is learned, is distinct from shared instinctive behavior.

---

[11]Bodley, J. H. (1990). *Victims of progress* (3rd ed., p. 138). Mountain View, CA: Mayfield.

[12]Fox, R. (1968). *Encounter with anthropology* (p. 290). New York: Dell.

■ Although culture involves a group's shared values, ideas, and behavior, everything within a culture is not uniform. For instance, in all cultures there is some difference between the roles of men and women. Anthropologists use the term *gender* to refer to the cultural elaborations and meanings assigned to the biological differences between sexes. Age variation is also universal, and in some cultures there are other subcultural variations as well. A subculture (for example, the Amish) shares certain overarching assumptions of the larger culture, while observing its own set of distinct rules. Pluralistic societies are those in which two or more ethnic groups or nationalities are politically organized into one territorial state but maintain their cultural differences.

■ All cultures have the following characteristics: In addition to being shared, they are learned, with individual members learning the accepted norms of social behavior through the process of enculturation; culture is based on symbols—transmitted through the communication of ideas, emotions, and desires expressed in symbols, especially language; culture is integrated, so that all aspects function as an integrated whole (albeit not without tension, friction, and even conflict); finally, all cultures are dynamic and changeable.

■ As illustrated in the barrel model, all aspects of a culture fall into one of three broad, interrelated categories: infrastructure (the subsistence practices or economic system), social structure (the rule-governed relationships), and superstructure (the ideology or worldview).

■ Cultural adaptation has enabled humans to survive and expand into a wide variety of environments. Sometimes what is adaptive in one set of circumstances or over the short run is maladaptive over time. To endure, a culture must satisfy the basic biological and psychological needs of its members, provide some structure for reproduction to ensure their continuity, and maintain order among its members as well as between its members and outsiders.

■ Culture change takes place in response to such events as population growth, technological innovation, environmental crisis, intrusion of outsiders, or modification of values and behavior within the culture. Although cultures must change to adapt to new circumstances, sometimes the unforeseen consequences of change are disastrous for a society. As well, a society must strike a balance between the self-interest of individuals and the needs of the group.

■ Ethnocentrism is the belief that one's own culture is superior to all others. To avoid making ethnocentric judgments, anthropologists adopt the approach of cultural relativism, which requires suspending judgment in order to understand each culture in its own terms.

■ The least biased measure of a culture's success may be based on answering this question: How well does a particular culture satisfy the physical and psychological needs of those whose behavior it guides? These indicators provide answers: the nutritional status and general physical and mental health of the population, the incidence of violence, the stability of domestic life, and the group's relationship to its resource base.

Questions for Reflection

1. An often overlooked first step for developing an understanding of another culture is having knowledge and respect for one's own cultural traditions. Do you know the origins of the worldview commonly held by most people in your community? How do you think it developed over time and what makes it so accepted or popular in your group today?

2. Although all cultures across the world display some degree of ethnocentrism, some are more ethnocentric than others. In what ways is your own society ethnocentric? Considering today's globalization (as described in Chapter 1), do you think ethnocentrism poses more of a problem than in the past?

3. Like everyone else in the world, you are meeting daily challenges of survival through your culture. And since you are made "fully human" by your own culture, how do you express your individual identity in your own community? What do your hairstyle, clothes, shoes, jewelry, and so on communicate about who you are?

4. Many large modern societies are pluralistic. Are you familiar with any subcultures in your own society? Could you make friends with or even marry someone from another subculture? What kind of problems would you be likely to encounter?

5. The barrel model offers you a simple framework to imagine what a culture looks like from an analytical point of view. How would you apply that model to your own community?

Key Terms

culture	symbol
enculturation	social structure
society	infrastructure
gender	superstructure
subculture	cultural adaptation
ethnic group	ethnocentrism
ethnicity	cultural relativism
pluralistic society	

VISUAL ESSENCE

As social creatures dependent upon one another for survival, humans creatively design multiple ways to communicate meaningfully, using a variety of distinctive gestures, sounds, touches, and body postures. Our most sophisticated means of sharing large amounts of complex information is through language—a foundation stone of every human culture. Today, as shown in this image of indigenous New Guineans, modern technology enables people to communicate instantly across oceans, deserts, and mountains. But to make sense of messages, they must share a language, no matter how sophisticated their electronic gadgets.

Language and Communication

9

The human ability to communicate through language rests squarely on our biological makeup. We are "programmed" for language, be it through sounds or gestures. (Sign languages, such as the American Sign Language—ASL—used by the hearing impaired, are fully developed languages in their own right.) Beyond the cries of babies, which are not learned but which do communicate, humans must learn their language. So it is that any normal child from anywhere in the world readily learns the language of his or her culture.

Language is a system of communication using sounds and/or gestures that are put together according to certain rules, resulting in meanings that are intelligible to all who share that language. These sounds and gestures fall into the category of a *symbol* (defined as a sign, sound, gesture, or other thing that is arbitrarily linked to something else and represents it in a meaningful way). For example, the word *crying* is a symbol, a combination of sounds to which we assign the meaning of a particular action and which we can use to communicate that meaning, whether or not anyone around us is actually crying.

Signals, unlike culturally learned symbols, are instinctive sounds and gestures that have a natural or self-evident meaning. Screams, sighs, or coughs, for example, are signals that convey some kind of emotional or physical state. Today's language experts differ on how much credit to give to animals, such as various dolphin and ape species, for the ability to use symbols as well as signals. But it has become evident

> **language** A system of communication using sounds or gestures that are put together in meaningful ways according to a set of rules
> **signals** Instinctive sounds or gestures that have a natural or self-evident meaning

that these animals and many others communicate in remarkable ways.[1]

What are the implications for our understanding of the nature and evolution of language? No final answer will be evident until we gain more knowledge about the various systems of animal communication. Meanwhile, even as debate continues over how human and animal communication relate to each other, we cannot dismiss communication among nonhuman species as a set of simple instinctive reflexes or fixed action patterns.[2]

A remarkable example of the many scientific efforts under way on this subject is the story of an orangutan named Chantek, featured in the following Original Study. Among other things, it illustrates the creative process of language development and the capacity of a nonhuman primate to recognize symbols.

Original Study

Language and the Intellectual Abilities of Orangutans

H. Lyn White Miles

In 1978, after researchers began to use American Sign Language for the deaf to communicate with chimpanzees and gorillas, I began the first long-term study of the language ability of an orangutan named Chantek. There was criticism that symbol-using apes might just be imitating their human caregivers, but there is now growing agreement that orangutans, gorillas, and both chimpanzee species can develop language skills at the level of a 2- to 3-year-old human child.

The goal of Project Chantek was to investigate the mind of an orangutan through a developmental study of his cognitive and linguistic skills. It was a great ethical and emotional responsibility to engage an orangutan in what anthropologists call "enculturation," since I would not only be teaching a form of communication, I would be teaching aspects of the culture upon which that language was based. . . .

A small group of caregivers at the University of Tennessee, Chattanooga, began raising Chantek when he was 9 months old. They communicated with him by using gestural signs based on the American Sign Language for the deaf. After a month, Chantek produced his own first sign and eventually learned to use approximately 150 different signs, forming a vocabulary similar to that

of a very young child. Chantek learned names for people (LYN, JOHN), places (YARD, BROCK-HALL), things to eat (YOGURT, CHOCOLATE), actions (WORK, HUG), objects (SCREWDRIVER, MONEY), animals (DOG, APE), colors (RED, BLACK), pronouns (YOU, ME), location (UP, POINT), attributes (GOOD, HURT), and emphasis (MORE, TIME-TO-DO).

We found that Chantek's signing was spontaneous and nonrepetitious. He did not merely imitate his caregivers, but

rather he actively used signs to initiate communications and meet his needs. Almost immediately, he began using signs in combinations and modulated their meanings with slight changes in how he articulated and arranged his signs. He commented "COKE DRINK" after drinking his coke, "PULL BEARD" while pulling a caregiver's hair through a fence, and "TIME HUG" while locked in his cage as his caregiver looked at her watch. But, beyond using signs in this

© H. Lyn Miles, PhD, Chantek Foundation

Chantek beginning the sign for "tomato."

[1]Among many references on this, see Bekoff, M., et al. (Eds.). (2002). *The cognitive animal: Empirical and theoretical perspectives on animal cognition.* Cambridge, MA: MIT Press; Patterson, F. G. P., & Gordon, W. (2002). Twenty-seven years of Project Koko and Michael. In B. Galdikas et al. (Eds.), *All apes great and small* (vol. 1): *Chimpanzees, bonobos, and gorillas* (pp. 165–176). New York: Kluwer Academic.

[2]Armstrong, D. F., Stokoe, W. C., & Wilcox, S. E. (1993). Signs of the origin of syntax. *Current Anthropology 34,* 349–368; Burling, R. (1993). Primate calls, human language, and nonverbal communication. *Current Anthropology 34,* 25–53.

way, could he use them as symbols, that is, more abstractly to represent a person, thing, action, or idea, even apart from its context or when it was not present?

One indication of the capacity of both deaf and hearing children to use symbolic language is the ability to point, which some researchers argued that apes could not do spontaneously. Chantek began to point to objects when he was 2 years old, somewhat later than human children. First, he showed and gave us objects, and then he began pointing where he wanted to be tickled and to where he wanted to be carried. Finally, he could answer questions like WHERE HAT? WHICH DIFFERENT? and WHAT WANT? by pointing to the correct object.

As Chantek's vocabulary increased, the ideas that he was expressing became more complex, such as when he signed BAD BIRD at noisy birds giving alarm calls, and WHITE CHEESE FOOD-EAT for cottage cheese. He understood that things had characteristics or attributes that could be described. He also created combinations of signs that we had never used before.

In the way that a child learns language, Chantek began to over- or under-extend the meaning of his signs, which gave us insight into his emotions and how he was beginning to classify his world. For example, he used the sign DOG for actual dogs, as well as for a picture of a dog in his Viewmaster, orangutans on television, barking noises on the radio, birds, horses, a tiger at the circus, a herd of cows, a picture of a cheetah, and a noisy helicopter that presumably sounded like it was barking. For Chantek, the sign BUG included crickets, cockroaches, a picture of a cockroach, beetles, slugs, small moths, spiders, worms, flies, a picture of a graph shaped like a butterfly, tiny brown pieces of cat food, and small bits of feces. He signed BREAK before he broke and shared pieces of crackers, and after he broke his toilet. He signed BAD to himself before he grabbed a cat, when he bit into a radish, and for a dead bird.

We also discovered that Chantek could comprehend our spoken English (after the first couple of years we used speech as well as signing). When he was 2 years old, Chantek began to sign for things that were not present. He frequently asked to go to places in his yard to look for animals, such as his pet squirrel and cat, who served as playmates. He also made requests for ICE CREAM, signing CAR RIDE and pulling us toward the parking lot for a trip to a local ice cream shop.

We learned that an orangutan can tell lies. Deception is an important indicator of language abilities since it requires a deliberate and intentional misrepresentation of reality. In order to deceive, you must be able to see events from the other person's perspective and negate his or her perception. Chantek began to deceive from a relatively early age, and we caught him in lies about three times a week. He learned that he could sign DIRTY to get into the bathroom to play with the washing machine, dryer, soap, and so on, instead of using the toilet. He also used his signs deceptively to gain social advantage in games, to divert attention in social interactions, and to avoid testing situations and coming home after walks on campus.

On one occasion, Chantek stole a pencil eraser, pretended to swallow it, and "supported" his case by opening his mouth and signing FOOD-EAT, as if to say that he had swallowed it. However, he really held the eraser in his cheek, and later it was found in his bedroom where he commonly hid objects.

We carried out tests of Chantek's mental ability using measures developed for human children. Chantek reached a mental age equivalent to that of a 2- to 3-year-old child, with some skills of even older children. On some tasks done readily by children, such as using one object to represent another and pretend play, Chantek performed as well as children, but less frequently. He engaged in chase games in which he would look over his shoulder as he darted about, although no one was chasing him. He also signed to his toys and offered them food and drink.

By 4½ years of age, Chantek showed evidence of planning, creative simulation, and the use of objects in novel relations to one another to invent new meanings. For example, he simulated the context for food preparation by giving his caregiver two objects needed to prepare his milk formula and staring at the location of the remaining ingredient.

Chantek was extremely curious and inventive. When he wanted to know the name of something, he offered his hands to be molded into the shape of the proper sign. But language is a creative process, so we were pleased to see that Chantek began to invent his own signs. He invented: NO-TEETH (to show us that he would not use his teeth during rough play); EYE-DRINK (for contact lens solution used by his caregivers); and DAVE-MISSING-FINGER (a name for a favorite university employee who had a hand injury). Like our ancestors, Chantek had become a creator of language.

(Adapted from H. Lyn White Miles. (1993). Language and the orangutan: The old "person" of the forest. In P. Cavalieri & P. Singer (Eds.), The great ape project (pp. 45–50). New York: St. Martin's Press)

2008 UPDATE

My relationship and research with Chantek continue, through the Chantek Foundation and Animal Nation, Inc. of Kennesaw, Georgia. Chantek now uses several hundred signs and has invented some new ones of his own—for example, BOTTLED WATER (by combining the signs for CAR and WATER), and KATSUP (by combining TOMATO and TOOTHPASTE). He uses a computer and makes stone tools, paintings, and other arts and crafts, including small percussion instruments used in my Native American rock band Animal Nation. He even co-composes songs with the band. Chantek also makes unique jewelry and found art assemblages of semi-precious stones for the foundation, which helps to fund the research.

As someone of Abenaki Indian heritage, I believe that animals are "persons of the nonhuman kind." There is a growing movement across the globe for recognition of the intelligence, personhood, and even legal protection of all great apes, based on their culture in natural settings and on what we have learned from Chantek's abilities. Plans are in the making for Chantek and other enculturated apes to live in culture-based preserves where they have more range of choices and learning opportunities than zoos or research centers are willing to provide. An exciting new project under the auspices of Animal Nation, Inc. will give great apes an opportunity to communicate with one another via the Internet. As rock musician Peter Gabriel says in his song "Animal Nation" about communicating with apes, "Who knows where this will end?" (For more information, see www.chantek.org.)

For linguists studying language in the field, laptops and recording devices are indispensable tools. Here Tiffany Kershner of Kansas State University works with native Sukwa speakers in northern Malawi, Africa.

Courtesy of Tiffany Kershner

While language studies such as the one involving Chantek are fascinating and reveal much about primate cognition, the fact remains that human culture is ultimately dependent on an elaborate system of communication far more complex than that of any other species—including our fellow primates. The reason for this is the sheer amount of knowledge that must be learned by each person from other individuals in order to fully participate in society. Of course, a significant amount of learning can and does take place in the absence of language by way of observation and imitation, guided by a limited number of meaningful signs or symbols. However, all known human cultures are so rich in content that they require communication systems that not only can give precise labels to various classes of phenomena but also permit people to think and talk about their own and others' experiences and expectations—past, present, and future.

---

linguistics The modern scientific study of all aspects of language

phonetics The systematic identification and description of distinctive speech sounds in a language

phonology The study of language sounds

phonemes The smallest units of sound that make a difference in meaning in a language

morphology The study of the patterns or rules of word formation in a language (including such things as rules concerning verb tense, pluralization, and compound words)

morphemes The smallest units of sound that carry a meaning in language. They are distinct from phonemes, which can alter meaning but have no meaning by themselves

syntax The patterns or rules by which words are arranged into phrases and sentences

---

The central and most highly developed human system of communication is language. Knowledge of the workings of language, then, is essential to a full understanding of what culture is about and how it operates.

LINGUISTIC RESEARCH AND THE NATURE OF LANGUAGE

Any human language—Chinese, English, Swahili, or whatever—is a means of transmitting information and sharing with others both collective and individual experiences. It is a system that enables us to translate our concerns, beliefs, and perceptions into symbols that can be understood and interpreted by others.

In spoken language, this is done by taking sounds—no language uses more than about fifty—and developing rules for putting them together in meaningful ways. Sign languages, such as American Sign Language, do the same with gestures rather than sounds. The vast array of languages in the world—some 7,000 or so different ones—may well astound and mystify us by their great variety and complexity, yet language experts have found that all languages, as far back as we can trace them, are organized in the same basic way.

The roots of **linguistics**—the systematic study of all aspects of language—go back a long way, to the works of ancient language specialists in India more than 2,000 years ago. The European age of exploration, from the 16th through the 18th centuries, set the stage for a great leap forward in the scientific study of language. Explorers, invaders, and missionaries accumulated information about a huge diversity of languages from all around the world. An estimated 10,000 languages still existed when they began their inquiries.

Linguists in the 19th century, including anthropologists, made a significant contribution in discovering system, regularity, and relationships in the data and tentatively formulating laws and regular principles concerning language. In the 20th century, while still collecting data, they made considerable progress in unraveling the reasoning process behind language construction, testing and working from new and improved theories.

Insofar as theories and facts of language are verifiable by independent researchers looking at the same materials, it can now be said that we have a science of linguistics. This science has three main branches: descriptive linguistics, historical linguistics, and a third branch that focuses on language in relation to social and cultural settings.

DESCRIPTIVE LINGUISTICS

How can an anthropologist, a trader, a missionary, a diplomat, or any other outsider research a foreign language that has not yet been described and analyzed, or for which there are no readily available written materials? There are hundreds of such undocumented languages in the world. Fortunately, effective methods have been developed to help with the task. Descriptive linguistics involves unraveling a language by recording, describing, and analyzing all of its features. It is a painstaking process, but it is ultimately rewarding in that it provides deeper understanding of a language—its structure, its unique linguistic repertoire (figures of speech, word plays, and so on), and its relationship to other languages.

The process of unlocking the underlying rules of a spoken language requires a trained ear and a thorough understanding of the way multiple different speech sounds are produced. Without such know-how, it is extremely difficult to write out or make intelligent use of any data concerning a particular language. To satisfy this preliminary requirement, most people need special training in phonetics, discussed below.

Phonology

Rooted in the Greek word *phone* (meaning "sound"), **phonetics** is defined as the systematic identification and description of the distinctive sounds of a language. Phonetics is basic to **phonology**, the study of language sounds. In order to analyze and describe any language, one first needs an inventory of all its distinctive sounds.

While some of the sounds used in other languages may seem very much like those of the researcher's own speech pattern, others may be unfamiliar. For example, the *th* sound common in English does not exist in the Dutch language and is difficult for most Dutch speakers to pronounce, just as the *r* sound used in numerous languages is tough for Japanese speakers. And the unique "click" sounds used in Bushmen languages in southern Africa are difficult for speakers of just about every other language.

While collecting speech sounds or utterances, the linguist works to isolate the **phonemes**—the smallest units of sound that make a difference in meaning. This isolation and analysis may be done by a process called the minimal-pair test. The researcher tries to find two short words that appear to be exactly alike except for one sound, such as *bit* and *pit* in English. If the substitution of *b* for *p* in this minimal pair makes a difference in meaning, as it does in English, then those two sounds have been identified as distinct phonemes of the language and will require two different symbols to record. If, however, the linguist finds two different pronunciations (as when "butter" is pronounced "budder") and then finds that there is no difference in their meaning for a native speaker, the sounds represented will be considered variants of the same phoneme. In such cases, for economy of representation only one of the two symbols will be used to record that sound wherever it is found.

Morphology, Syntax, and Grammar

While making and studying an inventory of distinctive sounds, linguists also look into **morphology**, the study of the patterns or rules of word formation in a language (including such things as rules concerning verb tense, pluralization, and compound words). They do this by marking out specific sounds and sound combinations that seem to have meaning. These are called **morphemes**—the smallest units of sound that carry a meaning in a language.

Morphemes are distinct from phonemes, which can alter meaning but have no meaning by themselves. For example, a linguist studying English in a North American farming community would soon learn that *cow* is a morpheme—a meaningful combination of the phonemes *c, o,* and *w.* Pointing to two of these animals, the linguist would elicit the word *cows* from local speakers. This would reveal yet another morpheme—the *s*—which can be added to the original morpheme to indicate plural.

The next step in unraveling a language is to identify its **syntax**—the patterns or rules by which morphemes, or words, are arranged into phrases and sentences. The **grammar** of the language will ultimately consist of all observations about its morphemes and syntax.

One of the strengths of modern descriptive linguistics is the objectivity of its methods. For example, English-speaking anthropologists who specialize in this will not approach a language with the idea that it must have nouns, verbs, prepositions, or any other of the form classes identifiable in English. Instead they see what turns up in the language and attempt to describe it in terms of its own inner workings. This allows for unanticipated discoveries. For instance, unlike many other languages, English does not distinguish between feminine and masculine nouns. So it is that English speakers use the definite article *the* in front of any noun, while French requires two types of such definite articles: *la* for feminine nouns and *le* for masculine—as in *la lune* (the moon) and *le soleil* (the sun). German speakers go one step farther, utilizing three types of articles: *der* in front of masculine nouns, *die* for feminine, and *das* for neutral. It is also interesting to note that in contrast to their French neighbors, Germans consider the moon as masculine, so they say *der Mond,* and the sun as feminine, which makes it *die Sonne.* In another corner of the world, the highlands of Peru and Bolivia in South America, indigenous peoples who speak Quechua are not concerned about whether nouns are gendered or neutral, for their language has no definite articles.

HISTORICAL LINGUISTICS

While descriptive linguistics focuses on all features of a particular language as it exists at any one moment in time, historical linguistics deals with the fact that languages change. In addition to deciphering "dead" languages that are no longer spoken, specialists in this field investigate relationships between earlier and later forms of the same language, study older languages to track processes of change into modern ones, and examine interrelationships among older languages. For example, they attempt to sort out the development of Latin (spoken almost 1,500 years ago in southern Europe) into Italian, Spanish, Portuguese, French, and Romanian by identifying natural shifts in the original language, as well

as modifications brought on by direct contact during the next few centuries with Germanic-speaking invaders from northern Europe.

Historical linguists are not limited to the faraway past, for even modern languages are constantly transforming—adding new words, dropping others, or changing meaning. Over the last two decades, Internet use has widened the meaning of a host of existing English words—from *hacking* and *surfing* to *spam*. Entirely new words, such as *blogging* and *vlogging,* have been coined.

Especially when focusing on long-term processes of change, historical linguists depend on written records of languages. They have achieved considerable success in working out the relationships among different languages, and these are reflected in schemes of classification. For example, English is one of approximately 140 languages classified in the larger Indo-European language family (Figure 9.1). A **language family** is a group of languages descended from a single ancestral language. This family is subdivided into some eleven subgroups, which reflects the fact that there has been a long period (6,000 years or so) of **linguistic divergence** from an ancient unified language (reconstructed as Proto-Indo-European) into separate "daughter" languages. English is one of several languages in the Germanic subgroup (Figure 9.2), all of which are more closely related to one another than they are to the languages of any other subgroup of the Indo-European family.

So it is that, despite the differences between them, the languages of one subgroup share certain features when compared to those of another. As an illustration, the word for "father" in the Germanic languages always starts with an *f* or closely related *v* sound (Dutch *vader,* German *Vater,* Gothic *Fadar*). Among the Romance languages, by contrast, the comparable word always starts with a *p*: French *père,* Spanish and Italian *padre*—all derived from the Latin *pater*. The original Indo-European word for "father" was *p'tēr,* so in this case, the Romance languages have retained the earlier pronunciation, whereas the Germanic languages have diverged.

Processes of Linguistic Divergence

Studying modern languages in their specific cultural context can help us understand the processes of change that may have led to linguistic divergence. Clearly, one force for change is selective borrowing by one language from another. This is evident in the many French words present in the English language—and in the growing number of English words cropping up in languages all around the world due to globalization.

grammar The entire formal structure of a language, including morphology and syntax

language family A group of languages descended from a single ancestral language

linguistic divergence The development of different languages from a single ancestral language

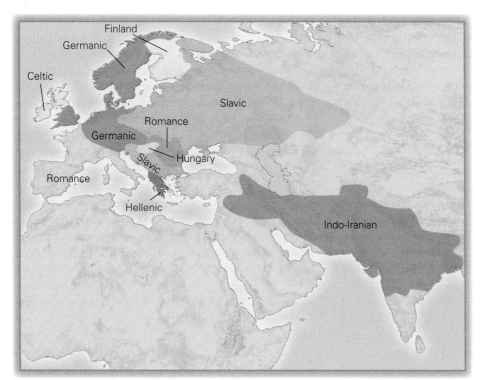

Figure 9.1 The Indo-European Languages
Not all languages spoken in Europe are part of the Indo-European family. For example, the languages spoken by most people in Finland and Hungary belong to the Uralic language family.

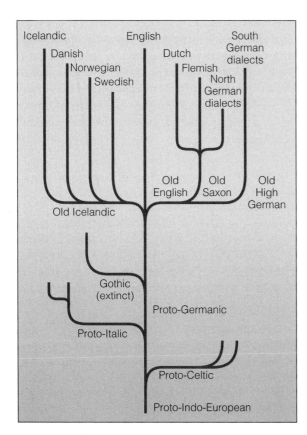

Figure 9.2
English is one of a group of languages in the Germanic subgroup of the Indo-European family. This diagram shows its relationship to other languages in the same subgroup. The root was Proto-Indo-European, an ancestral language originally spoken by early farmers and herders who spread north and west over Europe, bringing with them both their customs and their language.

Technological breakthroughs resulting in new equipment and products also prompt linguistic shifts. For instance, the electronic revolution that brought us radio, television, and computers has created entirely new vocabularies.

Increasing professional specialization is another driving force. We see one of many examples in the field of biomedicine where today's students must learn the specialized vocabulary and idioms of the profession—over 6,000 new words in the first year of medical school. There is also a tendency for any group within a larger society to create its own unique vocabulary, whether it is a street gang, sorority, religious group, prison inmates, or platoon of soldiers. By changing the meaning of existing words or inventing new ones, members of the in-group can communicate with fellow members while effectively excluding outsiders who may be within hearing range. Finally, there seems to be a human tendency to admire the person who comes up with a new and clever idiom, a useful word, or a particularly stylish pronunciation, as long as these do not seriously interfere with communication. All of this means that no language stands still.

Language Loss and Revival

Perhaps the most powerful force for linguistic change is the domination of one society over another, as demonstrated during 500 years of European colonialism. Such dominations persist today in many parts of the world, such as Taiwan's indigenous peoples being governed by Mandarin-speaking Chinese, Tarascan Indians by Spanish-speaking Mexicans, or Bushmen by English-speaking Namibians.

In many cases, foreign political control has resulted in linguistic erosion or even complete disappearance, sometimes leaving only a faint trace in old, indigenous names for geographic features such as hills and rivers. In fact, over the last 500 years about 3,000 of the world's 10,000 or so languages have become extinct as a direct result of warfare, epidemics, and forced assimilation brought on by colonial powers and other aggressive outsiders. Most of the remaining 7,000 languages are spoken by very few people, and many of them are losing speakers rapidly due to globalization. In fact, half have fewer than 10,000 speakers each, and a quarter have fewer than 1,000. In North America, for instance, only 150 of the original 300 indigenous languages still exist, and many of these surviving tongues are seriously endangered and moving toward extinction at an alarming rate.

Anthropologists predict that the number of languages still spoken in the world today will be cut in half by the year 2100, in large part because children born in ethnic minority groups no longer use the ancestral language when they go to school, migrate to cities, join the larger workforce, and are exposed to printed and electronic media. The printing press, radio, satellite television, Internet, and text messaging on cell phones are driving the need for a shared language that many understand, and increasingly that is English. In the past 500 years, this language—originally spoken by about 2.5 million people living only in part of the British Isles in northwestern Europe—has spread around the world. Today some 375 million people (6 percent of the global population) claim English as their native tongue. About 1.2 billion others (over 17 percent) speak it as a second or foreign language.

While a common language allows people from different ethnic backgrounds to communicate, there is the risk that a global spread of one language may contribute to the

disappearance of others. And with the extinction of each language, a measure of humankind's richly varied cultural heritage, including countless insights on life, is lost.

A key issue in language preservation efforts today is the impact of electronic media, such as the Internet, where content still exists in relatively few languages, and nearly 85 percent of regular Internet users are native speakers of just ten of the world's 7,000 languages. In 2001, the United Nations Educational, Scientific, and Cultural Organization (UNESCO) established Initiative B@bel, which uses information and communication technologies to support linguistic and cultural diversity. Promoting multilingualism on the Internet, this initiative aims to bridge the digital divide—to make access to Internet content and services more equitable for users worldwide (Figure 9.3).

Sometimes, in reaction to a real or perceived threat of cultural dominance by powerful foreign societies, ethnic groups and even entire countries may seek to maintain or reclaim their unique identity by purging their vocabularies of "foreign" terms. Emerging as a significant force for linguistic change, such **linguistic nationalism** is particularly characteristic of the former colonial countries of Africa and Asia today. It is by no means limited to those countries, however, as one can see by periodic French attempts to purge their language of such Americanisms as *le hamburger*. A recent example of this is France's decision to substitute the word *e-mail* with the newly minted government-approved term *couriel*.

For many ethnic minorities, efforts to counter the threat of linguistic extinction or to resurrect already extinct languages form part of their struggle to maintain

---

linguistic nationalism The attempt by ethnic minorities and even countries to proclaim independence by purging their language of foreign terms

sociolinguistics The study of the relationship between language and society through examining how social categories (such as age, gender, ethnicity, religion, occupation, and class) influence the use and significance of distinctive styles of speech

gendered speech Distinct male and female speech patterns, which vary across social and cultural settings

dialects Varying forms of a language that reflect particular regions, occupations, or social classes and that are similar enough to be mutually intelligible

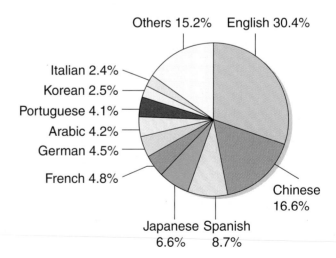

Figure 9.3

Although the world's digital divide is diminishing, it is still dramatic. As illustrated here, nearly 85 percent of today's Internet users are native speakers of just ten of the world's 7,000 languages. Notably, the use of Arabic on the Internet grew more than 2,000 percent in the first decade of the 21st century.

source: www.internetworldstats.com, 2008.

Makers of the feature film *Dances With Wolves* aimed for cultural authenticity by casting Native American actors and hiring a language coach to teach Lakota to those who did not know how to speak it. However, the lessons did not include the "gendered speech" aspect of Lakota—the fact that females and males follow different rules of syntax. Consequently, when native speakers of the language saw the film, they were amused to hear the actors who portrayed the Lakota warriors speaking like women.

a sense of cultural identity and dignity. A prime means by which powerful groups try to assert their dominance over minorities living within their borders is to actively suppress their languages.

LANGUAGE IN ITS SOCIAL AND CULTURAL SETTINGS

As discussed in the section on descriptive linguistics, language is not simply a matter of combining sounds according to certain rules to come up with meaningful utterances. It is important to remember that languages are spoken by people who are members of distinct societies. In addition to the fact that most societies have their own unique cultures, individuals within each society tend to vary in the ways they use language based on social factors such as gender, age, class, and ethnicity.

We choose words and sentences to communicate meaning, and what is meaningful in one community or culture may not be in another. Our use of language reflects, and is reflected by, the rest of our culture. For that reason, linguistic anthropologists also research language in relation to its various distinctive social and cultural contexts. This third branch of linguistic study falls into two categories: sociolinguistics and ethnolinguistics.

Sociolinguistics

Sociolinguistics, the study of the relationship between language and society, examines how social categories (such as age, gender, ethnicity, religion, occupation, and class) influence the use and significance of distinctive styles of speech.

Language and Gender

As a major factor in personal and social identity, gender is often reflected in language use, so it is not surprising that numerous thought-provoking sociolinguistic topics fall under the category of language and gender. These include research on **gendered speech**—distinct male and female speech patterns, which vary across social and cultural settings.

One of the first in-depth studies in this vein, done in the early 1970s, asserted that neither language nor gender could be studied independently of the socially constructed communities in which we live. Exploring the relationship of gender and power, it addressed specific issues including social factors said to contribute to North American women exhibiting less decisive speech styles than men. This study and a subsequent wave of related scholarly works have produced new insights about language as a social speech "performance" in both private and public settings.[3]

Gendered speech research also includes the study of distinct male and female syntax exhibited in various languages around the world, such as the Lakota language, still spoken at the Pine Ridge and Rosebud Indian reservations in South Dakota. When a Lakota woman asks someone, "How are you?" she says, "Tonikt*hkahe*?" But when her brother poses the same question, he says, "Tonikt*ukahwo*?" As explained by Michael Two Horses, "Our language is gender-specific in the area of commands, queries, and a couple of other things."[4]

---

[3]See Lakoff, R. T. (2004). *Language and woman's place.* M. Bucholtz (Ed.). New York: Oxford University Press.
[4]Personal communication, April 2003.

Social Dialects

Sociolinguists are also interested in **dialects**—varying forms of a language that reflect particular regions, occupations, or social classes and that are similar enough to be mutually intelligible.

Distinguishing dialects from languages and revealing the relationship between power and language, the noted linguist-political activist Noam Chomsky observed that a dialect is a language without an army.[5] Technically, all dialects are languages—there is nothing partial or sublinguistic about them—and the point at which two different dialects become distinctly different languages is roughly the point at which speakers of one are almost totally unable to communicate with speakers of the other.

Boundaries may be psychological, geographical, social, or economic, and they are not always very sharp. In the case of regional dialects, there is frequently a transitional territory, or perhaps a buffer zone, where features of both are found and understood, as between central and southern China. The fact is that if you learn the Chinese of Beijing, you will find that a Chinese person from Canton or Hong Kong will understand almost nothing of what you say, although both languages—or dialects—are usually lumped together as Chinese.

A classic example of the kind of dialect that may set one group apart from others within a single society is one spoken by many inner-city African Americans. Technically known as African American Vernacular English (AAVE), it has often been referred to as "black English" and "Ebonics." Unfortunately, there is a widespread misperception among non-AAVE speakers that this dialect is somehow substandard or defective. A basic principle of linguistics is that the selection of a so-called prestige dialect—in this case, what we may call Standard English as opposed to AAVE—is determined by social historical forces such as wealth and power and is not dependent on virtues or shortcomings of the dialects themselves. In fact, AAVE is a highly structured mode of speech with patterned rules of sounds and sequences like any other language or dialect. Many of its distinctive features stem from the retention of sound patterns, grammatical rules concerning verbs, and even words of the West African languages spoken by the ancestors of present-day African Americans.[6]

In many societies where different dialects or languages are spoken, individuals often know more than one and become skilled at switching back and forth, depending on the situation in which they are speaking. Without being conscious of it, we all do the same sort of thing when we switch from formality to informality in our speech, depending on where we are and to whom we are talking. The process of changing from one mode of speech to another as the situation demands, whether from one language to another or from one dialect of a language to another, is known as **code switching**, and it has been the subject of a number of sociolinguistic studies.

Ethnolinguistics

The study of the dynamic relationship between language and culture, and how they mutually influence and inform each other, is the domain of **ethnolinguistics**.

In this type of research, anthropologists may investigate how a language reflects the culturally significant aspects of a people's traditional natural environment. Among the Inuit in the Canadian Arctic, for instance, we find numerous words for different types of snow, whereas Americans in a city like Detroit most likely possess a rich vocabulary allowing them to precisely distinguish between many different types of cars, categorized by model, year, and manufacturer. This is an example of **linguistic relativity**—the idea that distinctions encoded in one language are unique to that language.

Another example concerns cultural categories of color. Languages have different ways of dividing and naming elements of the color spectrum, which is actually a continuum of multiple hues with no clear-cut boundaries between them. In English we speak of red, orange, yellow, green, blue, indigo, and violet, but other languages mark out different groupings. For instance, Indians in Mexico's northwestern mountains speaking Tarahumara have just one word for both green and blue—*siyoname*.

---

code switching Changing from one mode of speech to another as the situation demands, whether from one language to another or from one dialect of a language to another

ethnolinguistics A branch of linguistics that studies the relationships between language and culture and how they mutually influence and inform each other

linguistic relativity The idea that distinctions encoded in one language are unique to that language

linguistic determinism The idea that language to some extent shapes the way in which we view and think about the world around us

---

[5]See biographical entry for Chomsky in Shook, J. R., et al. (Eds.). (2004). *Dictionary of modern American philosophers, 1860–1960*. Bristol, England: Thoemmes Press. The saying is attributed to Yiddish linguist Max Weinreich.

[6]Monaghan, L., Hinton, L., & Kephart, R. (1997). Can't teach a dog to be a cat? The dialogue on ebonics. *Anthropology Newsletter, 38*(3), 1, 8, 9.

tones are used to distinguish among normally stressed syllables that are otherwise identical. Thus, depending on intonation, *ba* can mean "to uproot," "eight," "to hold," or "a harrow" (farm tool).[12] Cantonese, the primary language in southern China and Hong Kong, uses six contrasting tones, and some Chinese dialects have as many as nine. In nontonal languages such as English, tone can be used to convey an attitude or to change a statement into a question, but tone alone does not change the meaning of individual words as it does in Mandarin, where careless use of tones with the syllable *ma* could cause one to call someone's mother a horse!

THE ORIGINS OF LANGUAGE

Cultures all around the world have sacred stories or myths addressing the age-old question of the origin of human languages. Anthropologists collecting these stories have often found that cultural groups tend to locate the place of origin in their own ancestral homelands and believe that the first humans also spoke their language.

For example, the Incas of Peru tell the story of Pacha Camac ("Earth Maker"), the divine creator, who came to the valley of Tiwanaku in the Andean highlands in ancient times. As the myth goes, Pacha Camac drew people up from the earth, making out of clay a person of each nation, painting each with particular clothing, and giving each a language to speak and songs to sing. On the other side of the globe, ancient Israelites believed that it was Yahweh, the divine creator, who had given them Hebrew, the original tongue spoken in paradise. Later, when humans began building the high Tower of Babel to signify their own power and to link earth and heaven, Yahweh intervened. He created a confusion of tongues so that people could no longer understand one another, and he scattered them all across the face of the earth, leaving the massive tower unfinished.

Early scientific efforts to explain the origin of language suffered from a lack of solid data. Today, there is more scientific evidence, including genetic information, to work with—better knowledge of primate brains, new studies of primate communication, more information on the development of linguistic competence in children, more human fossils that can be used to tentatively reconstruct what ancient brains and vocal tracts were like, and a better understanding of the lifeways of early human ancestors. We still cannot conclusively prove how, when, and where human language first developed, but we can now theorize reasonably on the basis of

more and better information. The archaeological record shows that archaic humans known as Neandertals (living from 30,000 to 125,000 years ago in Europe and southwestern Asia) had the neurological and anatomical features necessary for speech. Fossilized brain casts from earlier members of the genus *Homo* provide evidence of specializations in the left hemisphere of the brain associated with the development of language. In addition, the observation that the earliest stone tools were made predominantly by right-handed individuals also supports the idea that lateral specialization had occurred by this time.

Because human language is embedded within a gesture-call system of a type that we share with nonhuman primates (especially great apes), anthropologists have gained considerable insight on human language by observing the communication systems of fellow primates, as we saw in the Original Study about Chantek at the beginning of the chapter. Like humans, apes are capable of referring to events removed in time and space, a phenomenon known as **displacement** and one of the distinctive features of human language.[13]

Since continuity exists between gestural and spoken language, the latter could have emerged from the former through increasing emphasis on finely controlled movements of the mouth and throat. This scenario is consistent with the appearance of neurological structures underlying language in the earliest representatives of the genus *Homo* and steady enlargement of the human brain 200,000 to 2.5 million years ago. The soft tissues of the vocal tract related to speech are not preserved in the fossil record. But as outlined in the Biocultural Connection, a comparison of the vocal anatomy of chimps and humans allows paleoanthropologists to identify the anatomical differences responsible for human speech that appeared over the course of human evolution.[14]

The advantage of spoken over gestural language to a species increasingly dependent on tool use for survival is obvious. To talk with your hands, you must stop whatever else you are doing with them; speech does

---

[12]Catford, J. C. (1988). *A practical introduction to phonetics* (p. 183). Oxford: Clarendon Press.

[13]For a discussion covering thirty years of chimpanzee sign language studies and some neurological and behavior data accounting for the similarity between human and nonhuman communication systems, see Fouts, R. S., & Waters, G. (2001). Chimpanzee sign language and Darwinian continuity: Evidence for a neurology continuity of language. *Neurological Research, 23,* 787–794.

[14]Leading evolutionary theorist Philip Lieberman argues that the human language ability is the confluence of a succession of separate evolutionary developments rigged together by natural selection for an evolutionarily unique ability. See Lieberman, P. (2006). *Toward an evolutionary biology of language.* Cambridge, MA: Belknap Press.

The Biology of Human Speech

While other primates have shown some capacity for language (a socially agreed upon code of communication), actual speech is unique to humans; this ability is linked to humans' unique anatomical development of the vocal organs.

Of particular importance are the positions of the human larynx (voice box) and the epiglottis. The larynx, situated in the respiratory tract between the pharynx (throat) and trachea (wind pipe), contains the vocal chords. The epiglottis is the structure that separates the esophagus or food pipe from the wind pipe as food passes from the mouth to the stomach. (See the figure for comparative diagrams of the anatomy of this region in chimps and humans.)

As humans mature and develop the neurological and muscular coordination for speech, the larynx and epiglottis shift to a downward position. The human tongue bends at the back of the throat and is attached to the pharynx, the region of the throat where the food and airways share a common path. Sound occurs as air exhaled from the lungs passes over the vocal cords and causes them to vibrate.

Through continuous interactive movements of the tongue, pharynx, lips, and teeth, as well as nasal passages, the sounds are alternately modified to produce speech—the uniquely patterned sounds of a particular language. Based on longstanding socially learned patterns of speech, different

languages stress certain distinctive types of sounds as significant and ignore others. For instance, languages belonging to the Iroquoian family, such as Mohawk, Seneca, and Cherokee, are among the few in the world that have no bilabial stops (*b* and *p* sounds). They also lack the labio-dental spirants (*f* and *v* sounds), leaving the bilabial nasal *m* sound as the only consonant requiring lip articulation.

It takes many years of practice for people to master the muscular movements needed to produce the precise sounds of any particular language. But no human could produce the finely controlled speech sounds without a lowered position of the larynx and epiglottis.

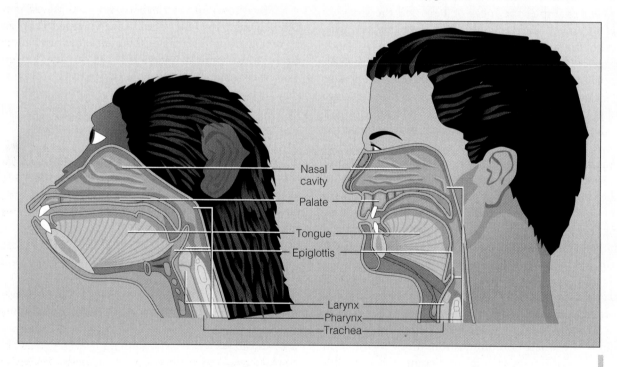

Nasal cavity
Palate
Tongue
Epiglottis
Larynx
Pharynx
Trachea

writing system A set of visible or tactile signs used to represent units of language in a systematic way
alphabet A series of symbols representing the sounds of a language arranged in a traditional order

not interfere with that. Other benefits include being able to talk in the dark, past opaque objects, or among speakers whose attention is diverted. Precisely when the changeover to spoken language took place is not known, although all would agree that spoken languages are at least as old as the species *Homo sapiens.*

Tac Yee Neen Ho Gar Ton (Red Indian) Emperor of the Six Nations 1710, Verelst. Johannes or Jan (b. 1648-fl. 1719)/Private Collection/The Bridgeman Art Library

Hendrick Tejonihokarawa ("Open the Door"), a Mohawk chief of the Iroquois Confederacy, holding a wampum belt made of hemp string and shell beads (quahog and whelk shells). Wampum designs were used to symbolize a variety of important messages or agreements, including treaties with other nations. (By Dutch painter Johannes Verelst in 1710. National Archives of Canada Collections.)

FROM SPEECH TO WRITING

When anthropology developed as an academic discipline over a century ago, it concentrated its attention on small traditional communities that relied primarily on personal interaction and oral communication for survival. Cultures that depend on talking and listening often have rich traditions of storytelling and speechmaking, which play a central role in education, conflict resolution, political decision making, spiritual or supernatural practices, and many other aspects of life.

Traditional orators (from the Latin *orare,* "to speak") are usually trained from the time they are very young. Their extraordinary memorization skills are often enhanced by oral devices such as rhyme, rhythm, and melody. Orators may also employ special objects to help them remember proper sequences and points to be made—memory devices such as notched sticks, knotted strings, bands embroidered with shells, and so forth. For example, traditional Iroquois Indian orators often performed their formal speeches with wampum belts made of hemp string and purple-blue and white shell beads woven into distinctive patterns that symbolized a variety of important messages or agreements, including treaties with other nations.

Thousands of languages, past and present, have existed only in spoken form, but many others have been documented in graphic symbols of some sort. Over time, visual representations in the form of simplified pictures of things (pictographs) evolved into more stylized symbolic forms.

Although different peoples invented a variety of graphic styles, anthropologists distinguish an actual **writing system** as a set of visible or tactile signs used to represent units of language in a systematic way. Recently discovered symbols carved into 8,600-year-old tortoise shells found in western China may represent the world's earliest evidence of elementary writing.[15]

A fully developed early writing system is Egyptian hieroglyphics, developed some 5,000 years ago and in use for about 3,500 years. Another very old system is *cuneiform,* an arrangement of wedge-shaped imprints developed primarily in Mesopotamia (southern Iraq), which lasted nearly as long. Cuneiform writing stands out among other early forms in that it led to the first phonetic writing system (that is, an **alphabet** or series of symbols representing the sounds of a language), ultimately spawning a wide array of alphabetic writing systems. About two millennia after these systems were established, others began to appear, developing independently in distant locations around the world.[16] The word *alphabet* comes from the first two letters in the Greek writing system, *alpha* and *beta.*

Literacy in Our Globalizing World

Thousands of years have passed since literacy first emerged, yet today nearly 800 million adults worldwide cannot read or write. Illiteracy condemns already disadvantaged people to ongoing poverty—migrant rural workers, refugees, ethnic minorities, and those living in rural backlands and urban slums throughout the world. For example, a third of India's adults are nonliterate, and 75 million children around the world are not enrolled in school.[17]

Declaring literacy a human right, the United Nations established September 8 as International Literacy Day and proclaimed the period 2003 to 2012 as the Literacy Decade with the objective of extending literacy to all humanity. Every September 8 during this decade, UNESCO awards prizes to individuals or groups making particularly effective contributions to the fight against illiteracy.[18]

[15]Li, X., et al. (2003). The earliest writing? Sign use in the seventh millennium BC at Jiahu, Henan Province, China. *Antiquity, 77,* 31–44.
[16]del Carmen Rodríguez Martínez, M., et al. (2006). Oldest writing in the New World. *Science, 313*(5793), 1610–1614.
[17]UNESCO Institute for Statistics. (2007). http://stats.uis.unesco.org
[18]www.unesco.org/education/litdecade

Chapter Summary

■ Anthropologists need to understand the workings of language, because it is through language that people in every society are able to share their experiences, concerns, and beliefs, over the past and in the present, and to communicate these to the next generation. Language makes communication of infinite meanings possible by employing a few sounds or gestures that, when put together according to certain rules, result in meanings that are intelligible to fellow speakers.

■ Today's language experts differ on how much credit to give to animals, such as various dolphin and ape species, for the ability to use symbols as well as signals, even though these animals and many others have been found to communicate in remarkable ways. Several chimpanzees, gorillas, and orangutans have been taught American Sign Language.

■ Linguistics is the systematic study of all aspects of language by anthropologists, psychologists, and other specialists. The three main branches of linguistics are descriptive linguistics, historical linguistics, and a third branch that focuses on language in relation to social and cultural settings.

■ Descriptive linguists mark out and explain the features of a language at a particular time in its history. Their work includes phonology (the study of language sound patterns) and the investigation of grammar—all rules concerning morphemes (the smallest units of meaningful combinations of sounds) and syntax (the principles according to which phrases and sentences are built).

■ Historical linguists investigate relationships between earlier and later forms of the same language—including identifying the forces behind the changes that have taken place in languages in the course of linguistic divergence. Their work provides a means of roughly dating certain migrations, invasions, and contacts of people.

■ Yet another group of linguists study language as it relates to society and culture—research areas known as sociolinguistics and ethnolinguistics. Sociolinguists study the relationship between language and society, examining how social categories (such as age, gender, ethnicity, religion, occupation, and class) influence the use and significance of distinctive styles of speech. Ethnolinguists study the dynamic relationship between language and culture and how they mutually influence and inform each other.

■ All languages change—borrowing terms from other languages or inventing new words for new technologies or social realities. A major cause of language change is the domination of one society over another, which over the last 500 years led to the disappearance of about 3,000 of the world's 10,000 languages. A reaction to this loss and to the current far-reaching spread and domination of the English language is linguistic nationalism—purging foreign terms from a language's vocabulary and pressing for the revitalization of lost or threatened languages.

■ A social dialect is the language of a group of people within a larger one, all of whom may speak more or less the same language.

■ All languages that have been studied are complex, sophisticated, and able to express a wide range of experiences.

■ Human language is embedded in a gesture-call system inherited from our primate ancestors that serves to "key" speech, providing the appropriate frame for interpreting linguistic form. The gestural component of the gesture-call system consists of facial expressions and body postures and motions that convey intended as well as subconscious messages. The method for notating and recording these motions is known as kinesics. Another aspect of body language is proxemics, the study of how people perceive and use space. The call component of the gesture-call system is represented by paralanguage, consisting of various voice qualities such as pitch and tempo and vocalizations such as giggling or sighing.

■ About 70 percent of the world's languages are tonal, in which the musical pitch of a spoken word is an essential part of its pronunciation and meaning.

■ Cultures around the world have sacred stories or myths about the origin of human languages. No firm scientific explanation of language origins has surfaced, but all agree that spoken languages are at least as old as the species *Homo sapiens*.

■ The first writing systems—Egyptian hieroglyphics and cuneiform—developed about 5,000 years ago. Recently discovered symbols carved into 8,600-year-old tortoise shells found in western China may represent the world's earliest evidence of elementary writing.

Questions for Reflection

1. In what ways do you feel prepared or unprepared to meet the challenge of communicating effectively in our increasingly globalized world?

2. Over 3,000 languages have disappeared over the last 500 years, most of them vanishing without a trace. Fewer than 7,000 languages remain. If the same rate of extinction continues, and just one or two languages exist in the year 2500, would that be a loss or a gain? How so?

3. Applying the principle of linguistic determinism to your own language, consider how your perceptions of objective reality might have been shaped by your language. How might your sense of reality be different if you grew up speaking Hopi?

4. What distinguishes us from apes like Chantek the orangutan? What words might Chantek choose to tell us about his confined existence as a subject of scientific research?

5. In the age of globalization, instant visual communication between all corners of the world occurs by means of electronic and digital media, in particular on the Internet. Since much of our communication takes place nonverbally, do you think that gestural messages are cross-culturally understood? What is the likelihood these are wrongly interpreted?

Key Terms

language	morphemes	gendered speech	kinesics
signals	syntax	dialects	proxemics
linguistics	grammar	code switching	paralanguage
phonetics	language family	ethnolinguistics	tonal language
phonology	linguistic divergence	linguistic relativity	displacement
phonemes	linguistic nationalism	linguistic determinism	writing system
morphology	sociolinguistics	gesture	alphabet

VISUAL ESSENCE

Throughout the world, people display their individual and collective social identity in a host of creative ways, including the apparel they wear. And every cultural group socializes its children, teaching the particular values and social codes that enable them to grow into functioning and contributing members in the community. This helps ensure that a society will reproduce itself culturally as well as biologically. Many traditional communities raise children in a gender-segregated cultural environment. Conditioning boys and girls for distinct social roles as men and women, adults make sure children have the proper clothes, headgear, and other essentials that may underscore gender differences. So it is among conservative Christian groups such as the Amish in the United States, the Wahabi Muslim fundamentalists in Arabia, and the Hasidim, pictured here. Originating in 18th-century Poland, this mystic Jewish movement is now widely dispersed, with large Hasidic ("pious") communities found in many urban centers around the world. Hasidim speak Yiddish (a Jewish-Germanic language developed in central Europe). The men wear unique hats and overcoats and usually grow full beards and long side-locks. Women, required to dress "modestly," wear headscarves and long skirts or dresses to cover their legs, necks, and elbows in public. This photo, representative of their unique conservative community, shows a Hasidic father and son in Jerusalem, where the orthodox sect is thriving.

Social Identity, Personality, and Gender

In 1690 English philosopher John Locke presented the *tabula rasa* theory in his book, *An Essay Concerning Human Understanding.* This notion held that a newborn human was like a blank slate, and what the individual became in life was written on the slate by his or her life experiences. The implication is that at birth all individuals are basically the same in their potential for personality development and that their adult personalities are exclusively the products of their postnatal experiences, which differ from culture to culture.

Locke's idea offered high hopes for the all-embracing impact of intellectual and moral instruction on a child's character formation, but it missed the mark, for it did not take into consideration what we now know: Based on recent breakthroughs in human genetic research, most anthropologists now recognize that an identifiable portion of our behavior is influenced by genetic factors.[1] This means each person is born with a particular set of inherited tendencies that help mark out his or her adult personality. While this genetic inheritance sets certain broad potentials and limitations, an individual's cultural identity and unique life experiences, particularly in the early years, also play a significant role in this formation.

Since different cultures handle the raising and education of children in different ways, these practices and their effects on personalities are important subjects of anthropological inquiry. Such cross-cultural studies gave rise to the specialization of psychological anthropology and are the subjects of this chapter.

ENCULTURATION: THE SELF AND SOCIAL IDENTITY

From the moment of birth, a person faces multiple survival challenges. Obviously, newborns cannot take care of their own biological needs. Only in myths and romantic

---

[1]Harpending, H., Cochran., G. (2002). In our genes. *Proceedings of the National Academy of Sciences of the United States of America, 99* (1), 10–12.

fantasies do we encounter stories about children successfully coming of age alone in the wilderness or accomplishing this feat having been raised by animals in the wild. Millions of children around the world have been fascinated by stories about Tarzan and the apes or the jungle boy Mowgli and the wolves. Moreover, young and old alike have been captivated by newspaper hoaxes about "wild" children, such as a 10-year-old boy reported found running among gazelles in the Syrian Desert in 1946.

Fanciful ideas aside, human children are biologically ill-equipped to survive without culture. This point has been driven home by several documented cases of feral children (*feral* comes from *fera,* which is Latin for "wild animal") who grew up deprived of human contact. None of them had a happy ending. For instance, there was nothing romantic about the girl Kamala, supposedly rescued from a wolf den in India in 1920: She moved about on all fours and could not feed herself. And everyone in Paris considered the naked "wild boy" captured in the woods outside Aveyron village in 1800 an incurable idiot. Clearly, the biological capacity for what we think of as human, which entails culture, must be nurtured to be realized.

Because culture is socially constructed and learned rather than biologically inherited, all societies must somehow ensure that culture is adequately transmitted from one generation to the next—a process we have already defined as *enculturation.* Since each group lives by a particular set of cultural rules, a child will have to learn the rules of his or her society in order to survive. Most of that learning takes place in the first few years when a child learns how to feel, think, speak, and, ultimately, act like an adult who embodies being Japanese, Kikuyu, Lakota, Norwegian, or whatever ethnic or national group into which it is born.

The first agents of enculturation in all societies are the members of the infant's household, especially the child's mother. (In fact, cultural factors are at work even before birth through what a pregnant mother eats, drinks, and inhales, as well as the sounds, rhythms, and activity patterns of her daily life.) Who the other members are depends on how households are structured in each particular society.

As the young person matures, individuals outside the household are brought into the enculturation process. These usually include other relatives and certainly the individual's peers. In some societies, professionals are brought into the process to provide formal instruction. In others, children are allowed to learn through observation and participation, at their own speed.

self-awareness The ability to identify oneself as an individual, to reflect on oneself, and to evaluate oneself
naming ceremony A special event or ritual to mark the naming of a child

Self-Awareness

Enculturation begins with the development of **self-awareness**—the ability to identify oneself as an individual creature, to reflect on oneself, and to evaluate oneself. Humans do not have this ability at birth, even though it is essential for their successful social functioning. It is self-awareness that permits one to assume responsibility for one's conduct, to learn how to react to others, and to assume a variety of roles in society. An important aspect of self-awareness is the attachment of positive value to one's self. Without this, individuals cannot be motivated to act to their advantage rather than disadvantage.

Self-awareness does not come all at once. In modern industrial and postindustrial societies, for example, self and non-self are not clearly distinguished until a child is about 2 years of age, lagging somewhat behind other cultures. Self-awareness develops in concert with neuromotor development, which is known to proceed at a slower rate in infants from industrial societies than in infants in many, perhaps even most, small-scale farming or foraging communities. The reasons for this slower rate are not yet clear, although the amount of human contact and stimulation that infants receive seems to play an important role.

In the United States, for example, infants generally do not sleep with their parents, most often being put in rooms of their own. This is seen as an important step in making them into individuals, "owners" of themselves and their capacities. As a consequence, they do not experience the steady stream of personal stimuli, including smell, movement, and warmth, that they would if co-sleeping. Private sleeping also takes away the opportunity for frequent nursing through the night.

In traditional societies, infants routinely sleep with their parents, or at least their mothers. Also, they are carried or held most other times, usually in an upright position. The mother typically responds to a cry or "fuss" within seconds, usually offering the infant her breast. So it is among traditional Ju/'hoansi (pronounced "zhutwasi") people of southern Africa's Kalahari Desert, whose infants breastfeed on demand in short, frequent bouts—commonly nursing about four times an hour, for 1 or 2 minutes at a time. Overall, a 15-week-old Ju/'hoansi infant is in close contact with its mother about 70 percent of the time (compared to 20 percent for home-reared infants in the United States). Moreover, they usually have considerable contact with numerous other adults and children of all ages.

This steady stream of varied stimuli is significant, for recent studies show that stimulation plays a key role in the "hard wiring" of the brain—it is necessary for development of the neural circuitry. Looking at breastfeeding in particular, studies show that the longer a child is breastfed, the higher he or she will score on cognitive

VISUAL COUNTERPOINT

Self-awareness is not restricted to humans. This chimpanzee knows that the individual in the mirror is himself and not some other chimp, just as the girl recognizes herself.

tests and the lower the risk of attention deficit hyperactivity disorder. Furthermore, breastfed children have fewer allergies, fewer ear infections, less diarrhea, and are at less risk of sudden infant death syndrome. Nonetheless breastfeeding tends to be relatively short-lived in the industrialized world, in part due to workplace conditions that rarely facilitate it.[2]

Social Identity Through Personal Naming

Personal names are important devices for self-definition in all cultures. It is through naming that a social group acknowledges a child's birthright and establishes its social identity. Without a name, an individual has no identity, no self. For this reason, many cultures consider name selection to be an important issue and mark the naming of a child with a special event or ritual known as a **naming ceremony**.

For example, Aymara Indians in the Bolivian highland community of Laymi do not consider an infant truly human until they have given it a name. And naming does not happen until the child begins to speak the Aymara language, typically around the age of 2. Once the child shows the ability to speak like a human, he or she is considered fit to be recognized as such with a proper name. A naming ceremony marks the child's social transition from a state of "nature" to "culture" and consequently to full acceptance into the Laymi community.

There are countless contrasting approaches to naming. Icelanders name babies at birth and still follow an ancient custom in which children use their father's personal given name as their last name. A son adds the suffix *sen* to the name and a daughter adds *dottir*. Thus, a brother and sister whose father is named Sven Olafsen would have the last names Svensen and Svendottir.

Among the Netsilik Inuit in Arctic Canada, women experiencing a difficult delivery would call out the names of deceased people of admirable character. The name being called at the moment of birth was thought to enter the infant's body and help the delivery, and the child would bear that name thereafter. Inuit parents may also name their children for deceased relatives in the belief that the spiritual identification will help shape their character.[3]

[2]Dettwyler, K. A. (1997, October). When to wean. *Natural History*, 49; Stuart-MacAdam, P., & Dettwyler, K. A. (Eds.). (1995). *Breastfeeding: Biocultural perspectives*. New York: Aldine de Gruyter.

[3]Balikci, A. (1970). *The Netsilik Eskimo*. Garden City, NY: Natural History Press.

Navajo babies begin to learn the importance of community at a special First Laugh Ceremony (*Chi Dlo Dil*). At this event, the person who prompted an infant's first laugh teaches the child (and reminds the community) about the joy of generosity by helping the baby give symbolic gifts of sweets and rock salt to each guest. Pictured here is the baby daughter of a pediatrician working at a remote clinic on the reservation. She celebrates her first laugh wearing a Navajo dress and jewelry given to her by her mother's Navajo patients.

In many cultures, a person receives a name soon after birth but may acquire new names during subsequent life phases. For instance, Navajo Indians from the southwestern United States name children at birth, but traditionalists often give the baby an additional ancestral clan name soon after the child laughs for the first time. Among the Navajo, laughter represents an infant's first expression of human language. It signals the beginning of life as a social being and is therefore an occasion for celebration. The person who prompted that very first laugh invites family and close friends to a First Laugh Ceremony (*Chi Dlo Dil*). At the gathering, the party sponsor holds and helps the child through an important social ritual: Placing rock salt in the baby's hand, he or she helps brush the salt all over the little one's body. Representing tears—of both laughter and crying—the salt is said to provide strength and protection, leading to a long, happy life. Then the ancestral name is given.

Next, because a central purpose of the occasion is to ensure that the child will become a generous and selfless adult, the sponsor helps the baby give sweets and a piece of salt to each guest as they step forward to greet and welcome the child into the embrace of the community. By accepting these symbolic gifts, guests also receive strength and protection. And by participating in the ceremony, young and old alike are reminded of the importance of generosity and sharing as traditional values in their community.[4]

Self and the Behavioral Environment

The development of self-awareness requires basic orientations that structure the psychological field in which the self acts. These include object orientation, spatial orientation, temporal orientation, and normative orientation.

---

personality The distinctive way a person thinks, feels, and behaves

[4]Authors' participant observation at traditional Navajo First Laugh ceremony of Wesley Bitsie-Baldwin; personal communication, LaVerne Bitsie-Baldwin and Anjanette Bitsie.

First, each individual must learn about a world of objects other than the self. Through this *object orientation,* each culture singles out for attention certain environmental features, while ignoring others or lumping them together into broad categories. A culture also explains the perceived environment. This is important, for a cultural explanation of one's surroundings imposes a measure of order and provides the individual with a sense of direction needed to act meaningfully and effectively.

Behind this lies a powerful psychological drive to reduce uncertainty—part of the common human need for a balanced and integrated perspective on the relevant universe. When confronted with ambiguity and uncertainty, people invariably strive to clarify and give structure to the situation; they do this, of course, in ways that their particular culture deems appropriate. Thus, we should not be surprised to find that observations and explanations of the universe are largely culturally constructed and mediated symbolically through language. In fact, everything in the physical environment varies in the way it is perceived and experienced by humans. In short, we might say that the world around us is perceived through a cultural lens.

The behavioral environment in which the self acts also involves *spatial orientation,* or the ability to get from one object or place to another. In all societies, the names and significant features of places are important references for spatial orientation. Finding your way to class, remembering where you left your car keys, directing someone to the nearest bus stop, and traveling through deep underground networks in subway tunnels are examples of highly complex cognitive tasks based on spatial orientation and memory. So is a desert nomad's ability to travel long distances from one remote oasis to another—determining the route by means of a mental map of the vast open landscape and gauging his location by the position of the sun in daytime, the stars at night, and even by the winds and smell of the air. Without these spatial orientations, navigating through daily life would be impossible.

Temporal orientation, which gives people a sense of their place in time, is also part of the behavioral environment. Connecting past actions with those of the present and future provides a sense of self-continuity. This is the function of calendars, for example. Just as the perceived environment of objects is organized in cultural terms, so too are time and space.

A final aspect of the behavioral environment is the *normative orientation.* Moral values, ideals, and principles, which are purely cultural in origin, are as much a part of the individual's behavioral environment as are trees, rivers, and mountains. Without them people would have nothing by which to gauge their own actions or those of others. In short, the self-evaluation aspect of self-awareness could not be made functional.

© James Akena/Reuters/Landov

Dark and foreboding to outsiders, the Ituri forest in the tropical heart of Africa is viewed with affection by the Mbuti foragers who live there. In their eyes, it is like a benevolent parent, providing them with all they ask for: sustenance, protection, security.

Normative orientation includes standards that indicate what ranges of behavior are acceptable for males and females in a particular society.

PERSONALITY

In the process of enculturation, we have seen that each individual is introduced to the ideas of self and the behavioral environment characteristic of his or her culture. The result is the creation of a kind of mental map of the world in which the individual will think and act. It is his or her particular map of how to run the maze of life. When we speak of someone's personality, we are generalizing about that person's cognitive map over time. Hence, personalities are products of enculturation, as experienced by individuals, each with his or her distinctive genetic makeup.

Personality does not lend itself to a formal definition, but for our purposes we may take it as the distinctive way a person thinks, feels, and behaves. Derived from the Latin word *persona,* meaning "mask," the term relates to the idea of learning to play one's role on the stage of daily life. Gradually, the "mask," as it is "placed" on the face of a child, begins to shape that person until there is little sense of the mask as a superimposed alien force. Instead it feels natural, as if one were born with it. The individual has successfully internalized the culture.

Personality Development

Although *what* one learns is important to personality development, most anthropologists assume that *how* one learns is no less important. Along with psychological theorists, anthropologists view childhood experiences as strongly influencing adult personality.

Psychological literature tends to be long on speculative concepts, clinical data, and studies that are culture-bound. Anthropologists, for their part, are most interested in studies that seek to prove, modify, or at least shed light on the cultural differences in shaping personality. For example, the traditional ideal in Western societies has been for men to be tough, aggressive, assertive, dominant, and self-reliant, whereas women have been expected to be gentle, passive, obedient, and caring. To many, these personality contrasts between the sexes seem so natural that they are thought to be biologically grounded and therefore fundamental, unchangeable, and universal. But are they? Have anthropologists identified any psychological or personality characteristics that universally differentiate men and women?

North American anthropologist Margaret Mead is well known as a pioneer in the cross-cultural study of both personality and gender. In the early 1930s she studied three ethnic groups in Papua New Guinea—the Arapesh, the Mundugamor, and the Tchambuli. This comparative research suggested that whatever biological differences exist between men and women, they are extremely malleable. Briefly put, she concluded biology is not destiny. Mead found that among the Arapesh, relations between men and women were expected to be equal, with both genders exhibiting what most North Americans traditionally consider feminine traits (cooperative, nurturing, and gentle). She also discovered gender equality among the Mundugamor (now generally called Biwat); however, in that community both genders displayed supposedly masculine traits (individualistic, assertive, volatile, aggressive). Among the Tchambuli (now called Chambri), however, Mead found that women dominated men.[5]

Recent anthropological research suggests that some of Mead's interpretations of gender roles were

incorrect—for instance, Chambri women do not dominate Chambri men, nor vice versa. Yet, overall her research generated new insights into the human condition, showing that male dominance is a cultural construct and, consequently, that alternative gender arrangements can be created. Although biological influence in male–female behavior cannot be ruled out (in fact, debate continues about the genetic and hormonal factors at play), it has nonetheless become clear that each culture provides different opportunities and has different expectations for ideal or acceptable behavior.[6]

To understand the importance of child-rearing practices for the development of gender-related personality characteristics, we may take another brief look at the already mentioned Ju/'hoansi, people native to the Kalahari Desert of Namibia and Botswana in southern Africa. Among those Ju/'hoansi who traditionally forage for a living, equality is stressed, and dominance and aggressiveness are not tolerated in either gender. Men are as mild-mannered as the women, and women are as energetic and self-reliant as the men. By contrast, among the Ju/'hoansi who have recently settled in permanent villages, men and women exhibit personality characteristics resembling those traditionally thought of as typically masculine and feminine in North America and other industrial societies.[7]

Among the Ju/'hoansi food foragers, each newborn child receives extensive personal care from its mother during the first few years of life, for the space between births is typically four to five years. This is not to say that mothers are constantly with their

---

dependence training Child-rearing practices that foster compliance in the performance of assigned tasks and dependence on the domestic group, rather than reliance on oneself

---

[5]Mead, M. (1950). *Sex and temperament in three primitive societies.* New York: New American Library. (orig. 1935)

[6]Errington, F. K., & Gewertz, D. B. (2001). *Cultural alternatives and a feminist anthropology: An analysis of culturally constructed gender interests in Papua New Guinea.* Cambridge, England, and New York: Cambridge University Press.

[7]Draper, P. (1975). !Kung women: Contrasts in sexual egalitarianism in foraging and sedentary contexts. In R. Reiter (Ed.), *Toward an anthropology of women* (pp. 77–109). New York: Monthly Review Press.

children. For instance, when women go to collect wild plant foods in the bush, they do not always take their offspring along. At such times, the children are supervised by their fathers or other community adults, one-third to one-half of whom are always found in camp on any given day. Because these include men as well as women, children are as much habituated to the male as to the female presence.

Neither boys nor girls are assigned chores. Children of both sexes do equally little work. Instead, they spend much of their time in playgroups that include members of both sexes of widely different ages. And when it comes to older children keeping an eye out for the younger ones, this is done spontaneously rather than as an assigned task, and the burden does not fall more heavily on girls than boys. In short, Ju/'hoansi children in traditional foraging groups have few experiences that set one gender apart from the other.

The situation is different among Ju/'hoansi who have been forced to abandon their traditional foraging life and now reside in permanent settlements: Women spend much of their time at home preparing food, doing other domestic chores, and tending the children. Men, meanwhile, spend many hours outside the household growing crops, raising animals, or doing wage labor. As a result, children are less habituated to their presence. This remoteness of the men, coupled with their more extensive knowledge of the outside world and their cash, tends to strengthen male influence in the household.

Within these village households, gender typecasting begins early. As soon as girls are old enough, they are

In traditional Ju/'hoansi society, fathers as well as mothers show great indulgence to children, who do not fear or respect men more than women.

© Anthony Bannister/Gallo Images/Corbis

expected to attend to many of the needs of their younger siblings, thereby allowing their mothers more time to deal with other domestic tasks. This shapes and limits the behavior of girls, who cannot range as widely or explore as freely as they could without little brothers and sisters in tow. Boys, by contrast, have little to do with babies and toddlers, and when they are assigned work, it generally takes them away from the household. Thus, the space that village girls occupy becomes restricted, and they are trained in behaviors that promote passivity and nurturance, whereas village boys begin to learn the distant, controlling roles they will later play as adult men.

Such comparisons help us see how a society's economy helps structure the way a child is brought up, and how this, in turn, influences the adult personality. It also shows that alternatives exist to the way that children are raised—which means that changing the societal conditions in which one's children grow up can alter significantly the way men and women act and interact.

Dependence Training

Some years after Margaret Mead's pioneering comparative research on gender in three Papua New Guinea communities, psychological anthropologists carried out a significant and more wide-ranging series of cross-cultural studies on the relationship between child rearing and personality. Among other things, their work distinguished two general patterns of child rearing. These patterns stem from a number of practices that, regardless of the reason for their existence, have the effect of emphasizing dependence on the one hand and independence on the other. Thus, for convenience, we may speak of "dependence training" and "independence training."[8]

Dependence training socializes people to think of themselves in terms of the larger whole. Its effect is to create community members whose idea of selfhood transcends individualism, promoting compliance in the performance of assigned tasks and keeping individuals within the group. This pattern is typically associated with extended families, which consist of several husband-wife-children units within the same household. It is most likely to be found in societies with an economy based on subsistence farming but also in foraging groups where several family groups may live together for at least part of the year. Big extended families are important, for they provide the labor force necessary to till the soil, tend whatever flocks are kept, and carry out other part-time economic pursuits considered necessary for existence.

These large families, however, have built into them certain potentially disruptive tensions. For example,

---

[8]Whiting, J. W. M., & Child, I. L. (1953). *Child training and personality: A cross-cultural study.* New Haven, CT: Yale University Press.

important family decisions must be collectively accepted and followed. In addition, the in-marrying spouses—husbands and/or wives who come from other groups—must conform themselves to the group's will, something that may not be easy for them.

Dependence training helps to keep these potential problems under control and involves both supportive and corrective aspects. On the supportive side, indulgence is shown to babies and toddlers, particularly in the form of breastfeeding, which is provided on demand and continues for several years. They may interpret this as a reward for seeking support within the family, the main agent in meeting their needs. Also on the supportive side, at a relatively young age children are assigned a number of child-care and domestic tasks, all of which make significant and obvious contributions to the family's welfare. Thus, they learn early on that family members should actively help and support one another.

On the corrective side, adults actively discourage selfish or aggressive behavior. Moreover, they tend to be insistent on overall obedience, which commonly inclines the individual toward being subordinate to the group. This combination of encouragement and discouragement in the socialization process teaches individuals to put the group's needs above their own—to be compliant, supportive, noncompetitive, and generally responsible, to stay within the fold and not do anything potentially disruptive. Indeed, a person's very definition of self comes from the individual being a part of a larger social whole rather than from his or her mere individual existence.

Independence Training

Independence training fosters individual independence, self-reliance, and personal achievement. It is typically associated with societies in which a basic social unit consisting of parent(s) and offspring fends for itself. Independence training is particularly characteristic of mercantile (trading), industrial, and postindustrial societies where self-sufficiency and personal achievement are important traits for success, if not survival—especially for men, and increasingly for women.

This pattern also involves both encouragement and discouragement. On the negative side, infant feeding is prompted more by schedule than demand. In North America, as already noted, babies are rarely nursed for more than a year, if that. Many parents resort to an artificial nipple or teething ring (pacifier) to satisfy the

independence training Child-rearing practices that foster independence, self-reliance, and personal achievement
modal personality The body of character traits that occur with the highest frequency in a culturally bounded population

baby's sucking instincts—typically doing so to calm the child rather than out of an awareness that infants need sucking to strengthen and train coordination in the muscles used for feeding and speech.

North American parents are comparatively quick to start feeding infants baby food and even try to get them to feed themselves. Many are delighted if they can prop their infants up in the crib or playpen so that they can hold their own bottles. Moreover, as soon after birth as possible, children are commonly given their own private space, away from their parents.

Collective responsibility is not pushed upon children; they are not usually given significant domestic tasks until later in childhood; and these are often carried out for personal benefit (such as to earn an allowance to spend as they wish) rather than as contributions to the family's welfare.

Displays of individual will, assertiveness, and even aggression are encouraged, or at least tolerated to a greater degree than where dependence training is the rule. In schools, and even in the family, competition and winning are emphasized. Schools in the United States, for example, devote considerable resources to competitive sports. Competition is fostered within the classroom as well—overtly through such devices as spelling bees and awards, covertly through such devices as grading on a curve. In addition, there are various popularity contests, such as crowning a prom queen and king or holding an election to choose the classmate who is "best looking" or "most likely to succeed." Thus, by the time individuals have grown up in U.S. society, they have received a clear message: Life is about winning or losing, and losing is equal to failure.

In sum, independence training generally encourages individuals to take control of their own lives and to seek and earn attention rather than give it. Such qualities are useful in societies with hierarchical social structures that emphasize personal achievement and where individuals are expected to look out for their own interests. Its socialization patterns match the competitive, materialist, and self-centered values, attitudes, and activities that promote and profit from the aggressive spread of global capitalism.

Combined Dependence/Independence Training

In actuality, dependence and independence training represent extremes along a continuum, and particular situations may include elements of both. This is the case in child-rearing practices in food-foraging societies, for example. "Share and share alike" is the order of the day, so competitive behavior, which can interfere with the cooperation on which all else depends, is discouraged. Thus, infants receive much in the way of positive, affectionate attention from adults, including extended breastfeeding from the mother. This, as well as low pressure for compliance and a lack of emphasis on competition, encourages individuals to be more supportive of one another than is often the case in modern industrial and postindustrial societies. At the same time, personal achievement and independence are encouraged, for those individuals most capable of self-reliance are apt to be the most successful in the food quest.

In North America the argument is sometimes made that "permissive" child rearing produces irresponsible adults. Yet the practices of food foragers seem to be about as "permissive" as they can get, and socially responsible adults are produced. The fact is that none of these child-rearing systems is inherently better or worse than any other; what matters is whether the system is functional or dysfunctional in the context of a particular society. If compliant adults who are accepting of authority are required, then independence training will not work well in that society. Nor will dependence training serve very well a society whose adults are expected to be self-reliant, questioning of authority, and ready to explore and embrace new ways of doing things.

Group Personality

From studies such as those reviewed here, it is clear that personality, child-rearing practices, and other aspects of culture are systemically interrelated. The existence of a close, if not causal, relationship between a group's child-rearing practices and personality development, coupled with cross-cultural variation in these practices, has led to a number of attempts to distinguish whole societies in terms of particular personality types. Indeed, common sense suggests that personalities fitting for one culture may be less suitable for others. For example, an egocentric, aggressive personality would be out of place where cooperation and sharing are the keys to success.

Unfortunately, common sense, like conventional wisdom in general, is not always the truth. A question worth asking is: Can we describe a group personality without falling into stereotyping? The answer appears to be a qualified yes; in an abstract way, we may speak of a generalized "cultural personality" for a society, as long as we do not expect to find a uniformity of personalities within that society. Put another way, each individual develops certain personality characteristics that, from common experience, resemble those of other people. Yet, each human being also acquires distinct personality traits because every individual is exposed to unique sets of experiences and may react to shared experiences in novel ways. Moreover, each person brings to these experiences a one-of-a-kind genetic potential (except in the case of identical twins) that plays a role in determining personality.

Yanomani men living in the Amazon rainforest of South America display their fierceness. While flamboyant, belligerent personalities are especially compatible with the Yanomami idea of male fierceness, some men are quiet and strong.

This is evident, if not obvious, in every society—including even the most traditional ones. Consider for example the Yanomami Indians, who subsist on foraging and horticulture in the tropical forests of northern Brazil and southern Venezuela. Commonly, Yanomami men strive to achieve a reputation for fierceness and aggressiveness, and they defend that reputation at the risk of serious personal injury and death. Yet, among the Yanomami there are men who have quiet and somewhat retiring personalities. It is all too easy for an outsider to overlook these individuals when other, more "typical" Yanomami are in the front row, pushing and demanding attention.

Modal Personality

Obviously, any productive approach to the problem of group personality must recognize that each individual is unique to a degree in both genetic inheritance and life experiences, and it must leave room for a range of different personality types in any society. In addition, personality traits that may be regarded as appropriate in men may not be so regarded in women, and vice versa. Given all this, we may focus our attention on the **modal personality** of a group, defined as the body of character traits that occur with the highest frequency in a culturally bounded population.

Modal personality is a statistical concept rather than the personality of an average person in a particular society. As such, it opens up for investigation the questions of how societies organize diversity and how diversity relates to culture change. Such questions are easily missed if one associates a certain type of personality with one particular culture, as did some earlier anthropologists. At the same time, modal personalities of different groups can be compared.

Data on modal personality are best gathered by means of psychological tests (such as the Rorschach or "ink blot" test) administered to a sample of the population in question. In addition, observing and recording the frequency of certain behaviors, collecting and analyzing life histories and dreams, and analyzing popular tales, jokes, legends, and traditional myths can yield useful data on modal personality.

While having much to recommend it, the concept of modal personality as a means of dealing with group personality nevertheless presents certain difficulties. One is the complexity of the measurement techniques, which may be difficult to do in the field. For instance, an adequate representative sample of subjects is necessary. The problem here is twofold: making sure the sample is really representative and having the time and personnel necessary to administer the tests, conduct interviews, and so on, all of which can be lengthy proceedings.

Also, the tests themselves constitute a problem, for those devised in one cultural setting may not be appropriate in another. Moreover, language differences or conflicting cultural values between the researcher and the individuals being studied may inhibit communication and/or lead to misinterpretation. For example, just what is aggression? Does everyone define it the same way? Is it an elemental analytical concept, or does it involve other variables?

National Character

Several years ago, Italy's tourism minister publicly commented on "typical characteristics" of Germans, referring to them as "hyper-nationalistic blondes" and "beer-drinking slobs" holding "noisy burping contests" on his country's beaches.[9] Outraged (and proud of his country's excellent beer), Germany's chancellor canceled his planned vacation to Italy and demanded an official apology. Of course, many Germans think of Italians as dark-eyed, hot-blooded spaghetti eaters. To say so in public, however, might cause an uproar.

Unflattering stereotypes about foreigners are deeply rooted in cultural traditions everywhere. Many Japanese believe Koreans are stingy, crude, and aggressive, while many Koreans see the Japanese as cold and arrogant. Similarly, we all have in mind some image, perhaps not well defined, of the typical citizen of Russia or Mexico or England. And many Americans traveling abroad are suprised or insulted that some Europeans hold the nega-tive image of loud, brash, and arrogant "Yankees"—immortalized in print as the *Ugly American* in the 1958 bestseller that also became a Hollywood movie starring Marlon Brando. Essentially, these are simply stereotypes. We might well ask, however, if these stereotypes have any basis in fact. In reality, does such a thing as *national character* exist?

Some anthropologists once thought that the answer might be yes. Accordingly, they embarked upon national character studies in the 1930s and 1940s, aiming to discover basic personality traits shared by the majority of the people of modern state societies. In what came to be known as the *culture and personality* movement, their research emphasized child-rearing practices and education as the factors theoretically responsible for such characteristics.

Early on it was recognized that the national character studies were flawed, mainly because they made over-generalized conclusions based on limited data, relatively small samples of informants, and questionable assumptions about developmental psychology.[10]

Core Values

An alternative approach to national character—one that allows for the fact that not all personalities will conform to cultural ideals—is that of Chinese American anthropologist Francis Hsu. His approach was to study **core values** (values especially promoted by a particular culture) and related personality traits. The Chinese, he suggested, value kin ties and cooperation above all else. To them, mutual dependence is the very essence of personal relationships and has been for thousands of years. Compliance and subordination of one's will to that of family and kin transcend all else, while self-reliance is neither promoted nor a source of pride.

Perhaps the core value held in highest esteem by North Americans of European descent is rugged individualism—traditionally for men but in recent decades for women as well. Each individual is supposed to be able to achieve anything he or she likes, given a willingness to work hard enough. From their earliest years, individuals are subjected to relentless pressures to excel, and as we have already noted, competition and winning are seen as crucial to this. Undoubtedly, this contributes to the restlessness and drive seen as characteristic for much of North American society today.

Also, to the degree that it motivates individuals to work hard and to go where the jobs are, it fits well

---

core values Those values especially promoted by a particular culture

---

[9]"Italy–Germany verbal war hots up." (2003, July 9). *Deccan Herald* (Bangalore, India).

[10]See Beeman, W. O. (2000). Introduction: Margaret Mead, cultural studies, and international understanding. In M. Mead & R. Métraux (Eds.), *The study of culture at a distance* (pp. xiv–xxxi). New York and Oxford: Berghahn Books.

The collectively shared core values of Chinese culture promote the integration of the individual into a larger group, as we see in this large gathering of Hong Kong residents doing Tai Chi together.

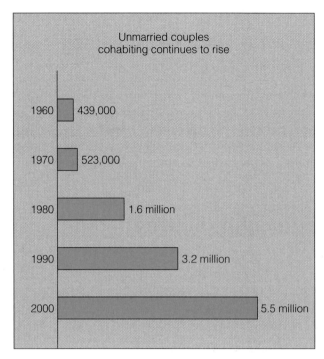

Unmarried couples cohabiting continues to rise

Year	Number
1960	439,000
1970	523,000
1980	1.6 million
1990	3.2 million
2000	5.5 million

Figure 10.1

Number of unmarried couples cohabiting in the United States, by year. According to the most recent national census, in the year 2000, 8.5 percent of all cohabiting couples in the United States were unmarried. That number continues to rise, thereby diminishing the legal obligations of partners. For American women with children, cohabitation may pose fewer financial burdens than single parenthood, but it is often less advantageous economically than marriage.

with the demands of a modern economy. Thus, while individuals in Chinese traditional society are firmly bound into a larger group to which they have lifelong obligations, most urban North Americans and western Europeans live isolated from relatives other than their young children and spouse—and even the commitment to marriage has lessened. Many people in western Europe, North America, and other industrial or postindustrial societies choose to remain single or postpone marriage. This growing individualism is also indicated by the rising rates of divorce—with close to 50 percent of marriages now failing.[11]

Other evidence of this individualizing trend is the growing number of couples choosing cohabitation without being married (Figure 10.1). Since 1960, the total number of cohabiting households in the United States is up more than twelvefold. For women with children, cohabitation often imposes disproportionate financial burdens. In wealthy countries of western Europe, cohabitation has also dramatically risen, particularly in Norway. In that Scandinavian country, over half of all live births now occur outside marriage. One reason for this is that Norwegian "cohabiting couples who have children together or have lived together for minimum two years will have many of the same rights and obligations to social security, pensions and taxation as their married counterparts."[12]

---

[11]Observations on North American culture in this section are drawn primarily from Natadecha-Sponsal, P. (1993). The young, the rich and the famous: Individualism as an American cultural value. In P. R. DeVita & J. D. Armstrong (Eds.), *Distant mirrors: America as a foreign culture* (pp. 46–53). Belmont, CA: Wadsworth. See also Whitehead, B. D., & Popenoe, D. (2004). *The state of our unions: The social health of marriage in America 2004*. Rutgers, NJ: Rutgers University National Marriage Project.

---

[12]Noack, T. (2001). Cohabitation in Norway: An accepted and gradually more regulated way of living. *International Journal of Law, Policy, and the Family, 15*(1),102–117.

ALTERNATIVE GENDER MODELS FROM A CROSS-CULTURAL PERSPECTIVE

As touched upon earlier, the gender roles assigned to each sex vary from culture to culture and have an impact on personality formation. But what if the sex of an individual is not self-evident, as revealed in the following Original Study? Written when its author was an undergraduate student of philosophy at Bryn Mawr College in Pennsylvania, this narrative offers a compelling personal account of the emotional difficulties associated with intersexuality and gender ambiguity, while making the important point that attitudes toward gender vary cross-culturally. However, some of the cultural information is overly generalized and therefore not quite accurate, including the idea that all or most Native American spiritual-religious worldviews were and are nonhierarchical.[13]

Original Study

The Blessed Curse

R. K. Williamson

One morning not so long ago, a child was born. This birth, however, was no occasion for the customary celebration. Something was wrong: something very grave, very serious, very sinister. This child was born between sexes, an "intersexed" child. From the day of its birth, this child would be caught in a series of struggles involving virtually every aspect of its life. Things that required little thought under "ordinary" circumstances were, in this instance, extraordinarily difficult. Simple questions now had an air of complexity: "What is it, a girl or a boy?" "What do we name it?" "How shall we raise it?" "Who (or what) is to blame for this?"

A FOOT IN BOTH WORLDS

The child referred to in the introductory paragraph is myself. As the great-granddaughter of a Cherokee woman, I was exposed to the Native American view of people who were born intersexed, and those who exhibited transgendered characteristics. This view, unlike the Euramerican one, sees such individuals in a very positive and affirming light. Yet my immediate family (mother, father, and brothers) were firmly fixed in a negative Christian Euramerican point of view. As a result, from a very early age I was presented with two different and conflicting views of myself. This resulted in a lot of confusion within me about what I was, how I came to be born the way I was, and what my intersexuality meant in terms of my spirituality as well as my place in society.

I remember, even as a small child, getting mixed messages about my worth as a human being. My grandmother, in keeping with Native American ways, would tell me stories about my birth. She would tell me how she knew when I was born that I had a special place in life, given to me by God, the Great Spirit, and that I had been given "a great strength that girls never have, yet a gentle tenderness that boys never know" and that I was "too pretty and beautiful to be a boy only and too strong to be a girl only." She rejoiced at this "special gift" and taught me that it meant that the Great Spirit had "something important for me to do in this life." I remember how good I felt inside when she told me these things and how I soberly contemplated, even at the young age of 5, that I must be diligent and try to learn and carry out the purpose designed just for me by the Great Spirit.

My parents, however, were so repulsed by my intersexuality that they would never speak of it directly. They would just refer to it as "the work of Satan." To them, I was not at all blessed with a "special gift" from some "Great Spirit," but was "cursed and given over to the Devil" by God. My father treated me with contempt, and my mother wavered between contempt and distant indifference. I was taken from one charismatic church to another in order to have the "demon of mixed sex" cast out of me. At some of these "deliverance" services I was even given a napkin to cough out the demon into!

In the end, no demon ever popped out of me. Still I grew up believing that there was something inherent within me that caused God to hate me, that my intersexuality was a punishment for this something, a mark of condemnation.

Whenever I stayed at my grandmother's house, my fears would be allayed, for she would once again remind me that I was fortunate to have been given this special gift. She was distraught that my parents were treating me cruelly and pleaded with them to let me live with her, but they would not let me stay at her home permanently. Nevertheless, they did let me spend a significant portion of my childhood with her. Had it not been for that, I might not have been able to survive the tremendous trials that awaited me in my walk through life.

---

intersexuals People born with reproductive organs, genitalia, and/or sex chromosomes that are not exclusively male or female

[13]For scholarly accounts of the issues presented here, readers may turn to several excellent books, including the one mentioned in the Original Study: Roscoe, W. (1991). *Zuni man-woman.* Albuquerque: University of New Mexico Press.

BLESSED GIFT: THE NATIVE AMERICAN VIEW

It is now known that most, if not all, Native American societies had certain individuals that fell between the categories of "man" and "woman." The various nations had different names for such people, but a term broadly used and recognized is *berdache*, a word of French origin that designated a male, passive homosexual. [The preferred term today is *two-spirit*.] Some of these individuals were born physically intersexed. Others appeared to be anatomically normal males, but exhibited the character and the manners of women—or vice versa. The way native people treated such individuals reveals some interesting insights into Native American belief systems.

THE SPIRIT

The extent to which Native Americans see spirituality is reflected in their belief that all things have a spirit: "Every object—plants, rocks, water, air, the moon, animals, humans, the earth itself—has a spirit. The spirit of one thing (including a human) is not superior to the spirit of any other.... The function of religion is not to try to condemn or to change what exists, but to accept the realities of the world and to appreciate their contributions to life. Everything that exists has a purpose."

This paradigm is the core of Native American thought and action. Because everything has a spirit, and no spirit is superior to that of another, there is no "above" or "below," no "superior" or "inferior," no "dominant" and "subordinate." These are only illusions that arise from unclear thinking. Thus, an intersexed child is not derided or viewed as a "freak of nature" in many traditional Native American cultures. Intersexuality (as well as masculinity in a female or effeminacy in a male) is seen as the manifestation of the spirit of the child, so an intersexed child is respected as much as a girl child or a boy child. It is the spirit of the child that determines what the gender of the child will ultimately be. According to a Lakota, Lame Deer, "the Great Spirit made them *winktes* [*two-spirit*], and we accepted them as such." In this sense, the child has no control over what her or his gender will be. It follows that where there is no choice, there can be no accountability on the part of the child. Indeed, the child who is given the spirit of a *winkte* is unable to resist becoming one.

"When an Omaha boy sees the Moon Being [a feminine Spirit] on his vision quest, the spirit holds in one hand a man's bow and arrow and in the other a woman's pack strap.... 'When the youth tried to grasp the bow and arrows, the Moon Being crossed hands very quickly, and if the youth was not very careful he seized the pack strap instead of the bow and arrows, thereby fixing his lot in later life. In such a case he could not help acting [like a] woman, speaking, dressing, and working just as ... women ... do.'"

THE CURSE: THE EURAMERICAN VIEW

In contrast to the view of respect and admiration of physical intersexuality and transgendered behavior traditionally held by Native Americans, the Europeans who came to "Turtle Island" (the Cherokee name for North America) brought with them their worldview, shaped by their Judeo-Christian beliefs. According to this religious perspective, there had to be, by mandate of God, a complete dichotomy of the sexes. . .

Will Roscoe, in his book *The Zuni Man-Woman*, reports (pp. 172–73): "Spanish oppression of 'homosexual' practices in the New World took brutal forms. In 1513, the explorer Balboa had some forty berdaches thrown to his dogs [to be eaten alive]—'a fine action by an honorable and Catholic Spaniard,' as one Spanish historian commented. In Peru, the Spaniards burned 'sodomites, . . . and in this way they frightened them in such a manner that they left this great sin.'"

It is abundantly clear that Christian Euramericans exerted every effort to destroy Native American culture: "In 1883, the U.S. Office of Indian Affairs issued a set of regulations that came to be known as the Code of Religious Offenses, or Religious Crimes Code. . . . Indians who refused to adopt the habits of industry, or to engage in 'civilized pursuits or employments' were subject to arrest and punishment. . . . By interfering with native sexuality [and culture], the agents of assimilation effectively undermined the social fabric of entire tribes" (Roscoe, p. 176).

A PERSONAL RESOLUTION

For me, the resolution to the dual message I was receiving was slow in coming, largely due to the fear and self-hatred instilled in me by Christianity. Eventually, though, the spirit wins out. I came to adopt my grandmother's teaching about my intersexuality. Through therapy, and a new, loving home environment, I was able to shed the constant fear of eternal punishment I felt for something I had no control over. After all, I did not create myself.

Because of my own experience, and drawing on the teaching of my grandmother, I am now able to see myself as a wondrous creation of the Great Spirit—but not only me. All creation is wondrous. There is a purpose for everyone in the gender spectrum. Each person's spirit is unique in her or his or her-his own way. It is only by living true to the nature that was bestowed upon us by the Great Spirit, in my view, that we are able to be at peace with ourselves and be in harmony with our neighbor. This, to me, is the Great Meaning and the Great Purpose . . .

(Adapted from R. K. Williamson (1995). The blessed curse: Spirituality and sexual difference as viewed by Euramerican and Native American cultures. The College News, *18(4). Reprinted with permission of the author)*

The biological facts of human nature are not always as clear-cut as most people assume. At the level of chromosomes, biological sex is determined according to whether a person's 23rd chromosomal set is XX (female) or XY (male). Some of the genes on these chromosomes control sexual development. This standard biological package does not apply to all humans, for a considerable number are **intersexuals**—people who are born with reproductive organs, genitalia, and/or sex chromosomes that are not exclusively male or female. These individuals do not fit neatly into a binary gender standard.[14]

For example, some people are born with a genetic disorder that results in them having only one X chromosome instead of the usual two. A person with this chromosomal complex, known as Turner syndrome, develops female external genitalia but has nonfunctional ovaries and is therefore infertile. Other individuals are born with the XY sex chromosomes of a male but have an abnormality on the X chromosome that affects the body's sensitivity to androgens (male hormones). This is known as androgen insensitivity syndrome (AIS). An adult XY person with complete AIS appears fully female with a normal clitoris, labia, and breasts. Internally, these individuals possess testes (up in the abdomen, rather than in their usual descended position in the scrotal sac), but they are otherwise born without a complete set of either male or female internal genital organs. They generally possess a short, blind-ended vagina.

"Hermaphrodites" comprise a distinct category of intersexuality—although the terms "male pseudohermaphrodite" and "female pseudohermaphrodite" are often used to refer to a range of intersex conditions. The name, objected to by many, comes from a figure in Greek mythology: Hermaphroditus (son of Hermes, messenger of the gods, and Aphrodite, goddess of beauty and love) who became half-male and half-female when he fell in love with a nymph, and his body fused with hers.

More obviously intersexed individuals ("true hermaphrodites") have both testicular and ovarian tissue. They may have a separate ovary and testis, but more commonly they have an ovotestis—a gonad containing both sorts of tissue. About 60 percent of these individuals possess XX (female) sex chromosomes, and the remainder may have XY or a mosaic (a mixture). Their external genitalia may be ambiguous or female, and they

may have a uterus or (more commonly) a hemi-uterus (half uterus).[15]

Intersexuality may be unusual, but it is not uncommon. In fact, about 1 percent of all humans are intersexed in some (not necessarily visible) way—in other words, over 60 million people worldwide.[16] Until recently, it was rarely discussed publicly in many societies. Since the mid-20th century, individuals with financial means in technologically advanced parts of the world have had the option of reconstructive surgery and hormonal treatments to alter such conditions, and many parents faced with raising a visibly intersexed child in a culture intolerant of such minorities have chosen this option for their baby. However, there is a growing movement to put off such irreversible procedures indefinitely or until the child becomes old enough to make the choice. Obviously, a society's attitude toward these individuals can affect their personality—their fundamental sense of self and how they express it.

In addition to people who are biologically intersexed, throughout history some individuals have been subjected to a surgical removal of some of their sexual organs. In many cultures, male prisoners or war captives have undergone forced castration, crushing or cutting the testicles. While castration of adult males does not eliminate the sex drive or the possibility of having an erection, it does put an end to the production of sperm necessary for reproduction.

Archaeological evidence from ancient Egypt, Iraq, Iran, and China suggests that the cultural practice of castrating war captives may have begun several thousand years ago. Young boys captured during war or slave-raiding expeditions were often castrated before being sold and shipped off to serve in foreign households, including royal courts. In the Ottoman Empire of the Turks, where they could occupy a variety of important functions in the sultan's household from the mid-15th century onward, they became known as eunuchs. As suggested by the original meaning of the word, which is Greek for "guardian of the bed," castrated men were often put in charge of a ruler's harem, the women's quarters in a household. Eunuchs could also rise to high status as priests and administrators and were even appointed to serve as

---

transgenders People who cross over or occupy a culturally accepted intermediate position in the binary male–female gender construction. Also identified as "third gender" people (or by various culturally specific names such as "two spirits," used in many Native American groups)

---

[14]This section is based on several sources: Chase, C. (1998). Hermaphrodites with attitude. *Gay and Lesbian Quarterly*, *4*(2), 189–211; Dumurat-Dreger, A. (1998, May/June). "Ambiguous sex" or ambivalent medicine? *The Hastings Center Report*, *28*(3), 2435 (posted on the Intersex Society of North America website: www.isna.org); Fausto-Sterling, A. (1993). The five sexes: Why male and female are not enough. *The Sciences*, *33*(2), 20–24; the Mayo Clinic website.

[15]Fausto-Sterling, A. (2000, July). The five sexes revisited. *The Sciences*, 20–24.

[16]Fausto-Sterling, A. (2003, August 2). Personal e-mail communication from this recognized expert on the subject. For published statistics, see her article co-authored with Blackless, M., et al. (2000). How sexually dimorphic are we? Review and synthesis. *American Journal of Human Biology*, *12*, 151–166.

army commanders. Some powerful lords, kings, and emperors kept hundreds of eunuchs in their castles and palaces.

In addition to forced castration, there were also men who engaged in self-castration or underwent voluntary castration. For example, early Christian monks in Egypt and neighboring regions voluntarily abstained from sexual relationships and sometimes castrated themselves for the sake of the kingdom of heaven. Such genital mutilation was also practiced among Coptic monks in Egypt and Ethiopia, until the early 20th century.[17]

In the late 15th century, Europe saw the emergence of a category of musical eunuchs known as castrati. These eunuchs sang female parts in church choirs after Roman Catholic authorities banned women singers on the basis of Saint Paul's instruction, "Let your women keep silence in the churches."[18]

Mapping the sexual landscape, anthropologists have come to realize that gender bending exists in many cultures all around the world, playing a significant role in shaping behaviors and personalities. For example, indigenous communities in the Great Plains and Southwest created social space for **transgenders**, people who cross over or occupy an alternative position in the binary male–female gender construction. The Lakota of the northern Plains had a third gender category of culturally accepted transgendered males who dressed as women and were thought to possess both male and female spirits. They called (and still call) these third-gender individuals *winkte,* applying the term to a male "who wants to be a woman." Thought to have special curing powers, *winktes* traditionally enjoyed considerable prestige in their communities. Among the neighboring Cheyenne, such a person was called *hemanah,* literally meaning "half-man, half-woman."[19] The preferred term among most North American Indians today is "two-spirits."

Such third-gender individuals are well known in Samoa, where males who take on the identity of females are referred to as *fa'afines* ("the female way"). Becoming a *fa'afine* is an accepted option for boys who prefer to dance, cook, clean house, and care for children and the elderly. In large families, it is not unusual to find two or three boys being raised as girls to take on domestic roles in their households. As North American anthropologist Lowell Holmes reported,

> In fact, they tend to be highly valued because they can do the heavy kinds of labor that most women find difficult. A Samoan nun once told me how fortunate it is to have a fa'afine in the family to help with the household chores. [There] is also the claim made that fa'afines never have sexual relations with each other but, rather, consider themselves to be "sisters." [They] are religious and go to church regularly dressed as women and . . . some are even Sunday school teachers. Fa'afines often belong to women's athletic teams, and some even serve as coaches.[20]

These transgendered cultural types cannot simply be lumped together as homosexuals. For example,

Transgendering occurs in many cultures, but it is not always publicly tolerated. Among Polynesians inhabiting Pacific Ocean islands such as Tonga and Samoa, however, such male transvestites are culturally accepted. Samoans refer to these "third-gender" individuals as *fa'afines* ("the female way").

[17]Abbot, E. (2001). *A history of celibacy.* Cambridge, MA: Da Capo Press.

[18]Taylor, G. (2000). *Castration: Abbreviated history of western manhood* (pp. 38–44, 252–259). New York: Routledge.

[19]Medicine, B. (1994). Gender. In M. B. Davis (Ed.), *Native America in the twentieth century.* New York: Garland; see also Gilley, B. J. (2007). *Becoming two-spirit: Gay identity and social acceptance in Indian Country.* Lincoln: University of Nebraska Press.

[20]Holmes, L. D. (2000). "Paradise Bent" (film review). *American Anthropologist, 102*(3), 604–605.

the Tagalog-speaking people in the Philippines use the word *bakla* to refer to a man who views himself "as a male with a female heart." These individuals cross-dress on a daily basis, often becoming more female than females in their use of heavy makeup, in the clothing they wear, and in the way they walk. Like the Samoan *fa'afafines,* they are generally not sexually attracted to other *bakla* but are drawn to heterosexual men instead.

In addition, some people are gender variants—permanent or incidental transvestites without being homosexuals—making it obvious that the cross-cultural sex and gender scheme is complex. Indeed, the late 19th-century "homosexuality" label is quite inadequate to cover the full range of sex and gender diversity.

In sum, human cultures in the course of thousands of years have creatively dealt with a wide range of inherited and artificially imposed sexual features. The importance of studying complex categories involving intersexuality and transgendering is that doing so enables us to recognize the existing range of gender alternatives and to debunk false stereotypes. It is one more piece of the human puzzle—an important one that prods us to rethink social codes and the range of forces that shape personality as well as each society's definition of normal.

NORMAL AND ABNORMAL PERSONALITY IN SOCIAL CONTEXT

The cultural standards that define normal behavior for any society are determined by that society itself. So it is that in mainstream European and North American societies, in contrast to those just noted, transgender behavior has traditionally been regarded as culturally abnormal. If a male in those societies dresses as a woman, he is still widely viewed as emotionally troubled, or even mentally ill, and his abnormal behavior may lead to psychiatric intervention. There are countless examples of the fact that what seems normal and acceptable (if not always popular) in one society is considered abnormal and unacceptable (ridiculous, shameful, and sometimes even criminal) in another.

Not only are the boundaries that distinguish the normal from the abnormal culturally variable (and thus neither absolute nor fixed), but so are the standards of what is socially acceptable. In other words, there are individuals in each society who deviate in appearance or behavior from general social standards or norms but who are not considered "abnormal"

in the strict sense of the word—and are not socially rejected, ridiculed, censured, condemned, jailed, or otherwise penalized. Quite to the contrary, some cultures tolerate or accept a much wider range of diversity than others and may even accord special status to the deviant or eccentric as unique, extraordinary, or even sacred.

Sadhus: Holy Men in Hindu Cultures

A fascinating ethnographic example of a culture in which abnormal individuals are socially accepted and even honored is provided by religious mystics in India and Nepal. Surrendering all social, material, and even sexual attachments to normal human pleasures and delights, these ascetic monks, or *sadhus,* dedicate themselves to achieving spiritual union with the divine or universal Soul. This is done through intense meditation (chanting sacred hymns or mystical prayer texts—mantras) and yoga (an ascetic and mystic discipline involving prescribed postures and controlled breathing). The goal is to become a fully enlightened soul, liberated from the physical limits of the individual mortal self, including the cycle of life and death.

The life of the *sadhu* demands extraordinary concentration and near superhuman effort, as can be seen in the most extreme yoga postures. This chosen life of suffering may even include self-torture as a form of extreme penance. For instance, some *sadhus* pierce their tongue or cheeks with a long iron rod, stab a knife through their arm or leg, or stick their head into a small hole in the ground for hours on end.

Most Hindus revere and sometimes even fear *sadhus.* When they encounter one—by a temple or cemetery, or perhaps near a forest, riverbank, or mountain cave—they typically offer him food or other alms. Sightings are not uncommon since an estimated

© Thomas L. Kelly

Shaivite *sadhu* of the Aghori subsect drinks from human skull bowl. He is a strict follower of the Hindu god Shiva, whose picture can be seen behind him. The practice of eating and drinking from a human skull is a daily reminder of human mortality. These ascetics remain naked and often wear a rosary made of bones around their neck. To become a *sadhu*, one must transform his personal identity, leave his place in the social order, and surrender all attachments to normal human pleasures.

5 million *sadhus* live in India and Nepal.[21] Of course, if one of these bearded, long-haired Hindu monks decided to practice his extreme yoga exercises and other sacred devotions in western Europe or North America, such a holy man would be viewed as severely mentally disturbed.

Mental Disorders Across Time and Cultures

No matter how eccentric or even bizarre certain behaviors might seem in a particular place and time, it is possible for the "abnormal" to become socially accepted in cultures that are changing. Such is the case with manic depression (now more properly called *bipolar disorder*) and attention deficit hyperactivity disorder (ADHD), both previously regarded as dreaded liabilities.

In western Europe and North America, the manic and hyperactivity aspects of these conditions are gradually becoming viewed as assets in the quest for success. More and more, they are interpreted as indicative of "finely wired, exquisitely alert nervous systems" that make one highly sensitive to signs of change, able to fly from one thing to another while pushing the limits of everything, and doing it all with an intense level of energy focused totally in the future. These are extolled as high virtues in the corporate world, where being considered "hyper" or "manic" is increasingly an expression of approval.[22]

Just as social attitudes concerning a wide range of both psychological and physical differences change over time within a society, they also vary across cultures—as is evident in this chapter's Biocultural Connection.

---

[21]See Kelly, T. L. (2006). *Sadhus*, the great renouncers. Photography exhibit, Indigo Gallery, Naxal, Kathmandu, Nepal. www.asianart .com/exhibitions/sadhus/index.html. See also Heitzman, J., & Wordem, R. L. (Eds.). (2006). *India: A country study* (sect. 2, 5th ed.). Washington, DC: Federal Research Division, Library of Congress.

[22]Martin, E. (1999). Flexible survivors. *Anthropology News, 40*(6), 5–7.

Biocultural Connection

Down Syndrome Across Cultures

Katherine A. Dettwyler

Biological anthropologist Katherine Dettwyler compares the cultural experience of Down syndrome, the biological state of having an extra 21st chromosome, in Peter, her son, and in Abi, a child she meets while doing fieldwork in Mali, West Africa. She writes:

Down syndrome children are often (though not always!) sweet, happy, and affectionate kids. Many families of children with Down syndrome consider them to be special gifts from God and refer to them as angels. . . .

A little girl had just entered the hut, part of a large family with many children. She had a small round head, and all the facial characteristics of a child with Down syndrome—Oriental-shaped eyes with epicanthic folds, a small flat nose, and small ears. There was no mistaking the diagnosis. Her name was Abi, and she was about 4 years old, the same age as Peter.

I knelt in front of the little girl. "Hi there, sweetie," I said in English. "Can I have a hug?" I held out my arms, and she willingly stepped forward and gave me a big hug.

I looked up at her mother. "Do you know that there's something 'different' about this child?" I asked, choosing my words carefully.

"Well, she doesn't talk," said her mother, hesitantly, looking at her husband for confirmation.

"That's right," he said. "She's never said a word."

"But she's been healthy?" I asked.

"Yes," the father replied. "She's like the other kids, except she doesn't talk. She's always happy. She never cries. We know she can hear, because she does what we tell her to. Why are you so interested in her?"

"Because I know what's the matter with her. I have a son like this." Excitedly, I pulled a picture of Peter out of my bag and showed it to them. They couldn't see any resemblance, though. The difference in skin color swamped the similarities in facial features. But then, Malians think all white people look alike. And it's not

true that all kids with Down syndrome look the same. They're "different in the same way," but they look most like their parents and siblings.

"Have you ever met any other children like this?" I inquired, bursting with curiosity about how rural Malian culture dealt with a condition as infrequent as Down syndrome. Children with Down syndrome are rare to begin with, occurring about once in every 700 births. In a community where thirty or forty children are born each year at the most, a child with Down syndrome might be born only once in twenty years. And many of them would not survive long enough for anyone to be able to tell that they were different. Physical defects along the midline of the body (heart, trachea, intestines) are common among kids with Down syndrome; without immediate surgery and neonatal intensive care, many would not survive. Such surgery is routine in American children's hospitals but nonexistent in rural Mali. For the child without any major physical defects, there are still the perils of rural Malian life to survive: malaria, measles, diarrhea, diphtheria, and polio. Some, like Peter, have poor immune systems, making them even more susceptible to childhood diseases. The odds against finding a child with Down syndrome, surviving and healthy in a rural Malian village, are overwhelming.

Not surprisingly, the parents knew of no other children like Abi. They asked if I knew of any medicine that could cure her. "No," I explained, "this condition can't be cured. But she will learn to talk, just give her time. Talk to her a lot. Try to get her to repeat things you say. And give her lots of love and attention. It may take her longer to learn some things, but keep trying. In my country, some people say these children are special gifts from God." There was no way I could explain cells and chromosomes and nondisjunction to them, even with a translator's help. And how, I thought to myself, would that have helped them anyway? They

just accepted her as she was.

We chatted for a few more minutes, and I measured the whole family, including Abi, who was, of course, short for her age. I gave her one last hug and a balloon and sent her out the door after her siblings. . . .

I walked out of the hut, . . . trying to get my emotions under control. Finally I gave in, hugged my knees close to my chest, and sobbed. I cried for Abi—what a courageous heart she must have; just think what she might have achieved given all the modern infant stimulation programs available in the West. I cried for Peter—another courageous heart; just think of what he might achieve given the chance to live in a culture that simply accepted him, rather than stereotyping and pigeonholing him, constraining him because people didn't think he was capable of more. I cried for myself—not very courageous at all; my heart felt as though it would burst with longing for Peter, my own sweet angel.

There was clearly some truth to the old adage that ignorance is bliss. Maybe pregnant women in Mali had to worry about evil spirits lurking in the latrine at night, but they didn't spend their pregnancies worrying about chromosomal abnormalities, the moral implications of amniocentesis, or the heart-wrenching exercise of trying to evaluate handicaps, deciding which ones made life not worth living. Women in the United States might have the freedom to choose not to give birth to children with handicaps, but women in Mali had freedom from worrying about it. Children in the United States had the freedom to attend special programs to help them overcome their handicaps, but children in Mali had freedom from the biggest handicap of all—other people's prejudice.

I had cried myself dry. I splashed my face with cool water from the bucket inside the kitchen and returned to the task at hand.

(Adapted from Katherine A. Dettwyler (1994). Dancing skeletons: Life and death in West Africa (ch. 8). Reprinted by permission of Waveland Press, Inc., Long Grove, IL)

Cultural Relativity of Abnormality

Is all of this to suggest that "normalcy" is a meaningless concept when applied to personality? Within the context of a particular culture, the concept of normal personality is quite meaningful. Irving Hallowell, a major figure in the development of psychological anthropology, somewhat ironically observed that it is normal to share the delusions traditionally accepted by one's society. Abnormality involves the development of a delusional system of which the culture does not approve.

If severe enough, culturally induced conflicts can produce psychosis and also determine the form of the psychosis. In a culture that encourages aggressiveness and suspicion, the insane person may be one who is passive and trusting. In a culture that encourages passivity and trust, the insane person may be the one who is aggressive and suspicious. Just as each society establishes its own norms, each individual is unique in his or her perceptions.

Many anthropologists see the only meaningful criterion for personality evaluation as the correlation between personality and social conformity. From their point of view, insanity is a culturally constructed mental illness, and people are considered insane when they fail to conform to a culturally defined range of normal behavior. This is not to say that psychosis is simply a matter of an especially bad fit between an individual and his or her particular culture.

Although it is true that each particular culture defines what is and is not normal behavior, the situation is complicated by findings suggesting that major categories of mental disorders may be universal types of human affliction. Take, for example, schizophrenia—probably the most common of all psychoses and one that may be found in any culture, no matter how it may manifest itself. Individuals afflicted by schizophrenia experience distortions of reality that impair their ability to function adequately, so they often withdraw from the social world into their own psychological shell. Although environmental factors play a role, evidence suggests that schizophrenia is caused by a biochemical disorder for which there is an inheritable tendency. One of its more severe forms is paranoid schizophrenia. Those suffering from it fear and mistrust nearly everyone. They hear voices that whisper dreadful things to them, and they are convinced that someone is "out to get them." Acting on this conviction, they engage in bizarre sorts of behaviors, which lead to their removal from society.

ethnic psychosis A mental disorder specific to a particular ethnic group

Ethnic Psychosis

An **ethnic psychosis** is a mental disorder specific to a particular cultural group. For example, anorexia nervosa is an ethnic psychosis, occurring most frequently among girls and young women—and now boys and young men as well—in Western countries. This psychosis is now spreading to other parts of the world, in part stimulated by compelling Western images of "sexy" thin fashion models and film celebrities. Featuring an excessive preoccupation with thinness and a refusal to eat, anorexia can result in death.

A historical example of an ethnic psychosis is Windigo psychosis, limited to northern Algonquian Indian groups such as the Cree and Ojibwa. In their traditional belief systems, these northern Indians recognized the existence of cannibalistic monsters called Windigos. Individuals afflicted by the psychosis developed the delusion that, falling under the control of these monsters, they were themselves transformed into Windigos, with a craving for human flesh. As this happened, the psychotic individuals saw people around them turning into various edible animals—fat, juicy beavers, for instance. Although there are no known instances where sufferers of Windigo psychosis actually ate another human being, they were acutely afraid of doing so, and people around them were genuinely fearful that they might.

Windigo psychosis may seem different from clinical cases of paranoid schizophrenia found in Euramerican cultures, but a closer look suggests otherwise. The disorder was merely being expressed in ways compatible with traditional northern Algonquian cultures. Ideas of persecution, instead of being directed toward other humans, were directed toward supernatural beings (the Windigo monsters); cannibalistic panic replaced panic expressed in other forms. Northern Algonquian Indians, like Euramericans, expressed their problems in terms compatible with the appropriate view of the self and its behavioral environment.

By contrast, the delusions of Irish schizophrenics draw upon the images and symbols of Irish Catholicism and feature virgin and savior motifs. Euramericans, on the other hand, tend toward secular or electromagnetic persecution delusions.

The underlying structure of the mental disorder is the same in all cases, but its expression is culturally specific. Anthropologists view all mental health issues in their cultural context, in recognition of the fact that each individual's social identity, unique personality, and overall sense of mental health is molded by the particular culture within which the person is born and raised to function as a valued member of the community.

Chapter Summary

■ Enculturation, the process by which individuals become members of their society, begins soon after birth. Its first agents are the members of an individual's household, but later, other members of society become involved. For enculturation to proceed, individuals must possess self-awareness, the ability to identify oneself as an individual, to reflect on oneself, and to evaluate oneself.

■ For self-awareness to emerge and function, four basic orientations are necessary to structure the behavioral environment in which the self acts: object orientation (learning about a world of objects other than the self), spatial orientation, temporal orientation, and normative orientation (an understanding of the values, ideals, and standards that constitute the behavioral environment).

■ A child's birthright and social identity are established through personal naming, a universal practice with numerous cross-cultural variations. A name is an important device for self-definition—without one, an individual has no identity, no self. Many cultures mark the naming of a child with a special ceremony.

■ Personality refers to the distinctive ways a person thinks, feels, and behaves. Along with psychologists, most anthropologists believe early childhood experiences play a key role in shaping adult personality. A prime goal of anthropologists has been to produce objective studies that test this theory. Cross-cultural studies of gender-related personality characteristics, for example, show that whatever biologically based personality differences exist between men and women, they are extremely malleable. A society's economy helps structure the way children are brought up, which in turn influences their adult personalities.

■ Psychological anthropologists, on the basis of cross-cultural studies, have established the interrelation of personality, child-rearing practices, and other aspects of culture. For example, dependence training, usually associated with traditional farming societies, stresses compliance in the performance of assigned tasks and dependence on the domestic group, rather than reliance on oneself. At the opposite extreme, independence training, typical of societies characterized by small, independent families, puts a premium on self-reliance, independent behavior, and personal achievement. Although a society may emphasize one sort of behavior over the other, it may not emphasize it to the same degree in both sexes. Some psychological anthropologists contend that child-rearing practices have their roots in a society's customs for meeting the basic physical needs of its members and that these practices produce particular kinds of adult personalities.

■ Gender behaviors and relations are malleable and vary cross-culturally. Each culture presents different opportunities and expectations concerning ideal or acceptable male–female behavior. In some cultures, male–female relations are based on equal status, with both genders expected to behave similarly. In others, however, male–female relations are based on

inequality and are marked by different standards of expected behavior. Anthropological research demonstrates that gender dominance is a cultural construct and, consequently, that alternative male–female social arrangements can be created if so desired.

■ Early on, anthropologists began to work on the problem of whether it is possible to delineate a group personality without falling into stereotyping. Each culture chooses, from the vast array of possibilities, those traits that it sees as normative or ideal. Individuals who conform to these traits are rewarded; the rest are not. The modal personality of a group is the body of character traits that occur with the highest frequency in a culturally bounded population. As a statistical concept, it opens up for investigation how societies organize the diverse personalities of their members, some of which conform more than others to the modal type.

■ National character studies have focused on the modal characteristics of modern countries. They have attempted to determine the child-rearing practices and education that shape such a group personality. Many anthropologists believe national character theories are based on unscientific and overly generalized data; others have chosen to focus on the core values promoted in particular societies while recognizing that success in instilling these values in individuals may vary considerably.

■ Intersexuals—individuals born with reproductive organs, genitalia, and/or sex chromosomes that are not exclusively male or female—do not fit neatly into either a male or female biological standard or into a binary gender standard. Numerous cultures in the course of history have created social space for intersexuals, as well as transgenders—physically male or female persons who cross over or occupy an alternative social position in the binary male–female gender construction.

■ What defines normal behavior in any culture is determined by the culture itself, and what may be acceptable, or even admirable, in one may not be in another. Abnormality involves developing personality traits not accepted by a culture. Culturally induced conflicts not only can produce psychological disturbance but can determine the form of the disturbance as well. Similarly, mental disorders that have a biological cause, like schizophrenia, will be expressed by symptoms specific to the culture of the afflicted individual. Ethnic psychoses are mental disorders specific to a particular ethnic group.

Questions for Reflection

1. Every society faces the challenge of humanizing its children, teaching them the values and social codes that will enable them to be functioning and contributing members in the community. What child-rearing practices did you experience that embody the values and social codes of your society?

2. Considering the cultural significance of naming ceremonies in so many societies, what do you think motivated your parents when they named you? Does that have any influence on your sense of self?

3. Do you fit within the acceptable range of your society's modal personality? How so?

4. Given that over 60 million people in today's world are intersexed, what do you think of societies that have created cultural space for a third-gender option?

5. Cross-cultural research on gender relations suggests that male dominance is a cultural construct and, consequently, that alternative gender arrangements can be created. Looking at your grandparents, parents, siblings, do you see any changes in your own family? What about your own community? Do you think such changes are positive?

Key Terms

self-awareness	modal personality
naming ceremony	core values
personality	intersexuals
dependence training	transgenders
independence training	ethnic psychosis

VISUAL ESSENCE

All humans depend on food, water, and shelter for survival. Beyond these basic subsistence needs, they enjoy many other things that make life comfortable, offer pleasure, provide prestige, or are otherwise desirable or important. As this photograph of a regional market in the highlands of Guatemala shows, Maya Indian farmers grow more food crops than they need to feed their families. They take the surplus to this traditional marketplace and barter what they have for merchandise they do not grow or make themselves—from sugar to blue jeans and rubber boots to plastic containers, steel axes, knives, shovels, and machetes. They also sell their produce for money to pay for goods and services, such as medicine and the bus or truck that carries them back to their mountain villages. To a knowing eye, the distinctly embroidered blouse (*huipile*) worn by each of these Maya women reveals where she lives and whether she is single or married. All around the world, at open marketplaces like this one, people from different places forge and affirm their social networks. These friendships, partnerships, and alliances, in turn, are essential in their search for safety and well-being.

Subsistence and Exchange

All living beings must satisfy certain basic needs to stay alive—including food, water, and shelter. Moreover, because these needs must be met on a regular basis, no creature could long survive if its relations with its environment were random and chaotic. People have a huge advantage over other animals in this regard. We have culture. With the passing of time, culture has become our primary means of adapting to the limitations and possibilities within any given environment.

ADAPTATION

In previous chapters, we noted that adaptation is the ongoing process organisms undergo to achieve a beneficial adjustment to a particular environment. What makes human adaptation unique among all other species is our capacity to produce and reproduce culture, enabling us to creatively adapt to an extraordinary range of radically different environments. The biological underpinnings of this capacity include large brains and a long period of growth and development.

How humans adjust to the burdens and opportunities presented in daily life is the basic concern of all cultures. As defined in Chapter 8, a people's *cultural adaptation* consists of a complex of ideas, activities, and technologies that enable them to survive and even thrive and that, in turn, affect their environment.

Through cultural adaptation, different human groups have managed to inhabit a diversity of natural environments, ranging from Arctic snowfields to Polynesian coral islands, from the Sahara Desert to the Amazon rainforest. Adaptation occurs not only when humans make all kinds of changes in their natural environment, but also when they are biologically changed by their natural environment, as illustrated in this chapter's Biocultural Connection.

Surviving in the Andes:
Aymara Adaptation to High Altitude

However adaptable we are as a species through our diverse cultures, some natural environments pose such extreme climatic challenges that the human body must make physical adaptations to successfully survive. The central Andean highlands of Bolivia offer an interesting example of complex biocultural interaction, where a biologically adapted human body type has emerged due to natural selection.

Known as the *altiplano,* this high plateau has an average elevation of 4,000 meters (13,000 feet). Many thousands of years ago, small groups of human foragers in the warm lowlands climbed up the mountain slopes in search of game and other food. The higher they climbed, the harder it became to breathe due to decreasing molecular concentration, or partial pressure, of oxygen in the air. However, upon reaching the cold and treeless highlands, they found herds of llamas and hardy food plants, including potatoes—reasons to stay. Eventually (about 4,000 years ago) their descendants domesticated both the llamas and the potatoes and developed a new way of life as high-altitude agropastoralists.

The llamas provided meat and hides, as well as milk and wool. And the potatoes, a rich source of carbohydrates, became their staple food. In the course of many centuries, the Aymara selectively cultivated more than 200 varieties of these tubers on small family-owned tracts of land. They boiled them fresh for immediate consumption and also freeze-dried and preserved them as *chuño,* which is the Aymara's major source of nutrition to this day.

Still surviving as highland subsistence farmers and herders, these Aymara Indians have adapted culturally and biologically to the cold and harsh conditions of Bolivia's altiplano.

© Victor Englebert

They live and go about their work at extremely high altitudes (up to 4,800 meters/15,600 feet), where partial pressure of oxygen in the air is far lower than most humans are biologically accustomed to.

Experiencing a marked hypoxemia (insufficient oxygenation of the blood), a person's normal physiological response to being active at such heights is quick and heavy breathing. Most outsiders visiting the altiplano typically need several days to acclimatize to these conditions. Going too high too quickly can cause *soroche* (mountain sickness), with physiological problems such as pulmonary hypertension, increased heart rates, shortness of breath, headaches, fever, lethargy, and nausea. These symptoms usually disappear when one becomes fully acclimated, but most people will still be quickly exhausted by otherwise normal physical exercise.

For the Aymara Indians whose ancestors have inhabited the altiplano

for many thousands of years, the situation is different. Through generations of natural selection, their bodies have become biologically adapted to the low oxygen levels. Short-legged and barrel-chested, their small bodies have an unusually large thoracic volume compared to their tropical lowland neighbors and most other humans. Remarkably, their expanded heart and lungs possess about 30 percent greater pulmonary diffusing capacity to oxygenate blood. In short, the distinctly broad chests of the Aymara Indians are evidence of their biological adaptation to the low-oxygen atmosphere of a natural habitat in which they survive as high-altitude agropastoralists.

(See P. Baker (Ed.). (1978). The biology of high altitude peoples. *London: Cambridge University Press; Rupert, J. L., & Hochachka, P. W. (2001). The evidence for hereditary factors contributing to high altitude adaptation in Andean natives: A review.* High Altitude Medicine & Biology, 2(2), 235–256)*

The Unit of Adaptation

The unit of adaptation includes both organisms and their environment. Organisms, including human beings, exist as members of a population; populations, in turn, must have the flexibility to cope with variability and change within the natural environment that sustains them. In biological terms, this flexibility means that different organisms within the population have somewhat differing genetic endowments. In cultural terms, it means that variation occurs among individual skills, knowledge, and personalities. Indeed, organisms and environments form dynamic interacting systems. And although environments do not determine culture, they do present certain possibilities and limitations: People might just as easily farm as fish, but we do not expect to find farmers in Siberia's frozen tundra or fishermen in the middle of North Africa's Sahara Desert.

Some anthropologists have adopted the ecologists' concept of **ecosystem**, defined as a system, or functioning whole, composed of both the natural environment and all the organisms living within it. The system is bound by the activities of the organisms, as well as by such physical processes as erosion and evaporation.

Adaptation in Cultural Evolution

Human groups adapt to their environments by means of their cultures. However, cultures may change over the course of time; they evolve. This is called **cultural evolution**. The process is sometimes confused with the idea of **progress**—the notion that humans are moving forward to a better, more advanced stage in their development toward perfection. Yet, not all changes turn out to be positive in the long run, nor do they improve conditions for every member of a society even in the short run. Complex urban societies are not more highly evolved than those of food foragers. Rather, both are highly evolved, but in quite different ways.

To fit into an ecosystem, humans (like all organisms) must have the potential to adjust to or become a part of it. A good example of this is the Comanche, whose history begins in the highlands of southern Idaho.[1] Living in that harsh, arid region, these North American Indians traditionally subsisted on wild plants, small animals, and occasionally larger game. Their material equipment was simple and limited to what they (and their dogs) could carry or pull. The size of their groups was restricted, and what little social power could develop was in the hands of the shaman, who was a combination of healer and spiritual guide.

At some point in their nomadic history, the Comanche moved east onto the Great Plains, attracted by enormous bison herds. As much larger groups could be supported by the new and plentiful food supply, the Comanche needed a more complex political organization. Eventually they acquired horses and guns from European and neighboring Indian traders. This enhanced their hunting capabilities significantly and led to the emergence of powerful hunting chiefs.

The Comanche became raiders in order to get more horses (which they did not breed for themselves), and their hunting chiefs evolved into war chiefs. The once materially poor and peaceful hunter-gatherers of the dry highlands became wealthy, and raiding became a way of life. In the late 18th and early 19th centuries, they dominated the southern plains (now primarily Texas and Oklahoma). In moving from one regional environment to another and in adopting a new technology, the Comanche were able to take advantage of existing cultural capabilities to thrive in their new situation.

Sometimes societies that developed independently of one another find similar solutions to similar problems. For example, the Cheyenne Indians moved from the woodlands of the Great Lakes region to the Great Plains and took up a form of Plains Indian culture resembling that of the Comanche, even though the cultural historical backgrounds of the two groups differed significantly. (Before they transformed into horse-riding bison hunters, the Cheyenne had cultivated crops and gathered wild rice, which fostered a distinct set of social, political, and religious practices.) This is an example of **convergent evolution**—the development of similar cultural adaptations to similar environmental conditions by different peoples with different ancestral cultures.

Especially interesting is that the Cheyenne gave up crop cultivation completely and focused exclusively on hunting and gathering after their move into the vast grasslands of the northern High Plains. Contrary to the popular notion of evolution as a progressive movement toward increased manipulation of the environment, this ethnographic example shows that cultural historical changes in subsistence practices do not always go from dependence on wild food to farming; they may go the other way as well.

Related to the phenomenon of convergent evolution is **parallel evolution**, in which similar cultural adaptations to similar environmental conditions are achieved by peoples whose ancestral cultures were already somewhat alike. For example, the development of farming in Southwest Asia and Mesoamerica (discussed in

---

ecosystem A system, or a functioning whole, composed of both the natural environment and all the organisms living within it

cultural evolution Culture change over time (not to be confused with progress)

progress The ethnocentric notion that humans are moving forward to a higher, more advanced stage in their development toward perfection

convergent evolution In cultural evolution, the development of similar cultural adaptations to similar environmental conditions by different peoples with different ancestral cultures

parallel evolution In cultural evolution, the development of similar cultural adaptations to similar environmental conditions by peoples whose ancestral cultures were already somewhat alike

---

[1]Wallace, E., & Hoebel, E. A. (1952). *The Comanches*. Norman: University of Oklahoma Press.

Chapter 5) took place independently, as people in both regions, whose lifeways were already comparable, became dependent on a narrow range of plant foods that required human intervention for their protection and reproductive success. Both developed intensive forms of agriculture, built large cities, and created complex social and political organizations.

It is important to recognize that stability as well as change is involved in cultural adaptation and evolution; episodes of major adaptive change may be followed by long periods of relative stability in a cultural system.

Moreover, not everybody benefits from changes, especially if change is forced upon them. As history painfully demonstrates, all too often humans have made changes that have had disastrous results, leading to the deaths of thousands, even millions, of people—not to mention other creatures—and to the destruction of the natural environment. In short, we must avoid falling into the ethnocentric trap of equating change with progress or seeing everything as adaptive.

MODES OF SUBSISTENCE

Human societies all across the world have developed a cultural infrastructure compatible with the natural resources they have available to them and within the limitations of their various habitats. Each mode of subsistence involves not only resources but also the technology required to effectively capture and utilize them, as well as the kinds of work arrangements that are developed to best suit a society's needs. In the next few pages, we will discuss the major types of cultural infrastructure, beginning with the oldest and most universal mode of subsistence: food foraging.

Food-Foraging Societies

Before the domestication of food plants and animals, all people supported themselves through **food foraging**,

---

food foraging A mode of subsistence involving some combination of hunting, fishing, and gathering wild plant foods
industrial society A society in which human labor, hand tools, and animal power are largely replaced by machines, with an economy primarily based on big factories
Neolithic revolution The profound culture change beginning about 10,000 years ago associated with the early domestication of plants and animals and settlement in permanent villages; sometimes referred to as the Neolithic transition
horticulture Cultivation of crops carried out with simple hand tools such as digging sticks or hoes
slash-and-burn cultivation An extensive form of horticulture in which the natural vegetation is cut, the slash is subsequently burned, and crops are then planted among the ashes; also known as swidden farming

---

a mode of subsistence involving some combination of hunting, fishing, and gathering wild plant foods. When food foragers had the earth to themselves, they had their pick of the best environments. But gradually areas with rich soils and ample supplies of water were appropriated by farming societies and, more recently, by **industrial societies**, in which human labor, hand tools, and animal power were largely replaced by machines. As a result, small foraging communities were edged out of their traditional habitats.

Today at most a quarter of a million people (less then 0.005 percent of the world population of over 6 billion) still support themselves mainly as foragers. They are found only in the world's most marginal areas—frozen Arctic tundra, deserts, and deep forests—and typically lead a migratory existence. As foraging cultures have nearly disappeared in areas having a natural abundance of food and fuel resources, anthropologists are necessarily cautious when it comes to making generalizations about the ancient human past based on in-depth studies of still-existing foraging groups that have adapted to more marginal habitats.

Characteristics of Food-Foraging Societies

Typically, foragers have ample and balanced diets and are less likely to experience severe famine than farmers. Their material possessions are limited, but so is their desire to amass things. Notably, they have plenty of leisure time for concentrating on family ties, social life, and spiritual development—apparently far more than people living in farming and industrial societies. Such findings clearly challenge the once widely held view that food foragers live a miserable existence.

Present-day people who subsist by hunting, fishing, and wild plant collection are not following an ancient way of life because they do not know any better. Rather, they have been forced by circumstances into situations where foraging is the best means of survival or they simply prefer to live this way. In fact, foraging constitutes a rational response to particular ecological, economic, and sociopolitical realities. Moreover, for at least 2,000 years, hunters, fishers, and gatherers have met the demands for commodities such as furs, hides, feathers, ivory, pearls, fish, nuts, and honey within larger trading networks. Like everyone else, most food foragers are now part of a larger system with social, economic, and political relations extending far beyond regional, national, or even continental boundaries.

The hallmarks of food-foraging societies (particularly those few that still, or until recently, survive in marginal areas that are not as naturally rich in food and fuel) include mobility and small group size. Food foragers move as needed within a circumscribed region that is their home range to tap into naturally available food sources. A crucial factor in this mobility is availability of water. The distance between the food supply and water must not be so great that more energy is required to fetch water than can be obtained from the food.

Another characteristic of the food-foraging adaptation is the small size of local groups, typically fewer than a hundred people. No completely satisfactory explanation for this has been offered, but both ecological and social factors are involved. Among the ecological factors is the number of people that the available resources can support at a given level of food-getting techniques. This requires adjusting to seasonal and long-term changes in resource availability. The population density of foraging groups surviving in marginal environments today rarely exceeds one person per square mile—a very low density.

Other key characteristics are egalitarianism, communal property, and flexible division of labor by gender—all discussed in the economics section of this chapter.

Food–Producing Societies

As described in Chapter 5, the domestication of plants and animals began about 10,000 years ago with the **Neolithic revolution**. This led to radical transformations in cultural systems, with foragers developing new social and economic patterns based on either plant cultivation or pastoralism. Although food production gave people alternative sources for nutrition and some control over vital resources, the new ways of life were not always more reliable than foraging.

Producing Food in Gardens: Horticulture

With the advent of plant domestication, some societies took up **horticulture** (from the Latin *hortus*, meaning "garden"), in which small communities of gardeners cultivate crops with simple hand tools, using neither irrigation nor the plow. Typically, horticulturists cultivate several varieties of food plants in small, hand-cleared gardens. Since they do not usually fertilize the soil, they use a given garden plot for only a few years before abandoning it in favor of a new one. Often, horticulturists can grow enough food for their subsistence, and occasionally they produce a modest surplus that can be used for purposes such as inter-village feasts and exchange. Although their major food supplies may come from their gardens, many horticulturalists will also fish, hunt game, and collect wild plants foods when need and opportunity arise.

One of the most widespread forms of horticulture, especially in the tropics, is **slash-and-burn cultivation**, or *swidden farming*, in which the natural vegetation is cut, the slash is subsequently burned, and crops are then planted among the ashes. This is an ecologically sophisticated and sustainable way of raising food, especially in the tropics, when carried out under the right conditions: low population densities and adequate amounts of land. It mimics the diversity of the natural ecosystem, growing several different crops in the same field. Mixed together, the crops are less vulnerable to pests and plant diseases than a single crop.

Not only is the system ecologically sound, but it is far more energy efficient than modern farming methods used in developed countries such as the United States, where natural resources such as land and fuel are still relatively cheap and abundant, and many farms operate with financial support in the form of government subsidies or tax breaks. While high-tech farming requires more energy input than it yields, slash-and-burn farming produces between 10 and 20 units of energy for every unit expended.

Here the process of slash-and-burn cultivation is carried out in the Amazon forest in Venezuela in preparation for new planting. Although it looks destructive, if properly carried out, slash-and-burn cultivation (also known as swidden farming) is an ecologically sound way of growing crops in the tropics.

© Jacques Jangoux/Alamy

Producing Food on Farms: Agriculture

In contrast to horticulture, **agriculture** (from the Latin *agri,* meaning "field") is growing food plants like grains, tubers, fruits, and vegetables in soil prepared and maintained for crop production. This form of more intensive food production involves using technologies other than hand tools, such as irrigation, fertilizers, and plows pulled by harnessed draft animals. In the so-called developed countries of the world, agriculture relies on fuel-powered tractors to produce food on larger plots of land. But the ingenuity of some early agriculturalists is illustrated in this chapter's Anthropology Applied feature, highlighting an ecologically sound mountain terracing and irrigation system established 1,000 years ago.

Among agriculturists, surplus crop cultivation is generally substantial—providing food not only for

---

Anthropology Applied

Agricultural Development and the Anthropologist

Ann Kendall

Gaining insight into the traditional practices of indigenous peoples, anthropologists have often been impressed by their ingenuity. This awareness has spread beyond the profession to the Western public at large, giving birth to the popular notion that indigenous groups invariably live in some sort of blissful oneness with the environment. But this was never the message of anthropologists, who know that traditional people are only human, and like all human beings, are capable of making mistakes. Yet, just as we have much to learn from their successes, so can we learn from their failures.

Archaeologist Ann Kendall is doing just this in the Patacancha Valley in the Andes Mountains of southern Peru. Kendall is director and founder of the Cusichaca Trust, near Oxford, England, a rural development organization that revives ancient farming practices. In the late 1980s, after working for ten years on archaeological excavations and rural development projects, she invited botanist Alex Chepstow-Lusty of Cambridge University to investigate climatic change and paleoecological data. His findings, along with Kendall's, provided evidence of intensive farming in the Patacancha Valley, beginning about 4,000 years ago. The research showed that over time widespread clearing to establish and maintain farm plots, coupled with minimal terracing of the hillsides, had resulted in tremendous soil loss through erosion. By 1,900 years ago, soil degradation and a cooling climate had led to a dramatic reduction in farming. Then, about 1,000 years ago, farming was

revived, this time with soil-sparing techniques.

Kendall's investigations have documented intensive irrigated terrace construction over two periods of occupation, including Inca development of the area. It was a sophisticated system, devised to counteract erosion and achieve maximum agricultural production. The effort required workers to haul load after load of soil up from the valley floor. In addition, they planted alder trees to stabilize the soil and to provide both firewood and building materials. So successful was this farming system by Inca times that the number of people living in the valley quadrupled to some 4,000, about

the same as it is now. However, yet another reversal of fortune occurred when the Spanish took over Peru, and the terraces and trees were allowed to deteriorate.

Armed with these research findings and information and insights gathered through interviews and meetings with locals, the Cusichaca Trust supported the restoration of the terraces and 5.8 kilometers of canal. The effort relied on local labor working with traditional methods and materials—clay (with a cactus mix to keep it moist), stone, and soil. Local families have replanted 160 hectares of the renovated preconquest terraces with maize, potatoes, and wheat, making the plots up to 10 times more productive than they were. Among other related accomplishments, 21 water systems have been installed, which reach more than 800 large families, and a traditional concept of home-based gardens has been adapted to introduce European-style vegetable gardens to improve diet and health and to facilitate market gardening. Since 1997, these projects have been under a new and independent local rural development organization known as ADESA.

The Cusichaca Trust is now continuing its pioneering work in areas of extreme poverty in Peru further to the north, such as Apurimac and Ayacucho, using proven traditional technology in the restoration of ancient canal and terrace systems.

(Adapted from K. Krajick. (1998). Greenfarming by the Incas? Science, 281, 323. The update and elaboration by textbook authors are based on personal communication with Kendall and Cusichaca Trust reports. For more information see www .cusichaca.org)

their own needs but also for those of various full-time specialists and nonproducing consumers. This surplus may be traded or sold for cash, or it may be coerced out of the farmers through taxes, rent, or tribute (forced gifts acknowledging submission or protection) paid to landowners or other dominant groups. These landowners and specialists—such as traders, carpenters, blacksmiths, sculptors, basket makers, and stonecutters—typically reside in substantial towns or cities, where political power is centralized in the hands of a socially elite class. Dominated by more powerful groups and markets, much of what the farmers do is governed by political and economic forces over which they have little control.

Characteristics of Crop-Producing Societies

One of the most significant correlates of crop cultivation was the development of fixed settlements, in which farming families reside together near their cultivated fields. The task of food production lent itself to a different kind of social organization. Because the hard work of some members of the group could provide food for all, others became free to devote their time to inventing and manufacturing the equipment needed for a new sedentary way of life. Tools for digging and harvesting, pottery for storage and cooking, clothing made of woven textiles, and housing made of stone, wood, or sun-dried bricks all grew out of the new sedentary living conditions and the altered division of labor.

The Neolithic revolution also brought important changes in social structure. At first, social relations were egalitarian and hardly different from those that prevailed among food foragers. As settlements grew, however, and large numbers of people had to share important resources such as land and water, society became more elaborately organized.

Herding Grazing Animals: Pastoralism

One of the more striking examples of human adaptation to the environment is **pastoralism**—breeding and managing large herds of domesticated herbivores (grazing and browsing animals), such as goats, sheep, cattle, horses, llamas, or camels.

Dependent on livestock for survival, families in pastoral cultures own herds of grazing animals whose needs for food and drink determine their everyday routines. Unlike crop cultivators who need to remain close to their fields, pastoral peoples do not usually establish permanent settlements since they must follow or drive their large herds to new pastures on a regular basis. Like their animals, most pastoralists must be mobile and have adjusted their way of life accordingly.

Nomadic pastoralism is an effective way of living—far more so than sheep or cattle ranching—in environments that are too dry, cold, steep, or rocky for farming, such as the vast, arid grasslands that stretch eastward from northern Africa through the Arabian Desert, across the plateau of Iran and into Turkistan and Mongolia. Today, in Africa and Asia alone, more than 21 million people are pastoralists, still migrating with their herds. These nomadic groups regard movement as a natural part of life.

Although pastoral nomads depend greatly on animals to meet their daily needs, they do trade surplus animals, leather, and wool (and various crafts such as woven rugs) with farmers or merchants. In exchange they receive crops and valued commodities such as flour, dried fruit, spices, tea, metal knives, pots and kettles, cotton or linen textiles, guns and (more recently) lightweight plastic containers, sheets, and so on. In other words, there are many ties that connect them to surrounding agricultural and industrial societies.

Labor division among pastoral nomads is mainly according to age and gender. Typically, the chief task of the adult men and older boys is tending the herds. Although women and older girls in many pastoral societies are involved in herding as well, they primarily cook, sew, weave, care for the children, and carry fuel and water.

Industrial Societies

Until about 200 years ago, human societies worldwide had developed a cultural infrastructure based on foraging, horticulture, agriculture, pastoralism, crafts, trade, or some combination of these. This changed with the invention of the steam engine in England, which brought about an industrial revolution that quickly spread to other parts of the globe. Machines and tools powered by water, wind, and steam (followed by oil, gas, and diesel fuel) replaced human labor, animal power, and hand tools, increasing factory production and facilitating mass transportation.

Throughout the 1800s and 1900s, this resulted in large-scale industrialization of many societies. Technological inventions utilizing oil, electricity, and (since the 1940s) nuclear energy brought about more dramatic changes in social and economic organization on a worldwide scale.

In the late 20th century, the electronic-digital revolution made the production and distribution of information and services the center of economic activity in some wealthy societies. This transition from an industrial to

agriculture Intensive crop cultivation, employing plows, fertilizers, and/or irrigation
pastoralism Breeding and managing large herds of domesticated herbivores (grazing and browsing animals), such as goats, sheep, cattle, horses, llamas, or camels

In the Zagros Mountains region of Iran, pastoral nomads follow seasonal pastures, migrating vast distances with their huge herds of goats and sheep over rugged terrain that includes perilously steep snowy passes and fast ice-cold rivers.

postindustrial society is taking place primarily in parts of the United States, Canada, Japan, and western Europe, where economies are becoming less dependent on large-scale production and distribution of machine-made commodities. Instead of big factories, these postindustrial economies are increasingly based on research and development of new knowledge and technologies, as well as providing information, services, and finance capital on a global scale.[2]

SUBSISTENCE AND ECONOMICS

An **economic system** is an organized arrangement for producing, distributing, and consuming goods. Since a people, in pursuing a particular means of subsistence, necessarily produces, distributes, and consumes things,

postindustrial society A society with an economy based on research and development of new knowledge and technologies, as well as providing information, services, and finance capital on a global scale
economic system An organized arrangement for producing, distributing, and consuming goods
technology Tools and other material equipment, together with the knowledge of how to make and use them

it is obvious that our discussion of subsistence patterns involves economic matters. Yet economic systems encompass much more than we have covered so far.

Although anthropologists have adopted theories and concepts from economists, most recognize that theoretical principles derived from the study of capitalist market economies have limited applicability to economic systems in societies that are not industrialized and where people do not produce and exchange goods for private profit. This is because, in these non-state societies, the economic sphere of behavior is not separate from the social, religious, and political spheres.

In every society, particular customs and rules govern the kinds of work done, who does the work, attitudes toward the work, how it is accomplished, and who controls the resources necessary to produce desired goods, knowledge, and services. The primary resources in any culture are raw materials, technology, and labor. The rules directing the use of these are embedded in a people's culture and determine the way the economy operates within any given natural environment.

Control of Land and Water Resources

All societies regulate allocation of valuable natural resources—especially land and water. Food foragers must determine who will hunt game and gather plants in their home range and where these activities take place. Groups that rely on fishing or growing crops need to make similar

[2]Ritzer, G. (2007). *The coming of post-industrial society* (2nd ed.). New York: McGraw-Hill.

decisions concerning who carries out which task on which stretch of water or land. Farmers must have some means of determining title to land and access to water supplies for irrigation. Pastoralists require a system that determines rights to watering places and grazing land, as well as to the areas through which they move their herds.

In Western capitalist societies, a system of private ownership of land and rights to natural resources generally prevails. For instance, although elaborate laws have been enacted to regulate the buying, owning, and selling of land and water resources, if individuals wish to re-allocate valuable farmland to some other purpose, they generally can.

In traditional nonindustrial societies, land is often controlled by kinship groups such as the family or band rather than by individuals. For example, among the Ju/'hoansi of the Kalahari Desert, each band of ten to thirty people lives on roughly 250 square miles of land, which they consider to be their territory—their own country. These territories are not defined by boundaries but in terms of water holes that are located within them. The land is said to be "owned" by those who have lived the longest in the band, usually a group of brothers and sisters or cousins. Their concept of landholding, however, is not something easily translated in modern Western terms of private ownership. Suffice it to say that within their traditional worldview, no part of their homeland can be sold for money or traded away for goods. Outsiders must ask permission to enter the territory—but denying the request would be unthinkable.

The practice of defining territories on the basis of *core features*—be they water holes (as among the Ju/'hoansi), watercourses (as among Indians of the northeastern United States), unique sites in the landscape where ancestral spirits are thought to dwell (as among the Aborigines in Australia), or whatever—is typical of food foragers. Territorial boundaries tend to be rather vaguely defined, and to avoid friction foragers may designate part of their territory as a buffer zone

between them and their neighbors. The adaptive value of this is obvious: The size of band territories, as well as the size of the bands, can adjust to keep in balance with availability of resources in any given place. Such adjustment would be more difficult under a system of individual ownership of clearly bounded land.

Technology Resources

All societies have some means of creating and allocating tools that are used to produce goods, as well as traditions concerning passing them on to succeeding generations. The number and kinds of tools a society uses—which, together with knowledge about how to make and use them constitute its **technology**—are related to the life-styles of its members. Food foragers and pastoral nomads who are frequently on the move are apt to have fewer and simpler tools than more settled peoples such as sedentary farmers. A great number of complex tools would hinder mobility. Thus, the average weight of an individual's personal belongings among the Ju/'hoansi foragers is just under 25 pounds, limited to the barest essentials such as implements for hunting, gathering, fishing, building, and cooking. Pastoral nomads, aided by pack animals, typically have more material possessions than foragers, but still less than people who live in permanent settlements.

Food foragers make and use a variety of tools, many of which are ingenious in their effectiveness. Some of these they make for their individual use, but codes of generosity are such that a person may not refuse to give or loan what is requested. Tools may be given or loaned to others in exchange for the products resulting from their use. For example, a Ju/'hoansi who gives his arrow to another hunter has a right to a share in any animals the hunter kills. Game is considered to "belong" to the man whose arrow killed it, even when he is not present on the hunt. In this context, it makes little sense for them to accumulate luxuries or surplus goods, and the fact that no one owns significantly more than another helps to limit status differences.

Among horticulturists, the axe, digging stick, and hoe are the primary tools. Since these are relatively easy to produce, almost everyone can make them. Whoever makes a tool has first rights to it, but when he or she is not using it, any family member may ask to use it, and the request is rarely denied. Refusal would cause people to treat the tool owner with scorn for this singular lack of concern for others. If a relative helps raise the crop traded for a particular tool, that relative becomes part owner of the implement, and it may not be traded or given away without his or her permission.

In permanently settled agricultural communities, tools and other productive goods are more complex, heavier, and costlier to make. In such settings, individual ownership tends to be more absolute, as are the conditions under which people may borrow and use such equipment. It is easy to replace a knife lost by a relative during palm cultivation but much more difficult to replace an iron plow or a diesel-fueled harvesting machine. Rights to the ownership of complex tools are more rigidly applied; generally the person who has funded the purchase of a complex piece of machinery is considered the sole owner and may decide how and by whom it will be used.

Labor Resources and Patterns

In addition to raw materials and technology, labor is a key resource in any economic system. A look around the world reveals many different labor patterns, but two features are almost always present in human cultures: a basic division of labor by gender and by age.

Division of Labor by Gender

Anthropologists have studied extensively the social division of labor by gender in cultures of all sorts. Whether men or women do a particular job varies from group to group, but typically work is divided into the tasks of either one or the other. For example, the practices most commonly regarded as "women's work" tend to be those that can be carried out near home and that are easily resumed after interruption. The tasks historically often regarded as "men's work" tend to be those requiring physical strength, rapid mobilization of high bursts of energy, frequent travel at some distance from home, and assumption of high levels of risk and danger.

Many exceptions occur, however, as in those societies where women regularly carry burdensome loads or put in long hours of hard work cultivating crops in the fields. In some societies, women perform almost three-quarters of all work, and in several societies they participate in combat. There are references to female warriors in ancient Ireland, and archaeological evidence indicates their presence among Vikings. In the 19th-century West African kingdom of Dahomey (in what is now called Benin), thousands of women served in the armed forces of the Dahomean king, and some considered the women to be better fighters than their male counterparts.

During World War II, tens of thousands of Russian and other Soviet women engaged in frontline combat defending their homeland against German invaders. Today, women serve in the military of most countries, but only Canada, Denmark, France, Germany, and a few others permit them to join combat units.

Instead of looking for key biological factors to explain the social division of labor, a more useful strategy is to examine the kinds of work that men and women do in the context of specific societies to see how it relates to other cultural and historical factors. Researchers find a continuum of patterns, ranging from flexible integration of men and women to rigid segregation by gender.[3]

The *flexible/integrated pattern* is exemplified by the Ju/'hoansi discussed above and is seen most often among food foragers (as well as communities where crops are traditionally cultivated primarily for family consumption). In such societies, men and women perform up to 35 percent of activities with approximately equal participation, and tasks deemed especially appropriate for one gender may be performed by the other without loss of face, as the situation warrants. Where these practices prevail, boys and girls grow up in much the same way, learn to value cooperation over competition, and become equally habituated to adult men and women, who interact with one another on a relatively equal basis.

Societies following a *segregated pattern* define almost all work as either masculine or feminine, so men and women rarely engage in joint efforts of any kind. In such societies, it is inconceivable that someone would even think of doing something considered the work of the opposite sex. This pattern is frequently seen in pastoral nomadic, intensive agricultural, and industrial societies, where men's work keeps them outside the home for much of the time. Typically, men in such societies are expected to be tough, aggressive, and competitive—and this often involves assertions of male superiority, and hence authority, over women. Historically, societies segregated by gender often have imposed their control on those featuring integration, upsetting the egalitarian nature of the latter.

In the third pattern of labor division by gender, sometimes called the *dual sex configuration,* men and women carry out their work separately, as in societies segregated by gender, but the relationship between them is one of balanced complementarity rather than inequality. Thus, as in integrated societies, neither gender exerts dominance over the other. The dual sex orientation may be seen among certain American Indian peoples whose economies were based upon subsistence farming, as well as among several West African kingdoms, including that of the aforementioned Dahomeans.

In postindustrial societies, the division of labor by gender becomes blurred and even irrelevant, resembling the flexible/integrated pattern of traditional foragers briefly discussed above. Although gender preferences

---

[3]Sanday, P. R. (1981). *Female power and male dominance: On the origins of sexual inequality* (pp. 79–80). Cambridge, England: Cambridge University Press.

Many children in the Third World enter the labor force when they are 6 or 7. In Pakistan, about 6 million children under the age of 10 are employed in wage labor, like these boys who work almost every day from dawn to dusk making mud bricks.

and discrimination in the workplace exist in societies making the economic transition, cultural ideas more fitting agricultural or industrial societies predictably change in due time, adjusting to postindustrial challenges and opportunities.

Division of Labor by Age

Division of labor according to age is also typical of human societies. Among the Ju/'hoansi, for example, children are not expected to contribute significantly to subsistence until they reach their late teens. Indeed, until they possess adult levels of strength and endurance, many "bush" foods are tough for them to gather.

The Ju/'hoansi equivalent of retirement comes somewhere around the age of 60. Elderly people, while they will usually do some foraging for themselves, are not expected to contribute much food. However, older men and women alike play an essential role in spiritual matters. Freed from food taboos and other restrictions that apply to younger adults, they may handle ritual substances considered dangerous to those still involved with hunting or having children. By virtue of their old age, they have memories of customary practices and events that happened far in the past. Thus, they are repositories of accumulated wisdom—the libraries of a nonliterate people—and are able to suggest solutions for problems younger adults have never before had to face. Considered useful for their knowledge, they are far from being unproductive members of society.

In many traditional farming societies, children as well as older people may make a greater contribution to the economy in terms of work and responsibility than is common in industrial or postindustrial societies. For instance, in Maya peasant communities in southern Mexico and Guatemala, children not only look after their younger brothers and sisters but also help with housework. Girls begin to make a substantial contribution to the work of the household by age 7 or 8. By age 11 they are constantly busy with an array of chores—grinding corn, making tortillas, fetching wood and water, sweeping, and so forth. Young boys have less to do but are given small tasks, such as bringing in the chickens or playing with a baby. However, by age 12 they are carrying toasted tortillas to the men out working in the fields and returning with loads of corn.[4]

Children also work in industrial societies, where poor families depend on every possible contribution to the household. There, however, economic desperation may easily lead to the cold exploitation of children in factory settings. The use of child labor has become a matter of increasing concern as large capitalist corporations count more and more on the low-cost manufacture of goods in the world's poorer countries. Reliable figures are hard to come by, but it is estimated that there are some 200 million child laborers under age 14, almost all living in Third World countries where their families

[4]Vogt, E. Z. (1990). *The Zinacantecos of Mexico: A modern Maya way of life* (2nd ed., pp. 83–87). Fort Worth: Holt, Rinehart & Winston.

depend on the extra income they bring home. Many enter the labor force when they are only 6 or 7 years old, working full-time, from dawn to dusk, for extremely low wages, which helps keep the labor costs down. Although the United States long ago passed laws prohibiting institutionalized child labor, the country imports at least $100 million worth of products manufactured by poorly paid children, ranging from rugs and carpets to clothing and soccer balls.[5]

Cooperative Labor

Cooperative work groups can be found everywhere—in foraging as well as food-producing and in nonindustrial as well as industrial societies. Often, if the effort involves the whole community, a festive spirit permeates the work.

In some parts of East Africa, work parties begin with the display of a pot of millet beer to be consumed after the tasks have been finished. Home-brewed from millet, their major cereal crop, the beer is not really payment for the work; indeed, the labor involved is worth far more than the beer consumed. Rather, drinking the low-alcohol but highly nutritious beverage together is more of a symbolic activity to celebrate the spirit of friendship and mutual support, whereas recompense comes as individuals sooner or later participate in work parties for others. In rural areas all around the world, farmers commonly help one another during harvest and haying seasons, often sharing major pieces of equipment.

In most human societies, the basic unit within which cooperation takes place is the household. It is a unit of both production and consumption; only in industrial societies have these two things been separated.

Task Specialization

In contemporary industrial and postindustrial societies, there is a great diversity of specialized tasks to be performed, and no individual can even begin to know

---

reciprocity The exchange of goods and services, of approximately equal value, between two parties
generalized reciprocity A mode of exchange in which the value of the gift is not calculated, nor is the time of repayment specified
balanced reciprocity A mode of exchange in which the giving and the receiving are specific as to the value of the goods and the time of their delivery
negative reciprocity A mode of exchange in which the aim is to get something for as little as possible. Neither fair nor balanced, it may involve hard bargaining, manipulation, outright cheating, or theft

---

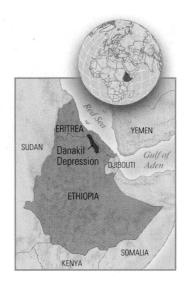

all of those customarily seen as fitting for his or her age and gender. However, although specialization has increased in these societies, modern technologies are making labor divisions based on gender less relevant. By contrast, in small-scale foraging and traditional crop-cultivating societies, where division of labor typically occurs along lines of age and gender, each person has knowledge and competence in all aspects of work appropriate to his or her age and gender. Yet, even in these nonindustrial societies there is a measure of task specialization.

An example of task specialization can be found among the Afar people of the Danakil Depression in the borderlands of Eritrea and Ethiopia, one of the lowest and hottest places on earth.[6] The desolate landscape features sulphur fields, smoking fissures, volcanic tremors, and vast salt plains. Since ancient times, groups of Afar men periodically mine the salt, hacking blocks from the plain's crust. The work is backbreaking, all the more so with temperatures soaring to 140 degrees Fahrenheit.

Along with the physical strength required for such work under the most trying conditions, successful mining demands specialized planning and organization skills for getting to and from the work site.[7] Pack camels have to be fed in advance, since importing sufficient fodder for them interferes with their ability to carry out salt. Food and water, packed by Afar women at the desert's edge, must be carried in for the miners, typically numbering thirty to forty per group. Travel is arranged for nighttime to avoid the scorching sun.

---

[5]"It's the law: Child labor protection." (1997, November/December). *Peace and Justice News*, 11.

[6]Nesbitt, L. M. (1935). *Hell-hole of creation*. New York: Knopf.
[7]Mesghinua, H. M. (1966). Salt mining in Enderta. *Journal of Ethiopian Studies, 4*(2); O'Mahoney, K. (1970). The salt trade. *Journal of Ethiopian Studies, 8*(2).

Scorching hot and dry, the Danakil Desert in northeast Africa lies some 370 feet below sea level—remains of what was once part of the Red Sea—with enormous salt flats. Afar nomads and their pack camels periodically travel to this desert, cutting blocks of this rock salt that they trade with peoples in the interior highlands. Here they adjust a camel load at Berahile, a stopover on the Danakil route.

DISTRIBUTION AND EXCHANGE

In societies without a money economy, the rewards for labor are usually direct. The workers in a family group consume what they harvest, eat what the hunter or gatherer brings home, and use the tools they themselves make. But even where no formal medium of exchange such as money exists, some distribution of goods takes place. Anthropologists often classify the cultural systems of distributing material goods into three modes: reciprocity, redistribution, and market exchange.[8]

Reciprocity

Reciprocity refers to the exchange of goods and services, of roughly equal value, between two parties. This may involve gift giving. Notably, individuals or groups in most cultures like to think that the main point of the transaction is the gift itself, yet what actually matters are the social ties that are created or reinforced between givers and receivers. Because reciprocity is about a relationship between the self and others, gift giving is seldom really selfless. The overriding (if unconscious) motive is

to fulfill social obligations and perhaps to gain a bit of prestige in the process.

Cultural traditions dictate the occasion, location, and manner of exchange. For example, when a group of Australian hunters kill an animal, the meat is divided among the hunters' families and other relatives. Each person in the camp gets a share, the size depending on the nature of the person's kinship tie to the hunters. The giving and receiving are obligatory, as is the particularity of the distribution. Such sharing of food reinforces community bonds and ensures that everyone eats. By giving away part of a kill, the hunters get social credit for a similar amount of food in the future. It is a bit like buying a collective insurance policy.

Reciprocity falls into several categories. The Australian food distribution example just noted constitutes an example of **generalized reciprocity**— exchange in which the value of what is given is not calculated, nor is the time of repayment specified. Gift giving, in the unselfish sense, also falls in this category. So, too, does the act of a kindhearted soul who stops to help a stranded motorist or someone else in distress and refuses payment with the admonition: "Pass it on to the next person in need."

Most generalized reciprocity, however, occurs among close kin or people who otherwise have very close ties with one another. Within such circles of intimacy, people give to others when they have the means and can count on receiving from others in time of need. Typically, participants will not consider such exchanges in economic terms but will couch them explicitly in terms of family and friendship social relations.

Balanced reciprocity differs in that it is not part of a long-term process. The giving and receiving, as well as the time involved, are more specific. One has a direct obligation to reciprocate promptly in equal value in order for the social relationship to continue. Examples of balanced reciprocity in contemporary North American society include such customary practices as hosting a baby shower for young friends expecting their first baby; giving presents at birthdays and various other culturally prescribed special occasions; and buying drinks when one's turn comes at a gathering of friends.

Negative reciprocity is a third form of exchange, in which the aim is to get something for as little as possible. The parties involved have opposing interests and are not usually closely related; they may be strangers or even enemies. They are people with whom exchanges are often neither fair nor balanced and are usually not expected to be such. It may involve hard bargaining, manipulation, or outright cheating. An extreme form of negative reciprocity is to take something by force, while realizing that one's victim may seek compensation or retribution for losses.

[8]Polanyi, K. (1968). The economy as instituted process. In E. E. LeClair, Jr., & H. K. Schneider (Eds.), *Economic anthropology: Readings in theory and analysis* (pp. 127–138). New York: Holt, Rinehart & Winston.

Trade and Barter

Exchanges that occur within a group of relatives or between friends generally take the form of generalized or balanced reciprocity. *Trade* refers to a transaction in which two or more people are involved in an exchange of something—a quantity of food, fuel, clothing, jewelry, animals, or money, for example—for something else of equal value. In such a transaction, the value of the trade goods can be fixed by previous agreements or negotiated on the spot by the trading partners. When there is no money involved in the transaction, and the parties negotiate a direct exchange of one trade good for another, we may speak of *barter*. In barter, arguing about the price and terms of the deal may well be in the form of negative reciprocity, with each party aiming to get the better end of the deal. Relative value is calculated, and despite an outward show of indifference, sharp trading is generally the rule, when compared to the more balanced nature of exchanges within a group.

Kula Ring: Gift Giving and Trading in the South Pacific

Balanced reciprocity can take more complicated forms, whereby mutual gift giving serves to facilitate social interaction, "smoothing" social relations between traders wanting to do business. One classic ethnographic example of balanced reciprocity between trading partners seeking to be friends and do business at the same time is the **Kula ring** in the southwestern Pacific Ocean. Involving thousands of seafarers going to great lengths to establish and maintain good trade relations, this centuries-old ceremonial exchange system continues to this day.[9]

Kula participants are men of influence who travel to islands within the Trobriand ring to exchange prestige

items—red shell necklaces (*soulava*), which are circulated around the ring of islands in a clockwise direction, and white shell armbands (*mwali*), which are carried in the opposite direction (Figure 11.1). Each man in the Kula is linked to partners on the islands that neighbor his own. To a partner residing on an island in the clockwise direction, he offers a *soulava* and receives in return a *mwali*. He makes the reverse exchange of a *mwali* for a *soulava* to a partner living in the counterclockwise direction. Each of these trade partners eventually passes the object on to a Kula partner further along the chain of islands.

Soulava and *mwali* are ranked according to their size, their color, how finely they are polished, and their particular histories. Such is the fame of some that, when they appear in a village, they create a sensation.

Traditionally, men make their Kula journeys in elaborately carved dugout canoes, sailing and paddling these 20- to 25-feet-long boats across open waters to shores some 60 miles or more away. The adventure is often dangerous and may take men away from their homes for several weeks, sometimes even months. Although men on Kula voyages may use the opportunity to trade for practical goods, acquiring such goods is not always the reason for these voyages—nor is Kula exchange a necessary part of regular trade expeditions.

Perhaps the best way to view the Kula is as an indigenous insurance policy in an economic order fraught with danger and uncertainty. It establishes and reinforces social partnerships between traders doing business on distant shores, ensuring a welcome reception from people who have similar vested interests. That

> **Kula ring** A form of balanced reciprocity that reinforces trade and social relations among the seafaring Trobriand people, who inhabit a large ring of islands in the southwestern Pacific Ocean off the eastern coast of Papua New Guinea, and other Melanesians
>
> **redistribution** A mode of exchange in which goods flow into a central place, where they are sorted, counted, and reallocated
>
> **conspicuous consumption** A showy display of wealth for social prestige
>
> **potlatch** On the northwestern coast of North America, a ceremonial event in which a village chief publicly gives away stockpiled food and other goods that signify wealth

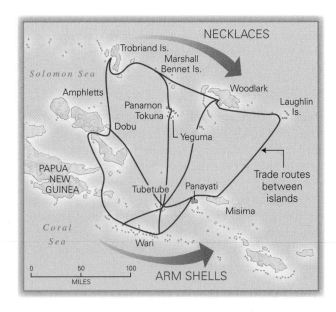

Figure 11.1

The ceremonial gift exchanges of shell necklaces and armbands in the Kula ring encourages trade and barter throughout the Melanesian islands.

[9]Malinowski, B. (1922). *Argonauts of the western Pacific* (p. 94). London: Routledge & Kegan Paul; Weiner, A. B. (1988). *The Trobrianders of Papua New Guinea* (pp. 139–157). New York: Holt, Rinehart & Winston.

said, this ceremonial exchange network does more than simply smooth or enhance the trade of foods and other goods essential for survival. Melanesians participating in the Kula ring have no doubt that their social position has to do with the company they keep, the circles in which they move. They derive their social prestige from the reputations of their partners and the valuables that they circulate. By giving and receiving armbands and necklaces that accumulate the histories of their travels and the names of those who have possessed them, men proclaim their individual fame and talent, gaining considerable influence for themselves in the process.

Like other forms of currency, *soulava* and *mwali* must flow from hand to hand; once they stop flowing, they may lose their value. A man who takes these valuables out of their inter-island circuit invites criticism. He not only may lose prestige or social capital as a man of influence, but may become a target of sorcery for unraveling the cultural fabric that holds the islands together as a functioning social and economic order.

As this example from the South Pacific illustrates, the potential tension between trading partners may be resolved or lessened by participation in a ritual of balanced reciprocity. As an elaborate complex of ceremony, political relationships, economic exchange, travel, magic, and social integration, the Kula ring illustrates how inseparable economic matters are from the rest of culture. Although perhaps difficult to recognize, this is just as true in modern industrial societies as it is in traditional Trobriand society—as evident when heads of state engage in ceremonial gift exchanges at official visits.

Redistribution

Redistribution is a form of exchange in which goods flow into a central place where they are sorted, counted, and reallocated. Commonly, it involves an element of power. In societies with a sufficient surplus to support some sort of government, goods in the form of gifts, tribute, taxes, and the spoils of war are gathered into storehouses controlled by a chief or some other type of leader. From there they are handed out again. The leadership has three motives in redistributing this income: The first is to gain or maintain a position of power through a display of wealth and generosity; the second is to assure those who support the leadership an adequate standard of living by providing them with desired goods; and the third is to establish alliances with leaders of other groups by hosting them at lavish parties and giving them valuable goods.

Taxes imposed by central governments of countries all around the world today are one form of redistribution—required payments commonly based on a percentage of one's income and property value. Typically, a portion of the taxes goes toward supporting the government itself, while the rest is redistributed either in cash (such as welfare payments and government loans or subsidies to businesses) or in the form of services (such as military defense, law enforcement, food and drug inspection, schools, highway construction, and the like). Tax codes vary greatly among countries. In many European countries, wealthy citizens pay considerably higher percentages of their incomes than those in the United States.

Spending Wealth to Gain Prestige

In societies where people devote most of their time to subsistence activities, gradations of wealth are small, kept that way through various cultural mechanisms and systems of reciprocity that serve to spread quite fairly what little wealth exists. It is a different situation in ranked societies where substantial surpluses are produced, and the gap between the have-nots and the have-lots can be considerable. In these societies, showy display for social prestige—known as **conspicuous consumption**—is a strong motivator for the distribution of wealth.

Obviously, excessive efforts to impress others with one's wealth or status also play a prominent role in industrial and postindustrial societies, as individuals compete for prestige. Indeed, many North Americans and Europeans spend much of their lives trying to impress others. This requires the display of symbolic prestige items—designer clothes, substantial jewelry, mansions, big cars, private planes—and fits neatly into an economy based on consumer wants.

A form of conspicuous consumption also occurs in some crop-cultivating and foraging societies—as illustrated by potlatches hosted by the chiefs of various American Indian groups living along the Pacific Northwest coast, including the Tlingit, Haida, and Kwakwaka'wakw (Kwakiutl) peoples. A **potlatch** is a ceremonial event in which a village chief publicly gives away stockpiled food and other goods that signify wealth. (The term comes from the Chinook Indian word *patshatl*, which means "gift.")

Traditionally, a chief whose village had built up enough surplus to host such a feast for other villages in the region would give away large piles of sea otter furs, dried salmon, blankets, and other valuables while making boastful speeches about his generosity, greatness, and glorious ancestors. While other chiefs became indebted to him, he reaped the glory of successful and generous leadership and saw his prestige rise. In the future, his own village might face shortages, and he would find himself on the receiving end of a potlatch. Should that happen, he would have to listen to the self-serving and pompous speeches of rival chiefs. Obliged to receive, he would temporarily lose prestige and status.

Among Native Americans living along the Pacific Northwest coast of North America, one gains prestige by giving away valuables at the potlatch feast. Here we see Tlingit clan members dressed in traditional Chilkat and Raven's Tail robes during a recent potlatch in Sitka, Alaska.

In extreme displays of wealth, chiefs even destroyed some of their precious possessions. This occurred with some frequency in the second half of the 19th century, after European contact triggered a process of culture change that included new trade wealth. Outsiders might view such grandiose displays as wasteful in the extreme. However, these extravagant giveaway ceremonies have played an ecologically adaptive role in a coastal region where villages alternately faced periods of scarcity and abundance and relied upon alliances and trade relations with one another for long-term survival. The potlatch provided a ceremonial opportunity to strategically redistribute surplus food and goods among allied villages in response to periodic fluctuations in fortune.

A strategy that features this sort of accumulation of surplus goods for the express purpose of displaying wealth and giving it away to raise one's status is known as a **prestige economy**. In contrast to conspicuous consumption in industrial and postindustrial societies, the emphasis is not on amassing goods that then become unavailable to others. Instead, it is on gaining wealth in order to give it away for the sake of prestige and status.

Leveling Mechanisms

The potlatch is an example of a **leveling mechanism**—a cultural obligation compelling prosperous members of a community to give away goods, host public feasts, provide free service, or otherwise demonstrate generosity so that no one permanently accumulates significantly more wealth than anyone else. With leveling mechanisms at work, greater wealth brings greater social pressure to spend and give generously. In exchange for such demonstrated altruism, a person not only increases his or her social standing in the community, but may also keep disruptive envy at bay.

prestige economy Creation of a surplus for the express purpose of displaying wealth and giving it away to raise one's status

leveling mechanism A cultural obligation compelling prosperous members of a community to give away goods, host public feasts, provide free service, or otherwise demonstrate generosity so that no one permanently accumulates significantly more wealth than anyone else

market exchange The buying and selling of goods and services, with prices set by rules of supply and demand

Underscoring the value of collective well-being over individual self-interest, leveling mechanisms are important in the long-term survival of traditional communities. The potlatch is just one of many cultural varieties of leveling mechanisms. Another example can be found in Maya Indian towns in the highlands of Guatemala and southern Mexico. In these traditional communities, the higher public offices are those of councilmen, judges, and mayors, in addition to various ceremonial leadership positions. Because the people who are called upon to fill these roles are not paid, the positions are known as *cargos* (Spanish for "burdens"). In fact, Maya Indian officeholders are expected to personally pay for the food, liquor, music, fireworks, or whatever is required for community festivals or for feast meals associated with their particular post. For some cargos, the cost can be as much as a man can earn in four years!

After holding a cargo position, a man usually returns to his normal life for a period, during which he may accumulate sufficient resources to campaign for a higher office. Each successful male citizen of the community is socially obliged to serve in the community's cargo system at least once, and the social pressure to do so drives individuals who have once again accumulated surplus wealth to apply for higher offices in order to raise their social status. Ideally, while some individuals gain appreciably more prestige than others in their community, no one has significantly more wealth in the long run than anyone else.

By pressuring members into sharing their wealth in their own community rather than hoarding it or privately investing it elsewhere, leveling mechanisms keep resources in circulation. They also reduce social tensions among relatives, neighbors, and fellow town folk, promoting a collective sense of togetherness. An added practical benefit is that they ensure that necessary services within the community are performed.

Market Exchange

To an economist, **market exchange** has to do with the buying and selling of goods and services, with prices set by rules of supply and demand. Personal loyalties and moral values are not supposed to play a role, but they often do. Since the actual location of the transaction is not always relevant in today's world, we must distinguish between the "marketplace" and "market exchange."

Typically, until well into the 20th century, market exchange was carried out in specific localities or *marketplaces.* This is still the case in much of the nonindustrial world and even in numerous centuries-old European and Asian towns and cities. In food-producing societies, marketplaces overseen by a centralized political authority provide the opportunity for farmers or peasants in the surrounding rural territories to exchange some of their livestock and produce for needed items manufactured in factories or in the workshops of craft specialists living (usually) in towns and cities. Thus, some sort of complex division of labor as well as centralized political organization is necessary for the appearance of markets.

The traditional market is local, specific, and contained. Prices are typically set on the basis of face-to-face bargaining rather than by unseen market forces wholly removed from the transaction itself. Notably, sales do not necessarily involve money; instead, goods may be directly exchanged through some form of barter among the specific individuals involved.

In industrializing and industrial societies, many market transactions still take place in a specific identifiable location—including international trade fairs such as the semi-annual Canton Trade Fair in Guangzhou, China. In spring 2007, 13,000 Chinese enterprises participated in the event, offering 150,000 products and generating over $36 billion in sales among 207,000 visitors.

Yet, it is increasingly common for people living in technologically wired parts of the world to buy and sell everything from cattle to cars without ever being in the same city, let alone the same space. For example, think of Internet companies such as eBay where all buying and selling occur electronically and irrespective of geographic distance. Thus, when people talk about a market in today's industrial or postindustrial world, the particular geographic location where something is bought or sold is often not important at all.

The faceless market exchanges that take place in industrial and postindustrial societies stand in stark contrast to experiences in the marketplaces of nonindustrial societies, which have much of the excitement of a fair. Traditional exchange centers are colorful places where a host of sights, sounds, and smells awaken the senses. Typically, vendors and/or their family members produced the goods they are selling, thereby personalizing the transactions. Dancers and musicians may perform, and feasting and fighting may mark the end of the day. In these markets social relationships and personal interactions are key elements, and noneconomic activities may overshadow economic ones. In short, such markets are gathering places where people renew friendships, see relatives, gossip, and keep up with the world, while procuring needed goods they cannot produce for themselves.[10]

[10]Plattner, S. (1989). Markets and marketplaces. In S. Plattner (Ed.), *Economic anthropology* (p. 171). Stanford, CA: Stanford University Press.

Money as Means of Exchange

Although there are marketplaces without money of any sort, money does facilitate trade. **Money** may be defined as something used to make payments for other goods and services as well as to measure their value. Its critical attributes are durability, transportability, divisibility, recognizability, and interchangeability. Items that have been used as money in various societies include salt, shells, precious stones, cacao beans, special beads, livestock, and of course valuable metals such as iron, copper, silver, and gold.

About 5,000 years ago, merchants and others in Mesopotamia (now part of Iraq) began using precious metal such as silver in transactions. Once they agreed on the value of these pieces as a means of exchange, or money, more complex commercial developments followed. As the means of exchange were standardized in terms of their value, it became easier to accumulate, lend, or borrow money for specified amounts and periods against payment of interest. In due time, some began to deal in money itself and became bankers.

As the use of money became widespread, the metal units were adapted to long-term use, easy storage, and long-distance transportation. In some cultures, such pieces of iron, copper, or silver were cast as miniature models of valuable implements like sword blades, axes, or spades. But some 2,600 years ago in the ancient kingdom of Lydia (southwestern Turkey), they were molded into small flat discs conforming to different sizes and weights.[11] Over the next few centuries, metal coins were also standardized in terms of the metal's purity and value, such as 100 units of copper equals 10 units of silver or 1 of gold.

By about 2,000 years ago, commercial use of such coins had spread throughout much of Europe and become common in parts of Asia and Africa, especially along trade routes and in urban centers. Thus, money set into motion radical economic changes in many traditional societies and introduced what has been called merchant capitalism in many parts of the world.[12]

> **money** Anything used to make payments for other goods and services as well as to measure their value; may be special purpose or multipurpose
> **informal economy** A network of producing and circulating marketable commodities, labor, and services that for various reasons escape government control

LOCAL ECONOMIES AND GLOBAL CAPITALISM

Failing to overcome cultural biases can have serious economic consequences, especially in this era of globalization. For example, it has led prosperous countries to impose inappropriate development schemes in parts of the world that they regard as economically underdeveloped. Typically, these schemes focus on increasing the target country's gross national product through large-scale production that all too often boosts the well-being of a few but results in poverty, poor health, discontent, and a host of other ills for many.

Among many examples of this is the global production of soy, which has grown enormously in many parts of the world, particularly in Paraguay. There, big landowners, coupled with large agribusinesses, most of which are owned by neighboring Brazilians, now produce genetically modified seeds, developed and marketed by foreign companies, especially the U.S.-based multinational corporation Monsanto. Although these large landowners and agribusinesses possess just 1 percent of the total number of Paraguayan farms, they now own almost 80 percent of the country's agricultural land. Exporting the soy, they make hefty profits because production costs are low and international demand is high for cattle feed and bio fuel. But the victims of progress are the rural poor—hundreds of thousands of small farmers, landless peasants, rural laborers, and their families. Traditionally growing much of their own food (plus a bit extra for the local market) on small plots, many of them have been edged out and forced to work for hunger wages or to migrate to the city, or even abroad, in order to survive. Those who stay face malnutrition and other hardships, for they lack enough fertile land to feed their families and do not earn enough to buy basic foodstuffs.[13]

Such failures are tied to the fact that every culture is an integrated system (as illustrated by the barrel model, see Chapter 8) and that a shift in the infrastructure, or economic base, affects interlinked elements of the society's social structure and superstructure. As the ethnographic examples of the potlatch and the Kula ring show, economic activities in traditional cultures are intricately intertwined with social and political relations and may also involve spiritual elements. Development programs that do not take such complexities into consideration may have unintended negative consequences on a society. Fortunately, there is now a growing awareness on

[11]Davies, G. (2005). *A history of money from the earliest times to present day* (3rd ed.). Cardiff: University of Wales Press.
[12]See also Wolf, E. R. (1982). *Europe and the people without history* (pp. 135–141). Berkeley: University of California Press.

[13]Fogel, R., & Riquelme, M. A. (2005). *Enclave sojero. Merma de soberania y pobreza*. Asuncion: Centro de Estudios Rurales Interdisciplinarias; Bodley, J. H. (1990). *Victims of progress* (3rd ed., p. 141). Mountain View, CA: Mayfield.

A crowd of protesters demonstrated against World Trade Organization (WTO) policies favoring rich countries over poor ones during the organization's December 2007 meeting in Hong Kong. Established in 1995 and headquartered in Geneva, the WTO is the only global international organization with rules of trade among its 150 member countries.

the part of development officials that future projects are unlikely to succeed without the expertise that anthropologically trained people can bring to bear.

Achieving a cross-cultural understanding of the economic organizations of other peoples that is not distorted or limited by the logic, hopes, and expectations of one's own society has also become important for corporate executives in today's world. Recognizing how the economic structures are intertwined with other aspects of a culture could help business corporations avoid problems of the sort experienced by Gerber, when it began selling baby food in Africa. As in the United States, Gerber's labels featured a picture of a smiling baby. Only later did company officials learn that, in Africa, businesses routinely put pictures of the products themselves on the outside label, since many people cannot read.[14]

As globalization increases so does corporate awareness of the cost of such cross-cultural miscues. So it is not surprising that business recruiters on college campuses in North America and elsewhere are now on the lookout for job candidates with the kind of cross-cultural understanding of the world anthropology provides.

When such work opportunities involve helping an enterprise more effectively exploit people for the sake of commercial gain, anthropologists have to deal with the profession's first ethical principle: Do no harm. It is important to note that powerful business corporations typically aim to make large profits—not to protect the weak, benefit the poor, support the sick, favor small producers, or save the environment. Their agenda is universally promoted through slogans such as "free trade," "free markets," and "free enterprise." The commercial success of such enterprises, foreign or domestic, does not come without a price, and all too often that price is paid by still surviving indigenous foragers, small farmers, herders, fishermen, local artisans such as weavers and carpenters, and so on. From their viewpoint, such slogans of freedom have the ring of "savage capitalism," a term now commonly used in Latin America to describe a world order in which the powerless are often condemned to poverty and misery.

Although political authorities in state-organized societies seek to govern and control economic activities for regulation and taxation purposes, they do not always succeed. Either because of insufficient government resources, bureaucratic mismanagement, and official corruption, or because of people seeking to escape from government regulations and tax collectors, state-organized societies also possess a largely undocumented **informal economy**—a network of producing and circulating marketable commodities, labor, and services that for various reasons escape government control (enumeration, regulation, or other types of public monitoring or auditing).

Such enterprises may encompass a range of activities: house cleaning, child care, gardening, repair or construction work, making and selling alcoholic beverages, street peddling, money lending, begging, prostitution, gambling, drug dealing, pick-pocketing, and labor by illegal foreign workers, to mention just a few.

---

[14]"Madison Avenue relevance." (1999). *Anthropology Newsletter,* *40*(4), 32.

These off-the-books or black market activities have been known for a long time but generally have long been dismissed by economists as of marginal importance. Yet, in many countries of the world, the informal economy is, in fact, more important than the formal economy. In many places, large numbers of under- and unemployed people who have only limited access to the formal economic sector in effect improvise, "getting by" on scant resources. Meanwhile, more affluent members of society may dodge various regulations in order to maximize returns and/or to vent their frustrations at their perceived loss of self-determination in the face of increasing government regulation.

And now that globalization is connecting national, regional, and local markets in which natural resources, commodities, and human labor are bought and sold, people everywhere in the world face new economic opportunities and confront new challenges. Not only are natural environments more quickly and radically transformed by means of new powerful technologies, but long-established subsistence practices, economic arrangements, social organizations, and associated ideas, beliefs, and values are also under enormous pressure.

Chapter Summary

■ Adaptation, essential for survival, is the ongoing process organisms undergo to achieve beneficial adjustments to a particular environment. Humans are unique in their capacity for cultural adaptation—the complex of ideas, activities, and technologies that enable people to survive in a certain environment and in turn affect the environment.

■ Cultural evolution (the changing of cultures over time) should not be confused with the idea of progress (the notion that humans are moving forward to a better, more advanced stage in their development toward perfection).

■ The food-foraging way of life, the oldest and most universal type of human adaptation, requires that people move their residence according to changing food sources. Local group size is kept small, possibly because small numbers fit the land's capacity to sustain the group. Obviously, a habitat rich in natural resources can sustain more people than marginal lands that are home to the world's few surviving foragers.

■ The shift from food foraging to food production, known as the Neolithic revolution, began about 10,000 years ago. With it came the development of permanent settlements as people practiced horticulture using simple hand tools. One common form of horticulture is swidden farming or slash-and-burn cultivation. Agriculture, a more complex activity, involves irrigation, fertilizers, and/or animal-powered plows. Pastoralism is a means of subsistence that relies on breeding and managing herds of domesticated herbivores, such as cattle, sheep, and goats. Pastoralists are usually nomadic, moving as needed to provide animals with pasture and water.

■ The industrial revolution began 200 years ago with the invention of the steam engine. It replaced human labor, animal power, and hand tools with machines and resulted in massive culture change in many societies. Today, in some parts of the world, we see the emergence of postindustrial societies with economies based on research and development of new knowledge and technologies, as well as providing information, services, and finance capital on a global scale.

■ An economic system is an organized arrangement for producing, distributing, and consuming goods. Studying the economics of nonliterate, nonindustrialized societies can be undertaken only in the context of the total culture of each society. Each society solves the problem of subsisting by allocating natural resources, technology, and labor according to its own priorities.

■ All societies regulate the allocation of land and other valuable resources. In nonindustrial societies, individual ownership of land is rare. Generally land is controlled by kinship groups, such as the band, which provides flexibility of land use, since the size of a band and its territories can be adjusted according to availability of resources in any particular place. The technology of a people, in the form of the tools they use and associated knowledge, is related to their mode of subsistence.

■ Labor is a major productive resource, and the allotment of work is commonly governed by rules according to gender and age. Only a few broad generalizations can be made covering the kinds of work performed by men and women cross-culturally. A more productive strategy is to examine the kinds of work that men and women do in the context of specific societies to see how it relates to other cultural and historical factors. The cooperation of many people working together is a typical feature of both nonindustrial and industrial societies. Task specialization is important even in societies with very simple technologies. Afar people who mine salt in Africa's Danakil Depression are one of countless examples of such specialization.

■ A characteristic of food-foraging societies is their egalitarianism. Since this way of life requires mobility, people accumulate only the material goods necessary for survival, so that status differences are limited to those based on age and gender. Status differences associated with gender, however, do not imply subordination of women to men. Food resources are distributed equally throughout the groups; thus, no individual can achieve the wealth or status that hoarding might bring. In food-foraging societies, codes of generosity promote free access to tools, even though individuals may have made these for their own use. Settled farming communities offer greater opportunities to accumulate material belongings, and inequalities of wealth may develop. In many such communities, though, a relatively egalitarian social order may be maintained through leveling mechanisms, such as the potlatch and the cargo system.

■ Nonindustrial peoples consume most of what they produce themselves, but they do exchange goods. The processes of distribution may be distinguished as reciprocity, redistribution, and market exchange. Reciprocity, the exchange of goods and services of roughly equal value between two parties, comes in three forms: (a) generalized (in which the value is not calculated, nor the time of repayment specified); (b) balanced (in which one has an obligation to reciprocate promptly); and (c) negative (in which the aim is to get something for as little as possible).

■ Trade refers to a transaction in which two or more people are involved in an exchange of something for something else of equal value. Trading exchanges have elements of reciprocity but involve a greater calculation of the relative value of goods exchanged. Barter is a form of trade in which no money is involved, and the parties negotiate a direct exchange of one trade good for another. It may well be in the form of negative reciprocity, with each party aiming to get the better end of the deal. A classic example of exchange that involves both balanced reciprocity and sharp trading is the Kula ring of the Trobriand Islanders.

■ Strong, centralized political organization is necessary for redistribution to occur. The government assesses a tax or tribute on each citizen, uses the proceeds to support the government and religious elite, and redistributes the rest, usually in the form of public services. The system of collecting taxes and delivering government services and subsidies in the United States is a form of redistribution.

■ Conspicuous consumption, or display for social prestige, is a motivating force in societies that produce a surplus of goods. The prestige comes from publicly divesting oneself of valuables, as in the potlatch ceremony, which is also an example of a leveling mechanism.

■ Exchange in the marketplace serves to distribute goods in a region. In nonindustrial societies, the marketplace is usually a specific site where produce, livestock, and material items the people make are exchanged. It also functions as a social gathering place and a news medium. Although market exchanges may take place without money through bartering and other forms of reciprocity, some form of money, at least for special transactions, makes market exchange more efficient. In market economies, the informal sector may become more important than the formal sector. The informal economy consists of those economic activities that escape official scrutiny and regulation.

■ The anthropological approach to economics has taken on new importance in today's world of international development and commerce. Without it, development schemes for so-called underdeveloped countries are prone to failure, and international trade is handicapped as a result of cross-cultural misunderstandings.

Questions for Reflection

1. Since the beginning of human history, our species has met the challenge of survival by adapting to different environments. In capturing essential natural resources, we have also modified these environments. Can you think of any examples of landscapes radically transformed for economic reasons? Who benefits from such environmental changes in the long run?

2. What was so radical about the Neolithic transition that prompted some to refer to it as a revolution? Are you aware of any equally radical changes in subsistence practices going on in the world today?

3. As the potlatch ceremony shows, prestige may be gained by giving away wealth. Does such a prestige-building mechanism exist in your own society? If so, how does it work?

4. As discussed in this chapter, economic relations in traditional cultures are usually wrapped up in social, political, and even spiritual issues. Can you come up with some examples in your own society in which the economic sphere is inextricably intertwined with other structures in the cultural system? Would tinkering with the economic sphere affect these other aspects of your culture?

5. What do you think is the future for the world's hundreds of millions of independent herders, farmers, and peasants trying to make a living off the land like their ancestors?

Key Terms

ecosystem	technology
cultural evolution	reciprocity
progress	generalized reciprocity
convergent evolution	balanced reciprocity
parallel evolution	negative reciprocity
food foraging	Kula ring
industrial society	redistribution
Neolithic revolution	conspicuous consumption
horticulture	potlatch
slash-and-burn cultivation	prestige economy
agriculture	leveling mechanism
pastoralism	market exchange
postindustrial society	money
economic system	informal economy

VISUAL ESSENCE

Every society has rules and customs concerning sexual relations, marriage, household and family structures, and child-rearing practices. These cultural constructs play important roles in establishing and maintaining the social alliances and continuity that help ensure a society's overall well-being. A wedding ceremony not only marks the marriage of individuals from different families, but also forges a link between relatives from both sides. As in many countries, weddings in Japan represent a mix of traditional Japanese and contemporary Western styles. Conforming to that nation's ancient tradition of Shinto ("the way of the spirits"), the bride and groom pictured here pose with close relatives and selected elders who serve as go-betweens in the ceremony. The groom wears a black kimono and gray *hakama* pants, traditional trousers designed to protect the legs of warriors on horseback. The bride wears a white hood, symbolically hiding "horns of jealousy" from her new mother-in-law, who will have authority over her in the household she is joining. The white color of her silk kimono professes purity. Other women also wear kimonos, black for those who are members of the bride's family. In the background is Tokyo's sacred Meiji shrine, a favorite wedding location, dedicated to the deified spirits of the ancestral emperor and his wife. After the Shinto priest ritually purifies the couple, they and their close relatives drink sake, an alcoholic beverage made of fermented rice, symbolizing the bonding of their families.

Sex, Marriage, and Family

Sexual behavior varies significantly from one society to another, for culture plays a role in determining when, how, and between whom sex takes place. For instance, in some societies, sexual intercourse during pregnancy is taboo, while in others it is looked upon positively as something that promotes the growth of the fetus. And while some societies sharply condemn same-sex relations, other societies accept them.

Marriage customs also vary across cultures—from the choosing of partners to the wedding rituals, marriage codes, and rules (or prohibition) of divorce. In some cultures weddings are private events, attended only by the couple, their close relatives, and a spiritual or political office-holder who formally confirms this bonding ritual. In others, they may involve all members of the community and sometimes even people from neighboring ones. When high-ranking leaders or famous entertainers marry, the event can turn into a public spectacle with thousands in attendance and millions viewing it on TV or the Web.

Whether private or public, sacred or secular, weddings reveal, confirm, and underscore important ideas and values of a culture. Symbolically rich, they usually feature particular speech rituals, along with prescribed apparel, postures and gestures, food and drink, songs and dances—all passed down through many generations.

CONTROL OF SEXUAL RELATIONS

In many parts of the world, sexual intercourse outside the marriage is normally disapproved—covered up, scandalized, or condemned. In a male-dominated society such as Japan, this cultural ideal applies to women (often more so than to men), as underscored by the color white in the bride's customary wear. Yet, preoccupation with a bride's sexual "purity" is by no means universal—and in recent decades it has diminished or disappeared in many societies.

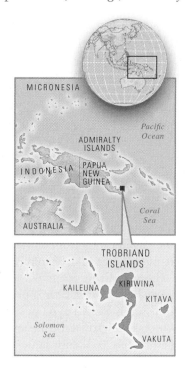

In contrast to individuals raised in traditional Shinto Japanese families, young single people in the Trobriand Islands of the southern Pacific are traditionally unconstrained in premarital sexual explorations. Attracting sexual partners is an important matter, and the Trobrianders spend a great deal of time making themselves look attractive and seductive. Youthful conversations during the day are loaded with sexual innuendo, and magical spells as well as small gifts are employed to entice a prospective sex partner to the beach at night or to the house in which boys sleep apart from their parents. Because girls, too, sleep apart from their parents, youths and adolescents have considerable freedom in arranging their love affairs. Boys and girls play this game as equals, with neither having an advantage over the other.[1]

Until the latter part of the 20th century, the Trobriand attitude toward adolescent sexuality was in marked contrast to that of most Western cultures in Europe and North America, where individuals were

marriage A culturally sanctioned union between two or more people that establishes certain rights and obligations between the people, between them and their children, and between them and their in-laws. Such marriage rights and obligations most often include, but are not limited to, sex, labor, property, child rearing, exchange, and status

incest taboo The prohibition of sexual relations between specified individuals, usually parent and child and sibling relations at a minimum

not supposed to have sexual relations before or outside of marriage. Since then, practices in much of Europe and North America have shifted toward those of the Trobrianders, even though the traditional ideal of premarital abstinence has not been abandoned entirely.

In addition to a wide range of different heterosexual practices, there are also many cross-cultural differences with respect to same-sex relations. Not infrequently, we also find mixtures of sexual relations, such as in many cultures in Melanesia, including New Guinea. There, certain male-to-male sexual acts are part of initiation rituals required of all boys to become respected adult men.[2] For example, some Papua communities in New Guinea consider the transmission of semen from older to younger boys, through oral sex, as vital for building up the strength needed to protect

To attract lovers, young Trobriand women and men must look as attractive and seductive as possible. This woman's beauty has been enhanced by face painting and adornments given by her father.

---

[1]Weiner, A. B. (1988). *The Trobrianders of Papua New Guinea* (p. 17). New York: Holt, Rinehart & Winston.

[2]Kirkpatrick, R. C. (2000). The evolution of human homosexual behavior, *Current Anthropology, 41,* 385.

against the supposedly debilitating effects of adult heterosexual intercourse.[3]

Marriage and the Regulation of Sexual Relations

In the absence of effective birth control devices, the usual outcome of sexual activity between fertile individuals of the opposite sex is that, sooner or later, the woman becomes pregnant. Given the intricate array of social responsibilities involved in rearing the children that are born of sexual relations—and the potential for violent conflict resulting from unregulated sexual competition—it is not surprising that all societies have cultural rules that seek to regulate those relations.

In much of Europe and North America, where sexual activity outside of marriage was traditionally taboo (especially for women in male-dominated societies), individuals were expected to establish a family through marriage; through marriage one gained an exclusive right of sexual access to another person. According to strict Judeo-Christian law prescribed in Leviticus (20:10), adultery was punishable by death: "And the man that committeth adultery with another man's wife . . ., the adulterer and the adulteress shall surely be put to death." Deuteronomy (22:24) adds: "Ye shall bring them both out unto the gate of that city, and ye shall stone them with stones that they die."

Many centuries later, among Christian colonists in 17th- and 18th-century New England, a woman's participation in adultery remained a serious crime. While it did not lead to stoning, women so accused were shunned by the community and could even be imprisoned. As recounted in *The Scarlet Letter* by Nathaniel Hawthorne, the adulteress was forced to have the letter "A" stitched on her dress, publicly signifying her transgression.

Such restrictions exist today in many traditional Muslim societies in northern Africa and western Asia, where age-old Shariah law continues or has been reinstated to regulate social behavior in strict accordance with religious standards of morality. Under this law, women found guilty of having sexual relations outside marriage can be sentenced to death by stoning. In northern Nigeria, for example, a Muslim woman who committed adultery and had a child outside marriage was sentenced to death in 2002. Her sentence was ultimately overturned by an Islamic appeals court, but it nonetheless drove home the rule of Shariah law. Turning legal transgressions into a public spectacle, authorities reinforce public awareness of the rules of social conduct.

A positive side effect of such restrictive rules is that they may limit the spread of sexually transmitted diseases. For instance, the global epidemic of HIV/AIDS has had dramatically less impact in North Africa's Muslim countries than in the non-Muslim states of sub-Saharan Africa, where the average infection rate among adults is almost 17 times higher. The statistics vividly illustrate the impact of religious and cultural prohibitions: The reported percentage of adults infected by the HIV/AIDS virus is 0.1 percent in Algeria, Morocco, and Tunisia, in contrast to 18.8 percent in South Africa, 24.1 percent in Botswana, and 33.8 percent in Swaziland.[4]

Most cultures in the world do not sharply regulate an individual's personal habits, including sexual practices. Indeed, a majority of all cultures are considered sexually permissive or semi-permissive (the former having few or no restrictions on sexual experimentation before marriage, the latter allowing some experimentation but less openly). A minority of known societies—about 15 percent—have rules requiring that sexual involvement take place only within marriage.

This brings us to an anthropological definition of **marriage**—a culturally sanctioned union between two or more people that establishes certain rights and obligations between the people, between them and their children, and between them and their in-laws. Such marriage rights and obligations most often include, but are not limited to, sex, labor, property, child rearing, exchange, and status. Thus defined, marriage is universal. Notably, our definition of marriage refers to "people" rather than "a man and a woman" because in some countries same-sex marriages are considered socially acceptable and allowed by law, even though opposite-sex marriages are far more common. We will return to this point later in the chapter.

Incest Taboo

Just as marriage in its various forms is found in all cultures, so is the **incest taboo**—the prohibition of sexual contact between certain close relatives. But, what is defined as "close" is not the same in all cultures. Moreover, such definitions may be subject to change over time. The scope and details of the taboo vary across cultures and time, but almost all societies past and present strongly forbid sexual relations at least between parents and children and nearly always between siblings. In some societies the taboo extends to other close relatives, such as cousins, and even some relatives linked through marriage.

---

[3]Herdt, G. H. (1993). Semen transactions in Sambia culture. In D. N. Suggs & A. W. Mirade (Eds.), *Culture and human sexuality* (pp. 298–327). Pacific Grove, CA: Brooks/Cole.

[4]AIDS Epidemic Update. (2007), p. 7. Geneva: Joint United Nations Program on HIV/AIDS (UNAID) and World Health Organization. www.unaids.org; see also Gray, P. B. (2004, May). HIV and Islam: Is HIV prevalence lower among Muslims? *Social Science & Medicine, 58*(9), 1751–1756.

Anthropologists have long been fascinated by the incest taboo and have proposed many explanations for its cross-cultural existence and variation. The simplest explanation, based on the idea of "human nature," is that our species has an "instinctive" repulsion for incest. It has been documented that human beings raised together have less sexual attraction for one another. However, by itself this "familiarity breeds contempt" argument may simply substitute the result for the cause. The incest taboo ensures that children and their parents, who are constantly in close contact, avoid regarding one another as sexual objects. Besides this, if an instinctive horror of incest exists, how do we account for the far from rare violations of the incest taboo? (In the United States, for instance, an estimated 10 to 14 percent of children under 18 years of age have been involved in incestuous relations.[5])

Moreover, so-called instinctive repulsion does not explain institutionalized incest, such as requiring that the divine ruler of the Inca empire in ancient Peru be married to his own (half) sister. Sharing the same father, both siblings belonged to the political dynasty that derived its sacred right to rule the empire from Inti, its ancestral Sun God. And by virtue of this royal lineage's godly origin, their children could claim the same sacred political status as their human god-father and god-mother. Ancient emperors in Egypt also practiced such religiously prescribed incest based on a similar claim to godly status.

Early students of genetics argued that the incest taboo prevents the harmful effects of inbreeding. While this is so, it is also true that, as with domestic animals, inbreeding can increase desired characteristics as well as detrimental ones. Furthermore, undesirable effects will show up sooner than without inbreeding, so whatever genes are responsible for them are quickly eliminated from the population. That said, a preference for a genetically different mate does tend to maintain a higher level of genetic diversity within a population, and in evolution this variation works to a species' advantage. Without genetic diversity a species cannot adapt biologically to environmental change.

The inbreeding or biological avoidance theory can be challenged on several fronts. Detailed census records made in Roman Egypt about 2,000 years ago show that brother–sister marriages were not uncommon among ordinary members of the farming class.[6] Moreover, in a sample of 129 societies, anthropologist Nancy Thornhill found that only fifty-seven had specific rules against parent–child or sibling incest. Twice that number (114) had explicit rules to control activity with cousins, in-laws, or both.[7]

Some anthropologists have argued that the incest taboo exists as a cultural means to preserve the stability and integrity of the family, which is essential to maintaining social order. Sexual relations between members other than the husband and wife would introduce competition, destroying the harmony of a social unit fundamental to social order. A truly convincing explanation of the incest taboo has yet to be advanced.

Endogamy and Exogamy

Whatever its cause, the utility of the incest taboo can be seen by examining its effects on social structure. Closely related to prohibitions against incest are cultural rules against **endogamy** (from Greek *endon*, "within," and *gamos*, "marriage"), or marriage within a particular group of individuals (cousins and in-laws, for example). If the group is defined as one's immediate family alone, then societies generally prohibit or at least discourage endogamy, thereby promoting **exogamy** (from Greek *exo*, "outside," and *gamos*, "marriage"), or marriage outside the group. Yet, a society that practices exogamy at one level may practice endogamy at another. Among the Trobriand Islanders, for example, each individual has to marry outside of his or her own clan and lineage (exogamy). However, since eligible sex partners are to be found within one's own community, village endogamy is commonly practiced.

Interestingly, societies vary widely concerning which relatives are or are not covered by rules of exogamy. For example, first cousins are prohibited from marrying each other in many countries where the Roman Catholic Church has long been a dominant institution. Such marriages are also illegal in thirty-one of the United States. Yet, in numerous other societies, first cousins are preferred spouses.[8] (See a discussion of U.S. marriage prohibitions in the Biocultural Connection.)

Early anthropologists suggested that our ancestors discovered the advantage of intermarriage as a means of creating bonds of friendship or alliances between distinct

endogamy Marriage within a particular group or category of individuals
exogamy Marriage outside the group

---

[5]Whelehan, P. (1985). Review of incest, a biosocial view. *American Anthropologist, 87*, 678. See also Langan, P., & Harlow, C. (1994). *Child rape victims, 1992*. Washington, DC: Bureau of Justice Statistics, U.S. Department of Justice.

---

[6]Leavitt, G. C. (1990). Sociobiological explanations of incest avoidance: A critical review of evidential claims. *American Anthropologist, 92*, 982.
[7]Thornhill, N. (1993). Quoted in W. A. Haviland & R. J. Gordon (Eds.), *Talking about people* (p. 127). Mountain View, CA: Mayfield.
[8]Ottenheimer, M. (1996). *Forbidden relatives: The American myth of cousin marriage* (pp. 116–133). Champaign: University of Illinois Press.

Biocultural Connection

Marriage Prohibitions in the United States

Martin Ottenheimer

In the United States, every state has laws prohibiting the marriage of some relatives. Every state forbids parent–child and sibling marriages, but there is considerable variation in prohibitions concerning more distant relatives. For example, although the majority of states ban marriage between first cousins, nineteen states allow it and others permit it under certain conditions. Notably, the United States is the only country in the Western world that has prohibitions against first-cousin marriage.

Many people in the United States believe that laws forbidding marriage between family members exist because parents who are too close biologically run the risk of producing children with mental and physical defects. Convinced that first cousins fall within this "too close" category, they believe laws against first-cousin marriage were established to protect families from the effects of harmful genes.

There are two major problems with this belief: First, cousin prohibitions were enacted in the United States long before the discovery of the genetic mechanisms of disease. Second, genetic research has shown that offspring of first-cousin couples do not have any significantly greater risk of negative results than offspring of very distantly related parents.

Why, then, do some North Americans maintain this belief? To answer this question, it helps to know that laws against first-cousin marriage first appeared in the United States right after the mid-1800s when evolutionary models of human behavior became fashionable. In particular, a pre-Darwinian model that explained social evolution as dependent upon biological factors gained popularity. It supposed that "progress from savagery to civilization" was possible when humans ceased inbreeding. Cousin marriage was thought to be characteristic of savagery, the lowest form of human social life, and it was believed to inhibit the intellectual and social development of humans. It became associated with "primitive" behavior and dreaded as a threat to a civilized America.

Thus, a powerful myth emerged in American popular culture, which has since become embedded in law. That myth is held and defended to this day, sometimes with great emotion despite being based on a discredited social evolutionary theory and contradicted by the results of modern genetic research.

Recently, a group of geneticists published the result of a study of consanguineous unions, estimating that there is "about a 1.7–2.8% increased risk for congenital defects above the population background risk."[a] Not only is this a high estimate, it is also well within the bounds of the margin of statistical error. But even so, it is a lower risk than that associated with offspring from women over the age of 40—who are not forbidden by the government to marry or bear children.

(By Martin Ottenheimer, Kansas State University)

[a]Bennett, R. L., et al. (2002, April). Genetic counseling and screening of consanguineous couples and their offspring: Recommendations of the National Society of Genetic Counselors. *Journal of Genetic Counseling, 11(2)*, 97–119.

communities. By widening the human network, a larger number of people could pool natural resources and cultural information, including technology and other useful knowledge.

Exogamy may also help build and maintain political alliances and promote trade between groups, thereby ensuring mutual protection and access to needed goods and resources not otherwise available. Forging wider kinship networks, exogamy also functions to integrate distinctive groups and thus potentially reduces violent conflict.

Distinction Between Marriage and Mating

Having defined marriage, in part, in terms of sexual access, we must make clear the distinction between marriage and mating. All mammals, including humans, form breeding pairs—some mate for life and some not, some with a single individual and some with several.

Mates are secured and held solely through individual effort and mutual consent. In contrast to mating, which is a personal issue between individuals, marriage is a culturally recognized relationship. Only marriage is backed by social, political, and ideological factors that regulate sexual relations as well as reproductive and property rights and obligations. Thus, while mating is biological, marriage is cultural. This is evident when we consider the various forms that marriage takes cross-culturally.

FORMS OF MARRIAGE

Within societies, and all the more so across cultures, we see contrasts in the constructs and contracts of marriage. Indeed, as evident in the definition of marriage given above, this institution comes in various forms—and these forms are distinct in terms of the number and gender of spouses involved.

Monogamy

Monogamy—marriage in which both partners have just one spouse—is the most common form of marriage worldwide. In North America and most of Europe, it is the only legally recognized form of marriage. Not only are other forms prohibited there, but also systems of inheritance, whereby property and wealth are transferred from one generation to the next, are based on the institution of monogamous marriage. In some parts of the world, such as North America and Europe where divorce and remarriage rates are high, an increasingly common form of marriage is **serial monogamy**, whereby an individual marries a series of partners in succession.

Polygamy

While monogamy is the most common marriage form worldwide, it is not the most culturally preferred. That distinction goes to **polygamy** (one individual having multiple spouses)—specifically to **polygyny**, in which a man is married to more than one woman (*gyne* is Greek for "woman" and "wife"). Favored in about 80 to 85 percent of the world's cultures, polygyny is commonly practiced in parts of Asia and much of sub-Saharan Africa.[9]

Although polygyny is the favored marriage form in these places, monogamy exceeds it, and the reason for this is economic rather than moral. In many polygynous societies, where a groom is usually expected to compensate a bride's family in cash or kind, a man must be fairly wealthy to be able to afford more than one wife. Recent multiple surveys of twenty-five sub-Saharan African countries where polygyny is common show that it declined by about half since the 1970s, but nonetheless remains highly significant with an overall average of 25 percent of married women in polygynous unions.[10]

> **monogamy** Marriage in which both partners have just one spouse
>
> **serial monogamy** A marriage form in which a man or a woman marries or lives with a series of partners in succession
>
> **polygamy** One individual having multiple spouses at the same time; from the Greek words *poly* ("many") and *gamos* ("marriage")
>
> **polygyny** Marriage of a man to two or more women at the same time; a form of polygamy
>
> **polyandry** Marriage of a woman to two or more men at one time; a form of polygamy

---

[9]Lloyd, C. B. (Ed.). (2005). *Growing up global: The changing transitions to adulthood in developing countries* (pp. 450–453). Washington, D.C.: National Academies Press, Committee on Population, National Research Council, and Institute of Medicine of the National Academies.

[10]Lloyd, pp. 450–453.

This dramatic decline of polygyny has many reasons, one of which is related to families making an economic transition from traditional farming and herding to urban areas where they primarily subsist on wage labor.

Polygyny is particularly common in traditional food-producing societies that support themselves by herding grazing animals or growing crops and where women do the bulk of cultivation. Under these conditions, women are valued both as workers and as child bearers. Because the labor of wives in polygynous households generates wealth, and little support is required from husbands, the wives have a strong bargaining position within the household. Often, they have considerable freedom of movement and some economic independence from the sale of crafts or crops. Wealth-generating polygyny is found in its fullest elaboration in parts of sub-Saharan Africa and southwestern Asia, though it is known elsewhere as well.[11]

In societies practicing wealth-generating polygyny, most men and women do enter into polygynous marriages, although some are able to do so earlier in life than others. This is made possible by a female-biased sex ratio and/or a mean age at marriage for females that is significantly below that for males. In fact, this marriage pattern is frequently found in societies where violence, including war, is common and where many young males lose their lives in fighting. Their high combat mortality results in a population where women outnumber men.

By contrast, in societies where men are more heavily involved in productive work, generally only a small minority of marriages are polygynous. Under these circumstances, women are more dependent on men for support, so they are valued as child bearers more than for the work they do. This is commonly the case in pastoral nomadic societies where men are the primary owners and tenders of livestock. This makes women especially vulnerable if they prove incapable of bearing children, which is one reason a man may seek another wife.

Another reason for a man to take on secondary wives is to demonstrate his high position in society. But where men do most of the productive work, they must work extremely hard to support more than one wife, and few actually do so. Usually, it is the exceptional hunter or male shaman ("medicine man") in a food-foraging society or a particularly wealthy man in a horticultural, agricultural, or pastoral society who is most apt to practice polygyny. When he does, it is usually of the *sororal* type, with the co-wives being sisters. Having lived their lives together before marriage, the sisters continue to do so with their husband, instead of occupying separate dwellings of

---

[11]White, D. R. (1988). Rethinking polygyny: Co-wives, codes, and cultural systems. *Current Anthropology, 29,* 529–572.

VISUAL COUNTERPOINT

A Christian polygamist with his three wives and children in front of their dormitory-style home in Utah, and a Baranarna man of Upper Guinea, West Africa, with his two wives and children.

their own. Polygyny also occurs in a few places in Europe. In 1972, for example, English laws concerning marriage changed to accommodate immigrants who traditionally practiced polygyny. Since that time polygynous marriages have been legal in England for some specific religious minorities, including Muslims and Sephardic Jews. According to one family law specialist, the real impetus behind this law change was a growing concern that "destitute immigrant wives, abandoned by their husbands, [were] overburdening the welfare state."[12]

Even in the United States, where it is illegal, somewhere between 20,000 and 60,000 people in the Rocky Mountain states live in households made up of a man with two or more wives.[13] Most consider themselves Mormons, even though the official Mormon Church does not approve of the practice. A growing minority, however, call themselves "Christian polygamists," citing the Bible as justification.[14] Despite its illegality, regional law enforcement officials have generally adopted a "live and let live" attitude toward polygyny in their region. One woman—a lawyer and one of nine co-wives—expresses her attitude toward polygyny as follows:

> I see it as the ideal way for a woman to have a career and children. In our family, the women

can help each other care for the children. Women in monogamous relationships don't have that luxury. As I see it, if this lifestyle didn't already exist, it would have to be invented to accommodate career women.[15]

Although monogamy and polygyny are the most common forms of marriage in the world today, other forms do occur. **Polyandry** (*andros* in Greek means "man" or "husband"), the marriage of one woman to two or more men simultaneously, is known in only a few societies, perhaps in part because a woman's life expectancy is usually longer than a man's, and female infant mortality is somewhat lower, so a surplus of women in a society is likely.

Fewer than a dozen societies are known to have favored this form of marriage, but they involve people as widely separated from one another as the eastern Eskimos (Inuit), Marquesan Islanders of the Pacific, and Tibetans in central Asia. In Tibet, where inheritance is in the male line and arable land is limited, the marriage of brothers to a single woman (*fraternal polyandry*) keeps the land together by preventing it from being repeatedly subdivided among sons from one generation to the next. Unlike monogamy, it also holds down population growth, thereby avoiding increased pressures on

---

[12]Cretney, S. (2003). *Family law in the twentieth century: A history* (pp. 72–73). New York: Oxford University Press.

[13]Egan, T. (1999, February 28). The persistence of polygamy. *New York Times Magazine*, 52.

[14]Wolfson, H. (2000, January 22). Polygamists make the Christian connection. *Burlington Free Press*, 2c.

[15]Johnson, D. (1996). Polygamists emerge from secrecy, seeking not just peace but respect. In W. A. Haviland & R. J. Gordon (Eds.), *Talking about people* (2nd ed., pp. 129–131). Mountain View, CA: Mayfield.

resources. Finally, among Tibetans who practice a mixed economy of farming, herding, and trading, fraternal polyandry provides the household with an adequate pool of male labor for all three subsistence activities.[16]

Group Marriage

Group marriage (also known as *co-marriage*) is a rare arrangement in which several men and women have sexual access to one another. Among Eskimos in northern Alaska, for instance, sexual relations between unrelated individuals implied ties of mutual aid and support. In order to create or strengthen such ties, a man could share his wife with another man for temporary sexual relationships:

> Thus, in attracting and holding members of a hunting crew, an umialik [whaleboat headman] could lend his wife to a crew member and borrow that man's wife in turn. These men thereafter entered into a partnership relationship, one virtually as strong as kinship. The children of such men, in fact, retained a recognized relationship to each other by virtue of the wife exchange of their parents.[17]

CHOICE OF SPOUSE

The Western egalitarian ideal that an individual should be free to marry whomever he or she chooses is a distinct arrangement, certainly not universally embraced. In many societies, marriage and the establishment of a family are considered far too important to be left to the whims of young people. The individual relationship of two people who are expected to spend their lives together and raise their children together is viewed as incidental to the more serious matter of making allies of two families through the marriage bond. Marriage involves a transfer of rights between families, including rights to property and rights over children, as well as sexual rights. Thus, marriages tend to be arranged for the economic and political advantage of the family unit.

Although arranged marriages are rare in North American society, they do occur. Among ethnic minorities, they may serve to preserve traditional values that people fear might otherwise be lost. Among families of wealth and power, marriages may be arranged by segregating their children in private schools and carefully steering them toward "proper" marriages. The following Original Study illustrates how marriages may be arranged in societies where such practices are commonplace.

Original Study

Arranging Marriage in India
Serena Nanda

Six years [after my first field trip to India] I returned to do fieldwork among the middle class in Bombay (Mumbai), a modern, sophisticated city. From the experience of my earlier visit, I decided to include a study of arranged marriages in my project. By this time I had met many Indian couples whose marriages had been arranged and who seemed very happy. Particularly in contrast to the fate of many of my married friends in the United States who were already in the process of divorce, the positive aspects of arranged marriages appeared to me to outweigh the negatives. In fact, I thought I might even participate in arranging a marriage myself. I had been fairly successful in the United States in "fixing up" many of my friends, and I was confident that my matchmaking skills could be easily applied to this new situation, once I learned the basic rules. "After all," I thought, "how complicated can it be?"

An opportunity presented itself almost immediately. A friend from my previous Indian trip was in the process of arranging for the marriage of her eldest son. Since my friend's family was eminently respectable and the boy himself personable, well educated, and nice looking, I was sure that by the end of my year's fieldwork, we would have found a match.

The basic rule seems to be that a family's reputation is most important. It is understood that matches would be arranged only within the same caste and general social class, although some crossing of subcastes is permissible if the class positions of the bride's and groom's families are similar. Although dowry is now prohibited by law in India,

[16]Levine, N. E., & Silk, J. B. (1997). Why polyandry fails. *Current Anthropology, 38,* 375–398.

[17]Spencer, R. F. (1984). North Alaska Coast Eskimo. In D. Damas (Ed.), *Arctic: Handbook of North American Indians* (vol. 5, pp. 320–337). Washington, DC: Smithsonian Institution.

group marriage Marriage in which several men and women have sexual access to one another. Also called co-marriage

extensive gift exchanges took place with every marriage. Even when the boy's family does not "make demands," every girl's family nevertheless feels the obligation to give the traditional gifts—to the girl, to the boy, and to the boy's family. Particularly when the couple would be living in the joint family—that is, with the boy's parents and his married brothers and their families, as well as with unmarried siblings, which is still very common even among the urban, upper-middle class in India—the girl's parents are anxious to establish smooth relations between their family and that of the boy. Offering the proper gifts, even when not called "dowry," is often an important factor in influencing the relationship between the bride's and groom's families and perhaps, also, the treatment of the bride in her new home.

In a society where divorce is still a scandal and where, in fact, the divorce rate is exceedingly low, an arranged marriage is the beginning of a lifetime relationship not just between the bride and groom but between their families as well. Thus, while a girl's looks are important, her character is even more so, for she is being judged as a prospective daughter-in-law as much as a prospective bride. . . .

My friend is a highly esteemed wife, mother, and daughter-in-law. She is religious, soft-spoken, modest, and deferential. She rarely gossips and never quarrels, two qualities highly desirable in a woman. A family that

has the reputation for gossip and conflict among its womenfolk will not find it easy to get good wives for their sons. . . .

Originally from North India, my friend's family had lived for forty years in Bombay, where her husband owned a business. The family had delayed in seeking a match for their eldest son because he had been an air force pilot for several years, stationed in such remote places that it had seemed fruitless to try to find a girl who would be willing to accompany him. In their social class, a military career, despite its economic security, has little prestige and is considered a drawback in finding a suitable bride. . . .

The son had recently left the military and joined his father's business. Since he was a college graduate, modern, and well traveled, from such a good family, and, I thought, quite handsome, it seemed to me that he, or rather his family, was in a position to pick and choose. I said as much to my friend. While she agreed that there were many advantages on their side, she also said, "We must keep in mind that my son is both short and dark; these are drawbacks in finding the right match." . . .

An important source of contacts in trying to arrange her son's marriage was my friend's social club in Bombay. Many of the women had daughters of the right age, and some had already expressed an interest in my friend's son. I was most enthusiastic about the possibilities of one particular family who had five daughters, all of whom were pretty, demure, and well educated. Their mother had told my friend, "You can have your pick for your son, whichever one of my daughters appeals to you most." I saw a match in sight. "Surely," I said to my friend, "we will find one there. Let's go visit and make our choice." But my friend held back; she did not seem to share my enthusiasm, for reasons I could not then fathom.

When I kept pressing for an explanation of her reluctance, she admitted, "See, Serena, here is the problem. The family has so many daughters, how will they be able to provide nicely for any of them? . . . Since this is our eldest son, it's best if we marry him to

a girl who is the only daughter, then the wedding will truly be a gala affair." I argued that surely the quality of the girls themselves made up for any deficiency in the elaborateness of the wedding. My friend admitted this point but still seemed reluctant to proceed.

Is there something else," I asked her, "some factor I have missed?" "Well," she finally said, "there is one other thing. They have one daughter already married and living in Bombay. The mother is always complaining to me that the girl's in-laws don't let her visit her own family often enough. So it makes me wonder, will she be that kind of mother who always wants her daughter at her own home? This will prevent the girl from adjusting to our house. It is not a good thing." And so, this family of five daughters was dropped as a possibility.

Somewhat disappointed, I nevertheless respected my friend's reasoning and geared up for the next prospect. This was also the daughter of a woman in my friend's social club. There was clear interest in this family and I could see why. The family's reputation was excellent; in fact, they came from a subcaste slightly higher than my friend's own. The girl, who was an only daughter, was pretty and well educated and had a brother studying in the United States. Yet, after expressing an interest to me in this family, all talk of them suddenly died down and the search began elsewhere.

What happened to that girl as a prospect?" I asked one day. "You never mention her anymore. She is so pretty and so educated, what did you find wrong?"

"She is too educated. We've decided against it. My husband's father saw the girl on the bus the other day and thought her forward. A girl who 'roams about' the city by herself is not the girl for our family." My disappointment this time was even greater, as I thought the son would have liked the girl very much. . . . I learned that if the family of the girl has even a slightly higher social status than the family of the boy, the bride may think herself too good for them, and this too will cause problems. . . .

[continued]

[continued]

After one more candidate, who my friend decided was not attractive enough for her son, almost six months had passed and I had become anxious. My friend laughed at my impatience: "Don't be so much in a hurry," she said. "You Americans want everything done so quickly. You get married quickly and then just as quickly get divorced. Here we take marriage more seriously. We must take all the factors into account. It is not enough for us to learn by our mistakes. This is too serious a business. If a mistake is made we have not only ruined the life of our son or daughter, but we have spoiled the reputation of our family as well. And that will make it much harder for their brothers and sisters to get married. So we must be very careful."

What she said was true and I promised myself to be more patient. I had really hoped and expected that the match would be made before my year in India was up. But it was not to be. When I left India my friend seemed no further along in finding a suitable match for her son than when I had arrived.

Two years later, I returned to India and still my friend had not found a girl for her son. By this time, he was close to 30, and I think she was a little worried. Since she knew I had friends all over India, and I was going to be there for a year, she asked me to "help her in this work" and keep an eye out for someone suitable. . . .

It was almost at the end of my year's stay in India that I met a family with a marriageable daughter whom I felt might be a good possibility for my friend's son. . . . This new family had a successful business in a medium-sized city in central India and were from the same subcaste as my friend. The daughter was pretty and chic; in fact, she had studied fashion design in college. Her parents would not allow her to go off by herself to any of the major cities in India where she could make a career, but they had compromised with her wish to work by allowing her to run a small dress-making boutique from their home. In spite of her desire to have a career, the daughter was both modest and home-loving and had had a traditional, sheltered upbringing.

I mentioned the possibility of a match with my friend's son. The girl's parents were most interested. Although their daughter was not eager to marry just yet, the idea of living in Bombay—a sophisticated, extremely fashion-conscious city where she could continue her education in clothing design—was a great inducement. I gave the girl's father my friend's address and suggested that when they went to Bombay on some business or whatever, they look up the boy's family.

Returning to Bombay on my way to New York, I told my friend of this newly discovered possibility. She seemed to feel there was potential but, in spite of my urging, would not make any moves herself. She rather preferred to wait for the girl's family to call upon them.

A year later I received a letter from my friend. The family had indeed come to visit Bombay, and their daughter and my friend's daughter, who were near in age, had become very good friends. During that year, the two girls had frequently visited each other. I thought things looked promising.

Last week I received an invitation to a wedding: My friend's son and the girl were getting married. Since I had found the match, my presence was particularly requested at the wedding. I was thrilled. Success at last! As I prepared to leave for India, I began thinking, "Now, my friend's younger son, who do I know who has a nice girl for him . . . ?"

(Excerpted from Serena Nanda. (1992). Arranging a marriage in India. In P. R. De Vita (Ed.), The naked anthropologist (pp. 139–143). Belmont, CA: Wadsworth)

Cousin Marriage

While cousin marriage is prohibited in some societies, certain cousins are the preferred marriage partners in others. A **parallel cousin** is the child of a father's brother or a mother's sister (Figure 12.1). In some societies, the preferred spouse for a man is his father's brother's daughter or, from the woman's point of view, her father's brother's son. This is known as *patrilateral parallel-cousin marriage*. Although not obligatory, such marriages have been favored historically among Arabs, the ancient Israelites, and the ancient Greeks. All of these societies are (or were) hierarchical in nature—that

is, some people are ranked higher than others because they have more power and property—and although male dominance and descent are emphasized, property of value to men is inherited by daughters as well as sons. Thus, when a man marries his father's brother's daughter (or a woman marries her father's brother's son), property is retained within the single male line of descent. In these societies, generally speaking, the greater the property, the more this form of parallel-cousin marriage is apt to occur.

A **cross cousin** is the child of a mother's brother or a father's sister (see Figure 12.1). Some societies favor *matrilateral cross-cousin marriage*—marriage of a man to his mother's brother's daughter, or a woman to her father's sister's son. This preference exists among food foragers (such as the Aborigines of Australia) and some farming cultures (including various peoples of South India). Among food foragers, who inherit relatively little in the way of property, such marriages help

parallel cousin Child of a father's brother or a mother's sister

cross cousin Child of a mother's brother or a father's sister

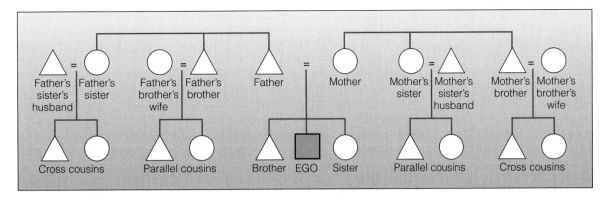

Figure 12.1

Anthropologists use diagrams of this sort to illustrate kinship relationships. This one shows the distinction between cross cousins and parallel cousins. In such diagrams, males are always shown as triangles, females as circles, marital ties by an equal sign (=), sibling relationships as a horizontal line, and parent–child relationships as a vertical line. Terms are given from the perspective of the individual labeled EGO, who can be female or male.

establish and maintain ties of solidarity between social groups. In agricultural societies, however, the transmission of property is an important determinant. In societies that trace descent exclusively in the female line, for instance, property and other important rights usually pass from a man to his sister's son; under cross-cousin marriage, the sister's son is also the man's daughter's husband.

Same-Sex Marriage

As noted earlier in this chapter, our definition of marriage refers to a union between "people" rather than between "a man and a woman" because in some societies same-sex marriages are socially acceptable and officially allowed by law. Marriages between individuals of the same sex may provide a way of dealing with problems for which opposite-sex marriage offers no satisfactory solution. This is the case with a woman–woman marriage, a practice that is permitted in many sub-Saharan African societies, although in none does it involve more than a small minority of all women.

Details differ from one society to another, but woman–woman marriages among the Nandi of western Kenya may be taken as representative of such practices in Africa.[18] The Nandi are a pastoral people who also do considerable farming. Control of most significant property and the primary means of production—livestock and land—is exclusively in the hands of men

and may only be transmitted to their male heirs, usually their sons. Since polygyny is the preferred form of marriage, a man's property is normally divided equally among his wives for their sons to inherit. Within the household, each wife has her own home in which she lives with her children, but all are under the authority of the woman's husband, who is a remote and aloof figure within the household. In such situations, the position of a woman who bears no sons is difficult; not only does she not help perpetuate her husband's male line—a major concern among the Nandi—but also she has no one to inherit the proper share of her husband's property.

To get around these problems, a woman of advanced age who bore no sons may become a female

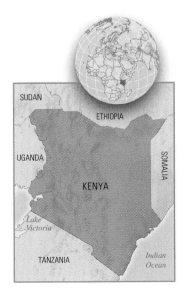

---

[18]The following is based on Obler, R. S. (1982). Is the female husband a man? Woman/woman marriage among the Nandi of Kenya. *Ethnology, 19,* 69–88.

husband by marrying a young woman. The purpose of this arrangement is for the young wife to provide the male heirs her female husband could not. To accomplish this, the woman's wife enters into a sexual relationship with a man other than her female husband's male husband; usually it is one of his male relatives. No other obligations exist between this woman and her male sex partner, and her female husband is recognized as the social and legal father of any children born under these conditions.

In keeping with her role as female husband, this woman is expected to abandon her female gender identity and, ideally, dress and behave as a man. In practice, the ideal is not completely achieved, for the habits of a lifetime are difficult to reverse. Generally, it is in the context of domestic activities, which are most highly symbolic of female identity, that female husbands most completely assume a male identity.

The individuals who are parties to woman–woman marriages enjoy several advantages. By assuming male identity, a barren or sonless woman raises her status considerably and even achieves near equality with men, who otherwise occupy a far more favored position in Nandi society than women. A woman who marries a female husband is usually one who is unable to make a good marriage, often because she (the female husband's wife) has lost face as a consequence of premarital pregnancy. By marrying a female husband, she too raises her status and also secures legitimacy for her children. Moreover, a female husband is usually less harsh and demanding, spends more time with her, and allows her a greater say in decision making than a male husband does. The one thing she may not do is engage in sexual activity with her marriage partner. In fact, female husbands are expected to abandon sexual activity altogether, including with their male husbands to whom they remain married even though the women now have their own wives.

In contrast to woman–woman marriages among the Nandi are same-sex marriages that include sexual activity between partners. Over the past decade, the legal recognition of such unions has become a matter of vigorous debate in some parts of the world.

---

bride-price Money or valuable goods paid by the groom or his family to the bride's family upon marriage. Also called bride wealth

bride service A designated period of time when the groom works for the bride's family

dowry Payment of a woman's inheritance at the time of her marriage, either to her or to her husband

---

Several countries—including Belgium, Canada, the Netherlands, Norway, South Africa, and Spain—have passed laws legalizing gay marriages. Meanwhile numerous U.S. states have adopted constitutional amendments barring same-sex marriage, while others—Connecticut and Massachusetts—now legally recognize these unions.

Among the arguments most commonly marshaled by opponents of same-sex unions is the belief that marriage has always been between males and females—but as we have just seen, this is not true. Same-sex marriages have been documented not only for a number of societies in Africa but in other parts of the world as well. As among the Nandi, they provide acceptable positions in society for individuals who might otherwise be marginalized.

MARRIAGE AND ECONOMIC EXCHANGE

Marriages in many human societies are formalized by some sort of economic exchange. This may take the form of a gift exchange known as **bride-price** or *bride wealth*, which involves payments of money or valuable goods to a bride's parents or other close kin. This usually happens in patrilineal societies where the bride will become a member of the household where her husband grew up; this household will benefit from her labor as well as from the offspring she produces. Thus, her family must be compensated for their loss.

Not only is bride-price not a simple "buying and selling" of women, but the bride's parents may use the money to purchase jewelry or household furnishings for her or to finance an elaborate and costly wedding celebration. It also contributes to the stability of the marriage, because it usually must be refunded if the couple separates. Other forms of compensation are an exchange of women between families—"My son will marry your daughter if your son will marry my daughter." Yet another is **bride service**, a period of time during which the groom works for the bride's family.

In a number of societies more or less restricted to the western, southern, and eastern margins of Eurasia, where the economy is based on agriculture, women often bring a dowry with them at marriage. A form of dowry in the United States is the custom of the bride's family paying the wedding expenses. In effect, a **dowry** is a woman's share of parental property that, instead of passing to her upon her parents' death, is given to her at the time of their marriage. This does not mean that she retains control of

© John Eastcott/Yva Momat/UK/ Woodfin Camp & Associates

In some societies, when a woman marries she receives her share of the family inheritance (her dowry), which she brings to her new family (unlike bride-price, which passes from the groom's family to the bride's family). Shown here are Slovakian women carrying the objects of a woman's dowry.

this property after marriage. In some European and Asian countries, for example, a woman's property traditionally falls exclusively under her husband's control. Having benefited by what she has brought to the marriage, however, he is obligated to look out for her future well-being, including her security after his death.

Thus, one of the functions of dowry is to ensure a woman's support in widowhood (or after divorce), an important consideration in a society where men carry out the bulk of productive work, and women are valued for their reproductive potential rather than for the work they do. In such societies, women incapable of bearing children are especially vulnerable, but the dowry they bring with them at marriage helps protect them against desertion. Another function of dowry is to reflect the economic status of the woman in societies where differences in wealth are important. It also permits women, with the aid of their parents and kin, to compete through dowry for desirable (that is, wealthy) husbands.

DIVORCE

Like marriage, divorce in most societies is a matter of great concern to the couple's families. Since marriage is less often a religious matter than it is an economic one, divorce arrangements can be made for a variety of reasons and with varying degrees of difficulty. Among the Gusii farmers of western Kenya, for instance, sterility and impotence are grounds for a divorce. Among Chenchu foragers inhabiting the thickly forested hills in central India, divorce was discouraged after children were born; couples usually were urged by their families to adjust their differences. By contrast, in the southwestern United States, a Hopi Indian woman in Arizona could divorce her husband at any time merely by placing his belongings outside the door to indicate he was no longer welcome.

An adult unmarried woman is very rare in most non-Western societies where a divorced woman usually soon remarries. In many societies, economic considerations are often the strongest motivation to wed. On the island of New Guinea, a man does not marry because of sexual needs, which he can readily satisfy out of wedlock, but because he needs a woman to make pots and cook his meals, to fabricate nets and weed his plantings. Likewise, women in communities that depend for security upon males capable of fighting need husbands who are raised to be able warriors as well as good hunters.

Although divorce rates may be high in various corners of the world, they have become so high in Western industrial and postindustrial societies that many worry about the future of what they view as traditional and familiar forms of marriage and the family. It is interesting to note that although divorce was next to impossible in Western societies between 1000 and 1800, few marriages lasted more than about ten or twenty years, due to high mortality rates caused in part by inadequate health care and medical expertise.[19] With increased longevity, separation by death has diminished, and separation by legal action has grown. In the United States today, some 50 percent of first marriages end in divorce—twice the 1960 divorce rate but slightly less than the high point in the early 1980s.[20]

Notably, in some societies marriage is a relatively marginal institution and is not considered central to the establishment and maintenance of family life and society. In recent decades, marriage has lost much of its traditional significance in societies where this institution was a central and deeply rooted social institution. Such is the case, for example, in the Scandinavian societies of Iceland, Norway, Sweden, and Denmark, in part due to changes in the political economy, more balanced gender relations, and the shared public benefits of these wealthy capitalist welfare states.

FAMILY AND HOUSEHOLD

Dependence on group living for survival is a basic human characteristic. We have inherited this from primate ancestors, although we have developed it in our own distinctly human way—through culture. However each culture may define what constitutes a family, this social unit forms the basic cooperative structure that ensures an individual's primary needs and provides the necessary care for children to develop as healthy and productive members of the group and thereby help ensure its future.

Comparative historical and cross-cultural studies reveal a wide variety of family patterns, and these patterns may change over time. Thus, the definition of **family** is necessarily broad: two or more people related by blood, marriage, or adoption. The family may take many forms, ranging from a single parent with one or more children, to a married couple or polygamous spouses with or without offspring, to several generations of parents and their children.

For purposes of cross-cultural comparison, anthropologists define the **household** as the basic residential unit where economic production, consumption, inheritance, child rearing, and shelter are organized and carried out. In the vast majority of human societies, most households are made up of families, but there are many other arrangements. For instance, among the Mundurucu Indians, a horticultural people living in the center of Brazil's Amazon rainforest, married men and women are members of separate households, meeting periodically for sexual activity. At age 13 boys join their fathers in the men's house. Meanwhile, their sisters continue to live with their mothers and the younger boys in two or three houses grouped around the men's house. Thus, the men's house constitutes one household inhabited by adult males and their sexually mature sons, and the women's houses, inhabited by adult women and prepubescent boys and girls, constitute others.

An array of other domestic arrangements can be found in other parts of the world, including situations in which co-residents of a household are not related biologically or by marriage—such as the service personnel in an elaborate royal household, apprentices in the household of craft specialists, or low-status clients in the household of rich and powerful patrons. So it is that *family* and *household* are not always synonymous.

Forms of the Family

To discuss the various forms families take in response to particular social, historical, and ecological circumstances, we must, at the outset, make a distinction between a **conjugal family** (in Latin *conjugere* means "to join together"), which is formed on the basis of marital ties, and a **consanguineal family** (based on the Latin word *consanguineus*, literally meaning "of the same blood"), which consists of related women, their brothers, and the women's offspring.

Consanguineal families are not common, but examples of this include the Musuo of southwestern China

---

family Two or more people related by blood, marriage, or adoption. The family may take many forms, ranging from a single parent with one or more children, to a married couple or polygamous spouses with, or without, offspring, to several generations of parents and their children

household The basic residential unit where economic production, consumption, inheritance, child rearing, and shelter are organized and carried out

conjugal family A family established through marriage

consanguineal family A family of "blood relatives" consisting of related women, their brothers, and the women's offspring

nuclear family A group consisting of one or two parents and dependent offspring, which may include a stepparent, stepsiblings, and adopted children. (Until recently this term referred only to the father, mother, and child(ren) unit)

---

[19]Stone, L. (1998). *Kinship and gender: An introduction* (p. 235). Boulder, CO: Westview Press.

[20]Whitehead, B. D., & Popenoe, D. (2004). *The state of our unions: The social health of marriage in America 2004*. Rutgers, NJ: Rutgers University National Marriage Project.

This is a celebration at the palace in the Yoruba City of Oyo, Nigeria. As is usual in societies with royal households, that of the Yoruba includes many individuals not related to the ruler, as well as the royal family.

and the Tory Islanders (a Roman Catholic, Gaelic-speaking fisherfolk living off the coast of Ireland). Typically, Tory Islanders do not marry until they are in their late 20s or early 30s. By then, commented one local woman,

> It's too late to break up arrangements that you have already known for a long time. . . . You know, I have my sisters and brothers to look after, why should I leave home to go live with a husband? After all, he's got his sisters and his brothers looking after him.[21]

Notably, since the community numbers but a few hundred people, husbands and wives are within easy commuting distance of each other.

According to a cross-cultural survey of family types in 192 cultures around the world, the extended family is most common, present in nearly half of those cultures, compared to the nuclear family at 25 percent, and polygamous at 22 percent.[22] Each of these is discussed below.

The Nuclear Family

The smallest family unit is known as the **nuclear family**, a group consisting of one or two parents and dependent offspring, which may include a stepparent, stepsiblings, and adopted children (Figure 12.2). Until recently, the term *nuclear family* referred only to the mother, father, and child(ren) unit—the family form that most North Americans, Europeans, and many others now regard as

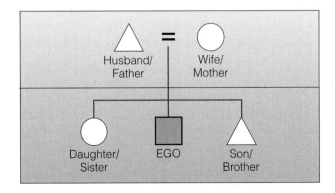

Figure 12.2

This diagram shows the relationships in a traditional nuclear family, a form that is common but declining in North America and much of Europe.

[21]Fox, R. (1981, December 3). [Interview]. Coast Telecourses, Inc., Los Angeles.

[22]Winick, C. (Ed.). (1970). *Dictionary of anthropology* (p. 202). Totowa, NJ: Littlefield, Adams.

the normal or natural nucleus of larger family units. In the United States, father, mother, and child(ren) nuclear family households reached their highest frequency around 1950, when 60 percent of all households conformed to this model.[23] Today such families comprise only one-quarter of U.S. households,[24] and the term *nuclear family* is used to cover the social reality of several types of small parent–child units, including single parents with children and same-sex couples with children.

Industrialization and market capitalism have played a historical role in shaping the nuclear family with which most of us are familiar today. One reason for this is that factories, mining and transportation companies, warehouses, shops, and other businesses generally only pay individual wage earners for the jobs they are hired to do. Whether these workers are single, married, divorced, have siblings or children is really not a concern to the profit-seeking companies. Because jobs may come and go, individual wage earners must remain mobile to adapt to the labor markets. And since few wage earners have the financial resources to support large numbers of relatives without incomes of their own, industrial or postindustrial societies do not favor the continuance of larger extended families (discussed below), which are standard in most societies traditionally dependent on pastoral nomadism, agriculture, or horticulture.

Interestingly, the nuclear family is also likely to be prominent in traditional foraging societies such as that of the Eskimo people who live in the barren Arctic environments of eastern Siberia, Alaska, Greenland, and Canada (where Eskimos are now known as Inuit). In the winter the traditional Inuit husband and wife, with their children, roam the vast Arctic Canadian snowscape in their quest for food. The husband hunts and makes shelters. The wife cooks, is responsible for the children, and makes the clothing and keeps it in good repair. One of her chores is to chew her husband's boots to soften the leather for the next day so that he can resume his quest for game. The wife and her children could not survive without the husband, and life for a man is unimaginable without a wife.

Similar to nuclear families in industrial societies, those living under especially harsh environmental conditions must be prepared to fend for themselves. Such isolation comes with its own set of challenges, including the difficulties of rearing children without

> **extended family** Two or more closely related nuclear families clustered together into a large domestic group

[23]Stacey, J. (1990). *Brave new families* (pp. 5, 10). New York: Basic Books.

[24]Irvine, M. (1999, November 24). Mom-and-pop houses grow rare. *Burlington Free Press; Current population survey.* (2002). U.S. Census Bureau.

multigenerational support and a lack of familial care for the elderly. Nonetheless, this form of family is well adapted to a mode of subsistence that requires a high degree of geographic mobility. For the Inuit in Canada, this mobility permits the hunt for food; for other North Americans, the hunt for jobs and improved social status requires a mobile form of family unit.

The Extended Family

When two or more closely related nuclear families cluster together into a large domestic group, they form a unit known as the **extended family**. This larger family unit, common in traditional horticultural, agricultural, and pastoral societies around the world, typically consists of siblings with their spouses and offspring, and often their parents. All of these kin, some related by blood and some by marriage, live and work together for the common good and deal with outsiders as a single unit.

Because members of the younger generation bring their husbands or wives to live in the family, extended families have continuity through time. As older members die off, new members are born into the family. Extended families have built into them particular challenges. Among these are difficulties that the in-marrying spouse is likely to have in adjusting to his or her spouse's family.

Nontraditional Families and Nonfamily Households

In North America and parts of Europe, increasing numbers of people live in nonfamily households, either alone or with nonrelatives. In fact, about one-third of households in the United States fall into this category. Many others live as members of what are often called *nontraditional families.*

Increasingly common are *cohabitation* households, comprised of unmarried couples. Since 1960, such

Extended family households exist in many parts of the world, including among the Maya people of Central America and Mexico.[25] In many of their communities, sons bring their wives to live in houses built on the edges of a small open plaza, on one edge of which their father's house already stands. Numerous household activities are carried out on this plaza—children play while adults weave, do some other productive work, or socialize with guests. The head of the family is the sons' father, who makes most of the important decisions. All members of the family work together for the common good and deal with outsiders as a single unit.

households have increased in number dramatically, especially among young couples in their 20s and early 30s in North America and parts of Europe. In Norway, over half of all live births now occur outside marriage, in part because Norwegian "cohabiting couples who have children together or have lived together for minimum two years will have many of the same rights and obligations to social security, pensions and taxation as their married counterparts."[26] For many, however, cohabitation represents a relatively short-lasting domestic arrangement, since most cohabiting couples either marry or separate within two years.[27]

Cohabitation breakup has contributed to the growing number of *single-parent* households—as have increases in divorce, sexual activity outside marriage, declining marriage rates among women of childbearing age, and the number of women preferring single motherhood.

In the United States, about one-third of all births occur outside of marriage. There, the percentage of single-parent households has grown to 9 percent, while the number comprised of married couples with children has dropped to 24 percent. Although single-parent households account for just 9 percent of all U.S. households, they are home to 28 percent of all children (under 18 years of age) in the country.[28] In the vast majority of cases, a child living in a single-parent household is with his or her mother.

Single-parent households headed by women are neither new nor restricted to industrial or postindustrial societies. They have been known and studied for a long time in the countries of the Caribbean Sea, where men historically have been exploited as a cheap source of labor on sugar, coffee, or banana plantations. In more recent decades, many of these men have taken up work as temporary migrant laborers in foreign countries, primarily in the United States—often living in temporary households comprised of fellow laborers.

[25]Vogt, E. Z. (1990). *The Zinacantecos of Mexico, A modern Maya way of life* (2nd ed., pp. 30–34). Fort Worth: Holt, Rinehart & Winston.

[26]Noack, T. 2001. Cohabitation in Norway: An accepted and gradually more regulated way of living. *International Journal of Law, Policy, and the Family, 15*(1),102–117.

[27]Forste, R. (2008). Prelude to marriage, or alternative to marriage? A social demographic look at cohabitation in the U.S. Working paper. Social Science Electronic Publishing, Inc. http://papers.ssrn.com/sol3/papers.cfm?abstract_id=269172.

[28]*Current population survey.*

RESIDENCE PATTERNS

Where some form of conjugal or extended family is the norm, family exogamy requires that either the husband or wife, if not both, must move to a new household upon marriage. There are five common patterns of residence that a newly married couple may adopt—the prime determinant being ecological circumstances, although other factors enter in as well. Thus, postmarital residence arrangements, far from being arbitrary, are adaptive in character. Here we will mention only the three most common arrangements.

Patrilocal residence is when a married couple lives in the husband's father's place of residence. This arrangement is favorable in situations where men play a predominant role in subsistence, particularly if they own property that can be accumulated, if polygyny is customary, if warfare is prominent enough to make cooperation among men especially important, and if an elaborate political organization exists in which men wield authority. These conditions are most often found together in societies that rely on animal husbandry and/or intensive agriculture for their subsistence. Where patrilocal residence is customary, the bride often must move to a different band or community. In such cases, her parents' family is not only losing the services of a useful family member, but they are losing her potential offspring as well. Hence, some kind of compensation to her family, most commonly brideprice, is usual.

Matrilocal residence, in which a married couple lives in the wife's mother's place of residence, is a likely result if cultural ecological circumstances make the role of the woman predominate for subsistence. It is found most often in horticultural societies, where political organization is relatively uncentralized and where cooperation among women is important. The Hopi Indians provide one example. Although it is the Hopi men who do the farming, the women control access to land and "own" the harvest. Indeed, men are not even allowed in the granaries. Under matrilocal residence, men usually do not move very far from the family in which they were raised so they are available to help out there from time to time. Therefore, marriage usually does not involve compensation to the groom's family.

Under **neolocal residence**, a married couple forms a household in a separate location. This occurs where the independence of the nuclear family is emphasized. In industrial societies such as the United States, where most economic activity occurs outside rather than inside the family and where it is important for individuals to be able to move where jobs can be found, neolocal residence is better suited than any of the other patterns.

MARRIAGE, FAMILY, AND HOUSEHOLD IN OUR GLOBALIZED AND TECHNOLOGIZED WORLD

In many countries the mosaic of marriage, family, and household forms has become more varied in recent decades. Many factors contribute to this, including global capitalism and large-scale emigration of peoples moving across cultural boundaries. Also significant are high rates of divorce and remarriage, resulting in *blended families* composed of a married couple together raising children from previous unions. And although it has not been uncommon for childless couples in many cultures throughout human history to adopt children, including orphans and even captives, today it is a transnational practice for adults from industrial and postindustrial countries to travel across the world in search of infants to adopt, regardless of their ethnic heritage. Other contributing factors to the diversity of families and households include *new reproductive technologies* (NRTs), such as in vitro fertilization, as well as surrogacy (substitute pregnancy) and open adoption, which make it possible for a child to have a relationship with both the biological and adoptive parents.

Also of note, worldwide, is the ever-growing number of households composed of temporary and migrant workers. Today, China alone has 114 million of them, mostly young people who have quit the peasant villages of their childhood and traveled to fast-growing cities to work in factories, shops, restaurants, and other such places. Some pile into apartments with friends or co-workers, others live in factory dormitories—new, single-generation households that stand in stark contrast to the multigeneration extended family households in which they were raised. Similar scenes are repeated all around the world as individuals in this transient workforce set up house together far away from home in order to make a living. Although many countries have passed legislation intended to provide migrants with protections concerning housing, as well

patrilocal residence A residence pattern in which a married couple lives in the husband's father's place of residence
matrilocal residence A residence pattern in which a married couple lives in the wife's mother's place of residence
neolocal residence A pattern in which a married couple establishes its household in a location apart from either the husband's or the wife's relatives

Many of China's 114 million migrant laborers work in factories and live in factory dormitories such as this.

as work conditions and pay (such as the 1983 Migrant and Seasonal Agricultural Worker Protection Act in the United States), living conditions for these workers are often miserable.[29]

As the various ethnographic examples in this chapter illustrate, our species has invented a wide variety of marriage, family, and household forms, each in correspondence with related features in the social structure and conforming to the larger cultural system. In the face of new challenges, we explore and tinker in search of solutions, sometimes resulting in finding completely new forms, and other times returning to time-tested formulas of more traditional varieties.

Chapter Summary

■ Every society has rules and customs concerning sexual relations, marriage, household and family structures, and child-rearing practices, all of which play important roles in establishing and maintaining the social alliances and continuity that help ensure a society's overall well-being.

■ A majority of cultures are sexually permissive and do not sharply regulate personal sexual practices. Others are restrictive and explicitly prohibit all sexual activity outside of marriage. Of these, a few punish adultery by imprisonment, social exclusion, or even death, as traditionally prescribed by some religious laws.

■ Marriage can be broadly defined as a culturally sanctioned union between two or more people that establishes certain rights and obligations between the people, between them and their children, and between them and their in-laws. Incest taboos forbid sexual relations between certain close relatives— usually between parent–child and siblings at a minimum. A truly convincing explanation of the incest taboo has yet to be advanced, but it is related to the practices of endogamy (marrying within a group of individuals) and exogamy (marrying outside a group).

■ Marriage, in contrast to mating, is backed by social, legal, and economic forces. It falls into several broad categories. Monogamy, or the taking of a single spouse, is the most common form of marriage, primarily for economic reasons. Serial monogamy, in which a man or woman marries a series of partners, has become common among Europeans and North Americans. Polygamy, in which one individual has multiple spouses, comes in two forms: polygyny and polyandry. A man must have a certain amount of wealth to be able to afford polygyny, or marriage to more than one wife at the same time. Yet in societies where women do most of the productive work, polygyny may serve as a means of generating wealth for a household. Although few marriages in a given society may be polygynous, it is regarded as an appropriate, and even preferred, form of marriage in the majority of the world's societies. Since few communities have a surplus of men, polyandry, or the custom of a woman having several husbands, is uncommon. Also rare is group marriage, in which several men and several women have sexual access to one another.

■ In industrial and postindustrial countries of the West, marriages are generally based on ideals of romantic love. Other

---

[29]Chang, L. (2005, June 9). A migrant worker sees rural home in new light. *Wall Street Journal.*

parts of the world do not risk marriages based on such youthful whims. In non-Western societies, economic considerations are of major concern in arranging marriages, and marriage serves to bind two families as allies.

■ Preferred marriage partners in many societies are particular cross cousins (mother's brother's daughter if a man; father's sister's son if a woman) or, less commonly, parallel cousins on the paternal side (father's brother's son or daughter). Cross-cousin marriage is a means of establishing and maintaining solidarity between groups.

■ Same-sex marriages exist in some societies. For example, woman–woman marriages as practiced in some African cultures provide a socially approved way to deal with problems for which heterosexual marriages offer no satisfactory solution. In recent years, some countries—notably Belgium, Canada, Spain, Norway, and the Netherlands—and some U.S. states have legalized same-sex marriage.

■ In many human societies, marriages are formalized by some sort of economic exchange—such as a reciprocal gift exchange between the bride's and groom's relatives. More common is bride-price, the payment of money or other valuables from the groom's to the bride's kin. Bride service occurs when the groom is expected to work for a period for the bride's family. A dowry is the payment of a woman's inheritance at the time of marriage to her or her husband. Its purpose is to ensure support for women in societies where men do most of the productive work, and women are valued primarily for their reproductive potential.

■ Divorce is possible in all societies, although reasons and frequency vary cross-culturally.

■ The family may take many forms, ranging from a single parent with one or more children, to a married couple or polygamous spouses with or without offspring, to several generations of parents and their children. A family is distinct from a household, which is the basic residential unit where economic production, consumption, inheritance, child rearing, and shelter are organized and carried out. In the vast majority of human societies, most households are made up of families or parts of families, but there are many other household arrangements.

■ The smallest domestic unit is the nuclear family—a group consisting of one or two parents and dependent offspring, which may include a stepparent, stepsiblings, and adopted children. Until recently, the term referred solely to the mother, father, and child(ren) unit. This family form is common in the industrial and postindustrial countries of North America and Europe and also in societies that live in harsh environments, as do the Inuit. It is well suited to the mobility required both in food-foraging groups and in industrial societies where job changes are frequent. The extended family consists of several closely related nuclear families living and often working together in a single household.

■ Three common residence patterns are patrilocal (in which a married couple lives in the locality of the husband's father's place of residence), matrilocal (living in the locality of the wife's mother's place of residence), and neolocal (living in a locality apart from the husband's or wife's parents).

■ In North America and parts of Europe, increasing numbers of people live in nonfamily households, either alone or with nonrelatives. This includes the fast-growing category of unmarried couples who cohabitate. Many others live as members of what are often called nontraditional families, including single-parent households and blended families. New reproductive technologies, surrogacy, and international adoptions are adding new dimensions to familial relationships.

Questions for Reflection

1. According to Shinto tradition in traditional Japanese society, the bridal dress is white as a symbolic expression of her purity. Many women living in less sexually restrictive societies also choose white bridal gowns. Why do you think that is, and how is it in your own family and community? Also, why do you think the prescribed dress color for Japanese grooms is black and gray? Is that also true for your own culture?

2. Members of traditional communities in countries where the state is either weak or absent depend on relatives to help meet the basic challenges of survival. In such traditional societies, why would it be risky to choose marriage partners exclusively on the basis of romantic love? Can you imagine other factors playing a role in the choice if the long-term survival of your community was at stake?

3. Although most women in Europe and North America probably view polygyny as a marriage practice exclusively benefiting men, women in cultures where such marriages are traditional may stress more positive sides of sharing a husband with several co-wives. Under which conditions do you think polygyny could be considered as relatively beneficial for women?

4. Why do you think your own culture has historically prescribed restrictive rules about sexual relations, not only with respect to heterosexual contact outside marriage, but also condemning same-sex relations? Do you expect economic and social changes in a society will further change ideas and attitudes toward sex and marriage? And if so, will they become more or less restrictive?

5. Many children in Europe and North America are raised in single-parent households. In contrast to the United States, where most children living with their unmarried mothers grow up in economically disadvantaged households, in Norway, relatively few children raised by unmarried mothers face poverty. Why do you think that is?

Key Terms

marriage	polygamy	bride-price	consanguineal family
incest taboo	polygyny	bride service	nuclear family
endogamy	polyandry	dowry	extended family
exogamy	group marriage	family	patrilocal residence
monogamy	parallel cousin	household	matrilocal residence
serial monogamy	cross cousin	conjugal family	neolocal residence

© Hugh Morton

As social creatures, humans create and maintain networks that reach beyond immediate family or household to provide security and support. On a basic level these associations are arranged by kinship. In the highlands of Scotland, as among many traditional peoples around the world, large kinship groups known as clans have been important units of social organization. Tracing descent exclusively through fathers from a distant founding male ancestor, clan members typically express their kinship by wearing kilts and shawls with a distinct tartan (plaid) pattern that identifies their particular group. Historically, there were several dozen Scottish clans, often identified with the prefix "Mac" or "Mc" (from an old Celtic word meaning "son of"). Over the past few centuries, many Scots emigrated from their homelands in search of economic opportunity. Today, their descendants are dispersed across the globe, especially in Australia, Canada, and the United States. Often aided by the Internet, widely scattered Scots seek to re-establish kinship ties, traveling long distances to clan gatherings, where they celebrate their cultural heritage, including traditional dancing and piping. Pictured here is a "parade of tartans"—a festive expression of group identity and ethnic pride during a gathering of the clans at Grandfather Mountain in North Carolina.

Kinship and Other Methods of Grouping

All societies rely on some form of family or household organization to meet basic human needs: securing food, shelter, and protection against danger, coordinating work, regulating sexual activities, and organizing child rearing. As efficient and flexible as these socioeconomic units may be for meeting such challenges, many societies confront problems that are beyond the coping ability of family and household organization.

For example, members of one independent local group often need some means of interacting with people outside their immediate circle for defense against natural disasters or outside aggressors and for securing vitally important natural resources for food, fuel, and shelter. A wider circle may also be necessary in forming a cooperative workforce for tasks that require more participants than households alone can provide.

Humans have come up with many ways to widen their circles of support to meet such challenges. One is through a formal political system, with personnel to make and enforce laws, keep the peace, allocate resources, and perform other regulatory and societal functions. But the predominant way to build this support in societies that are not organized as political states—especially foraging, crop-cultivating, and pastoral societies—is by means of **kinship**, a network of relatives within which individuals possess certain mutual rights and obligations.

DESCENT GROUPS

A common way of organizing a society along kinship lines is by creating what anthropologists call descent groups. Found in many societies, a **descent group** is any

kinship A network of relatives within which individuals possess certain mutual rights and obligations
descent group Any kinship group with a membership lineally descending from a real (historical) or fictional common ancestor

Biocultural Connection

Maori Origins: Ancestral Genes and Mythical Canoes

Anthropologists have been fascinated to find that oral traditions of Maori people in New Zealand fit quite well with scientific findings. New Zealand, an island country whose dramatic geography served as the setting for the *Lord of the Rings* film trilogy, lies in a remote corner of the Pacific Ocean some 1,200 miles southeast of Australia. Named by Dutch seafarers who landed on its shores in 1642, it was claimed by the British as a colony about 150 years later. Maoris, the country's indigenous people, fought back but were outgunned, outnumbered, and forced to lay down their arms in the early 1870s. Today, nearly 600,000 of New Zealand's 4.1 million citizens claim some Maori ancestry.

Maori have an age-old legend about how they came to Aotearoa ("Land of the Long White Cloud"), their name for New Zealand: More than twenty-five generations ago, their Polynesian ancestors arrived in a great fleet of sailing canoes from Hawaiki, their mythical homeland sometimes identified with Tahiti where the native language closely resembles their own. According to chants and genealogies passed down through the ages, this fleet consisted of at least seven (perhaps up to thirteen) seafaring canoes. Estimated to weigh about 5 tons, each of these large dugouts had a single claw-shaped sail and may have carried 50 to 120 people, plus food supplies, plants, and animals.

As described by Maori anthropologist Te Rangi Hiroa (Peter Buck), the seafaring skills of these voyagers enabled

them to navigate by currents, winds, and stars across vast ocean expanses.[a] Perhaps escaping warfare and tribute payments in Hawaiki, they probably made the five-week-long voyage around 1350 AD, although there were earlier and later canoes as well.

Traditional Maori society is organized into about thirty different *iwi* ("tribe"), grouped in thirteen *waka* ("canoe"), each with its own traditional territory. Today, prior to giving a formal talk, Maoris still introduce themselves by identifying their *iwi,* their *waka,* and the major sacred places of their ancestral territory. Their genealogy connects them to their tribe's founding ancestor who was a crew member or perhaps even a chief in one of the giant canoes mentioned in the legend of the Great Fleet.[b]

Maori oral traditions about their origins fit quite well with scientific data based on anthropological and more recent genetic research. Study by

outsiders can be controversial because Maori equate an individual's genes to his or her genealogy, which belongs to one's *iwi* or ancestral community. Considered sacred and entrusted to the tribal elders, genealogy is traditionally surrounded by *tapu* ("sacred prohibitions").[c] The Maori term for genealogy is *whakapapa* ("to set layer upon layer"), which is also a word for "gene." Thus, this Maori term captures something of the original *genous,* the Greek word for "begetting offspring." Another Maori word for gene is *ira tangata* ("life spirit of mortals"), and for them, a gene has *mauri* (a "life force"). Given these spiritual associations, genetic investigations of Maori human DNA could not proceed until the Maori themselves became actively involved in the research.

Together with other researchers, Maori geneticist Adele Whyte has examined maternally and paternally inherited genetic markers, namely, mitochondrial DNA in women and Y chromosomes in men.[d] She recently calculated that the number of Polynesian females required to found New Zealand's Maori population probably ranged between 170 and 230 women. If the original fleet sailing to Aotearoa consisted of seven large canoes, it may have carried a total of about 600 people (men, women, and children).

A comparison of the DNA of Maori with that of Polynesians across the Pacific Ocean and peoples from Southeast Asia reveals a genetic map of very ancient Maori migration

---

kinship group with a membership in the direct line of descent from a real (historical) or fictional common ancestor. The addition of a few culturally meaningful obligations and taboos acts as a kind of glue to help hold the structured social group together.

unilineal descent Descent that establishes group membership exclusively through either the male or female line
matrilineal descent Descent traced exclusively through the female line to establish group membership
patrilineal descent Descent traced exclusively through the male line to establish group membership

Although many important functions of the descent group are taken over by other institutions when a society becomes politically organized as a state, elements of such kin-ordered groups may continue. We see this with many traditional indigenous societies that have become part of larger state societies yet endure as distinctive kin-ordered communities.

So it is with the Maori of New Zealand, featured in this chapter's Biocultural Connection. Retaining key elements of their traditional social structure, they are still organized in about thirty large descent groups known as *iwi* ("tribe"), which form part of

Traditional Maori *waka* (ocean-going canoe).

routes. Mitochondrial DNA, which is passed along virtually unchanged from mothers to their children, provides a genetic clock linking today's Polynesians to southern Taiwan's indigenous coastal peoples, showing that female ancestors originally set out from that island off the southeast coast of China about 6,000 years ago.[e] In the next few thousand years, they migrated by way of the Philippines and then moved south and east, hopping from island to island.

Adding to their gene pool in the course of later generations, Melanesian males from New Guinea and elsewhere joined the migrating bands before arriving in Aotearoa. In short, Maori cultural traditions in New Zealand are generally substantiated by anthropological as well as molecular biological data.

[a]Buck, P. H. (1938). *Vikings of the Pacific*. Chicago: University Press of Chicago.

[b]Hanson, A. (1989). The making of the Maori: Culture invention and its logic. *American Anthropologist, 91*(4), 890–902.

[c]Mead, A. T. P. (1996). Genealogy, sacredness, and the commodities market. *Cultural Survival Quarterly, 20*(2).

[d]Whyte, A. L. H. (2005). Human evolution in Polynesia. *Human Biology, 77*(2), 157–177.

[e]"Gene study suggests Polynesians came from Taiwan." (2005, July 4). Reuters.

larger social and territorial units known as *waka* ("canoe").

Descent group membership must be sharply defined in order to operate effectively in a kin-ordered society. If membership is allowed to overlap, it is unclear where someone's primary loyalty belongs, especially when different descent groups have conflicting interests. Membership can be restricted in a number of ways. The most common way is what anthropologists refer to as *unilineal descent*.

Unilineal Descent

Unilineal descent (sometimes called *unilateral descent*) establishes descent group membership exclusively through the male or the female line. In non-Western societies, unilineal descent groups are quite common. The individual is assigned at birth to membership in a specific descent group, which may be traced either by **matrilineal descent** through the female line, or by **patrilineal descent** through the male line, depending on the culture. In matrilineal societies females are culturally recognized as socially significant, for they are considered responsible for the group's continued existence. In patrilineal societies, this responsibility falls on the male members of the group, thereby enhancing their social importance.

The two major forms of a unilineal descent group, be it patrilineal or matrilineal, are the lineage and the

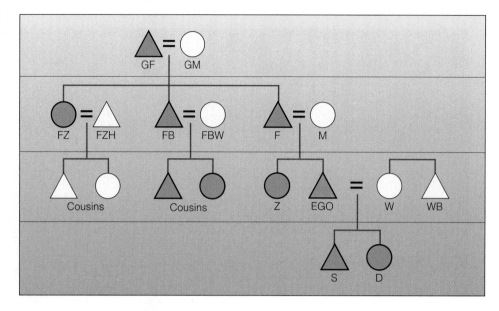

Figure 13.1 **Tracing Patrilineal Descent**

Only the individuals symbolized by a filled-in circle or triangle are in the same descent group as EGO (the central person from whom the degree of each kinship relationship is traced). The abbreviation F stands for father, B for brother, H for husband, S for son, M for mother, Z for sister, W for wife, D for daughter, and G for grand. Note that a woman cannot transmit descent to her own children.

clan. A **lineage** is a unilineal kinship group descended from a common ancestor or founder who lived four to six generations ago and in which relationships among members can be exactly stated in genealogical terms. A **clan** is an extended unilineal kinship group, often consisting of several lineages, whose members claim common descent from a remote ancestor, usually legendary or mythological.[1]

Patrilineal Descent and Organization

Patrilineal descent (sometimes called *agnatic* or *male descent*) is the more widespread of the two unilineal descent systems. Through forefathers, the male members of a patrilineal descent group trace their descent from a common ancestor (Figure 13.1). Brothers and sisters belong to the descent group of their father's father, their father, their father's siblings, and their father's brother's children. A man's son and daughter also trace their descent back through the male line to their common ancestor. In the typical patrilineal group, authority over the children rests with the father or his elder brother. A woman belongs to the same descent group as her father and his brothers, but her children cannot trace their descent through them.

> **lineage** A unilineal kinship group descended from a common ancestor or founder who lived four to six generations ago, and in which relationships among members can be exactly stated in genealogical terms
> **clan** An extended unilineal kinship group, often consisting of several lineages, whose members claim common descent from a remote ancestor, usually legendary or mythological

[1]See Hoebel, E. A. (1949). *Man in the primitive world: An introduction to anthropology* (pp. 646, 652). New York: McGraw-Hill.

Matrilineal Descent and Organization

As the term implies, matrilineal descent is traced exclusively through the female line (Figure 13.2), just as patrilineal descent is through the male line. However, the matrilineal pattern differs from the patrilineal in that it does not automatically confer gender authority.

Although descent passes through the female line and women may have considerable power, they do not hold exclusive authority in the descent group. They share it with men. Usually, these are the brothers, rather than the husbands, of the women through whom descent is traced. Apparently, the adaptive purpose of matrilineal systems is to provide continuous female solidarity within the female work group. Matrilineal systems are usually found in horticultural societies in which women perform much of the work in the house and nearby gardens. In part because women's labor as crop cultivators is regarded as so important to the society, matrilineal descent prevails.

In a matrilineal system, brothers and sisters belong to the descent group of the mother, the mother's mother, the mother's siblings, and the mother's sisters' children. Thus, every male belongs to the same descent group as his mother, and a man's own children belong to his wife's descent group, not his.

Although not true of all matrilineal systems, a common feature is the relative weakness of the social tie between wife and husband. A woman's husband lacks authority in the household they share. Her brother, and not the husband-father, distributes goods, organizes work, settles disputes, supervises rituals, and administers inheritance and succession rules. Meanwhile, her husband fulfills the same role in his own sister's household. Furthermore, his property and status are inherited by his sister's son rather than his own son. Thus, brothers and sisters maintain lifelong ties with one another, whereas marital ties are easily

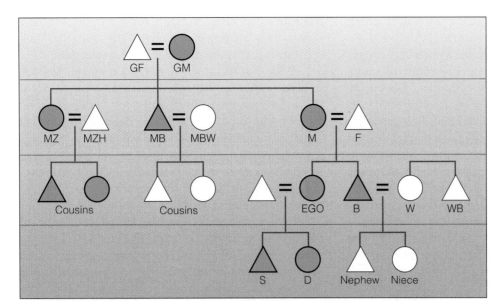

Figure 13.2 **Tracing Matrilineal Descent**

This diagram can be compared with patrilineal descent in Figure 13.1. The two patterns are virtually mirror images. Note that a man cannot transmit descent to his own children.

Unlike the Han, the dominant ethnic majority in China who are patrilineal, several ethnic minorities in southwestern China are matrilineal, including the Mosuo. The women in the Mosuo family shown here are blood relatives of one another, and the men are their brothers. Mosuo husbands live apart from their wives, in the households of their sisters.

severed. In matrilineal societies, unsatisfactory marriages are more easily ended than in patrilineal societies.

Other Forms of Descent

Among Samoan Islanders (and many other cultures in the Pacific as well as in Southeast Asia) a person has the option of affiliating with either the mother's or the father's descent group. Known as *ambilineal descent,* such a kin-ordered system provides a measure of flexibility. However, this flexibility also introduces the possibility of dispute and conflict as unilineal groups compete for members.

This problem does not arise under *double descent,* or double unilineal descent, a very rare system in which

descent is matrilineal for some purposes and patrilineal for others. Generally, where double descent is traced, the matrilineal and patrilineal groups take action in different spheres of society. For example, among the Yakö of eastern Nigeria, property is divided into both patrilineal possessions and matrilineal possessions.[2] The patrilineage owns perpetual productive resources, such as land, whereas the matrilineage owns consumable property, such as livestock. The legally weaker matriline is somewhat more important in religious matters than the

[2]Forde, C. D. (1968). Double descent among the Yakö. In P. Bohannan & J. Middleton (Eds.), *Kinship and social organization* (pp. 179–191). Garden City, NY: Natural History Press.

patriline. Through double descent, a Yakö might inherit grazing lands from the father's patrilineal group and certain ritual privileges from the mother's matrilineal group.

Finally, when descent derives from both the mother's and father's families equally, anthropologists use the term *bilateral descent*. In such a system people trace their descent from all ancestors, regardless of their gender or side of the family. We may recognize bilateral descent when individuals apply the same genealogical terms to identify similarly related individuals on both sides of the family. For instance, when they speak of a "grandmother" or "grandfather," no indication is given whether these relatives are on the paternal or maternal side of the family.

Bilateral descent exists in various foraging cultures and is also quite common in many contemporary state societies with agricultural, industrial, or postindustrial economies. For example, although most people in Europe, Australia, and North America typically inherit their father's family name (indicative of a culture's history in which patrilineal descent was the norm), they usually consider themselves as much a member of their mother's as their father's family.

DESCENT WITHIN THE LARGER CULTURAL SYSTEM

There is a close relationship between the descent system and a cultural system's infrastructure. Generally, patrilineal descent predominates where male labor is considered of prime importance, as among pastoralists and agriculturalists. Matrilineal descent predominates mainly among horticulturalists in societies where female work in subsistence is especially important. Numerous matrilineal societies are found in southern Asia, one of the earliest cradles of food production in the world. They are also prominent in parts of indigenous North America, South America's tropical lowlands, and parts of Africa.

In many societies an individual has no legal or political status except as a lineage member. Since "citizenship" is derived from lineage membership and legal status depends on it, political powers are derived from it as well. Because a lineage endures after the deaths of members with new members continually born into it, it has a continuing existence that enables it to act like a corporation, as in owning property, organizing productive activities, distributing goods and labor power, assigning status, and regulating relations with other groups. The descent group also may act as a repository of religious

---

traditions. Ancestor worship, for example, is often a powerful force acting to reinforce group solidarity. Thus, it is a strong, effective base of social organization.

Whatever form of descent predominates, the kin of both mother and father are important components of the social structure in all societies. Just because descent may be traced patrilineally, this does not mean that matrilineal relatives are necessarily unimportant. It simply means that, for purposes of group membership, the mother's relatives are excluded. Similarly, under matrilineal descent, the father's relatives are excluded for purposes of group membership.

By way of example, among the matrilineal Trobriand Islanders in the southern Pacific, discussed in Chapter 12, children belong to their mother's descent groups, yet fathers play an important role in their upbringing. Upon marriage, the bride and groom's paternal relatives contribute to the exchange of gifts, and, throughout life, a man may expect his paternal kin to help him improve his economic and political position in society. Eventually, sons may expect to inherit personal property from their fathers.

As a traditional institution in a kin-ordered society, the descent group often endures in state-organized societies where political institutions are ineffective or weakly developed. Such is the case in many countries of the world today, especially in remote mountain or desert villages difficult to reach by state authorities.

Also, because the cultural ideas, values, and practices associated with traditional descent groups may be deeply embedded, such patterns of culture often endure in *diasporic communities* (among immigrants who have relocated from their ancestral homelands and retain their distinct cultural identities as ethnic minority groups in their new host countries).

Lineage Exogamy

A common characteristic of lineages is *exogamy*. As defined in the previous chapter, this means that lineage members must find their marriage partners in other lineages. One advantage of exogamy is that competition for desirable spouses within the group is curbed, promoting the group's internal cohesiveness. Lineage exogamy also means that each marriage is more than a union between two individuals; it also forges or reaffirms an alliance between lineages. This helps to maintain them as components of larger social systems. Finally, lineage exogamy maintains open communication within a society, promoting the diffusion of knowledge from one lineage to another.

From Lineage to Clan

In the course of time, as generation succeeds generation and new members are born into the lineage, the kinship group's membership may become too large to manage or may outgrow the lineage's resources. When this

---

fission The splitting of a descent group into two or more new descent groups

totemism The belief that people are related to particular animals, plants, or natural objects by virtue of descent from common ancestral spirits

Tsimishian people of Metlakatla, Alaska, raise a memorial totem pole gifted to the community by noted carver David Boxley, a member of the Eagle clan. The tradition of erecting totem poles to commemorate special events endures in several Native American communities in the Pacific Northwest. Carved from tall cedar trees, these spectacular monuments display a clan or lineage's ceremonial property and are prominently positioned as frontal house posts, as markers at grave sites, or at some other place of significance. Often depicting legendary ancestors and mythological animals, the painted carvings symbolically represent a descent group's cultural status and associated privileges in the community.

happens, **fission** occurs; that is, the original lineage splits into new, smaller lineages. Usually the members of the new lineages continue to recognize their original relationship to one another. The result of this process is the appearance of a larger kind of descent group: the clan.

As already noted, a clan—typically consisting of several lineages—is an extended unilineal descent group whose members claim common descent from a distant ancestor (usually legendary or mythological) but are unable to trace the precise genealogical links back to that ancestor. This stems from the great genealogical depth of the clan, whose founding ancestor lived so far in the past that the links must be assumed rather than known in detail. A clan differs from a lineage in another respect: It lacks the residential unity generally—although not invariably—characteristic of a lineage's core members. As with the lineage, descent may be patrilineal, matrilineal, or ambilineal. Scots, such as those pictured in this chapter's opening, provide an example of patrilineal clans (or patriclans), which trace descent exclusively through men from a founding ancestor.

Because clan membership is dispersed rather than localized, it usually does not involve a shared holding of tangible property. Instead, it involves shared participation in ceremonial and political matters. Only on special occasions will the membership gather together for specific purposes.

Clans, however, may handle important integrative functions. Like lineages, they may regulate marriage through exogamy. Because of their dispersed membership, they give individuals the right of entry into local groups other than their own. Usually, members are expected to give protection and hospitality to others in the clan. Hence, these rights to benefits can be expected in any local group that includes people who belong to a single clan.

Clans, lacking the residential unity of lineages, frequently depend on symbols—of animals, plants, natural forces, colors, and special objects—to provide members with solidarity and a ready means of identification. These symbols, called *totems*, often are associated with the clan's mythical origin and reinforce for clan members an awareness of their common descent. The word *totem* comes from the Ojibwa American Indian word *ototeman*, meaning "he is a relative of mine." **Totemism** was defined by the British anthropologist A. R. Radcliffe-Brown as a set of customary beliefs and practices "by which there is set up a special system of relations between the society and the plants, animals, and other natural objects that are important in the social life."[3] For example, Hopi Indian matrilineal clans in Arizona bear such totemic names as Bear, Bluebird, Butterfly, Lizard, Spider, and Snake.

Phratries and Moieties

Larger kinds of descent groups are phratries and moieties (Figure 13.3). A **phratry** (after the Greek word for "brotherhood") is a unilineal descent group composed of at least two clans that supposedly share a common ancestry, whether or not they really do. Like individuals in the clan, phratry members cannot trace precisely their descent links to a common ancestor, although they firmly believe such an ancestor existed.

If the entire society is divided into only two major descent groups, whether they are equivalent to clans or phratries, each group is called a **moiety** (after the French word *moitié,* for "half"). Members of the moiety believe themselves to share a common ancestor but cannot prove it through definite genealogical links. As a rule, the feelings of kinship among members of lineages and clans are stronger than those of members of phratries and moieties. This is largely because of the much larger size and more diffuse nature of the latter groups.

Since feelings of kinship are often weaker between people from different clans, the moiety system is a cultural invention that keeps clan-based communities

together by binding the clans into a social network of obligatory giving and receiving. By institutionalizing reciprocity between groups of clans, the moiety system binds together families who otherwise would not be sufficiently invested in maintaining the commonwealth.

Like lineages and clans, phratries and moieties are often exogamous and so are bound together by marriages between their members. And like clans, they provide members rights of access to other communities. In a community that does not include one's clan members, one's phratry members are still there to turn to for hospitality. Finally, moieties may perform reciprocal services for one another. Among them, individuals turn to members of the opposite "half" in their community for the necessary mourning rituals when a member of their own moiety dies. Such interdependence between moieties, again, serves to maintain the cohesion of the entire society.

BILATERAL KINSHIP AND THE KINDRED

Important though descent groups are in many societies, they are not found in all societies, nor are they the only kinds of extended kinship groups to be found. *Bilateral kinship,* a characteristic of most contemporary European and American societies as well as a number of food-foraging cultures, affiliates a person with genetically close relatives (but not in-laws) through both sexes. In other words, the individual traces descent through both parents, all four grandparents, and so forth, recognizing multiple ancestors. Theoretically, one is associated equally with all "blood" relatives on both the mother's and father's sides of the family. Thus, this principle relates an individual lineally to all eight great-grandparents and laterally to all third and fourth cousins.

Since such a huge group is too big to be socially practical, it is usually reduced to a smaller circle of paternal and maternal relatives, called the kindred. The **kindred** may be defined as an individual's close blood relatives on the maternal and paternal sides of his or her family. It is laterally rather than lineally organized—that is, **EGO**, or the central person from whom the degree of each relationship is traced, is the center of the group (Figure 13.4). Thus, unlike a true descent group, the kindred is not composed of people with an ancestor in common, but rather those with a living relative in common.

Most North Americans are familiar with the kindred; those who belong are simply referred to as relatives. It includes those blood relatives on both sides of the family who are seen on important occasions, such as family weddings, reunions, and funerals. They can identify the members of their kindred up to grandparents and first, if not always second, cousins.

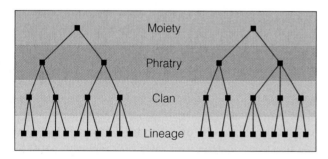

Figure 13.3

This diagram shows how lineages, clans, phratries, and moieties form an organizational hierarchy. Each moiety is subdivided into phratries, each phratry is subdivided into clans, and each clan is subdivided into lineages.

phratry A unilineal descent group composed of at least two clans that supposedly share a common ancestry, whether or not they really do
moiety Each group that results from a division of a society into two halves on the basis of descent
kindred An individual's close blood relatives on the maternal and paternal sides of his or her family
EGO The central person from whom the degree of each relationship is traced

[3]Radcliffe-Brown, A. R. (1931). Social organization of Australian tribes. *Oceana Monographs, 1,* 29.

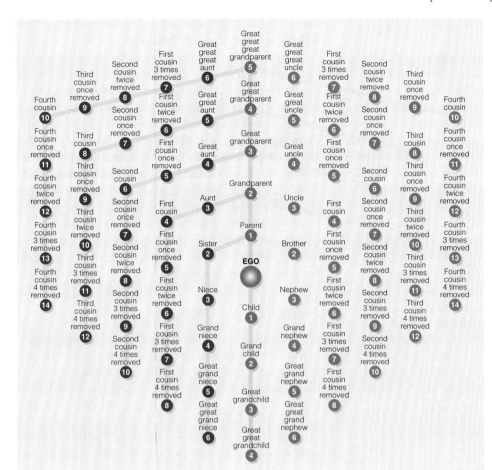

Figure 13.4 **EGO and His/Her Kindred**

The kindred designates a person's exact degree of being related by blood to other relatives in the family. This degree of blood relatedness determines not only one's social obligations toward relatives, but also one's rights. For instance, when a wealthy widowed great-aunt without children dies without a will, specific surviving members of her kindred will be legally entitled to inherit from her.

Because of its bilateral structure, a kindred is never the same for any two people except siblings (brothers and sisters). And it is not self-perpetuating—it ceases with EGO's death. Unlike a descent group, it has no constant leader, nor can it easily hold, administer, or pass on property. Because of its vagueness, temporary nature, and changing affiliation, the kindred cannot function as a group except in relation to EGO. In most cases, it cannot organize work, nor can it easily administer justice or assign status.

It can, however, be turned to for aid. In non-Western societies, for example, raiding or trading parties may be composed of kindreds. The group comes together to perform some particular function, shares the results, and then disbands. It also can act as a ceremonial group for rites of passage: initiation ceremonies and the like. Traditionally, the kindred is also of importance in many European cultures, where it may serve to help raise bail, compensate a victim's family, or carry out revenge for the murder or injury of a person in one's own kindred. Finally, kindreds also can regulate marriage through exogamy.

Kindreds are frequently found in industrial and postindustrial state societies where capitalist wage labor conditions bring on mobility and promote individualism, thereby weakening the importance of a strong kinship organization.

KINSHIP TERMINOLOGY AND KINSHIP GROUPS

Any system of organizing people who are relatives into different kinds of groups—whether kindreds, lineages, or clans—influences how relatives are labeled in any given society. Kinship terminology systems vary considerably across cultures, reflecting the positions individuals occupy within their respective societies and helping to differentiate one relative from another. Distinguishing factors include gender, generational differences, or genealogical differences. In the various systems of kinship terminology, any one of these factors may be emphasized at the expense of others.

By looking at the terms people in a particular society use for their relatives, an anthropologist can tell how kinship groups are structured, what relationships are considered especially important, and sometimes what the prevailing attitudes are concerning various relationships. For instance, a number of languages use the same term to identify a brother and a cousin, and others have a single word for cousin, niece, and nephew. Some cultures find it useful to distinguish an oldest brother from his younger brothers and have different words for these brothers. And unlike English, many languages distinguish between an aunt who is mother's sister and one who is father's sister.

Regardless of the factors emphasized, all kinship terminologies accomplish two important tasks. First, they classify similar kinds of individuals into single specific categories; second, they separate different kinds of individuals into distinct categories. Generally, two or more kin are merged under the same term when the individuals have more or less the same rights and obligations with respect to the person referring to them as such. Such is the case among most English-speaking North Americans, for instance, when someone refers to a mother's sister and father's sister both as an "aunt." As far as the speaker is concerned, both relatives possess a similar status.

Several different systems of kinship terminology result from the application of the above principles just mentioned, including the Eskimo, Hawaiian, Iroquois, Crow, Omaha, Sudanese, Kariera, and Aranda systems, each named after the ethnographic example first or best described by anthropologists. The last five of these systems are fascinating in their complexity and are found among only a few of the world's societies. However, to illustrate some of the basic principles involved, we will focus our attention on the first three systems.

Eskimo System

The Eskimo system, comparatively rare among all the world's systems, is the one used by Euramericans, as well as by a number of food-foraging peoples (including the Inuit and other Eskimos; hence the name). Sometimes referred to as the *lineal system,* the **Eskimo system** emphasizes the nuclear family by specifically identifying mother, father, brother, and sister while lumping together all other relatives into a few large categories (Figure 13.5). For example, the father is distinguished from the father's brother (uncle); but the father's brother is not distinguished from the mother's brother (both are called "uncle"). The mother's sister and father's sister are treated similarly, both called "aunt." In addition, all the sons and daughters of aunts and uncles are called "cousin," thereby making a generational

distinction but without indicating the side of the family to which they belong or even their gender.

Unlike other terminologies, the Eskimo system provides separate and distinct terms for the nuclear family members. This is probably because the Eskimo system is generally found in bilateral societies where the dominant kin group is the kindred, in which only immediate family members are important in day-to-day affairs. This is especially true of modern European and North American societies, where many families are independent, living apart from, and not directly involved with, other relatives except on special occasions. Thus, most North Americans (and others) generally distinguish between their closest kin (parents and siblings) but lump together (as aunts, uncles, cousins) other kin on both sides of the family.

Hawaiian System

The **Hawaiian system** of kinship terminology, common (as its name implies) in Hawaii and other islands in the southern central Pacific Ocean but found elsewhere as well, is the least complex system, in that it uses the fewest terms. The Hawaiian system is also called the *generational system,* since all relatives of the same generation and sex are referred to by the same term (Figure 13.6). For example, in one's parents' generation, the term used to refer to one's father is used as well for the father's brother and mother's brother. Similarly, one's mother, mother's sister, and father's sister are all lumped together under a single term. In EGO's generation, male and female cousins are distinguished by gender and are equated with brothers and sisters.

The Hawaiian system reflects the absence of strong unilineal descent, and members on both the father's and the mother's sides are viewed as more or less equal. Thus, someone's father's and mother's siblings are all recognized as being similar relations and are merged under a single term appropriate for their gender. In like manner, the children of the mother's and father's siblings are related to EGO in the same way brother and

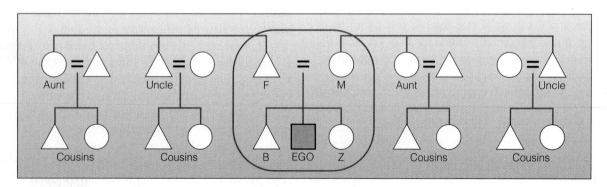

Figure 13.5 **Eskimo System**
The Eskimo system of kinship terminology emphasizes the nuclear family (circled). EGO's father and mother are distinguished from EGO's aunts and uncles, and siblings from cousins.

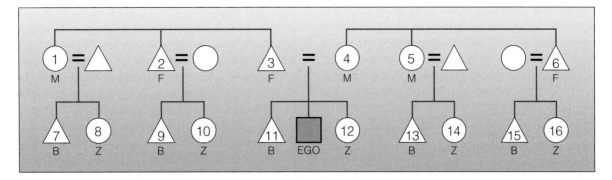

Figure 13.6 Hawaiian System

In the Hawaiian kinship system the men numbered 2 and 6 are called by the same term as father (3) by EGO; the women numbered 1 and 5 are called by the same term as mother (4). All cousins of EGO's own generation (7–16) are considered brothers (B) and sisters (Z).

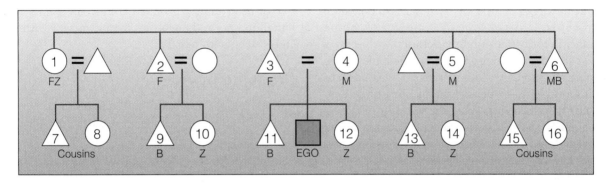

Figure 13.7 Iroquois System

According to the Iroquois system of kinship terminology, EGO's father's brother (2) is called by the same term as the father (3); the mother's sister (5) is called by the same term as the mother (4); but the people numbered 1 and 6 are each referred to by a distinct term. Those people numbered 9–14 are all considered siblings, but 7, 8, 15, and 16 are considered cousins.

sister are. Falling under the incest taboo, they are ruled out as potential marriage partners.

Iroquois System

In the **Iroquois system** of kinship terminology, the father and father's brother are referred to by a single term, as are the mother and mother's sister; however, the father's sister and mother's brother are given separate terms (Figure 13.7). In one's own generation, brothers, sisters, and parallel cousins (offspring of parental siblings of the same sex—that is, the children of the mother's sister or father's brother) of the same sex are referred to by the same terms, which is logical enough considering that they are the offspring of people who are classified in the same category as EGO's actual mother and father. Cross cousins (offspring of parental siblings of opposite sex—that is, the children of the mother's brother or father's sister) are distinguished by terms that set them apart from all other kin. In fact, cross cousins are often preferred as spouses, for marriage to them reaffirms alliances between related lineages or clans.

Iroquois terminology, named for the Iroquoian Indians of northeastern North America's woodlands, is in fact very widespread and is usually found with

unilineal descent groups. It was, for example, the terminology in use until recently in rural Chinese society.

Kinship Terms and New Reproductive Technologies

If systems of kinship reckoning other than one's own seem strange and complex, consider the implications of an event that took place in 1978: the production of the

Eskimo system Kinship reckoning in which the nuclear family is emphasized by specifically identifying the mother, father, brother, and sister, while lumping together all other relatives into broad categories such as uncle, aunt, and cousin. Also known as the lineal system
Hawaiian system Kinship reckoning in which all relatives of the same sex and generation are referred to by the same term. Also known as the generational system
Iroquois system Kinship reckoning in which a father and father's brother are referred to by a single term, as are a mother and mother's sister, but a father's sister and mother's brother are given separate terms. Parallel cousins are classified with brothers and sisters, while cross cousins are classified separately but not equated with relatives of some other generation

world's first test-tube baby, outside the womb, without sexual intercourse. Since then, thousands of babies have been created in this way, and all sorts of new technologies have become part of the reproductive repertoire. **New reproductive technologies (NRTs)** are alternative means of reproduction such as surrogate motherhood and in vitro fertilization.

These technologies have opened up a large—and sometimes mind-boggling—array of reproductive possibilities. For example, if a child is conceived from a donor egg, implanted in another woman's womb to be raised by yet another woman, who is its mother? To complicate matters even further, the egg may have been fertilized by sperm from a donor not married to, or in a sexual relationship with, any of these women. Indeed, it has been suggested that we need nearly a dozen different kinship terms to cover the concepts of mother and father in today's changing societies.[4]

Clearly, the new reproductive technologies are influencing traditional notions of kinship. Beyond transforming our sense of being human, they force us to redefine established ideas about the status of relatives—challenging us to rethink what being "related" to others is about and, specifically, what our rights and obligations are toward such unfamiliar categories of kin.

GROUPING BEYOND KINSHIP

Because ties of kinship and household are not always sufficient to handle all the challenges of human survival, people also form groups based on gender, age, common interest, and class or social rank.

Grouping by Gender

As shown in preceding chapters, division of labor along gender lines occurs in all human societies. In some cultures—the previously discussed Ju/'hoansi in southern Africa, for example—many tasks that men and women undertake may be shared. People may perform work normally assigned to the opposite sex without loss of face. In others, however, men and women are rigidly segregated in

what they do. Such is the case in many maritime cultures, where seafarers aboard fishing, whaling, and trading ships are usually men. For instance, we find temporary all-male communities aboard ships of coastal Basque fishermen in northwest Spain, Yupik Eskimo whalers in Alaska, and Swahili merchants sailing along the East African coast. These seafarers commonly leave their wives, mothers, and daughters and young sons behind in their home ports, sometimes for months at a time.

Clearly demarcated grouping by gender also occurs in many traditional horticultural societies. For instance, among the Mundurucu Indians of Brazil's Amazon rainforest, men and women work, eat, and sleep separately. From age 13 onward males live together in one large house, while women, girls, and preteen boys occupy two or three houses grouped around the men's house. For all intents and purposes, men associate with men, and women with women.

Grouping by Age

Age grouping is so familiar and so important that it and sex have been called the only universal factors that determine a person's positions in society. In North America today, for instance, a child's first friends are usually children of his or her own age. Starting preschool or kindergarten with age mates, children typically move through a dozen or more years in the educational system together. At specified ages they are allowed to see certain movies, drive a car, and do things reserved for adults, such as voting, drinking alcoholic beverages, and serving in the military. Ultimately, North Americans retire from their jobs at a specified age and, increasingly, spend the final years of their lives in retirement communities, segregated from the rest of society. As North Americans age, they are labeled "teenagers," "middle-aged," and "senior citizens," whether they like it or not and for no other reason than the number of years they have lived.

Age classification also plays a significant role in non-Western societies, which, at a minimum, make a distinction between immature, mature, and older people whose physical powers are waning. In these societies old age often has profound significance, bringing with it the period of greatest respect (for women it may mean the first social equality with men). Rarely are the elderly shunted aside or abandoned. Even the Inuit of the Canadian Arctic, who are often cited as a people who literally abandon their aged relatives, do so only in truly desperate circumstances, when the group's physical survival is at stake. In all oral tradition societies, elders are the repositories of accumulated wisdom for their people. Recognized as such and no longer expected to carry out many subsistence activities, they play a major role in passing on cultural knowledge to their grandchildren.

All human societies recognize a number of life stages. The demarcation and duration of these stages vary

---

new reproductive technologies (NRTs) Alternative means of reproduction such as surrogate motherhood and in vitro fertilization
age grade An organized category of people based on age; every individual passes through a series of such categories over his or her lifetime
age set A formally established group of people born during a certain time span who move through the series of age-grade categories together

---

[4]Stone, L. (1998). *Kinship and gender: An introduction* (p. 272). Boulder, CO: Westview Press.

across cultures. Each successive life stage provides distinctive social roles and comes with certain cultural features such as specific patterns of activity, attitudes, prohibitions, and obligations. In many cultures, the social position of an individual in a specific life stage is also marked by a distinctive outward appearance in terms of dress, hairstyle, body paint, tattoos, insignia, or some other symbolic distinction. Typically, these stages are designed to help the transition from one age to another, to teach needed skills, or to lend economic assistance. Often they are taken as the basis for the formation of organized groups.

Age Grade

An organized category of people with membership on the basis of age is known as an **age grade**. Entry into and transfer out of age grades may be accomplished individually, either by a biological distinction, such as puberty, or by a socially recognized status, such as marriage or childbirth. Whereas age-grade members may have much in common, may engage in similar activities, may cooperate with one another, and may share the same orientation and aspirations, their membership may not be entirely parallel with physiological age. A specific time is often ritually established for moving from a younger to an older grade. An example of this is the traditional Jewish ceremony of the *bar mitzvah* (a Hebrew term meaning "son of the commandment"), marking that a 13-year-old boy has reached the age of religious duty and responsibility. *Bat mitzvah,* meaning "daughter of the commandment," is the term for the equivalent ritual for a girl.

Although members of senior groups commonly expect deference from and acknowledge certain responsibilities to their juniors, this does not necessarily mean that one grade is seen as better, or worse, or even more important than another. There can be standardized competition (opposition) between age grades, such as that traditionally between first-year students and sophomores on U.S. college campuses.

Age Set

In addition to age grades, some societies feature age sets (sometimes referred to as *age classes*). An **age set**

Maasai subclans of western Kenya at the opening parade of the elaborate *eunoto* ceremony, marking the coming of age of *morans* (warriors). At the end of the ceremony, these men will be in the next age grade—junior adults—ready to marry and start families. Members of the same age set, they were initiated together into the warrior age grade as teenagers. They spent their warrior years raiding cattle (an old tradition that is now illegal, but nonetheless still practiced) and protecting their community homes and animal enclosures (from wild animals and other cattle raiders). The *eunoto* ceremony includes a ritual in which mothers shave the warrior's heads, marking the end of many freedoms and the passage to manhood.

is a formally established group of people born during a certain time span who move through the series of age-grade categories together. Age sets, unlike age grades, end after a specified number of years; age-set members usually remain closely associated throughout their lives. This is akin to but distinct from the broad and informal North American practice of identifying generation clusters composed of all individuals born within a particular time frame—such as baby boomers (1946–1960), gen-Xers (1961–1980), and the millennial or Internet generation (1981–2000) (year spans approximate).

The age-set notion implies strong feelings of loyalty and mutual support. Because such groups may possess property, songs, shield designs, and rituals and are internally organized for collective decision making and leadership, age sets are distinct from simple age grades. Although age is a criterion for group membership in many parts of the world, its most varied and elaborate use is found in several pastoral nomadic groups in East Africa.[5]

GROUPING BY COMMON INTEREST

The rise of urban, industrialized societies in which individuals are often separated from their kin has led to a proliferation of **common-interest associations**—associations that result from an act of joining and are based on sharing particular activities, objectives, values, or beliefs. Moreover, common-interest associations help people meet a range of needs from companionship to safe work conditions to learning a new language and customs upon moving from one country to another.

---

common-interest associations Associations that result from an act of joining based on sharing particular activities, objectives, values, or beliefs

stratified societies Societies in which people are hierarchically divided and ranked into social strata, or layers, and do not share equally in basic resources that support survival, influence, and prestige

egalitarian societies Societies in which everyone has about equal rank, access to, and power over basic resources

social class A category of individuals in a stratified society who enjoy equal or nearly equal prestige according to the system of evaluation

caste A closed social class in a stratified society in which membership is determined by birth and fixed for life

---

Because common-interest associations are by nature flexible, they have often been turned to, both in cities and in rural areas, as a way of meeting these needs. Common-interest associations are not, however, restricted to modernizing societies alone. They also are found in many traditional societies, and there is reason to believe they arose with the emergence of the first horticultural villages. Furthermore, associations in traditional societies may be just as complex and highly organized as those of countries such as the United States and Canada.

The variety of common-interest associations is astonishing. In the United States, they include such diverse entities as street gangs, private militias, sport and service clubs, religious groups, political parties, labor unions, environmental organizations, and women's and men's clubs of all sorts. Their goals may include the pursuit of friendship, recreation, and the promotion of certain values, as well as governing, seeking peace on a local or global scale, and the pursuit or defense of economic interests.

Associations also have served to preserve traditional songs, history, language, moral beliefs, and other customs among members of various ethnic minorities. So it is among North American Indians, who since the late 1960s have been experiencing a resurgence of ethnic pride after generations of forced assimilation and schooling designed to stamp out their cultural identity. A satisfying way of publicly expressing pride in their ethnic identity and cultural heritage is by way of ceremonial gatherings known as *powwows*, which take place not only on reservations but also in cities where most American Indians now live.[6]

Over the last decade or so, common-interest associations have had a boost in societies that have access to the Internet. The cyber world has seen an explosion of what are, in effect, virtual common-interest associations, all of which have their own particular rules on matters such as what members may or may not post and how they should behave online.

GROUPING BY SOCIAL RANK IN STRATIFIED SOCIETIES

Social stratification is a common and powerful structuring force in many of the world's societies. Basically, **stratified societies** are those in which people are hierarchically divided and ranked into social strata, or layers, and do not share equally in basic resources that support

---

[5]Among numerous references on this, see Sangree, W. H. (1965). The Bantu Tiriki of western Kenya. In J. L. Gibbs, Jr. (Ed.), *Peoples of Africa* (pp. 69–72). New York: Holt, Rinehart & Winston.

[6]Ellis, C. (2006). *A dancing people: Powwow culture on the southern plains.* Lawrence: University Press of Kansas.

VISUAL COUNTERPOINT

The range of common-interest associations is astounding, as suggested by these photos of Shriners and Crips. The Shriners are a secret fraternal order of middle-class males in the United States committed to "fun, fellowship, and service" and named after the Ancient Arabic Order of Nobles of the Mystic Shrine. The Crips are a violent urban gang, originating in poor Los Angeles neighborhoods. Their trademark is a blue bandana—in contrast to the red bandana of their rival gang, the Bloods. The notoriety of the Crips spread as a result of sensational stories in the media, spawning a network of independent satellite Crip gangs in other U.S. cities as well as in Europe and Central America.

survival, influence, and prestige. Members of low-ranked strata typically have fewer privileges and less power than those in higher ranked strata. In addition, the restrictions and obligations they face are usually more oppressive, and they must work harder for less reward.

In short, social stratification amounts to institutionalized inequality. Without ranking—high versus low—no stratification exists; social differences without this do not constitute stratification.

Stratified societies stand in sharp contrast to **egalitarian societies**, in which everyone has about equal rank as well as access to and power over basic resources. As we saw in earlier chapters, foraging societies are characteristically egalitarian, although there are some exceptions.

Social Class and Caste

A **social class** may be defined as a category of individuals in a stratified society who enjoy equal or nearly equal prestige according to the system of evaluation. The qualification "nearly equal" is important, for a certain amount of inequality may occur even within a given class. Class distinctions are not always clear-cut and obvious in societies that have a wide and continuous range of differential privileges.

A **caste** is a closed social class in a stratified society in which membership is determined by birth and fixed for life. The opposite of the principle that all humans are born equal, the caste system is based on the principle

that humans neither are nor can be equal. Castes are strongly endogamous, and offspring are automatically members of their parents' caste.

Traditional Hindu Caste System

The classic ethnographic example of a caste system is the traditional Hindu caste system of India (also found in other parts of Asia, including Nepal and Bali). Perhaps the world's longest surviving social hierarchy, it encompasses a complex ranking of social groups on the basis of "ritual purity." Each of some 2,000 different castes considers itself as a distinct community higher or lower than other castes, although their particular ranking varies among geographic regions and over time. The different castes are associated with specific occupations and customs, such as food habits and styles of dress, along with rituals involving notions of purity and pollution. Ritual pollution is the result of contact such as touching, accepting food from, or having sex with a member of a lower caste. For this reason, castes are always endogamous. Differences in caste rankings are traditionally justified by the religious doctrine of *karma*, a belief that one's status in this life is determined by one's deeds in previous lifetimes.

All of these castes, or *jatis*, are organized into four basic orders or *varnas* (literally meaning "colors"), distinguished partly by occupation and ranked in order of descending religious status of purity. The religious foundation for this social hierarchy is found in a sacred text known as the Laws of Manu, an ancient work

about 2,000 years old and considered by traditional Hindus as the highest authority on their cultural institutions. It defines the Brahmans as the purest and therefore highest *varna.* As priests and lawgivers, Brahmans represent the world of religion and learning. Next comes the order of fighters and rulers, known as the Kshatriyas. Below them are the Vaisyas (merchants and traders), who are engaged in commercial, agricultural, and pastoral pursuits. At the bottom are the Shudras (artisans and laborers), an order required to serve the other three *varnas* and who also make a living by handicrafts.

Falling outside the *varna* system is a fifth category of degraded individuals known as Dalits or "untouchables." Commonly discriminated against by fellow Hindus as "impure," these outcasts can own neither land nor the tools of their trade. They constitute a large pool of cheap labor at the beck and call of those controlling economic and political affairs. In an effort to bestow some dignity on these poverty-stricken victims of the caste system, Hindu nationalist leader Mahatma Gandhi renamed them *harijan* or "children of God."

Although India's national constitution of 1950 sought to officially abolish the caste system, and its faith-based discriminatory practices against Dalit untouchables, the caste system remains deeply entrenched in Hindu culture and is still widespread, especially in rural India. In what has been called India's "hidden apartheid," entire villages in many Indian states remain completely segregated by caste. Representing about 15 percent of India's population—nearly 170 million people—the widely scattered Dalits endure near complete social isolation, humiliation, and discrimination based exclusively on their birth status. Even a Dalit's shadow is believed to pollute the upper castes.

They may not cross the line dividing their part of the village from that occupied by higher castes, drink water from public wells, or visit the same temples as the higher castes. Dalit children are still often made to sit at the back of classrooms, and in rural areas some still lack access to education altogether.[7]

Castelike situations are known elsewhere in the world. In Bolivia, Ecuador, and several other South and Central American countries, for example, the wealthy upper class is almost exclusively of European descent and rarely intermarries with people of American Indian or African descent. In contrast, the lower class of working poor in those countries is primarily made up of darker-skinned laborers and peasants.

Segregation in the United States

Until quite recently, institutionalized racial segregation also officially existed in the United States, where the country's ruling upper class is historically composed exclusively of individuals of European ("Caucasian" or "white") descent. After the American Revolution, several states in New England joined Virginia and other southern states and made it illegal for American whites to marry blacks or American Indians. Although the U.S. federal government officially abolished slavery in 1863, these anti-miscegenation laws remained in force in numerous states from Maine to Florida for many more decades.

In 1924, Virginia's General Assembly passed the Racial Integrity Act to prevent light-skinned individuals with some African ancestry from "passing" as whites. Known as the *one drop rule,* it codified the idea of white racial purity by classifying individuals as black if just one of their multiple ancestors was of African origin ("one drop of Negro blood").

However light-skinned, they were subject to a wide range of discriminatory practices not applicable to whites. Such institutionalized racial discrimination continued for a century after slavery was abolished, and today self-segregation exists in many parts of the United States. The following Original Study painfully illustrates the effects of this institutionalized racism—while also showing the role public education can play in challenging stereotypes and inequities.

---

[7]Concluding observations of the Committee on the Elimination of Racial Discrimination, India (p. 3). (2007, March). Consideration of reports submitted by states parties under Article 9 of the International Convention on the Elimination of All Forms of Racial Discrimination, 70th Session. www2.ohchr.org/english/bodies/cerd/cerds70.htm; see also "Hidden apartheid: Caste discrimination against India's untouchables." (2007). Human Rights Watch and the Center for Human Rights and Global Justice. www.hrw.org/reports/2007/india0207.

Original Study

African Burial Ground Project

Michael Blakey

In 1991, construction workers in lower Manhattan unearthed what turned out to be part of a six-acre African burial ground containing remains of an estimated 10,000 enslaved African captives brought to New York in the 17th and 18th centuries to build the city and provide the labor for its thriving economy. The discovery sparked controversy as the African American public held protests and prayer vigils to stop the part of a federal building project that nearly destroyed the site. In 1993, the site was designated a National Historic Landmark, which opened the door to researching and protecting the site.

As a biological anthropologist and African American, I had a unique opportunity to work together with the descendant African American community to develop a plan that included both extensive biocultural research and the humane retention of the sacred nature of the site, ultimately through reburial and the creation of a fitting memorial. The research also involved archaeological and historical studies that used a broad African diasporic context for understanding the lifetime experiences of these people who were enslaved and buried in New York.

Studying a sample population of 419 individuals from the burial ground, our team used an exhaustive range of skeletal biological methods, producing a database containing more than 200,000 observations of genetics, morphology, age, sex, growth and development, muscle development, trauma, nutrition, and disease. The bones revealed an unmistakable link between biology and culture: physical wear and tear of an entire community brought on by the social institution of slavery.

We now know, based on this study, that life for Africans in colonial New York was characterized by poor nutrition, grueling physical labor that enlarged and often tore muscles, and death rates that were unusually high for 15- to 25-year-olds. Many of these young adults died soon after arriving on slaving ships. Few Africans lived past 40 years of age, and less than 2 percent lived beyond 55. Church records show strikingly different mortality trends for the Europeans of New York: About eight times as many English as Africans lived past 55 years of age.

Forty-percent of the remains unearthed were those of children under the age of 12. Skeletal research also showed that those Africans who died as children and were most likely to have been born in New York exhibited stunted and disrupted growth and exposure to high levels of lead pollution—unlike those who had been born in Africa (and were distinguishable because they had filed teeth). Fertility was very low among enslaved women in New York, and infant mortality was high. In these respects, this northern colonial city was very similar to South Carolina and the Caribbean to which its economy was tied—regions where conditions for African captives were among the harshest.

Individuals in this deeply troubling burial ground came from warring African states including Calibar, Asante, Benin, Dahomey, Congo, Madagascar, and many others—states that wrestled with the European demand for human slaves. They resisted their enslavement through rebellion, and they resisted their dehumanization by carefully burying their dead and preserving what they could of their cultures.

There is something about human remains that is so compelling. While many people find them disturbing, in the proper context science can give the public a chance to get close to these people, to imagine their lives, their era, their challenges—and what these have to tell us about our own lives and times.

The remains of certain individuals stood out to me and stirred my imagination. Among them is a man between 26 and 35 years old, who we labeled "101." His skull shape appears to be West African, and one of the chemicals we analyzed, strontium, points towards him having been born in Africa. And another chemical, lead, is somewhere intermediate between New York and West Africa. Given this and evidence of treponemal, a tropical disease, he may have been raised in the Caribbean. Also of note, he has elegant filed teeth, plus bone evidence of hard work and some healed fractures in his spine. But perhaps the most important thing about this particular individual is the heart-shaped symbol discovered on his coffin lid. That symbol nagged me for a while. I was sure that I had seen it somewhere before, but it was vague to me.

One day, early on in the project, I attended an African American cultural event at Howard University in Washington, DC. An image on the program cover grabbed my attention. It looked like the same symbol I had seen on 101's coffin. I asked a colleague at the New York burial ground lab to send me a drawing of the symbol found on the coffin. Then I took it to an art historian at Howard who specializes in this area—and tried my best not to appear excited. He too recognized it was a version of a symbol called the *sankofa*.

The meaning of this historic symbol is entirely fitting for an African burial site. It stands for the spiritual connection between the past and the present— the idea that we need to go back and search the past so that it can be a guide in the present. The *sankofa* symbolizes reverence for the ancestors and respect for elders. Disseminating knowledge of this symbol and its message, the African Burial Ground helps reverse the sort of historical amnesia that allows the repetition of social injustices.

As the largest bioarchaeological site of its kind, this African Burial Ground has provided significant opportunities

[continued]

[continued]

to raise public awareness of colonial African heritage, especially in northern states. Of particular note is the 2003 Rites of Ancestral Return—a ceremony in which the remains of the 419 individuals excavated from the site were re-interred. The ceremony began with a procession of about 2,500 people walking in silence to the burial ground. I joined the researchers behind several hundred children, mostly of primary school age. These youngsters, dressed in little dark red uniforms and walking with a kind of reverent orderliness, really touched me. "They're the future," I thought to myself. One day they'll tell their children and grandchildren about the African Burial Ground. They are part of another step toward a more complete understanding of African American history—a more complete understanding of themselves and a more complete identity.

(By Michael Blakey)

Despite U.S. civil rights laws passed in the 1960s (prohibiting discrimination in accommodations, schools, employment, and voting for reasons of color, race, religion, or national origin), ethnic inequality persists in which the typical African American household has 54 cents of income and 12 cents of wealth for every corresponding dollar in the typical "white" American household.[8] And, despite laws against it, discrimination continues, especially in former slave-holding states such as North Carolina. Recent research on that state's legal system showed that the life of a "white" person is more highly valued than a "non-white," as defendants whose victims are "white" are 3.5 times more likely to be sentenced to death than those with "non-white" victims.[9]

Social Class Indicators

Social classes are manifested in various ways, including *symbolic indicators*. For example, in the United States certain activities and possessions are indicative of class: occupation (a garbage collector has different class status than a medical specialist); wealth (rich people are generally in a higher social class than poor people); dress ("white collar" versus "blue collar"); form of recreation (upper-class people are expected to play golf rather than shoot pool down at the pool hall—but they can shoot pool at home or in a club); residential location (upper-class people do not ordinarily live in slums); kind of car; and so on. All sorts of status symbols are indicative of class position, including measures such as the number of bathrooms in a person's house. That said, class rankings do not fully correlate with economic status or pay scales. The local garbage collector or unionized car-factory laborer typically makes more money than an average college professor with a doctorate.

Maintaining Stratification

In any system of stratification, those who dominate proclaim their supposedly superior status, commonly asserting it through intimidation or propaganda (in the form of gossip, media, religious doctrine, and so forth) that presents their position as normal, natural, hereditary, divinely guided, or at least well-deserved. As U.S. anthropologist Laura Nader of the University of California, Berkeley, points out, "Systems of thought develop over time and reflect the interests of certain classes or groups in the society who manage to universalize their beliefs and values."[10]

So it is with certain religious ideologies that effectively assert that the social order is divinely fixed and therefore not to be questioned. In India, for example, Hindu belief in reincarnation and an incorruptible supernatural power that assigns people to a particular caste position, as a reward or punishment for the deeds and misdeeds of past lives, justifies one's position in this life. If, however, individuals faithfully perform the duties appropriate to their caste in this lifetime, then they can expect to be reborn into a higher caste in a future existence.

social mobility Upward or downward change in one's social class position in a stratified society

---

[8]Boshara, R. (2003, January/February). Wealth inequality: The $6,000 solution. *Atlantic Monthly*. See also Kennickell, A. B. (2003, November). *A rolling tide: Changes in the distribution of wealth in the U.S. 1989–2001*. Levy Economics Institute.

[9]Unah, I., & Boger, C. (2001, April). *Race and the death penalty in North Carolina*. www.common-sense.org/pdfs/NCDeath PenaltyReport2001.pdf.

---

[10]Nader, L. (1997). Controlling processes: Tracing the dynamic components of power. *Current Anthropology, 38*, 271.

In the minds of orthodox Hindus, then, one's caste position is something earned rather than the accident of birth as it appears to outside observers. Thus, although the caste system explicitly recognizes (and accepts as legitimate) inequality among people, an implicit assumption of ultimate equality underlies it. This contrasts with the situation in the United States, where the equality of all people is proclaimed even while various groups are repressed or otherwise discriminated against.

Social Mobility

Most stratified societies offer at least some **social mobility**—upward or downward change in one's social class position. The prospects of improving status and wealth help to ease the strains inherent in any system of inequality.

Social mobility is most common in societies made up of independent nuclear families where the individual is closely tied to fewer people—especially when neolocal residence is the norm, and it is assumed that individuals will leave their family of birth when they become adults. In such social settings, through hard work, occupational success, opportune marriage, and disassociation from the lower-class family in which they grew up, individuals can more easily move up in status and rank.

Societies that permit a great deal of upward and downward mobility are referred to as *open-class societies*—although the openness is apt to be less in practice than members hope or believe. In the United States, despite its rags-to-riches ideology, most mobility involves a move up or down only a notch, although if this continues in a family over several generations, it may add up to a major change. Nonetheless, U.S. society makes much of relatively rare examples of great upward mobility consistent with its cultural values and does its best to overlook the numerous cases of little or no upward (not to mention downward) mobility.

Caste societies exemplify *closed-class societies*, because of their severe institutionalized limits on social mobility. Yet, even the Hindu caste system, with its guiding ideology that all social hierarchies within it are eternally fixed, has a degree of flexibility and mobility. Although individuals cannot move up or down the caste hierarchy, whole groups can do so depending on claims they assert for higher ranking and on how well they can press, convince, or manipulate others into acknowledging their claims.

Although sharp differences in terms of wealth, status, and power continue in India and beyond

Photo by Oliver O'Hanlon

Despite India's formal abolition of "untouchability," Dalits continue to face segregation in housing, hospitals, education, water sources, markets, other public places—and in the work sphere. The most subservient jobs, such as waste removal, continue to be allocated to their miserable ranking in the underside of the caste system. Moreover, hygiene and illness prevention are low priorities for their employers who consider them "outcasts." Global outcry against this institutionalized discrimination is growing gradually through the United Nations High Commission on Human Rights, organizations such as Human Rights Watch, and the Center for Human Rights and Global Justice. There is also grassroots political action by the Dalits themselves. Aiming to end the humiliation and exploitation and claiming their rights as citizens in the world's largest democracy, they have recently emerged as a major force challenging the system that has long oppressed them.

(with new inequities emerging in many societies as a consequence of globalization), there are countries in which systemic discrimination has been successfully confronted. Such was the case in South Africa, for instance, where racial segregation (apartheid) was abolished, ending the legalized privileges of the country's ruling white minority in 1994.

■ ...ties, kinship groups commonly deal ...amilies and households cannot handle ...volving defense, resource allocation, and ...ative labor. As societies become larger and ...ormal political systems take over many of ... A common form of kinship group is the descent g... hich has as its criterion of membership descent from a common ancestor through a series of parent–child links. Unilineal descent establishes kin-group membership exclusively through the male or female line. Matrilineal descent is traced through the female line; patrilineal, through the male.

■ The descent system is closely tied to a society's economic base. Generally, patrilineal descent predominates where males do the majority of the primary productive work and matrilineal where females do it. Anthropologists recognize that in all societies the kin of both mother and father are important elements in the social structure, regardless of how descent group membership is defined.

■ The male members of a patrilineage trace their descent from a common male ancestor. In a patrilineage a female belongs to the same descent group as her father and his brother, but her children cannot trace their descent through them. Typically, authority over the children lies with the father or his elder brother. The requirements for younger men to defer to older men and for women to defer to men, as well as to the women of a household they marry into, are common sources of tension in a patrilineal society.

■ Matrilineal descent is traced exclusively through the female line, just as patrilineal descent is through the male line. However, the matrilineal pattern differs from the patrilineal in that it does not automatically confer gender authority.

■ Double descent is matrilineal for some purposes and patrilineal for others. Ambilineal descent provides a measure of flexibility in that an individual has the option of affiliating with either the mother's or father's descent group. When descent derives from both the mother's and father's families equally, anthropologists use the term *bilateral descent*.

■ A lineage is a unilineal descent group descended from a known ancestor, or founder, and in which relationships among members can be exactly stated in genealogical terms. Since lineages are commonly exogamous, sexual competition within the group is largely avoided. In addition, marriage of a group member represents an alliance of two lineages. Lineage exogamy also serves to maintain open communication within a society and fosters the exchange of information among lineages.

■ Fission is the splitting of a large lineage group into new, smaller ones, with the original lineage becoming a clan. Clan members claim common descent from a remote ancestor, usually legendary or mythological. Unlike lineages, clan residence is usually dispersed rather than localized. In the absence of residential unity, clan identification is often reinforced by totems: symbols from nature that remind members of their common ancestry. A phratry is a unilineal descent group of two or more clans that supposedly share a common ancestry. When a society is divided into two halves, each half consisting of one or more clans, these two major descent groups are called moieties.

■ In bilateral societies, such as industrial, postindustrial, and many food-foraging societies, individuals are affiliated equally with all relatives on both the mother's and father's sides. Such a large group is socially impractical and is usually reduced to a small circle of paternal and maternal relatives called the kindred. A kindred is never the same for any two people except siblings. Different types of descent systems appear in different societies. In those where the nuclear family predominates, bilateral kinship and kindred organization are likely to prevail.

■ In any society cultural rules dictate the way kinship relationships are defined. Factors such as gender and generational or genealogical differences help distinguish one kin from another. The Hawaiian system is the simplest system of kinship terminology, with all relatives of the same generation and gender referred to by the same term. The Eskimo system, also used by English-speaking North Americans and many others, emphasizes the nuclear family and merges all other relatives in a given generation into a few large, generally undifferentiated categories. In the Iroquois system, a single term is used for father and his brother and another for a mother and her sister. Parallel cousins are equated with brothers and sisters but distinguished from cross cousins.

■ With new reproductive technologies that separate conception from sexual intercourse and eggs from wombs, traditional notions of kinship and gender are being challenged, and new social categories are emerging.

■ Grouping by gender separates men and women to varying degrees in different societies; in some, they may be together much of the time, while in others they may spend much of their time apart, even to the extreme of eating and sleeping separately.

■ Age grouping is another form of association that may augment or replace kinship grouping. An age grade is a category of people organized by age. Some societies have not only age grades, but also age sets, composed of individuals who are initiated into an age grade at the same time and move together through a series of life stages. The most varied use of age grouping is found in African societies south of the Sahara. Among the Maasai of East Africa, for example, age sets pass through four successive age grades.

■ Common-interest associations are linked with rapid social change and urbanization. They have increasingly assumed the roles formerly played by kinship or age groups. In urban areas they help new arrivals cope with the changes demanded by the move. Common-interest associations also are seen in traditional societies, and their roots may be found in the first horticultural villages.

■ A stratified society is divided into two or more categories of people who do not share equally in wealth, influence, or prestige. Societies may be stratified by gender, age, social class, or caste. Class differences are not always clear-cut and obvious. Caste is a closed form of social class in which membership is determined by birth and fixed for life. Endogamy is particularly marked within castes, and children automatically belong to their parents' caste.

■ Social class is based on role differentiation, although this by itself is not sufficient for stratification. Also necessary are formalized positive and negative attitudes toward roles and restricted access to the more valued ones. Social classes are given expression in several ways. One is through symbolic indicators: activities and possessions indicative of class position.

■ Social mobility is present to a greater or lesser extent in all stratified societies. Open-class societies are those with the easiest mobility. In most cases, however, the move is limited to one rung up or down the social ladder. The degree of mobility is related to factors such as access to higher education or the type of family organization that prevails in a society. Where the extended family is the norm, mobility tends to be severely limited. The independent nuclear family makes mobility easier.

Questions for Reflection

1. People growing up in modern industrial and postindustrial societies generally treasure ideas of personal freedom, individuality, and privacy as essential in their pursuit of happiness. Considering the social functions of kinship relations in traditional non-state societies, why do you think that such ideas may be considered unsociable and even dangerously selfish?

2. Why do you think that one of the simplest kinship terminology systems imaginable, namely, the Eskimo system, is functionally adequate for most Europeans, North Americans, and others living in complex modern societies?

3. In some North American Indian languages, the English word for "loneliness" is translated as "I have no relatives." What does that tell you about the importance of kinship in these Native cultures?

4. When young adults leave their parental home to go to college or find employment in a distant part of the country, they face the challenge of establishing social relationships that are not based on kinship but on common interest. To which common-interest associations do you belong and why?

5. Do you think that members of an upper class or caste in a socially stratified system have a greater vested interest in the idea of law and order than those forced to exist on the bottom of such societies? Why or why not?

Key Terms

kinship	Hawaiian system
descent group	Iroquois system
unilineal descent	new reproductive
matrilineal descent	technologies (NRTs)
patrilineal descent	age grade
lineage	age set
clan	common-interest
fission	associations
totemism	stratified societies
phratry	egalitarian societies
moiety	social class
kindred	caste
EGO	social mobility
Eskimo system	

VISUAL ESSENCE

Political organization takes many forms, of which the state is just one. Often states are ruled by well-connected and wealthy individuals or groups possessing the resources (including money, weapons, and manpower) to manage and control inhabitants of a territory. Some of the smallest states today measure less than 1 square mile, while the largest cover over 6 million square miles. Every state, whatever its population, claims sovereign power over its territory and protects its borders. Throughout world history, neighboring states have had conflicts, often over boundaries. After the British empire pulled out of South Asia over sixty years ago, that subcontinent erupted in warfare between Muslims and Hindus. The region was then carved up along religious lines into Pakistan and India. Since then, these countries have fought three wars against each other. The tense political relations between these nuclear-armed rivals are symbolically displayed in the military border-closing ritual at Wagah, pictured here. Every evening, Pakistani Pathan guards, dressed in black uniforms and fan-tailed headgear of the same color, face India's border guards, dressed in khaki uniforms and hats adorned with scarlet fan-tails. Brandishing rifles and parading in goosestep, they greet each other, lock gates, and lower their national flags. In this territorial display, both nations also symbolically signal their objective of nonviolent coexistence.

Politics, Power, and Violence

14

Ironically, the groups formed to facilitate much-needed human cooperation also create dynamics that may lead to conflict within and between groups. Therefore, every society must have ways and means for resolving internal conflicts and preventing a breakdown of its social order. Moreover, each society must possess the capacity to deal with neighboring societies in peace and war. Today, throughout the world, state governments play a central role in maintaining social order.

Despite the predominance of state societies today, there are still groups where political organization consists of flexible and informal kinship systems whose leaders lack real **power**—the ability of individuals or groups to impose their will upon others and make them do things even against their own wants or wishes. Between these two polarities of kin-ordered and state-organized political systems lies a world of variety.

SYSTEMS OF POLITICAL ORGANIZATION

The term **political organization** refers to the way power is distributed and embedded in society, whether in organizing a giraffe hunt, managing irrigated farmlands, or raising an army. In short, it is the means through which a society creates and maintains social order. It assumes a variety of forms among the peoples of the world, but anthropologists have simplified this complex subject by identifying four basic kinds of

power The ability of individuals or groups to impose their will upon others and make them do things even against their own wants or wishes

political organization The way power is distributed and embedded in society; the means through which a society creates and maintains social order and reduces social disorder

TYPES OF POLITICAL ORGANIZATION

The symbol ➞ indicates that the attribute varies between less and more complex societies of that type.

	BAND	TRIBE	CHIEFDOM	STATE
MEMBERSHIP				
Number of people	Dozens and up	Hundreds and up	Thousands and up	Tens of thousands and up
Settlement pattern	Mobile	Mobile or fixed: 1 or more villages	Fixed: 2 or more villages	Fixed: Many villages and cities
Basis of relationships	Kin	Kin, descent groups	Kin, rank, and residence	Class and residence
Ethnicities and languages	1	1	1	1 or more
GOVERNMENT				
Decision making, leadership	"Egalitarian"	"Egalitarian" or Big Man	Centralized, hereditary	Centralized
Bureaucracy	None	None	None, or 1 or 2 levels	Many levels
Monopoly of force and information	No	No	No ➞ Yes	Yes
Conflict resolution	Informal	Informal	Centralized	Laws, judges
Hierarchy of settlement	No	No	No ➞ Paramount village or head town	Capital
ECONOMY				
Food production	No	No ➞ Yes	Yes ➞ Intensive	Intensive
Labor specialization	No	No	No ➞ Yes	Yes
Exchanges	Reciprocal	Reciprocal	Redistributive ("tribute")	Redistributive ("taxes")
Control of land	Band	Descent group	Chief	Various
SOCIETY				
Stratified	No	No	Yes, ranked by kin	Yes, by class or caste
Slavery	No	No	Some, small-scale	Some, large-scale
Luxury goods for elite	No	No	Yes	Yes
Public architecture	No	No	No ➞ Yes	Yes
Indigenous literacy	No	No	No ➞ Some	Often

Figure 14.1 Four Types of Political Systems

political systems: bands, tribes, chiefdoms, and states (Figure 14.1). The first two are uncentralized systems; the latter two are centralized.

Uncentralized Political Systems

Until recently, many non-Western peoples have had neither chiefs with established rights and duties nor any fixed form of government, as those who live in modern states understand the term. Instead, marriage and kinship have formed their principal means of social organization. The economies of these societies are primarily of a subsistence type, and populations are typically small.

Leaders do not have real power to force compliance with the society's customs or rules, but if individuals do not conform, they may become targets of scorn and gossip or even be banished. Important decisions are usually made in a collective manner by agreement among adults. Dissenting members may decide to act with the majority, or they may choose to adopt some other course of action, including leaving the group.

This egalitarian form of political organization provides great flexibility, which in many situations offers an adaptive advantage. Since power in these kin-ordered communities is shared, with nobody exercising exclusive control over collective resources or public affairs, individuals typically enjoy much more freedom than those who form part of larger and more complex political systems.

band A relatively small and loosely organized kin-ordered group that inhabits a specific territory and that may split periodically into smaller extended family groups that are politically independent

tribe In anthropology, refers to a range of kin-ordered groups that are politically integrated by some unifying factor and whose members share a common ancestry, identity, culture, language, and territory

Bands

The **band** is a relatively small and loosely organized kin-ordered group that inhabits a specific territory and that may split periodically into smaller extended family groups that are politically independent. Typically, bands are found among food foragers and other nomadic societies where people organize into politically autonomous extended-family groups that usually camp together, although the members of such families may periodically break up into smaller groups to forage for food or visit other relatives. The band is probably the oldest form of political organization, since all humans were once food foragers and remained so until the development of farming and pastoralism over the past 10,000 years.

Since bands are egalitarian and small, numbering at most a few hundred people, no real need exists for formal, centralized political systems. Because everyone is related to—and knows on a personal basis—everyone else with whom dealings are required, there is high value placed on "getting along." Conflicts that do arise are usually settled informally through gossip, ridicule, direct negotiation, or mediation. When negotiation or mediation is used, the focus is on reaching a solution considered fair by all concerned parties, rather than on conforming to some abstract law or rule.

Decisions affecting a band are made with the participation of all its adult members, with an emphasis on achieving consensus—a collective agreement—rather than a simple majority. Individuals become leaders by virtue of their abilities and serve in that capacity only as long as they retain the confidence of the community. They have no real power to force people to abide by their decisions. A leader who exceeds what people are willing to accept quickly loses followers.

An example of the informal nature of band leadership is found among the Ju/'hoansi of the Kalahari Desert mentioned in earlier chapters. Each Ju/'hoansi band is composed of a group of families that live together, linked through kinship to one another and to the headman (or, less often, headwoman). Although each band has rights to the territory it occupies and the resources within it, two or more bands may range over the same land. The head, called the *kxau,* or "owner," is the focal point for the band's claims on the territory. He or she does not personally own the land or resources but symbolically represents the rights of band members to them. If the head leaves the area to live elsewhere, people turn to someone else to lead them.

The head coordinates band migration when resources are no longer adequate for subsistence in a particular habitat. This leader's major duty is to plan when and where the group will move, and when the move begins his or her position is at the head of the line. The leader selects the site for the new settlement and has the first choice of a spot for his or her own fire.

There are few other material rewards or duties. For example, a Ju/'hoansi head is not a judge and does not punish other band members. Wrongdoers are judged and held accountable by public opinion, usually expressed by gossip—which can play an important role in curbing socially unacceptable behavior.

Another prime technique in small-scale societies for resolving disputes, or even avoiding them in the first place, is mobility. Those unable to get along with others of their group may choose or feel pressured to move to another group where existing kinship ties may give them rights of entry—or they may try to establish a new community of their own.

Tribes

The second type of uncentralized authority system is the tribe. In anthropology, the term **tribe** refers to a wide range of kin-ordered groups that are politically integrated by some unifying factor and whose members share a common ancestry, identity, culture, language, and territory. In these larger political entities, people sacrifice a degree of household and band autonomy in return for greater security. Tribes may develop when a number of bands group together, resolving conflicts between each other, for purposes of economic exchange and/or collective self-defense against common enemies.

Traditionally, a tribe has an economy based on some form of crop cultivation or herding. Since these subsistence methods usually yield more food than those of the food-foraging band, tribal membership is usually larger than band membership. While band population densities are usually less than one person per square mile, tribal population densities generally exceed that and may be as high as 250 per square mile. Greater population density brings a new set of problems to be solved as opportunities for bickering, begging, adultery, and theft increase markedly, especially among people living in permanent villages.

Shown here is a meeting of the Navajo Tribal Council, a nontraditional governing body created in response to requirements set by the U.S. government in order for the Navajo to exercise national sovereignty. Calling themselves Dineh ("the people"), the Navajo were traditionally organized in self-governing communities led by respected clan leaders known as *naat'áanii* ("the ones who orate"). These clan leaders led the collective decision-making process by their wise guidance and building consensus.

© Matt York/Associated Press

Each tribe consists of one or more self-supporting and self-governing local communities (including local groups earlier discussed as bands) that may then form alliances with others for various purposes. As in the band, political organization in the tribe is informal and temporary. Whenever a situation requiring political integration of all or several groups within the tribe arises—perhaps for defense, to carry out a raid, to pool resources in times of scarcity, or to capitalize on a windfall that must be distributed quickly lest it spoil—groups join to deal with the situation in a cooperative manner. When the problem is satisfactorily solved, each group then resumes autonomy.

In many tribal societies the organizing unit and seat of political authority is the clan, comprised of people who consider themselves descended from a common ancestor. Within the clan, elders or headmen and/or headwomen regulate members' affairs and represent their clan in interactions with other clans. As a group, the elders of all the clans may form a council that acts within the community or for the community in dealings with outsiders. Because clan members usually do not all live together in a single community, clan organization facilitates joint action with members of related communities when necessary.

Leadership in tribal societies is also relatively informal, as evident in a wide array of past and present examples. The Navajo Indians in the southwestern

United States, for example, traditionally did not think of government as something fixed and all-powerful, and leadership was not vested in a central authority. A local leader was a man respected for his age, integrity, and wisdom. Therefore, people sought his advice frequently, but he had no formal means of control and could not force any decision on those who asked for his help. Group decisions were made by public consensus, although the most influential man usually played a key role in reaching a decision. Social mechanisms that induced members to abide by group decisions included gossip, criticism, withdrawal of cooperation, and the belief that antisocial actions caused sickness and other misfortune.

Another example of tribal leadership is the "Big Man." Common in the South Pacific, such men are leaders of localized descent groups or of a territorial group. The Big Man combines a small amount of interest in his tribe's welfare with a great deal of cunning and calculation for his own personal gain. His authority is personal; he does not come to office in any formal sense, nor is he elected. His status is the result of acts that raise him above most other tribe members and attract to him a number of loyal followers.

The Kapauku of Western New Guinea typify this form of political organization. Among them, the Big Man is called the *tonowi*, or "rich one." To achieve this status, one must be male, wealthy, generous, and eloquent. Physical bravery and an ability to deal with the supernatural are also common *tonowi* characteristics, but they are not essential.

The *tonowi* functions as the headman of the village unit in a wide variety of situations within and beyond the community. He represents his group in dealing with

chiefdom A regional polity in which two or more local groups are organized under a single chief, who is at the head of a ranked hierarchy of people

outsiders and other villages and acts as negotiator and/or judge when disputes break out among his followers.

Notably, a *tonowi* who refuses to lend money to other villagers may be ostracized, ridiculed, and, in extreme cases, actually executed by a group of warriors. Such responses to tightfistedness ensure that economic wealth is distributed throughout the group. Also, since a *tonowi's* wealth comes from his success at breeding pigs (the focus of the entire Kapauku economy; see Chapter 8), it is not uncommon for a *tonowi* to lose his fortune rapidly due to bad management or bad luck with his pigs. Thus the Kapauku political structure shifts frequently; as one man loses wealth and consequently power, another gains it and becomes a *tonowi*. These changes confer a degree of flexibility on the political organization and prevent any one *tonowi* from holding political power for too long.

Political Integration Beyond the Kin Group

Age sets, age grades, and common-interest groups discussed in the previous chapter are among the mechanisms used by tribal societies as means of political integration. Cutting across territorial and kin groupings, these organizations link members from different lineages and clans. For example, among many Indian nations inhabiting North America's Great Plains in the 19th century, the band was the basic territorial and political unit. In addition, however, there were a number of military societies or warrior clubs.

Among the Cheyenne, for instance, there were seven such military societies. A boy might be invited to join one of them when he achieved warrior status, whereupon he became familiar with the society's particular insignia, songs, and rituals. Beyond military functions, the warrior groups also had ceremonial and social functions.

The Cheyenne warriors' daily tasks consisted of overseeing activities in the village, protecting families on the move to the next camping site, and enforcing buffalo hunting rules. In addition, each warrior society had its own repertoire of dances, performed on special ceremonial occasions. Since each Cheyenne band had identical military societies bearing identical names, the societies served to integrate the entire tribe for military and political purposes.[1]

Centralized Political Systems

In bands and tribes, political authority is not centralized, and each group is economically and politically autonomous. Political organization is vested in kinship, age, and common-interest groups. Populations are small and relatively homogeneous, with people engaged for the most part in the same sorts of activities throughout their lives. However, as a society's social life becomes more complex—as population rises, technology becomes more intricate, and specialization of labor and trade networks produce surplus goods—the opportunity increases for some individuals or groups to exercise control at the expense of others. In such societies, political authority and power are concentrated in a single individual (the chief) or in a body of individuals (the state).

Chiefdoms

A **chiefdom** is a regional polity in which two or more local groups are organized under a single ruling individual—the chief—who is at the head of a ranked hierarchy of people. An individual's status in such a polity is determined by the closeness of his or her relationship to the chief. Those closest are officially superior and receive deferential treatment from those in lower ranks.

The office of the chief is usually for life and often hereditary. Typically, it passes from a man to his son in patrilineal societies and from a man to his sister's son in matrilineal groups. However, sometimes, even in some patrilineal societies, the chief's position passes to the eldest daughter.

Unlike the headmen or headwomen in bands and tribes, the leader of a chiefdom is generally a true authority figure, whose authority serves to unite members in all affairs and at all times. For example, a chief can distribute land among community members and recruit people into military service.

Chiefdoms have a recognized hierarchy consisting of major and minor authorities who control major and minor subdivisions. Such an arrangement is, in effect, a chain of command, linking leaders at every level. It serves to bind groups in the heartland to the chief's headquarters, be it a mud and dung hut or a marble palace. Although leaders of chiefdoms are almost always men, in some cultures a politically astute wife, sister, or single daughter of a deceased male chief could inherit such a powerful position as well.

Chiefs usually control the economic activities of those who fall under their political rule. Typically,

---

[1]Hoebel, E. A. (1960). *The Cheyennes: Indians of the Great Plains.* New York: Holt, Rinehart & Winston.

chiefdoms involve redistributive systems, and the chief has control over surplus goods and perhaps even over the community's labor force. Thus, he (and sometimes she) may demand a quota of rice from farmers, which will then be redistributed to the entire community. Similarly, laborers may be recruited to build irrigation works, a palace, or a temple.

The chief may also amass a great amount of personal wealth and pass it on to offspring. Land, cattle, and luxury goods produced by specialists can be collected by the chief and become part of the power base. Moreover, high-ranking families of the chiefdom may engage in the same practice and use their possessions as evidence of noble status.

An example of this form of political organization may be seen among the Kpelle of Liberia in West Africa.[2] Among them is a class of *paramount chiefs*, each of whom presides over one of the Kpelle chiefdoms (and each of which is now a district of the Liberian state). Their traditional tasks include hearing disputes, preserving order, overseeing the upkeep of trails, and performing various other supervising functions. In addition, they are now salaried officials of the Liberian government, mediating between it and their own people.

state In anthropology, a centralized political system involving large numbers of people within a defined territory who are divided into social classes and organized and directed by a formal government that has the capacity and authority to make laws and to use force to defend the social order
nation A people who share a collective identity based on a common culture, language, territorial base, and history
pluralistic society A society in which two or more ethnic groups or nationalities are politically organized into one territorial state but maintain their cultural differences

[2]Gibbs, J. L., Jr. (1965). The Kpelle of Liberia. In J. L. Gibbs, Jr. (Ed.), *Peoples of Africa* (pp. 216–218). New York: Holt, Rinehart & Winston.

Also, a paramount chief receives government commissions on taxes and court fees collected within his chiefdom, plus a commission for furnishing the rubber plantations with laborers. Moreover, he gets a stipulated amount of rice from each household and gifts from people who come to request favors and intercessions. In keeping with his exalted station in life, a paramount chief has at his disposal uniformed messengers, a literate clerk, and the symbols of wealth: many wives, embroidered gowns, and freedom from manual labor.

In a ranked hierarchy beneath each Kpelle paramount chief are several lesser chiefs: one for each district within the chiefdom, one for each town within a district, and one for each quarter of all but the smallest towns. Each acts as a kind of lieutenant for his chief of the next higher rank and also serves as a liaison between him and those of lower rank. Unlike paramount or district chiefs, who are comparatively remote, town and quarter chiefs are readily accessible to people at the local level.

Traditionally, chiefdoms in all parts of the world have been highly unstable, with lesser chiefs trying to take power from higher-ranking chiefs or paramount chiefs vying with one another for supreme power. In precolonial Hawaii, for example, war was the way to gain territory and maintain power; great chiefs set out to conquer one another in an effort to become paramount chief of all the islands. When one chief conquered another, the loser and all his nobles were dispossessed of all property and were lucky if they escaped alive. The new chief then appointed his own supporters to positions of political power. As a consequence, there was very little continuity of governmental or religious administration.

State Systems

The **state** is a complex centralized political system involving large numbers of people within a defined territory who are divided in social classes and organized and directed by a formal government that has the capacity and authority to make laws and to use force to defend the social order. The most formal of political organizations, it represents one of the hallmarks of what is commonly referred to as *civilization*. From the perspective of the political elite in control of the state, its formation and endurance are typically represented as something positive—as progress. This view is not necessarily shared by those who exist on the political underside and do not possess much personal freedom to say and do as they please.

A large population in a state-organized society requires increased food production and wider distribution networks. Together, these lead to a transformation of the landscape by way of irrigation and terracing, carefully managed crop rotation cycles, intensive competition for clearly demarcated lands, roads, and enough farmers and other rural workers to support market systems and

A Kpelle chief in Liberia, West Africa, listens to a dispute in his district. Settling disputes is one of several ongoing traditional tasks that fall to paramount chiefs among Kpelle people.

a specialized urban sector. Under such conditions, corporate groups that stress exclusive membership proliferate, ethnic differentiation and ethnocentrism become more pronounced, and the potential for social conflict increases dramatically. Given these circumstances, state institutions—which minimally involve a bureaucracy, a military, and (usually) an official religion—provide the means for numerous and diverse groups to function together as an integrated whole.

Although their guiding ideology is that they are permanent and stable, since their first appearance some 5,000 years ago, states have been anything but permanent. Commonly unstable, many have disappeared in the course of time, some temporarily and others forever. Some were annexed by other states, and others collapsed or fragmented into smaller political units. Although some present-day states are very old—such as Japan, which has endured as a state for almost 1,500 years—few are older than the United States, an independent republic since the American Revolutionary War ended in success with the signing of the 1783 peace treaty with Great Britain. Nowhere have states even begun to show the staying power exhibited by less centralized political systems, the longest lasting social forms invented by humans.[3]

An important distinction to make at this point is between state and nation. As noted in Chapter 1, a **nation** is a people who share a collective identity based on a common culture, language, territorial base, and history.[4] Today, there are roughly 200 internationally recognized states in the world, most of which did not exist before the end of World War II (1945). By contrast, there are about 5,000 nations (including tribes), many of which have existed since "time immemorial." Rarely do state and nation coincide, as they do, for example, in Iceland, Japan, and Swaziland.

About 73 percent of the world's states are **pluralistic societies**, having within their boundaries peoples of more than one nation.[5] Often, smaller nations (including tribes) and other groups find themselves at the mercy of one or more dominant nations or ethnic groups controlling the state. Frequently facing discrimination, even repression, some minority nations seek to improve their political

[3]Diamond, J. (2005). *Collapse: How societies choose to fail or succeed.* New York: Viking Penguin.

[4]Clay, J. W. (1996). What's a nation? In W. A. Haviland & R. J. Gordon (Eds.), *Talking about people* (2nd ed., p. 188). Mountain View, CA: Mayfield.

[5]Van den Berghe, P. L. (1992). The modern state: Nation builder or nation killer? *International Journal of Group Tensions, 22*(3), 193.

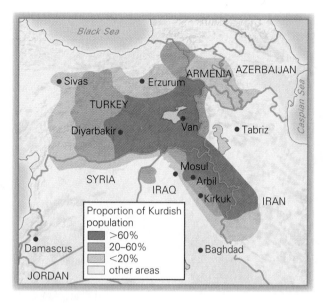

Figure 14.2

The Kurds—most of whom live in Turkey, Iran, and Iraq—are an example of a nation without a state. With a population of about 27 million, they are much more numerous than Australians, for example. In fact, the total population of the four Scandinavian countries—Denmark, Finland, Norway, and Sweden—is less than that of the Kurds who have no independent country of their own.

position by founding an independent state. In the process, they usually encounter stiff opposition, even violent confrontations.

So it is with the Kurdish people inhabiting the borderlands of Turkey, Iran, and Iraq (Figure 14.2), the Palestinians whose lands on the West Bank have been militarily occupied and controlled by Israel for several decades, and the Chechens in the Russian federation, to cite but a few examples. While the outcome of armed struggle may be the formation of a new state (such as Kosovo's split from Serbia), some nations have forged their own states without open violence. Papua New Guinea in the southern Pacific, which gained independence from Australia in 1975, is one example of this.

An important aspect of the state is its delegation of authority to maintain order within and outside its borders. Police, foreign ministries, war ministries, and other bureaucracies function to control and punish disruptive acts of crime, dissension, and rebellion. By such agencies the state asserts authority impersonally and in a consistent, predictable manner. Western forms of government, like that of the United States, of course, are state governments, and their organization and workings are undoubtedly familiar to most everyone.

legitimacy The right of political leaders to govern—to hold, use, and allocate power—based on the values a particular society holds

POLITICAL SYSTEMS AND THE QUESTION OF LEGITIMACY

Whatever a society's political system, it must find some way to obtain and retain the people's allegiance. In uncentralized systems, where every adult participates in all decision making, loyalty and cooperation are freely given, since each person is considered a part of the political system. As the group grows larger, however, and the organization becomes more formal, the problem of obtaining and keeping public support becomes greater.

Centralized political systems may rely upon coercion as a means of social control. This, however, carries a measure of risk since the personnel needed to apply force may be numerous and grow to be a political power. Also, the emphasis on force may create resentment and lessen cooperation. Thus, police states are generally short-lived; most societies choose less extreme forms of social coercion. In the United States, this is reflected in the increasing emphasis placed on cultural, as opposed to social, control, as will be discussed in the sections on internalized and externalized controls a bit later in this chapter.

Also basic to the political process is the concept of **legitimacy**, or the right of political leaders to govern—to lawfully hold, use, and allocate power. Like force, legitimacy is a form of support for a political system; unlike force, it is based on the socially accepted customs, rules, or laws that bind and hold a people together as a collective whole. For example, among the Kapauku of Western New Guinea discussed above, the legitimacy of the *tonowi's* power comes from his wealth; the kings of Hawaii, and of England and France before their revolutions, were thought to have a god-given right to rule; and the head of the traditional Dahomey state, in what is now the West African country Benin, acquired legitimacy through his age, as he was always the oldest living male.

Power based on legitimacy results in *authority*. It is distinct from power based solely on force: Obedience to authority results from the belief that obedience is "right"; compliance to power based on force results from fear of being deprived of liberty, physical well-being, life, or material property. Thus, power based on legitimacy is symbolic and depends upon the positive expectations of those who recognize and accept it. If the expectations are not met regularly (if the head of state fails to deliver economic prosperity or the leader is continuously unsuccessful in preventing or dealing with calamities), the legitimacy of the recognized power figure erodes or may collapse altogether.

POLITICS AND RELIGION

Religion is often intricately connected to politics. Frequently it is religion that legitimizes the political order and leadership. Religious beliefs may influence or

VISUAL COUNTERPOINT

In contrast to countries such as the United States, where religion and state are constitutionally separated, countries such as Iran and Great Britain permit a much closer relationship between political and religious affairs. For instance, Shiite Muslim religious leader Ayatollah Khamenei is not only Iran's supreme spiritual leader but also his country's highest political authority. In England, Queen Elizabeth is not only her country's nominal head of state but also "the Supreme Governor" of the Church of England, which entitles her to appoint the Anglican bishops in that state.

provide authoritative approval to customary rules and laws. For example, acts that people believe to be sinful are often illegal as well.

In both industrial and nonindustrial societies, belief in the supernatural is important and is reflected in people's political institutions. One place where the effect of religion on politics was well exemplified was in medieval Europe: Holy wars were fought over the smallest matter; labor was mobilized to build immense cathedrals in honor of the Virgin Mary and other saints; kings and queens ruled by "divine right" and pledged allegiance to the pope, asking his blessing in all important ventures, whether they were marital or martial.

In Peru, the divine ruler of the Inca empire proclaimed absolute authority based on the proposition that he was descended from the Sun God. Mexico's ancient Aztec state was also a politico-religious one, having a divine ruler and engaging in nearly constant warfare to procure captives for human sacrifices thought necessary to assuage or please the gods. Modern Iran was proclaimed an "Islamic republic," and its first head of state was the most holy of all Shiite Muslim holy men.

The fact that the president of the United States takes the oath of office by swearing on the Bible is another instance of the use of religion to legitimize political power, as is the phrase "one nation, under God" in the Pledge of Allegiance. On U.S. coins is the phrase "In God We Trust," many meetings of government bodies begin with a prayer or invocation, and the phrase "so help me God" is routinely used in legal proceedings. In spite of an official separation of church and state, religious legitimization of government lingers.

POLITICAL LEADERSHIP AND GENDER

Irrespective of cultural configuration or type of political organization, women hold important positions of political leadership far less often than men. Furthermore, when they do occupy publicly recognized offices, their power and authority rarely exceed those of men. But significant exceptions occur. Historically, one might cite the female chiefs, or *sachems,* of Algonquian Indian communities in southern New England, as well as powerful queens in several Asian, African, and European monarchies.

Liberian President Ellen Johnson Sirleaf inspects members of the Liberian police after taking the presidential oath in January 2006. The first female president on the African continent, Sirleaf is a Harvard-educated economist who took the world by surprise when she won the elected head office in her war-torn and poverty-stricken country. Since taking office, she has managed to cancel most of Liberia's international debt, promote investment in the country, and significantly increase its economic output. Serious challenges continue, but she has done much to change Liberia's course.

© AFP/Getty Images

Perhaps most notable is Queen Victoria, the long-reigning queen of England, Scotland, Wales, and Ireland. Also recognized as monarch in a host of colonies all over the world, Victoria even acquired the title Empress of India. Ruling the British empire from 1837 until 1901, she was perhaps the world's wealthiest and most powerful leader.

In addition to inheriting high positions of political leadership, a growing number of women have also been elected as presidents, chancellors, or prime ministers. Countries with elected female heads of state now or in recent years include Argentina, Indonesia, Ireland, Sri Lanka, Norway, India, Liberia, Chile, Germany, and the Philippines, to mention just a few. While such high-profile female leadership is still relatively rare, women regularly enjoy as much political power as men in a number of societies. In band societies, for example, it is common for females to have as much of a say in public affairs as males, even though more often than not men are the nominal leaders of their groups.

Among the Iroquois nations of New York State, all leadership positions above the household and clan level were, without exception, filled by men. Thus, men held all positions on the village and tribal councils, as well as on the great council of the Iroquois Confederacy. However, they were completely beholden to women, for only women could nominate men to high office. Moreover, women actively lobbied the men on the councils

and could have someone removed from office whenever it suited them.

Lower visibility in politics does not necessarily indicate that women lack power in political affairs. And just as there are various ways in which women play a role behind the scenes, so it is when they have more visible roles, as in the dual-sex system of the Igbo in Nigeria, West Africa. Among the Igbo, each political unit has separate political institutions for men and women, so that both have an autonomous sphere of authority, as well as an area of shared responsibility.[6] At the head of

cultural control Control through beliefs and values deeply internalized in the minds of individuals
social control External enforcement through open coercion

[6]Okonjo, K. (1976). The dual-sex political system in operation: Igbo women and community politics in midwestern Nigeria. In N. Hafkin & E. Bay (Eds.), *Women in Africa*. Stanford, CA: Stanford University Press.

each political unit was a male *obi*, considered the head of government although in fact he presided over the male community, and a female *omu*, the acknowledged mother of the whole community but in practice concerned with the female section of the community. Unlike a queen (though both she and the *obi* were crowned), the *omu* was neither the *obi's* wife nor the previous *obi's* daughter.

Just as the *obi* had a council of dignitaries to advise him and act as a check against any arbitrary exercise of power, the *omu* was served by a council of women in equal number to the *obi's* male councilors. The duties of the *omu* and her councilors involved such tasks as establishing rules and regulations for the community market (marketing was a woman's activity) and hearing cases involving women brought to her from throughout the town or village. If such cases also involved men, then she and her council would cooperate with the *obi* and his council.

In the Igbo system, then, women managed their own affairs, and their interests were represented at all levels of government. Moreover, they had the right to enforce their decisions and rules with sanctions similar to those employed by men, including strikes, boycotts, and "sitting on" someone, including a man:

> To "sit on" or "make war on" a man involved gathering at his compound, sometimes late at night, dancing, singing scurrilous songs which detailed the women's grievances against him and often called his manhood into question, banging on his hut with the pestles women used for pounding yams, and perhaps demolishing his hut or plastering it with mud and roughing him up a bit. A man might be sanctioned in this way for mistreating his wife, for violating the women's market rules, or for letting his cows eat the women's crops. The women would stay at his hut throughout the day, and late into the night if necessary, until he repented and promised to mend his ways.[7]

When the British imposed colonial rule on the Igbo in the late 1800s, they failed to acknowledge the autonomy and power of the women, in part because they were influenced by cultural values of their own male-dominated society. This is ironic because the long-reigning and powerful head of the British empire at the time was, as mentioned earlier, Queen Victoria.

Nevertheless, British colonial administrators introduced "reforms" that destroyed traditional forms of female autonomy and power without providing alternative forms in exchange. As a result, Igbo women lost much of their traditional equality and became politically subordinate to men.

POLITICAL ORGANIZATION AND THE MAINTENANCE OF ORDER

Political organization always includes means of maintaining order that ensure people behave in acceptable ways and define what action will be taken when they do not. In chiefdoms and states, some sort of authority has the power to regulate the affairs of society. In bands and tribes, however, people behave generally as they are expected to, without the direct intervention of any centralized political authority. To a large degree, gossip, criticism, fear of supernatural forces, and the like serve as effective deterrents to antisocial behavior.

Internalized Controls

Individuals who are well-socialized and enculturated members of their own society typically acquire an internalized set of shared beliefs and values about what is proper and what is not. These values are so deeply ingrained that each person becomes personally responsible for his or her own conduct. **Cultural control** may be thought of as an internalized form of self-control, as opposed to **social control**, which involves external enforcement through open coercion.

Cultural controls are embedded in our consciousness and may rely on deterrents such as fear of supernatural punishment—ancestral spirits sabotaging the hunting, for example—and magical retaliation. Like the devout Christian who avoids sinning for fear of hell, the individual expects some sort of punishment, even though no one in the community may be aware of the wrongdoing.

Cultural controls can also be framed in positive terms, with customary ways and means that encourage individual sacrifice for the common good. For example, many cultures honor traditions of giving to, or volunteering for, charitable or humanitarian institutions. Performed out of a desire to help those in need, such personal sacrifices may be motivated by a spiritual or religious worldview. Often deeply rooted in basic ideas of a wider community and reciprocity, there are also cultural controls against self-seeking, self-serving, greedy opportunism that threatens the well-being of a larger community.

---

[7]Van Allen, J. (1997). Sitting on a man: Colonialism and the lost political institutions of Igbo women. In R. Grinker & C. Steiner (Eds.), *Perspectives on Africa* (p. 450). Boston: Blackwell Press.

Formal sanctions may involve some form of regulated combat, seen here as armed dancers near Mount Hagen in New Guinea demand redress for murder.

Externalized Controls

Because internalized controls are not wholly sufficient even in bands and tribes, every society develops externalized social controls known as **sanctions** designed to encourage conformity to social norms. Operating within social groups of all sizes and involving a mix of cultural and social controls, sanctions may vary significantly within a given society, but they fall into one of two categories: positive or negative. Positive sanctions consist of incentives to conformity such as awards, titles, and recognition by one's neighbors. Negative sanctions consist of threats such as imprisonment, fines, corporal punishment, or ostracism from the community for violation of social norms.

For sanctions to be effective, they must be applied consistently, and they must be generally known among members of the society. If some individuals are not convinced of the advantages of social conformity, they are still more likely to obey society's rules than to accept the consequences of not doing so.

Sanctions may also be either formal or informal, depending on whether or not a legal statute is involved. In the United States, the man who goes shirtless in shorts to a church service may be subject to a variety of informal sanctions, ranging from disapproving glances from the clergy to the chuckling of other parishioners. If, however, he were to show up without any clothing at all, he would be subject to the formal negative sanction of arrest for indecent exposure. Only in the second instance would he have been guilty of breaking the law.

Formal sanctions, such as laws, are always organized, because they attempt to precisely and explicitly regulate people's behavior, whether they are peacefully trading with others or confronting others on a battlefield. Other examples of organized sanctions include, on the positive side, military decorations and monetary rewards. On the negative side are loss of face, exclusion from social life and its privileges, seizure of property, imprisonment, and even bodily mutilation or death.

Informal sanctions emphasize cultural control and are diffuse in nature, involving spontaneous expressions of approval or disapproval by members of the group or community. They are, nonetheless, very effective in enforcing a large number of seemingly unimportant customs. Because most people want to be accepted, they are willing to acquiesce to the rules that govern dress, eating, and conversation, even in the absence of actual laws.

SOCIAL CONTROL THROUGH LAW

Among the Inuit of northern Canada, all offenses are considered to involve disputes between individuals; thus, they must be settled between the disputants themselves. A traditional way of doing this is through a *song duel*, in

sanctions Externalized social controls designed to encourage conformity to social norms

Having a song duel is the traditional approach to dispute resolution among the Inuit of northern Canada.

which the individuals involved heap insults upon one another in songs specially composed for the occasion. Although society does not intervene, its interests are represented by spectators, whose applause determines the outcome. If, however, social harmony cannot be restored—and that is the goal, rather than assigning and punishing guilt—one or the other disputant may move to another band. Ultimately, there is no binding legal authority.

In Western society, by contrast, someone who commits an offense against another may become subject to a series of complex legal proceedings. In criminal cases the primary concern is to assign and punish guilt rather than to help out the victim. The offender will be arrested by the police; will be tried before a judge and, perhaps, a jury; and, depending on the severity of the crime, may be fined, imprisoned, or even executed. Rarely does the victim receive restitution or compensation.

Throughout this chain of events, the accused party is dealt with by police, judges, jurors, and jailers, who may have no personal acquaintance whatsoever with the plaintiff or the defendant. How strange this all seems from the standpoint of traditional Inuit culture!

Clearly, the two systems operate under distinctly different assumptions.

Definition of Law

Once two Inuit settle a dispute by engaging in a singing contest, the affair is considered closed; no further action is expected. Would we choose to describe the outcome of such a contest as a *legal* decision? If every law is a sanction but not every sanction is a law, how are we to distinguish between social sanctions in general and those to which we apply the label "law"?

Although rules enacted by an authorized legislative body and enforced by the judicial mechanisms of the state are fundamental features of Western jurisprudence, they are not the universal backbone of human law. Can any concept of law be applied to societies for whom the notion of a centralized judiciary is virtually meaningless? How shall we categorize Inuit song duels and other socially condoned forms of dispute resolution that seem to meet some but not all of the criteria of law?

Ultimately, it is always of greatest value to consider each case within its cultural context. After all, law reflects a society's basic postulates, so to understand any society's laws, one must understand the underlying values and assumptions. Nonetheless, a working definition of law is useful for purposes of discussion and cross-cultural comparison, and for this, **law** is adequately characterized as formal rules of conduct that, when violated, lead to negative sanctions.

Functions of Law

Anthropologists recognize three basic functions of law. First, it defines relationships among society's members and marks out proper behavior under specified circumstances. Knowledge of the law permits each person to know his or her rights and duties with respect to every other member of society.

Second, law allocates the authority to employ coercion in the enforcement of sanctions. In societies with centralized political systems, such authority is generally vested in the government and its judiciary system. In societies that lack centralized political control, the authority to employ force may be allocated directly to the injured party.

Third, law functions to redefine social relations and to ensure social flexibility. As new situations arise, law must determine whether old rules and assumptions retain their validity and to what extent they must be altered. Law, if it is to operate efficiently, must allow room for change.

In practice, law is never as neat as a written description about it. In any given society, the power to employ sanctions may vary from level to level within the larger group. Thus, the head of a Kapauku household in Papua New Guinea may punish a household member by slapping or beating, but the authority to confiscate property is vested exclusively in the headman of the lineage. Analogous distinctions exist in the United States among municipal, state, and federal jurisdictions. The complexity of legal jurisdiction within each society makes it difficult to generalize about law.

Crime

As we have observed, an important function of negative sanctions, legal or otherwise, is to discourage the breach of social norms. A person contemplating theft is aware of the possibility of being caught and punished. Yet, even in the face of severe sanctions, individuals in every society sometimes violate the norms and subject themselves to the consequences of their behavior.

In Western societies a clear distinction is made between offenses against the state and offenses against an individual. However, in non-state societies such as bands and tribes, all offenses are viewed as transgressions against individuals or kin-groups (families, lineages, clans, and so on).

Disputes between individuals or kin-groups may seriously disrupt the social order, especially in small groups where the number of disputants, though small in absolute numbers, may be a large percentage of the total population. For example, although the Inuit traditionally have no effective domestic or economic unit beyond the family, a dispute between two people will interfere with the ability of members of separate families to come to one another's aid when necessary and is consequently a matter of wider social concern. The goal of judicial proceedings in such instances is restoring social harmony rather than punishing an offender. When distinguishing between offenses of concern to the community as a whole and those of concern only to a few individuals, we may refer to them as *collective* or *personal*.

Basically, disputes are settled in one of two ways. First, disputing parties may, through argument and compromise, voluntarily arrive at a mutually satisfactory agreement. This form of settlement is referred to as **negotiation** or, if it involves the assistance of an unbiased third party, **mediation**. In bands and tribes a third-party mediator has no coercive power and thus cannot force disputants to abide by such a decision, but as a person who commands great personal respect, the mediator frequently may help bring about a settlement.

Second, in chiefdoms and states, an authorized third party may issue a binding decision that the disputing parties will be compelled to respect. This process is referred to as **adjudication**. The difference between mediation and adjudication is basically a difference in authorization. In a dispute settled by adjudication, the disputing parties present their positions as compellingly as they can, but they do not participate in the ultimate decision making. Although the adjudication process is not universally characteristic, every society employs some form of negotiation to settle disputes.

Often negotiation is a prerequisite or an alternative to adjudication. For example, in the resolution of U.S. labor disputes, striking workers may first negotiate with management, often with the mediation of a third party. If the state decides the strike constitutes a threat to the public welfare, the disputing parties may be forced to

---

law Formal rules of conduct that, when violated, lead to negative sanctions

negotiation The use of direct argument and compromise by the parties to a dispute to arrive voluntarily at a mutually satisfactory agreement

mediation Settlement of a dispute through negotiation assisted by an unbiased third party

adjudication Mediation with an unbiased third party making the ultimate decision

submit to adjudication. In this case, the responsibility for resolving the dispute is transferred to a presumably impartial judge.

The judge's work is difficult and complex. In addition to sifting through evidence presented, he or she must consider a wide range of norms, values, and earlier rulings to arrive at a decision intended to be considered just not only by the disputing parties but by the public and other judges as well.

Restorative Justice and Conflict Resolution

Punitive justice, such as imprisonment, may be the most common approach to justice in North America, but it has not proven to be an effective way of changing criminal behavior. There are cultural alternatives.

Indigenous communities in Canada successfully urged their federal government to reform justice services to make them more consistent with indigenous values and traditions.[8] In particular, they have pressed for restorative justice techniques such as the Talking Circle. For this, parties involved in a conflict come together in a circle with equal opportunity to express their views—one at a time, free of interruption. Usually, a "talking stick" (or eagle feather or some other symbolic tool) is held by whoever is speaking to signal that she or he has the right to talk at that moment, and others have the responsibility to listen.

In North America over the past three decades, there has been significant movement away from the courts of law in favor of outside negotiation and mediation to resolve a wide variety of disputes. Many jurists see this as a means to clear overloaded court dockets so as to concentrate on more important cases.

Today, leaders in the field of dispute resolution are finding effective ways to bring about balanced solutions to conflict. An example of this is discussed in the Anthropology Applied feature.

Anthropology Applied

Dispute Resolution and the Anthropologist

William Ury

In an era when the consequences of settling disputes with violence are more far-reaching than ever, conflict management is of growing importance. A world leader in this area is anthropologist William L. Ury, an independent negotiations specialist.

In his first year at graduate school, Ury began looking for ways to apply anthropology to practical problems, including conflicts of all dimensions. He wrote a paper about the role of anthropology in peacemaking and on a whim sent it to Roger Fisher, a law professor noted for his work in negotiation and world affairs. Fisher, in turn, invited the young graduate student to co-author a kind of how-to book for international mediators. The book they researched and wrote together turned out to have a far wider audience, for it presented basic principles of negotiation that could be applied to household spats, management–employee conflicts, or international crises. Titled *Getting to*

Yes: Negotiating Agreement Without Giving In (1981), it sold millions of copies, was translated into twenty-one languages, and earned the nickname "the negotiator's bible."

While working on *Getting to Yes,* Ury and Fisher co-founded the Program on Negotiation (PON) at Harvard Law School, pulling together an interdisciplinary group of academics interested in new approaches to and applications of the negotiation process. Today this applied research center is a multiuniversity consortium that trains mediators, businesspeople, and government officials in negotiation skills. It has four key goals: (1) design, implement, and evaluate better dispute resolution practices; (2) promote collaboration among practitioners and scholars; (3) develop education programs and materials for instruction in negotiation and dispute resolution; (4) increase public awareness and understanding of successful conflict resolution efforts.

In 1982, Ury earned his doctorate in anthropology from Harvard with a dissertation titled "Talk Out or Walk Out: The Role and Control of Conflict in a Kentucky Coal Mine." Afterward, he taught for several years while maintaining a leadership role at PON. In particular, he devoted himself to PON's Global Negotiation Project (initially known as the Project on Avoiding War). Today, having left his teaching post at Harvard, Ury continues to serve as director of the Global Negotiation Project, writing, consulting, and running regular workshops on dealing with difficult people and situations.

Utilizing a cross-cultural perspective sharpened through years of anthropological research, he specializes in ethnic and secessionist disputes, including those between white and black South Africans, Serbs and Croats, Turks and Kurds, Catholics and Protestants in Northern Ireland, and Russians and Chechens in the former Soviet Union.

[continued]

---

[8]Criminal Code of Canada, §718.2(e).

[continued]

Among the most effective tools in Ury's applied anthropology work are his books on dispute resolution. His 1999 book, *Getting to Peace: Transforming Conflict at Home, at Work, and in the World,* examines what he calls the "third side," which is the role that the surrounding community can play in preventing, resolving, and containing destructive conflict between two parties.[a]

His 2002 edited volume *Must We Fight?* challenges entrenched ideas that violence and war are inevitable and presents convincing evidence that human beings have as much inherent potential for cooperation and co-existence as they do for violent conflict. The key point in this book is that violence is a choice. In Ury's words, "Conflict is not going to end, but violence can."[b]

What Ury and others in this field are doing is helping create a culture of negotiation in a world where adversarial, win–lose attitudes are out of step with the increasingly interdependent relations between people.

[a]Pease, T. (2000). Taking the third side. *Andover Bulletin* (Spring).

[b]Ury, W. (2002). A global immune system. *Andover Bulletin* (Winter); see also www.PON.harvard.edu and www.thirdside.org.

VIOLENT CONFLICT AND WARFARE

Although the regulation of a society's internal affairs is an important function of any political system, it is by no means the sole function. Another is the management of external affairs—relations not just among different states but among different bands, lineages, clans, or whatever the largest autonomous political unit may be. And just as the threatened or actual use of force may be used to maintain order within a society, it also may be used in the conduct of external affairs.

Humans have a horrific track record when it comes to violence. Far more lethal than spontaneous and individual outbursts of aggression, organized violence in the form of war is responsible for enormous suffering and deliberate destruction of life and property.

Generally, we may distinguish among different motives, objectives, methods, and scales of warfare as organized violence. For instance, some societies engage in defensive wars only and avoid armed confrontations with others unless seriously threatened or actually attacked. Others initiate aggressive wars to pursue particular strategic objectives, including material benefits in the form of precious resources such as slaves, gold, or oil, as well as territorial expansion or control over trade routes. In some cultures, aggressive wars are waged for ideological reasons, such as spreading one's own worldview or religion and defeating "evil" ideas or heresies elsewhere.

The scope of violent conflict is wide, ranging from individual fights, local feuds, and raids to formally declared international wars fought by professional armed forces. In addition, we may distinguish among various civil wars (in which armies from different geographic sections, ethnic or religious groups, or political parties within the same state are pitted against each other) and low-intensity guerrilla warfare involving small-scale hit-and-run tactical operations instead of pitched battles.

Why War?

Why do wars occur? Some argue that males of the human species are naturally aggressive. However, as discussed in earlier chapters, warfare among humans, as well as aggressive group behavior among apes, may be situation specific rather than an unavoidable expression of biological predisposition (see this chapter's Biocultural Connection).

This is not to say that violence was unknown among ancient humans. Archaeological evidence, including the occasional discovery of stone spear points embedded in human skeletons, prove otherwise. In fact, armed conflicts in the form of deadly feuds and raids have long existed in stateless societies such as foraging bands, horticultural villagers, or nomadic herders.

Nevertheless, it is clear that war is not a universal phenomenon, for in various parts of the world there are societies that do not practice warfare as we know it. Examples include people as diverse as the Ju/'hoansi Bushmen and Pygmy peoples of southern and central Africa, the Arapesh of New Guinea, and the Jain of India, as well as the Amish of North America. Among societies that do practice warfare, levels of violence may differ dramatically.

We have ample reason to suppose that wars—not to be confused with more limited forms of deadly violence such as raids—have become a problem only in the last 10,000 years, since the invention of food-production techniques and especially since the formation of centralized states 5,000 years ago. Warfare has reached crisis proportions in the past 200 years, with the invention of modern weaponry and increased direction of violence against civilian populations.

Beginning in 1917 with military use of mustard gas—a chemical poison that causes blindness, large blisters on exposed skin, and (if inhaled) bleeding and blistering in mouth, throat, and lungs—the development of "weapons of mass destruction" has been lethally effective. Today, the chemical, biological, and atomic weapons arsenals stockpiled by many states are

Biocultural Connection

Gender, Sex, and Human Violence

At the start of the 21st century, war and violence are no longer the strictly male domains that they were in many societies in the past. War has become embedded in non-combatant life in many parts of the world and affects the daily lives of elderly people, women, and children. Moreover, women now serve in the military forces of numerous states, although their participation in actual battlefield operations remains limited. Some female soldiers in the United States argue that gender should not limit their participation in combat as they consider themselves as strong, capable, and well trained as their male counterparts. Others believe that biologically based sex differences make war a particularly male domain.

Scientists have long argued that males are biologically more suited to combat because natural selection has made them on average larger and more muscular than females. This idea, known as sexual selection, was first put forth by Charles Darwin in the 19th century. This British naturalist proposed that the physical specializations of males in animal species—such as horns, vibrant plumage, and, in the case of humans, intelligence and tool use—demonstrate selection acting upon males to aid in the competition for mates. In these scenarios, male reproductive success is thought to be optimized through a strategy of "spreading seed"—in other words, by being sexually active with as many females as possible.

Females, on the other hand, are considered "gatekeepers," who optimize their reproductive success through caring for individual offspring. According to Darwin's theory of sexual selection, in species where male–male competition is high, males will be considerably larger than females, and aggression will serve males well. In monogamous species, males and females will be of similar sizes.

British primatologist Richard Wrangham, a biological anthropologist at Harvard University, has taken the idea of sexual selection even further. In his book *Demonic Males,* he explores the idea that both male aggression and patriarchy have an evolutionary basis. He states that humans, like our close cousins the chimpanzees, are "party gang" species characterized by strong bonds among groups of males who have dominion over an expandable territory. These features "suffice to account for natural selection's ugly legacy, the tendency to look for killing opportunities when hostile neighbors meet."[a] Violence in turn generates a male-dominated social order: "Patriarchy comes from biology in the sense that it emerges from men's temperaments out of their evolutionarily derived efforts to control women and at the same time have solidarity with fellow males in competition against outsiders."[b]

Some feminist scholars have pointed out that such scientific models are "gendered" in that they incorporate the gender norms derived from the scientists' culture. Darwin's original model of sexual selection incorporated the Victorian gender norms of the passive female and active male. Wrangham's more recent *Demonic Males* theory appears to be similarly shaped by the author's culture. It incorporates the dominant world order (military states) and the gender norms (aggressive males) it values. In both cases, scientific theory has provided a nature-based argument for a series of culture-based social customs.

This does not mean that biological differences between the sexes cannot be studied in the natural world. Instead, scientists studying sex differences must be especially aware of how they may project cultural beliefs onto nature. Meanwhile, the attitudes of women soldiers continue to challenge generalizations regarding "military specialization" by gender.

[a]Wrangham, R., & Peterson, D. (1996). *Demonic males* (p. 168). Boston: Houghton Mifflin.

[b]Wrangham & Peterson, p. 125.

---

probably sufficient to wipe out all life on the planet, many times over.

Not surprisingly, given this development in the technology of death, casualties not just of civilians but also of *children* far outnumber those of soldiers. Indeed, because dangerous poisons, such as the anthrax bacterium or the nerve gas Sarin, are easy to produce and cheap, non-state groups, including terrorists, also seek to gain access to these modern weapons of mass destruction, if only to threaten to use them against more powerful opponents. Thus, war is not so much an age-old problem as it is a relatively recent one.

Among food foragers, with their uncentralized political systems, violence may erupt sporadically, but warfare was all but unknown until recent times. Since territorial boundaries and membership among food-foraging bands are usually fluid and loosely defined, a man who hunts with one band today may hunt with a neighboring band next month. This renders warfare impractical. So, too, does the systematic exchange of marriage partners among food-foraging groups, which makes it likely that someone in each band will have a sibling, parent, or cousin in a neighboring band. Moreover, the absence of a food surplus among foragers makes prolonged combat difficult. In sum, where populations are small, food surpluses are absent, property ownership is minimal, and no state organization exists, the likelihood of organized violence by one group against another is small.[9]

---

[9]Knauft, B. M. (1991). Violence and sociality in human evolution. *Current Anthropology, 32,* 391–409.

Despite the traditional view of the gardener or farmer as a peaceful tiller of the soil, it is among such people, along with pastoralists, that warfare becomes prominent. One reason may be that food-producing peoples have a far greater tendency to grow in population than do food foragers, whose numbers are generally maintained well below **carrying capacity** (the number of people that the available resources can support at a given level of food-getting techniques). This population growth, if unchecked, can lead to resource depletion—a problem commonly solved by seizing the resources of others.

In addition, the commitment to a fixed piece of land inherent in farming makes such societies somewhat less fluid in their membership than those of food foragers. Instead of marrying distantly, farmers marry locally, depriving them of long-distance kin networks. In rigidly matrilocal or patrilocal societies, each new generation is bound to the same territory, no matter how small it may be or how large the group trying to live within it.

The availability of unoccupied lands may not be sufficient to discourage the outbreak of war. Among swidden farmers, for example, competition for land cleared of old growth forest frequently leads to hostility and armed conflict. The centralization of political control and the possession of valuable property among farming people provide many more stimuli for warfare.

It is among such peoples, especially those organized into states, where the violence of warfare is most apt to result in indiscriminate mass killing. This development has reached its peak in modern states. Indeed, much (but not all) of the warfare that has been observed in recent stateless societies (so-called tribal warfare) has been induced by states as a reaction to colonial expansion.[10]

Although competition for scarce resources may turn violent and lead to war, the motivations and justifications for war are often embedded in a society's worldview—the collective body of ideas that members of a culture generally share concerning the ultimate shape and substance of their reality. There are many examples of this, ranging from the Crusades (a series of "Wars of the Cross" by European Christian armies between 700 and 900 years ago to push the Muslims out of Palestine, a territory they viewed as holy) to Aztec Indian warfare in Mexico (conducted some 500 years ago in part to capture people for sacrifice to Aztec gods).

Wars Today

Currently, there are several dozen wars going on in the world, often resulting in massive killing fields. And many contemporary wars are not between states but rather within countries where the government is either corrupt, ineffective, or without popular support. Notably, many armies around the world recruit not only men, but also women and children. Today, more than 250,000 child soldiers, many as young as 12 years old, are participating in armed conflicts around the world.[11]

The following examples offer some specific data. In the 1990s, between 2 and 3 million died due to warfare in southern Sudan. Another 5 million died in the recent war in Congo (1998–2003), which involved armies from a handful of neighboring states as well. Moreover, the Middle East is in political turmoil, especially since the U.S.-led invasion of Afghanistan and Iraq's oil-rich dictatorship in 2003. In addition to the many tens of thousands of fatalities, the vast majority of whom are noncombatant civilians, there is also massive destruction of the countries' infrastructure.

Beyond these wars there are numerous so-called low-intensity wars involving guerrilla organizations, rebel armies, resistance movements, terrorist cells, and a host of other armed groups engaged in violent conflict with official state-controlled armed forces. Every year, confrontations result in hundreds of hot spots and violent flashpoints, most of which are never reported in Western news media.[12]

As the above examples show, the causes of warfare are complex, involving economic, political, and ideological factors. The challenge of eliminating human warfare has never been greater—nor has the cost of *not* finding a way to do so.

In the age of globalization, a new category—crimes against humanity—has been adopted by most countries in order to punish those responsible for mass murder; these crimes may be prosecuted in an international court of justice.

---

carrying capacity The number of people that the available resources can support at a given level of food-getting techniques

acculturation Massive culture change that occurs in a society when it experiences intensive firsthand contact with a more powerful society

ethnocide The violent eradication of an ethnic group's collective cultural identity as a distinctive people; occurs when a dominant society deliberately sets out to destroy another society's cultural heritage

---

[10]Whitehead, N. L., & Ferguson, R. B. (1993, November). Deceptive stereotypes about tribal warfare. *Chronicle of Higher Education*, A48.

[11]"Study estimates 250,000 active child soldiers." (2006, July 26). Associated Press.

[12]icasualties.org.

DOMINATION AND REPRESSION

So far, we have discussed how societies have grown in size, from bands to states, and how political power has grown from noncoercive leadership in small kin-groups to dictatorial regimes governing millions of subjects with little or no rights of self-determination. Today, only a quarter of all internationally recognized countries are inhabited by just one ethnic group or nationality. All others are occupied by more than one ethnic group, some even by multiple formerly independent nations whose territories have been joined, either by peaceful political means or as a result of military conquest and annexation.

As noted earlier in this chapter, smaller or less powerful nations, as well as ethnic minorities, are often dominated by those who control the state and its armed forces. In such unequal power-sharing arrangements, ethnic or national minorities are often subjected to governmental political rules and practices they find discriminatory or even repressive. And although the heyday of colonialism is now behind us, powerful groups still expand and strengthen their control over societies and their territories far and near, primarily for coercive and exploitative purposes.

Acculturation

Acculturation is the massive culture change that occurs in a society when it experiences intensive firsthand contact with a more powerful society. It always involves an element of force, either directly, as in conquests, or indirectly, as in the implicit or explicit threat that force will be used if people refuse to make the demanded changes. Other variables include degree of cultural difference; circumstances, intensity, frequency, and hostility of contact; relative status of the agents of contact; who is dominant and who is submissive; and whether the nature of the flow is reciprocal or nonreciprocal.

In the course of cultural contact, any number of things may happen. Merger or fusion occurs when two cultures lose their separate identities and form a single culture, as historically expressed by the "melting pot" ideology in the United States. Sometimes, though, one of the cultures loses its autonomy but retains its identity as a subculture in the form of a caste, class, or ethnic group. This is typical of conquest or slavery situations, and the United States has examples of this in spite of its melting pot ideology—we need look no further than the nearest American Indian reservation.

The most extreme cases of forced culture change, or acculturation, occur as a result of military conquest or massive invasion and breaking up of traditional political structures by dominant newcomers who know or care nothing about the culture they control. The indigenous people—unable to effectively resist imposed changes and obstructed in carrying out many of their own social, religious, and economic activities—may be forced into new practices that tend to isolate individuals and destroy the integrity of their societies.

Ethnocide

A more vicious and radical form of acculturation is **ethnocide**—the violent eradication of an ethnic group's collective cultural identity as a distinctive people—occurs when a state or more dominant nation deliberately sets out to destroy another society's cultural heritage in order to erase its collective identity as a distinct people. This may take place when a powerful nation aggressively expands its territorial control by annexing neighboring peoples and their territories, incorporating the conquered groups as subjects.

A policy of ethnocide typically includes forbidding a subjugated nation's ancestral language, criminalizing their traditional customs, destroying their religion and demolishing sacred places and practices, breaking up their social organizations, and dispossessing or removing the survivors from their homelands. In essence, ethnocide includes everything short of physical extermination to remove all traces of a unique culture.

Among the many tragic examples of ethnocide is the experience of the Tibetan people in the Himalayan Mountains of Central Asia who could not defend themselves against an invasion by the Chinese communist army in 1950. The Chinese government then initiated ethnocidal policies by means of systematic attacks against traditional Tibetan culture. Seeking to stamp out deeply rooted religious beliefs and practices, it ordered the demolition of most Buddhist temples and monasteries. Following a mass uprising, hundreds of thousands of Tibetans were killed or forced into exile abroad.

Seeking to annihilate Tibetan identity, China sought to turn the surviving Tibetans into political subjects who would culturally identify themselves as

When China took the opportunity to host the 2008 Olympic Games, the world's biggest and most prestigious sporting event, it expected to showcase its status as an emerging global superpower. While impressing many with its festival flare and spectacular event settings, the Chinese also had to contend with negative publicity as political opponents of the communist state staged protest rallies throughout the world. Here we see Buddhist monks and other refugees exiled from Chinese-occupied Tibet protesting outside the United Nations office in Katmandu, the capital city of Tibet's neighboring country, Nepal. They demanded a UN investigation of a recent Chinese crackdown in Tibet. While many were arrested by Nepalese police, this political demonstration successfully attracted global media attention.

genocide The physical extermination of one people by another, either as a deliberate act or as the accidental outcome of activities carried out by one people with little regard for their impact on others

tradition Customary ideas and practices passed on from generation to generation, which in a modernizing society may form an obstacle to new ways of doing things

syncretism In acculturation, the creative blending of indigenous and foreign beliefs and practices into new cultural forms

rebellion Organized armed resistance to an established government or authority in power

revolution Radical change in a society or culture. In the political arena, it involves the forced overthrow of an old government and establishment of a completely new one

Chinese nationals.[13] Today, more than 130,000 Tibetans live in exile, primarily in India and Nepal. The flow of Tibetans escaping Chinese oppression continues to this day, with around 3,000 people fleeing their homes each year. They take great risks to do so—most crossing by foot over the dangerous Himalayas.

Genocide

Prior to European invasions of the Amazon rainforest, more than 700 distinct ethnic groups inhabited this vast tropical region in South America. Their combined total

---

[13]Turner, T. (1991). Major shift in Brazilian Yanomami policy. *Anthropology Newsletter, 32*(5), 1, 46.

population may have been as high as 5 million. However, after more than four centuries of colonial and capitalist pressures, the number of indigenous groups was down to about 270, and their collective total population had dwindled to some 200,000 people.[14]

This dramatic decline did not happen by itself, and it raises the troubling issue of **genocide**—the physical extermination of one people by another, either as a deliberate act or as the accidental outcome of activities carried out by one people with little regard for their impact on others. Genocide, like ethnocide, is not new in the world. In North America in 1637, for example, a deliberate attempt was made to destroy the Pequot Indians by setting fire to their village at Mystic, Connecticut, and then shooting down all those—primarily unarmed elderly people, women, and children—who sought to escape the fire. To ensure that even their very memory would be stamped out, colonial authorities forbade the mention of the Pequot name. Numerous other massacres of Indian peoples occurred thereafter, up until the last one at Wounded Knee, South Dakota, in 1890.

Of course, such acts were by no means restricted to the Americas. Among many now almost forgotten 19th-century acts of genocide is the extermination of the indigenous inhabitants of Tasmania, the large island just south of Australia.

The most widely known act of genocide in recent history was the attempt of the Nazis during World War II to wipe out European Jews and Gypsies (especially Roma and Sinti). Together with almost 5 million other individuals whom the Nazis deemed "abnormal" and "sub-human" (homosexuals, mentally ill, disabled, political and religious dissidents), these ethnic groups were targeted for extermination. About 500,000 Gypsies and 6 million Jews were all murdered in the name of "improving" the human species.

In addition to this much documented holocaust, there are many other recent mass murders. For example, in 1994 more than half a million Tutsi people were slaughtered by their Hutu neighbors in the African country of Rwanda,[15] and today a genocidal campaign is being waged against the non-Arab black peoples in the Darfur desert region of western Sudan. Estimates vary, but during the 20th century, as many as 83 million people died of genocide and tyranny.[16]

---

[14]http://www.savetibet.org/tibet/us/proceedings/ senatefrmauramoynihan.php. See also Avedon, J. F. (1997). *In exile from the land of snows: The definitive account of the Dalai Lama and Tibet since the Chinese conquest.* New York: Harper.

[15]www.hrw.org/reports/1999/rwanda.

[16]White, M. (2001). *Historical atlas of the twentieth century.* http:// users.erols.com/mwhite28/20centry.htm; see also Van den Berghe.

RESISTANCE TO DOMINATION AND REPRESSION

The reactions of indigenous peoples to the radical upheaval brought about by foreign aggressors invading their ancestral homelands have varied considerably. Some have responded by moving to the nearest available forest, desert, or other remote place in hopes of being left alone. In Brazil, a number of communities once located near the coast took this option a few hundred years ago and were successful until the great push to invade, exploit, and destroy the Amazon tropical wilderness began in the 1960s. Others, like many Indians of North America, took up arms to fight back but were ultimately forced to sign treaties and surrender much of their territory, after which they were reduced to an impoverished underclass in their own land. Today, they continue to fight through nonviolent means to retain their identities as distinct peoples and to regain control over natural resources on their lands.

In addition, ethnic groups may try to retain their distinctive identities by maintaining cultural boundaries such as holding on to traditional language, festive ceremonies, customary dress, ritual songs and dances, unique food, and so on. Indeed, in opposing modernization, people often seek cultural protection and emotional comfort from **tradition**—customary ideas and practices passed on from generation to generation, which in a modernizing society may form an obstacle to new ways of doing things. When people are able to hold on to some of their traditions in the face of powerful outside domination, the result may be **syncretism**—the creative blending of indigenous and foreign beliefs and practices into new cultural forms.

Violent Resistance: Rebellion and Revolution

When the scale of collective discontent and frustrated anger within a society reaches a critical level, the possibilities are high for **rebellion**—organized armed resistance to an established government or regime in power. For instance, there have been many peasant rebellions around the world in the course of history. Often, such rebellions are triggered by repressive regimes imposing new taxes on the already struggling small farmers unable to feed their families under such unacceptable levels of exploitation.

In contrast to rebellions, which have rather limited objectives, a **revolution**—a radical change in a society or culture—involves a more extreme transformation. Revolutions occur when the level of collective frustration, coupled with a lack of political representation, in a society is very high. In the political arena, revolution involves the forced overthrow of an old government and the establishment of a completely new one.

The question of why revolutions erupt, as well as why they frequently fail to live up to the expectations of the people initiating them, is unsolved. It is clear, however, that the colonial policies of countries such as Britain, France, Spain, Portugal, and the United States during the 19th and early 20th centuries have created a worldwide situation in which revolution is nearly inevitable.

Despite the political independence most colonies have gained since World War II, powerful countries continue to exploit many of these "underdeveloped" countries for their natural resources and cheap labor, causing a deep resentment of rulers beholden to foreign powers. Further discontent has been caused as governing elites in newly independent states try to assert their control over peoples living within their boundaries. By virtue of a common ancestry, possession of distinct cultures, persistent occupation of their own territories, and traditions of self-determination, the peoples they aim to control identify themselves as distinct nations and refuse to recognize the legitimacy of what they regard as a foreign government.

Thus, in many a former colony, large numbers of people have taken up arms to resist annexation and absorption by imposed state governments run by people of other nationalities. As they attempt to make their multi-ethnic states into unified countries, ruling elites of one nationality set about stripping the peoples of other nations within their states of their lands, resources, and particular cultural identities.

One of the most important facts of our time is that the vast majority of the distinct peoples of the world have never consented to rule by the governments of states within which they find themselves living.[17] In many newly emerging countries, such peoples feel they have no other option than to fight.

Of the hundreds of armed conflicts in the world today, almost all are in the economically poor countries of Africa, Asia, and Central and South America, many of

which were at one time under European colonial domination (Figure 14.3). Of these wars, the majority are between the state and one or more nations or ethnic groups within the state's borders who are seeking to maintain or regain control of their personal lives, communities, lands, and resources in the face of what they regard as repression or subjugation by a foreign power.[18]

Nonviolent Resistance: Revitalization Movements

Not all suppressed, conquered, or colonized people eventually rise up against established authority, although why they do not is debatable. When they do, however, their political resistance may be nonviolent, such as, for instance, **civil disobedience**—refusal to obey civil laws in an effort to induce change in governmental policy or legislation, characterized by the use of passive resistance or other nonviolent means. Other nonviolent forms of resistance go far beyond politics.

Such is the case with **revitalization movements**, which are efforts for radical culture reform in response to widespread social disruption and collective feelings of repression, anxiety, and despair. When primary ties of culture, social relationships, and activities are broken and meaningless activity is imposed by outside forces, individuals and groups characteristically react by rejecting newly introduced cultural elements, reclaiming historical roots and traditional identity, and sometimes mustering spiritual imagination.

In the United States, revitalization movements have occurred often—whenever significant segments of the population have found their conditions in life to be at odds with the values of the American Dream. For example, the 1960s saw the emergence of revitalization movements among young people of middle-class and even upper-class families. In their case, the professed cultural values of peace, equality, and individual freedom were seen to be at odds with the realities of persistent war, poverty, and constraints on individual action imposed by a variety of impersonal institutions. Youths countered these realities by advocating free love, joining hippie communes, celebrating new forms of rock and folk music, using mind-altering drugs, challenging authority, growing their hair long, and wearing unconventional clothes.

Today, there are a variety of revitalization movements in many parts of the world. These often arise where powerful forces of globalization have destabilized and culturally disrupted traditional societies without providing achievable alternatives for improving living standards for the majority of the populations so affected.

---

civil disobedience Refusal to obey civil laws in an effort to induce change in governmental policy or legislation, characterized by the use of passive resistance or other nonviolent means
revitalization movements Movements for radical cultural reform in response to widespread social disruption and collective feelings of great stress and despair

---

[17]Nietschmann, B. (1987). The third world war. *Cultural Survival Quarterly*, 11(3), 3.

[18]Nietschmann, p. 7.

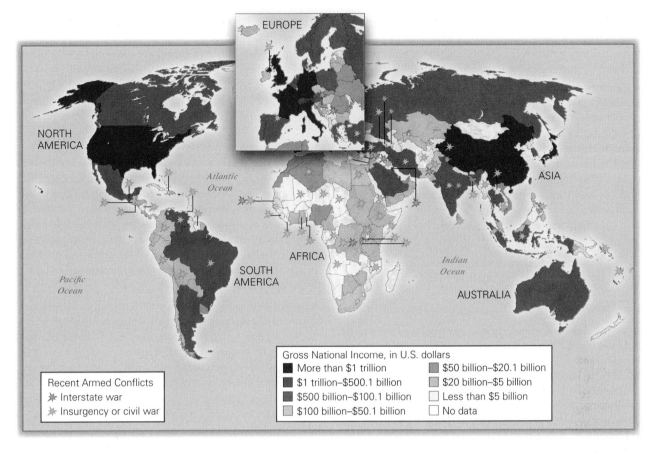

Figure 14.3

Today, the majority of armed conflicts are in the economically poor countries of Africa, Asia, and Central and South America, many of which were at one time under European colonial domination. Most are between the state and one or more nations or ethnic groups within the state's borders who are seeking to maintain or regain control over their lives, lands, and resources.

Chapter Summary

■ Through political organization, societies impose and maintain social order, manage public affairs, and reduce social disorder. No group can function without persuading or coercing its members to conform to agreed-upon rules of conduct.

■ Four basic types of political systems may be identified, ranging from uncentralized bands and tribes to centralized chiefdoms and states. The band is a relatively small and loosely organized kin-ordered group that inhabits a specific territory and that may split into smaller extended family groups that are politically independent. Political organization in bands is democratic, and informal control is exerted by public opinion in the form of gossip and ridicule. Band leaders are usually older men whose personal authority lasts only as long as members approve of their leadership.

■ In anthropology, tribe refers to a range of kin-ordered groups that are politically integrated by some unifying factor and whose members share a common ancestry, identity, culture, language, and territory. With an economy usually based

on crop cultivation or herding, the tribe's population is larger than that of the band, although family units within the tribe are still relatively autonomous and egalitarian. As in the band, political organization is transitory, and leaders have no coercive means of maintaining authority.

■ One type of authority in tribes is the Big Man, who builds up his wealth and political power until he must be reckoned with as a leader. In many tribal societies the organizing political unit is the clan, comprised of people who consider themselves descended from a common ancestor. A group of elders or headmen or headwomen regulate the affairs of members and represent their group in relations with other clans.

■ As societies include larger numbers of people and become more heterogeneous socially, politically, and economically, leadership becomes more centralized. A chiefdom is a regional polity in which two or more local kin-ordered groups are organized under a chief who heads a ranked hierarchy of people. An individual's status is determined by his or her position in a descent group and distance of relationship to the chief, whose role is to unite his community in all matters. The chief may accumulate great personal wealth, which enhances his power base and which he may pass on to his heirs.

■ The most centralized of political organizations is the state—a complex political institution involving large numbers of people within a defined territory. Its members are organized and directed by a formal government that has the capacity and authority to make laws and use force to maintain the social order. The state is found in diverse, stratified societies, with unequal distribution of wealth and power. States are inherently unstable and transitory and differ from nations, which are communities of people who share a collective identity based on a common culture, language, territorial base, and history.

■ Legitimacy, or the right of political leaders to hold, use, and allocate power, is required to govern with authority. Legitimate government may be distinguished from rule based on intimidation or force. To a greater or lesser extent, most governments use ideology, including religion, to legitimize political power.

■ Historical and contemporary evidence from across the world indicates that far fewer women than men have held important positions of political leadership. Nonetheless, in a number of societies, women have enjoyed political equality with men, as among the Iroquoian peoples in northeastern North America. Lower visibility in politics does not necessarily indicate that women lack power in political affairs. Today, a growing number of women have been elected as president, chancellor, or prime minister.

■ Two kinds of control exist: internalized and externalized. Internalized controls are cultural in nature, self-imposed by enculturated individuals who share beliefs and values about what is proper and what is not. Externalized controls known as sanctions mix cultural and social control (involving actions taken by others). Positive sanctions are rewards or recognition by others, whereas negative sanctions include threat of imprisonment, fines, corporal punishment, or loss of face. Sanctions are either formal, including actual laws, or informal, involving norms. Sanctions serve to assure conformity to group norms, including actual law, and to maintain the place of each social faction in a community.

■ Law, formal negative sanctions, defines relationships, prescribes and prohibits behavior among a society's members, and allocates authority to enforce sanctions. In centralized political systems, this authority rests with the government and court system, whereas uncentralized societies give this authority directly to the injured party.

■ In contrast to bands, tribes, and chiefdoms, state societies distinguish between crimes (offenses against the state) and offenses against an individual. A dispute may be settled in two ways: negotiation or adjudication. All societies use negotiation to settle individual disputes. In negotiation the parties to the dispute reach an agreement themselves, with or without the help of a third party. In adjudication, an authorized third party issues a binding decision.

■ Political systems also attempt to regulate external affairs, or relations between politically autonomous units. In doing

so they may resort to the threat or use of force. The scope of violent conflict is wide, ranging from individual fights, local feuds, and raids to formally declared international wars fought by professional armed forces. Some societies engage in defensive wars only and avoid armed confrontations with others unless seriously threatened or actually attacked. Others initiate aggressive wars to pursue material or ideological objectives. War is not a universal phenomenon.

■ Acculturation, the massive culture change that occurs in a society when it experiences intensive firsthand contact with a more powerful society, always involves an element of force. Ethnocide, the violent eradication of an ethnic group's collective identity as a distinctive people, occurs when a dominant society sets out to destroy another society's cultural heritage. Genocide is the physical extermination of one people by another, either as a deliberate act or as the accidental outcome of activities carried out by one people with little regard for the impact on others.

■ Reactions of indigenous peoples to imposed changes vary considerably. Some have retreated to inaccessible places in hopes of being left alone, while others have lapsed into apathy. Some have reasserted their traditional culture's values by modifying foreign practices to conform to indigenous values, a phenomenon known as syncretism.

■ When frustration and anger born of suppression and oppression reach a certain level within a society, the possibilities are high for rebellion—organized armed resistance to an established government or authority in power. And if the level of dissatisfaction rises even higher, it may lead to revolution—a radical change in a society or culture. In the political arena, revolution refers to the forced overthrow of an old government and the establishment of a new one.

■ Suppression and repression may spawn nonviolent civil disobedience and revitalization movements—collective efforts for radical cultural reform. Some revitalization movements try to speed up the acculturation process to get more of the benefits expected from the dominant culture. Others try to reconstitute a bygone but still remembered way of life. In other cases, a repressed group may try to introduce a new social order based on its ideology.

Questions for Reflection

1. Given the basic definition of politics presented in the beginning of this chapter, why do you think that power in egalitarian societies plays a relatively insignificant role?

2. In many states, political power is concentrated in the hands of a wealthy elite—the so-called have-lots. Imagine you belong to a group that is losing its traditional freedom or quality of life due to government policies but feel that your political representatives are unwilling or unable to defend your interests. How would you challenge the state authorities?

3. The 1992 book *Men Are from Mars, Women Are from Venus* became a bestseller in North America. Symbolically linking men to the ancient warrior god Mars, who was worshiped by Roman soldiers, this male stereotype suggests they are

natural-born killers. Considering that many states with powerful armies are headed by women as queens or presidents and that women now serve as soldiers and military officers, do you think women are inherently more peaceful and less likely to fight than men?

4. When your own government declares war against another country, on which basis does it seek to justify its decision to send soldiers into battle? Do you know the death ratio of noncombatants to soldiers in your country's most recent wars?

5. Powerful forces of globalization are disrupting the traditional way of life in many societies all across the world. Not capable of controlling the sweeping forces of rapid change, many fear a complete unraveling of their clutures. In reaction, they may seek to turn back the clock and rebuild cultural traditions as they remember them. Do you know of any reactionary, conservative, or revitalization movements in your own environment? What do you think motivates people who are active in such movements? Under which circumstances would you join one?

Key Terms

power
political organization
band
tribe
chiefdom
state
nation
pluralistic society
legitimacy
cultural control
social control
sanctions
law

negotiation
mediation
adjudication
carrying capacity
acculturation
ethnocide
genocide
tradition
syncretism
rebellion
revolution
civil disobedience
revitalization movements

Biocultural Connection

Peyote Art: Divine Visions among the Huichol

For generations, Huichol Indians living in Mexico's mountainous western Sierra Madre region have created art remarkable for its vibrant colors. They are especially noted for their spectacular beadwork and embroidery. Although many people appreciate the intricate beauty of Huichol art, most are probably unaware that the colorful designs express a religious worldview tied to the chemical substance of a sacred plant: a small cactus "button" known as peyote (*Lophophora williamsii*).[a]

Among the many Huichol gods and goddesses, all addressed in kinship terms, is Our Grandfather Fire. His principal spirit helper is Our Elder Brother Deer, a messenger between the gods and humans. Serving the Huichol as their spiritual guide, this divine deer is also the peyote cactus itself. Huichol Indians refer to peyote as *yawéi hikuri,* the "divine flesh of Elder Brother Deer." Guided by their shamans on a pilgrimage to harvest peyote, they "hunt" this "deer" in Wirikúta, the sacred desert highlands where their ancestor deities dwell. Having found and "shot" the first cactus button with an arrow, they gather many more, later to be consumed in fresh, dried, or liquid form.

Participating in a holy communion with the creator god, Huichol shamans consume peyote (the divine flesh) as a sacrament. Doing so, they enter into an ecstatic trance. With the help of peyote, their spiritual guide, they become hawks or eagles soaring high in the sky. Having visions extending far across the world, they interact directly with their gods and seek advice on behalf of those who need help in dealing with illness and other misfortunes.

From a purely chemical point of view, peyote contains a psychotropic substance identified by modern chemists as an alkaloid. By consuming some of this toxic organic substance, the Huichol move into an altered state of consciousness. In this dreamlike psychological state, which is also profoundly emotional, they experience religiously inspired, brilliantly colored visions from their spirit world.

These are reflected in Huichol art, such as the piece pictured here in which a stylized peyote button and deer have been rendered in rainbow-hued beading. The sacred cactus with its starlike shape is the most prominent symbolic design in Huichol art. Beaded

© Benjamin Chodroff

onto fabric and objects of all kinds or embroidered on clothing, shoulder bags, and so forth, it can be found in almost all of their artwork—much of it now produced for sale abroad.

[a]Schaeffer, S. B., & Furst, P. T. (Eds.). (1996). *People of the peyote: Huichol Indian history, religion, and survival.* Albuquerque: University of New Mexico Press.

---

as a "father" who had a divine "son" but do not entertain thoughts of God as a "mother" nor of a divine "daughter." Such male-privileging religions developed in traditional societies with economies based upon the

animism A belief that nature is enlivened or energized by distinct personalized spirit beings separable from bodies
animatism A belief that nature is enlivened or energized by an impersonal spiritual force or supernatural energy, which may make itself manifest in any special place, thing, or living creature

herding of animals or intensive agriculture carried out or controlled by men, who are dominating figures to their children.

Goddesses, by contrast, are likely to be most prominent in societies where women play a significant role in the economy, where women enjoy relative equality with men, and where men are less controlling figures to their wives and children. Such societies are most often those that depend upon crop cultivation carried out solely or mostly by women.

Ancestral Spirits

A belief in ancestral spirits is consistent with the widespread notion that human beings are made up of two closely intertwined parts: a physical body and some mental component or spiritual self. For example, traditional belief of the Penobscot Indians in Maine holds that each person has a vital spirit capable of traveling apart from the body. Given such a concept, the idea of the spirit being freed from the body in trance and dreams or by death, and having an existence thereafter, seems quite reasonable. Frequently, where a belief in ancestral spirits exists, these beings are seen as retaining an active interest and even membership in society.

Belief in ancestral spirits of one sort or another is found in many parts of the world, especially among people having unilineal descent systems with their associated ancestor orientation. In several such African societies, the concept is highly elaborate. Here one frequently finds ancestral spirits behaving just like humans. They are able to feel hot, cold, and pain, and they may be capable of dying a second death by drowning or burning. They even may participate in family and lineage affairs, and seats will be provided for them, even though the spirits are invisible. If they are annoyed, they may send sickness or death. Eventually, they are reborn as new members of their lineage, and, in societies that hold such beliefs, adults need to observe infants closely to determine just who has been reborn. Such beliefs provide a strong sense of continuity that links the past, present, and future.

Ancestor spirits played an important role in the patrilineal society of traditional China. For the gift of life, a boy was forever indebted to his parents, owing them obedience, deference, and a comfortable old age. Even after their death, he had to provide for them in the spirit world, offering them food, money, and incense on the anniversaries of their births and deaths. In addition, people collectively worshiped all lineage ancestors periodically throughout the year. Giving birth to sons was regarded as an obligation to the ancestors, because boys inherited their father's ancestral duties.

To fulfill his ancestors' needs for descendants (and his own need to be respectable in a culture that demanded satisfying the needs of one's ancestors), a man would go so far as to marry a girl who had been adopted into his family as an infant so she could be raised as a dutiful wife for him, even when this arrangement went against the wishes of both parties. Furthermore, a father readily would force his daughter to marry a man against her will. In fact, a female child raised to be cast out by her natal family might not find acceptance in her husband's family for years. Not until after death, when her vital spirit was carried in a tablet and placed in the shrine of her husband's family, was she an official member of it. As a consequence, once a son was born to her, a woman worked long and hard to establish the strongest possible tie between herself and her son to ensure she would be looked after in life.

Strong beliefs in ancestral spirits are particularly appropriate in a society of descent-based groups with their associated ancestor orientation. But, more than this, as noted above, these beliefs provide a strong sense of continuity that links the past, present, and future.

Animism

One of the most widespread concepts concerning supernatural beings is **animism**, a belief that nature is animated (enlivened or energized) by distinct personalized spirit beings separable from bodies. Spirits such as souls and ghosts are thought to dwell in humans and animals but also in human-made artifacts, plants, stones, mountains, wells, and other natural features. So too the woods may be full of a variety of unattached or free-ranging spirits.

The various spirits involved are a highly diverse lot. Generally speaking, though, they are less remote than gods and goddesses and are more involved in people's daily affairs. They may be benevolent, malevolent, or just plain neutral. They also may be awesome, terrifying, lovable, or mischievous. Since they may be pleased or irritated by human actions, people are obliged to be concerned about them.

Animism is typical of those who see themselves as being a part of nature rather than superior to it. This includes most food foragers, as well as those food-producing peoples who acknowledge little qualitative difference between a human life and any living entity from turtles to trees, or even rivers and mountains. In such societies, gods and goddesses are relatively unimportant, but the woods are full of spirits. Gods and goddesses, if they exist at all, may be seen as having created the world and perhaps making it fit to live in; but in animism, spirits are the ones to beseech when ill, the ones to help or hinder the shaman, and the ones who the ordinary hunter may meet when off in the woods.

Animatism

Although supernatural power is often thought of as being vested in supernatural beings, it does not have to be. Such is the case with **animatism**—the belief that nature is enlivened or energized by an impersonal spiritual force or supernatural energy, which may make itself manifest in any special place, thing, or living creature. This concept may not be universal, but it is found in cultures on every continent.

The Melanesians, for example, think of *mana* as a force inherent in all objects—not unlike the idea of a cosmic energy passing into and through everything, affecting both living and nonliving matter (similar to "the Force" in the *Star Wars* films). It is not in itself physical, but it can reveal itself physically. A warrior's success in fighting is not attributed to his own strength but to the *mana* contained in an amulet that hangs around his neck. Similarly, a farmer may know a great deal about horticulture, soil conditioning, and the correct time for sowing and harvesting but nevertheless depend upon *mana* for a successful crop, often building a simple altar to this power at one end of the field. If the crop is good, it is a sign that the farmer has in some way appropriated the necessary *mana*. Far from being a personalized spirit power, *mana* is abstract in the extreme, a force or energy lying always just beyond reach of the senses.

This concept of impersonal spirit force or energy was widespread among North American Indians. The Algonquins called it *manitou;* to the Mohawk it was *orenda;* to the Lakota, *wakonda*. In some cultures this energy is turned to for healing purposes. Notably, *animism* (as a belief in distinct spirit beings) and *animatism* (which lacks particular substance or individual form) are not mutually exclusive. They are often found in the same culture, as in Melanesian societies and also in the North American Indian societies just mentioned.

Why do people believe in the existence of supernatural beings or spiritual forces? While there are no easy answers, one explanation is that such metaphysical ideas are kindled and sustained by occurrences perceived as extraordinary and for which people do not have an acceptable realistic interpretation.

Given a belief in animatism and/or the powers of supernatural beings, one is predisposed to see what appear to be results of the application of such powers. For example, if a Melanesian warrior is convinced of his power because he possesses the necessary *mana* and he is successful, he is likely to interpret this success as proof of the efficacy of *mana*: "After all, I would have lost had I not possessed it, wouldn't I?" Beyond this, because of his confidence in his *mana*, he may be willing to take more chances in his fighting, and this indeed could mean the difference between success or failure.

priest or priestess A full-time religious specialist formally recognized for his or her role in guiding the religious practices of others and for contacting and influencing supernatural powers

Failures, of course, do occur, but they can be explained. Perhaps one's prayer was not answered because a deity or spirit was still angry about some past insult. Or perhaps the Melanesian warrior lost his battle because he was not as successful in bringing *mana* to bear or his opponent had more of it. In any case, humans generally emphasize successes over failures, and long after many of the latter have been forgotten, tales will still be told of striking cases of the workings of supernatural powers.

Sacred Places

In addition to revering special supernatural figures such as deities, ancestral spirits, and other special beings, some religious traditions consider certain geographic places to be spiritually significant or even sacred. Typically, such sites are rivers, lakes, waterfalls, islands, forests, caves, and—especially—mountains. Often, their status is due to some unique shape or outstanding feature, such as a conical volcano capped with snow. Numerous mountains around the world fall into this category. Often they are associated with origin myths as splendid abodes of the gods. Or they are revered as dwelling places for the spirits of the dead, heights where prophets received their divine directions, or retreats for prayer, meditation, and vision quests.

Three sacred mountains are shared by the Jewish, Christian, and Muslim traditions: Mount Ararat in the Caucasus Mountain range of northeast Turkey where the ark of the ancient patriarch Noah is said to have landed after the Great Flood; Mount Horeb, the "mountain of God" in the Sinai Desert where the prophet Moses received the stone tablets with the ten sacred rules of behavior from his god; and Mount Zion at the old city of Jerusalem where Solomon, the Israelite king, is believed to have been divinely ordered to build the Great Temple and where the Muslim sacred site Dome of the Rock (the spot where the prophet Muhammad, accompanied by the angel Gabriel, ascended to heaven) is also located.

Symbolic of the supreme being, or associated with various important deities or ancestral spirits, sacred mountains may feature in religious ceremonies or spiritual rituals. In some religious traditions, volcanic mountains are not only sacred but actually deified and worshiped as gods themselves—as is Kaata among Aymara people living in the Bolivian highlands of South America. Some mountains are places of worship, like shrines, or are sacred destinations for spiritual journeys or pilgrimages. For example, every year thousands of Buddhist and Hindu worshipers make a long pilgrimage to the foot of Mount Kailash in Tibet. They do

Pilgrims at Mount Kailash in Tibet. Rising 6,700 meters (about 22,000 feet), this mountain has been held sacred for thousands of years by Hindus, Buddhists, Jains, and followers of Bön (Tibet's indigenous religion). Year after year, pilgrims follow the ancient tradition of circling the mountain on foot. The rugged, 52-kilometer (32-mile) trek, known as *parikarma*, is seen as a holy ritual that removes sins and brings good fortune. The most devout pilgrims make the journey lying down: Prostrating their bodies full-length, they extend their hands forward and make a mark on the ground with their fingers; then they rise, pray, crawl ahead on hands and knees to the mark, and then repeat the process again and again.

not deify this peak, but they believe it to be the sacred abode of Lord Shiva, a member of the supreme divine trinity—so sacred that they would not even dream of trying to climb it.

PERFORMING RELIGION AND SPIRITUALITY

Much of religion's value comes from the activities called for by its prescriptions and rules. Participation in religious ceremonies may bring a sense of personal lift—a wave of reassurance, a feeling of overwhelming joy, and even a sense of moving into a trancelike state—or a feeling of closeness to fellow participants. The beliefs and ceremonial practices of religions vary considerably, as do the individuals who guide others in these.

Religious Specialists

All human societies include individuals who guide and supplement the religious practices of others. Such individuals are seen to be highly skilled at contacting and influencing supernatural beings and manipulating supernatural forces. Often their qualification for this is that they have undergone special training. In addition, they may display certain distinctive personality traits that make them particularly well suited to perform these tasks.

Priests and Priestesses

Within societies with the resources to support a full-time occupational specialist, a **priest or priestess** will have the role of guiding religious practices and influencing the supernatural. He or she is the socially initiated, ceremonially inducted member of a recognized religious organization, with a rank and function that belong to him or her as the holder of a position others have held before. The sources of power are the society and the institution within which the priest or priestess functions.

The priest, if not the priestess, is a familiar figure in Western societies; he is the priest, minister, imam, lama, rabbi, or whatever the official title may be in an organized religion. With their god defined historically in masculine, authoritarian terms, it is not surprising that, in the Judaic, Christian, and Islamic religions, the most important positions traditionally have been filled by men. Female religious specialists are likely to be found only in societies where women are acknowledged to contribute in a major way to the economy and where gods and goddesses are both recognized. In western Europe and North America, for instance, where women are now wage earners in almost every profession and occupy leadership positions in the workforce, they have an increasing presence in the leadership of many Judeo-Christian religious groups.[4]

Shamans

Societies that lack full-time occupational specialization have existed far longer than those with such specialization,

---

[4]Lehman, E. C., Jr. (2002). Women's path into the ministry. *Pulpit & Pew Research Reports, 1*(Fall), 4.

and they have always included individuals with special powers and skills that enable them to connect with and manipulate supernatural beings and forces. These powers have come to them through some personal experience, usually in solitude. In an altered state of consciousness, they receive a vision that empowers them to heal the sick, change the weather, control the movements of animals, and foretell the future. As they perfect these and related skills, they assume the role of shaman.

The word *shaman* originally referred to medical-religious specialists, or spiritual guides, among the Tungus and other Siberian pastoral nomads with animist beliefs. By means of various techniques such as fasting, drumming, chanting, or dancing, as well as hallucinogenic mushrooms, these Siberian shamans enter into a trance, or altered state of consciousness. While in this waking dream state, they experience visions of an alternate reality inhabited by spirit beings such as guardian animal spirits who may assist in the healing.

Cross-cultural research of shamanism shows that similar medical-religious healing practices also exist in traditional cultures outside Siberia. For that reason, the term *shaman* has also been applied to a variety of part-time spiritual leaders and traditional healers ("medicine men") active in North and South American indigenous communities and beyond.

As defined by U.S. anthropologist Michael Harner, famous for his participant observation among Shuar (or Jivaro) Indian shamans in the Amazon rainforest, a **shaman** is "a man or woman who enters an altered state of consciousness—at will—to contact and utilize an ordinarily hidden reality in order to acquire knowledge, power, and to help other persons. The shaman has at least one, and usually more, 'spirits' in his or her personal service."[5]

The term *shaman* has become so popular in recent decades that any non-Western local priest, healer, or diviner is often loosely referred to as one.[6] In addition to so-called new age enthusiasts, among whom shamanism is particularly popular, faith healers and other evangelists among fundamentalist Christians share many of the characteristics of shamanism.

---

shaman A person who enters an altered state of consciousness—at will—to contact and utilize an ordinarily hidden reality to acquire knowledge and power, and to help others

---

[5]Harner, M. (1980). *The way of the shaman: A guide to power and healing* (p. 20). San Francisco: Harper & Row.
[6]Kehoe, A. (2000). *Shamans and religion: An anthropological exploration in critical thinking.* Prospect Heights, IL: Waveland Press.

Typically, one becomes a shaman by passing through stages of learning and practical experience, often involving psychological and emotional ordeals brought about by isolation, fasting, physical torture, sensory deprivation, and/or hallucinations. These hallucinations (derived from the Latin word for "mental wandering") occur when the shaman is in a trance, which may occur spontaneously but can also be induced by drumming or consuming mind-altering drugs such as psychoactive vines or mushrooms.

Because shamanism is rooted in altered states of consciousness and the human nervous system that produces these trance states is universal, individuals involved in shamanism experience similarly structured visual, auditory, somatic (touch), olfactory (smell), and gustatory (taste) hallucinations. The widespread occurrence of shamanism and the remarkable similarities among shamanic traditions everywhere are consequences of this universal neurological inheritance. At the same time, the meanings ascribed to sensations experienced in altered states and made of their content are culturally determined; hence, despite their overall similarities, local traditions always vary in their details.

The shaman is essentially a religious go-between who acts on behalf of some human client, often to bring about healing or to foretell some future event. To do so, the shaman intervenes to influence or impose his or her will on supernatural powers. The shaman can be contrasted with the priest or priestess, whose "clients" are the deities. Priests and priestesses frequently tell people what to do; the shaman tells supernaturals what to do. In return for services rendered, the shaman may collect a fee—fresh meat, yams, or a favorite possession. In some cases, the added prestige, authority, and social power attached to the shaman's status are reward enough.

When a shaman acts on behalf of a client, he or she may put on something of a show—one that heightens the basic drama with a sense of danger. Typically, the shaman enters a trance state, in which he or she experiences the sensation of traveling to the alternate world and seeing and interacting with spirit beings. The shaman tries to impose his or her will upon these spirits, an inherently dangerous contest, considering the superhuman powers spirits usually are thought to possess.

An example of this can be seen in the trance dances of the Ju/'hoansi Bushmen of Africa's Kalahari Desert. Among the Ju/'hoansi, shamans constitute, on average, about half the men and a third of the older women in any group. Their most common reasons for going into a trance are to bring rain, control animals, and heal the sick. Healing is an important activity of shamans across cultures; the Original Study offers insight into shamanic healing as practiced among the Ju/'hoansi.

Original Study

Healing among the Ju/'hoansi of the Kalahari

Marjorie Shostak

One way the spirits affect humans is by shooting them with invisible arrows carrying disease, death, or misfortune. If the arrows can be warded off, illness will not take hold. If illness has already penetrated, the arrows must be removed to enable the sick person to recover. An ancestral spirit may exercise this power against the living if a person is not being treated well by others. If people argue with her frequently, if her husband shows how little he values her by carrying on blatant affairs, or if people refuse to cooperate or share with her, the spirit may conclude that no one cares whether or not she remains alive and may "take her into the sky."

Interceding with the spirits and drawing out their invisible arrows is the task of [Ju/'hoansi] healers, men and women who possess the powerful healing force called *n/um* [the Ju/'hoansi equivalent of *mana*]. *N/um* generally remains dormant in a healer until an effort is made to activate it. Although an occasional healer can accomplish this through solo singing or instrumental playing, the usual way of activating *n/um* is through the medicinal curing ceremony or trance dance. To the sound of undulating melodies sung by women, healers dance around and around the fire, sometimes for hours. The music, the strenuous dancing, the smoke, the heat of the fire, and the healers' intense concentration cause their *n/um* to heat up. When it comes to a boil, trance is achieved.

At this moment the *n/um* becomes available as a powerful healing force, to serve the entire community. In trance, a healer lays hands on and ritually cures everyone sitting around the fire. His hands flutter lightly beside each person's head or chest or wherever illness is evident; his body trembles; his breathing becomes deep and coarse; and he becomes coated with a thick sweat—also considered to be imbued with power. Whatever "badness" is discovered in the person is drawn into the healer's own body and met by the *n/um*

coursing up his spinal column. The healer gives a mounting cry that culminates in a soul-wrenching shriek as the illness is catapulted out of his body and into the air.

While in trance, many healers see various gods and spirits sitting just outside the circle of firelight, enjoying the spectacle of the dance. Sometimes the spirits are recognizable—departed relatives and friends—at other times they are "just people." Whoever these beings are, healers in trance usually blame them for whatever misfortune is being experienced by the community. They are barraged by hurled objects, shouted at, and aggressively warned not to take any of the living back with them to the village of the spirits.

To cure a very serious illness, the most experienced healers may be

Ju/'hoansi healers, when entering trance, are assisted by others among the trance dancers.

© Irven DeVore/Anthro-Photo

called upon, for only they have enough knowledge to undertake the dangerous spiritual exploration that may be necessary to effect a cure. When they are in a trance, their souls or vital spirits are said to leave their bodies and to travel to the spirit world to discover the cause of the illness or the problem. An ancestral spirit or a god is usually found responsible and asked to reconsider. If the healer is persuasive and the spirit agrees, the sick person recovers. If the spirit is elusive or unsympathetic, a cure is not achieved. The healer may go to the principal god, but even this does not always work. As one healer put it, "Sometimes, when you speak with God, he says, 'I want this person to die and won't help you make him better.' At other times, God helps; the next morning, someone who has been lying on the ground, seriously ill, gets up and walks again."

These journeys are considered dangerous because while the healer's soul is absent his body is in half-death. Akin to loss of consciousness, this state has been observed and verified by medical and scientific investigators. The power of other healers' *n/um* is all that is thought to protect the healer in this state from actual death. He receives lavish attention and care—his body is vigorously massaged, his skin is rubbed with sweat, and hands are laid on him. Only when consciousness returns—the signal that his soul has been reunited with his body—do the other healers cease their efforts.

(Excerpted from Marjorie Shostak. (1983). Nisa: The life and words of a !Kung woman (pp. 291–293). New York: Vintage)

In many human societies, sleight-of-hand tricks and ventriloquism occur at the same time as trancing. Among Arctic peoples, for example, a shaman may summon spirits in the dark and produce flapping noises and strange voices to impress the audience. Some Western observers regard this kind of trickery as evidence of the fraudulent nature of shamanism. However, those who have studied shamanic practices agree that even though shamans know perfectly well that they are manipulating people with their tricks, they really believe in their power to deal with supernatural forces and spirit beings. Their power, verified by the trance experience, gives them the right as well as the ability to manipulate people in minor technical matters. In short, the shaman regards his or her ability to perform extraordinary tricks as further proof of superior powers.

The importance of shamanism in a society should not be underestimated. It promotes, through the drama of performance, a trancelike feeling and a release of tension. And it provides psychological assurance that prevailing upon supernatural powers and spirits otherwise beyond human control can bring about invulnerability from attack, success at love, or the return of health. In fact, a frequent reason for a shamanic performance is poor health—a concept that is difficult to define effectively in cross-cultural terms. Not only do people in diverse cultures recognize and experience different types of illnesses, they may also view and explain them in different terms. The culturally defined diagnosis of an illness, in turn, determines how the patient will be treated according to the beliefs of the culture, in order to achieve healing.

Although the psychological effects of the shamanic treatment are not known, the connection between mind and body may contribute to the patient's recovery. From an anthropological perspective, shamanic healings can be understood by means of a three-cornered model: the *shamanic complex* (Figure 15.2). This triangle is created by the relationships among the shaman and the patient and the community to which both belong.

For healing to take place, the shaman needs to be convinced of the effectiveness of his or her spiritual powers and techniques. Likewise, the patient must see the shaman as a genuine healing master using appropriate techniques. Finally, to close the triangle's "magic field," the community within which the shaman operates on the patient must view the healing ceremony and its practitioner as potentially effective and beneficial.

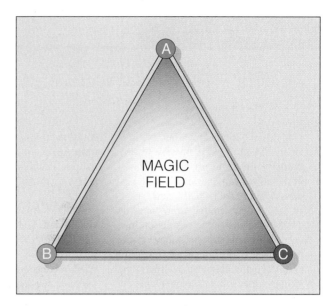

Figure 15.2 **The Shamanic Complex**
Shamanic healing takes place within a "magic field" created when the shaman (A) and patient (B), as well as their community (C), are all convinced that the shaman is a genuine healing master using appropriate techniques that are effective and beneficial. Similar psychological processes are involved in Western medical treatments.

Such dynamics are not unique to shamanic healing ceremonies, for similar social psychological processes are involved in Western medical treatments as well. Consider, for example, the *placebo effect*—the beneficial result a patient experiences after a particular treatment, due to his or her expectations concerning the treatment rather than from the treatment itself. Notably, some physicians involved in modern medicine work collaboratively with practitioners of traditional belief systems toward the healing of various illnesses.

Rituals and Ceremonies

Rituals, or ceremonial acts, are not all religious in nature (consider, for example, college graduation ceremonies in North America), but those that are play a crucial role in religious activity. Religious ritual is the means through which people relate to the supernatural; it is religion in action. Ritual serves to relieve social tensions and reinforce a group's collective bonds. More than this, it provides a means of marking many important events and lessening the social disruption and individual suffering of crises. One important type of ritual is the rite of passage.

Rites of passage are rituals that mark important stages in an individual's life cycle, such as birth, marriage, and death. In one of anthropology's classic works, French social scientist Arnold van Gennep analyzed the rites of passage that help individuals through the crucial crises or major social transitions in their lives, such as birth, puberty, marriage, parenthood, advancement to

rite of passage A ritual that marks an important stage in an individual's life cycle, such as birth, marriage, and death
separation In a rite of passage, the ritual removal of the individual from society
transition In a rite of passage, isolation of the individual following separation and prior to incorporation into society
incorporation In a rite of passage, reincorporation of the individual into society in his or her new status

Exiled Tibetan monks at Drepung Loseling monastery in India patiently create a mandala. Using narrow metal funnels, they spend many days placing millions of grains of fine, colored sand into a geometric design that has deep spiritual significance in their Buddhist worldview. An ancient Sanskrit word, mandala means "circle-circumference" or "completion," referring to the enlightened mind of the Buddha. The ritual provides a visual framework for meditation toward establishing that radiant mental state. It is a tool for spiritual teaching, trance induction, and for blessing the earth and all its creatures. Once complete, the sacred work is dismantled and the sand is disseminated (usually in a body of running water) to spread the blessings.

a higher class, occupational specialization, and death.[7] He found it useful to divide ceremonies for all of these life crises into three stages: **separation**, **transition**, and **incorporation**; the first being ritual removal of the individual from everyday society, followed by a period of isolation, and, finally, formal return and readmission back into society in his or her new status.

This sequence of stages is something that takes place in many forms in all cultures around the world, from military boot camps to college fraternity and sorority initiation ceremonies in the United States to a global array of puberty ceremonies that mark the transition from childhood to adulthood.

Male Initiation Rites among the Aborigines of Australia

The Aborigines of Australia provide an example of a male initiation rite into manhood. When the elders decide the time for initiation, the boys are taken from the village (separation), while the women cry and make a ritual show of resistance. At a place distant from the camp, groups of men from many villages gather. The elders sing and dance, while the initiates act as though they are dead. The climax of this part of the ritual is a bodily operation, such as circumcision or the knocking out of a tooth. Australian anthropologist A. P. Elkin comments:

> This is partly a continuation of the drama of death. The tooth-knocking, circumcision, or other symbolical act "killed" the novice; after this he does not return to the general camp and normally may not be seen by any woman. He is dead to the ordinary life of the tribe.[8]

In this transitional stage, the novice may be shown secret ceremonies and receive some instruction, but the most significant element is his complete removal from society. In the course of these Australian puberty rites, the initiate must learn the lore that all adult men are

---

[7]Van Gennep, A. (1960). *The rites of passage*. Chicago: University of Chicago Press.

[8]Elkin, A. P. (1964). *The Australian Aborigines*. Garden City, NY: Doubleday/Anchor Books.

expected to know; he is given, in effect, a "cram course." The trauma of the occasion is a pedagogical technique that ensures he will learn and remember everything; in a nonliterate society the perpetuation of cultural traditions requires no less, and so effective teaching methods are necessary.

On his return to society (incorporation), the novice is welcomed with ceremonies, as though he had returned from the dead. This alerts the society at large to the individual's new status—that people can expect him to act in certain ways, and in return they must act in the appropriate ways toward him. The individual's new rights and duties are thus clearly defined. He is spared, for example, the problems of a teenager in North America, a time when an individual is neither adult nor child, a person whose status is ill defined.

In the Australian case just cited, boys are prepared not just for adulthood but also for *manhood*. In their society, for example, courage and endurance are considered important masculine virtues, and the pain of tooth-knocking and circumcision help instill these in initiates. In a similar way, female initiation rites help prepare Mende girls in West Africa for womanhood.

Female Initiation Rites among the Mende of West Africa

After Mende girls have begun to menstruate, they are removed from society to spend weeks, or even months, in seclusion. There they discard the clothes of childhood, smear their bodies with white clay, and dress in short skirts and many strands of beads.

Shortly after entering this transitional stage, the girls undergo clitoridectomy, a removal of the clitoris, viewed as the feminine version of the penis. The girls (and Mende in general) believe this form of female circumcision enhances their reproductive potential. Until their incorporation back into society, they are trained in the moral and practical responsibilities of potential child bearers by experienced women in the Sande association, an organization to which the initiates will belong once their training has ended. This training is not all harsh, however, for it is accompanied by a good deal of singing, dancing, and storytelling, and the initiates are very well fed. Thus, they acquire both a positive image of womanhood and a strong sense of sisterhood. Once their training is complete, a medicine made by brewing leaves in water is used for a ritual washing, removing the magical protection that has shielded them during the period of their confinement.

Mende women emerge from their initiation as women in knowledgeable control of their sexuality, eligible for marriage and childbearing. The pain and danger of the surgery, endured in the context of intense social support from other women, serve as a metaphor for childbirth, which may well take place in the same place of seclusion, again with the support of women in the Sande association. It also has been suggested that, symbolically, clitoridectomy removes sexual ambiguity; having gone through this ritual, a traditional Mende woman knows she is "all woman."[9] Thus we have symbolic expression of gender as something important in people's cultural lives.

Clitoridectomy is the least extreme of several forms of female circumcision, all of which are often referred to as female genital mutilation (FGM) and most commonly practiced in Africa and Asia. Anthropological commitment to cultural relativism permits an understanding of FGM as part of female initiation rites. However, as discussed early on in this book, cultural relativism does not preclude the anthropologist from criticizing a given practice. Apart from the pain and the effect of the operation on a woman's future sexual satisfaction, significant numbers of young women die from excessive bleeding, shock, various infections, or damage to the urethra or anus brought on by the procedure. Others face later risks when giving birth as scar tissue tears.

Not surprisingly, female circumcision has been much condemned as a human rights violation in recent years. Committees to end the practice have been set up in twenty-two African countries.[10] (Notably, women's breast implant surgery has been compared to FGM as Western industrialized society's version of what it takes to be "all woman." The Original Study in Chapter 16 addresses this issue in detail.)

MAGIC

Among the most fascinating of ritual practices is application of the belief that supernatural powers can be compelled to act in certain ways for good or evil purposes by recourse to certain specified formulas. This is a

imitative magic Magic based on the principle that like produces like; sometimes called sympathetic magic

contagious magic Magic based on the principle that things or persons once in contact can influence each other after the contact is broken

witchcraft An explanation of events based on the belief that certain individuals possess an innate psychic power capable of causing harm, including sickness and death

divination A magical procedure or spiritual ritual designed to find out about what is not knowable by ordinary means, such as foretelling the future by interpreting omens

---

[9]MacCormack, C. P. (1977). Biological events and cultural control. *Signs, 3,* 98.
[10]"Female genital mutilation." (2000). Fact sheet no. 241. World Health Organization; Dirie, W., & Miller, C. (1998). *Desert flower: The extraordinary journey of a desert nomad* (pp. 218, 219). New York: William Morrow.

classical anthropological notion of magic. Many societies have magical rituals to ensure good crops, the replenishment of game, the fertility of domestic animals, and the avoidance or healing of illness in humans.

Although many Western peoples today—seeking to objectify and demythologize their world—have tried to suppress magic mysteries in their own consciousness, they continue to be fascinated by them. Not only are books and films about demonic possession and witchcraft avidly devoured and discussed, but horoscope columns are a regular feature of daily newspapers in the United States. And magical rituals are still commonly practiced by many Westerners seeking some "luck" where the outcome is in doubt or beyond factual influence—from lighting a votive candle for someone going through a hard time, to wearing lucky boxers on a hot date, to the curious gesturing baseball pitchers do before each throw.

In the 19th century British anthropologist Sir James George Frazer made a useful distinction between two fundamental principles of magic. The first principle, that "like produces like," he named **imitative magic** (sometimes called *sympathetic magic*). In Burma (Myanmar) in Southeast Asia, for example, a rejected lover might engage a sorcerer to make an image of his would-be love. If this image were tossed into water, to the accompaniment of certain charms, it was expected that the hapless girl would go mad. Thus, the girl would suffer a fate similar to that of her image.

Frazer called the second principle of thought on which magic is based **contagious magic**—the idea that things or persons once in contact can influence each other after the contact is broken. The most common example of contagious magic is the permanent relationship between an individual and any part of his or her body, such as hair, fingernails, or teeth. Frazer cited the Basutos of Lesotho in southern Africa, who were careful to conceal their extracted teeth, because these might fall into the hands of certain mythical beings who could harm the owners of the teeth by working magic on them. Related to this is the custom, in Western societies, of treasuring things that have been touched by special people. Such things range from a saint's relics to possessions of other admired or idolized individuals, such as the U.S. basketball star Michael Jordan or rock musician Mick Jagger of the Rolling Stones.

WITCHCRAFT

In Salem, Massachusetts, 200 innocent citizens suspected of being witches were arrested in 1692; of these, thirteen women and six men were hanged, and one 80-year-old farmer was tortured to death. Even though damages were awarded to descendants of some of the victims nineteen years later, it was not until 1957 that the last

© SSPL/The Image Works

A hundred-year-old fetish from the Congo in central Africa, believed to possess harmful spirit power. Known as a *nkondi*, the wooden carving's power comes in part from magic herbs hidden behind the mirror. During a special ritual (reflecting the principle of imitative magic), iron nails were driven into this figure to activate its power to destroy hostile evil spirits or hunt down wrongdoers and take vengeance.

of the Salem witches were exonerated by the Massachusetts legislature. **Witchcraft** is an explanation of events based on the belief that certain individuals possess an innate psychic power capable of causing harm, including sickness and death. It involves **divination**, a magical procedure or spiritual ritual designed to find out about what is not knowable by ordinary means, such as foretelling the future by interpreting omens.

Although many North Americans suppose it to be something that belongs to a less enlightened past, witchcraft is alive and well in the United States today. Indeed, starting in the 1960s, a neo-pagan "witch cult" known as Wicca began to undergo something of a boom, including among highly educated segments of U.S. society. Inspired by various pre-Christian western European beliefs, in particular the idea of a sacred Mother Earth, Wicca is a nature-centered religion. And, contrary to widespread but false rumor, its self-styled "witches" do not worship Satan and are not concerned with "working evil." In fact, Wicca's core ethical statement, known as the Wiccan Rede, states, "If it harm none, do what you will."

Ibibio Witchcraft

North Americans are by no means alone in having a contemporary interest in witchcraft. For example, as the Ibibio of Nigeria have become increasingly exposed to modern education and scientific training, their reliance on witchcraft as an explanation for misfortune has increased.[11] Furthermore, it is often the younger, more educated members of Ibibio society who accuse others of bewitching them. Frequently, the accused are older, more traditional members of society; thus, we have an expression of the intergenerational hostility that often exists in fast-changing traditional societies.

Ibibio witchcraft beliefs are highly developed and longstanding—as they are among most traditional peoples of sub-Saharan Africa. A rat that eats a person's crops is not really a rat but a witch that changed into one; if a young and enterprising man cannot get a job or fails an exam, he has been bewitched; if someone's money is wasted or if the person becomes sick, is bitten by a snake, or is struck by lightning, the reason is always the same—witchcraft.

Indeed, traditional Ibibio attribute virtually all misfortune, illness, or death to the malevolent activity of witches. The modern Ibibio's knowledge about the role microorganisms play in disease has little impact on this; after all, it says nothing about why these were sent to the afflicted individual. Although Ibibio religious beliefs provide alternative explanations for misfortune, those carry negative connotations and do not elicit nearly as much sympathy from others. Thus, if evil befalls a person, witchcraft is a far more satisfying explanation than something such as offspring disobedience or violation of a taboo.

Ibibio witches are thought to be men or women who have within them a special substance acquired from another established witch. From swallowing this substance—made up of needles, colored threads, and other ingredients—one is believed to become endowed with a special power that causes injury, even death, to others regardless of whether its possessor intends harm or not. The power is purely psychic, and witches do not perform rites or make use of "bad medicine." It is believed to give them the ability to transform into animals and travel any distance at incredible speed to get at their unsuspecting victims, whom they may torture or kill by transferring the victim's soul or vital spirit into an animal, which is then eaten.

To identify a witch, an Ibibio looks for any person living in the region whose behavior is considered odd, out of the ordinary, immoral, or unsocial. Witches are apt to look and act mean and to be socially disruptive people in the sense that their behavior exceeds the range of variance considered acceptable.

The Ibibio make a distinction between *sorcerers,* whose acts are especially diabolical and destructive, and benign *witches,* whose witchcraft is relatively harmless, even though their powers are thought to be greater than those of their malevolent counterparts. Sorcerers are the very embodiment of a society's conception of evil— beings that flout the rules of sexual behavior and disregard every other standard of decency. Benign witches are often the community's nonconformists. Typically, they are morose, arrogant, and unfriendly people who keep to themselves but otherwise cause little disturbance. Such witches are thought to be dangerous when offended— likely to retaliate by causing sickness, death, crop failure, cattle disease, or any number of lesser ills. Not surprisingly, people viewed as witches are usually treated with considerable caution, respect, and even fear.[12]

Functions of Witchcraft

Why witchcraft? We might better ask, why not? In a world where there are few proven techniques for dealing with everyday crises, especially sickness, a belief in witches is not foolish; it is indispensable.[13] No one wants to resign oneself to illness, and if the malady is caused by a witch's curse, then magical countermeasures should cure it.

Not only does the idea of personalized evil answer the problem of unmerited suffering, but it also provides an explanation for many happenings for which no cause can be discovered. Witchcraft, then, cannot be refuted.

[11]Offiong, D. (1985). Witchcraft among the Ibibio of Nigeria. In A. C. Lehmann & J. E. Myers (Eds.), *Magic, witchcraft, and religion* (pp. 152–165). Palo Alto, CA: Mayfield.

[12]See Mair, L. (1969). *Witchcraft* (p. 37). New York: McGraw-Hill.
[13]Mair.

A Sufi *sema* (prayer dance) in Istanbul, Turkey. Sufism, a mystical Muslim movement that emerged in the late 10th century, borrowing ideas from Buddhism, Christianity, and Neoplatonism, emphasizes the surrender of individual ego and attachment to worldly things in order to be receptive to God's grace. Known as "Whirling Dervishes," these Sufi dancers are part of the Mevlevi brotherhood founded by Mevlana Rumi in the 13th century. According to Mevlevi tradition, during the *sema* the soul is freed from earthly ties and able to jubilantly commune with the divine. (*Dervish* literally means "doorway" and is thought to be an entrance from the material world to the spiritual.) The felt hat represents personal ego's tombstone, and the wide skirt symbolizes its shroud.

Even if we could convince a person that his or her illness was due to natural causes, the victim would still ask, as the Ibibio do, Why me? Why now? Such a view leaves no room for pure chance; everything must be assigned a cause or meaning. Witchcraft offers an explanation and, in so doing, also provides both the basis and the means for taking counteraction.

Nor is witchcraft always entirely harmful. Its positive functions are noted in many African societies where people traditionally believe sickness, death, or other harm may be caused by witches. If people in the community agree that evildoing magic is in play, the ensuing search for the perpetrator of the misfortune becomes, in effect, a communal probe into dysfunctional social behavior. A witch-hunt is, in fact, a systematic investigation, through a public hearing, into all social relationships involving the victim of the sickness or death. Was a husband or wife unfaithful or a son lacking in the performance of his duties? Were an individual's friends uncooperative, or was the victim guilty of any of these wrongs? Accusations are reciprocal, and before long just about every unsocial or hostile act that has occurred in that society since the last outbreak of witchcraft (as manifested in sickness, death, or some other misfortune) is brought into the open.[14]

Through such periodic public scrutiny of everyone's behavior, people are reminded of what their society regards as both strengths and weaknesses of character. This encourages individuals to suppress as best they can those personality traits that are looked upon with disapproval, for if they do not, they at some time may be accused of being a witch. A belief in witchcraft thus serves as a broad control on antisocial behavior.

Consequences of Witchcraft

Anthropological research suggests that witchcraft, in spite of its often negative image, frequently functions in a very positive way to manage tensions within a society. Nonetheless, events may get out of hand, particularly in crisis situations, when widespread accusations may cause great suffering. This certainly was the case in the Salem witch trials, but even those pale in comparison to the half a million individuals executed as witches in Europe from the 15th through the 17th centuries. This was a time of profound change in European societies, marked by a good deal of political and religious conflict. At such times, it is all too easy to search out scapegoats to blame for what people believe are undesirable changes.

REVITALIZATION MOVEMENTS

No anthropological consideration of religion is complete without some mention of *revitalization movements*. As noted in the previous chapter, these are movements for radical culture reform in response to widespread social disruption and collective feelings of great stress and despair. Many such movements developed in indigenous societies where European colonial exploitation caused enormous upheaval.

[14]Turnbull, C. M. (1983). *The human cycle* (p. 181). New York: Simon & Schuster.

Among the various types of revitalization movements is the **cargo cult**—a spiritual movement (especially noted in Melanesia in the Southwest Pacific) in reaction to disruptive contact with Western capitalism, promising resurrection of deceased relatives, destruction or enslavement of white foreigners, and the magical arrival of utopian riches. Indigenous Melanesians referred to the white man's wealth as "cargo" (pidgin English for European trade goods). In times of great social stress, native prophets emerged, predicting that the time of suffering would come to an end, and a new paradise on earth would soon arrive. Their deceased ancestors would return to life, and the rich white man would magically disappear—swallowed by an earthquake or swept away by a huge wave. However, their cargo would be left for the prophets and their cult followers who performed rituals to hasten this supernatural redistribution of wealth.[15]

One of many cargo cults took place in 1931 at Buka, in the Solomon Islands (in the Pacific Ocean). A native religious movement suddenly emerged there when prophets predicted that a deluge would soon engulf all whites, and a ship would then arrive filled with Western industrial commodities. The prophets told their followers to construct a storehouse for the goods and to prepare themselves to repulse the colonial police. They also spread word that the ship would come only after the natives had used up all their own supplies, and for this reason believers ceased working in the fields. Although the leaders of the movement were arrested, the cult continued for some years.

As deliberate efforts to construct a more satisfying culture, revitalization movements aim to reform not just the religious sphere of activity but an entire cultural system. Such drastic measures are taken when a group's anxiety and frustration have become so intense that the only way to reduce the stress is to overturn the entire social system and replace it with a new one. From the cargo cults of Melanesia to the 1890 Ghost Dance of many North American Indians to the Mau Mau of the Kikuyu in Kenya in the 1950s, extreme and sometimes violent religious reactions to European domination are so common that anthropologists have sought to formulate their underlying causes and general characteristics.

Revitalization movements are by no means restricted to the colonial world, and in the United States alone hundreds of them have sprung up. These range from Mormonism, which began in the 19th century, to the more recent Unification Church led by Reverend Sun Myung Moon, the Branch Davidians led by Seventh-Day Adventist prophet David Koresh, and the Black Muslims led by Prophet Elijah Muhammad. Recent U.S. revitalization movements also include the American Indian revival of the spectacular Sun Dance ceremony, now held each summer at various reservations in the Great Plains.

Sometimes the movement will be so out of touch with existing circumstances that it is doomed to failure from the beginning. This was the case with the Branch Davidians, whose hostility toward government authorities prompted an official assault on the cult's compound in Waco, Texas. In reaction, cult members set fire to their own headquarters, sending their movement and their lives up in flames.

More rarely, a movement may tap long-dormant adaptive forces underlying a culture, and an enduring religion may result. Such was the case with Mormonism. Though heavily persecuted at first and hounded from place to place, Mormons adapted to the point that their religion thrives in the United States today. Indeed, revitalization movements lie at the root of all known religions—Judaism, Christianity, and Islam included.

In Africa, during and following the period of foreign colonization and missionization, indigenous groups resisted or creatively revised Christian teachings and formed culturally appropriate religious movements. Since the 1970s, thousands of indigenous Christian churches have been founded, often born of alternative theological interpretations, new divinely inspired revelations, or cultural disagreements between African Christians and European or North American missionaries over the extent to which traditional African practices (such as animism, ancestor worship, and polygamy) were permissible. Today the African continent is as religiously diverse as ever. Although at least 40 percent of the population is Christian and more than another 40 percent is Muslim, African indigenous religious traditions persist and are often merged with Christianity and Islam.

PERSISTENCE OF RELIGION AND SPIRITUALITY

From the ongoing need to make sense of their existence, humans continue to explore metaphysically or spiritually as well as scientifically. As chronicled in this chapter, we continue to see indications of spiritual curiosity, the search for deeper meanings, and faith in forces beyond empirical observation or scientific scrutiny all around the globe. These signs are apparent from religious gatherings, witchcraft accusations, spiritual healing ceremonies, buildings and other structures created for religious purposes, natural places that people have designated as sacred sites, and the list goes on.

---

cargo cult A spiritual movement (especially noted in Melanesia) in reaction to disruptive contact with Western capitalism, promising resurrection of deceased relatives, destruction or enslavement of white foreigners, and the magical arrival of utopian riches

---

[15]For more on cargo cults, see Lindstrom, L. (1993). *Cargo cult: Strange stories of desire from Melanesia and beyond.* Honolulu: University of Hawaii Press; and Worsley, P. (1957). *The trumpet shall sound: A study of "cargo" cults in Melanesia.* London: Macgibbon & Kee.

Chapter Summary

■ Religion, an organized system of ideas about spiritual reality, or the supernatural, is a key part of every culture's worldview. It consists of beliefs and practices by which people try to interpret and control aspects of the universe otherwise beyond their control. Among food-foraging peoples, religion is intertwined in everyday life. As societies become more complex, religion may be restricted to particular occasions.

■ Spiritual or religious beliefs and practices fulfill numerous social and psychological needs, such as reducing anxiety by providing an orderly view of the universe and answers to existential questions, including those concerning suffering and death. A traditional religion reinforces group norms, provides moral sanctions for individual conduct, and furnishes the ideology of common purpose and values that support social solidarity and the well-being of the community. Also of note, people often turn to religion or spirituality in the hope of reaching a specific goal, such as the healing of physical, emotional, or social ills.

■ Religion is characterized by a belief in supernatural beings and forces, which can be appealed to for aid through prayer, sacrifice, and other rituals. Supernatural beings may be grouped into three categories: major deities (gods and goddesses), ancestral spirits, and other sorts of spirit beings. Gods and goddesses are great but remote beings that control the universe or a specific part of it. Whether people recognize gods, goddesses, or both has to do with how men and women relate to each other in everyday life. Belief in ancestral spirits is based on the idea that human beings are made up of a body and a soul or vital spirit. Freed from the body at death, the spirit continues to participate in human affairs. This belief is characteristic of descent-based groups with their associated ancestor orientation.

■ Animism, common among peoples who see themselves as part of nature, is a belief that nature is animated or energized by distinct personalized spirit beings separable from bodies. Closer to humans than gods and goddesses, these spirit beings are intimately concerned with human activities. Animatism, sometimes found alongside animism, is a belief that nature is enlivened or energized by an impersonal spiritual force or supernatural energy, which may make itself manifest in any special place, thing, or living creature.

■ Belief in supernatural beings and powers is maintained through what people perceive as manifestations of power. Belief is also fueled by the fact that supernatural beings seem real because they possess certain attributes that are familiar to people. Finally, belief is explained and reinforced by myths.

■ All human societies have specialists—priests and priestesses and/or shamans—to guide religious practices and to intervene with the supernatural world. Shamans are individuals skilled at contacting and manipulating supernatural beings and powers through altered states of consciousness. Their performances promote a release of tension among individuals in a society, and the shaman can help to maintain social control. The benefits of shamanism for the shaman are prestige, sometimes wealth, and an outlet for artistic self-expression.

■ Religious rituals are religion in action. Through ritual acts, social bonds are reinforced. Rituals carried out to mark important stages in an individual's life cycle are rites of passage and include three stages: separation, transition, and incorporation.

Magic, which can be viewed as a ritual practice that makes supernatural powers act in certain ways, can be differentiated into imitative magic and contagious magic.

■ Witchcraft functions as an effective way for people to explain away personal misfortune without having to shoulder any personal blame. Even malevolent witchcraft may function positively in the realm of social control. It may also provide an outlet for feelings of hostility and frustration without disturbing the norms of the larger group.

■ Revitalization movements, which can happen in any culture, arise when people seek radical cultural reform in response to widespread social disruption and collective feelings of anxiety and despair. Among Melanesian islanders radically disturbed by Western colonization and capitalism, these movements have often taken the form of cargo cults, which have appeared spontaneously at different times since the beginning of the 20th century. No matter where they occur, revitalization movements follow a common sequence, and all religions stem from such movements.

Questions for Reflection

1. Beyond biological survival, humans need to find meaning in their existence. Do you ever ponder questions such as the meaning of your life and big issues such as the origin or destiny of the human species? How does your culture, including your religious or spiritual beliefs, offer you guidance in finding meaningful answers to such big questions?

2. You have read about female genital mutilation as a rite of passage in some cultures. Do you know of any genital mutilation practices in your society? Why are so many boys in the United States circumcised immediately after birth?

3. Do the basic dynamics of the shamanic complex also apply to preachers or priests in modern churches and medical doctors working in modern hospitals? Can you think of some similarities among the shaman, preacher, and medical doctor in terms of their respective fields of operation?

4. Revitalization movements occur in reaction to the upheavals caused by rapid colonization and modernization. Do you think that the rise of Christian fundamentalism in the North American Bible Belt today is a response to such upheavals as well?

5. In postindustrial societies such as western Europe, the United States, and Canada, there is growing interest in shamanism and alternative healing techniques. Is there any relationship between globalization and this phenomenon?

Key Terms

worldview	rite of passage
religion	separation
spirituality	transition
myth	incorporation
polytheism	imitative magic
pantheon	contagious magic
animism	witchcraft
animatism	divination
priest or priestess	cargo cult
shaman	

VISUAL ESSENCE

Since the beginning of the industrial revolution about two centuries ago, modern technology has radically increased or improved production, transportation, and communication throughout the world. During this period, humankind's population increased from 1 billion to nearly 7 billion, and a worldwide web of interconnectivity emerged. In pursuit of natural resources (food, fuel, and other raw materials), as well as markets for industrial products, people work, trade, collaborate, and compete with one another—transforming their cultures and their environments in the process. The Olympic Games are unique among the many strands in this global web. Inspired by the ancient Greek sporting event held at Olympia 2,000 years ago, the games have become a global spectacle, with thousands of athletes from all around the world competing in a different country every four years. In today's world—where powerful states have conquered and destroyed many smaller nations and also tens of millions have been killed in warfare worldwide—this global sports gathering is a crucial ritual, celebrating international peace in a friendly rivalry for medals and prestige. Pictured here is the opening ceremony of the 2008 Olympics in China.

Global Changes and the Role of Anthropology

16

Anthropology is superficially described by those who know little about it as an exotic discipline interested mainly in what happened long ago and far away. The most popular stereotype is that anthropologists devote all of their attention to digging up the past and describing the last surviving tribal communities with traditional ways of life. Yet, as noted throughout this book, anthropologists also investigate the ways and workings of industrial and postindustrial societies. Indeed, anthropologists are interested in the entire range of human cultures past and present—in their similarities and differences and in the multiple ways they influence one another.

In this current era, marked by rapid and radical change all around the world, many anthropologists wonder what today's globalizing processes will create and what will be transformed, disrupted, or damaged beyond repair. When traditional communities are exposed to intense contact with technologically empowered groups, their cultures typically change with unprecedented speed, often for the worse, becoming both less supportive and less adaptive. Since globalization is speeding along, we are compelled to ask: How can the thousands of different societies respond successfully to the radical changes hurled at them?

MODERNIZATION IN THE AGE OF GLOBALIZATION

One of the most frequently used terms to describe social and cultural changes as they are occurring today is **modernization**. This is most clearly defined as an

modernization The process of economic change, whereby developing societies acquire some of the social and political characteristics of Western industrial societies. It features five key subprocesses: technological development, agricultural development, urbanization, industrialization, and telecommunication

all-encompassing process of economic change, whereby developing societies acquire some of the social and political characteristics common to Western industrial societies.

The dominant idea behind this concept is that "becoming modern" is becoming like western European, North American, and other wealthy industrial or postindustrial societies, with the implication that not to do so is to be stuck in the past—backward, inferior, and needing to be improved. It is unfortunate that the term *modernization* continues to be so widely used. The best we can do here is to recognize its culture-bound bias, even as we continue to use it.

The process of modernization in societies all across the globe may be best understood as consisting of five subprocesses, all interrelated with no fixed order of appearance:

- *Technological development:* In the course of modernization, traditional knowledge and techniques give way to the application of scientific knowledge and techniques borrowed mainly from the industrialized West.
- *Agricultural development:* This is represented by a shift in emphasis from subsistence farming to commercial farming. Instead of raising crops and livestock for their own use, people turn with growing frequency to the production of cash crops, with increased reliance on a cash economy and on global markets for selling farm products and purchasing goods.
- *Urbanization:* This subprocess is marked particularly by population movements from rural settlements into cities.
- *Industrialization:* Here human and animal power becomes less important, and greater emphasis is placed on material forms of energy—especially fossil fuels—to drive machines.
- *Telecommunication:* The fifth and most recent subprocess involves electronic and digital media processing and sharing of news, commodity prices, fashions, and entertainment, as well as political and religious opinions. Information is widely dispersed to a mass audience, far across national borders.

Throughout the so-called underdeveloped regions of the world, in Africa, Asia, South and Central America, and elsewhere, whole countries are in the throes of radical political and economic change and overall cultural transformation. In fact, inventions and major advances in industrial production, mass transportation, and communication and information technologies are transforming societies in Europe and North America as well. As discussed in Chapter 1, this worldwide process of accelerated modernization in which all parts of the earth are becoming interconnected in one vast interrelated and all-encompassing system is known as *globalization,* evidenced in global movements of natural resources, trade goods, human labor, finance capital, information, and infectious diseases.

All around the globe we are witnessing the removal of economic activities—or at least their control—from the family and community setting. And we are seeing family structures alter in the face of the changing labor market: young children relying increasingly on parents alone for affection, instead of on the extended family; parental authority generally declining; schools replacing the family as the primary educational unit; old people spending their last days in nursing homes rather than with family members; the elimination of many customary rights and duties connected to kinship; and many other changes.

In many societies, this modernization process is now happening very fast, often without the necessary time to adjust gradually. Changes that took generations to accomplish in Europe and North America are attempted within the span of a single generation in developing countries. In the process cultures frequently face unforeseen disruptions and a rapid erosion of dearly held values they had no intention of giving up. Anthropologists doing fieldwork in distant communities throughout the world witness how these traditional cultures have been influenced, and often destroyed, by powerful global forces.

A GLOBAL TRANSNATIONAL CULTURE?

Despite vast geographic distance, human populations have always interacted. Almost five centuries ago, the first sailing ship successfully circumnavigated the entire globe—an almost three-year journey that was completed in 1522, but at great cost. Four of the five Spanish ships perished, as did most of the crew, as well as the seafarer Ferdinand Magellan who led this epic voyage of discovery.

Since then, peoples inhabiting every far-flung corner of the world have come in contact with one another, directly or indirectly. Many benefited from the new opportunities and prospered, enjoying the new commodities, such as sugar, spices, tobacco, silk, and other exotic luxuries. Millions, however, died in terrible epidemics or brutal warfare or were forced into slave labor.

About two centuries ago, the invention of steam engines and other machinery brought about the industrial revolution, with large-scale factory production and an expanding transportation network of steam-powered trains and ships. Modern mass transportation, along with recent revolutions in telecommunication technology (from print media to telegraph and telephone to radio, television, satellites, and the Internet), makes it possible to exchange more information, commodities, and services with more people faster and over greater distances. Obviously, this global flow of humans, their products, and their ideas plays a major role in culture change.

A popular belief since the mid-1900s has been that in the future there will be a single homogeneous world culture. This idea is based largely on the observation that technological developments in communication, transportation, and trade are causing peoples of the world to increasingly watch the same television programs, read the same newspapers, eat the same foods, wear the same types of clothes, play the same sports, listen to the same music, and communicate via satellites and the Internet.

Certainly it is striking—the extent to which items such as Western-style clothing, music, films, fast food, and soft drinks have spread to virtually all parts of the world. And many countries—Japan, for example—appear to have gone a long way toward becoming Westernized. Moreover, looking back over the past 5,000 years of human history, we see that political units have tended to become larger, more all-encompassing, and fewer in number. The logical outcome of this trend would be a further reduction of autonomous political units into a single one taking in the entire globe.

However, informed by comparative historical and cross-cultural research, anthropologists call attention to something that all large states throughout time have had in common: a tendency to come apart. Not only have the great empires of the past, without exception, broken up into numbers of smaller independent units, but states in virtually all parts of the world today show this same tendency to fragment, usually along major geographic and ethnic divisions.

The threat of political collapse is ever-present in multi-ethnic states, especially when these countries are large, difficult to travel, and lack major unifying cultural forces such as a common national language. Such has been the case, for instance, with Afghanistan. This vast, mountainous country is inhabited by several major ethnic groups, including Pashtun who live mainly in the south, and Tajik, Uzbek, Hazara, and Turkmen who live mainly in the north. Although the Pashtun are greatest in number and most dominant during the last 200 years, they were never able to successfully impose their political will on the other ethnic groups, who maintain a great deal of independence. Nor did they succeed in making their own native tongue, Pashto, the country's national language.

The tendency of multi-ethnic states to break apart has been especially noteworthy since the end of the Cold War between the United States and the former Soviet Union around 1990. For example, 1991 saw the dramatic breakup of the Soviet Union into about a dozen independent republics—Russia, Kazakhstan, Ukraine, and Georgia, among others. In 2008, about seventeen years after Georgia gained its own independence as an internationally recognized state, this multi-ethnic republic diminished in size when two of its ethnically distinct

The worldwide spread of such products as Pepsi is taken by some as a sign that a homogeneous world is developing. Pepsi beverages include not only cola, but Mountain Dew, Lipton's Iced Tea, Tropicana juices, and Aquafina water—generating more than $39 billion in sales in 2007.

©Allen Green/Photo Researchers, Inc.

regions, South Ossetia and Abkhazia, officially split after years of separatist pressure. Declaring independence, Abkhazia and Southern Ossetia both seek international recognition as small sovereign republics.

The splintering tendency of multi-ethnic states can also be seen in separatist movements such as that of French-speaking peoples in Canada, Basques in Spain, Tibetans in China, the Karen in Burma (Myanmar), Tamils in Sri Lanka, Kurds in Turkey, Iran, and Iraq, and so on—this list is far from exhaustive. Nor is the United States immune, as can be seen in Native American nations seeking to secure greater political self-determination on their reservations.

We may be reaching a point where the tendency for political units to increase in size while decreasing in number is being canceled out by the tendency for such units to fragment into a greater number of smaller ones. Despite these examples, there are also a few instances of reunification. Best known among these is the 1990 reunification of Germany, divided since the end of World War II as East and West Germany, into one large federal republic. Another notable exception is the recent integration of twenty-seven European countries into the European Union—however hindered by linguistic differences, distinctive cultural traditions, and bureaucratic red tape.

Also, many global integrative mechanisms have been developed to counter the divergent or centrifugal forces at work. (These include international sporting events from Wimbledon to the Olympics, plus organizations ranging from UNESCO to Rotary Clubs, Boy Scouts, and Girl Guides, as well as humanitarian aid organizations such as Doctors Without Borders and Save the Children.) Notably, while mechanisms such as these connect people all around the world, they do not represent a global transnational culture.

The Problem of a Global Culture

The idea of a global culture shared by most, if not all, peoples of the world today may have popular appeal in certain circles. A common language, for instance, would greatly facilitate international exchange, and a shared ideology (with everyone having similar political ideals and religious beliefs) might lessen cross-cultural misunderstandings and conflicting viewpoints that have led so often to violence over the past several hundred years.

However, anthropologists greet this prognosis with skepticism, suspecting that distinctive worldviews will

multiculturalism Public policy for managing cultural diversity in a multi-ethnic society, officially stressing mutual respect and tolerance for cultural differences within a country's borders

persist, even in the face of massive changes. Moreover, new worldviews are emerging, and those that are changing are not necessarily changing in the same fashion. In fact, given the intensified interactions among people in the world today, especially where competing interests are involved, it is more likely that the potential for serious conflict is actually growing.

Although the forces of globalization affect (almost) every society, not all peoples react the same way to the changes on their doorstep. Those who are willing and able to make the required adjustments may actually benefit from the transformation in their cultures, whereas others less well positioned for the changes may resist and/or have a deeply troubling experience. In short, globalization is a complex and dynamic process with a vast range of national, regional, and even local cultural reactions and adjustments.

Some have argued that perhaps a global culture would be desirable in the future, because some traditional cultures may be too specialized to adjust to a changed environment. For instance, when Amazonian Indians pursuing traditional ways of life that are well adapted to South America's tropical rainforest are confronted with sudden, radical changes brought on by foreign invaders, their long-established cultures often collapse. The reason for this, it is argued, is that the forest dwellers' traditions and political and social organizations are not adapted to modern ways and that they are naturally destined to give way to the new.

A problem with this argument is that, far from being unable to adapt, such traditional peoples have been robbed repeatedly of the opportunity to work out their own social and cultural adaptations based on their own agendas. Their hardships are caused not by laws of nature but rather by the political, economic, and ideological choices of powerful outsider forces.

Pluralistic Societies and Multiculturalism

If a single homogeneous global culture is not necessarily the wave of the future, what is? Some predict a world in which ethnic groups will become more nationalistic in response to globalization, each group stressing its unique cultural heritage and emphasizing differences with neighboring groups. But not all ethnic groups organize themselves politically as distinctive nations with their own state. In fact, it has been common for two or more neighboring ethnic groups or nations to draw together in a loose political union while maintaining their particular cultural identities. However, because such *pluralistic societies* lack a common cultural identity and heritage, and often do not share the same language or religion, political relationships between them can be fraught with tension. When feelings of ethnonationalism are near the surface, pressure may build up and result in political separation and independence.

One way of curbing divisive pressures in pluralistic or multi-ethnic societies is the adoption of a public policy based on mutual respect and tolerance for cultural differences. Known as **multiculturalism**, such an official policy or doctrine asserts the value of different cultures co-existing within a country and stresses the reciprocal responsibility of all citizens to accept the rights of others to freely express their views and values. In contrast to state policies in which a dominant ethnic group uses its power to impose its own culture as the national standard, forcing other groups within the same state to assimilate, multiculturalism involves a public policy for managing a society's cultural diversity. Examples of long-established multiculturalism may be seen in states such as Switzerland (where German-, French-, Italian-, and Romansh-speaking peoples co-exist under the same government) and Canada (where French- and English-speaking Canadians, as well as dozens of indigenous nations live side by side).

Although few pluralistic societies have successfully implemented multiculturism, several are now moving toward this goal and have changed their official "melting pot" ideology and associated policies of assimilation. One example of a country that is moving toward multiculturalism is the United States, which now has over 120 different ethnic groups within its borders (in addition to hundreds of federally recognized American Indian groups). Another is Australia, now counting over a hundred ethnic groups and with eighty languages spoken within its territorial boundaries. Similar changes are also under way in many European countries where millions of foreign immigrants have settled during the past few decades. Such changes are not easy and often engender protests along the way. In many pluralistic societies, however, governments lack the ideological commitment or political capacity to successfully structure a national cultural system.

We cannot ignore the fact that historically what has been called "nation building" in all parts of the world almost always involves attempts by those in control of a country's government to suppress or destroy the traditional cultures of peoples whose ethnic heritage or nationalities differ from their own.[1] The price tag for these repressive efforts is extremely high. During the last two decades of the 20th century, states were borrowing more money to fight peoples within their own boundaries than for all their other programs combined. Nearly all state debt in Africa and nearly half of all other debt in "underdeveloped" countries comes from the cost of weapons purchased by states to fight their own citizens.[2] The more divergent cultural traditions are, the more difficult it is to make pluralism work.

Pluralistic Societies and Ethnocentrism

A major obstacle to the successful functioning of a pluralistic society is the loyalty each ethnic group has toward its distinctive language and unique cultural traditions, from which its members derive psychological support and a firm social bond to their community. Such ethnic pride is often tied to the belief that the ways of one's own culture are the only proper ones. To overcome this kind of cultural superiority complex or *ethnocentrism*, a pluralistic society may have to develop a common superstructure with an ideological force that binds different peoples together with a collective sense of shared identity and destiny.

As illustrated again and again in this book, it is all too easy to turn ethnic pride and loyalty into a charter for denigrating people with different cultural practices and exploiting them for the benefit of one's own group. Although this is not an inevitable result, when it does occur, unrest, hostility, and violence commonly ensue.

In the world today, powerful governments frequently operate on the basis of the political idea that no group has the right to stand in the way of "the greater good for the greater number." This concept is commonly used to justify the expropriation of natural resources in regions traditionally occupied by subsistence farmers, pastoral nomads, or food foragers—without any respect for the rights, concerns, or wishes of these peoples. But is it truly the greater good for the greater number?

STRUCTURAL POWER IN THE AGE OF GLOBALIZATION

A new form of expansive international capitalism has emerged since the mid-1900s. Operating under the banner of globalization, it builds on earlier cultural structures of worldwide trade networks, and it is the successor to a system of colonialism in which a handful of powerful, mainly European, capitalist states ruled and exploited foreign nations inhabiting distant territories.

Enormously complex and turbulent, globalization is a dynamically structured process in which individuals, business corporations, and political institutions actively rearrange and restructure the political field to

---

[1]Van den Berghe, P. (1992). The modern state: Nation builder or nation killer? *International Journal of Group Tensions, 22*(3), 191–207.

[2]*Cultural Survival Quarterly.* (1991). *15*(4), 38.

their own competitive advantage, vying for increasingly scarce natural resources, cheap labor, new commercial markets, and ever-larger profits. In the age of globalization, this restructuring occurs in a vast arena spanning the entire globe. Doing this, of course, requires a great deal of power.

As discussed in Chapter 14, power refers to the ability of individuals or groups to impose their will on others and make them do things even against their own wants or wishes. Power may be applied to impose and maintain law and order, by means of which collective behavior is coordinated, regulated, and controlled within—and beyond—a particular community or society.

There are different levels of power within societies, as well as among societies. Austrian-American anthropologist Eric Wolf pointed out the importance of understanding a macro level of power that he referred to as **structural power**—power that organizes and orchestrates the systemic interaction within and among societies, directing economic and political forces on the one hand and ideological forces that shape public ideas, values, and beliefs on the other.[3] The concept of structural power not only applies to political organizations, such as chiefdoms or states, but also captures the complex new global forces currently restructuring and reshaping societies and environments everywhere on earth.

Joseph Nye, a political scientist, international security specialist, and former assistant secretary of defense in the U.S. government, refers to these two major interacting forces in the worldwide arena as "hard power" and "soft power."[4] **Hard power** is the kind of coercive power that is backed up by economic and military force. **Soft power** is co-optive rather than coercive, pressing others through attraction and persuasion to change their ideas, beliefs, values, and behaviors. Although propaganda is a form of soft power, the exercise of ideological influence (the global struggle for hearts and minds) also operates through more subtle means, such as foreign aid, international diplomacy, news media,

sports, entertainment, museum exhibits, and academic exchanges.

Military Hard Power

Today the United States has more hard power at its disposal than any of its allies or rivals worldwide. It is the global leader in military expenditure, spending $711 billion in 2008, followed by Europe ($289 billion) and China ($122 billion). In fact, as the world's still dominant superpower, the United States is responsible for almost half of the nearly $1.5 trillion spent on arms worldwide[5] (Figure 16.1).

Moreover, although there are seven other nuclear weapons states (Britain, France, and China, as well as Israel, India, Pakistan, and now also North Korea, collectively possessing about 900 active nuclear warheads), Russia and the United States have by far the largest nuclear arsenals at their disposal—minimally 5,830 and 5,735 operational warheads, respectively. (There are also nearly 16,000 intact but nonoperational warheads, almost all in the hands of the United States and Russia.[6])

In addition to military might, hard power involves the use of economic strength as a political instrument of coercion or intimidation in the global structuring process. Among other things, this means that economic size and productivity, technological capability, and

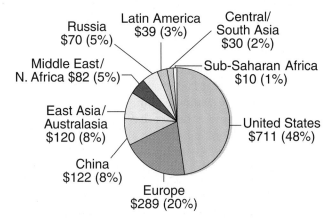

U.S. Military Spending vs. the World, 2008 (in billions of U.S. dollars)

Figure 16.1

The United States is responsible for nearly half of the $1.473 trillion spent on arms worldwide.

Source: Center for Arms Control and Non-Proliferation, February 20, 2008.

---

structural power Power that organizes and orchestrates the systemic interaction within and among societies, directing economic and political forces on the one hand and ideological forces that shape public ideas, values, and beliefs on the other
hard power Coercive power that is backed up by economic and military force
soft power Co-optive power that presses others through attraction and persuasion to change their ideas, beliefs, values, and behaviors

---

[3]Wolf, E. R. (1999). *Envisioning power: Ideologies of dominance and crisis* (p. 5). Berkeley: University of California Press.
[4]Nye, J. (2002). *The paradox of American power: Why the world's only superpower can't go it alone.* New York: Oxford University Press.

[5]www.globalissue.org.
[6]Norris, R. S., & Kristensen, H. M. (2006, July/August). Global nuclear stockpiles, 1945–2006. *Bulletin of the Atomic Scientists, 62*(4), 64–66.

finance capital may be brought to bear on the global market, forcing weaker states to break down trade barriers protecting their workers, natural resources, and local markets.

As the world's largest economy and leading exporter, the United States has long pushed for free trade for its corporations doing business on a global scale. Sometimes it uses military power to impose changes on a foreign political landscape by means of armed interventions or full-scale invasions.

Through history, the United States (like several other powerful countries, including Russia, Britain, and France) has engaged in such military interventions around the world. Because of this, many see the United States as an ever-present threat, apt to use overwhelming military force in order to benefit its corporate interests from fruit to fuel, from microchips to automobiles. The corporations, in turn, wield enormous political and financial power over governments and international organizations, including the World Trade Organization, headquartered in Geneva, and global banking institutions such as the International Monetary Fund (IMF) and World Bank, both based in Washington, DC.

As home base to more global corporations than any other country, the United States is endeavoring to protect its interests by investing in what it refers to as a *global security environment*. Numerous other countries, unable to afford expensive weapons systems (or blocked from developing or acquiring them), have invested in biological or chemical warfare technology. Still others, including relatively powerless political groups, have resorted to guerrilla tactics or terrorism as part of their local, regional, or even global warfare strategies.

Economic Hard Power: The Rise of Global Corporations

Global corporations, rare before the latter half of the 20th century, now are a far-reaching economic and political force in the world. Modern-day business giants such as General Electric, Shell, and Toyota are actually clusters of several corporations joined by ties of common ownership and responsive to a common management strategy. Usually tightly controlled by a head office in one country, these enterprises organize and integrate production across the international boundaries of different countries for interests formulated in corporate boardrooms, irrespective of whether these are consistent with the interests of people in the countries where they operate. These megacorporations are the products of the technological revolution, for without fast mass transportation, sophisticated data-processing equipment, and

telecommunication, they could not adequately oversee their worldwide operations.

Though typically thought of as responding impersonally to outside market forces, large corporations are in fact controlled by an increasingly smaller number of wealthy capitalists who benefit directly from their operations. Yet, unlike political leaders, the world's largest individual stockholders and most powerful directors are virtually unknown to the general public. For that matter, most people cannot even name the world's ten leading global corporations, which include Wal-Mart, Shell, and Toyota (Figure 16.2). Each of the top ten business giants currently generates annual revenues above $160 billion, and three of them are well above the $300 billion mark.[7]

So great is the power of large businesses operating all across the globe that they increasingly thwart the wishes of national governments or international organizations such as the United Nations, Red Cross, and the International Court of Justice. Because the information megacorporations process is kept from flowing in a meaningful way to the population at large, or even to lower levels within the organization, it becomes difficult for governments to get the information they need for informed policy decisions. It took years for the U.S. Congress to extract the information it needed from tobacco companies to decide what to do about tobacco legislation—and it is nearly as slow-going today getting energy and media companies to provide data needed for regulatory purposes.

Beyond this, global corporations have repeatedly shown they can overrule foreign policy decisions. While some might see this as a hopeful signal for getting beyond national vices and rivalries, it raises the unsettling issue of whether or not the global arena should be controlled by immensely large and powerful private corporations interested only in financial profits. According to one market research organization,

> Today, the top 100 companies control 33 percent of the world's assets, but employ only one percent of the world's workforce. General Motors is larger than Denmark, Wal-Mart bigger than South Africa. The mega-corporations roam freely around the globe, lobbying legislators, bankrolling elections and playing governments off against each other to get the best deals. Their private hands control the bulk of the world's news and information flows.[8]

---

[7]Forbes Global 500 List. www.forbes.com.
[8]www.adbusters.org, accessed January 10, 2003. See also Hertz, N. (2001). *The silent takeover: Global capitalism and the death of democracy* (p. 43). New York: Arrow Books.

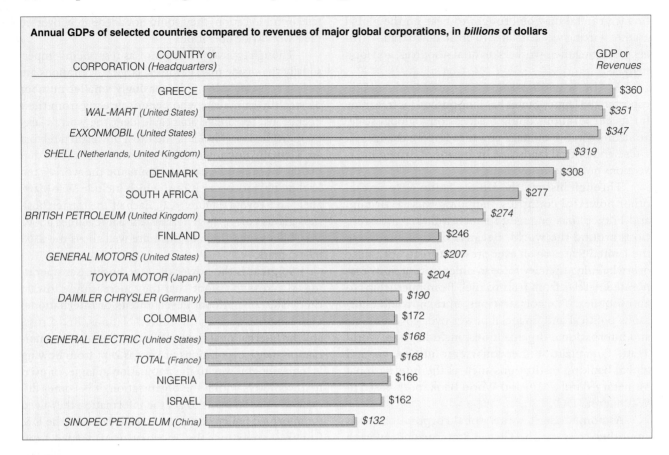

Annual GDPs of selected countries compared to revenues of major global corporations, in *billions* of dollars

COUNTRY or CORPORATION (Headquarters)	GDP or Revenues
GREECE	$360
WAL-MART (United States)	$351
EXXONMOBIL (United States)	$347
SHELL (Netherlands, United Kingdom)	$319
DENMARK	$308
SOUTH AFRICA	$277
BRITISH PETROLEUM (United Kingdom)	$274
FINLAND	$246
GENERAL MOTORS (United States)	$207
TOYOTA MOTOR (Japan)	$204
DAIMLER CHRYSLER (Germany)	$190
COLOMBIA	$172
GENERAL ELECTRIC (United States)	$168
TOTAL (France)	$168
NIGERIA	$166
ISRAEL	$162
SINOPEC PETROLEUM (China)	$132

Figure 16.2

In today's consumer-driven world, it is not uncommon for the yearly revenues of large multinational corporations to equal and even exceed the total value of all goods and services produced within a country per year, known as a country's gross domestic product (GDP). This graph shows the annual GDPs of selected countries alongside the annual revenues of leading global corporations. (Note: GDP says nothing about the unequal distribution of wealth within a country.)

Source: Based on 2007 Global 500 sales figures listed on www.forbes.com and 2007 GDP figures provided on www.worldbank.org.

Global corporations are changing the shape of the world and the lives of individuals from every walk of life, including those they employ. In the never-ending search for cheap labor, these megacorporations have returned to a practice once common in the textile mills of 19th-century Britain and New England, but now on a much larger scale. More than ever before, they have come to favor women for low-skilled assembly jobs. In so-called underdeveloped countries, as subsistence farming gives way to mechanized agriculture for production of crops for export, women are less able to contribute to their families' survival. Together with the devaluation of domestic work, this places pressure on women to seek jobs outside the household to contribute to its support. Since most women in these countries do not have the time or resources to get an education or to develop special job skills, only low-paying jobs are open to them.

Big business has created problems for consumers as well as workers. In a ten-year intensive study of relations between producers and consumers of products and services, anthropologist Laura Nader found repeated and documented offenses by North American businesses that could not be handled by existing complaint mechanisms, either in or out of court.[9]

Faceless relations between producers and consumers, among whom there is a grossly unequal distribution of power, have exacted a high cost: a terrible sense of indifference, apathy, even a loss of faith in the dehumanized—and dehumanizing—system itself. When workers do not trust their bosses, and bosses do not trust each other, production and trade relations on every level will be harmed or even ruined. Because these systems, in the final analysis, are made and maintained by humans, this alienation, or estrangement, may ultimately lead to a systemic breakdown. Now

[9]Nader, L. (Ed.). (1981). *No access to law: Alternatives to the American judicial system.* New York: Academic Press.

that production, trading, and banking operations are part of a globalized system, the breakdown in one part of the system may trigger a worldwide chain reaction of failures. Such was the global crisis triggered by the bankruptcy of a handful of mismanaged Wall Street firms in 2008.

Soft Power: A Global Media Environment

In addition to reliance on military and economic hard power in the global quest for dominance and profit, competing states and corporations utilize the ideological persuasion of soft power as transmitted through electronic and digital media, communication satellites, and other information technology. One of the major tasks of soft power is to package and sell the general idea of globalization as something positive and progressive (as "freedom," "free" trade, "free" market) and to frame or brand anything that opposes capitalism in negative terms.

Global mass media corporations like Cable News Network (CNN) possess enormous soft power. This U.S.-based private company produces and distributes news and other information through transnational cable and satellite networks, as well as websites. With bureaus in over thirty countries, its 24-hour news coverage is available to more than 1.5 billion people all over the world. Like even larger media giants, such as the British Broadcasting Corporation (BBC), CNN not only reports news, but also selects the visual imagery and determines what to stress or repress. By means of their awesome soft power, these corporations influence public perception and action ("hearts and minds").

The far-reaching capabilities of modern electronic and digital technologies have led to the creation of a new global media environment that plays a major role in how individuals and even societies view themselves and their place in the world. People today live in this media environment—a new, boundless cultural space that Indian anthropologist Arjun Appadurai refers to as a "global mediascape."[10]

In recent years, the power of corporations has become all the greater through media expansion. Over the past two decades, a global commercial media system has developed, dominated by a few megacorporations (such as General Electric and Disney), most based in the United States. Having control of television and other

© Harald E. L. Prins

The poorest people in the world, such as this Maka Indian woman in Paraguay, often wear clothing discarded by those who are better off—and people from all walks of life can be found wearing clothes with corporate logos. The power that big business (such as the Disney media corporation) has over individuals is illustrated by the ability of corporations to get consumers to pay for goods that advertise corporate products.

media, as well as the advertising industry, gives global corporations enormous influence on the ideas and behavior of hundreds of millions of ordinary people across the world in ways most people little suspect and can hardly imagine.

Consider, for example, the powerful marketing messages that shape cultural standards concerning the ideal human body. The widespread nature of this concern is evident in the abundance of TV infomercials selling workout equipment and "age-defying" cosmetic products, as well as in the highly popular TV drama *NipTuck* and the much-watched reality program *Dr. 90210* (which follows the stories of plastic surgery patients and doctors in Beverly Hills, California). The following Original Study offers details on what has become a lucrative cosmetic surgery industry.

---

[10]Appadurai, A. (1990). Disjuncture and difference in the global cultural economy. *Public Culture, 2,* 1–24.

Original Study

Standardizing the Body: The Question of Choice

by Laura Nader

The question of choice is central to the story of how medicine and business generate controlling processes in the shaping of women's bodies. Images of the body appear natural within their specific cultural milieus. For example, breast implants are not seen as odd within the cultural milieu of the United States, and female circumcision and infibulation (also known as female genital mutilation or FGM) are not considered odd among people from the Sudan and several other African countries. However, many feminist writers differentiate FGM from breast implantation by arguing that North American women *choose* to have breast implants whereas in Africa women are presumably subject to indoctrination since they experience circumcision as young girls.

One of the most heated debates arising from the public health concern over breast implants is whether the recipients are freely situated—that is, whether their decision is voluntary or whether control is disguised as free will.

An informed response to the free choice argument requires knowing how the beauty-industrial complex works. Toward this end, corporate accountability researcher Linda Coco carried out fieldwork in multiple sites, gaining insights into the inner workings of a multibillion-dollar industry that segments the female body and manufactures commodities of and for the body.

Coco's research shows how some women get caught in the official beauty ideology, and in the case of silicone-gel breast implants some hundreds of thousands of women have been ensnared. But who gets caught and when are important to an understanding of the ecology of power. The average age of a woman having breast implantation is 36 years, and she has an average of two children. She is the beauty industry's insecure consumer recast as a patient with an illness the industry defines as hypertrophy (small breasts).

Coco quotes a past president of the American Society of Plastic and Reconstructive Surgery (ASPRS): "There is substantial and enlarging medical knowledge to the effect that these [small breasts] deformities are really a disease which result in the patient's feelings of inadequacies, lack of self-confidence, distortion of body image, and a total lack of well-being due to a lack of self-perceived femininity. . . . Enlargement . . . is therefore . . . necessary to ensure the quality of life for the patient." In other words, cosmetic surgery is necessary to the patient's psychological health.

The plastic surgeon regards the construction of the official breast as art, the aim being to reform the female body according to the ideals of classic Western art. One surgeon pioneering procedures for correcting deformity took as his ideal female figure that of ancient Greek statues, which he carefully measured, noticing the exact size and shape of the breasts, their vertical location between the third and seventh ribs, the horizontal between the line of the sternal (breast bone) border and the anterior axillary line, and so forth. In Coco's analysis the exercise of the plastic surgeon's technoart recreates a particular static, official breast shape and applies this creation ostensibly to relieve women's mental suffering. The surgeon becomes a psychological healer as well as an artist.

Along with art and psychology, there is, of course, the business of organized

PROCEDURE	NUMBER DONE PER YEAR	PERCENT DONE FOR WOMEN
Facial skin resurfacing (chemical peel, laser, etc.)	1,543,620	92%
Eyelid surgery	240,763	87%
Nose reshaping	151,796	79%
Botox injection	2,775,176	88%
Face lift	138,152	91%
Breast enlargement	399,440	100%
Tummy tuck	185,335	97%
Liposuction	456,828	87%

Selected cosmetic surgical and nonsurgical procedures in the United States (2007) and the percentage carried out for women. *In total, more than 2 million cosmetic surgeries were done and nearly 10 million nonsurgical procedures (chemical peels, Botox injections, etc.), at a total cost of about $13 billion. From 1997 to 2007, the number of cosmetic procedures performed increased 457 percent.*

Source: American Society for Aesthetic Plastic Surgery, 2008.

plastic surgery, which responds to the demands and opportunities of market economics (see figure). By the late 1970s and early 1980s there was a glut of plastic surgeons. The ASPRS began to operate like a commercial enterprise instead of a medical society, saturating the media with ads and even providing low-cost financing. The discourse became a sales pitch. Women "seek" breast implants to keep their husbands or their jobs, to attract men, or to become socially acceptable. Coco calls this "patriarchal capitalism" and questions whether this is free choice or "mind colonization."

Understanding "choice" led Coco to an examination of the power both in the doctor–patient relationship and in the control of information. She found that women "were told by the media, plastic surgeons, women's magazines, other women, and the business world that they could enhance their lives by enhancing their bust lines . . . the social imperative for appearance was personalized, psychologized, and normalized." Social surveys indicate that, to the extent that women internalize the social imperative, they feel they are making the decision on their own.

Not surprisingly, women whose surgery resulted in medical complications often came to recognize the external processes of coercive persuasion that had led them to seek implants. In some ways, they resembled former cult members who had been deprogrammed: Their disillusionment caused them to question the system that had encouraged them to make the decision in the first place. The result was a gradual building of protest against the industry, expressed in networks, newsletters, support groups, workshops, and seminars. As have some former cult members, women have brought suit, testified before lawmakers, and challenged in other ways some of the largest corporations and insurance companies in the land.

The choice of implants, they learn, is part of a matrix of controlling processes in which women are subjects. Given the right circumstances it could happen to anyone. In the Sudan, the young girl is told that FGM procedures are done for her and not to her. In the United States the mutilation of natural breasts is also done for the recreation of femininity. Although power is exercised differently in these two cases, Coco notes the similarity: "The operation on the female breast in [North] America holds much of the same social symbolism and expression of cultural mandate as does FGM in Sudan. Thus, the question of why women choose breast augmentation becomes moot."

Breast implantation is now spreading elsewhere, most notably to China. Will it become a functional equivalent to footbinding in China as part of the competition between patriarchies East and West? Whatever the answer, many social thinkers agree that people are always more vulnerable to intense persuasion during periods of historical dislocation—a break with structures and symbols familiar to the life cycle—in which the media can bring us images and ideas originating in past, contemporary, or even imaginary worlds.

Feminist researchers have sought to crack controlling paradigms such as those that define women's capacities and those that construct a standardized body shape and determine what is beautiful in women. Some of their writings are attempts to free the mind from the beauty constructions of cosmetic industries and fashion magazines. Others relay how the one model of Western beauty is affecting members of ethnic groups who aspire to look the way advertisements say they should. Choice is an illusion, since the restructuring of taste is inextricably linked to shifts in the organization of consumption.

(Adapted from Laura Nader. (1997). Controlling processes: Tracing the dynamics of power. Current Anthropology, 38, 715–717)

PROBLEMS OF STRUCTURAL VIOLENCE

Structural power and its associated concepts of hard and soft power enable us to better understand the wider field of force in which local communities throughout the world are now compelled to operate. To comprehend it is to realize how unequal the distribution of wealth, health, and power is in today's global arena.

Indeed, globalization does more than create a worldwide arena in which megacorporations reap megaprofits. It also wreaks havoc in many traditional cultures and disrupts long-established social organizations everywhere. Considering existing cultural differences, political divisions, and competing economic interests, combined with growing worldwide resistance against superpower domination, the emerging world system is inherently unstable, vulnerable, and unpredictable, not to mention inequitable.

By the early 21st century, the global trend of economic inequality is becoming clear: The poor are becoming poorer, and the rich are becoming richer. For the many thousands of big winners or have-lots, there are many millions of losers or have-nots.

Not only are multinational megacorporations, including banks and investment companies, accused of being insensitive to the political, economic, and environmental consequences of the projects they support, but global finance institutions, such as the IMF and the World Bank, have been similarly chastised for the projects they support. For example, the World Bank approved a $40 million loan to the Chinese government to relocate some of the country's poorest Han Chinese farmers to more fertile land in Qinghai, territory that Tibetans consider part of their homeland. Tibetans protested that the World Bank was supporting China's effort to dilute the Tibetan ethnic minority population in that region.

Based on their capacity to harness, direct, and distribute global resources and energy flows, heavily armed states, megacorporations, and very wealthy elites use their coercive and co-optive powers to structure or rearrange the emerging world system and direct global processes to their own competitive advantage. When such structural power undermines the well-being of others, we may speak of **structural violence**—physical and/or psychological harm (including repression, environmental destruction, poverty, hunger, illness, and premature death) caused by impersonal, exploitative, and unjust social, political, and economic systems.

Clearly, the current structures are positioned in a way that leads to more wealth, power, comfort, and glory for the happy few and little more than poverty, subservience, suffering, and death for multitudes. Every day millions of people around the world face famine, ecological disasters, health problems, political instability, and violence rooted in development programs or profit-making maneuvers directed by powerful states or global corporations.

A useful baseline for identifying structural violence is provided by the Universal Declaration of Human Rights, officially adopted by all members of the United Nations in 1948. Anthropologists played a key role in drafting this important document. The declaration's preamble begins with the statement that "recognition of the inherent dignity and of the equal and inalienable rights of all members of the human family is the foundation of freedom, justice, and peace in the world."[11] Generally speaking, structural violence concerns the impersonal systemic violation of the human rights of individuals and communities to a healthy, peaceful, and dignified life.

Although human rights abuses are nothing new, globalization has enormously expanded and intensified structural violence. For instance, it is leading to an ever-widening gap between the wealthiest and poorest peoples, the powerful and powerless. In 1960 the average income for the twenty wealthiest countries in the world was fifteen times that of the twenty poorest. Today it is thirty times higher.[12]

More remarkable is the fact that the world's 225 richest individuals have a combined wealth equal to the annual income of the poorest 47 percent of the entire world population. In fact, half of all people in the world get by on less than $2 per day, and more than 1.2 billion people live on just $1 a day. Measuring the gap in another way reveals that the poorest 80 percent of the human population make do with 14 percent of all goods and services in the world, the poorest 20 percent with a mere 1.3 percent. Meanwhile, the richest 20 percent enjoy 86 percent.[13]

Structural violence has countless manifestations in addition to widespread poverty. These range from the cultural destruction already indicated to hunger and obesity, and environmental degradation, all discussed in the remaining pages of this chapter.

Overpopulation and Poverty

In 1750, 1 billion people lived on earth. Over the next two centuries our numbers climbed to nearly 2.5 billion. And between 1950 and 2000 the world population soared above 6 billion. Today, India and China each have more than 1 billion inhabitants. Such increases are highly significant because population growth increases the scale of hunger and pollution—and the many problems tied to these two big issues. Although controlling population growth does not by itself make the other problems go away, it is unlikely those other problems can be solved unless population growth is stopped or even reversed.

Despite progress in population control, the number of humans on earth continues to grow overall. Population projections are extremely tricky, given variables such as AIDS, but current projections suggest that global population will peak around 2050 at about 9.37 billion people.

The problem's severity becomes clear when it is realized that the present world population of nearly 7 billion people can be sustained only by using up nonrenewable resources such as oil, which is like living off income-producing capital. It works for a time, but once the capital is gone, so is the possibility of even having an income to live on.

Hunger and Obesity

As frequently dramatized in media reports, hundreds of millions of people face hunger on a regular basis, leading to a variety of health problems, premature death, and other forms of suffering. Today, over a quarter of the world's countries do not produce enough food to feed their populations and cannot afford to import what is needed. The majority of these countries are in sub-Saharan Africa.

structural violence Physical and/or psychological harm (including repression, environmental destruction, poverty, hunger, illness, and premature death) caused by impersonal, exploitative, and unjust social, political, and economic systems

---

[11]www.ccnmtl.columbia.edu/projects/mmt/udhr.

[12]www.worldbank.org/poverty. (2003 statistics).

---

[13]Kurth, P. (1998, October 14). Capital crimes. *Seven Days*, 7; Swaminathan, M. S. (2000). Science in response to basic human needs. *Science, 287,* 425. See also Human Development Report. (2002). *Deepening democracy in a fragmented world.* United Nations Development Program.

© AFP/Getty Images

Hunger afflicts much of the world. It is caused not only by drought and pests, but also by violent ethnic, religious, or political conflicts that uproot families and by global food production and a distribution system geared to satisfy the needs and demands of the world's most powerful countries. Without adequate nutrition, humans lose their ability to resist diseases. And without access to adequate health care, many of the poverty-stricken sick have little chance to survive. For the poor, especially in refugee camps, slums, and other places with miserable living conditions, suffering is a normal condition of life, and death looms everywhere. Here we see displaced people lined up for water at a refugee camp in Sudan's ethnic war-torn Darfur region. Since 2003, the conflict in Sudan has claimed a half-million lives and chased more than 2.5 million people from their homes to camps such as this, where hunger, thirst, and disease are daily threats.

All told, about 1 billion people in the world are undernourished. Some 6 million children aged 5 and under die every year due to hunger, and those who survive often suffer from physical and mental impairment.[14] For the victims of this situation, the effect is violent, even though it was not caused by the deliberate hostile act of a specific individual. The source of the violence may have been the unplanned yet devastatingly real impact of structural power—for instance, through the collapse of local markets due to subsidized foreign imports—and this is what structural violence is all about.

Ironically, while many millions of people in some parts of the world are starving, many millions of others are overeating—quite literally eating themselves to death. In fact, the number of overfed people now exceeds those who are underfed. According to the World Watch Institute in Washington, DC, more than 1.1 billion people worldwide are now overweight. And 300 million of these are obese (but still often malnourished in that their diets lack certain nutrients).

Seriously concerned about the sharp rise in associated health problems (including stroke, diabetes, cancer, and heart disease), the World Health Organization classifies obesity as a global epidemic. Overeating is particularly unhealthy for individuals living in societies where machines have eased the physical burdens of work and other human activities, which helps explain why more than half of the people in some industrial and postindustrial countries are overweight.

However, the obesity epidemic is not due solely to excessive eating and lack of physical activity. A key ingredient is the high sugar and fat content of mass-marketed foods. The problem is spreading and has become a serious concern even in some developing countries. In fact, the highest rates of obesity in the world now exist among Pacific Islanders living in places such as Samoa and Fiji. On the island of Nauru, up to 65 percent of the men and 70 percent of the women are now classified as obese. (That said, not all people who are overweight or obese are so because they eat too much junk food and do too little exercise. In addition to cultural factors, being overweight or obese can also have genetic or other biological causes.)

As for hunger cases, about 10 percent of them can be traced to specific events—droughts or floods, as well as various social, economic, and political disruptions, including warfare. During the 20th century, 44 million people died due to human-made famine.[15] For example, in several sub-Saharan African countries plagued by chronic civil strife, it has been almost impossible to raise and harvest crops, for hordes of hungry refugees, roaming militias, and underpaid soldiers constantly raid fields.

Another problem is that millions of acres in Africa, Asia, and Latin America once devoted to subsistence farming have been given over to the raising of cash crops for export. This has enriched members of elite social classes in these parts of the world, while satisfying the appetites of people in the developed countries for coffee, tea, chocolate, bananas, and beef. Those who used to farm the land for their own food needs have been relocated—either to urban areas, where all too often there is no employment for them, or to areas ecologically unsuited for farming.

---

[14]Hunger Project. (2003); see also Swaminathan.

[15]Hunger Project; see also White, M. (2001). *Historical atlas of the twentieth century.* http://users.erols.com/mwhite28/20centry.htm.

Malé is one of many low-lying islands threatened by rising sea levels brought on by global warming. It is the capital island of the Maldives, an Indian Ocean archipelago composed of 1,200 low-lying islands (199 inhabited), home to about 375,000 people. Climate change and rising sea levels are of great concern to the Maldivians, since their country is only 8 feet above sea level at its highest point. As global warming causes the polar ice caps to melt and sea levels to rise, the entire country could disappear. In recent years, the government had a $60 million seawall built around Malé and undertook the construction of a nearby artificial island where the land and buildings are several feet higher than the rest of the Maldives.

In Africa, such lands are often occupied seasonally by pastoral nomads, and turning them over to cultivation has reduced pasture available for livestock and led to overgrazing. The increase in cleared land, coupled with overgrazing, has depleted both soil and water, with disastrous consequences to nomad and farmer alike. So it is that more than 250 million people can no longer grow crops on their farms, and 1 billion people in 100 countries are in danger of losing their ability to grow crops.[16]

Pollution and Global Warming

The impact of pollution on people and their environment is another key aspect of structural violence brought on by the world's most powerful countries who are the greatest producers and consumers of energy. During the past 200 years, global cultural development has relied on burning increasing quantities of fossil fuels (coal, oil, and gas), which has had dire results: Massive deforestation and desertification, along with severe air, water, and soil pollution, now threaten the health of all life. Fossil fuel use has dramatically increased carbon dioxide levels, trapping more heat in the earth's atmosphere.

Most atmospheric scientists believe that the efficiency of the atmosphere in retaining heat—the so-called greenhouse effect—is being enhanced by increased carbon dioxide, methane, and other gases produced by industrial and agricultural activities. The result, a period of global warming, threatens to dramatically alter climates in all parts of the world.

Rising temperatures are causing more and greater storms, droughts, and heat waves, devastating populations in vulnerable areas. And if the massive meltdown of Arctic ice now under way continues, rising sea levels will inundate low coastal areas worldwide. Entire islands may soon disappear, including thousands of villages and even large cities.

Experts also predict that global warming will lead to an expansion of the geographic ranges of tropical

---

[16]Godfrey, T. (2000, December 27). Biotech threatening biodiversity. *Burlington Free Press*, 10A.

diseases and increase the incidence of respiratory diseases due to additional smog caused by warmer temperatures. Also, they expect an increase in deaths due to heat waves, as witnessed in the 52,000 deaths attributed to the 2003 heat wave in Europe.[17]

Especially since the industrial revolution took off about two centuries ago, societies began to experience the negative side effects of environmental degradation. Much of this degradation is caused by ever-increasing amounts of non-biodegradable waste and toxic emissions into the soil, water, and air. Until very recently, much of this pollution was officially tolerated for the sake of maximizing profits that primarily benefit select individuals, groups, and societies. Today, industries in many parts of the world are producing highly toxic waste at unprecedented rates. Pollutants such as various oxides of nitrogen or sulfur cause the development of acid precipitation, which damages soil, vegetation, and wildlife. Air pollution in the form of smog is often dangerous for human health.

Moreover, poisonous smokestack gases are clearly implicated in acid rain, which is damaging lakes and forests all over northeastern North America. Air containing water vapor with a high acid content is, of course, harmful to the lungs, but the health hazard is greater than this. As ground and surface water becomes more acidic, the solubility of lead, cadmium, mercury, and aluminum, all of them toxic, rises sharply. For instance, aluminum contamination is high enough on 17 percent of the world's farmland to be toxic to plants—and has been linked to senile dementia, Alzheimer's, and Parkinson's disease, three major health problems in industrial countries.

Finding their way into the world's oceans, toxic substances also create hazards for seafood consumers. For instance, Canadian Inuit face health problems related to eating fish and sea mammals that feed in waters contaminated by industrial chemical waste such as polychlorinated biphenyls (PCBs) (see the Biocultural Connection).[18] Obviously, environmental poisoning affects peoples all across the globe (Figure 16.3). Also of great concern are harmful chemicals in plastics used for water bottles, baby bottles, and can linings, as discussed in Chapter 7.

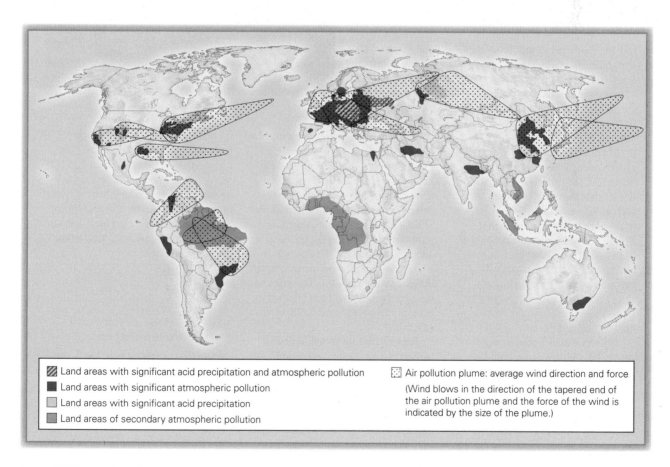

Figure 16.3 **Global Pollution**

Source: Student Atlas of Anthropology by J. L. and A. C. Shalinsky, p.123. © 2003 McGraw-Hill/Duskin Publishing.

---

[17]Larsen, J. (2006, July 28). *Setting the record straight*. Earth Policy Institute, Eco-economy updates.

[18]Inuit Tapiirit Kanatami. http://www.tapirisat.ca/english_text/itk/departments/enviro/ncp.

Toxic Breast Milk Threatens Arctic Culture

Asked to picture the Inuit people inhabiting the Arctic coasts of Canada, Greenland, and Labrador, you are likely to envision them dressed in fur parkas and moving across a pristine, snow-covered landscape on dogsleds—perhaps coming home from hunting seal, walrus, or whale.

Such imaginings are still true—except for the pristine part. Although Inuit live nearer to the North Pole than to any city, factory, or farm, they are not isolated from the pollutants of modern society. Chemicals originating in the cities and farms of North America, Europe, and Asia travel thousands of miles to Inuit territories via winds, rivers, and ocean currents. These toxins have a long life in the Arctic, breaking down very slowly due to icy temperatures and low sunlight. Ingested by zooplankton, the chemicals spread through the seafood chain as one species consumes another. The result is alarming levels of pesticides, mercury, and industrial chemicals in Arctic animals—and in the Inuit people who rely on fishing and hunting for food.

Of particular note are toxic chemicals known as PCBs (polychlorinated biphenyls), used widely over several decades for numerous purposes, such as industrial lubricants, insulating materials, and paint stabilizers. Research shows a widespread presence of PCBs in the breast milk of women around the globe. But nowhere on earth is the concentration higher than among the Inuit—on average seven times that of nursing mothers in Canada's biggest cities.[a]

PCBs have been linked to a wide range of health problems, from liver damage to weakened immune systems to cancer. Studies of children exposed to PCBs in the womb and through breast milk show impaired learning and memory functions. Beyond having a destructive impact on the health of humans (and other animal species), PCBs are affecting the economy, social organization, and psychological well-being of Arctic peoples. Nowhere is this more true than among the 450 Inuit living on Broughton Island, near Canada's Baffin Island. Here, word of skyrocketing PCB levels cost the community its valuable market for Arctic char fish. Other Inuits refer to them as "PCB people," and it is said that Inuit men now avoid marrying women from the island.[b]

The suggestion that the answer to these problems is a change of diet is soundly rejected by Inuit people, who have no real alternatives for affordable food. Abandoning the consumption of traditional seafood would destroy a 4,000-year-old culture based on hunting and fishing. Countless aspects of traditional Inuit culture—from worldview and social arrangements to vocabularies and myths—are linked to Arctic animals and the skills it takes to rely on them for food and so many other things. As one Inuit put it: "Our foods do more than nourish our bodies. They feed our souls. When I eat Inuit foods, I know who I am."[c]

The manufacture of PCBs is now banned in many Western countries (including the United States), and PCB levels are gradually declining worldwide. However, because of their persistence (and widespread presence in remnant industrial goods such as fluorescent lighting fixtures and electrical appliances), they are still the highest-concentration toxins in breast milk, even among mothers born after the ban.

© Bryan & Cherry Alexander/Arctic Photos

And even as PCBs decline, other commercial chemicals are finding their way northward. To date, about 200 hazardous compounds originating in industrialized regions have been detected in the bodies of Arctic peoples.[d] Global warming is fueling the problem, because as glaciers and snow melt, long-stored toxins are released.

[a]Colborn, T., et al. (1997). *Our stolen future* (pp. 107–108). New York: Plume (Penguin Books).

[b]AMAP. (2003). *AMAP assessment 2002: Human health in the Arctic* (pp. xii–xiii, 22–23). Oslo: Arctic Monitoring Assessment Project.

[c]Ingmar Egede, quoted in Cone, M. (2005). *Silent snow: The slow poisoning of the Arctic* (p. 1). New York: Grove Press.

[d]Additional sources: Johansen, B. E. (2002). The Inuit's struggle with dioxins and other organic pollutants. *The American Indian Quarterly, 26*(3), 479–490; Natural Resources Defense Council. (2005, March 25). *Healthy milk, healthy baby: Chemical pollution and mother's milk*. www.NRDC.org; Williams, F. (2005, January 9). Toxic breast milk? *New York Times Magazine.*

Structural violence also manifests itself in the shifting of manufacturing and hazardous waste disposal from developed to developing countries. In the late 1980s, a tightening of environmental regulations in industrialized countries led to a dramatic rise in the cost of hazardous waste disposal. Seeking cheaper ways to get rid of the wastes, "toxic traders" began shipping hazardous waste to eastern Europe and especially to poor and underdeveloped countries in western Africa—thereby passing on the health risks of poison cargo to the world's poorest people.

When news of these practices became public, international outrage led to the drafting and adoption of the Basel Convention to prohibit the export of hazardous wastes and minimize their generation. Today, the scope of the convention is severely limited by the fact that the United States, the largest toxic residue producer in the world, has not ratified the agreement.[19] Moreover, unscrupulous entrepreneurs and corrupt government officials in destitute countries receiving waste have found ways to circumvent the treaty obligations.

Given a general awareness of the causes and dangers of pollution and global warming, why is it that the human species as a whole is not committed to controlling practices that foul its own nest? At least part of the answer lies in philosophical and theological traditions. As we saw in the chapter on politics, Western industrialized societies accept the biblical assertion (found in the Koran as well) of human dominion over the earth, interpreting that it is their task to subdue and control the earth and all its inhabitants. These societies are the biggest contributors to global pollution. For example, on average, one North American consumes hundreds of times the resources of a single African, with all that implies with respect to waste disposal and environmental degradation (Figure 16.4). Moreover, each person in North America adds, on average, 20 tons of carbon dioxide (a greenhouse gas) a year to the atmosphere.

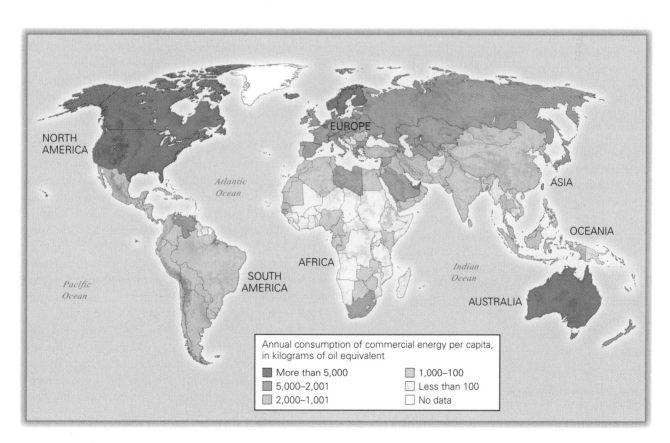

Figure 16.4 Global Energy Consumption

Most of the world's highest energy consumers are in North America and western Europe where at least 100 gigajoules of commercial energy per year are consumed by each person. (A gigajoule is the equivalent of about 3.5 metric tons of coal.) In some of these countries, such as the United States and Canada, the consumption rates are in the 300 gigajoule range. At the other end of the scale are low-income countries, whose consumption rates are often less than 1 percent of those in the United States. (These figures do not include the consumption of noncommercial energy—the traditional fuels of firewood, animal dung, and other organic matter widely used in the less developed parts of the world.)

Source: Student Atlas of Anthropology by J. L. Allen and A. C. Shalinsky, p.126. © 2004, McGraw-Hill/Dushkin Publishing.

---

[19]Hazardous waste trafficking. www.Choike.org.

In "underdeveloped" countries, less than 3 tons per person are emitted.[20] According to botanist Peter Raven, "if everyone lived like Americans, you'd need three planet earths . . . to sustain that level of consumption."[21]

REACTIONS TO GLOBALIZATION

No matter how effectively a dominant state or corporation combines its hard and soft power, globalization does run into opposition. Pockets of resistance exist within the wealthy industrial and postindustrial states as well as elsewhere in the world. This resistance may be manifested in the rise of traditionalisms and revitalization movements—efforts to return to life as it was (or how people think it was) before the familiar order became unhinged and people became unsettled. Some of these reactionary movements may take the form of resurgent ethnonationalism or religious fundamentalist movements. Others may find expression in alternative grassroots movements from radical environmental groups to peace groups.

While it is true that states and big corporations have expanded their power and influence through electronic communication technologies, it is also true that these same technologies present opportunities to individuals and groups that have traditionally been powerless. They provide a means of distributing information and promoting activities that are distinct from or in opposition to those of dominant society.

One striking case of a cultural reaction to globalization is the Taliban, a group of Muslim religious fundamentalists in Afghanistan. The Taliban (the Pashto word for "students," specifically of Islam) helped to force the Russian army out of their country and end the subsequent civil war; then they rose to power in the 1990s and imposed a radical version of traditional Islamic law (Shariah) in an effort to create an Islamic republic based on strict religious values.

In the United States, there has been a similar, though less radical, reaction against modernity. "Born

internal migration Movement within the boundaries of a country
external migration Movement from one country to another; can be voluntary (involving people seeking better conditions and opportunities), involuntary (involving those who have been taken as slaves or prisoners, or driven from their homelands by war, political unrest, religious persecution, or environment disasters), or imposed (not entirely forced but made advisable by the circumstances

again" and other fundamentalist citizens seek to shape or transform not only their towns but also states and even the entire country by electing politicians committed to forging a national culture based on what they see as American patriotism, English-only legislation, and traditional Christian values.[22]

Ethnic Minorities and Indigenous Peoples: Struggles for Human Rights

Throughout this book, we have discussed a wide range of cultures all across the globe. Many of our examples involve peoples who see themselves as members of distinct nations by virtue of their birth and their cultural and territorial heritage—nations over whom peoples of some other ethnic background have tried to assert political control. An estimated 5,000 such national groups exist in the world today, as opposed to a mere 192 states formally admitted as members of the United Nations (up from fewer than fifty in the 1940s).[23] Although some of these ethnic groups are small in population and area—100 or so people living on a few acres—many others are quite large. The Karen people inhabiting southern Burma (Myanmar), for example, number some 4.5 to 5 million, exceeding the population of nearly half of the countries in the world. And Kurds, living in Turkey, Iran, and Iraq, number about 30 million.

The reactions of such groups to forced annexation and domination by state regimes controlled by people of other nations range all the way from the nonviolence of the Saami in Scandinavia, Inuit of Nunavut in northern Canada, or Maori of New Zealand to bloody fights for national independence by Basque separatists in Spain, the Karen in eastern Burma, Chechens in southern Russia, or Palestinians in the Middle East. In pursuit of self-determination, national autonomy, independence, or whatever their political objectives, many struggles have been going on for years, often even decades.

Since the mid-1900s, global institutions such as the United Nations have tried to address the problem of discrimination, repression, and crimes against humanity, in particular genocide. For example, even though it often fails to act on it, the UN General Assembly's 1966 Covenant of Human Rights states unequivocally:

> In those states in which ethnic, religious or linguistic minorities exist, persons belonging to such minorities shall not be denied the rights, in community with the other members

[20]Broecker, W. S. (1992, April). Global warming on trial. *Natural History*, 14.
[21]Quoted in Becker, J. (2004, March). *National Geographic*, 90.

[22]Marsella, J. (1982). Pulling it together: Discussion and comments. In S. Pastner & W. A. Haviland (Eds.), *Confronting the creationists* (pp. 79–80). *Northeastern Anthropological Association, Occasional Proceedings*, 1.
[23]*Cultural Survival Quarterly*. (1992). *15*(4), 38.

of their group, to enjoy their own culture, to profess and practice their own religion or to use their own language.[24]

This covenant applies not only to minority groups, but also to the world's indigenous peoples, who comprise about 5 percent of humanity's population. Nearly all indigenous groups are relatively small nations. Typically, they have suffered repression or discrimination by ethnically different, more powerful, and almost always more heavily populated groups that have gained control over their ancestral homelands.

In the early 1970s indigenous peoples began to organize self-determination movements, resisting acculturation and challenging violations of their human rights. Joining forces across international borders, they established the World Council of Indigenous Peoples in 1975.

In 2007, after many years of popular media campaigns, political lobbying, and diplomatic pressure by hundreds of indigenous leaders and other activists all around the globe, the UN General Assembly finally adopted the Declaration of the Rights of Indigenous Peoples. A foundational document in the global human rights struggle, it contains some 150 articles urging respect for indigenous cultural heritages, calling for official recognition of indigenous land titles and rights of self-determination, and demanding an end to all forms of oppression and discrimination as a principle of international law.

Global Migrations: Refugees, Migrants, and Diasporic Communities

Structural power and structural violence may both be involved in human migration. Throughout human history, individuals, families, and sometimes entire communities have migrated in pursuit of food, safety, and opportunity. Migration has always had a significant effect on world social geography, contributing to culture change and development, to the diffusion of ideas and innovations, and to the complex mixture of peoples and cultures found in the world today.

Internal migration occurs within the boundaries of a country. Often unable to sustain themselves in the rural backlands, people all over the world continue to move to large urban areas, hoping to find a better life. All too often they live out their days in poor, congested, and diseased slums while attempting to achieve what is usually beyond their reach.

External migration is movement from one country to another. Such migration may be *voluntary* (people seeking better conditions and opportunities), but all too often it may be *involuntary, forced, or imposed* (people who have been taken as slaves or prisoners, or driven from their homelands by war, political unrest, religious persecution, or environment disasters) (Figure 16.5).

Today, about 35 million people in almost half of the world's countries either are internally displaced or have crossed international borders as refugees.

In 1982 the United Nations Sub-Commission on the Promotion and Protection of Human Rights established a Working Group on Indigenous Populations (WGIP). Eleven years later WGIP completed a draft of the Declaration of the Rights of Indigenous Peoples, ratified in 2007. Here we see delegates from Japan's ethnic Ainu community in the UN assembly hall at a recent WGIP gathering.

© EPA/Laurent Gilleron/Corbis

---

[24]Quoted in Bodley, J. H. (1990). *Victims of progress* (3rd ed., p. 99). Mountain View, CA: Mayfield.

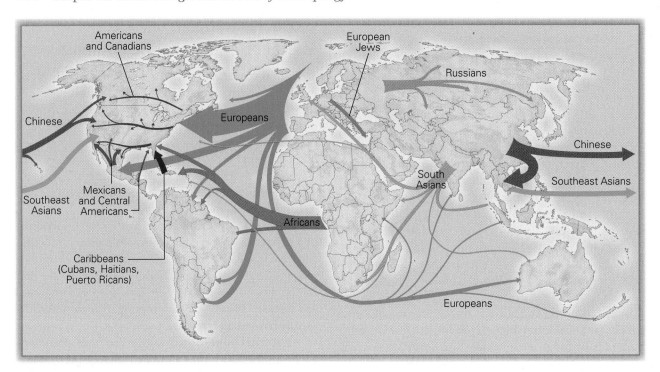

Figure 16.5 **World Migrations**

Migration has had and continues to have a significant effect on world social geography, contributing to culture change and development, to the diffusion of ideas and innovations, and to the complex mixture of people and cultures found in the world today. Internal migration occurs within the boundaries of a country. External migration, illustrated here, is movement from one country or region to another.

Source: Student Atlas of Anthropology by J. L. Allen and A. C. Shalinsky, p.73. © 2003 McGraw-Hill/Dushkin Publishing

Some 9 million of these unfortunates have been forced outside their countries, most of them suffering in make-shift camps where they cannot make a living. In some cases, a large proportion of an ethnic group's entire population finds itself forced to abandon their homes and flee for their lives. For instance, some 18 million Africans are currently uprooted. In war-torn Sudan alone, more than 2.5 million people have been driven from their homes.

In addition to such forced displacements, tens of thousands of people migrate to wealthy countries every year in search of wage labor and a better future for themselves and their offspring. While most cross inter-national borders as legal immigrants, seeking work per-mits and ultimately citizenship in their new homeland, untold numbers of others are illegal and do not enjoy many important rights and benefits.

Legal or not, many of these immigrants face great challenges as poor newcomers in these societies—all the more so because they may encounter racism and dis-crimination. As a consequence, many newcomers form or join communities of people who have come from the same part of the world. Modern transportation and tele-communication technology make it possible for these *diasporic communities*, which exist all across the globe, to remain in contact with relatives and friends who have

settled elsewhere, as well as with their country of origin. Indicative of this aspect of globalization is that today at least 175 million people (2.5 percent of the world's population) live outside their countries of birth—not as refugees or immigrants, but as transnationals who earn their living in one country while remaining citizens of another.

One fascinating aspect of this global movement is the electronic transfer of money in the form of remit-tances to relatives and friends still living in ancestral cit-ies or villages abroad. For example, Mexicans working in the United States send an estimated $25 billion of their savings by means of money transfer firms such as Western Union, banks, and international credit cards. Without these payments, many local communities throughout Mexico would face major economic prob-lems. Worldwide, remittances total some $250 billion per year.[25]

Over the past few decades, mass migration across international borders has dramatically changed the

[25]http://econ.worldbank.org/WBSITE/EXTERNAL/EXTDEC/ EXTDECPROSPECTS/0,contentMDK:21121930~menu PK:3145470~pagePK:64165401~piPK:64165026~theSitePK:47688 3,00.html.

ethnic composition of affluent societies in western Europe and North America. For instance, there are now at least 1.5 million Africans living in the United States, with an estimated 500,000 in the greater New York City area alone. About 1.5 million Africans and another 2 million people from other parts of the world, mainly from former colonial territories, now live in France. England is now home to over 1.5 million South Asians, plus another 1.3 million people of African descent, also primarily hailing from the former British colonies. And almost 2.5 million people of Turkish origin now reside in western Germany. Although the migrants may experience hardship, disappointment, and sometimes failure in their new countries, those who remain trapped in their troubled homelands often face worse challenges: malnutrition, hunger, chronic disease, and violence, resulting in a short life expectancy for many.

CONCLUDING REMARKS

As defined in Chapter 1, anthropology is the comparative study of humankind everywhere and throughout time. It seeks to produce reliable knowledge about different peoples and cultures, their ideas and behaviors. Since the beginning of the discipline in the mid-1800s, generations of anthropologists have studied our species in all its cultural and biological variation. In the process, they described in great detail an enormous number and range of human biology, beliefs, and practices. They also collected a staggering volume of ethnographic artifacts and documented and recorded the sounds and sights of hundreds of different cultures.

Today, many of the cultures studied by the earliest anthropologists more than a century ago have changed profoundly in response to powerful outside influences

© Monica Almeida/The New York Times/Redux

Gila River Indian community canal. In the 19th century Pima Indians in southwest Arizona, who call themselves Akimel O'otham, or "river people," lost the river that had for generations sustained their farming culture when white farmers upstream siphoned it off. The theft of the river—combined with U.S. federal government rations of lard (pig fat), canned meats, and sugary processed foods—unhinged traditional Pima life and conspired with genetic anomalies to sow an obesity epidemic that has left this reservation community with among the highest diabetes rates in the world. In 2004, after decades of litigation, the Pima and neighboring Maricopa Indians achieved the largest Indian water-rights settlement ever. Water is once again beginning to flow by way of irrigation canals, making it possible to re-establish vegetable farms with the hope of boosting Pima economy and restoring a healthier lifestyle. The question is whether this can repair the damage of generations of structural violence.

and internal dynamics. Others have disappeared as a result of deadly epidemics, violent conflicts, acculturation, ethnocide, or genocide. All too often, the only detailed records we now possess of these altered and vanished cultures are those that some visiting anthropologist was able to document before it was too late.

But, anthropologists do much more than try to preserve precious information about distinctive peoples and cultures. As chronicled in the pages of this book, they also try to explain why cultures are similar or different, why and how they did or did not change. Moreover, they try to identify the particular knowledge and insights that each culture holds concerning the human condition—including contrasting views about humankind's place in the world, how natural resources are used and treated, and how one relates to fellow humans and other species.

Anthropologists are trained to understand and explain economic, social, political, and ideological, as well as biological and environmental features and processes as parts of interrelated dynamic systems. Theoretical concepts, such as structural power and structural violence, illustrate how these phenomena are related and interdependent. The anthropological perspective on local communities in the age of globalization makes key contributions to our understanding of such troubling problems as overpopulation, poverty, food shortages, environmental destruction, and disease. The value of this perspective has been confirmed by international organizations that now employ anthropologists for their professional insights. For example, after a series of ill-conceived and mismanaged development projects that harmed more than helped local populations, the World Bank contracted dozens of anthropologists for projects all around the world. The same is true for other international organizations, as well as some global corporations and state government agencies.

Some anthropologists go beyond just studying different cultures and reach out to assist besieged groups that are struggling to survive in today's rapidly changing world. In so doing, they seek to put into practice their own knowledge about humankind—knowledge deepened through the comparative perspective of anthropology, which is cross-culturally, historically, and biologically informed.

The idea that anthropological research is fascinating in itself and also has the potential of helping solve practical problems on local and global levels has drawn and continues to draw a unique group of people into the discipline. Most of these individuals are inspired by the old but still valid idea that anthropology must aim to live up to its ideal as the most liberating of the sciences. As stated by noted anthropologist Margaret Mead, "Never doubt that a small group of committed people can change the world; indeed it is the only thing that ever has."

Chapter Summary

■ Modernization (an all-encompassing and global process of political and socioeconomic change, whereby developing societies acquire some of the cultural characteristics common to Western industrial societies) has five subprocesses: technological development, agricultural development, urbanization, industrialization, and telecommunication. Today we see a worldwide process of accelerated modernization known as globalization, in which all parts of the earth are becoming interconnected in one vast interrelated and all-encompassing system.

■ Some believe that rapid developments in communication, transportation, and world trade are leading toward a single world culture that could lessen chances for conflict. Most anthropologists are skeptical of this because comparative historical and cross-cultural research show the persistence of distinctive worldviews and the tendency of large multi-ethnic states tend to come apart.

■ Ethnic tension, common in pluralistic societies, sometimes turns violent, leading to formal separation. To manage cultural diversity within such societies, some countries have adopted multiculturalism, an official public policy of mutual respect and tolerance for cultural differences.

■ Structural power refers to the global forces that direct economic and political institutions and shape public ideas and values. Hard power is backed up by economic and military force, and soft power is ideological persuasion. The world's largest corporations are almost all based in a small group of wealthy and powerful states, which also dominate international trade and finance organizations.

■ Cutting across international boundaries, global corporations are a powerful force for worldwide integration despite the political, linguistic, religious, and other cultural differences that separate people. Their power and wealth, often exceeding that of national governments, have increased dramatically through media expansion. Major players in the globalization process, these megacorporations have enormous influence on the ideas and behavior of hundreds of millions of people worldwide. In pursuit of wealth and power, states and corporations now compete for increasingly scarce natural resources, cheap labor, new commercial markets, and ever-larger profits in a huge political arena spanning the entire globe.

■ Globalization provides megaprofits for large corporations but often wreaks havoc in many traditional cultures and disrupts long-established patterns of social organizations.

By means of soft power, globalization is marketed as positive and progressive for everyone, but the poor are becoming poorer even as the rich get richer. Globalization also engenders worldwide resistance against superpower domination. For this reason, the emerging world system is inherently unstable, vulnerable, and unpredictable.

■ One result of globalization is worldwide and growing structural violence—physical and/or psychological harm (including repression, cultural and environmental destruction, poverty, hunger and obesity, illness, and premature death) caused by impersonal, exploitative, and unjust social, political, and economic systems.

■ Reactions against the structural violence of globalization include the rise of traditionalism and revitalization movements—efforts to return to life as it was (or how people think it was) before the familiar order became unhinged and people became unsettled. These may take the form of resurgent ethnonationalism or religious fundamentalist movements.

■ Structural power and structural violence can both play a role in human migration. Internal migration occurs within the boundaries of a country. Often unable to sustain themselves in the rural backlands, people move to the large urban areas, hoping to find a better life. External migration is movement from one country to another; it can be voluntary, involuntary, or imposed.

■ Some dramatic changes in cultural values and motivations, as well as in social institutions and the types of technologies we employ, are required if humans are going to realize a sustainable future for generations to come. The shortsighted emphasis on consumerism and individual self-interest so characteristic of the world's affluent countries needs to be abandoned in favor of a more balanced social and environmental ethic. Trained in what has been called the most liberating of the sciences, anthropologists have a contribution to make in bringing about this shift. They are well versed in the dangers of culture-bound thinking, and they bring a holistic biocultural and comparative historical perspective to the challenge of understanding and balancing the sometimes conflicting needs and desires of local communities in the age of globalization.

Questions for Reflection

1. When societies become involved in the modernizing process, all levels of their cultural systems are affected by these changes. Do you think that people are fully aware of the long-term consequences of the changes they themselves may have welcomed? Can you come up with any examples of unforeseen changes in your own community or neighborhood?

2. No matter how divided peoples of the world are on economic, political, and ideological issues, all face the collective challenge of maintaining the long-term integrity of the planet we depend upon for survival. Do you think individuals like yourself can influence the current course toward environmental destruction that threatens all species, including our own? What steps do you think need to be taken individually and collectively to deal with this issue?

3. Considering the relationship between structural power and structural violence, does your own lifestyle in terms of buying clothes and food, driving cars, and so on reflect or have an effect on the globalization process?

4. In the global mediascape, television viewers and Internet users not only are consumers of news and entertainment but are also exposed to soft power. Can you think of an example of soft power in your daily life? And at which point does such influence turn into propaganda or manipulation?

5. The World Health Organization, UNESCO, Oxfam, and Amnesty International are global institutions concerned with structural violence and human rights violations. Confronted with genocidal conflicts, famines, epidemics, and torture of political prisoners, people active in these organizations try to improve the human condition. Why do you think that an anthropological perspective on such worldwide problems might be of practical use? Can you think of an example?

Key Terms

modernization	soft power
multiculturalism	structural violence
structural power	internal migration
hard power	external migration

GLOSSARY

absolute or chronometric dating In archaeology and paleoanthropology, dates for archaeological materials based on solar years, centuries, or other units of absolute time.

acculturation Massive culture change that occurs in a society when it experiences intensive firsthand contact with a more powerful society.

action theory The theory that self-serving actions by forceful leaders play a role in civilization's emergence.

adaptation A series of beneficial adjustments to the environment.

adjudication Mediation with an unbiased third party making the ultimate decision.

age grade An organized category of people based on age; every individual passes through a series of such categories over his or her lifetime.

age set A formally established group of people born during a certain time span who move through the series of age-grade categories together.

agriculture Intensive crop cultivation, employing plows, fertilizers, and/or irrigation.

alleles Alternate forms of a single gene.

alphabet A series of symbols representing the sounds of a language arranged in a traditional order.

anagenesis A sustained directional shift in a population's average characteristics.

analogies In biology, structures possessed by different organisms that are superficially similar due to similar function, without sharing a common developmental pathway or structure.

animatism A belief that nature is enlivened or energized by an impersonal spiritual force or supernatural energy, which may make itself manifest in any special place, thing, or living creature.

animism A belief that nature is enlivened or energized by distinct personalized spirit beings separable from bodies.

anthropoids A subdivision within the primate order that includes New World Monkeys, Old World monkeys, and apes (including humans).

anthropology The study of humankind in all times and places.

applied anthropology The use of anthropological knowledge and methods to solve practical problems, often for a specific client.

arboreal Living in the trees.

archaeology The study of human cultures through the recovery and analysis of material remains and environmental data.

Archaic cultures Term used to refer to Mesolithic cultures in the Americas.

artifact Any object fashioned or altered by humans.

Australopithecus The genus including several species of early bipeds from southern and eastern Africa living between about 1.1 and 4.3 million years ago, one of whom was directly ancestral to humans.

balanced reciprocity A mode of exchange in which the giving and the receiving are specific as to the value of the goods and the time of their delivery.

band A relatively small and loosely organized kin-ordered group that inhabits a specific territory and that may split periodically into smaller extended family groups that are politically independent.

binocular vision Vision with increased depth perception from two eyes set next to each other allowing their visual fields to overlap.

bioarchaeology The archaeological study of human remains emphasizing the preservation of cultural and social processes in the skeleton.

biocultural Focusing on the interaction of biology and culture.

bipedalism A special form of locomotion on two feet found in humans and their ancestors.

brachiation Using the arms to move from branch to branch, with the body hanging suspended beneath the arms.

bride-price Money or valuable goods paid by the groom or his family to the bride's family upon marriage. Also called bride wealth.

bride service A designated period of time when the groom works for the bride's family.

Bronze Age In the Old World, the period marked by the production of tools and ornaments of bronze; began about 5,000 years ago in China and Southwest Asia and about 500 years earlier in Southeast Asia.

cargo cult A spiritual movement (especially noted in Melanesia) in reaction to disruptive contact with Western capitalism, promising resurrection of deceased relatives, destruction or enslavement of white foreigners, and the magical arrival of utopian riches.

carrying capacity The number of people that the available resources can support at a given level of food-getting techniques.

caste A closed social class in which membership is determined by birth and fixed for life.

chiefdom A regional polity in which two or more local groups are organized under a single chief, who is at the head of a ranked hierarchy of people.

chromatid One half of the "X" shape of chromosomes visible once replication is complete. Sister chromatids are exact copies of each other.

chromosomes In the cell nucleus, the structures visible during cellular division containing long strands of DNA combined with a protein.

civil disobedience Refusal to obey civil laws in an effort to induce change in governmental policy or legislation, characterized by the use of passive resistance or other nonviolent means.

civilization In anthropology a type of society marked by the presence of cities, social classes, and the state.

cladogenesis Speciation through a branching mechanism whereby an ancestral population gives rise to two or more descendant populations.

clan An extended unilineal kinship group, often consisting of several lineages, whose members claim common descent from a remote ancestor, usually legendary or mythological.

clines Gradual changes in the frequency of an allele or trait over space.

code switching Changing from one mode of speech to another as the situation demands, whether from one language to another or from one dialect of a language to another.

common-interest associations Associations that result from an act of joining based on sharing particular activities, objectives, values, or beliefs.

community A unit of primate social organization composed of fifty or more individuals who inhabit a large geographical area together.

conjugal family A family established through marriage.

consanguineal family A family of "blood relatives" consisting of related women, their brothers, and the women's offspring.

conspicuous consumption A showy display of wealth for social prestige.

contagious magic Magic based on the principle that things or persons once in contact can influence each other after the contact is broken.

continental drift According to the theory of plate tectonics, the movement of continents embedded in underlying plates on the earth's surface in relation to one another over the history of life on earth.

convergent evolution In cultural evolution, the development of similar cultural adaptations to similar environmental conditions by different peoples with different ancestral cultures.

core values Those values especially promoted by a particular culture.

cross cousin Child of a mother's brother or a father's sister.

cultural adaptation A complex of ideas, activities, and technologies that enable people to survive and even thrive in their environment.

cultural anthropology Also known as social or sociocultural anthropology. The study of customary patterns in human behavior, thought, and feelings. It focuses on humans as culture-producing and culture-reproducing creatures.

cultural control Control through beliefs and values deeply internalized in the minds of individuals.

cultural evolution Culture change over time (not to be confused with progress).

cultural relativism The idea that one must suspend judgment of other people's practices in order to understand them in their own cultural terms.

cultural resource management A branch of archaeology concerned with survey and/or excavation of archaeological and historical remains threatened by construction or development and policy surrounding protection of cultural resources.

culture A society's shared and socially transmitted ideas, values, and perceptions, which are used to make sense of experience and generate behavior and are reflected in that behavior.

culture-bound Theories about the world and reality based on the assumptions and values of one's own culture.

datum point The starting, or reference, point for a grid system.

dependence training Child-rearing practices that foster compliance in the performance of assigned tasks and dependence on the domestic group, rather than reliance on oneself.

descent group Any kinship group with a membership lineally descending from a real (historical) or fictional common ancestor.

dialects Varying forms of a language that reflect particular regions, occupations, or social classes and that are similar enough to be mutually intelligible.

diffusion The spread of certain ideas, customs, or practices from one culture to another.

discourse An extended communication on a particular subject.

displacement Referring to things and events removed in time and space.

diurnal Active during the day and at rest at night.

divination A magical procedure or spiritual ritual designed to find out about what is not knowable by ordinary means, such as foretelling the future by interpreting omens.

DNA Deoxyribonucleic acid. The genetic material consisting of a complex molecule whose base structure directs the synthesis of proteins.

doctrine An assertion of opinion or belief formally handed down by an authority as true and indisputable.

domestication An evolutionary process whereby humans modify, either intentionally or unintentionally, the genetic makeup of a population of plants or animals, sometimes to the extent that members of the population are unable to survive and/or reproduce without human assistance.

dominance The ability of one allele for a trait to mask the presence of another allele.

dominance hierarchies An observed ranking system in primate societies ordering individuals from high (alpha) to low standing corresponding to predictable behavioral interactions including domination.

dowry Payment of a woman's inheritance at the time of her marriage, either to her or to her husband.

economic system An organized arrangement for producing, distributing, and consuming goods.

ecosystem A system, or a functioning whole, composed of both the natural environment and all the organisms living within it.

egalitarian societies Societies in which everyone has about equal rank, access to, and power over basic resources.

EGO The central person from whom the degree of each relationship is traced.

eliciting devices Activities and objects used to draw out individuals and encourage them to recall and share information.

empirical Based on observations of the world rather than on intuition or faith.

enculturation The process by which a society's culture is passed on from one generation to the next and individuals become members of their society.

endogamy Marriage within a particular group or category of individuals.

Eskimo system Kinship reckoning in which the nuclear family is emphasized by specifically identifying the mother, father, brother, and sister, while lumping together all other relatives into broad categories such as uncle, aunt, and cousin. Also known as the lineal system.

ethnic group People who collectively and publicly identify themselves as a distinct group based on cultural features such as common origin, language, customs, and traditional beliefs.

ethnicity This term, rooted in the Greek word *ethnikos* ("nation") and related to *ethnos* ("custom"), is the expression of the set of cultural ideas held by an ethnic group.

ethnic psychosis A mental disorder specific to a particular ethnic group.

ethnocentrism The belief that the ways of one's own culture are the only proper ones.

ethnocide The violent eradication of an ethnic group's collective cultural identity as a distinctive people; occurs when a dominant society deliberately sets out to destroy another society's cultural heritage.

ethnography A detailed description of a particular culture primarily based on fieldwork.

ethnolinguistics A branch of linguistics that studies the relationships between language and culture and how they mutually influence and inform each other.

ethnology The study and analysis of different cultures from a comparative or historical point of view, utilizing ethnographic accounts and developing anthropological theories that help explain why certain important differences or similarities occur among groups.

evolution Changes in allele frequencies in populations. Also known as microevolution.

exogamy Marriage outside the group.

extended family Two or more closely related nuclear families clustered together into a large domestic group.

external migration Movement from one country to another; can be voluntary (involving people seeking better conditions and opportunities), involuntary (involving those who have been taken as slaves or prisoners, or driven from their homelands by war, political unrest, religious persecution, or environment disasters), or imposed (not entirely forced but made advisable by the circumstances).

family Two or more people related by blood, marriage, or adoption. The family may take many forms, ranging from a single parent with one or more children, to a married couple or polygamous spouses with, or without, offspring, to several generations of parents and their children.

fieldwork The term anthropologists use for on-location research.

fission The splitting of a descent group into two or more new descent groups.

food foraging A mode of subsistence involving some combination of hunting, fishing, and gathering wild plant foods.

forensic anthropology Subfield of applied physical anthropology that specializes in the identification of human skeletal remains for legal purposes.

formal interview A structured question–answer session, carefully notated as it occurs and based on prepared questions.

fossil The preserved remains of plants and animals that lived in the past.

founder effects A particular form of genetic drift deriving from a small founding population not possessing all the alleles present in the original population.

gender The cultural elaborations and meanings assigned to the biological differentiation between the sexes.

gendered speech Distinct male and female speech patterns, which vary across social and cultural settings.

gene flow The introduction of alleles from the gene pool of one population into that of another.

gene pool All the genetic variants possessed by members of a population.

generalized reciprocity A mode of exchange in which the value of the gift is not calculated, nor is the time of repayment specified.

genes Portions of DNA molecules that direct the synthesis of specific proteins.

genetic drift Chance fluctuations of allele frequencies in the gene pool of a population.

genocide The physical extermination of one people by another, either as a deliberate act or as the accidental outcome of activities carried out by one people with little regard for their impact on others.

genome The complete structure sequence of DNA for a species.

genotype The alleles possessed for a particular trait.

genus, genera (pl.) In the system of plant and animal classification, a group of like species.

gestures Facial expressions and body postures and motions that convey intended as well as subconscious messages.

globalization Worldwide interconnectedness, evidenced in global movements of natural resources, trade goods, human labor, finance capital, information, and infectious diseases.

gracile australopithecines Members of the genus *Australopithecus* possessing a more lightly built chewing apparatus; likely had a diet that included more meat than that of the robust australopithecines.

grammar The entire formal structure of a language, including morphology and syntax.

grave goods Items such as utensils, figurines, and personal possessions, symbolically placed in the grave for the deceased person's use in the afterlife.

grid system A system for recording data in three dimensions from an archaeological excavation.

grooming The ritual cleaning of another animal's coat to remove parasites and other matter.

group marriage Marriage in which several men and women have sexual access to one another. Also called co-marriage.

haplorhines A subdivision within the primate order based on shared genetic characteristics; includes tarsiers, New World monkeys, Old World monkeys, and apes (including humans).

hard power Coercive power that is backed up by economic and military force.

Hawaiian system Kinship reckoning in which all relatives of the same sex and generation are referred to by the same term. Also known as the generational system.

hemoglobin The protein that carries oxygen in the red blood cells.

heterozygous Refers to a chromosome pair that bears different alleles for a single gene.

holistic perspective A fundamental principle of anthropology, that the various parts of human culture and biology must be viewed in the broadest possible context in order to understand their interconnections and interdependence.

Homo erectus "Upright man." A species within the genus *Homo* first appearing just after 2 million years ago in Africa and ultimately spreading throughout the Old World.

Homo habilis "Handy man." The first fossil members of the genus *Homo* appearing 2.5 million years ago, with larger brains and smaller faces than australopithecines.

homologies In biology, structures possessed by two different organisms that arise in similar fashion and pass through similar stages during embryonic development, though they may possess different functions.

homozygous Refers to a chromosome pair that bears identical alleles for a single gene.

horticulture Cultivation of crops carried out with simple hand tools such as digging sticks or hoes.

household The basic residential unit where economic production, consumption, inheritance, child rearing, and shelter are organized and carried out.

Human Relations Area Files (HRAF) A vast collection of cross-indexed ethnographic, biocultural, and archaeological data catalogued by cultural characteristics and geographic location. Archived in about 300 libraries (on microfiche or online).

hydraulic theory The theory that explains civilization's emergence as the result of the construction of elaborate irrigation systems, the functioning of which required full-time managers whose control blossomed into the first governing body and elite social class.

hypothesis A tentative explanation of the relation between certain phenomena.

imitative magic Magic based on the principle that like produces like; sometimes called sympathetic magic.

incest taboo The prohibition of sexual relations between specified individuals, usually parent and child and sibling relations at a minimum.

incorporation In a rite of passage, reincorporation of the individual into society in his or her new status.

independence training Child-rearing practices that promote independence, self-reliance, and personal achievement.

industrial society A society in which human labor, hand tools, and animal power are largely replaced by machines, with an economy primarily based on big factories.

informal economy Network of producing and circulating marketable commodities, labor, and services that for various reasons escape government control.

informal interview An unstructured, open-ended conversation in everyday life.

informed consent Formal recorded agreement to participate in the research. Federally mandated for all research in the United States and Europe.

infrastructure The economic foundation of a society, including its subsistence practices and the tools and other material equipment used to make a living.

innovation Any new idea, method, or device that gains widespread acceptance in society.

internal migration Movement within the boundaries of a country.

intersexuals People born with reproductive organs, genitalia, and/or sex chromosomes that are not exclusively male or female.

Iroquois system Kinship reckoning in which a father and father's brother are referred to by a single term, as are a mother and mother's sister, but a father's sister and mother's brother are given separate terms. Parallel cousins are classified with brothers and sisters, while cross cousins are classified separately but not equated with relatives of some other generation.

key consultants Members of the society being studied who provide information that helps the researchers understand the meaning of what they observe. Early anthropologists referred to such individuals as informants.

kindred An individual's genetically close blood relatives on the maternal and paternal sides of his or her family.

kinesics A system of notating and analyzing postures, facial expressions, and body motions that convey messages.

kinship A network of relatives within which individuals possess certain mutual rights and obligations.

Kula ring A form of balanced reciprocity that reinforces trade and social relations among the seafaring Trobriand people, who inhabit a large ring of islands in the southwestern Pacific Ocean off the eastern coast of Papua New Guinea, and other Melanesians.

lactase An enzyme in the small intestine that enables humans to assimilate lactose.

lactose A sugar that is the primary constituent of fresh milk.

language A system of communication using sounds or gestures that are put together in meaningful ways according to a set of rules.

language family A group of languages descended from a single ancestral language.

law Formal rules of conduct that, when violated, effectuate negative sanctions.

law of independent assortment The Mendelian principle that genes controlling different traits are inherited independently of one another.

law of segregation The Mendelian principle that variants of genes for a particular trait retain their separate identities through the generations.

legitimacy The right of political leaders to govern—to hold, use, and allocate power—based on the values a particular society holds.

leveling mechanism A cultural obligation compelling prosperous members of a community to give away goods, host public feasts, provide free service, or otherwise demonstrate generosity so that no one permanently accumulates significantly more wealth than anyone else.

lineage A unilineal kinship group descended from a common ancestor or founder who lived four to six generations ago, and in which relationships among members can be exactly stated in genealogical terms.

linguistic anthropology The study of human languages.

linguistic determinism The idea that language to some extent shapes the way in which we view and think about the world around us.

linguistic divergence The development of different languages from a single ancestral language.

linguistic nationalism The attempt by ethnic minorities and even countries to proclaim independence by purging their language of foreign terms.

linguistic relativity The idea that distinctions encoded in one language are unique to that language.

linguistics The modern scientific study of all aspects of language.

Lower Paleolithic Old Stone Age beginning with the earliest Oldowan tools spanning from about 200,000 or 250,000 to 2.6 million years ago.

macroevolution Evolution above the species level.

mammals The class of vertebrate animals distinguished by bodies covered with fur, self-regulating temperature, and in females milk-producing mammary glands.

market exchange The buying and selling of goods and services, with prices set by rules of supply and demand.

marriage A culturally sanctioned union between two or more people that establishes certain rights and obligations between the people, between them and their children, and between them and their in-laws. Such marriage rights and obligations most often include, but are not limited to, sex, labor, property, child rearing, exchange, and status.

material culture The durable aspects of culture such as tools, structures, and art.

matrilineal descent Descent traced exclusively through the female line to establish group membership.

matrilocal residence A residence pattern in which a married couple lives in the wife's mother's place of residence.

mediation Settlement of a dispute through negotiation assisted by an unbiased third party.

medical anthropology A specialization in anthropology that brings theoretical and applied approaches from cultural and biological anthropology to the study of human health and disease.

meiosis A kind of cell division that produces the sex cells, each of which has half the number of chromosomes found in other cells of the organism.

Mesoamerica The region encompassing southern Mexico and northern Central America.

Mesolithic The Middle Stone Age of Europe, Asia, and Africa beginning about 12,000 years ago.

microlith A small blade of flint or similar stone, several of which were hafted together in wooden handles to make tools; widespread in the Mesolithic.

middens A refuse or garbage disposal area in an archaeological site.

mitosis A kind of cell division that produces new cells having exactly the same number of chromosome pairs, and hence copies of genes, as the parent cell.

modal personality The body of character traits that occur with the highest frequency in a culturally bounded population.

modernization The process of economic change, whereby developing societies acquire some of the social and political characteristics of Western industrial societies. It features five key subprocesses: technological development, agricultural development, urbanization, industrialization, and telecommunication.

moiety Each group that results from a division of a society into two halves on the basis of descent.

molecular anthropology A branch of biological anthropology that uses genetic and biochemical techniques to test hypotheses about human evolution, adaptation, and variation.

money Anything used to make payments for other goods and services as well as to measure their value; may be special purpose or multipurpose.

monogamy Marriage in which both partners have just one spouse.

morphemes The smallest units of sound that carry a meaning in language. They are distinct from phonemes, which can alter meaning but have no meaning by themselves.

morphology The study of the patterns or rules of word formation in a language (including such things as rules concerning verb tense, pluralization, and compound words).

Mousterian The tool industry of the Neandertals and their contemporaries of Europe, Southwest Asia, and northern Africa from 40,000 to 125,000 years ago.

multiculturalism Public policy for managing cultural diversity in a multiethnic society, officially stressing mutual respect and tolerance for cultural differences within a country's borders.

multiregional hypothesis The hypothesis that modern humans originated through a process of simultaneous local transition from *Homo erectus* to *Homo sapiens* throughout the inhabited world.

mutation Chance alteration of genetic material that produces new variation.

myth A sacred narrative that explains the fundamentals of human existence—where we and everything in our world came from, why we are here, and where we are going.

naming ceremony A special event or ritual to mark the naming of a child.

nation A people who share a collective identity based on a common culture, language, territorial base, and history.

Natufian culture A Mesolithic culture living in the lands that are now Israel, Lebanon, and western Syria, between about 10,200 and 12,500 years ago.

natural selection The evolutionary process through which factors in the environment exert pressure, favoring some individuals over others to produce the next generation.

Neandertals A distinct group within the genus *Homo* inhabiting Europe and Southwest Asia from approximately 30,000 to 125,000 years ago.

negative reciprocity A mode of exchange in which the aim is to get something for as little as possible. Neither fair nor balanced, it may involve hard bargaining, manipulation, outright cheating, or theft.

negotiation The use of direct argument and compromise by the parties to a dispute to arrive voluntarily at a mutually satisfactory agreement.

Neolithic The New Stone Age; prehistoric period beginning about 10,000 years ago in which peoples possessed stone-based technologies and depended on domesticated crops and/or animals.

Neolithic revolution The profound culture change beginning about 10,000 years ago associated with the early domestication of plants and animals and settlement in permanent villages; sometimes referred to as the Neolithic transition.

neolocal residence A pattern in which a married couple establishes its household in a location apart from either the husband's or the wife's relatives.

new reproductive technologies (NRTs) Alternative means of reproduction such as surrogate motherhood and in vitro fertilization.

nocturnal Active at night and at rest during the day.

nuclear family A group consisting of one or more parents and dependent offspring, which may include a stepparent, stepsiblings, and adopted children. (Until recently this term referred only to the father, mother, and child(ren) unit.)

Oldowan The first stone tool industry, beginning between 2.5 and 2.6 million years ago.

opposable Able to bring the thumb or big toe in contact with the tips of the other digits on the same hand or foot in order to grasp objects.

ovulation Moment when an egg released from the ovaries into the womb is receptive for fertilization.

paleoanthropology The study of the origins and predecessors of the present human species.

pantheon The several gods and goddesses of a people.

paralanguage Voice effects that accompany language and convey meaning. These include vocalizations such as giggling, groaning, or sighing, as well as voice qualities such as pitch and tempo.

parallel cousin Child of a father's brother or a mother's sister.

parallel evolution In cultural evolution, the development of similar cultural adaptations to similar environmental conditions by peoples whose ancestral cultures were already somewhat alike.

participant observation In ethnography, the technique of learning a people's culture through social participation and personal observation within the community being studied, as well as interviews and discussion with individual members of the group over an extended period of time.

pastoralism Breeding and managing migratory herds of domesticated grazing animals, such as goats, sheep, cattle, llamas, or camels.

patrilineal descent Descent traced exclusively through the male line to establish group membership.

patrilocal residence A residence pattern in which a married couple lives in the husband's father's place of residence.

personality The distinctive way a person thinks, feels, and behaves.

phenotype The observable or testable appearance of an organism that may or may not reflect a particular genotype due to the variable expression of dominant and recessive alleles.

phenotypic inheritance Two or more genes contribute to the phenotypic expression of a single characteristic.

phonemes The smallest units of sound that make a difference in meaning in a language.

phonetics The systematic identification and description of distinctive speech sounds in a language.

phonology The study of language sounds.

phratry A unilineal descent group composed of at least two clans that supposedly share a common ancestry, whether or not they really do.

physical anthropology Also known as biological anthropology. The systematic study of humans as biological organisms.

pluralistic society A society in which two or more ethnic groups or nationalities are politically organized into one territorial state but maintain their cultural differences.

political organization The way power is distributed and embedded in society; the means through which a society creates and maintains social order and reduces social disorder.

polyandry Marriage of a woman to two or more men at one time; a form of polygamy.

polygamy One individual having multiple spouses at the same time; from the Greek words *poly* ("many") and *gamos* ("marriage").

polygenetic inheritance Two or more genes contribute to the phenotypic expression of a single characteristic.

polygyny Marriage of a man to two or more women at the same time; a form of polygamy.

polytheism Belief in several gods and/or goddesses (as contrasted with monotheism—belief in one god or goddess).

population In biology, a group of similar individuals that can and do interbreed.

postindustrial society A society with an economy based on research and development of new knowledge and technologies, as well as providing information, services, and finance capital on a global scale.

potlatch On the northwestern coast of North America, a ceremonial event in which a village chief publicly gives away stockpiled food and other goods that signify wealth.

power The ability of individuals or groups to impose their will upon others and make them do things even against their own wants or wishes.

prehensile Having the ability to grasp.

prehistory A conventional term used to refer to the period of time before the appearance of written records. Does not deny the existence of history, merely of *written* history.

prestige economy Creation of a surplus for the express purpose of displaying wealth and giving it away to raise one's status.

priest or priestess A full-time religious specialist formally recognized for his or her role in guiding the religious practices of others and for contacting and influencing supernatural powers.

primary innovation The creation, invention, or chance discovery of a completely new idea, method, or device.

primates The group of mammals that includes lemurs, lorises, tarsiers, monkeys, apes, and humans.

primatology The study of living and fossil primates.

progress The ethnocentric notion that humans are moving forward to a higher, more advanced stage in their development toward perfection.

prosimians A subdivision within the primate order that includes lemurs, lorises, and tarsiers.

proxemics The cross-cultural study of humankind's perception and use of space.

punctuated equilibria A model of macroevolutionary change that suggests evolution occurs via long periods of stability or stasis punctuated by periods of rapid change.

race In biology, the taxonomic category of subspecies that is not applicable to humans because the division of humans into discrete types does not represent the true nature of human biological variation. In some societies race is an important social category.

racism A doctrine of superiority by which one group justifies the dehumanization of others based on their distinctive physical characteristics.

rebellion Organized armed resistance to an established government or authority in power.

recent African origins hypothesis The hypothesis that all modern people are derived from one single population of archaic *H. sapiens* from Africa who migrated out of Africa after 100,000 years ago, replacing all other archaic forms due to their superior cultural capabilities. Also called the Eve or out of Africa hypothesis.

recessive An allele for a trait whose expression is masked by the presence of a dominant allele.

reciprocity The exchange of goods and services, of approximately equal value, between two parties.

redistribution A mode of exchange in which goods flow into a central place, where they are sorted, counted, and reallocated.

relative dating In archaeology and paleoanthropology, designating an event, object, or fossil as being older or younger than another.

religion An organized system of ideas about the spiritual sphere or the supernatural, along with associated ceremonial practices by which people try to interpret and/or influence aspects of the universe otherwise beyond their control.

revitalization movements Movements for radical cultural reform in response to widespread social disruption and collective feelings of great stress and despair.

revolution Radical change in a society or culture. In the political arena, it involves the forced overthrow of an old government and establishment of a completely new one.

rite of passage A ritual that marks an important stage in an individual's life cycle, such as birth, marriage, and death.

robust australopithecines Several species within the genus *Australopithecus*, who lived from 1.1 to 2.5 million years ago in eastern and southern Africa; known for the rugged nature of their chewing apparatus (large back teeth, large chewing muscles, and a bony ridge on their skull tops for the insertion of these large muscles).

sanctions Externalized social controls designed to encourage conformity to social norms.

secondary innovation A new and deliberate application or modification of an existing idea, method, or device.

self-awareness The ability to identify oneself as an individual, to reflect on oneself, and to evaluate oneself.

separation In a rite of passage, the ritual removal of the individual from society.

serial monogamy A marriage form in which a man or a woman marries or lives with a series of partners in succession.

shaman A person who enters an altered state of consciousness—at will—to contact and utilize an ordinarily hidden reality in order to acquire knowledge, power, and to help others.

sickle-cell anemia An inherited form of anemia caused by a mutation in the hemoglobin protein that causes the red blood cells to assume a sickle shape.

signals Instinctive sounds or gestures that have a natural or self-evident meaning.

slash-and-burn cultivation An extensive form of horticulture in which the natural vegetation is cut, the slash is subsequently burned, and crops are then planted among the ashes; also known as swidden farming.

social class A category of individuals who enjoy equal or nearly equal prestige according to the system of evaluation.

social control External control through open coercion.

social mobility Upward or downward change in one's social class position in a stratified society.

social structure The rule-governed relationships—with all their rights and obligations—that hold members of a society together. This includes households, families, associations, and power relations, including politics.

society An organized group or groups of interdependent people who generally share a common territory, language, and culture and who act together for collective survival and well-being.

sociolinguistics The study of the relationship between language and society through examining how social categories (such as age, gender, ethnicity, religion, occupation, and class) influence the use and significance of distinctive styles of speech.

soft power Co-optive power that presses others through attraction and persuasion to change their ideas, beliefs, values, and behaviors.

soil marks Stains that show up on the surface of recently plowed fields that reveal an archaeological site.

speciation The process of forming new species.

species The smallest working unit in the system of classification. Among living organisms, species are populations or groups of populations capable of interbreeding and producing fertile viable offspring.

spirituality Concern with the sacred, as distinguished from material matters. In contrast to religion, spirituality is often individual rather than collective and does not require a distinctive format or traditional organization.

state In anthropology, a centralized polity involving large numbers of people within a defined territory who are divided into social classes and organized and directed by a formal government that has the capacity and authority to make laws and to use force to defend the social order.

stereoscopic vision Complete three-dimensional vision (or depth perception) from binocular vision and nerve connections that run from each eye to both sides of the brain allowing nerve cells to integrate the images derived from each eye.

stratified Layered; said of archaeological sites where the remains lie in layers, one upon another.

stratified societies Societies in which people are hierarchically divided and ranked into social strata, or layers, and do not share equally in basic resources that support survival, influence, and prestige.

strepsirhines A subdivision within the primate order based on shared genetic characteristics; includes lemurs and lorises.

structural power Power that organizes and orchestrates the systemic interaction within and among societies, directing economic and political forces on the one hand and ideological forces that shape public ideas, values, and beliefs on the other.

structural violence Physical and/or psychological harm (including repression, environmental destruction, poverty, hunger, illness, and premature death) caused by impersonal, exploitative, and unjust social, political, and economic systems.

subculture A distinctive set of ideas, values, and behavior patterns by which a group within a larger society operates, while still sharing common standards with that larger society.

superstructure A society's shared sense of identity and worldview. The collective body of ideas, beliefs, and values by which a group of people makes sense of the world—its shape, challenges, and opportunities—and their place in it. This includes religion and national ideology.

swidden farming An extensive form of horticulture in which the natural vegetation is cut, the slash is subsequently burned, and crops are then planted among the ashes. Also known as slash-and-burn cultivation.

symbol A sign, sound, emblem, or other thing that is arbitrarily linked to something else and represents it in a meaningful way.

syncretism In acculturation, the creative blending of indigenous and foreign beliefs and practices into new cultural forms.

syntax The patterns or rules by which words are arranged into phrases and sentences.

taxonomy The science of classification.

technology Tools and other material equipment, together with the knowledge of how to make and use them.

theory In science, an explanation of natural phenomena, supported by a reliable body of data.

thrifty genotype Human genotype that permits efficient storage of fat to draw on in times of food shortage and conservation of glucose and nitrogen.

tonal language A language in which the sound pitch of a spoken word is an essential part of its pronunciation and meaning.

tool An object used to facilitate some task or activity.

totemism The belief that people are related to particular animals, plants, or natural objects by virtue of descent from common ancestral spirits.

tradition Customary ideas and practices passed on from generation to generation, which in a modernizing society may form an obstacle to new ways of doing things.

transgenders People who cross over or occupy a culturally accepted intermediate position in the binary male–female gender construction. Also identified as "third gender" people (or by various culturally specific names such as "two spirits," used in many Native American groups).

transition In a rite of passage, isolation of the individual following separation and prior to incorporation into society.

tribe In anthropology, a range of kin-ordered groups that are politically integrated by some unifying factor and whose members share a common ancestry, identity, culture, language, and territory.

unilineal descent Descent that establishes group membership exclusively through either the male or female line.

Upper Paleolithic The last part (10,000 to 40,000 years ago) of the Old Stone Age, featuring tool industries characterized by long slim blades and an explosion of creative symbolic forms.

vegeculture The cultivation of domesticated root crops, such as yams and taro.

witchcraft An explanation of events based on the belief that certain individuals possess an innate psychic power capable of causing harm, including sickness and death.

worldview The collective body of ideas that members of a culture generally share concerning the ultimate shape and substance of their reality.

writing system A set of visible or tactile signs used to represent units of language in a systematic way.

BIBLIOGRAPHY

Abbot, E. (2001). *A history of celibacy*. Cambridge, MA: Da Capo Press.

Abu-Lughod, L. (1986). *Veiled sentiments: Honor and poetry in a Bedouin society*. Berkeley: University of California Press.

Adams, R. E. W. (1977). *Prehistoric Mesoamerica*. Boston: Little, Brown.

Adams, R. M. (1966). *The evolution of urban society*. Chicago: Aldine.

Adams, R. M. (2001). Scale and complexity in archaic states. *Latin American Antiquity, 11*, 188.

Adbusters. www.adbusters.org. Accessed January 10, 2003.

AIDS Epidemic Update. (2007), p. 7. Geneva: Joint United Nations Program on HIV/AIDS (UNAID) and World Health Organization. www.unaids.org.

Alland, A., Jr. (1971). *Human diversity*. New York: Columbia University Press.

Allen, J. L., & Shalinsky, A. C. (2004). *Student atlas of anthropology*. New York: McGraw-Hill.

Allen, J. S., & Cheer, S. M. (1996). The non-thrifty genotype. *Current Anthropology, 37*, 831–842.

Alvard, M. S., & Kuznar, L. (2001). Deferred harvest: The transition from hunting to animal husbandry. *American Anthropologist, 103*(2), 295–311.

AMAP. (2003). *AMAP assessment 2002: Human health in the Arctic*. Oslo: Arctic Monitoring Assessment Project.

Ambrose, S. H. (2001). Paleolithic technology and human evolution. *Science, 291*, 1748–1753.

American Anthropological Association. (1998). Statement on "race." www.ameranthassn.org.

Amiran, R. (1965). The beginnings of pottery-making in the Near East. In F. R. Matson (Ed.), *Ceramics and man* (pp. 240–247). Viking Fund Publications, In *Anthropology*, no. 41.

Andrews, L. B., & Nelkin, D. (1996). The bell curve: A statement. *Science, 271*, 13.

Appadurai, A. (1990). Disjuncture and difference in the global cultural economy. *Public Culture, 2*, 1–24.

Appadurai, A. (1996). *Modernity at large: Cultural dimensions of globalization*. Minneapolis: University of Minnesota Press.

Appenzeller, T. (1998). Art: Evolution or revolution? *Science, 282*, 1451–1454.

Armstrong, D. F., Stokoe, W. C., & Wilcox, S. E. (1993). Signs of the origin of syntax. *Current Anthropology, 34*, 349–368.

Ashmore, W. (Ed.). (1981). *Lowland Maya settlement patterns*. Albuquerque: University of New Mexico Press.

Aureli, F., & de Waal, F. B. M. (2000). *Natural conflict resolution*. Berkeley: University of California Press.

Avedon, J. F. (1997). *In exile from the land of snows: The definitive account of the Dalai Lama and Tibet since the Chinese conquest*. New York: Harper.

Baker, P. (Ed.). (1978). *The biology of high altitude peoples*. London: Cambridge University Press.

Balandier, G. (1971). *Political anthropology*. New York: Pantheon.

Balikci, A. (1970). *The Netsilik Eskimo*. Garden City, NY: Natural History Press.

Balter, M. (1998). Why settle down? The mystery of communities. *Science, 282*, 1442–1444.

Balter, M. (1999). A long season puts Çatalhöyük in context. *Science, 286*, 890–891.

Balter, M. (2001). Did plaster hold Neolithic society together? *Science, 294*, 2278–2281.

Balter, M. (2001). In search of the first Europeans. *Science, 291*, 1724.

Banton, M. (1968). Voluntary association: Anthropological aspects. In *International encyclopedia of the social sciences* (vol. 16, pp. 357–362). New York: Macmillan.

Barber, B. (1957). *Social stratification*. New York: Harcourt.

Barham, L. S. (1998). Possible early pigment use in South-Central Africa. *Current Anthropology, 39*, 703–710.

Barnard, A. (1995). Monboddo's *Orang Outang* and the definition of man. In R. Corbey & B. Theunissen (Eds.), *Ape, man, apeman: Changing views since 1600* (pp. 71–85). Leiden: Department of Prehistory, Leiden University.

Barnett, H. (1953). *Innovation: The basis of cultural change*. New York: McGraw-Hill.

Barnouw, V. (1985). *Culture and personality* (4th ed.). Homewood, IL: Dorsey Press.

Barr, R. G. (1997, October). The crying game. *Natural History*, 47.

Barth, F. (1961). *Nomads of South Persia: The Basseri tribe of the Khamseh confederacy*. Boston: Little, Brown (series in anthropology).

Barth, F. (1962). Nomadism in the mountain and plateau areas of South West Asia. *The problems of the arid zone* (pp. 341–355). Paris: UNESCO.

Bar-Yosef, O. (1986). The walls of Jericho: An alternative interpretation. *Current Anthropology, 27*, 160.

Bar-Yosef, O., Vandermeersch, B., Arensburg, B., Belfer-Cohen, A., Goldberg, P., Laville, H., Meignen, L., Rak, Y., Speth, J. D., Tchernov, E., Tillier, A-M., & Weiner, S. (1992). The excavations in Kebara Cave, Mt. Carmel. *Current Anthropology, 33*, 497–550.

Bascom, W. (1969). *The Yoruba of southwestern Nigeria*. New York: Holt, Rinehart & Winston.

Becker, J. (2004, March). *National Geographic*, 90.

Bednarik, R. G. (1995). Concept-mediated marking in the Lower Paleolithic. *Current Anthropology, 36*, 606.

Beeman, W. O. (2000). Introduction: Margaret Mead, cultural studies, and international understanding. In M. Mead & R. Métraux (Eds.), *The study of culture at a distance* (pp. xiv–xxxi). New York and Oxford: Berghahn Books.

Behrensmeyer, A. K., Todd, N. E., Potts, R., & McBrinn, G. E. (1997). Late Pliocene faunal turnover in the Turkana basin, Kenya, and Ethiopia. *Science, 278*, 1589–1594.

Bekoff, M., et al. (Eds.). (2002). *The cognitive animal: Empirical and theoretical perspectives on animal cognition*. Cambridge, MA: MIT Press.

Bell, D. (1997). Defining marriage and legitimacy. *Current Anthropology, 38*, 241.

Belshaw, C. S. (1958). The significance of modern cults in Melanesian development. In W. Lessa & E. Z. Vogt (Eds.), *Reader in comparative religion: An anthropological approach*. New York: Harper & Row.

Benedict, R. (1959). *Patterns of culture*. New York: New American Library.

Bennett, R. L., et al. (2002, April). Genetic counseling and screening of consanguineous couples and their offspring: Recommendations of the National Society of Genetic Counselors. *Journal of Genetic Counseling, 11*(2), 97–119.

Berdan, F. F. (1982). *The Aztecs of Central Mexico*. New York: Holt, Rinehart & Winston.

Bermúdez de Castro, J. M., Arsuaga, J. L., Cabonell, E., Rosas, A., Martinez, I., & Mosquera, M. (1997). A hominid from the lower Pleistocene of Atapuerca,

Spain: Possible ancestor to Neandertals and modern humans. *Science, 276,* 1392–1395.

Bernal, I. (1969). *The Olmec world.* Berkeley: University of California Press.

Bernard, H. R. (2002). *Research methods in anthropology: Qualitative and quantitative approaches* (3rd ed.). Walnut Creek, CA: Altamira Press.

Berra, T. M. (1990). *Evolution and the myth of creationism.* Stanford, CA: Stanford University Press.

Berreman, G. D. (1968). Caste: The concept of caste. *International Encyclopedia of the Social Sciences* (vol. 2, pp. 333–338). New York: Macmillan.

Bicchieri, M. G. (Ed.). (1972). *Hunters and gatherers today: A socioeconomic study of eleven such cultures in the twentieth century.* New York: Holt, Rinehart & Winston.

Binford, L. R. (1972). *An archaeological perspective.* New York: Seminar Press.

Binford, L. R., & Chuan, K. H. (1985). Taphonomy at a distance: Zhoukoudian, the cave home of Beijing man? *Current Anthropology, 26,* 413–442.

Birdsell, J. H. (1977). The recalibration of a paradigm for the first peopling of Greater Australia. In J. Allen, J. Golson, & R. Jones (Eds.), *Sunda and Sahul: Prehistoric studies in Southeast Asia, Melanesia, and Australia* (pp. 113–167). New York: Academic Press.

Blackless, M., et al. (2000). How sexually dimorphic are we? Review and synthesis. *American Journal of Human Biology, 12,* 151–166.

Blakey, M. (2003, October 29). Personal communication. *African Burial Ground Project.* Department of Anthropology, College of William & Mary.

Blok, A. (1974). *The mafia of a Sicilian village 1860–1960.* New York: Harper & Row.

Blumer, M. A., & Byrne, R. (1991). The ecological genetics and domestication and the origins of agriculture. *Current Anthropology, 32,* 30.

Boas, F. (1962). *Primitive art.* Gloucester, MA: Peter Smith.

Boas, F. (1966). *Race, language and culture.* New York: Free Press.

Bodley, J. H. (1985). *Anthropology and contemporary human problems* (2nd ed.). Palo Alto, CA: Mayfield.

Bodley, J. H. (1990). *Victims of progress* (3rd ed.). Mountain View, CA: Mayfield.

Bodley, J. H. (1998). *Victims of progress* (4th ed.). San Francisco: McGraw-Hill.

Bodley, J. H. (2000). *Anthropology and contemporary human problems* (4th ed.). Palo Alto, CA: Mayfield.

Boehm, C. (2000). The evolution of moral communities. *School of American Research, 2000 Annual Report,* 7.

Bohannan, P. (Ed.). (1967). *Law and warfare: Studies in the anthropology of conflict.* Garden City, NY: Natural History Press.

Bohannan, P., & Dalton, G. (Eds.). (1962). *Markets in Africa.* Evanston, IL: Northwestern University Press.

Bohannan, P., & Middleton, J. (Eds.). (1968). *Kinship and social organization.* Garden City, NY: Natural History Press (American Museum Source Books in Anthropology).

Bohannan, P., & Middleton, J. (Eds.). (1968). *Marriage, family, and residence.* Garden City, NY: Natural History Press (American Museum Source Books in Anthropology).

Bolinger, D. (1968). *Aspects of language.* New York: Harcourt.

Bongaarts, J. (1998). Demographic consequences of declining fertility. *Science, 182,* 419.

Bonvillain, N. (2000). *Language, culture, and communication: The meaning of Messages* (3rd ed.). Upper Saddle River, NJ: Prentice-Hall.

Bordes, F. (1972). *A tale of two caves.* New York: Harper & Row.

Bornstein, M. H. (1975). The influence of visual perception on culture. *American Anthropologist, 77*(4), 774–798.

Boshara, R. (2003, January/February). Wealth inequality: The $6,000 solution. *Atlantic Monthly.*

Brace, C. L. (1981). Tales of the phylogenetic woods: The evolution and significance of phylogenetic trees. *American Journal of Physical Anthropology, 56,* 411–429.

Brace, C. L. (2000). *Evolution in an anthropological view* (p. 341). Walnut Creek, CA: Altamira Press.

Brace, C. L., Nelson, H., & Korn, N. (1979). *Atlas of human evolution* (2nd ed.). New York: Holt, Rinehart & Winston.

Bradford, P. V., & Blume, H. (1992). *Ota Benga: The pygmy in the zoo.* New York: St. Martin's Press.

Braidwood, R. J. (1960). The agricultural revolution. *Scientific American, 203,* 130–141.

Braidwood, R. J. (1975). *Prehistoric men* (8th ed.). Glenview, IL: Scott, Foresman.

Brain, C. K. (1968). Who killed the Swartkrans ape-men? *South African Museums Association Bulletin, 9,* 127–139.

Brain, C. K. (1969). The contribution of Namib Desert Hottentots to an understanding of australopithecine bone accumulations. *Scientific Papers of the Namib Desert Research Station,* 13.

Branda, R. F., & Eatoil, J. W. (1978). Skin color and photolysis: An evolutionary hypothesis. *Science, 201,* 625–626.

Brettell, C. B., & Sargent, C. F. (Eds.). (2000). *Gender in cross-cultural perspective* (3rd ed.). Upper Saddle River, NJ: Prentice-Hall.

Brew, J. O. (1968). *One hundred years of anthropology.* Cambridge, MA: Harvard University Press.

Broecker, W. S. (1992, April). Global warming on trial. *Natural History,* 14.

Brothwell, D. R., & Higgs, E. (Eds.). (1969). *Science in archaeology* (rev. ed.). London: Thames & Hudson.

Brown, B., Walker, A., Ward, C. V., & Leakey, R. E. (1993). New *Australopithecus boisei* calvaria from East Lake Turkana, Kenya. *American Journal of Physical Anthropology, 91,* 137–159.

Brown, D. E. (1991). *Human universals.* New York: McGraw-Hill.

Brown, P., et al. (2004). A new small-bodied hominin from the Late Pleistocene of Flores, Indonesia. *Nature, 431,* 1055–1061.

Brunet, M., et al. (2002). A new hominid from the Upper Miocene of Chad, Central Africa. *Nature, 418,* 145–151.

Buck, P. H. (1938). *Vikings of the Pacific.* Chicago: University Press of Chicago.

Burling, R. (1970). *Man's many voices: Language in its cultural context.* New York: Holt, Rinehart & Winston.

Burling, R. (1993). Primate calls, human language, and nonverbal communication. *Current Anthropology, 34,* 25–53.

Byers, D. S. (Ed.). (1967). *The prehistory of the Tehuacan Valley: Vol. 1. Environment and subsistence.* Austin: University of Texas Press.

Cachel, S. (1997). Dietary shifts and the European Upper Paleolithic transition. *Current Anthropology, 38,* 590.

Callaway, E. (2007, December 3). Chimp beats students at computer game. Published online: *Nature,* doi:10.1038/news.2007.317.

Carneiro, R. L. (1970). A theory of the origin of the state. *Science, 169,* 733–738.

Caroulis, J. (1996). Food for thought. *Pennsylvania Gazette, 95*(3), 16.

Carroll, J. B. (Ed.). (1956). *Language, thought and reality: Selected writings of Benjamin Lee Whorf.* Cambridge, MA: MIT Press.

Cartmill, M. (1998). The gift of gab. *Discover, 19*(11), 64.

Cashdan, E. (1989). Hunters and gatherers: Economic behavior in bands. In S. Plattner (Ed.), *Economic anthropology* (pp. 21–48). Stanford, CA: Stanford University Press.

Catford, J. C. (1988). *A practical introduction to phonetics.* Oxford: Clarendon Press.

Cavalli-Sforza, L. L. (1977). *Elements of human genetics.* Menlo Park, CA: W. A. Benjamin.

Chagnon, N. A. (1988). *Yanomamo: The fierce people* (3rd ed.). New York: Holt, Rinehart & Winston.

Chagnon, N. A., & Irons, W. (Eds.). (1979). *Evolutionary biology and human social behavior.* North Scituate, MA: Duxbury Press.

Chan, J. W. C., & Vernon, P. E. (1988). Individual differences among the peoples of China. In J. W. Berry (Ed.), *Human abilities in cultural context* (pp. 340–357). Cambridge, England: Cambridge University Press.

Chang, K. C. (Ed.). (1968). *Settlement archaeology.* Palo Alto, CA: National Press.

Chang, L. (2005, June 9). A migrant worker sees rural home in new light. *Wall Street Journal.*

Chase, C. (1998). Hermaphrodites with attitude. *Gay and Lesbian Quarterly, 4*(2), 189–211.

Chicurel, M. (2001). Can organisms speed their own evolution? *Science, 292,* 1824–1827.

Childe, V. G. (1951). *Man makes himself.* New York: New American Library. (orig.1936).

Childe, V. G. (1954). *What happened in history.* Baltimore: Penguin.

Cigno, A. (1994). *Economics of the family.* New York: Oxford University Press.

Ciochon, R. L., & Fleagle, J. G. (Eds.). (1987). *Primate evolution and human origins.* Hawthorne, NY: Aldine.

Ciochon, R. L., & Fleagle, J. G. (1993). *The human evolution source book.* Englewood Cliffs, NJ: Prentice-Hall.

Clark, E. E. (1966). *Indian legends of the Pacific Northwest.* Berkeley: University of California Press.

Clark, G. (1967). *The Stone Age hunters.* New York: McGraw-Hill.

Clark, G. (1972). *Starr Carr: A case study in bioarchaeology.* Reading, MA: Addison-Wesley.

Clark, G. A. (1997). Neandertal genetics. *Science, 277,* 1,024.

Clark, G. A. (2002). Neandertal archaeology: Implications for our origins. *American Anthropologist, 104*(1), 50–67.

Clark, J. G. D. (1962). *Prehistoric Europe: The economic basis.* Stanford, CA: Stanford University Press.

Clark, W. E. L. (1960). *The antecedents of man.* Chicago: Quadrangle Books.

Clark, W. E. L. (1966). *History of the primates* (5th ed.). Chicago: University of Chicago Press.

Clark, W. E. L. (1967). *Man-apes or ape-men? The story of discoveries in Africa.* New York: Holt, Rinehart & Winston.

Clarke, R. J. (1998). First ever discovery of a well preserved skull and associated skeleton of *Australopithecus. South African Journal of Science, 94,* 460–464.

Clarke, R. J., & Tobias, P. V. (1995). Sterkfontein member 2 foot bones of the oldest South African hominid. *Science, 269,* 521–524.

Clay, J. W. (1996). What's a nation? In W. A. Haviland & R. J. Gordon (Eds.), *Talking about people* (2nd ed., pp. 188–189). Mountain View, CA: Mayfield.

Clough, S. B., & Cole, C. W. (1952). *Economic history of Europe* (3rd ed.). Lexington, MA: Heath.

Coe, S. D. (1994). *America's first cuisines.* Austin: University of Texas Press.

Coe, W. R. (1967). *Tikal: A handbook of the ancient Maya ruins.* Philadelphia: University of Pennsylvania Museum.

Coe, W. R., & Haviland, W. A. (1982). *Introduction to the archaeology of Tikal.* Philadelphia: University Museum.

Cohen, M. N. (1977). *The food crisis in prehistory.* New Haven, CT: Yale University Press.

Cohen, M. N. (1995). Anthropology and race: The bell curve phenomenon. *General Anthropology, 2*(1), 1–4.

Cohen, M. N., & Armelagos, G. J. (1984). *Paleopathology at the origins of agriculture.* Orlando: Academic Press.

Cohen, M. N., & Armelagos, G. J. (1984). Paleopathology at the origins of agriculture: Editors' summation. In *Paleopathology at the origins of agriculture* (p. 594). Orlando: Academic Press.

Colburn, T., Dumanoski, D., & Myers, J. P. (1996). Hormonal sabotage. *Natural History, 3,* 45–46.

Colburn, T., et al. (1997). *Our stolen future.* New York: Plume (Penguin Press).

Collier, J., & Collier, M. (1986). *Visual anthropology: Photography as a research method.* Albuquerque: University of New Mexico Press.

Collier, J., Rosaldo, M. Z., & Yanagisako, S. (1982). Is there a family? New anthropological views. In B. Thorne & M. Yalom (Eds.), *Rethinking the family: Some feminist questions* (pp. 25–39). New York: Longman.

Collier, J. F., & Yanagisako, S. J. (Eds.). (1987). *Gender and kinship: Essays toward a unified analysis.* Stanford, CA: Stanford University Press.

Columbia Center for Media Teaching and Learning. www.ccnmtl.columbia.edu/projects/mmt/udhr.

Committee on the Elimination of Racial Discrimination, India. (2007, March).

Cone, M. (2005). *Silent snow: The slow poisoning of the Arctic.* New York: Grove Press.

Conner, M. (1996). The archaeology of contemporary mass graves. *SAA Bulletin, 14*(4), 6, 31.

Conroy, G. C. (1997). *Reconstructing human origins: A modern synthesis.* New York: Norton.

Consideration of reports submitted by states parties under Article 9 of the International Convention on the Elimination of All Forms of Racial Discrimination, 70th Session. www2.ohchr.org/english/bodies/cerd/cerds70.htm.

Coon, C. S., Garn, S. N., & Birdsell, J. (1950). *Races: A study of the problems of race formation in man.* Springfield, IL: Charles C. Thomas.

Cooper, A., Poinar, H. N., Pääbo, S., Radovci, C. J., Debénath, A., Caparros, M., Barroso-Ruiz, C., Bertranpetit, J., Nielsen-March, C., Hedges, R. E. M., & Sykes, B. (1997). Neanderthal genetics. *Science, 277,* 1021–1024.

Coppa, A., et al. (2006). Early Neolithic tradition of dentistry. *Nature, 440,* 755–756.

Coppens, Y., Howell, F. C., Isaac, G. L., & Leakey, R. E. F. (Eds.). (1976). *Earliest man and environments in the Lake Rudolf Basin: Stratigraphy, paleoecology, and evolution.* Chicago: University of Chicago Press.

Corbey, R. (1995). Introduction: Missing links, or the ape's place in nature. In R. Corbey & B. Theunissen (Eds.), *Ape, man, apeman: Changing views since 1600* (p.1). Leiden: Department of Prehistory, Leiden University.

Cornwell, T. (1995, November 10). Skeleton staff. *Times Higher Education,* 20.

Corruccini, R. S. (1992). Metrical reconsideration of the Skhul IV and IX and Border Cave I crania in the context of modern human origins. *American Journal of Physical Anthropology, 87,* 433–445.

Cottrell, L. (1963). *The lost pharaohs.* New York: Grosset & Dunlap.

Courlander, H. (1971). *The fourth world of the Hopis.* New York: Crown.

Cowgill, G. L. (1997). State and society at Teotihuacan, Mexico. *Annual Review of Anthropology, 26,* 129–161.

Cretney, S. (2003). *Family law in the twentieth century: A history.* New York: Oxford University Press.

Criminal Code of Canada, § 718.2(e).

Crocker, W. A., & Crocker, J. (1994). *The Canela, bonding through kinship, ritual, and sex.* Fort Worth, TX: Harcourt Brace.

Culbert, T. P. (Ed.). (1973). *The Classic Maya collapse*. Albuquerque: University of New Mexico Press.

Culotta, E. (1995). New hominid crowds the field. *Science, 269,* 918.

Culotta, E., & Koshland, D. E., Jr. (1994). DNA repair works its way to the top. *Science, 266,* 1926.

Cultural Survival Quarterly. (1991). *15*(4), 38. *Current population survey.* (2002). U.S. Census Bureau.

Dalton, G. (Ed.). (1967). *Tribal and peasant economics: Readings in economic Anthropology.* Garden City, NY: Natural History Press.

Dalton, G. (1971). *Traditional tribal and peasant economics: An introductory survey of economic anthropology.* Reading, MA: Addison-Wesley.

Daniel, G. (1970). *The first civilizations: The archaeology of their origins.* New York: Apollo Editions.

Daniel, G. (1975). *A hundred and fifty years of archaeology* (2nd ed.). London: Duckworth.

Darwin, C. (1936). *The descent of man and selection in relation to sex.* New York: Random House (Modern Library). (orig. 1871).

Darwin, C. (1887). *Autobiography.* Reprinted in *The life and letters of Charles Darwin* (1902). F. Darwin (Ed.), London: John Murray.

Darwin, C. (1967). *On the origin of species.* New York: Atheneum. (orig. 1859).

Davenport, W. (1959). Linear descent and descent groups. *American Anthropologist, 61,* 557–573.

Davies, G. (2005). *A history of money from the earliest times to present day* (3rd ed.). Cardiff: University of Wales Press.

Deetz, J. (1967). *Invitation to archaeology.* New York: Doubleday.

Deetz, J. (1977). *In small things forgotten: The archaeology of early American life.* Garden City, NY: Anchor Press / Doubleday.

del Carmen Rodríguez Martínez, M., et al. (2006). Oldest writing in the New World. *Science, 313*(5793), 1610–1614.

d'Errico, F., Zilhão, J., Julien, M., Baffier, D., & Pelegrin, J. (1998). Neandertal acculturation in Western Europe? *Current Anthropology, 39,* 521.

Dettwyler, K. A. (1994). *Dancing skeletons: Life and death in West Africa.* Prospect Heights, IL: Waveland Press.

Dettwyler, K. A. (1997, October). When to wean. *Natural History,* 49.

DeVore, I. (Ed.). (1965). *Primate behavior: Field studies of monkeys and apes.* New York: Holt, Rinehart & Winston.

de Waal, F. (1996). *Good natured: The origins of right and wrong in humans and other animals.* Cambridge, MA: Harvard University Press.

de Waal, F. B. M. (2000). Primates—A natural heritage of conflict resolution. *Science, 28,* 586–590.

de Waal, F. B. M. (2001). *The ape and the sushi master.* New York: Basic Books.

de Waal, F. B. M. (2001). Sing the song of evolution. *Natural History, 110*(8), 77.

de Waal, F. B. M., & Johanowicz, D. L. (1993). Modification of reconciliation behavior through social experience: An experiment with two macaque species. *Child Development, 64,* 897–908.

de Waal, F., Kano, T., & Parish, A. R. (1998). Comments. *Current Anthropology, 39,* 408, 410, 413.

Diamond, J. (1994). How Africa became black. *Discover, 15*(2), 72–81.

Diamond, J. (1994). Race without color. *Discover, 15*(11), 83–89.

Diamond, J. (1997). *Guns, germs, and steel.* New York: Norton.

Diamond, J. (1998). Ants, crops, and history. *Science, 281,* 1974–1975.

Diamond, J. (2005). *Collapse: How societies choose to fail or succeed.* New York: Viking Penguin.

Dirie, W., & Miller, C. (1998). *Desert flower: The extraordinary journey of a desert nomad.* New York: William Morrow.

Dixon, J. E., Cann, J. R., & Renfrew, C. (1968). Obsidian and the origins of trade. *Scientific American, 218,* 38–46.

Dobyns, H. F., Doughty, P. L., & Lasswell, H. D. (Eds.). (1971). *Peasants, power, and applied social change.* London: Sage.

Dobzhansky, T. (1962). *Mankind evolving.* New Haven, CT: Yale University Press.

Dozier, E. (1970). *The Pueblo Indians of North America.* New York: Holt, Rinehart & Winston.

Draper, P. (1975). !Kung women: Contrasts in sexual egalitarianism in foraging and sedentary contexts. In R. Reiter (Ed.), *Toward an anthropology of women* (pp. 77–109). New York: Monthly Review Press.

Driver, H. (1964). *Indians of North America.* Chicago: University of Chicago Press.

Dubois, C. (1944). *The people of Alor.* Minneapolis: University of Minnesota Press.

Dubos, R. (1968). *So human an animal.* New York: Scribner.

Dumurat-Dreger, A. (1998, May / June). "Ambiguous sex" or ambivalent medicine? *The Hastings Center Report, 28*(3), 2435 (posted on the Intersex Society of North America website: www.isna.org).

Dundes, A. (1980). *Interpreting folklore.* Bloomington: Indiana University Press.

Durant, J. C. (2000, April 23). Everybody into the gene pool. *New York Times Book Review,* 11.

Duranti, A. (2001). Linguistic anthropology: History, ideas, and issues. In A. Duranti (Ed.), *Linguistic anthropology: A reader* (pp. 1–38). Oxford: Blackwell.

Durkheim, E. (1964). *The division of labor in society.* New York: Free Press.

Durkheim, E. (1965). *The elementary forms of the religious life.* New York: Free Press.

duToit, B. M. (1991). *Human sexuality: Cross-cultural readings.* New York: McGraw-Hill.

Eastman, C. M. (1990). *Aspects of language and culture* (2nd ed.). Novato, CA: Chandler & Sharp.

Eaton, S. B., Konner, M., & Shostak, M. (1988). Stone-agers in the fast lane: Chronic degenerative diseases in evolutionary perspective. *American Journal of Medicine, 84*(4), 739–749.

Edey, M. A., & Johannson, D. (1989). *Blueprints: Solving the mystery of evolution.* Boston: Little, Brown.

Edwards, J. (Ed.). (1999). *Technologies of procreation: Kinship in the age of assisted conception.* New York: Routledge (distributed by St. Martin's Press).

Edwards, S. W. (1978). Nonutilitarian activities on the Lower Paleolithic: A look at the two kinds of evidence. *Current Anthropology, 19*(1), 135–137.

Egan, T. (1999, February 28). The persistence of polygamy. *New York Times Magazine,* 52.

Eggan, F. (1954). Social anthropology and the method of controlled comparison. *American Anthropologist, 56,* 743–763.

Eiseley, L. (1958). *Darwin's century: Evolution and the men who discovered it.* New York: Doubleday.

Eisenstadt, S. N. (1956). *From generation to generation: Age groups and social structure.* New York: Free Press.

El Guindi, F. (2004). *Visual anthropology: Essential method and theory.* Walnut Creek, CA: Altamira Press.

Elkin, A. P. (1964). *The Australian aborigines.* Garden City, NY: Doubleday / Anchor Books.

Ellis, C. (2006). *A dancing people: Powwow culture on the southern plains.* Lawrence: University Press of Kansas.

Ember, C. R., & Ember, M. (1996). What have we learned from cross-cultural research? *General Anthropology, 2*(2), 5.

Enard, W., et al. (2002). Molecular evolution of FOXP2, a gene involved in speech and language. *Nature, 418,* 869–872.

Erickson, P. A., & Murphy, L. D. (2003). *A history of anthropological theory* (2nd ed.). Peterborough, Ontario: Broadview Press.

Errington, F. K., & Gewertz, D. B. (2001). *Cultural alternatives and a feminist anthropology: An analysis of culturally constructed gender interests in Papua New Guinea.* Cambridge, England, and New York: Cambridge University Press.

Ervin-Tripp, S. (1973). *Language acquisition and communicative choice.* Stanford, CA: Stanford University Press.

Esber, G. S., Jr. (1987). Designing Apache houses with Apaches. In R. M. Wulff & S. J. Fiske (Eds.), *Anthropological praxis: Translating knowledge into action* (pp.187–196). Boulder, CO: Westview Press.

Evans, W. (1968). *Communication in the animal world.* New York: Crowell.

Evans-Pritchard, E. E. (1968). *The Nuer: A description of the modes of livelihood and political institutions of a Nilotic people.* London: Oxford University Press.

Fagan, B. M. (1995). *People of the earth* (8th ed.). New York: HarperCollins.

Fagan, B. M. (1995). The quest for the past. In L. L. Hasten (Ed.), *Annual Editions 95/96, Archaeology* (p. 10). Guilford, CT: Dushkin.

Fagan, B. M. (1999). *Archaeology: A brief introduction* (7th ed.). New York: Longman.

Fagan, B. M. (2000). *Ancient lives: An introduction to archaeology* (pp. 125–133). Englewood Cliffs, NJ: Prentice-Hall.

Falk, D. (1975). Comparative anatomy of the larynx in man and the chimpanzee: Implications for language in Neanderthal. *American Journal of Physical Anthropology, 43*(1), 123–132.

Falk, D. (1989). Ape-like endocast of "Ape Man Taung." *American Journal of Physical Anthropology, 80,* 335–339.

Falk, D. (1993). A good brain is hard to cool. *Natural History, 102*(8), 65.

Falk, D. (1993). Hominid paleoneurology. In R. L. Ciochon & J. G. Fleagle (Eds.), *The human evolution source book.* Englewood Cliffs, NJ: Prentice-Hall.

Falk, D., et al. (2005). The brain of LB1, *Homo floresiensis. Science, 308,* 242–245.

Farmer, P. (1992). *AIDS and accusation: Haiti and the geography of blame.* Berkeley: University of California Press.

Fausto-Sterling, A. (1993, March/April). The five sexes: Why male and female are not enough. *The Sciences, 33*(2), 20–24.

Fausto-Sterling, A. (2000, July/August). The five sexes revisited. *The Sciences, 40*(4), 19–24.

Fausto-Sterling, A. (2003, August 2). Personal e-mail communication.

Fedigan, L. M. (1986). The changing role of women in models of human evolution. *Annual Review of Anthropology, 15,* 25–56.

"Female genital mutilation." (2000). Fact sheet no. 241. World Health Organization.

Ferrie, H. (1997). An interview with C. Loring Brace. *Current Anthropology, 38,* 851–869.

Finkler, K. (2000). *Experiencing the new genetics: Family and kinship on the medical frontier.* Philadelphia: University of Pennsylvania Press.

Firth, R. (1952). *Elements of social organization.* London: Watts.

Firth, R. (1957). *Man and culture: An evaluation of Bronislaw Malinowski.* London: Routledge.

Firth, R. (Ed.). (1967). *Themes in economic anthropology.* London: Tavistock.

Fisher, R., & Ury, W. L. (1991). *Getting to yes: Negotiating agreement without giving in* (2nd ed.). Boston: Houghton Mifflin.

Flannery, K. V. (1973). The origins of agriculture. In B. J. Siegel, A. R. Beals, & S. A. Tyler (Eds.), *Annual review of anthropology* (vol. 2, pp. 271–310). Palo Alto, CA: Annual Reviews.

Flannery, K. V. (Ed.). (1976). *The Mesoamerican village.* New York: Seminar Press.

Fogel, R., & Riquelme, M. A. (2005). *Enclave sojero. Merma de soberania y pobreza.* Asuncion: Centro de Estudios Rurales Interdisciplinarias.

Folger, T. (1993). The naked and the bipedal. *Discover, 14*(11), 34–35.

Forbes, J. D. (1964). *The Indian in America's past.* Englewood Cliffs, NJ: Prentice-Hall.

Forbes Global 500 List. www.forbes.com.

Forde, C. D. (1955). The Nupe. In D. Forde (Ed.), *Peoples of the Niger-Benue confluence.* London: International African Institute (Ethnographic Survey of Africa. Western Africa, part 10).

Forde, C. D. (1968). Double descent among the Yakö. In P. Bohannan & J. Middleton (Eds.), *Kinship and social organization* (pp. 179–191). Garden City, NY: Natural History Press.

Forste, R. (2008). Prelude to marriage, or alternative to marriage? A social demographic look at cohabitation in the U.S. Working paper. Social Science Electronic Publishing, Inc. http://papers.ssrn.com/sol3/papers.cfm?abstract_id=269172.

Fortes, M. (1950). Kinship and marriage among the Ashanti. In A. R. Radcliffe-Brown & C. D. Forde (Eds.), *African systems of kinship and marriage.* London: Oxford University Press.

Fortes, M. (1969). *Kinship and the social order: The legacy of Lewis Henry Morgan.* Chicago: Aldine.

Fortes, M., & Evans-Pritchard, E. E. (Eds.). (1962). *African political systems.* London: Oxford University Press. (orig.1940).

Fossey, D. (1983). *Gorillas in the mist.* Burlington, MA: Houghton Mifflin.

Foster, G. M. (1955). Peasant society and the image of the limited good. *American Anthropologist, 67,* 293–315.

Fouts, R. S., & Waters, G. (2001). Chimpanzee sign language and Darwinian continuity: Evidence for a neurology continuity of language. *Neurological Research, 23,* 787–794.

Fox, R. (1967). *Kinship and marriage in an anthropological perspective.* Baltimore: Penguin.

Fox, R. (1968). *Encounter with anthropology.* New York: Dell.

Fox, R. (1981, December 3). [Interview]. Coast Telecourses, Inc., Los Angeles.

Frake, C. O. (1992). Lessons of the Mayan sky. In A. F. Aveni (Ed.), *The sky in Mayan literature* (pp. 274–291). New York: Oxford University Press.

Frankfort, H. (1968). *The birth of civilization in the Near East.* New York: Barnes & Noble.

Fraser, D. (1962). *Primitive art.* New York: Doubleday.

Fraser, D. (Ed.). (1966). *The many faces of primitive art: A critical anthology.* Englewood Cliffs, NJ: Prentice-Hall.

Frayer, D. W. (1981). Body size, weapon use, and natural selection in the European Upper Paleolithic and Mesolithic. *American Anthropologist, 83,* 57–73.

Frazer, Sir J. G. (1961 reissue). *The new golden bough.* New York: Doubleday, Anchor Books.

Freeman, J. D. (1960). The Iban of western Borneo. In G. P. Murdock (Ed.), *Social structure in Southeast Asia.* Chicago: Quadrangle Books.

Freeman, L. G. (1992). *Ambrona and Torralba: New evidence and interpretation.* Paper presented at the 91st Annual Meeting, American Anthropological Association.

Fried, M. (1967). *The evolution of political society: An essay in political anthropology.* New York: Random House.

Fried, M. (1972). *The study of anthropology.* New York: Crowell.

Fried, M., Harris, M., & Murphy, R. (1968). *War: The anthropology of armed conflict and aggression.* Garden City, NY: Natural History Press.

Friedl, E. (1975). *Women and men: An anthropologist's view.* New York: Holt, Rinehart & Winston.

Friedman, J. (Ed.). (2003). *Globalization, the state, and violence.* Walnut Creek, CA: Altamira Press.

Frye, D. P. (2000). Conflict management in cross-cultural perspective. In F. Aureli & F. B. M. de Waal, *Natural conflict resolution* (pp. 334–351). Berkeley: University of California Press.

Frye, M. (1983). *Sexism. In The politics of reality* (pp. 17–40). New York: Crossing Press.

Gamble, C. (1986). *The Paleolithic settlement of Europe.* Cambridge: Cambridge University Press.

Garn, S. M. (1970). *Human races* (3rd ed.). Springfield, IL: Charles C. Thomas.

Geertz, C. (1963). *Agricultural involution: The process of ecological change in Indonesia.* Berkeley: University of California Press.

Geertz, C. (1984). Distinguished lecture: Antirelativism. *American Anthropologist, 86,* 263–278.

"Gene study suggests Polynesians came from Taiwan." (2005, July 4). Reuters.

Gibbons, A. (1997). Ideas on human origins evolve at anthropology gathering. *Science, 276,* 535–536.

Gibbs, J. L., Jr. (1965). The Kpelle of Liberia. In J. L. Gibbs, Jr. (Ed.), *Peoples of Africa* (pp. 216–218). New York: Holt, Rinehart & Winston.

Gierstorfer, C. (2007). Peaceful primates, violent acts. *Nature, 447,* 7.

Gilley, B. J. (2007). *Becoming two-spirit: Gay identity and social acceptance in Indian Country.* Lincoln: University of Nebraska Press.

Ginsburg, F. D., Abu-Lughod, L., & Larkin, B. (Eds.). (2002). *Media worlds: Anthropology on new terrain.* Berkeley: University of California Press.

Gleason, H. A., Jr. (1966). *An introduction to descriptive linguistics* (rev. ed.). New York: Holt, Rinehart & Winston.

Gledhill, J. (2000). *Power and its disguises: Anthropological perspectives on politics* (2nd ed.). Boulder, CO: Pluto Press.

Godfrey, T. (2000, December 27). Biotech threatening biodiversity. *Burlington Free Press,* 10A.

Goodall J. (1986). *The chimpanzees of Gombe: Patterns of behavior.* Cambridge, MA: Belknap Press.

Goodall, J. (1990). *Through a window: My thirty years with the chimpanzees of Gombe.* Boston: Houghton Mifflin.

Goodall, J. (2000). *Reason for hope: A spiritual journey.* New York: Warner Books.

Goode, W. (1963). *World revolution and family patterns.* New York: Free Press.

Goodenough, W. (Ed.). (1964). *Explorations in cultural anthropology: Essays in honor of George Murdock.* New York: McGraw-Hill.

Goodenough, W. (1965). Rethinking status and role: Toward a general model of the cultural organization of social relationships. In M. Benton (Ed.), *The relevance of models for social anthropology.* New York: Praeger (ASA Monographs I).

Goodenough, W. H. (1990). Evolution of the human capacity for beliefs. *American Anthropologist, 92,* 601.

Goodman, A., & Armelagos, G. J. (1985). Death and disease at Dr. Dickson's mounds. *Natural History, 94*(9), 12–18.

Goody, J. (1969). *Comparative studies in kinship.* Stanford, CA: Stanford University Press.

Goody, J. (Ed.). (1972). *Developmental cycle in domestic groups.* New York: Cambridge University Press (Papers in Social Anthropology, No. 1).

Goody, J. (1976). *Production and reproduction: A comparative study of the domestic domain.* Cambridge: Cambridge University Press.

Goody, J. (1983). *The development of the family and marriage in Europe.* Cambridge, MA: Cambridge University Press.

Gordon, R. J. (1992). *The Bushman myth: The making of a Namibian underclass.* Boulder, CO: Westview Press.

Gordon, R. J., & Megitt, M. J. (1985). *Law and order in the New Guinea highlands.* Hanover, NH: University Press of New England.

Gould, S. J. (1983). *Hen's teeth and horses' toes.* New York: Norton.

Gould, S. J. (1989). *Wonderful life.* New York: Norton.

Gould, S. J. (1991). *Bully for brontosaurus.* New York: Norton.

Gould, S. J. (1991). *The flamingo's smile: Reflections in natural history.* New York: Norton.

Gould, S. J. (1994). The geometer of race. *Discover, 15*(11), 65–69.

Gould, S. J. (1996). *Full house: The spread of excellence from Plato to Darwin* (pp. 176–195). New York: Harmony Books.

Gould, S. J. (1996). *The mismeasure of man* (rev. ed.). New York: Norton.

Gould, S. J. (1997). *Questioning the millennium.* New York: Crown.

Gould, S. J. (2000). What does the dreaded "E" word mean anyway? *Natural History, 109*(1), 34–36.

Gray, P. B. (2004, May). HIV and Islam: Is HIV prevalence lower among Muslims? *Social Science & Medicine, 58*(9), 1751–1756.

Greenberg, J. H. (1968). *Anthropological linguistics: An introduction.* New York: Random House.

Grine, F. E. (1993). Australopithecine taxonomy and phylogeny: Historical background and recent interpretation. In R. L. Ciochon & J. G. Fleagle (Eds.), *The human evolution source book,* Englewood Cliffs, NJ: Prentice-Hall.

Grün, R., & Thorne, A. (1997). Dating the Ngandong humans. *Science, 276,* 1575.

Guthrie, S. (1993). *Faces in the clouds: A new theory of religions.* New York: Oxford University Press.

Gutin, J. A. (1995). Do Kenya tools root birth of modern thought in Africa? *Science, 270,* 1118–1119.

Hafkin, N., & Bay, E. (Eds.). (1976). *Women in Africa.* Stanford, CA: Stanford University Press.

Hager, L. (1989). The evolution of sex differences in the hominid bony pelvis. Ph.D. dissertation, University of California, Berkeley.

Hahn, R. A. (1992). The state of federal health statistics on racial and ethnic groups. *Journal of the American Medical Association, 267*(2), 268–271.

Hall, E. T. (1959). *The silent language.* Garden City, NY: Anchor Press/Doubleday.

Hamblin, D. J., & the Editors of Time-Life. (1973). *The first cities.* New York: Time-Life.

Hamburg, D. A., & McGown, E. R. (Eds.). (1979). *The great apes.* Menlo Park, CA: Cummings.

Hammond, D. (1972). *Associations.* Reading, MA: Addison-Wesley.

Hanson, A. (1989). The making of the Maori: Culture invention and its logic. *American Anthropologist, 91*(4), 890–902.

Harlow, H. F. (1962). Social deprivation in monkeys. *Scientific American, 206,* 1–10.

Harner, M. (1980). *The way of the shaman: A guide to power and healing.* San Francisco: Harper & Row.

Harpending, J. H., & Harpending, H. C. (1995). Ancient differences in population can mimic a recent African origin of modern humans. *Current Anthropology, 36,* 667–674.

Harris, M. (1968). *The rise of anthropological theory: A history of theories of culture.* New York: Crowell.

Harris, M. (1989). *Cows, pigs, wars, and witches: The riddles of culture.* New York: Vintage Books/Random House.

Harrison, G. G. (1975). Primary adult lactase deficiency: A problem in anthropological genetics. *American Anthropologist, 77,* 815–819.

Hart, C. W., Pilling, A. R., & Goodale, J. (1988). *Tiwi of North Australia* (3rd ed.). New York: Holt, Rinehart & Winston.

Hart, D., & Sussman, R. W. (2005). *Man the hunted: Primates, predators, and human evolution.* Boulder, CO: Westview Press.

Hartwig, W. C., & Doneski, K. (1998). Evolution of the Hominid hand and toolmaking behavior. *American Journal of Physical Anthropology, 106,* 401–402.

Hatcher, E. P. (1985). *Art as culture, an introduction to the anthropology of art.* New York: University Press of America.

Haviland W. (1967). Stature at Tikal, Guatemala: Implications for ancient Maya, demography, and social organization. *American Antiquity, 32,* 316–325.

Haviland, W. (1970). Tikal, Guatemala and Mesoamerican urbanism. *World Archaeology, 2,* 186–198.

Haviland, W. A. (1972). A new look at Classic Maya social organization at Tikal. *Ceramica de Cultura Maya, 8,* 1–16.

Haviland, W. A. (1974). Farming, seafaring and bilocal residence on the coast of Maine. *Man in the Northeast, 6,* 31–44.

Haviland, W. A. (1975). The ancient Maya and the evolution of urban society. *University of Northern Colorado Museum of Anthropology, Miscellaneous Series, 37.*

Haviland, W. A. (1997). Cleansing young minds, or what should we be doing in introductory anthropology? In C. P. Kottak, J. J. White, R. H. Furlow, & P. C. Rice (Eds.), *The teaching of anthropology: Problems, issues, and decisions* (p. 35). Mountain View, CA: Mayfield.

Haviland, W. A. (1997). The rise and fall of sexual inequality: Death and gender at Tikal, Guatemala. *Ancient Mesoamerica, 8,* 1–12.

Haviland, W. A. (2002). Settlement, society and demography at Tikal. In J. Sabloff (Ed.), *Tikal.* Santa Fe: School of American Research.

Haviland, W. A. (2003). *Tikal, Guatemala: A Maya way to urbanism.* Paper prepared for 3rd INAH / Penn State Conference on Mesoamerican Urbanism.

Haviland, W. A., et al. (1985). *Excavations in small residential groups of Tikal: Groups 4F-1 and 4F-2.* Philadelphia: University Museum.

Haviland, W. A., & Moholy-Nagy, H. (1992). Distinguishing the high and mighty from the hoi polloi at Tikal, Guatemala. In A. F. Chase & D. Z. Chase (Eds.), *Mesoamerican elites: An archaeological assessment.* Norman: Oklahoma University Press.

Haviland, W. A., & Power, M. W. (1994). *The original Vermonters* (2nd ed.). Hanover, NH: University Press of New England.

Hays, H. R. (1965). *From ape to angel: An informal history of social anthropology.* New York: Knopf.

Hazardous waste trafficking. www.choike.org.

Heilbroner, R. L. (1972). *The making of economic society* (4th ed.). Englewood Cliffs, NJ: Prentice-Hall.

Heilbroner, R. L., & Thurow, L. C. (1981). *The economic problem* (6th ed.). Englewood Cliffs, NJ: Prentice-Hall.

Heitzman, J., & Wordem, R. L. (Eds.). (2006). *India: A country study* (sect. 2, 5th ed.). Washington, DC: Federal Research Division, Library of Congress.

Helm, J. (1962). The ecological approach in anthropology. *American Journal of Sociology, 67,* 630–649.

Henry, D. O., et al. (2004). Human behavioral organization in the Middle Paleolithic: Were Neandertals different? *American Anthropologist, 107*(1), 17–31.

Henry, J. (1965). *Culture against man.* New York: Vintage Books.

Herdt, G. H. (1993). Semen transactions in Sambia culture. In D. N. Suggs & A. W. Mirade (Eds.), *Culture and human sexuality* (pp. 298–327). Pacific Grove, CA: Brooks / Cole.

Herskovits, M. J. (1952). *Economic anthropology: A study in comparative economics* (2nd ed.). New York: Knopf.

Herskovits, M. J. (1964). *Cultural dynamics.* New York: Knopf.

Hertz, N. (2001). *The silent takeover: Global capitalism and the death of democracy.* New York: Arrow Books.

Hewes, G. W. (1973). Primate communication and the gestural origin of language. *Current Anthropology, 14,* 5–24.

"Hidden apartheid: Caste discrimination against India's untouchables." (2007). Human Rights Watch and the Center for Human Rights and Global Justice. www.hrw.org/reports/2007/india0207.

Hodgen, M. (1964). *Early anthropology in the sixteenth and seventeenth centuries.* Philadelphia: University of Pennsylvania Press.

Hoebel, E. A. (1949). *Man in the primitive world: An introduction to anthropology.* New York: McGraw-Hill.

Hoebel, E. A. (1958). *Man in the primitive world: An introduction to anthropology.* New York: McGraw-Hill.

Hoebel, E. A. (1960). *The Cheyennes: Indians of the Great Plains.* New York: Holt, Rinehart & Winston.

Hoebel, E. A. (1972). *Anthropology: The study of man* (4th ed.). New York: McGraw-Hill.

Holden, C. (1999). Ancient child burial uncovered in Portugal. *Science, 283,* 169.

Hole, F. (1966). Investigating the origins of Mesopotamian civilization. *Science, 153,* 605–611.

Hole, F., & Heizer, R. F. (1969). *An introduction to prehistoric archeology.* New York: Holt, Rinehart & Winston.

Holloway, R. L. (1980). The O. H. 7 (Olduvai Gorge, Tanzania) hominid partial brain endocast revisited. *American Journal of Physical Anthropology, 53,* 267–274.

Holloway, R. L. (1981). The Indonesian Homo erectus brain endocast revisited. *American Journal of Physical Anthropology, 55,* 503–521.

Holloway, R. L. (1981). Volumetric and asymmetry determinations on recent hominid endocasts: Spy I and II, Djebel Jhroud 1, and the Salb Homo erectus specimens, with some notes on Neanderthal brain size. *American Journal of Physical Anthropology, 55,* 385–393.

Holloway, R. L., & de LaCoste-Lareymondie, M. C. (1982). Brain endocast asymmetry in pongids and hominids: Some preliminary findings on the paleontology of cerebral dominance. *American Journal of Physical Anthropology, 58,* 101–110.

Holmes, L. D. (2000). "Paradise Bent" (film review). *American Anthropologist, 102*(3), 604–605.

Hopkin, M. (2007, February 22). Chimps make spears to catch dinner. Published online: *Nature,* doi:10.1038 / news070219–11.

Hostetler, J., & Huntington, G. (1971). *Children in Amish society.* New York: Holt, Rinehart & Winston.

Houle, A. (1999). The origin of platyrrhines: An evaluation of the Antarctic scenario and the floating island model. *American Journal of Physical Anthropology, 109,* 554–556.

Howell, F. C. (1970). *Early man.* New York: Time-Life.

Hsu, F. L. (1961). *Psychological anthropology: Approaches to culture and personality.* Homewood, IL: Dorsey Press.

Hsu, F. L. K. (1979). The cultural problems of the cultural anthropologist. *American Anthropologist, 81,* 517–532.

Hubert, H., & Mauss, M. (1964). *Sacrifice.* Chicago: University of Chicago Press.

Human Development Report. (2002). *Deepening democracy in a fragmented world.* United Nations Development Program.

Hunger Project. (2003). www.thp.org.

Hymes, D. (1964). *Language in culture and society: A reader in linguistics and anthropology.* New York: Harper & Row.

Hymes, D. (Ed.). (1972). *Reinventing anthropology.* New York: Pantheon.

Hymes, D. (1974). *Foundations in sociolinguistics: An ethnographic approach.* Philadelphia: University of Pennsylvania Press.

icasualties.org

Inda, J. X., & Rosaldo, R. (Eds.). (2001). *The anthropology of globalization: A reader.* Malden, MA, and Oxford: Blackwell.

Ingmanson, E. J. (1998). Comment. *Current Anthropology, 39,* 409.

Inkeles, A., & Levinson, D. J. (1954). National character: The study of modal personality and socio-cultural systems. In G. Lindzey (Ed.), *Handbook of social psychology.* Reading, MA: Addison-Wesley.

Inoue, S., & Matsuzawa, T. (2007). Working memory of numerals in chimpanzees. *Current Biology, 17,* 23, 1004–1005.

Inuit Tapiirit Katami. http://www.taprisat.ca/english-text/itk/departments/enviro/ncp.

Irvine, M. (1999, November 24). Mom-and-pop houses grow rare. *Burlington Free Press.*

"Italy–Germany verbal war hots up." (2003, July 9). *Deccan Herald.* (Bangalore, India).

"It's the law: Child labor protection." (1997, November/December). *Peace and Justice News,* 11.

Jacobs, S. E. (1994). Native American two-spirits. *Anthropology Newsletter, 35*(8), 7.

Jacoby, R., & Glauberman, N. (Eds.). (1995). *The Bell Curve debate.* New York: Random House.

Jennings, F. (1976). *The invasion of America.* New York: Norton.

Jennings, J. D. (1974). *Prehistory of North America* (2nd ed.). New York: McGraw-Hill.

Johansen, B. E. (2002). The Inuit's struggle with dioxins and other organic pollutants. *The American Indian Quarterly, 26*(3), 479–490.

Johanson, D., & Shreeve, J. (1989). *Lucy's child: the discovery of a human ancestor.* New York: Avon.

Johanson, D. C., & Edey, M. (1981). *Lucy, the beginnings of humankind.* New York: Simon & Schuster.

Johanson, D. C., & White, T. D. (1979). A systematic assessment of early African hominids. *Science, 203,* 321–330.

John, V. (1971). Whose is the failure? In C. L. Brace, G. R. Gamble, & J. T. Bond (Eds.), *Race and intelligence.* Washington, DC: American Anthropological Association (Anthropological Studies No. 8).

Johnson, D. (1996). Polygamists emerge from secrecy, seeking not just peace but respect. In W. A. Haviland & R. J. Gordon (Eds.), *Talking about people* (2nd ed., pp. 129–131). Mountain View, CA: Mayfield.

Jolly, A. (1985). *The evolution of primate behavior* (2nd ed.). New York: Macmillan.

Jolly, A. (1991). Thinking like a vervet. *Science, 251,* 574.

Jolly, C. J. (1970). The seed eaters: A new model of hominid differentiation based on a baboon analogy. *Man, 5,* 5–26.

Jolly, C. J., & Plog, F. (1986). *Physical anthropology and archaeology* (4th ed.). New York: Knopf.

Jones, S., Martin, R., & Pilbeam, D. (1992). *Cambridge encyclopedia of human evolution.* New York: Cambridge University Press.

Joukowsky, M. A. (1980). *A complete field manual of archeology: Tools and techniques of field work for archaeologists.* Englewood Cliffs, NJ: Prentice-Hall.

Joyce, C. (1991). *Witnesses from the grave: The stories bones tell.* Boston: Little, Brown.

Kahn, H., & Wiener, A. J. (1967). *The year 2000.* New York: Macmillan.

Kaiser, J. (1994). A new theory of insect wing origins takes off. *Science, 266,* 363.

Kalwet, H. (1988). *Dreamtime and inner space: The world of the shaman.* New York: Random House.

Kaplan, D. (1972). *Culture theory.* Englewood Cliffs, NJ: Prentice-Hall (Foundations of Modern Anthropology).

Kaplan, D. (2000). The darker side of the original affluent society. *Journal of Anthropological Research, 53*(3), 301–324.

Kaplan, M. (2007, May 31). Upright orangutans point way to walking. Published online: doi:10.1038/news070528–8.

Kaplan, M. (2008, August 5). Almost half of primate species face extinction. Published online: *Nature,* doi:10.1038/news.2008.1013.

Karavani, I., & Smith, F. H. (2000). More on the Neanderthal problem: The Vindija case. *Current Anthropology, 41,* 839.

Kardiner, A. (1939). *The individual and his society: The psycho-dynamics of primitive social organization.* New York: Columbia University Press.

Kardiner, A., & Preble, E. (1961). *They studied men.* New York: Mentor.

Kay, R. F., Fleagle, J. G., & Simons, E. L. (1981). A revision of the Oligocene apes of the Fayum Province, Egypt. *American Journal of Physical Anthropology, 55,* 293–322.

Kay, R. F., Ross, C., & Williams, B. A. (1997). Anthropoid origins. *Science, 275,* 797–804.

Keen, B. (1971). *The Aztec image in western thought.* New Brunswick, NJ: Rutgers University Press.

Kehoe, A. (2000). *Shamans and religion: An anthropological exploration in critical thinking.* Prospect Heights, IL: Waveland Press.

Kelly, T. L. (2006). *Sadhus, the great renouncers.* Photography exhibit, Indigo Gallery, Naxal, Kathmandu, Nepal. www.asianart.com/exhibitions/sadhus/index.html.

Kennickell, A. B. (2003, November). *A rolling tide: Changes in the distribution of wealth in the U.S. 1989–2001.* Levy Economics Institute.

Kenyon, K. (1957). *Digging up Jericho.* London: Ben.

Key, M. R. (1975). *Paralanguage and kinesics: Nonverbal communication.* Metuchen, NJ: Scarecrow Press.

Kirkpatrick, R. C. (2000). The evolution of human homosexual behavior. *Current Anthropology, 41,* 384.

Kleinman, A. (1976). Concepts and a model for the comparison of medical systems as cultural systems. *Social Science and Medicine, 12*(2B), 85–95.

Kluckhohn, C. (1970). *Mirror for Man.* Greenwich, CT: Fawcett.

Kluckhohn, C. (1994). Navajo witchcraft. *Papers of the Peabody Museum of American Archaeology and Ethnology, 22*(2).

Knauft, B. (1991). Violence and sociality in human evolution. *Current Anthropology, 32,* 391–409.

Koch, G. (1997). Songs, land rights, and archives in Australia. *Cultural Survival Quarterly, 20*(4).

Konner, M., & Worthman, C. (1980). Nursing frequency, gonadal function, and birth spacing among !Kung hunter-gatherers. *Science, 207,* 788–791.

Koufos, G. (1993). Mandible of *Ouranopithecus macedoniensis* (hominidae: primates) from a new late Miocene locality in Macedonia (Greece). *American Journal of Physical Anthropology, 91,* 225–234.

Krader, L. (1968). *Formation of the state.* Englewood Cliffs, NJ: Prentice-Hall (Foundation of Modern Anthropology).

Krajick, K. (1998). Greenfarming by the Incas? *Science, 281,* 323.

Kramer, P. A. (1998). The costs of human locomotion: maternal investment in child transport. *American Journal of Physical Anthropology, 107,* 71–85.

Kraybill, D. B. (2001). *The riddle of Amish culture.* Baltimore: Johns Hopkins University Press.

Kroeber, A. (1958). Totem and taboo: An ethnologic psycho-analysis. In W. Lessa & E. Z. Vogt (Eds.), *Reader in comparative religion: An anthropological approach.* New York: Harper & Row.

Kroeber, A. L. (1939). Cultural and natural areas of native North America. *American Archaeology and Ethnology* (Vol. 38). Berkeley: University of California Press.

Kroeber, A. L. (1963). *Anthropology: Cultural processes and patterns.* New York: Harcourt.

Kroeber, A. L., & Kluckhohn, C. (1952). *Culture: A critical review of concepts and definitions.* Cambridge, MA: Harvard University Press (*Papers of the Peabody Museum of American Archaeology and Ethnology, 47*).

Kruger, J., et al. (2005, December). Egocentrism over e-mail: Can people communicate as well as they think? *Journal of Personality and Social Psychology, 89*(6), 925–936.

Kuhn, T. (1968). *The structure of scientific revolutions.* Chicago: University of Chicago Press (International Encyclopedia of Unified Science, 2[27]).

Kummer, H. (1971). *Primate societies: Group techniques of ecological adaptation.* Chicago: Aldine.

Kunnie, J. (2003). *Africa's fast growing indigenous churches.* http://coh.arizona.edu/newandnotable/kunnie/kunnie.html.

Kunzig, R. (1999). A tale of two obsessed archaeologists, one ancient city and nagging doubts about whether science can ever hope to reveal the past. *Discover, 20*(5), 84–92.

Kuper, H. (1965). The Swazi of Swaziland. In J. L. Gibbs (Ed.), *Peoples of Africa* (pp. 479–511). New York: Holt, Rinehart & Winston.

Kurth, P. (1998, October 14). Capital crimes. *Seven Days, 7.*

Kurtz, D. V. (2001). *Political anthropology: Paradigms and power.* Boulder, CO: Westview Press.

Kushner, G. (1969). *Anthropology of complex societies.* Stanford, CA: Stanford University Press.

La Barre, W. (1945). Some observations of character structure in the Orient: The Japanese. *Psychiatry, 8.*

LaFont, S. (Ed.). (2003). *Constructing sexualities: Readings in sexuality, gender, and culture.* Upper Saddle River, NJ: Prentice-Hall.

Lai, C. S. L., et al. (2001). A forkhead-domain gene is mutated in severe speech and language disorder. *Nature, 413,* 519–523.

Lakoff, R. T. (2004). *Language and woman's place.* Mary Bucholtz (Ed.). New York: Oxford University Press.

Lampl, M., Velhuis, J. D., & Johnson, M. L. (1992). Saltation and statsis: A model of human growth. *Science, 258*(5083), 801–803.

Lancaster, J. B. (1975). *Primate behavior and the emergence of human culture.* New York: Holt, Rinehart & Winston.

Landau, M. (1991). *Narratives of human evolution.* New Haven, CT: Yale University Press.

Landes, R. (1982). Comment. *Current Anthropology, 23,* 401.

Lang, I. A., et al. (2008). Association of urinary bisphenol A concentration with medical disorders and laboratory abnormalities in adults. *Journal of the American Medical Association, 300*(11), 1303–1310.

Langan, P., & Harlow, C. (1994). *Child rape victims, 1992.* Washington, DC: Bureau of Justice Statistics, U.S. Department of Justice.

Lanning, E. P. (1967). *Peru before the Incas.* Englewood Cliffs, NJ: Prentice-Hall.

Lanternari, V. (1963). *The religions of the oppressed.* New York: Mentor.

Larsen, J. (2006, July 28). *Setting the record straight.* Earth Policy Institute, Eco-economy updates.

Lasker, G. W., & Tyzzer, R. (1982). *Physical anthropology* (3rd ed.) New York: Holt, Rinehart & Winston.

Laughlin, W. S., & Osborne, R. H. (Eds.). (1967). *Human variation and origins.* San Francisco: Freeman.

Laurel, K. (1990). In the company of witches. *Natural History, 92.*

Lawler, A. (2001). Writing gets a rewrite. *Science, 292,* 2419.

Layton, R. (1991). *The anthropology of art* (2nd ed.). Cambridge, England: Cambridge University Press.

Leach, E. (1961). *Rethinking anthropology.* London: Athione Press.

Leach, E. (1962). The determinants of differential cross-cousin marriage. *Man, 62,* 238.

Leach, E. (1962). On certain unconsidered aspects of double descent systems. *Man, 214,* 13–34.

Leach, E. (1965). *Political systems of highland Burma.* Boston: Beacon Press.

Leach, E. (1982). *Social anthropology.* Glasgow: Fontana Paperbacks.

Leacock, E. (1981). *Myths of male dominance: Collected articles on women cross culturally.* New York: Monthly Review Press.

Leacock, E. (1981). Women's status in egalitarian society: Implications for social evolution. In *Myths of male dominance: Collected articles on women cross culturally.* New York: Monthly Review Press.

Leakey, L. S. B. (1965). *Olduvai Gorge, 1951–1961* (Vol. 1). London: Cambridge University Press.

Leakey, L. S. B. (1967). Development of aggression as a factor in early man and prehuman evolution. In C. Clements & D. Lundsley (Eds.), *Aggression and defense.* Los Angeles: University of California Press.

Leakey, L.S. B., Tobias, P. B., & Napier, J. R., (1964). A new species of the genus *Homo* from Olduvai Gorge. *Nature, 202,* 7–9.

Leakey, M. D. (1971). *Olduvai Gorge: Excavations in Beds I and II. 1960–1963.* London and New York: Cambridge University Press.

Leakey, M. G., Spoor, F., Brown, F. H., Gathogo, P. N., Kiare, C., Leakey, L. N., & McDougal, I. (2001). New hominin genus from eastern Africa shows diverse middle Pliocene lineages. *Nature, 410,* 433–440.

Leap, W. L. (1987). Tribally controlled culture change: The Northern Ute language revival project. In R. M. Wulff & S. J. Fiske (Eds.), *Anthropological praxis: Translating knowledge into action* (pp. 197–211). Boulder, CO: Westview Press.

Leavitt, G. C. (1990). Sociobiological explanations of incest avoidance: A critical review of evidential claims. *American Anthropologist, 92,* 982.

Leclerc-Madlala, S. (2002). Bodies and politics: Healing rituals in the democratic South Africa. In V. Faure (Ed.), *Les cahiers de l'IFAS,* no. 2. Johannesburg: The French Institute.

Lee, R. (1993). *The Dobe Ju/hoansi.* Ft. Worth, TX: Harcourt Brace.

Lee, R. B., & Daly, R. H. (1999). *The Cambridge encyclopedia of hunters and gatherers.* New York: Cambridge University Press.

Lee, R. B., & DeVore, I. (Eds.). (1968). *Man the hunter.* Chicago: Aldine.

Leeds, A., & Vayda, A. P. (Eds.). (1965). *Man, culture and animals: The role of animals in human ecological adjustments.* Washington, DC: American Association for the Advancement of Science.

Lees, R. (1953). The basis of glottochronology. *Language, 29,* 113–127.

Lehman, E. C., Jr. (2002). Women's path into the ministry. *Pulpit & Pew Research Reports, 1*(fall), 4.

Lehmann, A. C., & Myers, J. E. (Eds.). (1993). *Magic, witchcraft and religion: An anthropological study of the supernatural* (3rd ed.). Mountain View, CA: Mayfield.

Lehmann, W. P. (1973). *Historical linguistics, An introduction* (2nd ed.). New York: Holt, Rinehart & Winston.

Leigh, S. R., & Park, P. B. (1998). Evolution of human growth prolongation. *American Journal of Physical Anthropology, 107,* 331–350.

Leinhardt, G. (1964). *Social anthropology*. London: Oxford University Press.

LeMay, M. (1975). The language capability of Neanderthal man. *American Journal of Physical Anthropology, 43*(1), 9–14.

Lenski, G. (1966). *Power and privilege: A theory of social stratification*. New York: McGraw-Hill.

Leroi-Gourhan, A. (1968). The evolution of Paleolithic art. *Scientific American, 218*, 58ff.

Lestel, D. (1998). How chimpanzees have domesticated humans. *Anthropology Today, 12*(3).

Lett, J. (1987). *The human enterprise: A critical introduction to anthropological theory*. Boulder, CO: Westview Press.

Levine, N. E., & Silk, J. B. (1997). Why polyandry fails. *Current Anthropology, 38*, 375–398.

Levine, R. (1973). *Culture, behavior and personality*. Chicago: Aldine.

Lévi-Strauss, C. (1963). The sorcerer and his magic. In *Structural anthropology*. New York: Basic Books.

Lewellen, T. C. (2002). *The anthropology of globalization: Cultural anthropology enters the 21st century*. Westport, CT: Greenwood Publishing Group/Bergin & Garvey.

Lewin, R. (1983). Is the orangutan a living fossil? *Science, 222*, 1223.

Lewin, R. (1985). Tooth enamel tells a complex story. *Science, 228*, 707.

Lewin, R. (1986). New fossil upsets human family" *Science, 233*, 720–721.

Lewin, R. (1987). Debate over emergence of human tooth pattern. *Science, 235*, 749.

Lewin, R. (1987). The earliest "humans" were more like apes. *Science, 236*, 1062–1063.

Lewin, R. (1987). Four legs bad, two legs good. *Science, 235*, 969.

Lewin, R. (1987). Why is ape tool use so confusing? *Science, 236*, 776–777.

Lewin, R. (1988). Molecular clocks turn a quarter century. *Science, 235*, 969–971.

Lewin, R. (1993). Paleolithic paint job. *Discover, 14*(7), 64–70.

Lewis, I. M. (1965). Problems in the comparative study of unilineal descent. In M. Banton (Ed.), *The relevance of models for social organization* (A.S.A. Monograph No. 1). London: Tavistock.

Lewis, I. M. (1976). *Social anthropology in perspective*. Harmondsworth, England: Penguin.

Lewis-Williams, J. D. (1990). *Discovering southern African rock art*. Cape Town and Johannesburg: David Philip.

Lewis-Williams, J. D., & Dowson, T. A. (1988). Signs of all times: Entoptic phenomena in Upper Paleolithic art. *Current Anthropology, 29*, 201–245.

Lewis-Williams, J. D., & Dowson, T. A. (1993). On vision and power in the Neolithic: Evidence from the decorated monuments. *Current Anthropology, 34*, 55–65.

Lewis-Williams, J. D., Dowson, T. A., & Deacon, J. (1993). Rock art and changing perceptions of Southern Africa's past: Ezeljagdspoort reviewed. *Antiquity, 67*, 273–291.

Lewontin, R. C. (1972). The apportionment of human diversity. In T. Dobzhansky, et al. (Eds.), *Evolutionary biology* (pp. 381–398). New York: Plenum Press.

Lewontin, R. C., Rose, S., & Kamin, L. J. (1984). *Not in our genes*. New York: Pantheon.

Li, X., Harbottle, G., Zhang, J., & Wang, C. (2003).The earliest writing? Sign use in the seventh millennium BC at Jiahu, Henan Province, China. *Antiquity, 77*, 31–44.

Lieberman, P. (2006). *Toward an evolutionary biology of language*. Cambridge, MA: Belknap Press.

Lindenbaum, S. (1978). *Kuru sorcery: Disease and danger in the New Guinea highlands*. New York: McGraw-Hill.

Lindstrom, L. (1993). *Cargo cult: Strange stories of desire from Melanesia and beyond*. Honolulu: University of Hawaii Press.

Little, K. (1964). The role of voluntary associations in West African urbanization. In P. van den Berghe (Ed.), *Africa: social problems of change and conflict*. San Francisco: Chandler.

Livingstone, F. B. (1973). The distribution of abnormal hemoglobin genes and their significance for human evolution. In C. Loring Brace & J. Metress (Eds.), *Man in evolutionary perspective*. New York: Wiley.

Lloyd, C. B. (Ed.). (2005). *Growing up global: The changing transitions to adulthood in developing countries*. Washington, DC: National Academies Press, Committee on Population, National Research Council and Institute of Medicine of the National Academies.

Lochhead, Carolyn. (2004, February 5). Court says same-sex marriage is a right. *San Francisco Chronicle*.

Lock, M. (2001). *Twice dead: Organ transplants and the reinvention of death*. Berkeley: University of California Press.

Lorenzo, C., Carretero, J. M., Arsuaga, J. L., Gracia, A., & Martinez, I. (1998). Intrapopulational body size variation and cranial capacity variation in middle Pleistocene humans: The Sima de los Huesos sample (Sierra de Atapuerca, Spain). *American Journal of Physical Anthropology, 106*, 19–33.

Lovejoy, C. O. (1981). Origin of man. *Science, 211*(4480), 341–350.

Lowie, R. H. (1948). *Social organization*. New York: Holt, Rinehart & Winston.

Lowie, R. H. (1956). *Crow Indians*. New York: Holt, Rinehart & Winston. (orig. 1935).

Lowie, R. H. (1966). *Culture and ethnology*. New York: Basic Books.

Lucy, J. A. (1997). Linguistic relativity. *Annual Review of Anthropology, 26*, 291–312.

Lustig-Arecco, V. (1975). *Technology strategies for survival*. New York: Holt, Rinehart & Winston.

MacCormack, C. P. (1977). Biological events and cultural control. *Signs, 3*, 93–100.

MacLarnon, A. M., & Hewitt, G. P. (1999). The evolution of human speech: The role of enhanced breathing control. *American Journal of Physical Anthropology, 109*, 341–363.

MacNeish, R. S. (1992). *The origins of agriculture and settled life*. Norman: University of Oklahoma Press.

"Madison Avenue relevance." (1999). *Anthropology Newsletter, 40*(4), 32.

Mair, L. (1969). *Witchcraft*. New York: McGraw-Hill.

Mair, L. (1971). *Marriage*. Baltimore: Penguin.

Malefijt, A. de W. (1969). *Religion and culture: An introduction to anthropology of religion*. London: Macmillan.

Malefijt, A. de W. (1974). *Images of man*. New York: Knopf.

Malinowski, B. (1922). *Argonauts of the western Pacific*. London: Routledge & Kegan Paul.

Malinowski, B. (1945). *The dynamics of culture change*. New Haven, CT: Yale University Press.

Mann, A., Lampl, M., & Monge, J. (1990). Patterns of ontogeny in human evolution: Evidence from dental development. *Yearbook of Physical Anthropology, 33*, 111–150.

Mann, C. C. (2002).The real dirt on rainforest fertility. *Science, 297*, 920–923.

Mann, C. C. (2005). *1491: New revelations of the Americas before Columbus*. New York: Knopf.

Marcus, J., & Flannery, K. V. (1996). *Zapotec civilization: How urban society evolved in Mexico's Oaxaca Valley*. New York: Thames & Hudson.

Marks, J. (1995). *Human biodiversity: Genes, race and history*. Hawthorne, NY: Aldine.

Marks, J. (2000, April 8). A feckless quest for the basketball gene. *New York Times*.

Marks, J. (2000, May 12). 98% alike (what our similarity to apes tells us about our understanding of genetics). *Chronicle of Higher Education*, B7.

Marks, J. (2002). *What it means to be 98 percent chimpanzee: Apes, people, and their genes.* Berkeley: University of California Press.

Marsella, J. (1982). Pulling it together: Discussion and comments. In S. Pastner & W. A. Haviland (Eds.), *Confronting the creationists* (pp. 79–80). *Northeastern Anthropological Association, Occasional Proceedings, 1.*

Marshack, A. (1972). *The roots of civilization: A study in prehistoric cognition; the origins of art, symbol and notation.* New York: McGraw-Hill.

Marshack, A. (1976). Some implications of the Paleolithic symbolic evidence for the origin of language. *Current Anthropology, 17*(2), 274–282.

Marshack, A. (1989). *Evolution of the human capacity: The symbolic evidence. Yearbook of physical anthropology* (vol. 32, pp. 1–34). New York: Alan R. Liss.

Marshall, L. (1961). Sharing, talking and giving: Relief of social tensions among !Kung bushmen. *Africa, 31,* 231–249.

Marshall, M. (1990). Two tales from the Trukese taproom. In P. R. DeVita (Ed.), *The humbled anthropologist* (pp. 12–17). Belmont, CA: Wadsworth.

Martin, E. (1994). *Flexible bodies: Tracking immunity in American culture-from the days of polio to the age of AIDS.* Boston: Beacon Press.

Martin, E. (1999). Flexible survivors. *Anthropology News, 40*(6), 5–7.

Martorell, R. (1988). Body size, adaptation, and function. *GDP, 335–347.*

Mascia-Lees, F. E., & Black, N. J. (2000). *Gender and anthropology.* Prospect Heights, IL: Waveland Press.

Mason, J. A. (1957). *The ancient civilizations of Peru.* Baltimore: Penguin.

Matson, F. R. (Ed.). (1965). *Ceramics and man.* New York: Viking Fund Publications in Anthropology, no. 41.

Maybury-Lewis, D. (1960). Parallel descent and the Apinaye anomaly. *Southwestern Journal of Anthropology, 16,* 191–216.

Maybury-Lewis, D. (1984). The prospects for plural societies. *1982 Proceedings of the American Ethnological Society.*

Maybury-Lewis, D. (1993, fall). A new world dilemma: The Indian question in the Americas. *Symbols,* 17–23.

Maybury-Lewis, D. (1993). A special sort of pleading. In W. A. Haviland & R. J. Gordon (Eds.), *Talking about people* (2nd ed.). Mountain View, CA: Mayfield.

Maybury-Lewis, D. (2001). *Indigenous peoples, ethnic groups, and the state* (2nd ed.). Boston: Allyn & Bacon.

McCorriston, J., & Hole, F. (1991). The ecology of seasonal stress and the origins of agriculture in the Near East. *American Anthropologist, 93,* 46–69.

McDermott, L. (1996). Self-representation in Upper Paleolithic female figurines. *Current Anthropology, 37,* 227–276.

McGrew, W. C. (2000). Dental care in chimps. *Science, 288,* 1747.

McHenry, H. (1975). Fossils and the mosaic nature of human evolution. *Science, 190,* 425–431.

McHenry, H. M. (1992). Body size and proportions in early hominids. *American Journal of Physical Anthropology, 87,* 407–431.

McKenna, J. (1999). Co-sleeping and SIDS. In W. Trevathan, E. O. Smith, & J. J. McKenna (Eds.), *Evolutionary medicine.* London: Oxford University Press.

McKenna, J. J. (2002, September–October). Breastfeeding and bedsharing. *Mothering,* 28–37.

Mead, A. T. P. (1996). Genealogy, sacredness, and the commodities market. *Cultural Survival Quarterly, 20*(2).

Mead, M. (1928). *Coming of age in Samoa.* New York: Morrow.

Mead, M. (1950). *Sex and temperament in three primitive societies.* New York: New American Library. (orig. 1935).

Mead, M. (1963). *Sex and temperament in three primitive societies* (3rd ed). New York: Morrow. (orig.1935).

Mead, M. (1970). *Culture and commitment.* Garden City, NY: Natural History Press, Universe Books.

Medicine, B. (1994). Gender. In M. B. Davis (Ed.), *Native America in the twentieth century.* New York: Garland.

Melaart, J. (1967). *Catal Hüyük: A Neolithic town in Anatolia.* London: Thames & Hudson.

Mellars, P. (1989). Major issues in the emergence of modern humans. *Current Anthropology, 30,* 356–357.

Meltzer, D., Fowler, D., & Sabloff, J. (Eds.). (1986). *American archaeology: Past & future.* Washington, DC: Smithsonian Institution Press.

Merin, Y. (2002). *Equality for same-sex couples: The legal recognition of gay partnerships in Europe and the United States.* Chicago: University of Chicago Press.

Merrell, D. J. (1962). *Evolution and genetics: The modern theory of genetics.* New York: Holt, Rinehart & Winston.

Merriam, A. P. (1964). *The anthropology of music.* Chicago: Northwestern University Press.

Mesghinua, H. M. (1966). Salt mining in Enderta. *Journal of Ethiopian Studies, 4*(2).

Michaels, J. W. (1973). *Dating methods in archaeology.* New York: Seminar Press.

Miles, H. L. W. (1993). Language and the orangutan: The "old person" of the forest. In P. Cavalieri & P. Singer (Eds.), *The great ape project* (pp. 45–50). New York: St. Martin's Press.

Millon, R. (1973). *Urbanization of Teotihuacán, Mexico: Vol. 1, Part 1. The Teotihuacán map.* Austin: University of Texas Press.

Mintz, S. (1996). A taste of history. In W. A. Haviland & R. J. Gordon (Eds.), *Talking about people* (2nd ed., pp. 81–82). Mountain View, CA: Mayfield.

Mitchell, W. E. (1978). *Mishpokhe: A study of New York City Jewish family clubs.* The Hague: Mouton.

Molnar, S. (1992). *Human variation: Races, types and ethnic groups* (3rd ed.). Englewood Cliffs, NJ: Prentice-Hall.

Monaghan, L., Hinton, L., & Kephart, R. (1997). Can't teach a dog to be a cat? The dialogue on ebonics. *Anthropology Newsletter, 38*(3), 1, 8, 9.

Montagu, A. (1964). *The concept of race.* London: Macmillan.

Montagu, A. (1964). *Man's most dangerous myth: The fallacy of race* (4th ed.) New York: World Publishing.

Montagu, A. (1975). *Race and IQ.* New York: Oxford University Press.

Morgan, L. H. (1877). *Ancient society.* New York: World Publishing.

Moscati, S. (1962). *The face of the ancient orient.* New York: Doubleday.

Murdock, G. P. (1965). *Social structure.* New York: Free Press.

Murdock, G. P. (1971). How culture changes. In H. L. Shapiro (Ed.), *Man, culture and society* (2nd ed.). New York: Oxford University Press.

Murphy, R., & Kasdan, L. (1959). The structure of parallel cousin marriage. *American Anthropologist, 61,* 17–29.

Mydens, S. (2001, August 12). He's not hairy, he's my brother. *New York Times,* sec. 4, 5.

Nader, L. (Ed.). (1969). *Law in culture and society.* Chicago: Aldine.

Nader, L. (Ed.). (1981). *No access to law: Alternatives to the American judicial system.* New York: Academic Press.

Nader, L. (Ed.). (1996). *Naked science: Anthropological inquiry into boundaries, power, and knowledge.* New York: Routledge.

Nader, L. (1997). Controlling processes: Tracing the dynamics of power. *Current Anthropology, 38,* 715–717.

Nanda, S. (1990). *Neither man nor woman: The hijras of India.* Belmont, CA: Wadsworth.

Nanda, S. (1992). Arranging a marriage in India. In P. R. De Vita (Ed.), *The naked anthropologist* (pp. 139–143). Belmont, CA: Wadsworth.

Natadecha-Sponsal, P. (1993). The young, the rich and the famous: Individualism as an American cultural value. In P. R. DeVita & J. D. Armstrong (Eds.), *Distant mirrors: America as a foreign culture* (pp. 46–53). Belmont, CA: Wadsworth.

Natural Resources Defense Council. (2005, March 25). *Healthy milk, healthy baby: Chemical pollution and mother's milk.* www.NRDC.org.

Neer, R. M. (1975). The evolutionary significance of vitamin D, skin pigment, and ultraviolet light. *American Journal of Physical Anthropology, 43,* 409–416.

Nesbitt, L. M. (1935). *Hell-hole of creation.* New York: Knopf.

Nettl, B. (1956). *Music in primitive culture.* Cambridge, MA: Harvard University Press.

Newman, P. L. (1965). *Knowing the Gururumba.* New York: Holt, Rinehart & Winston.

Nietschmann, B. (1987). The third world war. *Cultural Survival Quarterly, 11*(3), 1–16.

Noack, T. (2001). Cohabitation in Norway: An accepted and gradually more regulated way of living. *International Journal of Law, Policy, and the Family, 15*(1),102–117.

Norbeck, E., Price-Williams, D., & McCord, W. (Eds.). (1968). *The study of personality: An interdisciplinary appraisal.* New York: Holt, Rinehart & Winston.

Normile, D. (1998). Habitat seen as playing larger role in shaping behavior. *Science, 279,* 1454.

Norris, R. S., & Kristensen, H. M. (2006, July/August). Global nuclear stockpiles, 1945–2006. *Bulletin of the Atomic Scientists, 62*(4), 64–66.

Nye, J. (2002). *The paradox of American power: Why the world's only superpower can't go it alone.* New York: Oxford University Press.

Oakley, K. P. (1964). *Man the tool-maker.* Chicago: University of Chicago Press.

O'Barr, W. M., & Conley, J. M. (1993). When a juror watches a lawyer. In W. A. Haviland & R. J. Gordon (Eds.), *Talking about people* (2nd. ed., pp. 42–45). Mountain View, CA: Mayfield.

Oboler, R. S. (1980). Is the female husband a man? Woman/woman marriage among the Nandi of Kenya. *Ethnology, 19,* 69–88.

O'Carroll, E. (2008, June 27). Spain to grant some human rights to apes. *Christian Science Monitor.*

Offiong, D. (1985). Witchcraft among the Ibibio of Nigeria. In A. C. Lehmann & J. E.

Myers (Eds.), *Magic, witchcraft, and religion* (pp. 152–165). Palo Alto, CA: Mayfield.

Okonjo, K. (1976). The dual-sex political system in operation: Igbo women and community politics in midwestern Nigeria. In N. Hafkin & E. Bay (Eds.), *Women in Africa.* Stanford, CA: Stanford University Press.

Olszewski, D. I. (1991). Comment. *Current Anthropology, 32,* 43.

O'Mahoney, K. (1970). The salt trade. *Journal of Ethiopian Studies, 8*(2).

Ong, A. (1999). *Flexible citizenship: The cultural logics of transnationality.* Durham, NC: Duke University Press.

Ortiz, A. (1969). *The Tewa world.* Chicago: University of Chicago Press.

Oswalt, W. H. (1972). *Habitat and technology.* New York: Holt, Rinehart & Winston.

Oswalt, W. H. (1972). *Other peoples other customs: World ethnography and its history.* New York: Holt, Rinehart & Winston.

Otten, C. M. (1971). *Anthropology and art: Readings in cross-cultural aesthetics.* Garden City, NY: Natural History Press.

Ottenheimer, Martin. (1996). *Forbidden relatives: The American myth of cousin marriage.* Champaign: University of Illinois Press.

Parker, S., & Parker, H. (1979). The myth of male superiority: Rise and demise. *American Anthropologist, 81*(2), 289–309.

Parkin, R. (1997). *Kinship: An introduction to basic concepts.* Cambridge, MA: Blackwell.

Partridge, W. (Ed.). (1984). *Training manual in development anthropology.* Washington, DC: American Anthropological Association.

Patterson, F., & Linden, E. (1981). *The education of Koko.* New York: Holt, Rinehart & Winston.

Patterson, F. G. P., & Gordon, W. (2002). Twenty-seven years of Project Koko and Michael. In B. Galdikas et al. (Eds.), *All apes great and small, volume I: Chimpanzees, bonobos, and gorillas* (pp. 165–176). New York: Kluwer Academy.

Patterson, T. C. (1981). *Archeology: The evolution of ancient societies.* Englewood Cliffs, NJ: Prentice-Hall.

Pease, T. (2000). Taking the third side. *Andover Bulletin* (spring).

Pelto, G. H., Goodman, A. H., & Dufour, D. L. (Eds.). (2000). *Nutritional anthropology: Biocultural perspectives on food and nutrition.* Mountain View, CA: Mayfield,

Penniman, T. K. (1965). *A hundred years of anthropology.* London: Duckworth.

Pennisi, E. (1999). Genetic study shakes up out of Africa theory. *Science, 283,* 1828.

Peters, C. R. (1979). Toward an ecological model of African Plio-Pleistocene hominid adaptations. *American Anthropologist, 81*(2), 261–278.

Petersen, J. B., Neuves, E., & Heckenberger, M. J. (2001). Gift from the past: *Terra preta* and prehistoric American occupation in Amazonia. In C. McEwan and C. Barreo (Eds.), *Unknown Amazon* (pp. 86–105). London: British Museum Press.

Peterson, F. L. (1962). *Ancient Mexico, An introduction to the pre-Hispanic cultures.* New York: Capricorn Books.

Pfeiffer, J. E. (1977). *The emergence of society.* New York: McGraw-Hill.

Pfeiffer, J. E. (1978). *The emergence of man.* New York: Harper & Row.

Pfeiffer, J. E. (1985). *The creative explosion.* Ithaca, NY: Cornell University Press.

Piddocke, S. (1965). The potlatch system of the southern Kwakiutl: A new perspective. *Southwestern Journal of Anthropology, 21,* 244–264.

Piggott, S. (1965). *Ancient Europe.* Chicago: Aldine.

Pilbeam, D. (1987). Rethinking human origins. In *Primate evolution and human origins.* Hawthorne, NY: Aldine.

Pilbeam, D., & Gould, S. J. (1974). Size and scaling in human evolution. *Science, 186,* 892–901.

Pinker, S. (1994). *The language instinct: How the mind creates language.* New York: William Morrow.

Piperno, D. R., & Fritz, G. J. (1994). On the emergence of agriculture in the new world. *Current Anthropology, 35,* 637–643.

Plattner, S. (1989). Markets and market places. In S. Plattner (Ed.), *Economic anthropology.* Stanford, CA: Stanford University Press.

pluralism.org (The Pluralism Project, Harvard University).

Pohl, M. E. D., Pope, K. O., & von Nagy, C. (2002). Olmec origins of Mesoamerican writing. *Science, 298,* 1984–1987.

Polanyi, K. (1968). The economy as instituted process. In E. E. LeClair, Jr., & H. K. Schneider (Eds.), *Economic anthropology: Readings in theory and analysis* (pp. 127–138). New York: Holt, Rinehart & Winston.

Pollan, M. (2001). *The botany of desire: A plant's-eye view of the world.* New York: Random House.

Population Reference Bureau and UNAIDS. (2008). UC San Francisco, http://hivinsite.ucsf.edu/InSit.

Pospisil, L. (1963). *The Kapauku Papuans of west New Guinea.* New York: Holt, Rinehart & Winston.

Woolfson, P. (1972). Language, thought, and culture. In V. P. Clark, P. A. Escholz, & A. F. Rosa (Eds.), *Language.* New York: St. Martin's Press.

World almanac. (2004). New York: Press Publishing Co.

World Bank. (1982). *Tribal peoples and economic development.* Washington, DC: World Bank.

World Bank. (2003). www.worldbank.org/poverty. Accessed January 2003.

World Health Organization. http://www.who.int/about/definition/en/.

World Meteorological Organization. (2003). Increasing heat waves and other health hazards. greenpeaceusa.org/climate/index.fpl/7096/article/907. html. Accessed December 2003.

Worsley, P. (1957). *The trumpet shall sound: A study of "cargo" cults in Melanesia.* London: Macgibbon & Kee.

Worsley, P. (1959). Cargo cults. *Scientific American, 200* (May), 117–128.

Wrangham, R., & Peterson, D. (1996). *Demonic males.* Boston: Houghton Mifflin.

Wright, R. (1984). Towards a new Indian policy in Brazil. *Cultural Survival Quarterly, 8*(1).

Wright, R. M. (1997). Violence on Indian day in Brazil 1997: Symbol of the past and future. *Cultural Survival Quarterly, 21*(2), 47–49.

Wulff, R. M., & Fiske, S. J. (1987). *Anthropological praxis: Translating knowledge into action.* Boulder, CO: Westview Press.

www.globalissue.org.

www.healthanddna.com/behavioralgenetics.html www.savetibet.org/tibet/us/proceedings/senatefrmauramoynihan.php.

Yip, M. (2002). *Tone.* New York: Cambridge University Press.

Young, A. (1981). The creation of medical knowledge: Some problems in interpretation. *Social Science and Medicine, 17,* 1205–1211.

Young, W. (Ed.). (2000). Kimball award winner. *Anthropology News, 41*(8), 29.

Zeder, M. A., & Hesse, B. (2000). The initial domestication of goats (*Capra hircus*) in the Zagros Mountains 10,000 years ago. *Science, 287,* 2254–2257.

Zilhão, J. (2000). Fate of the Neandertals. *Archaeology, 53*(4), 30.

Zimmer, C. (1999). New date for the dawn of dream time. *Science, 284,* 1243.

Zohary, D., & Hopf, M. (1993). *Domestication of plants in the Old World* (2nd ed.). Oxford: Clarenden Press.

PHOTO CREDITS

Chapter 1 page 2: © New York Times/ Stephanie Sinclair/VII Network; page 4 (left): © Michael Newman/PhotoEdit; page 4 (right): © Marie-Stenzel/National Geographic Images; page 7: © Associated Press; page 8: © Susan Meiselas/Magnum Photos; page 14: © Eurelios/Photo Researchers, Inc.; page 17: © Kerry Cullinan; page 24: © The Canadian Press (Kevin Frayer)

Chapter 2 page 28: © Susan Van Etten/ PhotoEdit; page 30: From *Lindauer Bilderbogen* no. 5, edited by Friedrich Boer. Jan Thorbecke Verlag. Sigmaringen. West Germany; page 34: © Vittorio Luzzati/ National Portrait Gallery, London; page 35: © Leonard Lessin/Peter Arnold, Inc.; page 41: 20th Century Fox/The Kobal Collection/ Hayes, Kerry; page 43: © Meckes/Ottowa/ Photo Researchers, Inc.

Chapter 3 page 48: © Fotostock/SuperStock; page 50: © Associated Press; page 51: © Gerald Hinde/Getty Images; page 53: © Irven DeVore/AnthroPhoto; page 56 (top): © Carlo Dani/Jeske/Animals Animals; page 56 (bottom): © Michael Dick/Animals Animals; page 57: © Ingo Arndt/Minden Pictures/Getty; page 58: © Peter Drowne/ Color-Pic, Inc.; page 60: © Amy Parish/ Anthro-Photo; page 65: © Martin Harvey/ Peter Arnold, Inc.

Chapter 4 page 70: © The Natural History Museum, London; page 77: © Andrew Hill/ Anthro-Photo; page 78 (top left): © Associated Press; page 78 (bottom right): © 1985 David L. Brill; page 80: 1999 David L. Brill; page 83: © National Museums of Kenya; page 84 (left and right): William A. Haviland; page 86 (left & right): © David L. Brill; page 89: Rock painting of a bull and horses, ca. 17,000 BC Prehistoric Caves of Lascaux, Dordogne, France/The Bridgeman Art Library/Copyright status: out of copyright

Chapter 5 page 94: © Tavid Bingham and Amory Ledyard; page 98: Illustration by W. C. Galinat, Reprinted with Permission from W. C. Galinat, "The origin of maize: grain of humanity," *Economic Botany*, vol. 49, pp. 3–12, fig. 24-c, copyright 1995 The New York Botanical Garden; page 108: The Metropolitan Museum of Art/Art Resource, NY; page 110 (top and bottom): © Alan H. Goodman, Hampshire College

Chapter 6 page 114: © Aladin Abdel Naby/ Reuters/Landov; page 119: © Nishan Bingham; page 121: © Rolex Awards for Enterprise, Susan Gray; page 122: © Robert Holmes/Corbis; page 123: © Anita de Laguna Haviland; page 125: © Tavid Hingham; page 126: Cahokia Mounds State Historic Site; page 127: © AFP/Getty Images

Chapter 7 page 130: © Bettmann/Corbis; page 134 left: © Getty Images; page 134 (left): Laurence Dutton/Getty Images; page 134 (right): © Eugene Hoshiko/ Associated Press; page 135: © Schalkwijk/ Art Resource, NY; page 136: © blickwinkel/ Alamy; page 142: © Terrol Dew Johnson

Chapter 8 page 146: © Namit Arora; page 149 (left): © Jim McGuire/Index Stock Imagery; page 149 (right): © Richard Lord; page 150: © Randy Duchaine/Alamy; page 151: © Ian Adams Photography; page 158: © Tony Karumba/AFP/Getty Images; page 159: © Time/Getty Images; page 160: © Clay McLachlan/Reuters/Corbis

Chapter 9 page 162: © Bill Bachman/Painet; page 164: © H. Lyn Miles, PhD., Chantek Foundation; page 166: Courtesy of Tiffany Kirschner; page 171: © Orion Pictures Corporation/Everett Collection; page 174: © Kazuyoshi Nomachi/Corbis; page 175 (left): © Frank Pedrick/The Image Works; page 175 (right): © Robert Azzi/Woodfin Camp & Associates; page 179: Tac Yec Neen Ho Gar Ton (Red Indian) Emperor of the Six Nations 1710, Vereist, Johannes or Jan (b 1648-fl 1718)/Private Collection/ The Bridgeman Art Library

Chapter 10 page 182: © Photo by Evan Reader; page 185 (left): © James Balog; page 185 (right): © Laura Dwight/Corbis; page 186: © Robert H. Rothman/Harvard Medical School; page 187: © James Akena/ Reuters/Landov; page 189: © Anthony Bannister/Gallo Images/Corbis; page 191: © N. Chagnon/Anthro-Photo; page 193: © Simon Kwong/Corbis; page 197: © Photography Hugh Hartshorne/ReAngle Pictures; page 199: © Thomas L. Kelly

Chapter 11 page 204: © Louis-Layrent/ The Image Bank/Getty Images; page 206: © Victor Englebert; page 209: © Jacques Jangous/Alamy; page 212: © S. Iras Images & Stories, Turkey; page 215: © Jahangir

Khan/Reuters/Corbis; page 217: © John Warburton-Lee Photography/ Alamy; page 220: © AP Images/Daily Sitka Sentinel/James Poulson; page 223: © Irwin Fedriansyiah/Associated Press

Chapter 12 page 226: © Sean Sprague/ SpraguePhoto.com; page 228: © Hideo Haga/HAGA/The Image Works; page 233 (left): © Associated Press; page 233 (right): © Lauren Goldsmith/The Image Works; page 239 © John Eastcott/Yva Momatluk/ Woodfin Camp & Associates; page 241 © Aldona Sabalis/Photo Researchers, Inc.; page 243 © Joe Cavanaugh/DDB Stock Photo; page 245 © Edward Burtynsky

Chapter 13 page 248: © Hugh Morton; page 251: © Graeme Matthews/Photo New Zealand; page 253: © Gai Ming-Sheng/ HK China Tourism Press; page 255: © Lawrence Migdale/PIX; page 261: © Louise Gubb/Corbis; page 263 (left): © Malcolm Lightner/Corbis; page 263 (right): © Reuters/Lucas Jackson/Landov; page 267: Photo by Oliver O'Hanlon

Chapter 14 page 270: © Reuters/Corbis; page 274: © Matt York/Associated Press; page 277: © Jacques Jangoux/Peter Arnold, Inc.; page 279 (left): © Reuters/Corbis; page 279 (right): © K. Prouse/Pressnet/Topham/ The Image Works; page 280: © AFP/Getty Images; page 282: © Fred McConnaughey/ Photo Researchers, Inc.; page 283: © Bryan & Cherry Alexander/Arcticphoto

Chapter 15 page 296: © Michele Falzone Photography; page 298: © Ed Kashi/Corbis; page 302: © Benjamin Chodroff; page 305: © Images & Stories, Turkey; page 307: © Irven DeVore/Anthro-Photo; page 309: Waltraud Grubitzsch/DPA/Landov; page 311: SSPL/The Image Works; page 313: © Francois Daburon/Corbis

Chapter 16 page 316: © Guo Dayue/ Xinhua/Landov; page 319: © Allen Green/ Photo Researchers, Inc.; page 325: © Harald E. L. Prins; page 329: © AFP/Getty Images; page 330: © Yann Arthus-Bertrand/Corbis; page 332: © Bryan & Cherry Alexander/ Arcticphoto; page 335: © EPA/Laurent Gilleron/Corbis; page 337: © Monica Almeida/The New York Times/Redux

INDEX